The
Kennedy
Neurosis

The
Kennedy
Neurosis

Nancy Gager Clinch

With a Foreword by Bruce Mazlish

GROSSET & DUNLAP
A National General Company

Publishers   New York

Library of Congress Catalog Card Number: 72-77097
ISBN: 0-448-01313-4

Fourth Printing
Printed in the United States of America

The author wishes to express her gratitude for permission to reprint material from the following:

The Bridge at Chappaquiddick by Jack Olsen. Copyright © 1970 by Jack Olsen and Sue Olsen. By permission of Little, Brown and Co. and John Cushman Associates. *The Cuban Invasion* by Tad Szulc and Karl E. Meyer. By permission of Praeger Publishers, Inc. *85 Days: The Last Campaign of Robert Kennedy* by Jules Witcover. Copyright © by Jules Witcover. Reprinted by permission of G. P. Putnam's Sons. *The Founding Father: The Story of Joseph P. Kennedy* by Richard Whalen. Copyright © 1964 by Richard Whalen. Reprinted by permission of William Morris Agency, Inc. *The Heir Apparent* by William V. Shannon. Copyright © 1967 by William V. Shannon. Reprinted with permission of The Macmillan Company. *In a Time of Torment*, by I. F. Stone. Copyright © 1967 by I. F. Stone. Reprinted by permission of Random House, Inc., and Jonathan Cape, Ltd. *J.F.K.: The Man and the Myth* by Victor Lasky. © Victor Lasky 1963. Reprinted with permission of The Macmillan Company and Julian Bach Literary Agency, Inc. *John F. Kennedy: A Political Profile*, © 1959 by James MacGregor Burns. Reprinted by permission of Harcourt Brace Jovanovich, Inc. *The Kennedy Doctrine* by Louise FitzSimons. Copyright © 1972 by Louise FitzSimons. Reprinted by permission of Random House, Inc. *The Lost Prince* by Hank Searls. Copyright © 1969 by Hank Searls. Reprinted by arrangement with The New American Library, Inc., New York, and by permission of the author and the author's agents, Scott Meredith Literary Agency, Inc., 528 Fifth Avenue, New York, N.Y. 10036. "Money in America" by Robert Lekachman. Copyright © by Minneapolis Star and Tribune Co., Inc. Reprinted from the August 1970 issue of *Harper's Magazine* by permission of the author. *My Twelve Years with John F. Kennedy* by Evelyn Lincoln. Copyright © 1965 by Evelyn Lincoln, published by David McKay Co., Inc. Reprinted by permission of the publisher. *The Mythmakers: An Essay on Power and Wealth* by Bernard Nossiter. Copyright © 1964 by Bernard D. Nossiter. Reprinted by permission of the publisher Houghton Mifflin Company. *The Next Kennedy* by Margaret Laing. Copyright © 1968 by Margaret Laing. Reprinted by permission of Collins-Knowlton-Wing, Inc. *The Remarkable Kennedys* by Joe McCarthy. Copyright © 1960 by Joe McCarthy. Reprinted by permission of the publisher, The Dial Press, and William Morris Agency, Inc. *Robert Kennedy: A Memoir* by Jack Newfield. Copyright © 1969 by Jack Newfield. Published by E. P. Dutton & Co., Inc., and Jonathan Cape, Ltd., and used with their permission. *A Thousand Days* by Arthur M. Schlesinger, Jr. Copyright © 1965 by Arthur M. Schlesinger, Jr. Reprinted by permission of the publisher Houghton Mifflin Company and André Deutsch, Ltd. *White Power, Black Freedom* by Arnold Schuchter. Reprinted by permission of Beacon Press, Inc. *Cold War and Counterrevolution* by Richard J. Walton. Copyright © 1972 by Richard J. Walton. Reprinted by permission of The Viking Press, Inc. *R.F.K.* by Dick Schaap. Copyright © 1967 by Dick Schaap. Reprinted by arrangement with The New American Library, Inc., New York, and A.D. Peters and Company.

To my daughters Lucia and Tyler

Something we were withholding made us weak
Until we found out that it was ourselves.

—ROBERT FROST
"The Gift Outright"

CONTENTS

ACKNOWLEDGMENTS

Although the views and opinions expressed in this book are entirely my own, I am deeply indebted to two close friends for constant help on this project—Dr. Dorothy Camara, whose knowledge as a psychologist and insights as a humanist added immeasurably to my psychological understanding of the Kennedys and our era, and my historical colleague, Colonel Brooke Nihart, without whose sustained interest, advice, encouragement, and support this study might well never have been finished.

Other friends and acquaintances, some of them known to the Kennedy family as well, aided in various ways. Many understandably do not wish to be publicly identified in a note of thanks. But I wish to acknowledge the help of Jarle Brors, B.D., for his challenging psychological interpretations, and of Louise FitzSimons, who generously shared with me her political conclusions prior to the publication of her own excellent study, *The Kennedy Doctrine*. And I was fortunate to have as a college mentor in international relations Dr. M. Margaret Ball, then head of the Political Science Department at Wellesley College, an outstanding teacher who combined rigorous scholarship and tough-mindedness with an unfailing humanity. To all these, and many more, I am lastingly grateful.

Finally, I am indebted, and owe thanks as well, to the many writers, identified in the notes at the back of this book, who, responding to the public interest, have followed the careers of the Kennedys, in public and private, and so have provided a more than ample record of their thoughts, speech, and actions.

FOREWORD

by Bruce Mazlish

1

The Kennedy Neurosis is undoubtedly an important book; and, indeed, there is a very good chance that it will end up as a landmark in political biography, in spite of certain flaws.

There are at least three major contributions that make this an exceptional book. The first is that it substitutes history for myth, and in this it fulfills a task placed before historians and political scientists ever since Thucydides. The history that it offers is of a special sort: psychological history, or, as Ms. Clinch calls it, psychohistory. This approach is especially fitting because psychoanalysis, the basis of psychohistory, takes as one of its own tasks the analysis of myth.

The second contribution is to psychohistory itself. Until now, most of the work in this area has been individual life histories, of a Luther, a Gandhi. Ms. Clinch offers us the life history of a family. The Kennedys saw themselves, as indeed did others, as a dynasty, entitled to rule in Camelot. Now we can see that they were also characters in a Greek tragedy, doomed because of a family curse. As Ms. Clinch perceptively notes, the Kennedy curse, translated from the language of myth into that of psychohistory, can be seen for what it is: a "Kennedy neurosis," handed down from grandparents to parents to children.

The third contribution is the argument that the Kennedy neurosis mirrors a desperate strain in the American character. As the author puts it, "The Kennedy neurosis . . . grew not only out of the Kennedy family history but also out of a centuries-old cultural neurosis: America's obsessive drive to material success, belief in national omnipotence, and sense of crusading mission. . . ."

Taken together, these three contributions make a potent claim on our attention. When one adds that the book is written in a clear and compelling style — indeed, there is a mounting dramatic intensity to the presentation — pleasure joins importance in urging us on to its reading.

2

What is Ms. Clinch's thesis? Very briefly, it is that all the Kennedys, including JFK, who became President, sought power for their own inner needs rather than out of a desire to serve their fellowmen. The rhetoric, in which the Kennedys consciously believed, said otherwise; but the reality, in which their unconscious drives manifested themselves, betrayed a different story. As Irish immigrants, the Kennedy and Fitzgerald grandparents had begun the climb to competitive success in America. The sole aim was to win. Joseph Kennedy Sr. won in a big way: he became a multimillionaire. Yet his success was soured, for he was not accepted by the Boston Brahmins in whose midst he had grown up.

Joseph Kennedy determined that his children, all of them, would claw their way to the top socially and politically as he had done financially. Rather than a desire for "equality, love, and sharing," his aim was power and dominance over others: this is part of what Ms. Clinch calls the "Kennedy neurosis." For the children, this meant that they were not loved by the parents for themselves, but only as they fulfilled their parents' need for success, now projected onto them. The result in JFK and his siblings was a feeling of fundamental rejection, a doubting of inner worth, and a desperate need continuously to compete and to prove their courage. The consequence for American politics was pathological, as the politically adept Kennedys acquired office and power only to use them as vehicles to play out their neurotic needs. Both for themselves and for America, the result was dangerous and destructive — and left as its heritage the seeds of our present crisis in America.

It is obvious that this precis only skims the surface of Clinch's detailed and informed argument. The above are mere assertions; the detail and demonstration that she offers are the test of her work, and there can be no substitution for them here.

3

Ms. Clinch calls her work psychohistory; it is important therefore to look at the psychological context in which she works. Freud is the starting point, but Ms. Clinch quickly turns her back on him and appeals to some of his dissenting disciples. For her, Freud was too pessimistic in seeing human nature as "essentially hostile and self-destructive"; he was too "gloomy and mechanistic"; and, it follows from Ms. Clinch's women's liberation position, he was too sexist (as well as overemphasizing the sex drive). Instead, Clinch turns to what she calls "psychohumanism," to the views espoused by such Freudian disciples as Horney, Fromm, and Sullivan, and by such humanistic psychologists as Maslow, May, and Allport. Here the emphasis is on the power of love and on the way in which character is formed by the social environment. Thus *The Kennedy Neurosis* often appears to be a specific illustration of Horney's *Neurotic Personality of Our Time*.

Freud, as the founder of psychoanalysis, did see libido as fundamental to the dynamics of the unconscious, and he did tend to look at patients as if removed from the outer world. Some of his disciples moved to correct what they considered to be these overemphases. Thus, for example, Harry Stack Sullivan stressed instead that man must be viewed primarily as a socially interacting organism, though he is biologically rooted; that he develops and changes in a continuous process; and that his psychic states, anxiety, for example, are the result primarily of interpersonal relations (which are determined largely by his particular society and its socialization processes) rather than intrapsychic conflict.

At this point, of course, the analyst's view of his particular society becomes crucial; his own values begin to intrude more openly on the situation. Erich Fromm writes *Escape from Freedom*, borrowing heavily from sociological and Marxist theory, and indicting the marketing and authoritarian personalities produced by capitalism. Karen Horney analyzes the neurotic personality *of our time*, that is, as a time-bound phenomenon. Ms. Clinch places herself squarely in this tradition. She makes no effort to hide her own values, but rather seeks to use them to inform and illuminate her analysis. In my view, such an approach raises serious and subtle questions of methodology, which cannot be adequately argued here. While it brings gains, it also runs serious risks, and sometimes, I believe, falls victim to them.

Ms. Clinch's work also sets itself clearly apart, for better or worse, from one of the main directions hitherto taken by psychohistory, that of Erik Erikson. Erikson has analyzed "great men," seeking to show how their efforts to solve their own problems, their "neuroses," offered solutions to the problems of their fellowmen. Ms. Clinch is skeptical of "great men" — she obviously distrusts all leaders — and wants to make sure that they are genuinely great men — and women. She asks for conscious coldness toward those in power over us rather than an unconscious resonance to their psychic qualities. Erikson uses a scheme of psychosexual stages in his analysis of the life histories of his great men. In Ms. Clinch's eyes, this tars him with the Freudian brush, and she dismisses him as basing his work "on the repression of instinctive demons, and this considerably limits his understanding of human drives and potentials."

In a moment we shall examine this argument a bit further. Here we might conclude our account of the psychological background employed by Ms. Clinch to note a problem: her use of the term "neurosis." For my part, her usage is too vague. At one point she tells us that the neurotic "is emotionally centered on himself"; at another she informs us that all neuroses exhibit "dual feelings of aggressive power and predestined helplessness"; that "a personal sense of omnipotence . . . and a hypersensitivity to others' opinions are part of a neurotic whole"; and that "neurosis is a human sickness which prevents the victim from achieving his own humanity and thus from fulfilling his capacity for ethical living."

Is neurosis really one thing, or are there different kinds of neuroses (hysteria, phobias, obsessional states)? Do different kinds of neurotics, therefore, exhibit different kinds of characteristic behavior? As a clinical picture, Ms. Clinch's definition leaves something to be desired. Are not all of us neurotic to some degree, and does not the working through of neurosis in fact serve as the basis of our highest achievements? Surely Sigmund Freud (not to mention Harry Stack Sullivan) was neurotic; did this prevent him from achieving his own humanity and living ethically? Such questions suggest that Ms. Clinch might have given deeper thought to her use of this key term.

4

In spite of gestures toward balance and an acknowledgment of the Kennedy's creative qualities, Ms. Clinch comes dangerously close to writing psychopathology rather than psychohistory. The general tone of the work resembles Freud and Bullitt's *Woodrow Wilson*, where a similar disenchantment with a supposedly idealistic American President led to an extremely critical analysis. There is a kind of irony that Ms. Clinch's psychological humanism seems to lead her to a sort of inhuman treatment of the Kennedys that would distress, I am sure, someone such as Erik Erikson, whom she accuses of being mechanistic.

Because she would have people be more rational in their attitudes to authority figures, in my view Ms. Clinch underestimates or ignores the extent to which all political leadership depends partly on illusion, on rhetorically advanced ego ideals, and on psychological attraction. For instance, she gives short shrift to the Kennedys' psychological effect as what I shall call Catholic emancipators. In winning for themselves, the Kennedys won for all Catholics, allowing them to see themselves through identification as the equals of anyone in America, and taking them out of their psychological ghettos once and for all. The Kennedy neurosis in this sense can be seen as creative and even humanistic, and a psychohistorian could also note and analyze this achievement without overlooking the price attached to it.

Yet, with these qualifications, and others that could be made, I repeat, *The Kennedy Neurosis* is a major work, a highly important and, overall, successful book. As the great historian Jacob Burckhardt said of his history of the Renaissance, even if all of his individual facts were wrong, his general interpretation was right. Ms. Clinch is not only writing psychohistory, she is writing revisionist history. As she remarks with great self-awareness, "If my emphasis seems generally negative, it is largely because the lavish praise of the Kennedys has been so irrational and untrue that a revisionist must inevitably feel the weight of writing against an enormous tide of published opinion." In her new version of "debunking" or muckraking history, necessarily one-sided, Ms. Clinch gets the general picture right. She is best, it seems to me, where it counts: after the first few chapters, when she hits her stride with JFK and his political decisions. Her scholarship and acumen here are impressive, and her fusion of policy and personality convincing.

Ms. Clinch is the first to write openly about the Kennedy men and their sexual attitudes. She examines their need to compete, to win at any cost, and always to appear "strong." It is striking how similar in compulsive obedience to these imperatives both Lyndon Johnson and Richard Nixon have been. Our choosing of this triumvirate of recent Presidents at least suggests a correlation between their psychic needs and those of a broad segment of the American population. If there is a Kennedy neurosis, it is an American neurosis.

Much of what has come to be called the counterculture is a revulsion against this "neurosis." The counterculture seeks to change the values the Kennedys represented. Manliness in an atomic age is seen as a form of madness; and boys wear long hair like girls to symbolize the acceptance of "womanliness" and its fusion with "manliness." Competition gives way to community. Winning the world is seen as losing one's soul. The constant effort to seem "strong" is perceived as the outer disguise of an inner fear of "weakness." Without passing judgment on these attempted value changes, it should be clear that Ms. Clinch's book must be seen as a part of this movement. She wishes not only to analyze the Kennedys, but to offer treatment to the "American psyche."

Her desired value change may well have been part of what was at the heart of the 1972 election. Ted Kennedy may not have grown or been able to free himself from the Kennedy neurosis, according to Ms. Clinch. Had McGovern? Was the New Politics the political counterpart of the counterculture? In spite of the overt election results, was the landscape of American politics fundamentally changed? *The Kennedy Neurosis* cannot immediately answer these questions, though it throws a light ahead of itself onto them. It can, however, definitely convince us that personality in a President is as important as his policies, and not detachable from them. More importantly, it demonstrates this truth overwhelmingly in the specific case of the Kennedys. As a result, Ms. Clinch has irrevocably changed the landscape of the Kennedy phenomenon. We can no longer be innocents in Camelot.

Chapter 1

THE KENNEDYS AND PSYCHOHISTORY: THE ANATOMY OF AN ILLUSION

In the White House, character and personality are extremely important because there are no other limitations which govern a man's conduct. Restraint must come from within the presidential soul and prudence from within the presidential mind. The adversary forces which temper the actions of others do not come into play until it is too late to change course.
—George E. Reedy, *The Twilight of the Presidency*

The psyche of the President of the United States is a fit subject for public discussion and debate . . . the state of his emotions and nerves when the phone rings in the middle of the night is a very political question.
—Michael Harrington, "Does Nixon Have the Stuff?"
Washington *Evening Star*

The public wants to know and understand the quality of mind, temper, and personal background of a man who seeks the Presidency.
—William V. Shannon, *The Heir Apparent* ‍ℓ 418

The sins of the fathers are indeed visited upon the children, but there is nothing of a supernatural or theological character in this visitation. Its mechanism can be well enough understood, if we take the trouble to disentangle the separate emotional elements whereby neurosis is transmitted within the ties of the family from one generation to the next.
—Ronald V. Sampson, *The Psychology of Power*

Daddy was always very competitive. The thing he always kept telling us was that coming in second was just no good. The im-

1

portant thing was to win—don't come in second or third—that
doesn't count—but win, win, win.
                                        —Eunice Kennedy Shriver

. . . today Kennedy dead has infinitely more force than Kennedy living. Though his administration was not a success, he himself has become a world touchstone of political excellence. Part of
this phenomenon is attributable to the race's need for heroes, even
in deflationary times. But mostly the legend is the deliberate creation of the Kennedy family and its clients. Wanting to regain
power, it is now necessary to show that once upon a time there was
indeed a Camelot beside the Potomac, a golden age forever lost
unless a second Kennedy should become the President.
                        —Gore Vidal, "The Holy Family," *Esquire*

ℭ

ONCE UPON A time there was a country in which white men were often
able to work very hard and acquire great personal fortunes, depending
upon their individual circumstances and energies. There came to this
country a poor man who died poor, but whose son labored long and shrewdly and became both a successful businessman and a political leader in his
part of the land (there being no kings or queens, but instead a complicated
and not always honest system in which each person cast a vote for a leader).

The son of this first son was well educated at the best schools, and also
worked very hard and very shrewdly, in accordance with his father's
wishes. So great were his business talents, in fact, that this grandson of the
first immigrant became one of the richest men in the country. He did not,
however, believe in giving to the poor; instead, he decided to become as
rich as he possibly could, which was very rich indeed. But this rich grandson
soon became discontented with his lot as one of the richest men in the
country. He wanted to be accepted as an equal by people who had been
rich and important in the country for a very long time, and even not so
long a time. For, sad to relate, although this country prided itself upon
being a great democracy, most people in the country tended to look down
on certain other people for various reasons, such as the years they had lived
in the country, the size of their fortunes, their religions, the shape of their
noses, or the color of their skins.

The rich grandson did not like being looked down on by anybody for
any reason. It made him exceedingly angry. And although the President
of this great democracy had given the grandson several important jobs,
including making him a very important ambassador, the rich grandson
had angered many people by the way he got his money (which was, truth

to tell, not always scrupulous) and by the way he boasted about his fortune. Therefore few people wanted to elect him to be their political leader. The rich grandson decided that if he himself could not become a great political leader, one of his sons would. Since he had four sons, all of them intelligent, handsome, mannerly, and energetic, and since his own fortune was by now enormous, this seemed like a not impossible idea.

So the rich grandson set out to train his four sons to do everything he taught them to do and to work as hard as they possibly could at everything they did so that they would always win first prize. (The grandson also trained his five daughters, but being female they could never become leaders.) Winning, he told his children, was the most important thing in life. Fortunately for the rich grandson, his children were obedient—other than for a few childish pranks—and they worked very hard most of the time to do exactly what he wanted. The rich grandson also had a very hard-working wife who disciplined the children carefully when he was away making money, which at first was much of the time, and who scarcely ever disagreed with him.

Before long, the grandson's second son was elected a member of the national legislature. (Unhappily, the first son had been killed on a highly dangerous mission during a war.) The whole family worked as hard as they could, the father spent much of his fortune very cleverly, and in a few years the second son was in the Senate of the national legislature, which was almost as high as one could go. By now the whole family knew a great deal about winning elections; in fact, probably more than any other family in the country. But despite their riches and their fame, they still were not accepted by the "best people." So they decided that if only they could rule the country themselves, everybody who mattered would see that they were exceedingly important people.

To make a long story short, the second son, with the help of his rich father, his family, and his beautiful aristocratic wife, soon was elected the President of the country. Now the rich grandson was happy. He urged the second son, the President, to make the third son an important government official, and it was done. Then it occurred to the rich grandson that the fourth son should be important too. So he gathered the family together again to elect the fourth son to the Senate. This, as you can imagine, was soon accomplished.

Meanwhile the grandson's second son, the President, made a great many wonderful promises to the people of his country. Soon they could see that he was not only very handsome and very intelligent, but also an aristocrat, because only an aristocrat could use such marvelous words and live in such elegance with such an elegant wife, who indeed seemed to become more elegant every month. Although some thought it curious that the

President's promises came to very little, the common people knew that their dreams would come true once they had elected him President again. Because, after all, it takes time to do wonderful things. To the people's great horror, however, a madman killed the President. Then everyone saw that the grandson's second son had been not only a great leader, but even as one chosen by the gods to reside among the immortals.

Now the grandson's third son realized it was his turn to assume the task of national leadership, which by now included the gift of magical powers, or so it seemed to many. Soon the third son was elected to the Senate, where he joined the youngest brother. Joyous was the heart of the father, the rich grandson, even though he had become old and ill and was unable to help the sons directly. But his mind was at peace, we can assume, for he and his family were now famous throughout the whole world as great and even godlike people.

The third son was not certain the time would arrive when he should seek the office of Great Leader. But when he saw how unpopular was the President who had succeeded the dead brother, he decided to wait no longer. Imagine, then, the shock and consternation of his supporters when another madman shot and killed the third brother! Truly did a curse seem to be hanging over an illustrious family.

But the fourth son, hearing the cries and lamentations of the populace and his relatives, knew it was his duty to raise the banner of the immortal family. Besides, the mother told him he must do so. (The father, increasingly feeble, soon died.) So the fourth son worked hard in the Senate and made many wonderful promises to the people, as had the brothers before him.

Then one night there befell the fourth son a terrible and mysterious accident in which a young girl was drowned, and it seemed to many that the fourth son had behaved badly. The fourth son apologized to the people, and after a while they began to say again that he should one day be President. Some people wondered whether he might find a way not to be President, for it seemed to them that he had lost heart. But other people said, "Oh, yes, he must become President, because no one else can fulfill all those wonderful promises the brothers made to us." And the fourth son's mother, who was greatly admired by everyone for her courage and beauty, even though by this time she was very old, said to all these people who wanted him to be President, "You are entirely right."

I have cast this familiar and unfinished story in the style of a fairy tale to set the Kennedy legend in new perspective. Seen in this way, is there not something curiously childlike, primitive, and repetitive to the pattern of triumph and tragedy? Is there not something strangely—even ominously—

childish in the widespread acceptance of the Kennedy saga at face value? In the millions of words written about the Kennedys, has not something vital been omitted? The missing factor is occasionally hinted at or briefly mentioned, but the story has usually remained two-dimensional, for, to date, no one has published a consistent study of the essential element of the Kennedy story—the psychological element. Without it there can be no rational explanation of the Kennedys' ambitions, successes, and failures and of their extraordinary popularity in the minds and fantasies of millions of Americans.

The Kennedy Neurosis, although intended as a psychobiography in varying depths of the Kennedy family, has a broader purpose. The title itself is meant to symbolize this purpose, for as every person's emotional problems are in many ways uniquely his own, so they cannot be entirely comprehended under any pseudo-clinical heading such as *a* Kennedy neurosis. In a wider sense, this is a study of Americans living in the second half of the twentieth century. Thus the Kennedys are analyzed not only for their individual characteristics, but also, and more importantly, for their significance as factual and symbolic exemplars of emotional and social maladies that afflict an entire nation. We are all, in this sense, victims in differing ways of the "Kennedy neurosis."

From a historical overview, similar neuroses have existed throughout history. From this perspective, today's conflicted people are seen as the "victims of victims," suffering from emotional distortions passed on to them by grandparents and parents, distortions reshaped by their own social definitions and transmitted to their children. This neurotic conditioning, however, is not inevitable, unless one shares Freud's pessimistic view of human nature as essentially hostile and self-destructive, a perpetual tug-of-war between the life instinct, especially the sex drive, and the death instinct. I do not share that gloomy, mechanistic view. Rather, I agree with the psychological humanists who find human nature constantly striving toward loving relationships, social cooperation, and self-actualization.

Put most simply, the universally recurring human sickness that I have called the "Kennedy neurosis" is a drive to power and dominance of others rather than a drive for equality, love, and sharing. A British political scientist, Ronald V. Sampson, stated this hypothesis in *The Psychology of Power:* "The moral law rests on the fact that it is possible for every human being to develop in greater or lesser degree in one direction or another. He may seek to order his life and his relations with others on the basis of love or on the basis of power. . . . To the extent that the forces of love in men triumph over the forces of power, equality among men prevails. And conversely, to the extent that the forces of power prevail over the forces of love, domination and subjection characterize human relations . . . of necessity, everyone at all times and in all positions stands in a relation with other men which will be predominantly of one category or the other. In this sense, what happens in the world, what happens in history, inevitably reflects the contribution, active or passive, of everybody who participates in the vast web of human inter-relations. There are not diverse planes of reality to be judged by different standards. . . ."

In this definition of power-seeking as an essentially negative force, Professor Sampson is not talking of the creative powers within ourselves, the power of love, or the legitimate power of leadership through competence. These definitions are often confused in our minds. A predominant drive to love rather than to dominate does not mean that one then becomes weak and subservient. To the contrary, it is only the strong person, not the weak one, who is emotionally capable of loving rather than controlling. The pathological, neurotic drive to power is the opposite of the healthy development of one's leadership potential. The former is based on competition, the latter on competence.

Erich Fromm, a pioneering humanistic psychoanalyst, made this distinction in his interpretation of the inseparable link between ethics and character analysis. In *Man for Himself*, Dr. Fromm wrote, "When we speak of authority do we mean rational or irrational authority? *Rational authority* has its source in *competence*. The person whose authority is respected functions competently in the task with which he is entrusted by those who conferred it upon him. He need not intimidate them nor arouse their admiration by magic qualities; as long as and to the extent to which he is competently helping, instead of exploiting, his authority is based on rational grounds and does not call for irrational awe. Rational authority not only permits but requires constant scrutiny and criticism of those subjected to it; it is always temporary, its acceptance depending on its performance.

"The source of *irrational authority*, on the other hand, is always power over people. This power can be physical or mental, it can be realistic or only relative in terms of the anxiety and helplessness of the person submitting to this authority. Power on the one side, fear on the other, are always the buttresses on which irrational authority is built. Criticism of the authority is not only not required but forbidden. Rational authority is based upon the equality of both authority and subject, which differ only with respect to the degree of knowledge or skill in a particular field. Irrational authority is by its very nature based upon inequality, implying difference in value."

Dr. Samuel J. Warner, a psychotherapist, has also described the vital difference between competition, the "craving for prestige and dominance which Alfred Adler termed the 'most prominent evil of our civilization,'" and a healthy sense of competence. The former arises out of anxiety and weakness, the latter out of strength. As Dr. Warner commented in *Self-*

Realization and Self-Defeat, ". . . by the 'striving for power,' as we employ the term, we do not mean the realistic and mature desire for competence and reasonable self-sufficiency which Harry Stack Sullivan termed the 'power motive.' We mean, rather, an immature craving for omnipotence, a nebulous hunger for unlimited power over all others in the universe, which in Sullivan's terminology is the 'power drive'. . . ." Dr. Warner found that the "neurotic striving for power" differs from "the healthful wish for competence" in two essentials: the power wish is unlimited and insatiable; and the neurotic seeks power for the sake of power itself "rather than for the increased capacity to serve some living thing."

A chief argument of *The Kennedy Neurosis* is that Kennedy authority has rested far more upon the attributes of irrational than rational authority. Rather than being based upon competence and the scrutiny of those who submitted to it, the Kennedy political power was based on the irrational fears and desires of much of the voting public, and came to rest more and more on the creation of illusions and the assertion of magical qualities rather than on actual performance. The development and propagation of the Kennedy mystique, in which the Kennedys themselves came to believe, can be explained only by understanding the characterology of the Kennedys and of the society that helped form and then "bought" this mystique.

All politics are based upon a psychology; that is, upon a particular view of human nature and human society. What, in essence, does one want out of life, and what does one believe life can offer? Before learning about the Kennedys' effect on history, we must first find out what the Kennedys wanted out of history, on both the conscious and the unconscious levels of thought and feeling. We must ask three essential questions: How did the Kennedys see themselves? How did their society see them? And how realistic in terms of psychological truth and historical fact was each of these views?

My study of the Kennedys' characterology is based on a form of psychohistory which I call psychohumanism. The underlying theory is similar to that formulated by humanistically-oriented psychoanalysts such as Erich Fromm, Karen Horney, Harry Stack Sullivan, and Viktor Frankl, and by humanistic psychologists such as Abraham Maslow, Rollo May, and Gordon Allport. In this view, human behavior is determined primarily by a person's character development set within a social environment. Character is shaped by a person's relationships to himself, to other people, and to things (nature, culture, ideas). The energy motivating an individual's drives and passions does not come from an instinctive sex drive (which is only one of many physiological needs), but from those psychic relationships and needs that go far beyond the basic physiological needs (food, water, oxygen, sleep, shelter, sex). Once these survival needs are met (or sometimes even when they are not met), other psychological needs come into play:

first the needs for safety and belonging, for love and affection, for self-esteem and respect from others; then the needs for growth, development, and utilization of potential—in effect, the self-actualizing needs. Dr. Maslow, who most clearly articulated this "hierarchy" of needs, phrased this uniquely human pull as "the desire to become, more and more what one is, to become everything that one is capable of becoming."

Thus while a person has biological and unconscious motivations, they are far from rigidly predetermined, and they contain large elements of autonomy, self-direction, and freedom. Freedom, of course, is never complete, for choice may be severely constricted by learned patterns of self-defeat as well as by severe environmental limitations. Each of us arrives in the world with an individual temperament and physical constitution set within an individual parental pattern, which in turn exists within a specific cultural milieu. All these conditions act upon one another to form the particular human being who, it is hoped, will be helped by his parents and his society to make increasingly responsible choices in the direction of his life.

Through a close study of the Kennedys' express purposes and their recorded actions, I conclude that as a family they suffered in varying degrees from the form of emotional illness that psychologists call a "neurosis." In brief, a neurosis is a self-defeating defense pattern of feeling and behaving. It results largely from repeated childhood rejection, in which the child is made to feel that his own natural self is unacceptable to others. To find emotional acceptance, the neurotic develops a pseudo-self and a pattern of relating to himself and to others that make him feel most safe. This is what is meant by a confused identity. The threatened child dares not be himself, since this brings only rejection from the parents, who are themselves neurotic. Therefore an artificial identity becomes necessary for sheer survival. But because the individual's genuine strivings have been repressed, he no longer knows what he feels or wants. His basic anxiety—stemming from his original rejection—generates in him unconscious hostility against his parents, other people, and himself. In addition, society may constantly reinforce his initial sense of rejection. The neurotic's fearful emotions eventually produce a behavior pattern that is self-defeating. In extreme cases, it can become self-destructive.

In the case of the Kennedy parents, Joe and Rose, I believe that their excessive demands for perfection and social success helped produce in their children neuroses that had many similarities of cause and effect. Since the parental pressures for material achievement have been strongest on the sons in our male-oriented society, and since the Kennedy sons all tried to carry out the impossible demands of their parents, my analysis focuses upon Joe Junior, Jack, Bobby, and Teddy. Joseph Patrick Kennedy, the so-called founding father, once said, "There are no accidents in politics." Such a belief explains Joseph Kennedy's repeated and highly successful strategy of concentrating his enormous material and manipulative resources to assure political victory. In psychology, there is a close parallel. It was Sigmund Freud, in *The Psychopathology of Everyday Life*, who first uncovered how many supposed "accidents" are actually caused by our unconscious emotions. The Kennedys have been victims of an extraordinary number of accidents and disasters. While many genuine accidents do occur in life, it is also true that some people, for psychological reasons, are "accident prone."

Part of my thesis is that the Kennedys are among these afflicted people who, for deeply unconscious reasons, suffer a strong urge toward their own frustration, punishment, and even destruction, an urge that conflicts with their healthy, self-affirming drives. This is not to claim that the Kennedy accidents and the murders were in any way planned by the victims, which in light of the known facts would be absurd. But, very definitely, when a person is driven by unconscious emotional conflicts toward self-suffering, he will tend to bring about the circumstances that may eventually cause this suffering.

The evidence of recurrent Kennedy recklessness, indifference to danger, and bodily self-injury is too clear to be ignored. Disaster may come whether we wish it or not. But if part of us is unconsciously drawn to the pain or destruction of the disliked self, sooner or later disaster will almost certainly be ours. Some form of self-punishment is always present in a neurotic emotional pattern, although it may be well disguised from the casual observer, and most often from the victim himself. When the neurotic is also a national leader, his self-defeating impulses may seriously affect not only his fate, but the fate of his country and fellow citizens as well. This constant danger I seek to demonstrate in the individual Kennedy portraits.

It is my purpose to analyze what the historical record seems to reveal: that the Kennedy drive to power was largely neurotic in origin and thus largely neurotic in goal; and that when power was obtained, the Kennedys were severely limited in the use of their authority for positive aims because of emotional conflicts and ambivalences. The peculiar paralysis of power suffered by the Kennedys was never obvious, but eventually it became apparent to many observers despite their aura of glamor. In essence, the New Frontier rarely found purposeful direction or effective expression because, on the personal level, the old frontiers of inner stress and anxiety had never been breached.

The Kennedy powerlessness has both mirrored and added to the curious sense of powerlessness that we find in contemporary America. Hannah Arendt, among others, has given "examples to demonstrate the curious contradictions inherent in impotence of power." In *On Violence*, she noted, "Because of the enormous effectiveness of teamwork in the sciences, which is perhaps the outstanding American contribution to modern science, we can control the most complicated processes with a precision that makes trips to the moon less dangerous than ordinary weekend excursions; but the allegedly 'greatest power on earth' is helpless to end a war, clearly disastrous for all concerned, in one of the earth's smallest countries. It is as though we have fallen under a fairyland spell which permits us to do the 'impossible' on the condition that we lose the capacity of doing the possible, to achieve fantastically extraordinary feats on the condition of no longer being able to attend properly to our everyday needs."

The Kennedys, like American scientists, achieved the "impossible" through teamwork in their election triumphs. But once elected, they seemed to "fall under a fairyland spell" that kept them from accomplishing any significant part of their professed aims. This "spell" is really not mysterious in either the Kennedys or the nation, although its fabric is tortuously woven. In both cases, it seems evident that a "spell" of neurotic conflict has prevented the achievement of real and great potentials. While this book cannot undertake a thorough analysis of American society, a separate task, the problems of the Kennedys cannot be separated from the national condition and the problems of all Americans. I will briefly explore this theme of a reinforcing social neurosis in my final chapter.

Dr. Karen Horney was one of the earliest psychoanalysts to discover the neurotic roots of this sense of powerlessness in both individuals and societies, and the ways in which they are interrelated. In her first book, *The Neurotic Personality of Our Time*, Dr. Horney saw that "these contradictions embedded in our culture are precisely the conflicts which the neurotic struggles to reconcile: his tendencies toward yielding; his excessive demands and his fear of never getting anything; his striving toward self-aggrandizement and his feeling of personal helplessness. . . . It seems that the person who is likely to become neurotic is one who has experienced the culturally determined difficulties in an accentuated form, mostly through the medium of childhood experiences, and who has consequently been unable to solve them, or has solved them only at great cost to his personality. We might call him a stepchild of our culture." We will see in subsequent chapters how the highly competitive milieu of the Kennedys' childhood both reflected and intensified the emotional conflicts and contradictions of American society.

In many ways the Kennedys present a curious paradox in contemporary American politics. On the one hand, they have been hated and feared by many conservatives for their supposed desires to forward egalitarianism in American society. Although this condemnation is usually rationalized as a dislike of the Kennedys' overweening ambition, disapproval of political ambition becomes suspect when not also applied to equally driven conservatives, such as Richard M. Nixon. On the other hand, the Kennedys have been exalted by both liberal intellectuals and the dispossessed lower classes for this same supposed egalitarianism.

I believe the record amply shows that the Kennedys were as conservative, opportunistic, and narrowly motivated as many of their expressly status-quo opponents; and that to the Kennedys egalitarianism, far from being a belief, has actually been a risk generally to be avoided, although a useful and often politically necessary rhetorical device. Thus, to make my position clear, I stand with those liberals and liberal-radicals who criticize the Kennedys not for the humanistic promises they so articulately made, but for the preponderant lack of fulfillment of such promises and for the self-centered arrogance that so often underlay the assumption, spoken or not, that only the Kennedys could lead the nation toward the "American dream."

I do not see the Kennedy failures in performance as caused mainly by bad luck or by the vagaries of politics and human nature. Rather, the factual failures were largely the result of psychohistorical circumstances that existed for the Kennedy sons even before they were born and that strongly affected the shaping of their individual characters. In each son, unconscious emotional conflicts developed that were bound to disrupt their attitudes and actions as national leaders. This is not to excuse them from personal responsibility, but rather to suggest the restrictions on personal choice. Ethical behavior is, in essence, the freedom both to choose responsibly and then to decide to do so. Thus, at heart, the question of political leadership is both a psychological and a moral one. The problem is whether the leaders we choose, or those who cause themselves to be chosen, have sufficient psychic health to help us direct and develop our society for human, life-giving purposes or whether they are themselves ruled by immature and thwarting emotions.

Yet the Kennedys are fascinating not only for the lessons we may draw from them, but also as a family unmatched for dramatic interest. The barest facts are enough to test the imagination. In less than ten years, this family produced a President of the United States, three United States Senators, a U.S. Attorney General, and two additional presidential contenders. One of these candidates, but for the intervention of tragedy, might have been elected, and the second may yet have his hour. In addition, all of these national leaders were almost unprecedentedly young.

But the shining coin of success had its dark side. Of four Kennedy sons, three are dead: one by wartime disaster and two by assassination. The fourth son was nearly killed in a plane crash; and half a decade later, he disgraced himself in the eyes of millions by contributing to the death of a young woman under ambiguous circumstances, severely, if not irreparably, damaging his presidential ambitions. One daughter was killed in a plane crash. Another daughter has been confined since young adulthood in a home for the mentally retarded. Thus, of the nine heirs, only four have survived as functioning adults: one son and three daughters.

Peripheral tragedies have occurred through the years—a startling number for one family. The husband of the dead daughter was killed before his wife. Both parents of a Kennedy daughter-in-law died in a plane crash; her brother died in another plane accident. Subsequently, the brother's widow choked to death at a dinner celebrating a Kennedy political victory. Two Kennedy wives have had multiple miscarriages. One daughter's marriage ended in divorce—hardly a comparable tragedy, but serious enough in the eyes of staunch Roman Catholics.

Surely such an epic would tax any writer's credibility. As the Greek tragedy of the twentieth century, the Kennedy story has unfolded with a speed that contrasts with the far slower triumphs and tragedies of the Adams family of New England and the two related Roosevelt clans, the other great American political dynasties. The Kennedys have been true children of their century, not only in outlook and style, but also in the velocity of their rise and fall. At the pinnacle of success and power, they enjoyed a richness of life that is denied to all but a handful of human beings. The founding father not only made an enormous fortune, estimated at half a billion dollars, but gave considerable amounts to his children during his lifetime so that all were early multimillionaires. This fabulous wealth enabled both the father and the sons to develop the remarkable Kennedy aptitude for politics. In addition to having money and talents, the Kennedys have been consistently intelligent, good-looking, and extremely hard-working. Above all, each has been motivated by intense ambition, and loyalty to family has enabled the Kennedys to achieve their goal—political victory and power.

Many people, viewing the astonishing achievements on the one hand and the recurrent disasters on the other, have seen the Kennedys as victims of a mysterious curse. A second more intellectualized superstition interprets the Kennedys as suffering the fate of all mortals who aspire too high—they are punished. This is the ancient Greek concept of *hubris*, or excessive pride and arrogance, which offends the gods. The opposing humanistic view, that man's fate turns primarily on his own attitudes and actions rather than on those of spirits or gods, has an equally venerable lineage. This is the fundamental outlook of such visionaries as Socrates, Jesus, Confucius, Gautama, Tolstoy, Mill, and Kierkegaard, though their emphases often differed. This is also the basic view of post-Freudian psychoanalysis and psychology, psychohistory, and psychohumanism. In essence, each person is the decisive force shaping his own life and meeting his own death. That forces beyond our control affect us goes without saying. But the root force of humanity is the freedom, broad or narrow, with which we decide how to meet the external and internal forces both within and beyond our immediate control.

However, the neurotic, self-rejecting individual is not fully free to use his innately human powers. His natural energies, instead of going into the realization of his abilities, tend to go toward building defenses and patterns of retaliation that drive him away from his real needs. As Dr. Rollo May put it in *Man's Search for Himself*, "If any organism fails to fulfill its potentialities, it becomes sick. . . . This is the essence of neurosis—the person's unused potentialities, blocked by conditions in the environment (past or present) and by his own internalized conflicts, turn inward and cause morbidity." Dr. Horney found that all neuroses contained two factors: an illusion of omnipotence accompanied by an underlying sense of powerlessness; and a gap between real ability and actual achievement.

In the Kennedy sons, we can discern the outlines of these neurotic trends. All the Kennedys were raised within a childhood pattern centering on three negative dynamics: patriarchy, competition, and sexism. The first destructive dynamic was the overwhelming dominance of the father, who not only set neurotically perfectionistic goals in his offsprings' childhood, but also continued to assert his preeminence throughout their adult lives. In effect, the boys became what Dad wanted them to become. No amount of rhapsodizing over Kennedy successes can hide the fact that the chief life task of each son, especially the older sons, was to attain the peaks of social success, acceptability, and prominence that eluded the father.

That the chosen route was politics does not alter the central goal. I do not believe, as many have, that Joseph Kennedy wanted political power for his sons because he wished to shape the nation's destiny. He lacked the social imagination for such an ambition. Rather, the evidence shows that the founding father's ambition was far simpler and narrower: to achieve a mammoth triumph over the prejudiced WASPs who had so often snubbed and despised him as the son of an Irish ex-bartender. It also seems clear that while much of Joe Kennedy's hypersensitivity was socially justified, this reality was greatly exaggerated by his own emotional childhood rejection at the hands of an excessively demanding father. The Kennedy matriarch, Rose Kennedy, grew up in similar circumstances of acute sensitivity to the social limitations of an Irish-Catholic family in Protestant-dominated Boston and to aspersions on her Irish-politician father. Thus her social ambitions equaled her husband's. With his death, she has emerged on the American social and political scene as a force in herself, one that may yet compel the last son to seek the presidency.

The second neurotic attitude drilled into the children was the imperative of competitive success as the primary value in life. Although the Kennedy children were raised in a strict Roman Catholic household under the watchful eye of a devout and disciplinarian mother, there is no indication that the Christian catechism they learned ever interfered with the achievement of more worldly goals. The contradiction between unremitting competition and Christian ethics was reconciled by a fervent family conviction that the Kennedys deserved to win because they actually were superior to others.

The third area in which the Kennedy neurosis and the neurotic contradictions of American society as a whole converged was in what could be termed the Kennedys' "masculine mystique"—or, in contemporary language, the male chauvinism exhibited by all the Kennedys. Basically, this sexist mystique rested on the assumption that men are by nature superior to women. This assumption led to two primary patterns of attitude and behavior: (1) only the Kennedy sons were considered for political careers, despite the superior political talents of at least one daughter; and (2) all the Kennedy men were sexually promiscuous and tended to regard their wives as little more than attractive possessions and providers of "bed and board," giving emotional support when needed, bearing the full responsibility of raising offspring, and engaging in the political activity considered appropriate to a supportive wife. In essence, the Kennedy men, as prime examples of the virility-success cult so evident in American society, always put themselves first. The acceptance by the Kennedy women of passive, secondary, inferior roles only indicates the depth of their feminine socialization by religion and culture.

In support of this thesis, one can cite the well-known relationship of Joseph P. Kennedy with a film star; the extramarital sexual activities of John F. Kennedy, which apparently continued after his election to the presidency; and the sexual activities of the other brothers. The reactions of the Kennedy wives to their husbands' promiscuity have, of course, been largely concealed from public view. But gossipy memoirs of former Kennedy servants and retainers, and a few increasingly frank biographies, offer enough evidence to indicate the response of these dependent women— outer aloofness and a feigned ignorance, along with a good deal of repressed inner rage.

If irrational power is corrupting, the striving to attain such power is equally so. Joe Kennedy's extreme emphasis on competitive triumph— capsuled in such dictums as "Don't play unless you can be captain," and "Second place is failure"—was bound to create patterns of neurotic conflict and hostility in his driven children. For, as both humanists and psychologists have recognized, every human being must be free to develop his own potentialities. If forced to develop along lines arbitrarily set by others, the individual's growth will inevitably be stunted.

As Dr. Horney put it, "Only the individual himself can develop his

given potentialities. But, like any other living organism, the human in-
dividuum needs favorable conditions for his growth 'from acorn into oak
tree'; he needs an atmosphere of warmth to give him both a feeling of inner
security and the inner freedom enabling him to have his own feelings and
thoughts to express himself. He needs the good will of others, not only
to help him in his many needs but to guide and encourage him to become
a mature and fulfilled individual. He also needs healthy friction with the
wishes and wills of others. If he can thus grow *with* others, in love and in
friction, he will also grow in accordance with his real self."

The friction encountered within the Kennedy family was, more often
than not, far from healthy. While a superficial self-reliance was encouraged,
there was no genuine escape from the all-encompassing family. The purpose
of a family is to protect, nourish, and gently guide the child when he is
nearly helpless, and to support him emotionally and physically when he is
older. Firm limitations are necessary, but they should expand realistically
as the child grows. For the parents must also enable the child gradually to
outgrow the family and become a self-reliant, mature individual. No one in
the Kennedy clan has ever been allowed to outgrow the family. This means
that each one has been kept a child in some major aspects of his development. Such an immaturity was apparent not only in the identical life
directions accepted by the sons, but also in the continuing dependency of all
on the father's financial direction (including JFK when he was President of
the United States), even though the father had given them material independence.

True independence, however, must be emotional as well as material.
While the Kennedy sons could oppose their father on specific, limited
issues, it seems beyond doubt that Joseph Kennedy had early cast them in
emotional molds that continued to shape them all their adult years toward
narrowly constricted ends. Thus the basic anxiety caused by parental
dominance generated tensions in each son that gradually turned into
avenging furies. In Joe Junior, the furies led him to undertake a near-
suicidal mission that became truly suicidal. In Jack, they racked his body
with repeated pain and illness. In Bobby, they drove him in upon himself
in moody withdrawals and later outward in obsessive attacks on others.
In Teddy, they pushed him into reckless flying and driving and, perhaps,
off the bridge.

Camelot has often been used as a symbol for the Kennedys, but Franz
Kafka's Castle would be more appropriate. The Kennedy Camelot was
more an illusion of power than a reality, a dreamworld doomed to betrayal
from within. Kafka's story expresses the tragic powerlessness of a man out
of touch with reality and his own powers. As Fromm described it in *Escape
from Freedom*, "In his *Castle* he [Kafka] describes the man who wants to get

in touch with the mysterious inhabitants of a castle, who are supposed to tell him what to do and show him his place in the world. All his life consists in his frantic effort to get into touch with them, but he never succeeds and is left alone with a sense of utter futility and helplessness." The inhabitants, psychologically speaking, are the hero's own psychic resources, with which he can no longer communicate. Like Kafka's hero, the Kennedys, in pursuing the illusory Camelot of omnipotence, succeeded only in erecting a Castle that imprisoned their true selves.

The Kennedy epic could aptly be called *Profiles in Illusion*, after the title of Jack Kennedy's famous book, *Profiles in Courage*. The more they have sought acceptance and adulation from the crowd, the more has each Kennedy become mired in illusions of grandeur and separated from the truth about himself and others. The political life need not lead inevitably to such separation. But the political life—or any life—pursued so relentlessly and opportunistically can only result in inner defeat and loss, no matter how loud the cheers of a deceived populace. In such a transaction, the deceiver must also deceive himself, and so end by little knowing who he is or what he genuinely believes. The less he actually believes, the more passionately he must proclaim his "beliefs." Yet by their deeds and lack of deeds, the Kennedys repeatedly revealed the predominant hollowness of their protestations.

The Kennedys undeniably achieved enormous success and power, but so have countless other famous figures throughout history whom we now regard as neurotic or even psychotic. Success is no touchstone of emotional and moral strength and independence. By their proclaimed but illusory actions, the Kennedys impressed millions as the finest examples of imaginative, courageous, independent leaders. One of this book's primary contentions is that none of the Kennedy sons acted with true independence or originality, and that in them the humility of genuine strength was notable for its absence. Brilliant rhetoric (usually produced by hired minds) and the dazzling swirl of events largely obscured the basic patterns of their lives and careers. But, as I will trace, the three sons who achieved public office never transcended to any great degree the emotional straitjackets binding them to rigid responses and policies.

Although the Kennedy sons mastered the rhetoric of morality (despite Joseph Kennedy's open advice not to "play by the rules," a ruthless cynicism which would not win popular elections), their actions and nonactions constantly revealed the shallowness of their words. The gap between abilities and achievements, which many psychologists have found to be a persistent part of neurosis, was apparent in all the Kennedys. Once in office, the sons were largely unable to develop important creative ideas or to put their ideas into effect.

The Kennedys had the chance to achieve in their time and place what Erik Erikson calls "psychohistorical actuality"—an encounter between a great leader (such as Martin Luther or Gandhi) and his people that actualizes or releases fruitful new potentialities in both. America responded strongly to the Kennedy promise partly because that promise seemed to meet a deep national need. But the promise was illusory, and the need is still unmet. The Kennedys possessed the necessary intelligence, energy, and single-minded concentration. But the crucial moral vision—the essence of courage—was repeatedly shown to be missing. Their goal, being a neurotic self-gratification rather than a genuine self-fulfillment, kept them emotionally separated from the people they professed to lead.

The centuries-old relationship between psychology and political history has been noted by Dr. Arnold Rogow in *The Psychiatrists:* ". . . the effort to make psychiatry and psychoanalysis relevant to public affairs is not new. . . . Benjamin Rush, regarded as the father of American psychiatry, was as much a political activist as he was a physician, and since his time a number of leaders in psychiatry have stressed the connection between mental health and the social condition. . . . Many psychiatrists and analysts, however, while agreeing in principle that their professions must take an interest in the social and political context of mental health problems, nevertheless have difficulty specifying the exact content and form of such an interest. No doubt psychiatric illness in high office should be safeguarded against, but how, and by whom? Given the difficulties in diagnosing and prescribing for psychological problems, would anything be gained by having psychiatrists screen candidates for office, or, in accordance with one suggestion, by including a psychiatrist among the President's physicians?"

These are assuredly difficult questions, but the specialists have missed two important points. One is that persons who are trained and experienced in both psychological and socio-political fields may be able to make more relevant analyses of political persons and issues than specialists in either field. The second point is that the ordinary American citizen, when educated in the new concepts of a psychohistorical approach to public affairs, is capable of making more sensible and insightful assessments than many of those made by specialists. This comment is not meant to belittle the many deeply concerned social scientists who seek interdisciplinary rapprochement. It is an expression of faith in the innate ability of American citizens to evaluate political leaders intelligently and perceptively and so fulfill the democratic ideal. *The Kennedy Neurosis* is intended above all as a suggestion —one by no means approaching completeness—of the kinds of considerations we may use in the future when weighing our potential leaders.

A brief word on the development of psychohistory may prove useful. The roots of psychohistory go far back in time and are linked to the evolutionary development of philosophies and methods of historians and their increased understanding—often highly intuitive—of human psychology. In the strict sense, psychohistory as it is referred to today grew directly out of Freud's theories of psychoanalysis and his own pioneering efforts to link the interpretation of politics and history with the analysis of individual personality (notably in his studies of Leonardo da Vinci, Moses, and Woodrow Wilson). Unfortunately, Freud's strongly deterministic theories of personality and his unscientific philosophy of history were inadequate to the task. But in the 1920s and 1930s, pioneers in this developing field took inspiration and direction from Freud's example. Several notable writers were political scientist Harold Lasswell, who as early as 1930 published *The Psychopathology of Politics* and *World Politics and Personal Insecurity;* and Alexander and Juliette George, who in 1956 produced an illuminating psychoanalytic biography of President Wilson (clearly a fertile figure for exploration).

In more recent years, Erik H. Erikson has become the preeminent figure in the rapidly growing field of psychohistory (and indeed may have coined the term). Erikson's highly acclaimed interpretations of Martin Luther and Mohandas Gandhi gave psychohistory a newly reputable standing, and many have found his insights both provocative and stimulating (as was his earlier *Childhood and Society*). While I am indebted to Erikson for much stimulation, I find his theories less convincing than his insights, because I do not subscribe to his psychoanalytic basis. Erikson largely follows Freud's view of history, which is based on the repression of instinctive demons, and this considerably limits his understanding of human drives and potentials.

In concluding this introduction, an excerpt from historian William Willcox's study of British general Henry Clinton seems especially relevant to my analysis of the Kennedy sons. Clinton was the British commander-in-chief in America during much of the Revolutionary War. Wrote Professor Willcox, ". . . Clinton as an adult had a particularly intense craving for authority of his own, because at some deep level he was still trying to free himself from that of his parents. In the eyes of the world he succeeded, for at the peak of his career he had authority in full measure; and much of the time he used it with apparent self-assurance. But the assurance was precarious. Part of him insisted, at the same deep level, that he was a usurper guilty of intruding on the parental domain. The insistence was sometimes too faint to be perceptible, and then he could function effectively. At other times it was clamorous, as a result of pressures inside and outside himself; and then he was so torn between his craving and his guilt that he could not exercise the authority he had."

A major part of my theme is that the Kennedy demand for power grew out of neurotic competition far more than from genuine competence; that an obsessive-compulsive need for power and social recognition basically motivated the Kennedy triumphs; that this need arose from a profound sense of powerlessness and rejection in individual Kennedys and in the family as a whole; and that, therefore, the glorious promises, because of their largely neurotic origins, remained largely unfulfilled and unfulfillable.

The Kennedy story is an epic of personal and national illusion. Political dynasties have appeared before, at other places, in other ages, and they will undoubtedly appear again. But whereas families may be able to endure repeated tragedies, modern industrial societies may not. Science and technology have precipitated a situation where the risks of executive compulsions and illusions become potentially more dangerous every year. In short, it is imperative that we search out within ourselves and within our leaders the neurotic conflicts that could mean the difference between national survival and national extinction. What follows is written to contribute to this effort.

Chapter 2
GROWING UP COMPETITIVE: LIFE WITH FATHER

I don't think much of people who have it in them to be first, but who finish second. If you've got a second choice, then you haven't got a first choice.

The measure of a man's success is not the money he has made. It's the kind of family he has raised. In that, I've been mighty lucky.

Remember, if you can't be captain, don't play.

For the Kennedys, it's either the outhouse or the castle—no in-between.

—Joseph Patrick Kennedy

. . . the true virtue of human beings is fitness to live together as equals; claiming nothing for themselves but what they as freely concede to everyone else; regarding command of any kind as an exceptional necessity, and in all cases a temporary one; and preferring, whenever possible, the society of those with whom leading and following can be alternate and reciprocal. . . . What is needed is, that it [the family] should be a school of sympathy in equality, of living together in love, without power on one side or obedience on the other.

—John Stuart Mill, *The Subjection of Women*

The founding father of the Kennedy clan is clearly one of the most remarkable men of our times, although hardly a lovable one. . . . Until Franklin Roosevelt appointed him chairman of the Securities & Exchange Commission and then Ambassador to the Court of St. James, Kennedy's career was characterized by a succession of those brilliant strokes of the dedicated moneyman that inspire not only our admiration but also our fervent thanks

20

that we are not as they. The grave robber may be loved by his
wife and children but he does not have a large circle of admirers,
and financial grave-robbing was the field in which Kennedy's
particular genius lay. . . .

—Kenneth Lamott, *The Moneymakers*

ꑇ

IT IS A general psychological principle that neurotic individuals had neurotic parents, just as basically healthy and mature adults very probably
had basically mature and accepting parents (or else, in relatively rare
instances, were able to outgrow their crippling childhoods). The parental
attitudes that largely shape one's childhood are a decisive factor in favoring
or thwarting a person's growth from dependency to maturity and self-
respect. Thus before examining the Kennedy children, we must take a
closer look at the Kennedy parents and their origins if we are to understand
the historical basis of the general emotional difficulties I have, somewhat
symbolically, termed the "Kennedy neurosis."

The dominant Kennedy goal guiding the founding father, Joseph Patrick
Kennedy, has been stated with unmistakable emphasis and clarity by both
Kennedy and his biographers. In essence, the principle can be summed up
in a word: Win. At all costs. As Joe Kennedy himself said again and again,
the only important thing was victory. The only real victory was first place.
In Kennedy's philosophy, as his life history revealed, other qualities, such
as honesty, moral principle, generosity, fair play, and sportsmanship,
were not only expendable but actually undesirable if they interfered with
winning.

It is not difficult to see the Hobbesian-Darwinian core of such a belief
(life is a jungle, sharp of tooth and red of claw) or the essential pessimism
of so cynical a view of life. We must, however, recall that this outlook was
the prevalent nineteenth-century philosophy of the survival of the fittest.
Joe Kennedy's particular genius lay in the ability to adapt this crude world
view to changing social currents and technologies without ever losing his
deep belief in the need for and inevitability of Kennedy triumph. His view
of human nature was fundamentally negative, but his view of Kennedy
ability was extraordinarily optimistic. The Kennedys, the founding father
felt, could do anything. These grand illusions, neurotic in origin and
development, would result in both huge successes and huge disappointments for Joseph Kennedy and his sons.

Joseph Patrick's passion was to attain enormous wealth, power, and
social recognition—an intensified version of his father's life tenets, according
to Kennedy biographers and the evidence of the Kennedys' lives and at-

titudes. Patrick Joseph Kennedy ("P.J."), the father of Joseph and son of the original Kennedy immigrant, believed that winning meant coming in first and that the man who came in second was a loser. The development of this philosophy is further traceable to P.J.'s experience as a self-made success. His father, Patrick Kennedy, had emigrated from Ireland during the terrible potato famine of 1848 and had arrived penniless at Boston in an age when America was as much a land of rejection as a land of opportunity for many of its immigrant minorities. The Irish suffered more than many, being despised by the earlier Americans for their ignorance, superstition, and Catholicism. Young Patrick Kennedy, however, was enterprising. Finding work as a barrel-maker, he managed to earn enough to marry Bridget Murphy and father three daughters (Mary, Margaret, and Johanna) and, on January 8, 1858, a son, the future grandfather of a United States President. Less than a year later, at the age of thirty-five, the unfortunate Patrick died of cholera, leaving his widow with no money, three young daughters, and an infant son.

Bridget Murphy Kennedy was a determined and tough-fibered woman. Working hard in a notions shop and then as a hairdresser at Jordan Marsh, she held the family together. Young P.J., raised by his sisters while his mother worked, attended a neighborhood Catholic school run by the Sisters of Notre Dame. Afternoons and Saturdays, he aided his mother at the store. Then, in his early teens, he quit school to work as a stevedore to help support the family.

P.J. was different from the other hard-drinking, brawling laborers around him. He had formed a determination to rise above a life of remorseless drudgery. Boston at that time offered few opportunities for the oppressed Irish, but P.J. found a chance to escape the social trap. With carefully hoarded savings, he bought a saloon and gradually built it into a flourishing business. P.J.'s temperament and training suited him to his new occupation. Reserved and soft-spoken, but as muscular and tough as any of his former co-workers, P.J. could keep order in the saloon and yet maintain a friendly atmosphere that attracted customers and kept the police away.

As the years went by, P.J.'s interests expanded into other saloons, wholesale whiskey, coal-dealing, and—the central topic of Irish gossip—politics. With his elegantly curled moustache and dignified air, the blue-eyed and fair-skinned P.J. commanded respect. Soon he was running East Boston as a miniature welfare state after the old-time political formula by providing local residents with food, clothing, and shelter. Life for the Boston Irish in the late 1800s was barely above the subsistence level. Most Irish workers were only a few weeks away from starvation and even the smallest help—a bucket of coal, a small loan, a round of drinks—won gratitude and votes from families, relatives, and friends. In a short time, the canny P.J. acquired a large and loyal following that elected him to the Massachusetts House of Representatives at age twenty-eight, in 1886, and to the state Senate six years later.

But P.J. disliked campaigning and holding office. What he relished was power—the knowledge that he could grant public office to others or withhold it from them. Like his son and grandsons, he was primarily concerned with power for power's sake. What the holder of power could achieve for other people and his society seemed of little genuine concern to him. Thus it was P.J.'s knowledge of how to acquire power, not how to use it, that was passed along to his only son, Joseph Patrick. As veteran Boston political reporter Joseph Dinneen viewed the dominant Kennedy ethos, "Three generations of Kennedys have lived according to a tradition established by Patrick Joseph Kennedy. . . . As he saw it there was room for only one at the top. A contender who placed second was a loser." Joseph Patrick Kennedy, an only son in a family that lived by a credo of obsessive-compulsive perfectionism and unremitting efforts to rise in society, not only followed but expanded upon his father's dictates.

P.J.'s accomplishments were in many ways remarkable. By his intelligence and drive he had raised himself out of poverty to affluence and a dominant position in Boston politics and Irish-Catholic society. His son attended the *ne plus ultra* of the Protestant Brahmins, Harvard University, married the daughter of the mayor of Boston, fathered an American President, and became Ambassador to the Court of St. James's. Despite the immense barriers of initial poverty and continuing prejudice—and also partly because of them—the Kennedys in three generations leaped from the bottom of the immigrant class to the pinnacle of national power, wealth, and prestige.

Yet such a leap exacted a high price. It may seem contradictory to see neurosis (emotional conflicts and immaturities) in such an enormously successful family; but, indeed, it is among life's most paradoxical ironies that neurosis may actually bring great material success (this is not, of course, to rule out the successes of healthier drives). Thus a single-minded devotion to the acquisition of wealth and power that excludes other human goals may result in their attainment, but at the cost of profound failures in other areas of life.

Joseph Patrick Kennedy—the so-called founding father—was born on September 6, 1888, when his father was already East Boston's ward boss and a state representative. Like P.J., Joseph Patrick was the sole son in a family of girls (two), his only brother having died in infancy. P.J. ran his family on the common patriarchal model of that Victorian era. "A severe look from him was sufficient to quiet the children and enforce his absolute authority in the household," wrote one biographer. The male head of the family could do no wrong; his word and his actions were beyond question. His wife and children existed primarily to obey and serve him. Such a system, as we now know, often results in outer conformity and family unity, but great inner emotional distress for the repressed individuals.

The neurotically destructive effect of domestic inequality on both parents and children has been pointed out by Ronald V. Sampson in *The Psychology of Power:* ". . . this egocentric assumption that the male is more important than those who are dependent upon him is self-perpetuating. The male child in the family subject to the *patria potestas* feels the brunt in his own person, but he is quick to detect that his subjection is temporary only. For one day he too will become eligible to join this privileged class of male adults. The seeds of superiority consciousness and consequent corruption are thus sown very early in the mind of the male child. Since his entire culture is saturated in assumptions of male superiority, he is permeated with its implications from his earliest days." I will trace the corroding effect of this sexual inequality in various Kennedy marriages.

The Kennedys followed the main chance in their marriages as well as in their careers. Young Joe's mother, the former Mary Hickey, came from a Boston family of higher social elevation than his father's, a pattern that all the dominant Kennedy males would repeat with their wives (both Joe and his son John Fitzgerald married socially above themselves). Mary Kennedy, like her husband, was a strong-minded individual who oversaw the children's general discipline and upbringing according to the general American-Catholic principles of the day.

Both parents were ambitious for their only son and pleased by early demonstrations of his lifelong zeal for making money (such as hawking candy on sightseeing boats and selling captured city pigeons). The boy's political education also began young, as he made electioneering rounds with his father and witnessed the political supplicants who besieged the Kennedy household. Although P.J. had an unusual reputation for being personally above the flagrant corruption of Boston politics, his lieutenants were adept in the usual tricks of the trade. Joe remembered ward heelers reporting to his pleased father. "Pat," boasted one proud pair, "we voted one hundred and twenty-eight times today." It was a practical but hardly an ethical education.

Young Joseph Kennedy, after attending Catholic primary schools, was enrolled by his ambitious father in the famous Boston Latin School, "where the boy knew he was expected to compete hard for a place in the society that had been closed to his father," in the words of one biographer. We can see the familiar pattern of a parent projecting his own thwarted ambitions onto his son, a pattern that Joe Kennedy repeated with his own children.

Young Joe's unconscious rebellion against his parents took the form of neglecting his studies, also a common reaction in all generations. He flunked one year, but his parents made him stay in school rather than letting him drop out and get a job.

In other respects, however, Joe was a great success at the school. He became colonel of the cadet regiment, senior class president, and a baseball star. But in the sports he loved, the tall, redheaded Kennedy exhibited poor sportsmanship. A contemporary recalled, "The first time I saw Joe was in 1907, when he was playing first base for Boston Latin against Salem High on the Bridge Street grounds in Salem. Boston Latin was losing and the game was almost spoiled by Joe's constant bickering with the umpire. I can still see him, glaring at the umpire and slamming his fist in his glove." When a person's feeling of self-worth depends on winning, losing becomes unbearable and inadmissible.

From Boston Latin Joe went on to Harvard, at that time an unusual step for an Irish Catholic. But Pat Kennedy was to wrest every Yankee-Protestant advantage he could afford for his son. Joe Kennedy would later follow this same social-educational pattern for his own four sons. Fortunately, Joe had a flair for making friends as well as enemies. His exuberance, ready wit, and interest in sports were attractive qualities. Kennedy determinedly cultivated Harvard's socially elite and relaxed with students of a similar Irish background. Throughout his life he would work hard to pry open socially sacred portals, and be bitterly hurt when he failed. At Harvard, Joe received passable grades, but his obsession with success never extended to his academic career. This was very likely an unconscious way of getting back to some extent at an excessively demanding father.

While Joe Kennedy made many friends at Harvard, he also stirred up resentments by his determination to win at all costs. Although he was too slow to make the varsity baseball team, the captain put him into the final 1911 Harvard-Yale game, thus assuring Kennedy's letter in his junior year. When the game ended with his put-out of a man at first base, Kennedy refused to give the winning ball to the team captain. The Harvard captain later told another player that a few days before the game, some of P.J.'s friends had threatened to refuse him a movie theater license after graduation unless Joe received his letter. Young Joe may well have known of his father's action, or even requested it. According to this player, "Joe was the kind of guy who, if he wanted something bad enough, would get it, and he didn't care how he got it. He'd run right over anybody." This opinion would later be echoed by many former Kennedy business associates and clients. Twenty-six years later, Joe Kennedy would try to pressure a Harvard coach into putting his own son, Joe Junior, into a Harvard-Yale game for his letter. This time the technique backfired, and the furious coach refused.

P.J.'s political influence continued to be an important force in launching his son's career, although Joe often decided how best to use it. When Joe was an undergraduate, P.J. helped his son and a friend obtain part of a sightseeing bus franchise in Boston. After Harvard, young Kennedy secured an appointment as a state bank examiner, permitting him an invaluable self-education in the finances of Massachusetts banks. Because of his inside knowledge, Joe saved his father's bank from being taken over by other interests, and at twenty-five he became the state's (and perhaps the country's) youngest bank president.

Joe also became the husband of the oldest daughter of Boston's mayor. Rose Fitzgerald and Joe Kennedy had known each other for years, and the attraction had been mutual. Rose's father was Boston's famous John F. ("Honey Fitz") Fitzgerald, a frequent political ally of Pat Kennedy, although the two men were not personally close. Honey Fitz was P.J.'s temperamental opposite, an extroverted politician who loved to sing "Sweet Adeline" from tabletops, make speeches, and court publicity. When Joe wooed Rose, Honey Fitz had reached the zenith of his career, and he regarded young Kennedy as something of an upstart. But the bank presidency apparently helped change his mind, and Rose was both determined and her father's favorite. On October 7, 1914, Joe and Rose were married by Cardinal O'Connell of Boston.

Soon the children began to arrive, starting with Joseph Patrick Kennedy, Jr., on July 25, 1915. John Fitzgerald was born on May 29, 1917; Rosemary on September 13, 1918; Kathleen on February 20, 1920; Eunice on July 10, 1921; Patricia on May 6, 1924; Robert Francis on November 20, 1925; Jean on February 20, 1928; and Edward Moore on February 22, 1932.

While his family grew rapidly, the ambitious young father was quickly learning the inside ways of business, banking, and the stock market. During the war boom from 1917 to 1919, Joe Kennedy was assistant manager of a shipbuilding yard owned by Bethlehem Steel in Quincy, Massachusetts. When the 1918 Armistice ended the World War I shipbuilding program, he became Boston manager of a prominent investment banking firm. From 1919 to 1922, he worked for Hayden, Stone and Company, gaining an astute knowledge of investments and making valuable financial contacts. When Stone retired at the end of 1922, Kennedy struck out on his own. At thirty-four, he began to show the characteristics that would mark his business ventures throughout his life.

Joe Kennedy was essentially a lone operator with few trusted employees. He had strong nerves, a coolly calculating mind, a highly developed sense of timing for market and business fluctuations, and a cold-blooded acceptance of deceptive and ruthless manipulations. Although he remained basically aloof and emotionally withdrawn from most people, Kennedy nevertheless made friends easily when he wanted to. Unlike his father, who never used profanity, Joe sprinkled his conversation freely with pungent phrases, a likely assertion of his deep need to feel "manly."

In the next fifteen years, Joe Kennedy amassed a personal fortune, and Boston became too small an arena for his monetary and social ambitions. Realizing that he could never crack the social snobbery of the New England aristocracy no matter how brilliant his business successes, he packed the family aboard a private railroad car in 1926 and moved to New York, where an Irish *nouveau riche* family might be more acceptable. Perhaps, too, he wished to succeed on his own away from his father's native city.

Wall Street proved a congenial hunting ground for Joe Kennedy's predatory talents. In largely secret wheelings and dealings in the 1920s, Kennedy moved stocks up and down to change their values artificially so that he and his cronies could sell at enormous profits, leaving the duped investors holding the bag. This unscrupulous maneuver, at which Joe Kennedy was a master, was a favorite in that unregulated period, when thousands of naive buyers were persuaded to part with their life savings. Kennedy's ingrown pessimism saved his growing fortune when he sensed that the bubble would soon burst. Weeks before the 1929 Crash, he quietly sold himself out of the market. Thus in the 1930s, Kennedy had the cash, the contacts, and the experience to exploit new opportunities.

Hollywood's boom of the twenties also provided a lucrative outlet for Joe Kennedy's speculative talents and great organizational abilities. In Hollywood, Kennedy—who had bought a New England theater chain— quickly learned the secret of profitable film production: grind out cheap popular westerns and let other producers throw their money away on extravaganzas and experimental movies. But Kennedy did have the technological, if not the artistic or social, imagination to bring together film and sound developments in profitable mergers. He also dabbled intermittently in real estate, a field that would become a major source of profits in the 1940s and 1950s.

No business interested Kennedy for long, for he lacked the emotional steadiness to commit himself to any activity other than making money and pushing his family onward and upward. The end of Prohibition in 1933 brought a third great opportunity to the multimillionaire ex-saloonkeeper's son. By energetically supporting FDR in 1932, he had become a close friend of FDR's son James. In September, 1933, with the repeal of Prohibition imminent, he and Jimmy Roosevelt sailed to England, where Kennedy obtained import franchises from leading distillers. Many observers attributed Kennedy's huge coup to his influential companion. In addition, Kennedy's firms obtained immediate government "medicinal" whiskey import licenses so that Kennedy warehouses were well stocked when

Prohibition officially ended. Rumors spread that young Roosevelt had expected to receive part of the import firm, but that Kennedy had talked him out of it on the basis of his father's reputation. Joe later hotly denied using Jimmy's influence; the Roosevelts kept silent. Kennedy retained his liquor interests until 1946, when Jack ran for the U.S. Congress. Then he sold the business that had cost him an initial $100,000 for a reported $8 million.

A sidelight on this profitable transaction reveals Joe Kennedy's typical lack of generosity toward his employees. For decades, two men had built and loyally run Kennedy's liquor firm; when Joe sold out, he rewarded them with payments estimated at $25,000 to $37,500. All the Kennedys, as friends and journalists have noted, have reputations for being very tight-fisted with their employees and small creditors, but careless and often arrogant in their own claims on the purses of others. On the other hand, from time to time, Kennedy would secretly help out acquaintances, friends, and charities.

Psychologically, this apparent contradiction is understandable. Kennedy's insecurity seems much like that of many insecure persons who deeply resent what they feel are unreasonable "demands," even construing the legitimate claims of employees as such. On the other hand, Kennedy's occasional philanthropic gestures served to boost his weak ego and faltering sense of personal power. He may also, of course, have exhibited real generosity at times. But his insecurity and self-doubt kept him frequently out of touch with the humanity of people. It is the over-all pattern, not the exceptions, that reveal a person's general emotional makeup. In the case of Joseph Kennedy, that pattern was clearly self-protecting rather than self-giving.

In a general consideration of Joseph Kennedy's career as a businessman in his middle years—from 1910 to the mid-1930s—there can be no question of his administrative skill, practical intelligence, and capacity for work. What is disturbing to the social historian is the lack of ethical concern that he repeatedly demonstrated in his activities. His measure of achievement was always the self: What would he and his family get out of it? There was no evidence of regard for the effect of his actions on other people. While his extraordinary drive for material gain and his personal abilities eventually made him wealthy, his personal relationships were often stormy and his social vision remained narrow. In short, Joe Kennedy became a success, but at the price of attracting widespread hate and mistrust. In time, though, his reputation would mellow and fade sufficiently for a younger generation to accept his sons as national leaders.

It is also significant that the Kennedy fortune was based primarily on the gratification of human illusions and the unhealthy appetites of greed, sensationalism, and sense-dulling, rather than on the providing of socially useful goods and services. Kennedy developed his pre–World War II wealth from three main sources: the manipulation of stocks, the making of low-grade films, and the importation of liquor. As we consider the relevance and contribution of the Kennedys in the broadest social contexts, we come more and more to realize that they were among the greatest dream manufacturers of the twentieth century, and their native ability to fashion dream products satisfied the shifting American dream markets. Thus, after dealing in Wall Street (get-rich-quick) and Hollywood (romance-adventure) during the 1920s, Joe Kennedy moved to fulfill the alcoholic desires and fantasies of the 1930s, when Prohibition ended and many Americans thirsted to escape the disillusionment of the Great Depression.

Joe Kennedy's early backing of FDR, whom he had met when Roosevelt was Assistant Secretary of the Navy and Joe was working for Bethlehem's shipbuilding yard in Quincy, was one of the shrewdest moves of his entire career. Curiously enough, Kennedy's support was probably more the result of an emotional need for a personal savior than a calculated political judgment. Behind Kennedy's front of enormous self-confidence, he often revealed deep insecurities. One was his obsessive anxiety about money, an anxiety that led him to concentrate his whole life on amassing a fabulous fortune by almost any means available—within the generous latitude of the law. When Wall Street toppled in 1929, Joe suffered an attack of extreme anxiety that severely shook his already none-too-firm expectations of social and personal survival. As he later wrote, "I am not ashamed to record that in those days I felt and said I would be willing to part with half of what I had if I could be sure of keeping, under law and order, the other half. Then it seemed that I should be able to hold nothing for the protection of my family."

Kennedy turned to FDR as the strong leader with new ideas who could save the country and Kennedy personally. Roosevelt might well have been a father surrogate for Kennedy, the powerful parental figure who could quell the deep-seated fears that the Crash had brought to his semi-consciousness. Certainly it was not Roosevelt's liberalism that attracted Kennedy, for the speculator-turned-New-Dealer remained a social conservative whose conservatism increased with his years. As Richard Whalen analyzed Kennedy, "He had no political philosophy to speak of; his Democratic allegiance stemmed more from heredity than conviction. His father's professionalism, if anything, had helped drain politics of idealism, reducing it to an exciting but essentially cynical business in which office and advantage were all that mattered. As to the organization of society, the role of the individual and the place of the government, Kennedy's views were shapeless, little different from the shallow conservatism common to rich men."

The tremendous doubt and fear of life that seemed to be deeply buried

and disguised in Joseph Kennedy came to the surface on one other important occasion. This second time, Kennedy's unconscious drives caused his
downfall instead of pushing him in a fortunate direction. As U.S. Ambassador to Great Britain, he aroused widespread dismay on both sides of the
Atlantic by his blindness to the growing aggressions of Nazi Germany and
by his parallel inability to see the determination of the British people.
Kennedy's own Irish origins may have had something to do with his dis-
paraging of British strengths, although consciously he greatly enjoyed the
English people, a liking initially reciprocated. The approach of World War
II, however, seemed to bring out Kennedy's innermost dreads and insecur-
ities, and he strongly supported the Chamberlain government's policy of
appeasing Hitler in the futile hope of staving off war, a hope not shared by
President Roosevelt.

To add to the growing distrust between Kennedy and Roosevelt, in 1940
the Ambassador was mentioned in the press as a possible contender for the
Democratic presidential nomination. For a short time, Kennedy harbored
the idea that he might actually compete with Roosevelt. But FDR was too
strong, and Joe Kennedy was too contentious and controversial. As a former
stock manipulator with a shadowy reputation, and as a peppery, undiplo-
matic ambassador who had offended British sensibilities and alienated
many Americans by his international conservatism, Kennedy stood no real
chance with either the party politicians or the general electorate. Though
his presidential hopes were short-lived, he undoubtedly felt a keen disappointment that he was not even seriously considered for the office.
Joseph Kennedy's own thwarted presidential ambitions seem unquestionably to have been an element in the later development of obsessive political
ambitions for his sons.

The final rupture between Kennedy and FDR was occasioned by a press
interview in the fall of 1940 that Kennedy thought was off-the-record. In
what may well have been a gesture of unconscious retaliation against a
parental authority figure (FDR), a gesture also containing elements of
self-punishment, Kennedy freely voiced his outspokenly negative opinions
on England, United States policy, and even Mrs. Roosevelt. When the
interview was published, Kennedy's diplomatic usefulness was ended.
Although he was ready to leave the ambassadorship, which had been long
and increasingly frustrating, he must have suffered from the humiliating
manner of his abrupt dismissal. And while he continued to support FDR
and offered his services after Pearl Harbor, the President no longer had a
place for Joe Kennedy in his Administration.

Meanwhile Kennedy's children were growing up and venturing forth
into the world as young adults. The two oldest boys joined the U.S. Navy—

Joe Junior as a pilot flying patrols over the English Channel, and Jack as a PT boat skipper in the South Pacific. The oldest daughter, Rosemary, was congenitally retarded and finally was committed to a special home. But the next girl, Kathleen, soon followed her oldest brother to London as an American Red Cross worker. The five younger children—Eunice, Pat, Bobby, Jean and Teddy—were too young to participate in the war effort.

Joe had relentlessly trained his children after the precepts he had inherited: "Win at all costs" and "Second place is losing." Summers at the family home in Hyannis Port on Cape Cod's southern coast had been extremely active periods of both delight and pain for the Kennedy offspring. All the children (except for retarded Rosemary) were high-spirited and physically healthy, and took part in the arduous sailing, swimming, and tennis competitions that their father set for them. Joe Kennedy was a stern taskmaster, even trailing his children's sailboats in his power launch to note their mistakes. Those who erred and lost races were sharply scolded and sometimes sent in disgrace to eat dinner in the kitchen. Joe Junior and Eunice were daring and adroit sailors and Jack and Kathleen had to work hard to earn a claim to the family honor. Soon the Kennedy clan was well known for its many victories in local sailing contests.

While Cape Cod offered an ideal outdoor setting for the Kennedys' physical exuberance, the family also came up against some of the old social suspiciousness they had met so often elsewhere. Many Cape Codders, both year-rounders and summer residents, resented the Kennedys' brashness and their rapid and somewhat questionable rise to wealth and position. Part of this resentment undoubtedly came from native prejudices against newcomers; part probably grew out of the Kennedys' own immoderate self-assertiveness. The Kennedys, in turn, having been often snubbed, were ultrasensitive to real or imagined social rejection. Joe and Rose could vividly recall their own youthful ostracism from Boston's upper circles and, after marriage, such wounds as being kept out of the snobbish Cohasset Country Club. For the proud and insecure Kennedys, such slights were never forgotten, and in all probability played a large part in the intensity of family loyalties and aspirations.

Joe himself was always extremely sensitive to criticism and social disappointments. An indelible slight was Kennedy's failure to be elected to Harvard's Board of Overseers in 1928. Classmates pointed out that the voters were mainly older alumni whereas Kennedy was a comparatively recent graduate (1912), but the thin-skinned Irishman could see the election only as an example of Yankee prejudice. Kennedy was also hurt by Harvard's failure to award him an honorary degree after his ambassadorship. He never forgot these oversights, and refused to donate money to

Harvard Medical School and other college programs. As the patriarch once admitted to a thick-hided politician, "I can't take criticism; I don't see how you can."

Although he possessed considerable personal charm, Kennedy was not always able or willing to use it, and certainly he often acted callously toward others in both business and personal relationships. At Hyannis Port, according to one Cape Cod historian, Joe was considered "stand-offish and abrupt at the golf club, where he played his game and left without usual locker-room camaraderie with other members. . . ." For Joe and Rose, the production of their own large family may well have been an unconscious defense against further rejection. At least, the Kennedys must often have felt, they always had each other in the face of a frequently hostile world.

Thus in Hyannis Port, when the Kennedys' strong competitiveness and obvious need to win caused some reaction among other residents who found them too "pushy," the family tended to turn inward toward each other for protectiveness and companionship. The children did have many friends, but as one childhood playmate recalled, "No matter what anyone else had done, the Kennedy children always praised each other's accomplishments to the skies. While it was amusing and touching for a time, it got to be rather tiresome after a while." The Kennedys, however, while somewhat ingrown, were also gregarious and not "snotty and stuck on themselves like a lot of other rich summer kids," according to some Cape Codders. On the other hand, others felt like "sparring partners" and "just somebody for the Kennedys to play against." The Kennedys' graceless losing of races also clouded their reputation, as did the discovery that Joe Junior once used an oversized sail in a race. As many witnesses saw it, there would "be hell to pay if they didn't win every race."

Joe Kennedy brought his boys up not only to be winners and tough, but also to be assured men of the world. The senior Kennedy became fairly notorious as a successful womanizer, especially after his connection with Hollywood queen Gloria Swanson. Among the social elite word spread that Kennedy had taken Miss Swanson and subsequently other glamorous women to house parties without his wife. Among many American upper-crust sophisticates, he was often gossiped about as an upstart who simply did not know the proper rules of behavior: although a gentleman might have discreet liaisons, he never appeared for weekends with a person other than his spouse. Miss Swanson visited once at Hyannis Port and even accompanied the Kennedys on a trip to Europe. After that, rumor had it that Rose Kennedy put her foot down.

Whatever the truth or malicious dishonesty in the stories of the wandering Kennedy eye that continue to go the rounds, the general Kennedy attitude of masculine dominance and virility seems quite evident from the family history. Even so devoted a Kennedy worshiper as Pearl Buck took a cool view of the men's sexual shenanigans, commenting in *The Kennedy Women*, "Rose Kennedy showed for years a steadfast loyalty to her husband while he continued a long relationship with a beautiful film actress. Outwardly, she maintained a proud silence. But the inner struggle must have left its mark upon the children. . . . The Kennedy men were never celebrated for faithfulness to their wives, but their wives found it worthwhile to continue as wives and mothers."

By both example and precept, the founding father introduced his boys to the customs of male prerogatives. At Cape Cod, the Kennedys hired a series of "skippers" to manage the various boats as the children were growing up. One of these, a hard-drinking, hard-swearing young Norwegian, apparently gave the Kennedy boys a worldly view of life. The boys must have been apt learners, for in the mid-1930s Joe Junior and Jack spent a night in the cramped Edgartown jail after an overly boisterous celebration in an Edgartown hotel of their regatta victory. Decades later, a Kennedy grandson, Joseph P. Kennedy III (Bobby's oldest son), would also arouse the Edgartown police by his rowdiness. Soon afterwards, the tragedy at Chappaquiddick on July 29, 1969, put Edgartown on the world map.

Kennedy sexism is a subject that has been largely ignored by most writers, but no psychohistorian can bypass it. The mystique of masculine sexual conquest seems to be an integral part of the Hemingwayesque Kennedy ethos as practiced by Joseph Kennedy and his sons. This belief says, in effect, that to be tough guy, one must also be a ruler of women and a possessor of many women. It is part of the overvaluation of the masculine role known as *machismo*, which produces feelings of aggression (both sexual and physical) and often militarism. Politics necessitated the playing-down of the Kennedy males' private Don Juanism, but Chappaquiddick brought the reality to national attention. Since then, the Kennedy escapades have been more freely mentioned both in conversation and in print. In 1971, an adulatory women's magazine article on Rose Kennedy even mentioned that FDR had told Joseph Kennedy to stop seeing a certain woman; Kennedy reportedly retorted that Roosevelt would first have to get rid of his secretary, Missy Lehand.

On the psychological level, Joe Kennedy's promiscuity could have served the emotional neurotic needs similarly involved in his pursuit of wealth and power. His extramarital activities may have been a means of relieving anxieties, channeling hostilities, expressing unacceptable longings, keeping safe distances while seeking human relationships, and even punishing the despised self. It is not hard to see his sexual pursuits as part of an over-all need for triumph, power, conquest, self-vindication, and even a deeply repressed desire to punish his parents. In addition, there is the special obsession with sex produced by both Victorianism and the Catholic Church and their double sexual standard for men and women—the convention of public virtue within the marriage vows and private permissiveness for the males. A man such as Joseph Kennedy, who broke unspoken ethical rules in other areas of his life and who was under enormous psychic pressures from his parents, would be likely to turn to sexual affairs as an outlet for his repressed needs. Manliness has been an essential ingredient of the Kennedy life style, but the Kennedy definition of manliness has not often included compassion, empathy, gentleness, and humility. Even Bobby Kennedy, who is often held up as the most sensitive Kennedy male, derided other men of whom he disapproved as "womanly." For a man to be deemed like a woman, in the Kennedy lexicon, was a term of profound contempt.

Joe Kennedy wanted his four sons to mirror himself, and in this he was not disappointed. The oldest, Joe Junior, patterned himself after his father in every way, and even outshone his father academically and athletically. Thus it seemed natural to the harassed parents—one busy making a fortune, the other burdened with many children—to set up the younger Joe as a model for the other children to follow and give him the task of disciplining the younger brothers and sisters. While superficially logical, this is not a wise idea; for it raises a sibling rival into a preeminence difficult to challenge and fixes in the other children the firm idea of their own inferiority. Each child is an individual and should be treated as such. But the Kennedys were victims of their own parents, their social ethos, and their own particular compensatory mystique. So Joe Junior was raised to be President of the United States, an idea he found more and more attractive and one that gradually turned into a family heirloom to be passed along automatically, like a priceless treasure, to the eldest male.

Then, in 1944, Joe Senior suffered the most staggering blow of his life, the loss of his oldest son. In August of that year, word came from England that young Joe had been killed on a dangerous mission. The son he had molded in his own image and on whom he had lavished the greatest care was dead. The news was like a sword thrust deep into Joseph Kennedy's heart, an agony from which he never fully recovered. Years later, even the mention of young Joe could cause Kennedy to burst into long, racking sobs. A second terrible blow followed in 1948, when Kennedy's favorite daughter, Kathleen, was killed in a plane crash. But if there was great need, there was also great courage and an ability to endure suffering. The father absorbed his grief, turned his face to the future, and kept going.

During the war years, the Midas-touched multimillionaire never stopped adding to his enormous fortune. Real estate captured his sporadic interest in the early postwar years. In New York, he bought land and buildings for low down payments and sold them at huge profits. The hard side of his character emerged again in these business dealings. When tenants complained to the city's welfare committee of sudden steep rent hikes, New York City responded by setting twenty-year controls on commercial rents, and Kennedy sold out and moved on. According to Kenneth Lamott, Kennedy's real estate profits, "the larger part of the Kennedy fortune," resulted from the Ambassador's pessimistic miscalculation that the war would be followed by a financial crash. "With the thought of cutting his losses he went into real estate, trading Manhattan properties to great profit. The war, however, was followed not by a crash but by general prosperity, and Kennedy, even though he had bet on the wrong horse, was turned into a winner in spite of himself." The founding father's biggest acquisition was the 1945 purchase of Chicago's gigantic Merchandise Mart, the world's largest commercial building. Kennedy bought the Mart for almost $13 million ($12.5 million of which was borrowed from an insurance company), and over two decades it rose in value to $75 million, with rentals alone soaring to $13 million annually (Lamott figures of 1969). The Chicago Mart remains a keystone of the Kennedy fortune.

While the 1940s were personally tragic, although materially profitable, the 1950s became increasingly triumphant for Joe Kennedy's self-glorification and illusions of omnipotence. In 1946, he forced his oldest surviving son, Jack, who was still weak from wartime injuries, to run for the U.S. House of Representatives from Massachusetts. The expertly directed campaign was entirely the father's operation. Although the family pitched in wholeheartedly, as they had been trained to do, it was the ex-Ambassador who devised the strategy, handled the money, picked the key workers, and spent hundreds of hours phoning influential friends, politicians, and editors. Kennedy approached politics with the administrative skill of a highly successful businessman, and this was the key to his repeated victories, a knowledge he passed on to his sons. Besides brains and experience, he brought great wealth to bear on each election. The pattern was set in the 1946 campaign, which included what has been described as "the most elaborate professional advertising effort ever seen in a Massachusetts congressional election."

In retrospect, we can sense the immense impatience of Joseph Kennedy, a man who had been kept out of wartime service by his own indiscretions, who had lost his favorite son, and who intensely needed a fresh triumph to assuage his seared spirits. Joe's exploitation of Jack has been generally forgotten in the triumphant transformation of the reluctant politician into an eager young statesman. On the positive side, Kennedy Senior gave his sons opportunity to enter the national arena of politics and power. But on the negative side, as this book will try to demonstrate, the father quite callously, and without the slightest indication that he understood what he was doing, destroyed the selves these young men might have developed. Very possibly they would have been far more worthwhile and mature individuals who would have known the satisfactions of living their own lives. The parent did not help the boys grow in fruitful directions of their personal choosing; rather, he forced them into the confines of his own frustrated desires. If the sons gradually internalized the father's desires so that they seemed to be their own, this does not change the basic pattern of dominance-rejection (as opposed to the far healthier assistance-acceptance). Internalization simply closed the trap.

In 1946, Jack scored a thumping victory, to no one's great surprise. At fifty-eight, Joe Kennedy finally had a son in a nationally elective office. The sweet taste of victory and his own advancing age made the patriarch increasingly restless. Six years later, in 1952, he urged Jack to run for the Senate against the famous incumbent, Republican Henry Cabot Lodge, with the words, "When you've beaten him, you've beaten the best." While the outcome of such a contest appeared doubtful to outsiders, Kennedy Senior rarely acted impetuously. He had already carefully sampled the electorate with private polls, and the findings were favorable; the giant, he felt, could be toppled. Kennedy had already laid the groundwork; for three years Jack had given speeches up and down the state, and the organization was ready.

And Jack was no longer reluctant. The role of U.S. Congressman had given him a new confidence in his own abilities. Also, the constant shadow of Joe Junior had been removed from Jack's life, although in a psychological sense that shadow may well have been fastened on him forever, for now he had the double burden of filial and brotherly guilt to help propel him into the presidency. By 1952, Jack seemed to have assumed the psychological identity of his dead brother and to have fully internalized the family's ambitions.

Once again, the patriarch supplied the campaign's primary direction, although the two older brothers, the candidate and his twenty-six-year-old campaign manager, Bobby, were the Kennedys with high public visibility. The JFK legend has largely obscured Joe Kennedy's part in this decisive 1952 senatorial election, which paved the way to the White House. A strategy participant recalled, "The father was the distinct boss in every way. He dominated everything, even told everyone where to sit. They [were] just children in that house." A speech writer observed, "The Ambassador worked around the clock. He was always consulting people, getting reports, looking into problems. Should Jack go on TV with this issue? What kind of an ad should he run on something else? He'd call in experts, get opinions, have ideas worked up."

The result of the founding father's work in 1952 has been called "the most methodical, the most scientific, the most thoroughly detailed, the most intricate, the most disciplined and smoothly working statewide campaign in Massachusetts history—and possibly anywhere else." Once again, Joe Kennedy's insatiable capacity for perfectionism gave him victory: Jack upset Lodge by more than 70,000 votes. The family's emotional investment in the election was vividly revealed when Rose Fitzgerald Kennedy commented, "At last, the Fitzgeralds have evened the score with the Lodges!" For Joe Kennedy—who had never liked Rose's father, Honey Fitz, whom Lodge's father had beaten in 1916—the election must have seemed more a case of, "At last, the Kennedys have evened the score with those stiff-necked, Irish-hating, son-of-a-bitch Yankees!"

The ex-Ambassador's controversial past had been raised during the 1952 campaign, and now he retreated farther into the background. The labels "stock juggler," "whiskey peddler," "Nazi appeaser," and "Jew hater" clung to the father. While he himself denied any anti-Semitism, regarded his financial dealings as honest, and saw his past diplomacy as common-sense logic, Kennedy also knew that millions of Americans did not agree. As the family's smartest politician, and the political and financial mentor of his sons, Kennedy knew he was a potential liability. To avoid future damage to Jack, Joe quietly withdrew from public view.

Joe's boys were also changing rapidly from political neophytes into tough professionals. At times their ambitions even soared impatiently ahead of his own. In 1956, Jack and Bobby went against their father's advice and tried to win Jack the vice presidential nomination. Kennedy Senior had warned against this temptation. "I knew Adlai Stevenson was going to take a licking," he said, "and I was afraid Jack might be blamed because he was a Catholic. That would have made it much more difficult for another Catholic in years to come." And for Jack. After the ambitious young Senator was narrowly defeated, he apologized by phone to his father, then on the French Riviera. Joe replied that "God was still with him, that he would be President if he wanted to be and worked hard." By this time Jack needed little encouragement. "He was already working on it," the father later decided. Actually, as it turned out, Jack's impulsiveness was largely responsible for his meteoric rise to the presidency. His graceful acceptance of defeat at the 1956 convention brought him essential national attention and enormous publicity. Jack was lucky to lose the vice presidential nomination, and lucky that Stevenson lost the presidency. Of such luck, compounded with shrewdness and hard work, are Presidents made.

The way was gradually opening for the top race, and the Kennedys began to make the most of their chances. In 1957, the family went quietly and effectively to work in an unprecedented publicity buildup of Jack.

This time, they knew, if Jack won, they would all be winners. Again, Joe Kennedy industriously wooed publishers and writers. Unlike many professional politicos, the founding father was acutely aware of the new era of personality politics that the mass media had created. In 1959, he opined that "Jack is the greatest attraction in the country today"—and he was doing all he could to help Jack achieve that status. The father also began rounding up convention votes among his many influential acquaintances.

The Massachusetts senatorial election in 1958 played an essential part in the presidential campaign strategy. Jack's reelection was a foregone conclusion, but the Kennedys needed to convince the Democratic leaders of Jack's great popularity. As Joe Kennedy told a friend, "If we can get a plurality of a half million, they can't stop us for the Presidency." Joe kept out of sight but in touch with Jack's campaign headquarters from his own Beacon Street command post. Again, the well-oiled and brilliantly managed Kennedy machine produced results—an astonishing plurality of nearly 875,000 votes, the biggest landslide in Massachusetts history.

Joe Kennedy was now in his seventies and had definitely retired to the sidelines. Although he had relinquished command to Jack and Bobby, he still retained his authority as senior political statesman. After Jack announced his presidential candidacy in January, 1960, Joe began gathering New York delegate votes. When one party chairman commented adversely on Jack's youth, Joe admitted he was a little young to be President, "but I'm seventy-two and I want to be around to enjoy it." At Joe's insistence, Jack entered the Wisconsin primary against Senator Hubert Humphrey. Joe also urged Jack to enter the California primary, but he refused. The son, surer now than ever of his own political competence, was becoming the chief decision-maker.

Joe and Rose Kennedy were on hand for Jack's triumph at the Democratic convention in Los Angeles, staying secretly at the Beverly Hills mansion of ex-movie star Marion Davies, the companion of Joe's old friend William Randolph Hearst. With a poolside battery of telephones, Joe kept in touch with Kennedy headquarters at the Biltmore Hotel eleven miles away. Even after Jack's nomination, Joe remained invisible and flew alone to New York to try to win Henry Luce's backing (in which he failed). The patriarch had disappeared so effectively that Republicans jibed, "Jack and Bob will run the show, while Ted's in charge of hiding Joe."

While circumstances and age limited Joe's direct contribution to Jack's presidential election, his fortune and the political lessons he had taught his sons were largely responsible for the victory. Kennedy Senior continued to entertain politicians discreetly, but his direction was no longer needed. Jack and Bobby had learned their lessons well. Joe offered them frequent advice and encouragement, but otherwise he kept out of their way. Only once did he express pique at revived rumors of his anti-Semitism and promise a future comment; but Jack's cultivated image as another FDR soothed Jewish fears, and Joe remained silent.

After Jack's election, his father expressed surprise at the narrowness of the razor-thin victory. "I didn't think it would be that close," said Joe. "I was wrong on two things. First, I thought he would get a bigger Catholic vote than he did. Second, I did not think so many would vote against him because of his religion." There is an element of unconscious humor in Kennedy's feeling that only religious prejudice could explain a vote against Jack, while he approved of the religious prejudice that brought votes to his son. The father never seemed to realize, let alone transcend, the narrowness of his own fiercely parochial views and loyalties. Many commentators feel, in fact, that Jack's Catholicism won him the election.

Now Joe Kennedy could appear in public with his son. The supreme goal had been reached: a Kennedy was President of the United States. It was also Joe who demanded Robert Kennedy's appointment as Attorney General, which both Jack and Bobby at first opposed. But their father insisted that the new President would need a relative close at hand. In Joe's tribal ethos, no Kennedy could trust anyone completely except another Kennedy. The elder Kennedy was also behind the key Cabinet choices of Defense Secretary Robert McNamara and Secretary of State Dean Rusk, according to biographer Whalen. These two conservatives, while completely loyal to the Kennedys, helped lead JFK into his fatal decisions to enlarge the Vietnam war with the militaristic advice they later continued to give Lyndon Johnson.

The father, now approaching his mid-seventies, was semi-retired, but he kept busy at a variety of interests. Movies still fascinated him, and he personally supervised the production of *PT-109*, the film made from the book glorifying Jack's wartime experiences. Joe still spoke for the family on all important business dealings. When Bobby signed a studio contract for the filming of his book about crime investigation, *The Enemy Within*, the patriarch phoned to revise the agreement. A startled executive replied that his son, the Attorney General, had been satisfied. Joe Senior snapped back, "What the hell does he know about it?" Joe, as usual, got his way.

Then, on December 19, 1961, a stroke partially paralyzed the seventy-three-year-old man. During his annual winter vacation at Palm Beach, Florida, Kennedy collapsed on the golf course and had his niece drive him home. He refused to call a doctor, but when he immediately worsened, the family rushed him to the hospital. Kennedy had had warnings of a stroke but had refused to take the prescribed anticoagulants. This irrational attitude was typical of all the Kennedy men, who apparently wished to prove themselves supermen, but also probably felt a deeply buried need to punish themselves for their manifold ingrown guilts and anxieties. Joe Kennedy had suffered past physical symptoms of great nervous tension, ulcers and neuritis. Now, desperately ill, he was given the last rites of his church.

Kennedy had an inoperable blood clot on an artery of the brain. He was paralyzed on his right side and unable to speak. "Long a figure of boundless energy and roaring authority," wrote a biographer, "he now was mute and crippled and massively frustrated." But old Joe, like Jack, refused to be defeated. For months he struggled impatiently with intensive physical therapy. Finally, two and a half years after the stroke, the patriarch began to walk and talk haltingly, although he remained a semi-invalid for the last eight years of his life. Only an iron determination kept him alert and partially active. His son-in-law, Steve Smith, who ran the Kennedy New York office, told a visitor, "He comes in and listens to business. And, don't worry, if he wants to say no to something, he can make himself known."

Kennedy was able to make his wishes known less than a year after his stroke. While the Ambassador's success thus far might have seemed to most people not only complete but excessive, it was not enough for him, because neurotics are never satisfied. He had still another son to place in high position (apparently he never considered running his daughters, although Eunice was politically talented and Kennedy could very likely have put her in Congress, perhaps even in the Senate). In 1962, Ted Kennedy, the last son and youngest child, would be thirty—old enough to enter the U.S. Senate.

Ted and the family had first considered the Massachusetts governorship, but Joe wanted another heir on the national stage. Reportedly, he laid down the law to a reluctant Jack and Bobby, telling them, "Look, I spent a lot of money for that Senate seat. It belongs in the family." In the interim, the Kennedys had cleverly had Jack's ex-roommate, Ben Smith, appointed to hold the seat for the family. The time had come, and in 1962, the now thoroughly polished political techniques of the Kennedy organization swept Teddy into office, despite his total lack of experience or qualifications. On election night, the victorious new Senator was asked whether he had talked yet to his brothers, the President and the Attorney General. No, he replied. Had he spoken with his father? Yes, he was extremely excited.

Despite this brief final satisfaction, cruel blows lay just ahead. Crippled and only a shadow of his former commanding self, Joseph Kennedy lived on to see Jack struck down in 1963 and Bobby in 1968. And when former President Eisenhower was buried in April, 1969, the press reported that a confused Joe Kennedy at first thought the funeral was for his last son, Teddy. Yet Joe was still clinging to life when disaster did come to Ted. Had the Kennedy father retained enough strength, it is doubtful that Teddy would have blundered so badly in his actions and statements after the Chappaquiddick accident. But the family's shrewdest adviser was nearly gone.

On November 18, 1969, at the age of eighty-one, the Kennedy founding father died peacefully at his summer home in Hyannis Port. At the funeral, Ted read a tribute written by Bobby in 1965, which said in part, "He has called on the best that was in us. There was no such thing as half-trying. Whether it was running a race or catching a football, competing in school— we were to try. And we were to try harder than anyone else. We might not be the best, and none of us were, but we were to make the effort to be the best. 'After you have done the best you can,' he used to say, 'the hell with it.'"

Unfortunately, no one raised with such neurotic compulsions can ever really say, "The hell with it." Bobby also lauded his father for putting his children's advancement ahead of his own and for not visualizing "himself as a sun around which satellites would circle, or in the role of a puppet master. He wanted us, not himself, to be the focal points." Bobby, however, could not voice the essential direction of his father's ambitions. It was not necessary that Joe Kennedy be the visible focal point, since he could unconsciously project his needs and longings onto his sons. To see dominance and control only in obvious terms is to miss the real meaning of neurotic need and its manifold outlets. There were clear historical and psychological reasons why Kennedy pushed his sons into prominence in his own place and why he did not need to be a "puppet master" once they had achieved power. From a practical point of view, when Kennedy ended his public career by his own ambassadorial ineptitude, he was too old and publicly distrusted to begin a new political career. But his sons were growing up at just the right ages to provide the fresh faces and "new look" for his dynastic ambitions. By unconsciously living in and through them, Kennedy could reach the pinnacle of power.

Power and universal recognition for the Kennedys was the aim, it seems clear, not any particular program Joseph Kennedy wished to put into effect. He had no social ideas or ideals. Once he had steered his willing "puppets" onto the national stage, the "puppet master" could relax; they would dance their dance. The social recognition of power always seemed to be Kennedy's goal, not the social use of power, despite the Kennedy avowals of "public service." While the patriarch was capable of making valuable public efforts, such as his short service as chairman of the Securities and Exchange Commission and the Maritime Commission, these were narrow administrative jobs with specific concrete tasks set by the President, FDR. But in dealing with his intellectual and social equals or superiors, Kennedy's emotional hypersensitivities made him anxious. As Roosevelt was once said to have remarked of Kennedy, "You always had to hold his hand." When Joe Kennedy entered the wider arena of ambassadorial socio-political judgment and understanding, his lack of insights and sympathies finally brought him total failure and the harsh condemnation of former admirers.

An intimate summed up the driving force that the patriarch revealed to the world: "I like Joe Kennedy, but I have no illusions about him. He understands power. Everywhere he went, from Brahmin Boston to the Court of St. James, he saw great hypocrisy about the philosophy of those who rule. Power is the end. What other delight is there but to enjoy the sheer sense of control? He would say, 'Let me see any other motive in the people who command.' Joe thinks like a king, and kings aren't always nice guys."

A different explanation is more likely. Power and control are only apparent ends. For all power-hungry people, the underlying motivation is security. The need for power and the domination of others is the outward manifestation of a particular neurotic defense system. There are many varieties of such self-defense, but all of them contain a neurotic search for glory, unrealistic claims on life and the self, self-hate, and "a fundamental uncertainty about the feeling of identity." Unconsciously, every neurotic wonders who he really is. "Am I the proud superhuman being—or am I the subdued, guilty, and rather despicable creature?"

Since nobody is the perfect superhuman he would like to be, the neurotic must constantly deny his failures to himself by putting up an unconscious bluff. As Dr. Horney wrote in *Neurosis and Human Growth*, "He may be extremely proud, consciously or unconsciously, of his faculty of fooling everybody—and in his arrogance and contempt for others believes that he actually succeeds in this. Conversely, he is most afraid of being fooled himself and may feel it as a profound humiliation if he is. . . ." I have noted Joe Kennedy's pervasive distrust of anyone outside his family, his many expressions of "arrogance and contempt for others," and his extreme sensitivity to criticism. The Kennedy fortune was founded essentially on bluff and illusion: the artificial inflation of stocks and real estate, and the fantasy-escape worlds of movies and alcohol. In his political successes, Kennedy continued to use his profitable bluffing techniques to create the images and pseudo-events that elected his candidate-sons.

The distinct impression is conveyed that Kennedy unconsciously feared that his outer bluffs merely hid a weak and constantly threatened self. As one observer put it, "Kennedy had a pessimistic view of human nature. One who had pulled many a sharp trade, he was always wary of having the tables turned on him. Even the smallest deception that might make him appear foolish would arouse violent anger." It is interesting to note that Kennedy once told his future son-in-law, actor Peter Lawford, that he disliked actors, an understandable reaction in someone who unconsciously felt he was always playing a role.

Kennedy's profound insecurity and anxiety about life itself—its very basis and meaning—were shown in his lifelong "pessimism." The 1929 stock market collapse gave him a feeling of near panic, even though he had safely pulled out and conserved his fortune. The approach of World War II aroused his fears of an impending apocalypse. Such a man has little or no faith in human nature, for he lacks genuine faith in himself. Instead, the neurotic who feels life as an overwhelming threat must throw up a defense strong enough to hold back disaster. This seems to be the psychological basis of the fantastic energies that Kennedy displayed in realizing his ambitions. His ambitions, in essence, had to be equal to his fears. This is the core of self-glorification.

The neurotic's constant need for such exaggerated vindication inevitably poisons his relations with others. Since he lacks the ability to accept others as autonomous individuals, he strongly resents even their simple wishes and opinions or any doubts they may voice about his shortcomings. This constant resentment of the normal expectations of others, which are often felt as unbearable demands, may explode in a burst of rage, with the neurotic thereafter seeking someone who will "understand" him better. The result of such unsatisfactory relationships, however, is frequent loneliness.

Kennedy, a notorious "loner" in all his business operations, was assisted only by a close ring of intensely loyal employees (most notably his personal secretary for many years, Edward Moore, after whom Kennedy named his youngest son). He was also well known for his frequent breaks with friends and for his angry outbursts both outside and within his own family. A family adviser noted, "If Joe liked you, you were tops—no matter what anybody else thought. If he stopped liking you, you simply didn't exist any more."

Had Joseph Kennedy not been so absorbed in his neurotic needs, he might have become the great man his abilities often suggested. He possessed keen intelligence, enormous energy, and a capacity for intense concentration. But he was unable to commit himself for long to any endeavor not centered on his own interests. Such a commitment would have been too emotionally threatening. When one is committed, the potential pain of failure or rejection is that much greater. The already vulnerable ego of the neurotic simply cannot endure such a danger.

Unfortunately for all the Kennedys, the founding father's grand design for his sons and family contained a basic inescapable flaw: it is psychologically and historically impossible for any human being to impose his pattern of life upon another human being in the way he intends. Each person must discover and achieve his own life. This is the real meaning of human freedom. Any other result can only be a pseudo-identity created at enormous personal cost for both artificer and artifact. Kennedy's tragedy was a double one. Although he reached the heights of material and social success, his castle was built on illusion. He used his immense fortune to little purpose aside from the glorification of himself and his family. Today Joe Kennedy is remembered not for any social achievements, but as the very rich father of a President of the United States. Even his political brilliance is largely forgotten, eclipsed by Jack's success.

Secondly, while Kennedy did raise his offspring to become doers and manipulators in their own right, the history they made has proved largely ephemeral and in some instances actually destructive, instead of significantly constructive. Since the Kennedy sons were predominantly driven by unresolved parental conflicts rather than by their own desires, they largely lacked the inner maturity that alone brings genuine happiness. The Kennedys did not believe that it was "better to be right than be President," as Henry Clay put it. Joseph Kennedy taught his children that it was better to be President than anything. This was the greatest tragedy of all: in seeking to achieve himself through neurotic means, Kennedy not only lost much of his own human potential, he also passed on to his children a crippling inheritance.

Chapter 3

GROWING UP DISCIPLINED:
LIFE WITH MOTHER

I grew up in a very strict house where there were no free riders.

We soon learned that competition in the family was a kind of dry run for the world outside.

—John Fitzgerald Kennedy

We would try to instill into them the idea that no matter what you did, you should try to be first. . . . The competition between the two boys was very good, as it is good for any children. . . .

Whatever his religion, with faith, a child knows exactly why he was created, he has well-defined obligations to God and man. He has sure direction, ever-courageous because he knows God is directing him for his ultimate destiny. . . . If the children have been properly motivated, they will have a strong will power.

—Rose Fitzgerald Kennedy

In the America of today it is usually the mother whose all-pervasive presence and brutal decisiveness of judgment—although her means may be the sweetest—precipitate the child into a fatal struggle for his own identity: the child wants to be blessed by the one important parent, not for what he does and accomplishes, but for what he *is*, and he often puts the parent to mortal tests. The parent, on the other hand, has selected this one child, because of an inner affinity paired with an insurmountable outer distance, as the particular child who must *justify the parent*. Thus the parent asks only: What have you *accomplished?* and what have you done for *me?*

—Erik H. Erikson, *Young Man Luther*

45

I'm going to be eighty and I want to see another son in the White House. Ted, will you promise to try? Your promise will be my birthday gift.

—Attributed to Rose Fitzgerald Kennedy

The authentic child is the one who develops in freedom, thereby to become whole.

—Dr. Alan DeWitt Button, *The Authentic Child*

ƆⱭ

THERE IS a fine irony in the emergence of Rose Fitzgerald Kennedy as the world's most famous mother and grandmother and the matriarch of the Kennedy "dynasty." With the deaths of her three oldest sons and of her husband, Rose has become the moral and actual head of the clan in a way that was never possible when the men dominated the family. In addition, she has maintained her health and good looks to a remarkable degree, so that, in her eighties, she is able to step into the limelight on her own. As one of the world's wealthiest women and a lover of *haute couture* and jet travel, Rose Kennedy has zoomed into the headlines and onto covers of the world press with a zest scarcely imaginable a few years ago. In fact, Rose is even starting to compete with her former daughter-in-law and still the world's most famous woman, Jackie Kennedy Onassis.

None of this is out of character, for Rose Kennedy, although a figure in the background during her husband's and sons' rise to fortune and fame, has always been an intensely ambitious woman. She has also been a person of great self-control, maintaining her youthful good looks through the rearing of nine children by programs of sports, grooming, and discipline, so successfully that one diplomat, upon being introduced to the svelte Rose, quipped in astonishment, "At last—I believe in the stork!" And with her immediate responsibilities now greatly reduced, she is traveling more than ever, especially between the fashion centers of Paris and New York City, where she maintains a stylish apartment.

But Rose's growing fame rests on more than her position as wife and mother of four of the world's most famous men, on more than her dazzling of the "beautiful people." From beneath the brilliant façade of fame, wealth, and elegance there emerges the more important fact of Rose Kennedy's undiminished social and political ambition. According to close Kennedy watchers, Rose is determined to put Teddy into the White House. Or, if this should fail, to see her oldest grandson, Joseph Patrick Kennedy III (Bobby's handsome and energetic son), launched in the political footsteps of his father and uncles.

Right now, Rose's gaze seems to be set firmly on Teddy as the next Kennedy President. Friends say that Rose regards the White House as being currently "between Kennedys." To the goal of carrying on the Kennedy dynastic claims, the Kennedy matriarch is reportedly willing to devote a considerable portion of her fortune and expects other members of the family to do the same. "Teddy will be President," Rose has said more than once. And there is every evidence that the Kennedy matriarch is determined to make this dream come true. The possibility of a 1972 presidential goal was evident in Ted's exceptionally vigorous campaign for reelection to the Senate from Massachusetts in November, 1970, against an underdog opponent. Since then, Rose, Ted, and the other Kennedys have continued to make frequent appearances and headlines.

What manner of person is this extraordinary woman? Until very recently, Rose Kennedy was vastly overshadowed by her sons and her husband, although she was by no means an obscure person. As the daughter of a colorful Boston politician who served three terms in the U.S. Congress and two as Boston's mayor, Rose Fitzgerald Kennedy was accustomed from childhood to the hustle and bustle and unpredictable ups and downs of political life. She early took her place by her father's side as his hostess, for Rose's mother was shy and disliked political life. Thus in later years, Rose was prepared to enter wholeheartedly into her various roles as the wife of a U.S. Ambassador and the mother of congressional, senatorial, and presidential candidates. In addition, her often frustrated social ambitions were increasingly gratified by the rise of her husband and sons to national prominence. The Kennedys, who for decades were considered "out of society" among the snobbish non-Irish upper classes, by 1961 had become "society" for most Americans.

To understand the Kennedys and their meaning for America, it is essential to understand the importance of Rose Kennedy as both a partial perpetrator of the obsessive-compulsive success pattern that shows so plainly in the lives of her children, and as a contributor to the Kennedy dynastic fantasy of omnipotence. We can see the enormity of this fantasy in Rose's unshakable assumption that Teddy, despite his all-too-evident personal problems, is intended by God and nature to become President of the United States. While this fantasy has an element of reality, in that the Kennedys can still command huge wealth and political expertise, and enough popularity to make their dreams come true, on a nonopportunistic level I believe that the Kennedy "dream" has strong neurotic elements in that none of the sons, and particularly Teddy, has possessed sufficient genuine maturity and leadership qualities to lead this nation in a time of crisis.

To include Rose Kennedy in a "Kennedy neurosis" is certain to offend many people, for she alone of the Kennedys has aroused almost universal respect and admiration, even among otherwise harsh critics of the family. The tragic multiple blows that Rose has had to endure, and the tremendous courage, dignity, and resilience with which she has met each blow, are undeniable and undeniably admirable. She has repeatedly shown herself to be a strong, stoical woman with an apparently unlimited ability to sustain great loss, recover, and continue to enjoy life with enthusiasm. Apparently Rose Kennedy has a strong self-identity that never fails her, and a deep religious faith that has upheld her through all adversity.

Nevertheless, the mother of the Kennedy sons must be included in my thesis of general Kennedy obsessiveness with power and position. Mothers have a crucial, and often the most important, influence on their children's emotional life patterns. What is too often overlooked is that these mothers have been shaped by their own parents and by the intense molding pressures of a male-dominated society. Thus our fervent admiration for a dramatically strong and dedicated mother such as Rose Kennedy may well contain elements of expiation for the unconscious, repressed wrath many of us feel toward our own too absorbing or too remote mothers (both are forms of rejection).

In general, insufficient attention has been given to Rose Kennedy's role in the forming of the Kennedy sons. There is no doubt about Joseph Kennedy's great importance in influencing their lives and decisions, but, until very recently, Rose's true significance was concealed by the enormous material success and vocal personality of her husband, as well as by the still largely patriarchal pattern of American society. The influence of the mother in every family, even though exercised behind the scenes, can be even more decisive than that of the outwardly visible father. Had Rose Kennedy opposed the compulsive success pattern of her husband and exerted opposite influences, it is probable that the over-all "Kennedy neurosis" would have been greatly weakened or perhaps countered altogether.

Unhappily, it is a general psychological rule that neurotic people marry each other and all too often reinforce each other's neuroses and the effect of these neuroses on their children. Rose Kennedy grew up in an obsessive-compulsive success pattern centering on politics and wealth very similar to that of Joe Kennedy's childhood. Both Rose and Joe suffered the rejections and humiliations of being Irish Catholics in a Yankee-Protestant-dominated society. Each also underwent similar parental demands of particularized, concrete success, although the form of that success was more material for the male Joe than for the female Rose. The exact details of these demands can only be guessed at, but the subsequent emotional patterns revealed by both Kennedy parents strongly suggest the general nature of their origins.

Neurotic individuals also tend to marry their childhood patterns. In the case of Joe and Rose, Joe married a strong-minded, self-disciplined religious woman much like his mother, a woman who kept a tight emotional hold on her children. Rose married an intensely ambitious man who would be absent much of the time, like her politician-father, and who would leave the early raising of the children primarily to her. Also like her father, her husband had a vigorous, down-to-earth, outgoing personality (although a far less cheerful one) and a lack of scruples about the sources of his income. And, again like her father, Rose's husband indulged a wandering eye for female beauty and a belief in the double sexual standard for men and women. Again, like her mother, Rose maintained the outward decorum and devotion taught her by her church and late-Victorian society.

But Rose's mother could hardly have avoided feeling a secret resentment against her husband for his constant absences and obvious preference for the "real world" of politics and elective office. This resentment was vividly revealed in a pathetic incident when Fitzgerald was serving his second term as Boston's mayor in 1912. That May he announced with mistaken pride, "I have yet to spend a weekday night at home with my family since I have been Mayor." Soon afterwards Honey Fitz decided to spend one night at home, and to celebrate this unusual occasion he invited the press to attend his fireside party. "I am to spend the evening with you, children, so proceed to make merry," said Fitzgerald. Mrs. Fitzgerald told a reporter, "You must not mind what happens in this household tonight. You see, we don't have Mr. Fitzgerald often with us on a week-day evening, so it means a great deal to every member of the family." But Fred, age eight, commented, "I don't know about Dad. If he is sick, why doesn't he go to bed, and if he is well, why doesn't he go to work?"

One reporter who observed this scene found His Honor the opposite of a domesticated man. "If I were to meet him at a horse race," she said, "he would impress me as a Boston dandy of the smart set, a man who believes in keeping thoroughly in style." Fitzgerald trooped into the library with his six children—Fred, Eunice, Tom, John, Jr., Agnes, and Rose, the oldest (then almost twenty-two). Honey Fitz danced, sang, and played games with his children, boasted about his progeny, and had pictures taken. Then his wife observed with a smile, "John, it does indeed seem refreshing to have you here. I am not sorry you are to have photographs taken to mark the evening. I am going to frame one and place a card over it on which I will write: 'Taken on his one evening at home.'" Fitzgerald clearly felt the sarcasm of his wife's remark, for he replied, "Now you will make Miss Burt think I neglect my family if you keep on." Then he told the reporter, "I spend every Sunday with them, Miss Burt, and I have them each in town at least once a week. I am a family man. And the reason I am such is because I was one of many children. I took care of my brothers, did all the buying for the family, and was father and mother in one. [Fitzgerald was orphaned when he was eighteen.] This early training enabled me to shop wisely. Why, I think nothing of buying hats and coats for my little girls. . . ." His wife added, "I'm never surprised when he brings me home a suit. I will admit that although he doesn't spend many evenings at home with us during the week, he seems to have us on his mind a great deal."

But such veiled "peace offerings" could hardly compensate for the real absence, both physical and emotional, of a man whose deepest interests evidently lay elsewhere. Fitzgerald had an enormous fund of natural energy (which seemed to be inherited by Rose), and was widely regarded as Boston's most energetic, if not most effective, mayor. In his first term (1906–1907) a newspaper called the rambunctious, fun-loving "Fitzy" (another popular nickname) "a bundle of dynamos that never seem to run down. Tireless? Why, in the first two years of his first term he averaged two dinners and three dances a night, to say nothing of six speeches. In all, he attended 1200 dinners, 1500 dances, 200 picnics, and a thousand meetings. He made 3000 speeches and gave some 5000 girls the proud recollection of a dance apiece with Fitzy." Fitzgerald's amazing nocturnal schedules did not interfere with his official duties, for he was a strong, stocky man who needed only five or six hours of sleep a night.

The John F. Fitzgeralds, whatever emotional ambivalences husband and wife may have felt toward each other, generally kept up a public appearance of sweet harmony. In words that sounded nearly identical to those echoed by her daughter Rose in later years, Mary Josephine Fitzgerald would tell inquiring writers, "I want my home to be a place of inspiration and encouragement to all my family. I am a home woman in every way, and my one ambition is to make the home the most happy and attractive place for my husband and children. I try to go about quite a bit with Mr. Fitzgerald. When I attend the theatre I always call for him after the performance and we ride home together. And I am not a stranger at his office in City Hall." Despite these meager disclaimers, the fact was that Mrs. Fitzgerald, while quietly active in her own club and social circles, attended few functions with her exuberant and flamboyant husband. As the years went by, the Fitzgerald daughters, especially Rose, increasingly appeared in the public limelight with their father.

Nevertheless, Grandmother Fitzgerald had the satisfaction of outliving her husband by many years. She was an alert, erect ninety-five when her grandson Jack was elected President; Honey Fitz died in 1950 before Jack had even reached the Senate. While Rose acquired a taste for politics from her father, she inherited from her mother longevity, a serene temperament, and unusually youthful good looks. An amusing anecdote has a reporter checking Rose's identity at a reception and asking, "The young lady over there, in pink, is Miss Agnes, your sister?" "Yes," replied Rose. "And the very slim one in blue—which of the daughters is she?" asked the reporter. Rose laughed. "Her name? Why don't you know? Her name is Mother!"

A recent biographer of Rose Kennedy gives us additional insight into the neurotic patterns of the Fitzgerald family. As Gail Cameron describe's Rose's childhood: "In the well-established Irish-Victorian home, Rose was already organized, methodical, and precisely scheduled. . . . She became a dogged and persistent teacher of the younger children, but though Agnes could take her conscientiousness with benign indulgence, the boys could not, and a serious jealousy began to develop. 'What I remember most about Rosie when we were growing up,' said her late brother Tom, 'was that she was always nagging me about studying Latin and playing the violin.' He and the other boys became 'extremely jealous' of Rose, a jealousy that persisted, through many 'absurd incidents' into adulthood. It is no wonder, for Honey Fitz doted on his eldest daughter. The boys never became good students. They disappointed John and 'nearly broke their mother's heart.' One eventually 'drank himself to death'; another served as a toll collector on the Mystic River Bridge as his nephew prepared to run for the Presidency. Johnny Fitz was such an overwhelming figure in his own household, such a colorful and very public figure, and doted so much on his beautiful daughters that the boys were never allowed to develop their own styles . . . the boys remained subservient to him all their lives . . . ."

Rose Kennedy's father, John Francis Fitzgerald, was born on February 11, 1863, the third of seven sons born to Thomas Fitzgerald of County Wexford, Ireland, and Rose Mary Murray, who had also emigrated from Ireland in the 1840s. Tom Fitzgerald first worked on a farm in South Acton, Massachusetts, but later settled in Boston's North End near Paul Revere's old house, becoming a genial proprietor of a grocery and liquor store. Little Johnny Fitz, or "Fitzie," was born in a four-story red-brick tenement in the bustling, colorful neighborhood which he ever after referred to lovingly in innumerable speeches as the "dear old North End" (this finally led to the inhabitants being called the "Dearos").

Fitzie was well known for his skill in sports (like his son-in-law, Joe Kennedy), his eloquence on the rostrum, and his leadership ideas that kept him busy in dozens of social and athletic organizations. Also like the future Kennedy, young Fitzgerald attended Boston Latin School, where he managed the baseball team and captained the football team. After graduation, Fitzgerald entered the Harvard Medical School. But the future of Boston politics was changed when Fitzgerald's father died of pneumonia in 1881 (his wife had died three years earlier), and the boys were orphaned. Honey Fitz left medical school to care for his brothers and earn a living in the Custom House. (This story, with different variations, was told on many occasions by Fitzgerald with, as his biographer put it, "chokingly senti-mental details with just the proper quaver of voice.")

From the Custom House, Honey Fitz entered the insurance business, where his wide circle of friends and easy Irish "blarney" made him pros-perous. Democratic politics was the natural route to success for a Boston Irishman with Fitzgerald's outgoing personality, huge drive, and irre-pressible gift of gab. Starting as a boss of the North End's Ward Six and as a leader of many political and social organizations, Fitzgerald won a seat on the Common Council in 1892. Young Fitzie's slogan was "Work harder than anyone else," and he soon had a park for his constituents and many jobs for his supporters. Fitzgerald, like Joe Kennedy's father P.J. and other successful Boston politicians, based his winning formula on his own public-welfare state, dispensing food baskets, rent, coal, picnics, funerals, and constant amounts of "Fitzblarney," as well as patronage. Soon Fitzgerald was elected to the state Senate; then in 1894, the ruddy, handsome, blue-eyed showman, who could weep as easily as he could laugh, won a seat in the U.S. House of Representatives. Reelected in 1896 and again in 1898, he was at that time the only Democratic Congressman from New England. In those days, Capitol Hill was often the way to Boston's City Hall, a goal Honey Fitz finally reached in 1906.

As a politician and public "servant," Fitzgerald was a product of his time and environment, being no better and no worse than scores of other men who used their offices more for their own advancement, and that of their friends, than for idealistic and public-spirited purposes. The dominant political philosophy of the time (and to a large degree of our own time) was later expressed by Thomas G. Corcoran, FDR's White House assistant, who maintained, "The President must deceive, misrepresent, leave false im-pressions, even, sometimes, lie . . . and trust to charm, loyalty, and the result to make up for it. . . . A great man cannot be a good man." JFK, Fitzgerald's grandson, also subscribed to this view, but the results did not "make up for it."

Fitzgerald's main aim seemed to be his constant reelection, for he was a man who truly enjoyed the excitement and challenge of campaigning in that rowdy era of high jinks and low tricks, as well as the thrill of election and pride of office. While Honey Fitz prospered sufficiently to live com-fortably, his goal was never the amassing of great wealth, but rather the amassing of great popularity. To achieve that end Fitzgerald indulged in the customary graft and political tricks of the trade (which in his era covered almost every imaginable sort of fakery), but he was often vigorous in supporting public necessities, such as schools, parks, streets, and housing. Like his frequent enemy and sometimes ally, James Michael Curley, Fitz-gerald's record could most generally be seen as "checkered." He never matched Curley's histrionics, but neither did he ever quite match Curley's political chicanery. True, he was removed from the U.S. House of Representatives in 1916 because of an alleged voting fraud, but there is evidence that the other side used equal skullduggery, a common occurrence.

The flavor of Honey Fitz's freewheeling era is suggested by a few entertaining passages of history. "According to the quixotically honest City Clerk Wilfred Doyle," wrote Boston chronicler Francis Russell, "in Honey's day everybody in City Hall from department head to scrubwoman had to kick back. Honey Fitz, the host of the old Woodcock Hotel, was brazen. Elderly politicians in the city can still today repeat limericks about his blond friend, 'Toodles' Ryan." In the 1917 mayoralty campaign Curley, then Boston's mayor, announced, "I am preparing three addresses which, if necessary, I shall deliver in the fall and which, if a certain individual had the right to restrict free speech, I would not be permitted to deliver. One of these addresses is entitled: 'Graft, Ancient and Modern,' another, 'Great Lovers from Cleopatra to Toodles,' and last, but not least interesting, 'Libertines: From Henry VIII to the Present Day.' " That same day, Honey Fitz dropped his candidacy.

Fitzgerald was his own greatest admirer, a trait he shared with his son-in-law Joe Kennedy. One witty political toastmaster introduced Honey Fitz with appropriate satire: "Fitzie discovered Niagara Falls, conceived the High School of Commerce, built City Hall Annex, put an end to the Spanish and First World Wars, planned the Chamber of Commerce, freed Ireland, and invented the Ku Klux Klan to save the Irish from being bored in America."

In purpose and personality, Fitzgerald was in many ways the opposite of the Kennedy grandfather, P.J. While both were skillful political leaders and manipulators, one sought the pleasures of public popularity, the other disliked publicity and enjoyed only the secretive maneuvers of behind-the-scenes power. We can see these same attitudes reflected in their children, Rose and Joe. Rose, like her father and sons, enjoyed the stimulation of personal contact with masses of people (which, of course, is a superficial contact) and the excitement of the campaign trail. But Joe, like his father, was not attracted by personal politicking, preferring to be the invisible operator, manager, and superstrategist.

Thus the Kennedy sons inherited, politically speaking, the best of both worlds. As candidates, they were raised by a mother who had learned from childhood much of the adroitness of the wily politician who could be "all things to all men." As political planners, they were nurtured by a father who had been taught the secrets of manipulating voters and who carried this knowledge over into the fields of finance and politics.

Yet while these skills gained elective office and public fame and power for the Kennedy sons, such techniques could not fulfill the sons' unconscious needs for parental approval and acceptance. In effect, the Kennedys were trying to satisfy a basic human need—self-acceptance—by means that would not satisfy it. Political channels could temporarily gain the parents' approval, but the psychological channels that would have led to real personal satisfaction and self-actualization were largely blocked. The Kennedy sons gained high office, but once elected they suffered a paralysis of will, nerve, and vision that made them incapable of achieving genuinely productive policies.

Rose Elizabeth Fitzgerald Kennedy was born in Boston on July 22, 1890, the first of six children, including three daughters. While slim and self-contained like her mother, Rose was darker (all three girls were pretty) and temperamentally more extroverted like her father. The Fitzgerald daughters Rose, Agnes (two years younger), and Eunice (seven years younger), were raised to be devout Catholics, a teaching that Rose thoroughly absorbed. Rose was also a dedicated student, and at fifteen she was graduated from Dorchester High as the youngest graduate in the school's history. Her classmates also voted her the prettiest senior. After attending the Convent of the Sacred Heart in Boston, Rose entered New York's Manhattanville College of the Sacred Heart (where her own daughter Jean would one day room with a future Kennedy in-law, Ethel Skakel).

In addition to being the eldest Fitzgerald, Rose learned an early self-confidence from her political travels with her exuberant father. When she was seven, Honey Fitz (then in Congress) took Rose and Agnes to the White House to meet President William McKinley. This visit seems to have been somewhat spoiled by the President's thoughtless comparison of the two little girls. As Rose recalled the incident, "He looked at us both, turned to my sister and said, 'You are the prettiest little girl who has entered the White House.' I thought this was a wonderful story until one of my children looked at me and said, 'Why didn't he say it to you, Mother?'" Despite her outwardly modest self-deprecation, Rose in fact later named none of her four daughters for her sister Agnes, although one was named for sister Eunice. Eunice Fitzgerald died at twenty-three and this could have motivated Rose's naming of her third oldest daughter. Her first daughter she named for herself.

Rose's hurt feelings could hardly have been soothed by her father's frequent recounting of the White House incident. As Honey Fitz told it, McKinley presented his boutonniere to five-year-old Agnes, saying, "I want to present this flower to the prettiest child I have ever seen." The father, in his typical fashion, had elevated the level of his daughter's beauty. If this anecdote seems unimportant, we should remember that of such apparently trivial happenings are the emotional threads of adult character woven. In view of Honey Fitz's constant pushing forward of himself and his children, such destructive comparisons between the children may well have occurred often. Certainly Rose recalled this one clearly.

Fortunately, Fitzgerald was genuinely proud of all his daughters, even if sometimes tactless, and Rose seems to have become his closest female political supporter. In her teens, she accompanied him on trips to Latin America and Europe. Then for one apparently happy year, Rose and Agnes attended a Catholic school in Prussia, the Convent of the Sacred Heart in Blumenthal. Talented in languages and music, Rose won a gold medal for her piano playing. But when she returned to Boston, she encountered the cutting snobbery that excluded Irish girls, no matter how cultivated, from the highest Brahmin social circles. When Rose was refused admission to the Junior League, she joined the Irish Cecilian Guild and formed her own exclusive group, the Ace of Clubs, for Irish young ladies who had studied abroad and spoke French (the latter requirement was not strictly imposed).

But Rose had interests other than imitating the Yankee *grandes dames* and their daughters. At twenty, she was appointed the youngest member of the Boston Public Library Examining Committee. She also taught Sunday School, and is remembered as a painstaking teacher and firm disciplinarian who prodded her students to win annual catechism competitions. Rose, like her future husband, had learned early the importance of winning. She was also active with her father whenever election time rolled around. From her teens, she had taken a keen interest in attending political rallies and banquets, ship launchings, building dedications, and many of the endless functions contrived by Honey Fitz, the indefatigable booster of a "Bigger, Better, Busier Boston."

Rose had met young Joseph Patrick Kennedy as a child when her father and P.J. Kennedy conferred in East Boston. When Rose was at Dorchester High and Joe at Boston Latin, they had dated quietly, knowing of Honey Fitz's disapproval. The Fitzgeralds were rising faster socially than the Kennedys, an eminence crowned by Honey Fitz's 1910 triumph in the mayoralty race over a Yankee-backed candidate. In January, 1911, an exquisitely-gowned Rose made her debut and became the belle of Irish Boston. With other wealthy Boston suitors available, Joe Kennedy was not regarded as a suitable husband. But Rose preferred Joe; and when young Kennedy became a bank president in late 1913, Fitzgerald's objections were overcome. In October, 1914, the couple was married by Cardinal O'Connell in a widely publicized nuptial Mass. The newlyweds honeymooned at the Greenbrier at White Sulphur Springs, and then moved into a modest gray frame house in Brookline.

Rose soon had her hands full with a fast-growing family. In a single decade, from 1915 to 1925, the first seven of her nine children were born. The family was concluded with Jean in 1928 and Teddy in 1932, when Rose was not yet forty-two. Fortunately for Rose, her husband's fortune expanded at an even greater rate, and soon she had a sizable staff of cooks, nurses, and, later, governesses to help her with the children. But Rose always took full responsibility for the general supervision of her young charges, and was closely attentive to their physical and spiritual needs, although the results were not exactly what she must have anticipated. Her religious devotion is well known. As Rose is often quoted as saying, "On pleasant days I took the children for walks. I wheeled one in a baby carriage and two or three toddled along with me. I made it a point each day to take them into church for a visit. I wanted them to form a habit of making God and religion a part of their daily lives, not something to be reserved for Sundays." She believed in both authoritarian religion and firm authority at home, physically applied if necessary. "I used to have a ruler around, and paddled them occasionally, because when they're young that's all they understand."

This sort of spare-the-rod, spoil-the-child discipline was, of course, the prevalent child-raising belief of Rose's generation. Today psychologists and many parents, including the Kennedy daughters-in-law, find the results more negative than useful. Physical punishment is as humiliating for children as it would be for adults if still permitted (and socially-approved wife-beating is not far distant). Spanking or whipping destroys the respect of a child for his parent and plants the seeds of future unconscious hostility. While Rose Kennedy's intentions were, at least consciously, undoubtedly for the best, her severe methods of discipline contributed to the emotional difficulties of the children. Certainly such rigid discipline failed to inculcate self-control in the boys (the girls are less reported on), for they were as messy as most children in their personal habits. Jack, Bobby, and Teddy carried much of this over into their adult lives. (Jack was notoriously sloppy until he married Jackie and unpunctual even as President; Bobby, like Jack, expected other people to pick up after him; Teddy's frequent lack of self-discipline has been well publicized.) Only in Bobby, among the boys, did the mother's religious precepts appear to take deep root; but unfortunately his character seemed to hold stronger elements of fanaticism than the tolerance and humility that mark the genuinely religious person, no matter of what church or belief. It has been noted that Bobby was spanked quite often by his mother, though he could not recall ever being spanked by his father. "Hot water was my department," said Rose. "Business was Joe's department."

Joe Kennedy's frequent absences, especially in the early years, threw the major responsibilities of child-rearing onto Rose's capable shoulders. She was not completely alone, however, for her parents lived nearby, as did the

Kennedy in-laws. But Rose was diligent in her maternal duties, as her mother had been, reading to the children, taking them on sightseeing and shopping expeditions, and regularly hearing their prayers and Friday catechism lessons. As a friend observed, "She would leave any party early to be home in time for a baby's feeding." Servants never took the place of motherly concern. As Rose later told the Queen of England in a conversation that became a standard Kennedy anecdote, she kept a card index on each child recording his or her childhood diseases, vaccinations, physical examinations, and trips to the dentist.

Rose herself attended early-morning Mass daily, a habit she has continued all her life. Her stoicism showed in her refusal to admit her own discomfort, a trait that was learned by her children. Her husband once said proudly, "I don't think I know anyone who has more courage than my wife. In all the years that we have been married, I have never heard her complain. Never. Not even once. That is a quality that children are quick to see." But fortitude, while often admirable, can also be part of a general emotional pattern of exaggerated stoicism and self-sacrifice. The stoic may feel a secret pride in his silent suffering and endurance. For emotionally withdrawn and inhibited people, stoicism can also conceal an inability to communicate, as well as a useful ability to tolerate inescapable ills. This is not to belittle Rose Kennedy's undoubted courage, but rather to suggest other facets of her personality that could have caused a disproportionate need in her children to display courage and hardihood. For example, it is one thing to bear pain as bravely as possible, although a taboo against showing any grief is not necessarily the healthiest response. It is quite another matter to seek out unconscious opportunities for displaying and feeling one's bravery. A total lack of complaint in any marriage also strongly suggests an unhealthy lack of communication, for part of maturity is the ability to express what one dislikes as well as what one likes. Only deeply threatened people must constantly remain silent.

The Kennedy parents led curiously separate lives, which hinted at an unconscious emotional separation. But since neither partner made too many demands on the other, they were able to maintain a harmonious relationship within the apparent confines of unconscious prohibitions. In terms of their society's current attitudes, such sexually based divisions of labor and sharing (Rose knew almost nothing about Joe's businesses) were not regarded as peculiar or inhibiting. From the perspective of today's more generally open relationships, the situation seems intolerable, except for people who secretly do not wish to see too much of each other. Such may well have been the case with the Kennedys. It is interesting to recall that all the sons' marriages followed much the same pattern, with the politician-husband frequently absent from home. In Jack's case, the rela-

tively more independent Jackie also felt free to travel without husband or
children, a pattern consistent with her own upbringing by divorced parents.

The Kennedys' parental control often extended far beyond reasonable
bounds of careful supervision. In the late thirties Rose told an interviewer,
"Years ago, we decided that our children were going to be our best friends
and that we never could see too much of them. Since we couldn't do both, it
was better to bring up our family than to go out to dinners. The Kennedys
are a self-contained unit. If any of us wants to sail or play golf or go walking
or just talk, there's always a Kennedy eager to join in." There is a deep pathos in this revelation of Kennedy insecurities and social rejections. The sad
truth seems to have been that the parents felt so snubbed by the social class
they longed to join that they turned to their numerous children for emotional consolation. Such parental intensity could only have detrimental
effects upon the offspring.

Like her husband, Rose Kennedy longed for the social acceptance and
status that the Boston Yankee Brahmins would never confer on the "upstart" Irish Kennedys. Once, when Jack was a Harvard student, Rose
plaintively asked a friend of his, a member of Boston's best society, "Tell
me, when are the nice people of Boston going to accept us?" Vindication
and triumph finally came when President Franklin Roosevelt—himself an
aristocrat, but one who could laugh at his class—delightedly shocked New
England's blue bloods by naming Joe Kennedy as U.S. Ambassador to the
Court of St. James's, America's top diplomatic post.

Rose was clearly impressed with the Kennedys' new importance. With
rather guileless pride, she commented later, "Obviously we had a superior
entry to nearly everything. If we went to the races we watched from the
owners' boxes. We all had tea with the Queen. The children got a great
deal out of it." So, one may assume, did the parents. As Joe reportedly remarked to Rose one night as they dressed for dinner at Buckingham Palace,
"Well, Rose . . . this is a helluva long way from East Boston, isn't it?" The
Kennedys made the most of their long-sought opportunities. With the
family's size, good looks, and natural exuberance, they were the hit of
London society. Everything they did caused a sensation in the English
press, especially the presentation at Court of Rose and her two oldest
daughters, Rosemary and Kathleen. For this grandly formal occasion,
Mrs. Kennedy wore a beautiful Molyneux gown of silver- and gold-
embroidered lace over white satin, set off by a diamond-and-rubies tiara
and a white ostrich fan. (More than two decades later, she wore the same
gown—without alterations—to her son's presidential inaugural ball.) The
Second World War cut short this blissful period of social celebrity, and the
Kennedys, minus the Ambassador, sailed for home in the fall of 1939.

Child care and homemaking continued to occupy much of Rose Kennedy's time, as well as her church circles and work for the mentally retarded. While Rose thoroughly enjoyed society and had a poised, self-assured charm, her personality was far more restrained than that of her husband, who was excitable in both his enthusiasms and angers. Her emotional detachment was noted by Jack, the son who temperamentally most resembled her: "She was terribly religious. She was a little removed and still is, which I think is the only way to survive when you have nine children." A friendly writer described her dismay at leaving Boston in 1926: "If anybody in the family was reluctant to leave Boston, it was Rose Kennedy who is closely attached to her family there and whose only intimate friends over the years are a few Boston women whom she has known since girlhood." Many writers over the years have noticed Rose Kennedy's reticence and reserve, despite her public surface ease of manner. An interviewer meeting her in her seventies found Rose "reserved and shy at first, avoiding your eye." Like many politicians, the Kennedy matriarch often seems more at home with crowds than with individuals or small groups.

There also seemed to be a large degree of prudery in Rose Kennedy's makeup. While Joe's strain of coarseness is often mentioned, Rose is invariably portrayed as the "perfect lady." The extreme to which this self-image carried her, as well as the unspoken strains such prudery could have put on her family, is suggested by an amusing anecdote. A close friend once exuded, "If I tried to tell you how kind and gentle Rose Kennedy is, you wouldn't believe it. In all the years I've known her, I've never heard her say an unkind word about anybody, and how many women are like that? I remember one time playing bridge with her when that hot news about King Edward and Wally Simpson was beginning to be passed around. One of the girls at the table brought it up. Rose stopped her and said she wouldn't have it discussed in her house because it was slander." The probability that the Kennedy children, who were taught far less restraint by the patriarch, would rebel against such puritanism is evinced by a Kennedy maid's later description of the uninhibited discussions of sexual pursuits among the children.

Emotional display was also strongly repressed. Rose taught her children to hide their feelings from the world and to meet pain and grief with stoicism, which may be admirable qualities in balance and moderation. Unfortunately with the Kennedys, self-control and emotional dissembling seemed to turn into repression of the spontaneous self.

Emotional repression under extreme stress can be a useful psychological dynamic and help one to "carry on" in the face of overwhelming tragedy. But in moments of crisis, such repression has not always served the Kennedys well. (For example, Ted Kennedy displayed an inability to function well after the Chappaquiddick accident, although he seemed superficially rational; and in the 1962 missile crisis, as I will examine, John F. Kennedy might have acted more rationally had he allowed himself to feel the reality of the threat of annihilation to much of humanity, instead of the threat to his personal prestige.) Burke Marshall, assistant attorney general under JFK, gives a hint of this dynamic in his impression of Ted Kennedy shortly after Chappaquiddick. Marshall found Teddy "obviously disoriented, but he appeared coherent." And he added this general observation: "The Kennedys have a way of seeming fine, going forward without interruption under stress — I remember them all at the time of Bobby's funeral — but inside a great deal is blocked off." It is part of my thesis that a great deal of the authentic self has been "blocked off" in all the Kennedys. The emotional pressures of competitive success, which were built up so fiercely by the father and less overtly by the mother, were bound to burst out somewhere: in "accidents" (all the boys), ill health (Jack), rages against others and oneself (Bobby and Teddy), and similar self-punishing trends. Above all, the parental pressures and rigidities produced an evident inability to believe wholeheartedly in anything outside the feudalistic assumptions of an intensely ambitious family. Commitments to people and causes outside immediate blood ties means risk and the danger of further rejection, which the insecure Kennedys could never emotionally afford. Safety lay in running fast and never looking back or within, in obeying parental strictures and a parental God, and in never searching one's own soul and goals with humble doubt.

After Rose's husband returned home from England and resigned as Ambassador in late 1940, he took a more direct part in guiding the children. He had never been an entirely absent father, having often encouraged and admonished the children both in person and by letter. The major family decisions, such as the choice of schools for the boys, had always been made by Joe. Only in education did Mrs. Kennedy oppose him, wishing the sons as well as the daughters to attend Catholic schools. But Joe Kennedy felt that the best nonsecular education would equip the boys better for competing with their peers, so the sons went to Choate, Canterbury, Harvard, and the University of Virginia.

The war years were trying for all the family. First Rosemary, having finally become unmanageable, had to be sent away to a home for retarded children. Contrary to popular belief, retarded children do not become unmanageable if accepted. Mental retardation is not progressive. But a neurotic and hard-driving family would unconsciously signal rejection to a child such as Rosemary. She would sense the undercurrent of conflict in the family and that her existence was a problem. It seems impossible that this power-obsessed family of highly intelligent people could have truly integrated any retarded person. The Kennedys' monomania for constant triumph precluded genuine acceptance of a retarded family member.

Thus, although the Kennedys' conscious intentions for Rosemary were good, their neurotic drives unwittingly made her condition worsen to the point where she had to be removed. On an unrecognized level, the family had resolved the problem of a burdensome handicap. The Kennedys' atonement for their unconscious rejection of Rosemary can be seen in their subsequent passion for the relief of mental retardation, the only large-scale philanthropic cause embraced by this extremely wealthy family.

The Second World War brought an even harder blow. In 1943, Jack was reported missing in action in the South Pacific. Joe Kennedy shielded his wife from the news until Jack's rescue was known. But in the summer of 1944, it was the father who had to be helped, for the shattering news of Joe Junior's death was almost unbearable. Young Joe was his favorite son. Rose, although grieving deeply, has never been as stricken by the deaths of sons as was Joseph Kennedy. This is understandable in light of her religious creed of stoicism and belief in God's ultimate goodness, as well as her natural unconscious jealousy of the boys' preeminence with her husband and her culture. Rose could not have escaped the emotional deprivation and inevitable inner rage at her subservience as a woman, no matter how thoroughly conditioned she may have been to a "woman's place." Religion offered both consolation and the pride of endurance, an endurance she needed often. Only four years later, the Kennedys' second oldest daughter, Kathleen (who had been widowed by the war), was killed in a plane crash. Before that sad event, however, the Kennedys had entered elective politics.

In the first Kennedy campaign, Jack's election to Congress in 1946, Rose Kennedy was in her element. Having been raised in the great game of politics, she took to the campaign with a temperamental zest and skill that came straight from Honey Fitz. Like her father, she knew how to adapt her personality and appearance to her audience. With Italian women in Boston's North End, Rose appeared as the devoted homemaker and mother of nine, sharing recipes and domestic lore. She would greet her audience in Italian, then show them her famous card index file on the children. Her outfit would be deliberately simple, perhaps a plain black dress with one strand of pearls. Then off Rose would go to a meeting of Chestnut Hill matrons, deftly donning en route the dazzling jewelry and mink stole appropriate to an Ambassador's wife. Honey Fitz had used the same tricks of quick dress changes between his political appearances. In a taxi he would shift from a business suit into a tuxedo, or vice versa, and he always removed his fur coat before entering Charlestown, where the voters resented "fancy duds." This family conditioning reappeared at JFK's inaugural, when the new President doffed coat and hat to read his address in the biting cold.

The Kennedys also applied an old Fitzgerald (and Republican) technique of mingling politics and social snobbery. When invitations were sent to "meet the Kennedys" at receptions and teas, thousands of eager women put on their best gowns and lined up to shake hands with the ex-Ambassador and his famous family. As old Henry Cabot Lodge had once remarked of Honey Fitz, "There was not a more resourceful or adaptable political leader in Massachusetts than the King of the Dearos in making social and society functions important aids in political campaigns." While the conservative Boston blue bloods still turned up their noses at the Kennedys, the average voters were only too delighted to be invited to a Kennedy reception. The invitation lists were carefully compiled to cover wide cross-sections where word would quickly spread among the excited women and their families and friends.

Rose also knew exactly what to say to win the attention and sympathy of her audience. In the elite sections of Boston, she would speak briefly about Jack, and then say, "Now, let me tell you about the new dresses I saw in Paris last month." The women loved it. In the important 1952 campaign to put Jack in the Senate, Rose gave one of her typically effective "speeches" in Cape Cod's New Bedford Hotel. Wearing a brilliant red crepe dress from Paris, long black gloves, and a small red-and-black hat, the slender and attractive mother of the candidate modestly told her audience:

"I'm tremendously excited about all this. It is something that never has happened to me before. When I was a girl, my father John F. Fitzgerald was Mayor of Boston and any little talk by me was out of the question. When my husband became Ambassador to Britain, any public talk by me was even more out of the question. And now, I'll tell you something you may find interesting. I have just come home from Paris, and skirts are longer and tighter there!" According to a witness, "The roar of appreciative and surprised laughter and applause that greeted this superb change of pace was testimony to her skill as a public speaker, experienced or not." Rose, of course, was far more experienced than she wished people to know, being in many ways a veteran in politics. When the applause died down, she added, "You are wonderful to come out on this very hot night as you have to see us." It would be hard for the most critical to resist such a charming appearance.

In Jack's 1960 presidential campaign, Rose was once again an eager and close observer of events. According to Ted Sorensen, one of Jack's closest aides, the matriarch would often phone after watching her son on television and comment on some word he had misused or mispronounced. "She's a natural politician," Jack remarked to Sorensen with astonished pride after one long-distance call. "She wanted to know the political situation and nationalities in each of the states she's visiting this fall."

The Kennedy matriarch's political talents were well recognized by JFK's press secretary, Pierre Salinger, who had watched Rose in two campaigns. "She damn well knows all the nuts and bolts of politics," said Salinger, "She knows how to get the votes out, how you make the phone calls, raise money, and all that; and as a speaker, she's an absolute spellbinder. I mean, people are just riveted by her and she never talks about the issues; the issues are a total void with her, I think. She always talks about family." As Gail Cameron commented, "But for Rose, family and politics had always been synonymous, and when she reared her own children, she did so with politics in mind, just as she used carefully fashioned family stories as her primary stumping device.

As a vote-getter, Rose was recognized by the Kennedy strategists as a major resource. A decade later, when Teddy was fighting a hot battle in the 1962 Democratic primary for Jack's old Senate seat, Rose was a significant feature of his campaign. She spoke to Catholic Holy Name societies, appeared on television, and was hostess at receptions and teas. Rose clearly believed in the right of family dynasties to participate in democratic politics. She publicly praised the Adams family and said, "There is no more rewarding career than that of public service. My father and husband spent many years in public service and enjoyed it immensely." She hoped her children would continue this tradition, "and my children's children."

In 1968, with other Kennedy women, this seventy-eight-year-old mother worked for Bobby in the Indiana and Nebraska primaries with her usual energy and radiant smile. In one of the few political gaffes of her career, Rose responded to criticism of the huge sums being spent by the Kennedy forces in the Indiana primary by saying it was their money and they had a right to spend it as they chose. While undeniably true in the material if not moral sense, it was highly impolitic to remind voters how great wealth can be used to swing elections.

Yet, ironically, it was not political triumph but tragedy that brought Rose Kennedy the greatest measure of public acclaim. First came the terrible shock of Jack's assassination in November, 1963. This she endured with a fortitude and a quiet resignation, deeply rooted in religious faith, that won her the sympathetic admiration of the world. It was that dreadful event which abruptly swept both the Kennedy mother and a Kennedy wife, Jacqueline, to a popular fame that for the first time gave them images nearly equal to, and in some ways outdistancing, the Kennedy men they had faithfully served. The Kennedy legend was born at the moment of Jack's death, a legend in which both Rose and Jackie figured significantly.

The tragedy also brought Rose and Jackie to a new mutual sympathy and respect. The women had never been close, being temperamental opposites in many ways and having different outlooks on life, although each secretly treasured popular acclaim, social recognition, and the glamor of clothes, jewelry, travel, and celebrity status that great wealth and Kennedy prestige brought them. But Rose, being of an older generation, had accepted the socially required trait of feminine compliance with far greater patience than had Jackie, in whom one can sense a restless urge for a strong identity of her own.

In the days of Camelot, relations between the two women had been something of an intra-Administration joke. Jackie did not share the mother-in-law's inner imperative that demanded making the right political gesture at all times. On one occasion, Jackie refused to leave her room in Palm Beach—being in one of her withdrawn moods—to have lunch with some important guests, despite her mother-in-law's specific request. At the White House, it became standard to expect the mother as soon as the wife had departed on one of her periodic trips. Yet death dulls many resentments. Even though Rose was probably disappointed when Jackie abandoned the role of "keeper of the flame," in later years she often visited her in Greece and apparently accepted Jackie's new identity as Mrs. Onassis.

A logically based guess is that, essentially, Rose Kennedy and Jackie Kennedy Onassis are both lonely women who seek a constant reaffirmation of their importance to other people and to themselves. Each is a compulsive letter writer, sending huge quantities of mail to distant friends. Unconsciously, each may well see in the other an image of her repressed self. Rose may secretly enjoy Jackie's impulsiveness, since impulsiveness is precisely the characteristic that Rose has so throughly repressed in herself. Jackie, on the other hand, may unconsciously be attracted to the qualities of political drive and determined organization in Rose that she has never cultivated in herself.

A second great blow came to the matriarch five years after Jack's death when Bobby Kennedy was murdered. Rose was not in California with her third son when he was shot, nor at his bedside when he died. But at the all-night vigil in New York's St. Patrick's Cathedral before the requiem Mass, she appeared with her usual calm dignity with the rest of the family. There was a touching moment when the mother came once more to pray quietly and shared a prayer book with a young soldier. When Bobby was buried near Jack in Arlington Cemetery, her grief was contained in tearless composure.

Only a year later Rose suffered two more griefs: the accidental death of Mary Jo Kopechne at Chappaquiddick in July, 1969, and Teddy's disgrace; and then, in November, 1969, the death of her crippled husband, Joseph Kennedy. Again and again, Rose Kennedy's immense fortitude, self-containment, and ability to recover from repeated blows has amazed and moved people everywhere. Whatever else she may be, the Kennedy matriarch is undoubtedly a woman of indomitable courage and stoicism.

Rose Kennedy's philosophy for meeting tragedy has often been quoted in her own words: "This is a good life. God does not send us a cross any heavier than we can bear." After Chappaquiddick, Mrs. Kennedy commented, "How you cope is the important thing, not the events themselves." At least outwardly, her faith in her last surviving son has not faltered. "Teddy has been so magnificent under a tremendous strain which people don't know about. He has been overly conscientious about his father and about me and about Ethel—in addition to his own obligations. He has been so faithful in caring about us all. It has really been unfair—the burden." Even shortly after the 1969 accident, Rose's hopes for the Kennedy political future were not diminished. "I'm sure Ted can rise above all this," his mother said repeatedly.

Since Chappaquiddick, journalists have reported both that Rose persuaded—or ordered—Ted to keep his sights focused on the presidency and that she did no such thing, that she did not really want him to be President. The truth of such intimate interchanges remains veiled, for obvious reasons. But what is clear to the observer is the continued public political activity of both Ted Kennedy and his mother. If it is true that Teddy does not want the presidency and that his mother does not want her last son in that vulnerable position, then their outward behavior is contradictory. For the visible reality is that throughout 1971 and into 1972, until the attempted assassination of George Wallace, Ted behaved like a frenetically active presidential candidate, while Rose Kennedy appeared at political and social functions.

All the Kennedys rallied as usual behind Ted's campaign for reelection to the U.S. Senate in 1970. At a Boston fund-raising event in May, 1970, an irreverent reporter described Rose as "regal in white," and entering "with usual pomp, to the strains of the 'Star-Spangled Banner' . . . on the arm of Cardinal Cushing. . . . She is magnificent at eighty, listing the family's political accomplishments—from her father Honey Fitz in Boston's City Council through her husband the ambassador to son Jack, who (*crescendo*) held the greatest office in the *world:* 'And I come tonight with Ted, my son, my only son, my last son, and I find loyalty . . . response.' Shivers run up and down thousand-dollar spines. Joan has said, in print, that the Kennedy women don't want Ted to be President; but Rose is *not* talking about peanuts." Teddy was returned to the Senate by a large majority.

Rose was also said to have been instrumental in Teddy's physical improvement after Pearl Buck visited him in his office and wrote some unflattering comments on his dissipated and untidy appearance. Teddy lost his excess weight by cutting down heavily on his eating and drinking, and, reportedly, he stopped his compulsive woman-chasing. As one friend put it, "Ann-Margret could walk by Ted's desk smiling madly and he would not take a second look. A few months ago—wow!—he'd have taken off like a moonshot." Rose calmly explained her son's transformation in light of his new responsibilities. As she saw it, "Whenever there are older boys in a house, the younger boys are apt to be frivolous. When Joe was alive Jack was apt to goof off in a debonair fashion. That was natural."

If the reports are true that Rose is the moving force behind Ted Kennedy's possible drive for the White House, this development would only be a continuation of the basic Kennedy attitude that the children's major goal in life is to fulfill the family's claims to greatness. Let us review once more what this means in psychological terms. At heart, this particular family pattern is not so very different from that of many ordinary families in America and other countries. A major ingredient is the partial emotional rejection of the child by the parent, or parents, because of parental needs and fantasies. The neurotic parent is unconsciously largely obsessed with his own obstacles in reaching a genuine self-identity. Because of this, he often turns to his children and tries to mold them into unconscious alter egos and identity projections. In effect, the parent (again, usually unconsciously) wishes the child or children to attain what he himself was unable to reach. His search for identity has two levels: the profound universal human quest for a realization of one's finest human potentials; and, within an often harmful social context, the neurotic quest for the glorified self who seems to embody one's deepest desires.

Thus children in today's families often matter more to their parents as fulfillers of parental dreams than as autonomous individuals accepted simply for themselves. This is a disguised but common form of parental rejection. The intensity of rejection depends largely on the intensity of the parent's own unfulfilled needs and his dependence on his progeny as ego substitutes. In simplest terms, there is all too often a strong element of unrecognized parental need in the way children are "prepared" for life. Too many parents need to control and dominate their children in order to feel important and respected themselves in a society that offers far too few opportunities for individual self-realization. Such neurotically-based "discipline" is bound to create reactions of fear, frustration, and rage in the children, who always sense—though they cannot understand—the secret and dishonest aim behind the outward demands for obedience.

There is a genuinely helpful and healthy form of discipline and structure that all children basically need. But there are also dishonest and highly destructive forms, which may look superficially very much like the real thing. Much of this distinction is behind the current confusion over the so-called schools of discipline and permissiveness in child-rearing. The distinction is a false one, for there need be no conflict in providing both a disciplined framework for the child's needs and healthy areas of permissiveness which enable the child to grow as his abilities grow.

The essential factor is the parent's acceptance of himself as a worthwhile human being, in which case he will quite naturally and spontaneously accept his child as another worthwhile human being. Then the parent, although she or he will inevitably make mistakes, will provide the child with the general atmosphere of acceptance that is essential to healthy growth. The child, in effect, will feel genuinely loved; not loved for artificial, self-serving reasons on the part of the parent, but simply because he is a child and that parent's child. Unfortunately, both our society and our own upbringings have made this sort of natural and loving giving and receiving between all ages extraordinarily difficult. And as we become more confused, conflicted, and defensive ourselves, we all tend to contribute to these difficulties. Too often the vicious circle of neurotic rejection goes on from generation to generation to generation. In that sense we become, as I have pointed out, the "victims of victims."

That something of this sort happened to Rose Kennedy seems quite clear from her personal history and the way it helped determine her attitudes toward her children. Although the Kennedy parents ostensibly demanded "excellence" from their children, their definition of excellence turned out in fact to be public triumph and social vindication. As far as her social philosophy went, the mother was always as conservative and conventional as her husband.

From the many descriptions of Rose Kennedy her chief characteristics emerge with general consistency. As a mother, she was organized, strict, inflexible, self-disciplined, perfectionistic, and firmly in control. She gave her children a great deal of attention and kindness, yet she also believed in the value of competition, hard work, and punishment. Emotionally, she seems kindly but not warm, a person much aware of her dignity and preferring to hold herself somewhat aloof. This fits into a general pattern of rigid inner self-control and emotional inhibitions. From girlhood, Rose looked to her religion as a major consolation and guide, and was quite puritanical and conforming in both social and religious milieus. In brief, Rose Kennedy as a wife and mother believed thoroughly in energetic self-discipline and self-denial without complaint, constant effort, and strict rules strongly enforced. She was also socially ambitious and felt rebuffs keenly. It is this combination of considerable unconscious self-rejection combined with overt social rejection that has basically fed the Kennedy matriarch's apparently insatiable hunger for political prominence and triumph.

In addition to finding deep satisfactions from her sons' successes, evidence suggests that Rose Kennedy's outward strength has been rooted in a second ambivalent self-image: an unconscious conviction that she herself is super-woman. "I will never allow myself to be vanquished or annihilated," she has proudly affirmed. Her conscious feelings of mastery and superiority rest primarily on an ironclad stoical acceptance of all that life might bring. This acceptance itself is very probably based on a deep-rooted unacknowl-edged fear, and a hope of warding off this fear through the magic of total discipline, dedication, and a fatalistic acceptance. Unconsciously, the Ken-nedy mother could feel that the tragic blows life dealt her were special tests by a divine providence to prove her toughness and self-discipline. Both Kennedy parents greatly valued the quality of toughness. But while Joe's toughness was directed at other men, Rose's has been directed primarily at fate. She tried to make her children follow her standards as much as possible, but her fulfillment came only partially in their triumphs. Rose Kennedy's greatest fulfillment, according to the psychohistorical evidence, came from feeling herself as her own ideal.

Pushing her sons on to greater achievements could also be an unconscious way of punishing them for their masculine dominance, as well as a way of arranging for herself newly satisfying tests of strength and endurance. All such ambivalent needs, I can hardly repeat too often, would be totally repressed from mental consciousness. And if we look deeply within our own feelings, most of us may well find similar ambivalent impulses toward our own children. The more we recognize such impulses, the more we can accept and control them, and the weaker they will eventually become in both our unconscious and conscious lives.

The type of neurotic perfectionism exhibited by Rose Kennedy is whole-heartedly supported by the tenets of the Roman Catholic Church. Rose's lifelong close adherence to this church is probably the second reason—along with an inner taboo on emotional weakness—why family tragedy did not destroy her stability. Above all, the Catholic Church teaches the acceptance of God's will as revealed through the Church's teachings. Resignation, submission, and guilt are the emotional values most emphasized for Catholic women. The Church's authoritarian legalism fitted perfectly into the psychic necessities of a neurotic demand for behavioral perfectionism, puritanical standards, and an absolution of guilt. While the Church's ex-treme emphasis on "mortal sin" and guilt add to the already great burden of guilt present in every neurotic, the Church also provides a means of expiation and forgiveness through confession and the sacraments. Thus the neurotic guilt can be projected onto the religious guilt and, on the conscious level, comfortably taken care of by the method psychoanalysts call "ex-ternalization" of inner conflicts.

For a devout Catholic such as Rose Kennedy, the daily ritual she rigorously followed would help keep repressed neurotic pangs and disturbances within bounds. Death, of course, is fully provided for by the Church, as is all of life. The grieving mother could take pride and comfort in her belief that her dead children were now eternally secure in a heaven she had helped provide. These comments are not meant to detract from the genuineness of her loss and courage. But they are intended to suggest the artificiality of that solace, and the toll it exacted on both mother and children by ruling their emotions and reason with a thinly gloved fist.

Yet, one might ask, even if this is all true, what is wrong with it? If perfectionistic standards and resignation can support a person through life's tragedies and give him the strength to endure staggering blows with dignity and hope, are not these valuable and admirable qualities? The answer is that *non*-neurotic patterns of feeling and behavior can provide equally admirable qualities of strength, hope, and endurance, but without exacting a terrible cost in emotional spontaneity and fulfillment. The basic difference between neurotic and non-neurotic responses is that the first constrict life to a narrow, suffocating channel, while the second open up life to awesome human possibilities. Neurosis disables; maturity enables.

Although a neurotic perfectionist may meet crisis and tragedy with tremendous courage and dignity, there is inevitably a pathos to the timidity with which he approaches the less dramatic areas of life. Invariably, one finds a narrowness of view, an overconcern with meaningless trivia, and an inability to transcend a limited outlook and add to the manifold variety of human existence. For all of her philanthropic works (mainly in the area of mental retardation), Mrs. Kennedy has revealed no deep commitment other than to her family and her own standards of upright, impeccable behavior. With access to millions of dollars and to many influential people, she has failed to use either for other worthy causes. One could well wish for a little less will power and dignity and a little more imaginative humanity.

Neurotic people who have deep ambivalences toward themselves often show conflicting behavior. Kind and considerate to her friends and family, Mrs. Kennedy could apparently be stingy and thoughtless to her servants. She ran her household in a surprisingly casual and disorganized way for a person so concerned with rules and discipline. Yet, from a psychological viewpoint, this could well be the repressed side of Rose Kennedy that was bound to reveal its presence in some manner. The maltreated servants may also have served as unconscious projections of Rose's own feelings of worthlessness, as humble and partly helpless alter egos whom she could unconsciously punish and humiliate. While such suggestions may seem strained, and even cruel, similar psychic dynamics are commonplace; they operate in most of us at times.

To conclude this short assessment of the all-important mother, in Rose

Kennedy one cannot help but sense an unconscious arrogance, an assumption that God is on the side of the Kennedys. This feeling seems to go far beyond a simple "faith" in the essential goodness and mercy of God despite earthly suffering. For the Kennedy matriarch, faith means a conviction that the Kennedys are especially destined to be national leaders and that the White House will again be ruled by a Kennedy Administration. This feeling of omnipotence has been found to be inevitably present in neurotic personalities, as mentioned, though often deeply repressed and disguised. It is the exaggerated counterreflection of an inner sense of powerlessness and threat.

For Rose Kennedy, such insecurities were learned young, both as a female in a male-dominated culture where men were assumed to be the natural rulers and as an Irish Catholic in a society where Yankee Protestants were assumed to be the natural superiors. In the mind of the Kennedy founding mother, the old European idea of the "divine right of kings" has been transformed into a compensating "divine right of Kennedys," which apparently gratifies her deep hungers and unexpressed rebellions. While Rose Kennedy can hardly be condemned for her emotional development under such repressive conditions, the rest of us need not share her fantasies. The Kennedy sons have given no evidence of any extraordinary brilliance—their brilliance has been moot at best; and certainly their integrity, courage, and honesty have often been in doubt.

Chapter 4

JOSEPH PATRICK KENNEDY, JR.:
THE PRICE OF GLORY

The pyramid of sibling precedence, established by Kennedy, had at its apex his eldest son, "Little Joe." The vital, handsome, argumentative young man always was closest to his father's heart, and it was taken for granted that he would succeed him as the family's standard-bearer.
—Richard J. Whalen, *The Founding Father*

It was Joe who exemplified and insisted upon their father's rigorous code of values. Failure was not to be tolerated; passivity was a disgrace. Unremitting effort was the only door to respect.
—William V. Shannon, *The Heir Apparent*

I think that if the Kennedy children amount to anything now or ever amount to anything, it will be due more to Joe's behavior and his constant example than to any other factor.

He had a pugnacious personality. Later on it smoothed out but it was a problem in my boyhood.
—John Fitzgerald Kennedy

ℜℭ

FROM THE MOMENT Joe Junior was born in Nantasket, Massachusetts, on July 25, 1915, this first Kennedy son—the firstborn of nine children—was the father's favorite. It soon became evident that it would be young Joe's task in life to achieve the political and social successes his father had failed to win because of his temperamental liabilities. Some boys are slated for their father's prep school, the Ivy League, and eventual management of the family business; Joseph P. Kennedy's eldest son was intended for a grander destination—the presidency of the United States.

71

It is not unusual for a parent to want to realize his own dreams through a child's achievements, although this is never a healthy desire for either parent or child. But it is extremely unusual for a parent to choose the equivalent of installation on Mount Olympus as that dream. Yet Joe Senior's choice was not as fantastical as it may have seemed to those who did not comprehend the depth of his drives. Kennedy's political acumen, while apparently inhibited when it came to his personal advancement, seemed to operate fully at one emotional remove from his own ego needs, when focused on his sons. The drive toward the presidency was also supported by the political ambitions of Kennedy's father and father-in-law. (The latter, Honey Fitz, predicted upon Jack's election to Congress that he would one day occupy the White House.)

Joseph Kennedy had already achieved the preliminary goals of money and political influence, the latter a partial inheritance from relatives and in-laws, when he failed to realize his own presidential ambitions. Bested in 1940 by his parental surrogate, FDR, he still had an ideal son and namesake who could make it in his place. If the father could never sit in the famous oval room at 1600 Pennsylvania Avenue, he would work toward the next best—or, psychologically, the best—thing: an occupant who was name of his name and blood of his blood.

In Joe Junior, Joseph Kennedy had not only a substitute identity to win victories for him; he had also a surrogate father to preside over the family sessions and keep the other eight children in line during his frequent absences. While Rose Kennedy was a firm and dedicated mother, the parents felt that the children—especially the boys—needed a constant exemplar. As Rose put it, "I always felt that if the older children are brought up right, the younger ones will follow their lead. It was easy for all of the children to look up to Joe Junior because he was a good scholar, a good athlete, and popular with girls as well as men in every neighborhood where we lived."

To Rose this may have seemed ideal, but there are good reasons to believe that the practice is harmful. The exacerbation of sibling rivalry was constantly demonstrated in the Kennedy family—in Joe's furious rows with Jack, knock-down and drag-out fights witnessed in cowering fear by Bobby and vividly remembered by him years later. As far as the other boys were concerned, Joe's hot-tempered pugnacity and sexual prowess—traits exemplified by the father—may very well have contributed to serious defects in their personalities. In later years, both Bobby and Teddy showed difficulty in controlling their tempers, while Jack and Teddy, and, to a problematical degree, Bobby, became woman chasers.

Yet outwardly the heavens seemed to have smiled bountifully on Joseph P. Kennedy in his namesake, the mentor of Kennedy standards, the "standard-bearer." Young Joe was a model son in every way, patterning himself completely on his father. He imitated his father and absorbed his opinions, and in an argument his final authority was Joe Senior. He was everything that a father determined to put his name in the White House could hope for. And that was a good deal. Joe Junior was strong, healthy, handsome, extroverted, and intelligent. He was also a willing and dutiful son, an exceptional student, and a good athlete. He obeyed his parents completely, though without losing his high spirits, and apparently fully absorbed their constant drilling in discipline, loyalty, courage, competition, and, above all, winning. Only in small matters did the first son rebel against the father's authority—as in his liking for strong, black cigars. Kennedy Senior could not understand why anyone would waste money on tobacco. What the father failed to see was that smoking cigars can allow an immature young man to feel more masculine and virile. Later on, Jack, Bobby, and Teddy would all take up cigar smoking, the Freudian symbol of potency and power. (Freud himself was addicted to cigars even though he developed cancer of the throat.)

The family took it for granted that Joe Junior would carry the Kennedys to glory as successor to the father. With the confidence of an heir to enormous wealth who had his own natural talents and aptitudes, and driven by a dogged determination to succeed, there seemed little that the eldest Kennedy son could not accomplish. He was, in the current idiom, fully programmed for success.

As a baby, Joe had plenty of company besides his parents, including a nurse and assorted laundry girls. Soon he had family playmates, and shortly after the First World War the Kennedys moved from their crowded gray frame house at 83 Beals Street in Brookline to a much larger home a few blocks away on Naples Road and Abbottsford. Rose partitioned the huge front porch into individual play areas for the children, and there was domestic help to keep order while Joe Senior was away adding to the Kennedy millions.

Joe's childhood was typical for a boy of his background. His father made certain he went to the "right" schools. This meant non-Catholic schools at the upper levels if an Irish Catholic was to compete with patrician Protestants. Joe Junior's first school was Devotion School nearby in Brookline, a nonparochial institution named for Edward Devotion. Entering kindergarten in the fall of 1921, the little boy had trouble at first adjusting to the strange environment. But the next four years were easier and he earned good grades. Jack had entered a year behind Joe, and as the boys grew older their rivalry increased. Joe was gentle with his sisters and the younger children, for the most part, but Jack refused to defer to Joe's superior years and strength. In one now-famous incident, Joe and Jack raced their bikes around the block in opposite directions and collided head-on.

Joe was unhurt; Jack needed twenty-eight stitches. Both Joe and Jack learned how to charm and manipulate the Kennedy servants to get around their mother's small allowances and stern punishments for misbehavior. The use of charm and quick talk became one of Joe Junior's most distinctive traits. In later years, this ability, added to his good looks and natural talents, would make him irresistible to many people of both sexes.

By 1924, Joseph Kennedy's fortune had reached the point where he felt it was time for his sons to take a step up in the social and academic world. Not far from the Kennedy home, on St. Paul Street, stood the Brookline branch of Noble and Greenough School (later renamed Dexter), an old (1866) private school with strong ties to Harvard and students bearing distinguished Back Bay names. The school's uniformed sports gave Joe an outlet for his physical aggressiveness, and he worked hard at football and baseball. Unfortunately, like his father, young Joe bickered with umpires, and he shoved other infielders aside to go for fly balls. Joe Junior's pugnacity also showed up in Sunday School, where many Brookline Catholics remembered him as a "hell-raiser." According to some, he was the kind of boy who "couldn't pass a hat without squashing it in or leave an unprotected shin unkicked. He was cracked on the head by the Sisters with a catechism book so often, it was a wonder the top of his head wasn't flatter than a pancake."

Even in boyhood, Joe Junior often displayed an aggressive self-centeredness and arrogance very like his father's. He was rough, tough, and combative in sports, effective on the baseball field, especially as a pitcher; but he was also a bad loser (like Joe Senior) and definitely a "me-firster" with the other players. There is no mystery to this behavior, for Joe Junior was clearly raised to be intensely aggressive and, above all, a winner. Combative sports also offered effective arenas for discharging some of the hostility that would inevitably build up in a young man so driven by an overexpectant father. Later in life, beating up drunks, seducing women, and flying in a war would provide further socially and paternally acceptable outlets for Joe Junior's inner rages. This, of course, was not Joe's only side; but his hair-trigger temper and violent actions, which at times seemed to have sadistic elements, are a part of his personality too often overlooked in the laudatory praise of a dead hero. Unless we try to understand this less praiseworthy and smoldering side of Joe Junior, we will fail to understand the emotional conflicts that drove the Kennedys to their extraordinary successes and may well have helped drive young Joe to his death.

Young Joe had a ready target close at hand—his younger brother, Jack, an often infuriating rival for parental attention and approval. Jack was two years younger than Joe, wiry and slight where Joe was sturdy, no physical match in strength but a challenge in daring and quick-wittedness. Whereas the older, heavier Joe could use the head-on approach, Jack had to rely on impishness and sheer endurance to begin to hold his own. Many writers have viewed the Kennedy boys' fraternal battles as natural in strong, high-spirited sons, but sibling rivalry is not an instinctive trait, and does not exist in less competitive societies. Such competition is a learned pattern of behavior, a fight to win acceptability on socially and familially approved levels. In this context, we can see how the Kennedy neurosis and the general neuroses prevalent in America have many common roots and take similar forms.

Joe's constant attempts to dominate his younger brother and his apparently insatiable need for stardom strongly suggest a deep-seated ego lack, a need for public reaffirmation, identity, and applause. Such a probable lack is not hard to understand in view of the constant parental pressures, the ceaseless criticism (although tempered with praise), and the example of a father who established that ruthless activity is the sure route to success. Joe's father once called him the "star of our family," but the evidence points to a serious emotional uncertainty in Joe Junior that being the star of the family was a genuine or unshakable identity.

Because Joe Senior was frequently away on business and his mother was busy with Robert, Joe Junior turned to his grandfather, Honey Fitz, for paternal company. Soon young Joe was eating Sunday dinners with his grandparents and other relatives in their suite at the old Bellevue Hotel in Boston. Joe's unrequited longing for more parental attention is underlined by the subsequent observation of a college roommate, Ted Reardon (later Jack's Senate aide), that Joe's idea of a big night out was to sit in the Reardon kitchen while Ted's father cooked supper. It was a role unfamiliar to the Kennedy patriarch. Honey Fitz and Joe Junior became close friends, and the grandfather's huge fund of political lore and enthusiasm undoubtedly helped spark the oldest Kennedy son's precocious interest in politics. While the Kennedy father always had his sights set high for his boys, it is possible that Joe Junior actually thought of becoming the first Catholic President of the United States before his father. Indeed, such a grandiose goal could have been initially an unconscious way of competing with his all-powerful, incredibly successful father. According to some biographers, young Joe announced this goal to both his Brookline and prep school classmates. Certainly, he had made a firm decision before he entered Harvard, for the English socialist, Harold Laski, with whom Joe studied, well remembered Joe's determination to become President. That was in 1933, years before Joe Senior himself was mentioned for the presidency. But the older Kennedy disliked personal politicking, as he admitted to friends, and was probably delighted with the idea of a filial substitute. The way would have been clear for young Joe within the Kennedy domain had he returned from the war.

But at eleven, Joe Junior missed his father. When Kennedy *père* became thirty-eight, his oldest son sent him a loving birthday card, but the picture showed only the back of an armchair with a protruding pipe. Joe worked hard in school to win his father's approval. Then the time came for the Kennedys to move to a loftier address and a freer social atmosphere. In 1929, Joe Senior packed his family and servants aboard a private railroad car and moved to Riverdale, New York, only a few miles distant from Wall Street. Their new home, high above the Hudson River, was a grand slate-roofed mansion with sweeping grounds and woods which enticed Joe and Jack to adventurous explorations.

Joe Senior was still often absent on business and his oldest son tried hard to take his place. One morning, seeking to show his concern for the dollar, Joe Junior argued with Kathleen over a new schoolbag. "She doesn't need one," Joe decisively told his mother. But Kathleen fought back. Then Rose exerted her authority, telling Joe to go upstairs and write down "I must mind my own business" a hundred times. (As an ex-Sunday School teacher, Rose often used this disciplinary technique.) But Joe also spent many hours patiently playing with his sisters and youngest brothers, teaching them to catch footballs, somersault, swim, sail, and play tennis. He took his fatherly responsibilities seriously and seemed to derive a deep gratification as the commander of eight.

Occasionally, however, Joe's parental fervor carried him beyond reasonable bounds. When Teddy was two years old, Joe (then nineteen) decided to teach him to swim: he tied a rope around the chubby youngster and heaved him into the water. Fortunately, Teddy was used to the water and able to paddle back to safety. Teddy was Joe's favorite, but this did not protect him from brotherly challenges or wrath. Another time, Joe dared Teddy into diving from higher and higher points on the Riviera's Eden Roc, until Joe Senior called a halt. Brother Joe also once angrily threw Teddy overboard when he failed to understand a sailing command.

Eunice, six years younger than Joe, has commented on his easily aroused wrath and poor sportsmanship: ". . . he was very good, but he had quite a strong temper and would be cross as a billy goat and would blame somebody else when he didn't win."

In Riverdale, the Riverdale Country Day School provided an exclusive environment equal to the social stature and athletics of the Brookline school. Joe was a neat student, although messy at home, and soon received excellent grades even though, like Jack, he was usually late for the bus. Solidly built, Joe was also a star on the athletic field. The Kennedys became popular with both students and faculty, their home providing grounds for touch football games, Hollywood movies in the special basement projection room, and bootleg Scotch for the instructors. On Saturday afternoons, the absentee father would take his children into New York for lunch, the circus, a rodeo, or the movies. Joe Senior's prominence in the film world brought his off-spring introductions to many celebrities, and the young Kennedys grew used to moving with ease among the famous.

That same year, 1929, the founding father bought the Kennedy summer home in Hyannis Port, where other fast-rising businessmen were settling and the Puritan cool was less chilly than in patrician Cohasset. Joe Junior found old Brookline friends already summering there, and soon the Kennedy grounds were trampled by ambitious young athletes headed by Joe. At thirteen, Joe was the accepted family head when both parents were absent, carving the roast and presiding over the family table, assisted by a new young governess. In the next seven years, Rose Kennedy found relief from her lively brood by visiting Europe no less than seventeen times. In her absence, Joe Junior's decisions were final, even to an often reluctant Jack.

Kennedy home life at Hyannis Port in some ways resembled a rigorous summer camp. Children and parents went to bed early and rose early. The boys reported on the lawn at seven for vigorous calisthenics with their physical-education instructor. After breakfast, the children were released from duties for swimming and sailboating, although here, too, they had stiff lessons and goals to reach. Joe Junior was remembered by local residents as "rugged and fearless, full of restless energy," and a natural leader. Whether his leadership was entirely "natural" or not is a moot point; certainly it was acquired at a very early age.

But even relaxed Hyannis Port was not overly welcoming to the Irish Kennedys. Even so, the children held their own among the Yankee offspring, acquiring warm friends as well as gold medals. What the Kennedys lacked in lineage and social graces, they often made up for in charm, energy, and enthusiasm. While the Kennedys' tendency to count pennies, and the children's tendency to expect others to serve them and defer to their wishes, did not endear them to everyone, probably in these respects they were no worse than many of their rich neighbors; and in their general social unaffectedness and casualness, the Kennedys must have appealed to many of the younger crowd. For the Kennedys stayed at Hyannis Port. It became their favorite home, and later the site from which Jack Kennedy planned and won his campaign for the presidency.

At thirteen, Joe Junior found his first love in Hyannis, a California girl who was visiting an old Cape Cod family. She herself was immune to the widespread social snobbery that scorned the Irish *parvenus*, but the social ice that formed around her friendship with Joe proved too much. She and her mother returned home. Young Joe nursed his hurt and wrote ardent letters for many months, but he was too high-spirited to brood. Perhaps the dashing of these early hopes helped make him more cautious in future emotional attachments; not for another fifteen years did he fall in love. In between, he turned into a rather obsessive and highly skilled girl-chaser, a gallant young man who coolly played the field, dazzling with his good looks, wealth, charm, and social background, but never remaining attached to any one companion for long.

Joe also had other things on his mind that busy summer. The sparkling waters of Nantucket Sound off Hyannis Port offered even better sailing than at Cohasset, where the older boys had first learned to sail. Now Joe entered wholeheartedly into the sport that would remain his favorite, boat racing. As the daring leader of the Kennedy racing tribe, he set the aggressive standard for the other children. Eunice, like Joe, was a natural sailor, and Jack and Kathleen learned fast. With wild recklessness, but a sure sense of timing at the buoys and a feel for how much canvas the boat could stand, Joe made the Kennedy name prominent in local boating circles. Unfortunately, he also cast it in partial shadow when his professional skipper rigged the boat with a new mainsail larger than allowed by class regulations. Joe trained Jack as an able crewman, and the two often raced together to victory. But ashore they continued their intermittent battling, with Jack using nimble wit in an essentially hopeless fight against Joe's greater strength. Both boys competed in dead earnest, for, as Joe's biographer pointed out, "Behind his flashing smile and easy laugh Joe was steel and his status was always at stake."

But stronger competition lay just ahead. That fall of 1929, Joe Junior entered a still more exclusive world, the narrow but prestigious confines of Choate, one of America's most famous preparatory schools for boys. Located north of New Haven, the elegant Connecticut school stressed good manners and dress as well as high scholastic standards. Even though Joe's teeth earned him the nickname "Rat Face," he showed confidence in his new surroundings. Choate offered a wider arena for his combativeness; to Jack's huge delight, Joe also came in for his share of rough hazing. As Jack wrote their father about his older brother, "He was roughhousing in the hall a sixth former caught him he led him in and all the sixth formers had a swat or two. Did the sixth formers lick him. O Man he was all blisters, they almost paddled the life out of him. What I wouldn't have given to be a sixth former. They have some pretty strong fellows up there if blisters have anything to do with it."

At first Joe was frequently criticized by his house master for having his room generally out of order, making trouble for the sixth formers, and roughhousing with his roommate. His grades were poor, except in algebra, and the headmaster wrote the Kennedy parents, "Joe is still somewhat superficially childish. We like Joe so much that we want his best and Joe himself really wants to give it to us." Whether parental admonition was the exact cause is unknown, although it is likely, but at sixteen Joe Junior woke up and began to treat his life at Choate as an important race. Suddenly he was working hard, and his grades shot up. Joe also began to feel his relative insignificance on campus as a mere junior varsity guard. He started jogging through the rolling countryside to build stamina, meeting a fellow student en route who introduced him to Choate's ruling clique. Soon Joe was a school power, and he and his newfound friends delighted in schoolboy pranks and practical jokes. All his life, Joe would remain a confirmed practical joker and teaser, a trait charming in a teenager but somewhat suspect in an adult. We will see later where this tendency to get the better of others, sometimes not too subtly disguised by so-called humor, would lead him.

But at Choate all was well, despite occasional school punishments and speeding fines. Nor did Joe ever forget his evident primary interest, his family. He urged his parents to visit him at school, delighted in his trips home and in his new baby brother, Teddy. He even visited Jack at Canterbury School twenty-five miles away. Joe also kept up his religious training, kneeling regularly to pray and reporting to his mother each time he went to church. He was now yearbook editor and playing first-string football, with a growing reputation as an athlete-scholar. Choate's maturing effect on Joe caused the Kennedy parents to send Jack there also, for the second son was having problems at Canterbury. This decision was probably a mistake, as the direct competition was renewed and Jack fell farther behind. By his senior year, Joe was so outstanding that he won the Harvard Trophy, awarded to the graduate who best combined scholarship and sportsmanship (meaning, of course, playing skill rather than graceful losing on the field).

In November, 1933, with Joe Junior an eighteen-year-old six-footer fresh out of Choate, Joseph Senior was busy scoring more monetary coups. But his son's future was still uppermost in the father's mind. Rose Kennedy suggested a year at Oxford or Cambridge, but Joe Senior, after consulting with others, including Associate Supreme Court Justices Felix Frankfurter and Oliver Wendell Holmes, Jr., decided that young Joe could best learn to cope with the changing America of the Depression and the New Deal by studying under England's leading socialist, London School of Economics Professor Harold Laski. Laski was also a former Harvard professor, eased out after his support of the 1919 Boston Police Strike, and now a friend of FDR and New Deal leaders.

That fall, Joe Junior joined other American and British students attending Laski's seven weekly lectures and the afternoon teas in his flat. Professor Laski found Joe "adorably young and still more adorably unsophisticated," and later wrote, "He has often sat in my study and submitted with that smile that was pure magic to relentless teasing about his determination to be nothing less than President of the United States." Laski's widow, Frida Laski, remembered years later how "Joe would always come to the teas. He was tall and very good-looking. And argumentative, and very bright, but of course he was at a disadvantage. My husband would finish discussing some point and then he would turn to Joe, sitting on the floor, and say, 'Now Joe, what will you do about this when you are President?' "

Joe's London roommate, a fellow American named Aubrey Whitelaw, described Joe's typical response: "In a room full of experts . . . dead silence for only a second, and then Joe would tackle the problem in a completely logical manner and struggle through it until he had answered—not batting an eye or retreating from established positions either." Laski would often humorously deflate Joe's simplistic and naive answers, but Joe apparently took the good-natured ribbing in stride. He was a great kidder himself, constantly teasing people and taking off on their accents and peculiarities. Only when the butt of humor or criticism was a Kennedy relative did Joe Junior lose his self-possession. Then he could lash out with a volcanic fury. Later, a Harvard classmate disparaged Boston's ex-mayor Fitzgerald, not knowing that Honey Fitz was Joe's grandfather. The grandson leaped from a chair and floored the astonished speaker.

In London in those still-gay prewar years, Joe and "Whitey" found amusements to lighten their serious studies. Joe brought his roommate into the upper levels of society. He even took the astonished Whitey to an audience with the Pope in Rome, then on to Munich where Joe thumbed his nose at a Nazi poster. Using Kennedy Senior's letters of introduction to British filmdom, Joe and Whitey had no trouble filling their rooms at teatime with glamorous starlets and London debutantes. Joe also recruited his friend into his strenuous regimen of prebreakfast jogging and riding in Rotten Row. Every week, Joe phoned his family, and he kept a family photo placed "like a shrine" in the living room, Whitelaw recalled. The two young scholars also enjoyed tangling with the British in rugby, roughing up the game with bone-jarring, head-on tackles that the Englishmen could find no rules to outlaw. At the end of his studies, Joe traveled to Russia with the Laskis, visiting Moscow and Leningrad and getting a headache in the Anti-Religious Museum. For once, reported Frida Laski, Joe Kennedy did not want to argue. But later Joe urged his mother and Kathleen to visit Moscow and see the Museum for themselves, which they did the next year.

Back home, a somewhat older and more confident Joe entered Harvard in the autumn of 1934. Football again became a major interest in his life, as it would later be for Jack, Bobby, and Teddy at Harvard. The dominant Kennedy motif of the importance of being a football player, connected as it is to the central family theme of heroic glorification and tough virility, raises a delicate but not irrelevant psychological problem. This is the question of deeply repressed homosexual urges in the Kennedy sons. Such a subject is difficult to view dispassionately, since in our basically antisexual society, most Americans have a nearly hysterical fear of homosexuality. The psychobiological fact of the matter, however, is that all human beings have the potential for homosexual relationships. Whether the potential will ever be strongly felt or acted upon depends on a widely varying constellation of emotional and social factors that are different for each individual. For people suffering from serious neurotic conflicts, many psychologists have found, the latent homosexual potentials which all "normal" (that is, relatively non-neurotic) people possess usually become strong and often deeply feared and repressed urges. It is also widely known that men who engage in exaggeratedly violent or carnal activities are commonly partly motivated by conflicting homosexual fears and attractions. This does not mean that all football players are repressed homosexuals, although the excessive passion with which this brutal sport is regarded in America suggests some strong tendencies in that direction on the part of both players and audiences.

The prevalent dual Kennedy traits of frenetic physical activity, including a constant pull toward contact body sports, and obsessive sexual activity lead inevitably to the suspicion that constant proof of virility was so badly needed by the Kennedys because the dread of its absence was so compelling (virility in our society being simplistically equated with heterosexuality). Certainly the enormous demands put on all the sons by their largely emotionally rejecting parents, demands reinforced by a hypercompetitive society which also rejects women as less worthy than men, would have offered amply fertile ground for the planting of seeds of sexual confusion and torment.

At Harvard in 1934, Joseph Kennedy Junior, weighing 175 pounds and nearly six feet tall, made the freshman football squad despite the heavy competition ranged against him. Other players found Joe a little uncoordinated, but "the kind of guy," as one teammate put it, "who would spark a team, a guy you could depend on for the *big* play, if you let him in." In those brisk autumn afternoons by the chilly Charles River, young Joe joined the other Crimson "jocks" as they slammed into blocking sleds and dummies. Joe began carrying a football around the Yard, and asked "T.J." (Ted) Reardon, soon his closest friend, to throw to him. During his sophomore year, Joe offered to pay two thirds of T.J.'s room and board in Winthrop House, but Reardon refused. Another time, Joe wrote a check for T.J.'s tuition, but again his struggling classmate refused Kennedy's generosity and finally got a Student Council loan. But once Reardon made the mistake of teasing Joe about Honey Fitz—and was swiftly booted out of the room. Meanwhile Joe was undergoing various injuries from his football scrimmages. He tore his knee at practice and had to be operated on; then he broke his arm, and was seen driving his yellow Ford with a plaster cast; finally a blow to the head gave him a concussion. But nothing daunted Joe's determination. Indeed, such "battle scars" may well have given him a feeling of nobility.

Winthrop in Joe's era was the "jock" house, and Joe worked hard to make the Harvard varsity. But in football, Joe encountered more than a physical penchant for injuries; an even greater obstacle was his emotional distaste for Harvard's head coach, Dick Harlow. "Gentleman Dick," as this intelligent fat man was known, had an autocratic personality as well as the imagination to construct original football plays. Joe Junior, who argued hotly with his own autocratic and sharp-tempered father, found it hard to accept Harlow's domination. Harlow, in turn, sensed Joe's dislike. Joe also had the disadvantage of being a marginal player on a team of good ends. When success eluded him on the football field, he went out for rugby and scored the winning goal against Yale, earning him headlines in the New York newspapers.

Scholastically, Joe was an apt student. In his sophomore year he made the Dean's List and was appointed to the Tercentenary Celebration Committee, both advances in prestige that Joe Senior warmly applauded. The father also added his usual admonitions against financial laxity, for the nominal young millionaire was usually broke after spending his allowance. Young Joe tried to earn funds for himself, but he lacked his father's touch. In the summer of 1936, both Joe and Jack—who had entered Princeton instead of Harvard—spent several months at manual labor on the Arizona ranch of a Kennedy friend to toughen them up for the coming year.

Back at Harvard for his junior year, Joe was elected to Hasty Pudding and the Spee Club. By then he also had developed a lone-wolf technique of stealing other men's dates on college weekends, thus avoiding paying for the girls' transportation. Skiing was another sport that attracted the adventure-loving Joe, although he was too impatient to bother with lessons. He swam, sailed, and played golf, basketball, and intramural squash. In 1937, he was defeated for Student Council marshal, but decided to graduate from Harvard *cum laude*, which meant writing a thesis.

A less innocent side of Joe emerged during these undergraduate days. He and his fellow jocks would provoke brawls in East Boston saloons on Saturday nights for the pleasure of wreaking mayhem on drunken steelworkers. Although Joe's friends might be as drunk as the workers, Joe himself, like nearly all the Kennedys, drank little. Again, the facts suggest a need for violent outlet, fleshly contact, and the assuaging of an inner rage.

Joe was also befriended by his father's friend, Boston police commissioner Joe Timilty, and enjoyed watching the force at work after dark in the dives of South Boston. On one occasion he found a chivalrous target for his fighting impulses when he heard a woman screaming in a car. He beat up her attacker. Unfortunately, the police mistook his aim, and the furious youth spent a night in jail.

Joe Junior's biographer, Hank Searls, noted that Joe's tastes in female companionship ran more to showgirls and strippers than to Eastern college girls. But Joe, though bored—and probably unconsciously threatened—by Boston society, enjoyed New York's glamorous café society. His father's financial and theatrical empire gave him great advantages over the typical Harvard "girl collector." As Searls commented on Joe Junior's freewheeling amorous activities, "Today Joe would be a collegiate swinger; in the mid-thirties he was simply an active, handsome young student playing the field to keep himself free. His relations with the other sex required finesse and, Bilodeau [a classmate] recalls, considerable last-minute shuffling of the unhappy victims. He had vast energy and great impatience. . . ."

Joe was also famous for his wit and sense of humor, although some victims were never certain when the needling sarcasm was really meant. Jack Kennedy appreciated Joe's fast humor, but also saw in him "a slight detachment from things around him—a wall of reserve which few people ever succeeded in penetrating. I suppose I knew Joe as well as anyone and yet I sometimes wonder if I ever really knew him. He was very human and most certainly had his faults: a hot temper, intolerance for the slower pace of lesser men, and a way of looking—with a somewhat sardonic half smile—which could cut and prod more sharply than words. But these defects—if defects they were—were becoming smoothed with the passage of time." By this time, Jack was with Joe in Winthrop House (he had fallen ill at Princeton and transferred to Harvard) and the boys ate dinner together daily. Their rivalry seemed buried, but it still smoldered. Once Joe moved in on Jack when he was escorting a beautiful young singer at Harvard, and the flattered starlet found herself with two escorts. Another time, in New York, Joe spotted Jack with a glamorous date at the Stork Club, lured Jack to a phone, and pirated his girl.

In November, 1937, Joe's graduation with honors from Harvard the next June seemed assured, but he had not yet won the ardently desired Harvard football letter. It was Joe's last chance to win the coveted "H" by playing in a Harvard-Yale game. When the great day came that blustery November, Joe was still benched. But he and the other senior nonlettermen were confident Coach Harlow would put them into the game's last few seconds to earn their letters; it was an old Harvard tradition. Unfortunately for Joe, his father had taken precautions. Pessimism had served Kennedy Senior well in the stock market, but in dealing with people his lack of human insight led him to disaster. The day before the game, Kennedy had an important friend telephone Harlow and ask if Joe would get his letter. The ultrasensitive coach exploded and told his backfield coach, "Nobody's going to high-pressure me!" That night as Harlow slept in a hotel suite, Kennedy himself phoned, but an assistant coach detoured the call.

The next day, Coach Harlow sprang his surprise plays on Yale, and in the last quarter, with six minutes to go, Harvard held the lead. Everyone expected Harlow to send in the graduating players, but he made few substitutions; as the seconds ticked by, the ignored seniors fought back tears. When the game ended, at least eight, including Joe, had failed to earn their letters. Joe Senior furiously cursed Harlow, but he was helpless. It seems likely, from the known story, that Kennedy's own actions had prompted the proud, stubborn coach to exact this revenge on his son. (Years later, Harlow lost his coaching job in a player mutiny; he ended his Harvard career as the "Curator of Oology," overseeing the university's egg collection.) The Ambassador's bitter disappointment was doubled by Harvard's failure to award him an honorary degree. Joe Senior, as mentioned, never forgave his alma mater.

But Joe Junior was much younger, and fresh challenges healed old wounds. The next spring, he played rugby again for Harvard and was severely bashed about by Cambridge University's team. In June, 1938, the McMillan Cup sailing contest was held at Joe's own Wianno Yacht Club in Hyannis Port. For three days Joe and Jack raced in the familiar waters of Nantucket Sound, but in direct contradiction of most Kennedy literature, they did surprisingly poorly: neither scored on either the first or third days; on the second day, Jack was next to last in the fourth race, neither placed in the fifth, and in the sixth race Jack scored second and Joe fourth. But their combined points in the sixth race caused distorted headlines to credit the Kennedy boys with giving Harvard its victory over Williams. Actually, other Harvardmen had scored far more points, one man winning two victories, though this was barely mentioned. But Joe did win an "H" in sailing. And his thesis, "Intervention in Spain," which most likely took the Kennedy conservative position that America should stay neutral (the paper has since vanished), was judged worthy enough to merit a *cum laude* degree from Harvard.

In the summer of 1938, the new graduate, barely twenty-two, was eager to see European developments for himself. Hitler had seized Austria; Czechoslovakia had partly mobilized; and his father, representing the United States at the Court of St. James's, was a firm friend of Prime Minister Neville Chamberlain and his appeasement policies. Joe traveled to England with the Ambassador and Jack on the *Normandie*, and the boys spent their time en route dating girls. In Dublin, they paused for an honorary degree for Kennedy Senior and some emotional family touring, then headed for the Princes Gate residence in London where Joe became an embassy aide. On his first night in town, Joe joined the exclusive 400 Club and entered the golden world of that generation's "beautiful people." As an aristocratic English friend described him, "Joe liked the racetrack very much. And so did I. All of us were roughly the same age. Joe was more rugged than Jack. Joe very much *liked* being in England. He saw the point of this country, and one always likes to know that. Socially, and with the girls, he was a very great success." The young nobleman also remembered Joe and Jack competing for girls; but that fall Jack left for his junior year at Harvard.

In a family Christmas at Saint-Moritz, Joe discovered the dangerous thrills of bobsledding, dated a world skating champion, and broke his arm when he recklessly went skiing alone in the Alps, without benefit of instruction or practice. The Kennedy's family nurse helped drive him to the nearest hospital, three miles away. Joe's arm was bleeding badly, but Nurse Hennessy remembered that "Joe—like all of the Kennedys—had this high threshold of pain, and he never complained, except afterwards he'd say, 'Look at this! It sure looks awful, doesn't it?' "

For a glorious year, between enjoying the amenities of London and family vacations, Joe Junior traveled widely through Europe on a variety of exciting missions. First his father found him a temporary post in the U.S. Embassy in Paris, and right after the Munich pact of September, 1938, young Joe carried dispatches to the legation at Prague. From doomed Czechoslovakia, Joe journeyed to Warsaw, Poland, and then continued on to Leningrad, Stockholm, Copenhagen, Berlin, and back to Paris.

Joe was anxious to witness the last throes of the Spanish Republican government, which was being hammered into submission by Franco's Catholic legions, aided by Italian troops and German bombers. Like his father, Joe supported Franco, although his firsthand view of Spanish suffering gave him a human sympathy for the war's victims. By the time Joe reached Spain in late January, 1939, most American volunteers had left the Spanish Civil War or were dead or imprisoned. With his diplomatic connections, Joe saw Barcelona fall to Franco, on January 29, and then snagged a British destroyer to Valencia, the last Republican port. Valencia, with its hungry people living in rubble under deafening bombing, was a grim shock. By special Loyalist bus, Joe traveled to besieged Madrid, where he endured the terrors of air raids, Franco's artillery, and the fighting between Communist and non-Communist Loyalist factions which made the streets of the crumbling city highly dangerous. But the apparently fearless Joe got in touch with the Franco underground, and one night saved himself and his companions from being gunned down by militiamen in a dark street by showing his American passport. When Franco's troops marched into fallen Madrid, Joe was still there, busily sending reports to his proud but worried father. As the churches opened and Falangist bands paraded, Joe left for London via the French border; in a few weeks he returned for an auto tour with his sister Kathleen and a British friend. After a final Riviera vacation with the other Kennedys, Joe and Jack went to Berlin for a diplomatic assessment of the approaching war. Jack carried back the charge d'affaires' estimate of war within a week, and when German troops entered Poland on September 1, Joe Junior also left Berlin for London.

The prewar European adventures were over. After helping arrange sailings for American victims of a torpedoed British liner, Joe joined the other Kennedys as they returned home in different ships, traveling in cautious separation. In Manhattan, Joe was met by reporters and spoke on the radio. Then, leaving his temporary celebrity behind, Joe Junior headed for Cambridge, Massachusetts, to begin his new career at Harvard Law School. But Joe's international reputation had preceded him, and apparently he liked the flavor of fame; his biographer notes that when Joe's Spanish Civil War experiences paled with repetition, he began embellishing his adventures. Some of these tall tales now adorn the Kennedy saga, such as the story of his being jailed, stripped, and searched. Again, we can see the Kennedy need for heroic stature, an appetite which feeding only seemed to make larger.

While Harvard Law may at first have seemed dull next to wartime Europe, Joe Junior threw himself energetically into his work. Requirements were stiff, and a man either studied or flunked out. But young Kennedy also had the funds and personality for raucous good times. In his apartment, always shared with at least three other law students, Joe kept an alligator named Snooky in the bathtub, hired a houseman and a cook, and threw endless exuberant cocktail parties and songfests. He also gave play to his old passion for practical jokes. Once Joe set Ted Reardon's watch and the apartment clocks ahead three hours and sent T.J. speeding fearfully to a new job supposedly at noon instead of nine. Another day Kennedy urged a friend onto a horse he had chosen, started a race, and watched the other mount bolt and throw his classmate. One ex-flatmate described Joe as "Goodlooking, articulate, attractive, energetic. A very tough guy. Just a little bit unfeeling; he wouldn't have been elected the most popular man in the class." Even Tom Bilodeau, a very close friend, admitted, "Like the rest of the Kennedys he never felt he owed anybody anything." Joe still preferred models, singers, and working girls to debutantes and "nice Irish girls who wanted to get married." As Bilodeau recalled, "We had a terrible time trying to keep his girls apart." Joe also enjoyed playing bridge with Harvard Law professors, friends of his father; one housemate noted the subsequent improvement of his own marks. Like Jack, Joe loved to read, and his studies came easily. A classmate commented that "Joe was a born lawyer . . . sharp and aggressive. He could cut you apart—the best natural speaker of any of the Kennedys." Joe also worked on his style by taking courses in a Boston speech school.

Joe Junior still felt a political fever in his blood, and in the summer of 1940, between his two years in law school, he decided to have a preview of his future career. Roosevelt was cannily hedging on a third term, and Joe wanted to go to the Democratic convention as a Massachusetts delegate. Supposedly, he was a shoo-in, but, just to make sure, Joe campaigned hard —and won by a hair. Joe, like the other Massachusetts delegates, was pledged to support FDR's Postmaster General and National Committee Chairman, James A. Farley. In the stifling heat of Chicago in August, Kennedy found that Roosevelt was preparing to steamroll his way to a third-term nomination. Farley, who had been criticized by FDR, held out for the procedural vote. Prevoting pressure had been put on Joe, including calls to his father, who refused to interfere (by then the rift between Ambassador Kennedy and his former mentor, FDR, was deep, although they still maintained an outer amiability), and young Joe stuck to his pledge, the only Massachusetts delegate to call out his miniscule half-vote for Farley. In the stadium's rowdy and manipulated uproar, which disgusted Joe, the young novice politician had the satisfaction of feeling himself a man of honor.

After vacationing in California and a quick trip to Mexico City, Joe returned to Harvard Law for his second year. Three weeks later he registered for the draft, along with seventeen million other young Americans. Even that early, Joe had decided to try for naval aviation and a big patrol plane. The responsibility of a crew appealed to him rather than the freedom of a fighter. In light of his background, we can understand why Joe would wish to follow the pattern that in his youth had given him both security and a sense of authority. He had worked hard in Cambridge groups to keep America out of the war, but now that his country drew nearer to the conflict, Joe wanted his share of the action. Young Kennedy also campaigned for Roosevelt, as did his father, and introduced FDR to a Boston crowd when the President made his famous "You boys are not going to be sent into any foreign wars" speech. Five days later, Roosevelt squeaked back into office, and shortly afterward the Ambassador gave the indiscreet interview that ended his role in Roosevelt's Administration.

The pace toward war quickened. In March, 1941, Lend Lease was passed to help save Britain, and in April FDR extended the Atlantic Patrol. In May, with his graduation near, Joe Kennedy signed up for the Naval Aviation Cadet Program and passed the preliminary tests. Deferred until the end of the term, he was sworn in as a seaman second class on June 24; naval cadets did not become officers until graduation from flying school, a technicality that would make Jack senior to Joe when he signed on as an ensign several months later. According to Searls, Joe was proud of Jack but shattered "as previously undefeated contender for family honors. . . . For the first time Jack had passed him, and no matter how Joe strained, he could never catch up. He had a grim suspicion that if their paths crossed in uniform, his younger brother would never let him forget his seniority."

After preliminary check-outs at Squantum Naval Air Facility near Boston, Joe was sent to Jacksonville, Florida, for flight training. He loved to fly, although he found commands in the air hard to execute quickly. But he satisfied some of his repressed volatility (and hostility) by becoming president of the base Holy Name Society. This entitled him to wake up Catholics in the barracks for early Mass—which he did with a bucket of water at 5 A.M., including some Jews for good measure. Joe also outfinessed competition to become president of the Cadet Club, thereby gaining *carte blanche* for social invitations from local Floridians. But most of the time he spent sweating over navigation, mechanics, radio codes, and the demanding skills of flying the Navy's lumbering patrol boats. Joe graduated seventy-seventh out of a class of eighty-eight, but his fitness reports were above average and he was noted for his forceful character, likable personality, and cooperative attitude. With an attrition rate among naval air cadets of nearly 50 percent, Joe's was an achievement to be proud of. Ambassador Kennedy addressed the graduating cadets and broke down with emotion, but he pinned on Joe's golden wings.

From Jacksonville, Joe went in 1942 to Banana River, Florida—today renamed Cape Kennedy—for operational training. The nearest town, Cocoa, was sleepy in those days, so in his spare time Joe read, went fishing with a few pretty local girls, and phoned his family. To gain the air hours that would give him faster command of a plane, Joe requested instructor duty. For six months he taught pilots to fly the PBM Mariner. The plan worked. In January, 1942, after touring New York's night clubs on leave, Joe reported to San Juan, Puerto Rico, where in a few weeks he was given a plane, to the chagrin of others who did not know of his extra flying experience. At first there was some tension between Joe and his men. The squadron's chief found that "he stood for perfection in himself and expected the same from others. This at times led to a strained relation between him and his crew. At one time the relationship became so bad that it came to the attention of the squadron skipper." Apparently things straightened out, and Joe made friends among the other ensigns. The ocean patrols became longer, but no one spotted any U-boats. Off-duty, the naval officers enjoyed San Juan's country-club hospitality. Joe liked to gamble, take out the señoritas, and bar-hop with his buddies, though more for the sociability than the drink. Finally, with San Juan running out of air fuel, if not rum, Joe's outfit was ordered back to Norfolk, Virginia.

Joe was becoming increasingly impatient for the glory he had worked so hard to prepare for. Brother Jack was already a lieutenant (j.g.) slamming around the South Pacific in a PT boat. Joe heard of an actual sub sunk by a patrol plane off Newfoundland. Clearly, the North Atlantic was the place to hunt for action. But while he waited for more exciting duty, he diverted himself with the lonely Navy wives who filled Norfolk and with ex-showgirl friends from New York. Joe's biographer described the bachelor millionaire as "almost too handsome, just under six feet and broad-shouldered, with dark chestnut hair and the sapphire eyes of his family and a curving patrician nose and teeth straightened at Choate School. He had a remarkable lop-sided grin, devastating to women."

Joe rented an apartment and a car and began adding to his amorous reputation. Searls commented that "some of Joe's correspondence with Jack seems to hint that the brothers were engaged in a neck-and-neck international race for female conquests, but down deep Joe was emotional, vital, and honest with women, losing his arrogance when he truly cared." Despite Searls' chivalrous opinion, evidence is lacking that Joe often "cared." According to a close friend, Lorelle Hearst, Joe was "terribly sweet" with girls "and immediately made you feel very close to him and that you'd known him forever. He had a tremendous physical attraction and also there was a tough side to him. I don't know what would bring it out in him, but sometimes he could be cruel. He preferred girls a little older than himself because they had a little more sense. He never would have married anyone who wasn't socially prominent, mostly virginal, and Catholic, I think." We can see here other clues to Joe's repressed hostility toward women, a hostility that is evident in all the Kennedy men. This is not hard to understand in view of their social milieu, religious upbringing, and the dominance of a *machismo* father and a puritanical mother in a possessive family environment.

Finally, in June, 1943, a plane in Joe's squadron sighted a sub and dropped depth charges, though without effect. By this time Jack was in the thick of action, and even Kathleen Kennedy had reached London as a Red Cross worker. Joe's impatience grew, until suddenly, in mid-July, orders came for part of his squadron to report to England for training in antisubmarine work under the R.A.F. Coastal Command. The Navy was training its patrol pilots to fly B-24 Liberators for ocean and English Channel duty. Joe was overjoyed, the "most excited man in the room," according to his radioman. "He was bursting with enthusiasm." Another airman also noticed Kennedy's excitement. "I can recall quite well how enthused he was. . . . He was an eager beaver. He wanted to get with that war and get with it fast." Patrol flying might have seemed tame service to bomber and fighter pilots, but the dangers—even more from bad weather than from the enemy—were real. Joe's squadron would lose sixty-eight dead and a dozen planes, and win two Navy Crosses, four DFC's, twenty-seven Air Medals, and two Purple Hearts.

The group had six weeks to check out in their new craft. While Joe ferried aircraft from San Diego to the East Coast, Jack's PT-109 was cut in half by a Japanese destroyer, but, except for the Ambassador, none of the Kennedys knew this until Jack was rescued. Joe was deeply relieved when he heard the news, but also freshly motivated to win glory for himself. Now Jack was not only a battle veteran; he was a genuine hero. Joe's crewmen noticed their skipper's intensified ambition. His navigator complained, "When I tried to make casual conversation I got the positive impression that I was talking about firecrackers to a man valiantly trying to perfect the atom bomb before an impossible deadline." For Joe, the deadline was the end of the war.

A small incident illustrates just how important that deadline was to the Kennedy quondam "star." During his training for overseas, Joe went to Hyannis for his father's birthday. At the traditional Kennedy dinner, a prominent Massachusetts judge proposed a tactless toast that omitted Joe: "To Ambassador Joe Kennedy, father of our hero, our *own* hero, Lieutenant John F. Kennedy of the United States Navy!" According to Hank Searls, "Everyone waited, but that was all. The judge sat down. Joe Junior, face flaming and a sturdy grin plastered to his face, lifted his glass to his father and absent brother. But it was the final straw. That night as they turned in, he could hold in his frustration no longer and Timilty (who shared his room) could hear him crying in the other bed."

But soon Joe and his men were in Cornwall, England, fighting the dreary English weather and learning how to evade storms, enemy fighters, friendly flak, and barrage balloon cables in the crowded, hazardous air over the British Isles. Day after day the PB4Y's (converted Liberators) went out on ten- and twelve-hour patrols in eye-straining search of U-boats. Getting back to base was equally hard, for often the thick English fog had smothered their landing strip and the planes had to grope their way to unfamiliar bases, dodging the bursts of British gunners who had learned to fire at any strange aircraft. Planes and men crashed in bad weather or vanished at sea under the gunfire of the fast German fighters against whom they were nearly helpless. Joe Junior himself had several narrow escapes, once fighting off two Messerschmitts and another time sweating his way through hours of bad night weather, including being lost in a forest of balloon cables, before he landed in rain at another airdrome.

Yet life was not entirely the cold discomforts of the endless mud at Dunkeswell in Devon (where they had been sent from Cornwall), the boredom of the base, the monotony of long patrols, or the intermittent moments of horror when guns or weather brought violent death to unlucky flyers. Joe also had occasional passes to London, where "Kick" (Kathleen) was stationed; and there one day he met a woman described anonymously by his biographer as "the girl with the sky-blue eyes and a warm mischievous laugh." For the second time in his life, and perhaps really the first, Joe Kennedy apparently felt a passionate emotional attachment. Soon he was spending weekends with this woman and her aristocratic friends whenever he could get leave. Joe's new attachment was a member of the English nobility herself; her first husband was one of England's wealthiest peers. Married for the second time, she was the mother of several children, and her husband was a British artillery officer stationed in Italy. Joe and a few close officer friends visited her, along with Kick and other friends, in the country cottage where she had taken her children for safety. On the day Joe died, a year later, he had planned to join her there after returning from his last mission. Exactly what his intentions were, we perhaps will never know. From Searls' account of their many meetings and the constant phone calls Joe Junior made to this young woman, their feelings were apparently serious.

But through the rest of 1943 and early 1944, the war was Joe's major concern. He wanted to survive, but probably more than anything, he wanted to be a hero. Yet enemy targets were maddeningly elusive. Joe was known as a good and responsible pilot, even if a commander who insisted on unusual discipline and formality in flight. But as the end of his standard thirty-five missions neared, an element of desperation crept into his careful flying. He suggested using the PB4Y as a low-level bomber against surface ships; on his last patrol, he volunteered for a special mission searching for surface craft. But nothing happened, and Joe's crew had failed either to sink a sub, despite five contacts, or to shoot down an enemy plane. Joe's duty was over, but unlike Jack he had no decorations to show for it.

So, in the spring of 1944, with D-Day nearing, Joe Junior volunteered both himself and his crew for a second tour. Kennedy never asked the war-weary crew how they felt about staying. Probably few, or none, would have stayed, according to biographer Searls. Kennedy's thoughtless arrogance in volunteering his men for possible death or maiming is indicative of his neurotic need for heroic vindication, which made him emotionally callous about the fate of others. Like it or not, Joe's men were stuck for another twenty-five missions, the accepted number for a second tour.

That spring brought Joe a more personal duty. His sister Kick, after much soul-searching and long discussions with Joe, finally decided to marry the man she loved—an English Protestant and the heir to the Caven-dish fortune, William ("Billy") Hartington. Both sets of parents strongly disapproved of the marriage, but the determined couple decided to go

ahead anyway. Joe told Kick that if she were certain, he would stand by
her; and on May 6, 1944, he gave away the bride in the Chelsea Registry
Office. Afterwards Kathleen wrote of her oldest brother, "Never did anyone
have such a pillar of strength as I had in Joe in those difficult days before
my marriage. From the beginning, he gave me wise, helpful advice. When
he felt that I had made up my mind, he stood by me always. He constantly
reassured me and gave me renewed confidence in my own decision. Moral
courage he had in abundance and once he felt that a step was right for me,
he never faltered, although he might be held largely responsible for my
decision. He could not have been more helpful and in every way he was the
perfect brother, doing according to his own light the best for his sister with
the hope that in the end it would be the best for the family. How right he
was!" Joe Junior was never a coward, and once he had made a decision he
stuck by it. Unfortunately, as we shall see, flexibility is sometimes the better
part of valor.

   In that electric June of 1944, it became apparent that Joe Kennedy would
have his second chance to sink an enemy sub and earn the citation he seemed
to crave so deeply. The great fear of the Allied D-Day planners was that
German U-boats would destroy or scatter Eisenhower's invasion force. To
prevent such disastrous attacks, the U.S. Navy and R.A.F. patrol bombers
were to fly a tightly-woven surveillance over the English Channel's southern
end, through which the raiders would have to come from their French bases
on the Bay of Biscay. As June 6—D-Day—dawned, Joe and his crew began
the demanding patrols. Sub contacts were everywhere, but the Allied planes
harassed the U-boats so successfully that the subs exhausted their batteries
from endless crash dives and sank not a single ship on June 6. Joe's radioman
wrote in his diary during this period that Kennedy was a "no-nonsense guy
when on the job and expects the same of his crew. Yet his manner is at all
times democratic and engaging. Some of his crew find him a slavedriver
but their loyalty and respect is unwavering." The exhausted flyers began
drinking themselves into nightly insensibility under the constant strain, but
Joe usually took off for London or the country home of his young woman
companion. The weeks passed without a submarine kill, and Joe lost much
of his usual caution. Once he tried to hit a grounded E-boat, but was driven
off by heavy antiaircraft fire. Then he flew against orders so near to the
German-held island of Guernsey off Brest that his plane was hit by enemy
flak.

   Joe's second tour ended, still minus a victory. He turned down an offer
to be an assistant naval attaché in London; perhaps he feared his attachment to the woman was growing too strong. Already his squadron mates
thought he was engaged. Joe went to Plymouth and celebrated his promotion to full lieutenant with Navy friends. At Dunkeswell, he sent some of his
gear to the ship he intended to sail home in, one commanded by a friend.

For Joe, the European war seemed to be over; but the Pacific remained, and a chance for glory. Suddenly, before leaving, Joe was called in with other experienced pilots and asked to volunteer for a highly dangerous mission. According to Searls, Kennedy "volunteered immediately, demandingly, and with great enthusiasm."

Thanks to a diligent reporter, we know today many details of that top secret mission which were carefully concealed for nearly three decades. In the book *Aphrodite: Desperate Mission*, Jack Olsen describes the desperate efforts of American Army and Navy pilots to save London from the terrifying flying bombs that began devastating the city on June 13, 1944, a week after D-Day. The V-1 and V-2 missile programs were Hitler's last frightening scheme to save the crumbling Reich; German plans were even advanced for a missile to hit New York City. Allied military men and technicians frantically put together a jury-rigged scheme to have war-weary bombers loaded with explosives and flown by radio control into the apparently impregnable German V-1 sites on the French coast. Pilots were needed to lift the heavy planes off the ground and link them up with the radio system of the controlling mother ships; then the volunteers would parachute to safety. The risks were enormous: technical malfunctions were many, and the men had to bail out at high speed and low altitudes.

After six Army-piloted flights ended in total failure, the U.S. Navy, which had spent years using radio-controlled drones for target practice, took over the top-secret project. Joe Kennedy arrived at the secret English base of Fersfield on July 30, flying a new Navy PB4Y that would be packed with explosives. While Joe's plane was being readied, the Army got their doomed flights into the air, with alarming results: one pilot was killed, one lost an arm, one sprained his back and knocked four teeth down his throat, and only three—50 percent—escaped with minor injuries. None of the planes hit their targets.

But the Navy men were eager to go, and the officers vied with each other to be Joe's co-pilot. Finally, the Navy executive officer solved the problem by choosing himself. Lieutenant Wilford ("Bud") Willy was a pilot and experienced control technician, and he felt he had the best background. On August 12, 1944, at a little before six in the evening, Joe Kennedy's explosive-packed PB4Y took off for its target on a 150-mile zigzag route that would reach the V-1 site across the Channel near Calais at about 7 P.M. In the air, the mother aircraft took control, and Joe and Bud Willy began checking out instruments. Without warning, at 6:20 P.M. the plane exploded over England in two tremendous blasts one second apart. No trace of the bodies was ever found; the plane's debris was scattered over a wide area, although all four engines were later recovered. The huge blast damaged dozens of houses, but no one on the ground was hurt.

Hank Searls' account lists several possible causes of the accident but does not reach a conclusion. But Olsen's book is specific and startling. According to Olsen, who interviewed everyone connected with the disaster, a brilliant electronics officer working on the project, Lieutenant (j.g.) Earl Olsen (no apparent relation), discovered that the mission was almost certain to fail because of a poorly designed firing system. Horrified, Olsen told Willy, who was both his superior and a good friend. But Willy, who had himself installed a safety pin to ward off stray radio transmissions, refused to listen. Despite Lieutenant Olsen's careful explanation and insistence that the safety pin did not solve the electrical problem, Willy would not allow any changes. According to author Olsen's account, Bud Willy, who had come up from the ranks, was insecure in his new position and insisted on going by the book; the "experts" had designed the equipment, so it must be all right. Lieutenant Olsen, deeply alarmed by what he saw as a highly dangerous situation, went to a friend, autopilot expert Ensign Jimmy Simpson, and together they explained the problem to the base officer in charge of the Navy group, Commander James Smith. Smith listened with friendly interest, but like Willy he flatly refused to question the stateside experts. Ensign Simpson, who roomed with Kennedy and greatly admired the tall, devoted, self-contained pilot, tried to tell Joe of Lieutenant Olsen's worries. Here is Jack Olsen's account:

> " 'Joe,' he said, 'there's something serious I want to talk to you about.'
> " 'Serious about you, serious about me, or serious about the mission?'
> " 'Serious about the mission,' Simpson said.
> " 'Is it something we can do something about?'
> " 'Maybe *you* can.'
> "Kennedy was silent. 'Jimmy,' he said, fixing his narrow eyes on the other. 'I've been all around Robin Hood's barn about the mission. People have been asking me all kinds of things, suggesting all kinds of things, and I've developed a policy about the whole matter. And you know what that policy is.'
> " 'To keep quiet and obey orders?' Simpson said.
> " 'That's the way it is.'
> " 'And you won't change now?'
> " 'Nope,' Kennedy said. 'Not for you or anybody else.' "

On the day before the mission, Lieutenant Olsen "felt like crying or fighting or both. No one would listen. The PB4Y was almost fully loaded now; there would be 20,570 pounds of Torpex and 600 pounds of TNT demolition charges aboard, and on four hours' notice the whole deadly load could be ordered into the air, safetied by an amateurish arming panel and an improvised 'safety' pin that only made the device more dangerous."

Filled with forebodings, Earl Olsen saw Kennedy coming out of the hangar and impulsively hurried over. According to Jack Olsen, the lieutenant told Joe that the system wasn't working right. He had wanted to make changes, but no one would let him. Kennedy thanked him for his concern, but said he didn't have any say in the matter; he had just volunteered to be the pilot. Olsen replied that Kennedy had a big say, that he could refuse to fly unless changes were made. Kennedy could go to the skipper and tell him to fix up the plane. "Kennedy paused. 'No,' he said. 'I don't think I will. I think I'm gonna fly it.' He started to walk off, then turned and waved a friendly hand back toward the radio officer. 'Thanks, anyway, Oley,' he said. 'I know you mean well. I appreciate it.'" According to Simpson, Joe was upset and angry that evening, but only over the mission's postponement and his inability to tell his waiting friends, including his young woman, that he was delayed. Olsen's warnings had apparently been lightly dismissed. The next day, an outwardly cool Kennedy and a highly nervous Willy took off; half an hour later they were dead.

Joe Kennedy's death was an unnecessary folly, and the blame seems scattered among the incompetent technicians who designed the arming device (including a lieutenant present at the base who scorned Lieutenant Olsen's suggestions) and the fearful men, including the victims themselves, who worried more about questioning higher authority than about risking human lives in a highly dubious enterprise. By contrast, Joe's successor as Aphrodite pilot, a Navy captain's son, insisted on inspecting every detail of the project and refused a co-pilot; he bailed out safely, with minor bruises. Thus Lieutenant Olsen's claim that Joe could insist on last-minute precautions was not farfetched. Certainly in view of the Army pilots' repeated disasters, such questioning would not have seemed out of line. But young Joe Kennedy was not a man who questioned higher authority. Raised in an intensely patriarchal environment, he showed the ability to command men as he was commanded, but an unfortunate—and ultimately disastrous—tendency to let himself be dominated in the most important areas of his life. It was Joe's double misfortune to be caught in a situation with men whose emotional uncertainties about life seemed to equal—and even surpass—his own. The ability to stand by a decision can indicate a strong, integrated character in some situations; but under certain conditions, an element of emotional stubbornness and a taboo against changing one's mind can be a weakness and a sign of deep-seated insecurity rather than genuine strength. The final decision of Joe's life—to go on with the uncorrected mission despite serious warnings—falls, I believe, within the second category.

The final question raised by Joe Junior's death is why he volunteered for such a semi-suicidal mission at all after having served two dangerous tours of duty. Why, in fact, did this young man, who had an overriding ambition in life—to be the first Catholic President of the United States—and who had the enormous resources of wealth, family, influence, and talent to achieve that goal, risk his personal and family immortality on the sheerest chance? Several writers have argued that Joe Junior was motivated primarily by a desire to uphold the family's honor and restore the Kennedy name to glory and admiration in England, where his father's actions and opinions as Ambassador had cast it into disrepute. Many Britishers had even attributed cowardice to Joe Senior when he spent nights in the country during air raids (where a bomb nearly hit his house), surely a mortal insult to a Kennedy. From the psychohistorical point of view, these reasons are unconvincing. While gibes at the Kennedys could add to the son's determination, they seem minor factors. Such criticism was four years old and relatively insignificant in the fury of an all-out war. Meanwhile Kathleen and young Joe were warmly accepted members of wartime England and had numerous friends among the aristocracy. Indeed, Kathleen, "the girl on the bicycle," had already achieved public popularity by her uniformed rides as a Red Cross worker through wartorn London, and she soon married into the English nobility. Jack's wartime heroism had also been widely reported in England. Thus to reason that young Joe was stung by insults to his father into reckless action seems very farfetched.

There is another explanation of Joe's motivation that makes complete sense in light of his evident characterology and the Kennedy family history. This is the seemingly insatiable hunger in the Kennedys' oldest son for stardom and family triumph. When we look back at Joe's years of childhood, youth, and young maturity, we can see how this hunger wove like a crimson thread through all his activities. The constant need for glory and parental recognition seemed to be the vital umbilical cord that tied Joe to the athletic fields where he fought his way to repeated acceptance; to the daring adventures that carried him onto untested ski slopes, down icy toboggan ramps, and behind the lines in the Spanish Civil War; and that finally drove him into the cockpits of repeated war tours and a doomed flying bomb. As a substitute father to his younger brothers and sisters, Joe had to live up to the double expectations of ensuring the younger children's admiration, obedience, and respect, and of winning the parents' constant approval. He was scarcely allowed to be a child himself and to grow up at his own pace; premature maturity was expected of him and forced on him. If he reacted with secret aggressions against others and against himself, it is hardly surprising. Through these years, Joe was trailed by a younger brother, a sibling rival who constantly challenged his right to filial preeminence—and finally, unbelievably, actually surpassed him both in wartime rank and heroic achievement. Such a humiliation was intolerable. At any price, Joe had to regain his status in the family. This, I believe, is what drove Joe Junior to accept, despite misgivings and actual warnings of failure, the mission that killed him.

Joe Kennedy was posthumously recommended for the Congressional Medal of Honor, but both he and Bud Willy were instead awarded the next highest decoration, the Navy Cross. In addition, a new destroyer was named for young Joe, the U.S.S. *Joseph P. Kennedy, Jr.;* it was launched in the fall of 1945 and christened by Joe's favorite godchild, his sister Jean.

Apparently, a successful effort was made to keep the facts of Joe's death from the powerful Kennedys, for postmortem investigations totally supported Lieutenant Olsen's opinions. Both military and civilian electronics specialists concluded that the pilots had been killed by a faulty arming panel. As a final irony to the grim tale of futility, when the Allies overran the V-1 sites in France, the concrete domes were found to be empty, having been abandoned months before the Aphrodite project was organized. But the Kennedys never learned these disturbing facts, and undoubtedly found some comfort in a letter from a naval officer who had gone to Harvard with Joe. It read in part, "You may not have heard that he *was* successful and that through Joe's courage and devotion to what he thought was right, a great many lives have been saved."

The death of Joe Junior was a terrible shock to the father, one from which he never fully recovered. The only consolation was that, so far as the Kennedys knew, Joe had died a hero at a meaningful moment in history. There is no evidence that they ever doubted this fact. Heroic triumph and vindication were the foundation of the Kennedy ethos. To hear or believe a suggestion that the eldest son—the heir to a dynasty—could have died in a futile accident would have been inadmissible.

The oldest son was dead, but the family had a second young hero to carry on the Kennedy name and fulfill the father's ambitions. Jack was home safe, wounded and weakened, but recovering enough for his father to start planning for the future. There was still a chance that a Kennedy would become the first Catholic President of the United States.

Chapter 5

THE MAKING AND SELLING
OF JACK: 1917-1947

Jack hates to lose. He learned how to play golf, and he hates to
lose at that. He hates to lose at anything. That's the only thing
Jack gets really emotional about—when he loses. Sometimes, he
even gets cross.

—Eunice Kennedy Shriver

I thought everybody knows about that. Jack went into politics
because young Joe died. Young Joe was going to be the politician
in the family. When he died, Jack took his place.

I got Jack into politics, I was the one. I told him Joe was dead
and that it was therefore his responsibility to run for Congress.
He didn't want to. He felt he didn't have the ability and he still
feels that way. But I told him he had to.

—Joseph P. Kennedy

It was like being drafted. My father wanted his eldest son in
politics. "Wanted" isn't the right word. He demanded it. You
know my father.

—John F. Kennedy

We're going to sell Jack like soap flakes.

—Joseph P. Kennedy

୬୯

JOHN FITZGERALD KENNEDY, less than two years younger than the oldest
Kennedy son, Joe Junior, was born on May 29, 1917, in Brookline, Massachusetts. As a boy, Jack competed as was expected in games, sports, and
intellectual achievements both at home and at school. Like the other

eight children (except retarded Rosemary), he displayed the same furiously aggressive energies and physical recklessness, either in competition with his brothers and sisters or banded together with them against friends and enemies. And like the other Kennedy children, young Jack did not rebel overtly against the family code of never being satisfied with anything less than first place. While victory could only be intermittently achieved, what counted was the constant effort; only collapse ever put a Kennedy out of the running.

The rigor of the Kennedy constant-motion regime and competitive up-bringing is illustrated in a remark by Rose Kennedy about their domestic life: "The children argued about everything and among themselves in sports and games. They were taught to ski, play tennis, to swim and play golf. One of the chief problems for parents of large families is to keep the children occupied, particularly during the holidays. We always had a pro-gram prepared for them. They raced against one another and as a family team against others on foot, in swimming and in boats during the summer. Throughout the school year they had the same interests and engaged in the same sports as children in our neighborhood. We always lived in a house near a good school and a good playground. It was our idea that if they had to do something, they ought to learn how to do it well in order to compete with children in the neighborhood. All of them went to dancing schools and they began when they were quite young."

We have already seen what a keen interest Joseph Kennedy took in the victories and defeats of his children during the summer races at Hyannis Port, a keenness motivated far more by the spirit of win-at-all-costs than the healthier outlook that children should enjoy themselves. Jack strove hard to keep up with Joe Junior, though the slender younger boy could never hope to match his bigger, stronger brother. Often, however, they teamed together against other sailing opponents or, to test their own courage and endurance, against the elements. Once Jack and Joe took their boat out when storm warnings were up and all the other skippers had headed for shore; but the Kennedy boys were lucky—that day—and returned home safely. A sailing friend has recalled the boys' attitude toward seamanship: "Neither Jack nor Joe feared anything. The two boys would go sailing on days when it was so rough you could barely see the boat between the waves. One classic voyage occurred when the waves were running so high that no other boat in the harbor dared to leave its mooring, but Joe, Jack and two friends went out for a wild wet ride."

Touch football on the Kennedy grounds was another area of physical adventure where the young Kennedys sought to realize the ideal of heroic glory bred into them by their father, and on a deeply repressed emotional level could punish themselves, and others, for the sense of worthlessness which accompanies a childhood of constant criticism and parental pushing. A boyhood friend of Joe Junior, Tom Schriber, has described a typical game of Kennedy touch football: "You had to remember there were a lot of trees around the lawn at Bronxville. I always ran looking for the trees and the ball at the same time. But Joe and Jack and Bobby never did and WHANG! that was that. They were always knocking themselves out. I can remember many occasions when one or the other of the boys would be picked up unconscious; they were always bandaged and bruised all over."

As adults, the Kennedy men—and, to a lesser degree, the women—continued to draft their friends and acquaintances into games of touch football that often turned into opportunities for physical mayhem. One time Bobby Kennedy was so intent on running for a touchdown that he lunged headfirst into a barbed-wire fence and bounced off it, his face streaming with blood. Bobby scorned first aid and kept on playing. The day before Jack's wedding, the bridegroom engaged in a customary game of touch football and plowed into a rose bush; to the amazement of photographers, he marched down the aisle with the wounds of "valor" scratched into his face.

There is an excessiveness in such behavior that seems understandable only in light of the parents' own extreme attitudes toward danger and endurance. The dangerous recklessness that we find so often in all four Kennedy sons, both as boys and as adults, seems definitely to have been encouraged by the parents, who regarded it as a test and proof of the strength, courage, and ability to win that they valued above all else. Daring physical wounds and frequently suffering them would fulfill several neurotic obsessions: the need for heroic vindication and parental approval, the need for self-acceptance and a feeling of personal value, and a very secret need to remain a child, to be loved and cared for and comforted. The broken legs and arms and backs suffered by Joe, Jack, Bobby, and Teddy—injuries that were excessively courted, beyond the bounds of what could be considered fairly normal youthful activities—would have brought deep psychic satisfaction in all these emotional areas.

While Joe and Rose Kennedy indulged—and even encouraged—their sons' recklessness in the urgency of winning, there were other parts of life in which their excessive expectations took the form of strict supervision. Off the football fields and sailing decks, the boys were expected to be neat and orderly, to mind their manners and their elders. And yet while the Kennedy sons outwardly conformed, there is ample evidence that none of them ever took seriously their mother's constant admonitions of personal neatness and their father's demands for punctuality. Rose herself said of Jack as a child, "By and large, he wasn't any different from any other little boy in the neighborhood. He liked to play, and he had a terrible way of misplacing things like items of clothes. Sometimes he disobeyed, and then he was spanked. Sometimes I'd punish him by sending him off to bed with only bread and water. Then he'd slip downstairs and charm the cook into feeding him."

Jack's carelessness with personal possessions was to continue throughout his school years and into adulthood. A Choate classmate recalled that "the biggest complaints about him were that his room was never neat and he was always late to classes." A friendly biographer noted, "Before his marriage and his subsequent conversion into a fashion plate he would appear on Capitol Hill in khaki trousers and mismated socks." Another writer, less friendly, wrote that before his marriage "Jack was a notoriously sloppy dresser," one reason being his frequent absentmindedness. He often left suits behind in hotels, and had the habit on the House floor of pulling out his shirt tail to wipe his glasses and sometimes forgetting to retuck it. Kennedy was a popular bachelor among the social hostesses, but Pearl Mesta once said, "I wasn't prepared for Jack Kennedy to be wearing brown loafers with his tuxedo!" Only when Kennedy took aim at the White House did he give up his careless dressing habits and let himself be converted into a model of tailored elegance, a transformation which seems to have been caused by political necessity as much as by the tastes of his fastidious wife, Jacqueline.

Exaggerated personal carelessness and disorder can suggest some underlying emotional conflict. Consciously, there may be an indifference to other people's opinions, real or assumed. But since it is easier in life to be fairly orderly, both for the individual and for those around him, extreme sloppiness strongly implies a disturbed relationship with oneself and with others. The confusion outside can reflect the confusion within, as well as showing an unconscious desire to frustrate and defy others and one's own best interests. Even Kennedy's intensely loyal and dedicated secretary, Evelyn Lincoln, felt deeply irritated by his messy desk and other bad working habits when Kennedy served in the House of Representatives and the Senate. Mrs. Lincoln described Kennedy as "careless in keeping track of things. He had a habit of writing a telephone number on any stray slip of paper and then stuffing the paper in his wallet or pocket. Later, when he needed the number, he would dump dozens of such wrinkled slips out of his wallet, add still others from his various pockets, and scratch around in the pile. If he couldn't find the one he was seeking, he would call, 'Mrs. Lincoln, what's Tom's telephone number?' More often than not I didn't even know who Tom was, much less where I might find his number." Kennedy's poor handwriting was another trial for Mrs. Lincoln, until she gradually learned to decipher it. Jack, typically, seemed oblivious to the problem, and his secretary was amazed to learn from an old sixth-grade report card that one of his best grades had been in penmanship.

Kennedy was just as disorganized outside the office. According to Mrs. Lincoln (and many others), "He was always forgetting things, and I was continually tracking down some item, such as his overcoat or his briefcase. 'Where did I leave it this time?' he would ask. 'In the closet of the hotel,' I would reply." Mrs. Lincoln tried to look on the bright side. "I really didn't mind checking hotels and planes to locate his forgotten effects; that was something of a challenge." But, she admitted, "the condition of his desk was maddening. It seemed as if someone had taken a waste paper basket and turned it upside down on top of the desk. I tried to ignore it, but just couldn't. So, each time he left the office I would rush in, straighten up his desk, and file the papers that had accumulated there. When he came back from the Senate chamber, I would soon hear the buzzer being pressed angrily. 'How can you ever expect me to find anything? Why don't you leave my desk alone?' " Mrs. Lincoln wondered if she would ever adjust fast enough, especially when her boss said, "I don't believe you and I understand each other." But when the secretary looked crestfallen, Kennedy added, "See if you can't do a little better."

Kennedy's apparent lack of insight into his own self-created office difficulties is an example of "externalization," that is, attributing inner problems to outer conflicts caused by others. Externalization allows a neurotic person to blame others rather than himself for his problems. It also creates turmoil which serves to distract him from his deepest repressed anxieties. We can see this recurrent pattern of behavior throughout Kennedy's life, when staff members had to rush him to late appointments and retrieve his misplaced belongings. In another incident related by Mrs. Lincoln, Kennedy gave dictation to a typist when his secretary was on the phone with his father (usually she had to hang up immediately when Kennedy began dictating). The substitute emerged from his office and began transcribing her notes in a vague way, looking off into space. When the Senator asked her how she was coming, she typed frantically, then reluctantly gave him the transcript. "What in the world is this?" asked Kennedy. "It doesn't make sense." The girl had to confess that the Senator had talked so fast she couldn't get a word he said.

Such disorderliness and indifference to others (which is really arrogance) can be unconscious expressions of rebellion and revenge, revealing resentment against harsh and rigid parental expectations. It is useless to object that we are not actually rebelling against our parents, who may no longer be in our lives or at least not directly involved. The important point is whether our parents have taken permanent lodgings in our unconscious feelings, and if so to what degree. In Jack Kennedy's case, the supportive figures in both his personal and professional life, including even his secretary, seemed to act as indirect reminders of his deeply buried emotional feelings toward his parents, and thus often became unwitting targets of his anger and frustration. Arrogance (which all the Kennedy sons have displayed fairly often) can also express an unconscious demand that people accept the individual for himself rather than for appearances and achievements. It is a sign of both anger and longing, enabling the neurotic to cast all blame on others and vent his deep-seated rage at himself, his parents, and life in general. As we can see from these examples, Jack Kennedy often had a tendency to be inconsiderate of his office staff. On the other hand, he could also show warmth and kindness (for instance, it has been said that he could never bring himself to fire anyone for incompetence). As is well known, Jack developed considerable charm from boyhood on. Part of his charm seemed quite clearly a need to manipulate the authority figures in his life, but part gives the impression of a genuine warmth and liking for others.

Throughout this study of the Kennedys, we should remember that neurosis never blocks a person in all areas of his development, but only in certain directions, and in complex and varying degrees. If my emphasis seems generally negative, it is largely because the lavish praise of the Kennedys has been so irrational and untrue that a revisionist must inevitably feel the weight of writing against an enormous tide of published opinion. Thus the statement or suggestion of a negative characteristic is not meant to imply the absence of positive characteristics, but rather that in certain areas they were less dominant or prevalent, or at times inoperative.

Lateness was another problem that followed Jack into maturity. Again, compulsive lateness is usually a symptom of both a neurotic lack of control and a fear of and obsessive need for such control. By being late, a neurotic does at least five things: he releases hostility against others, as well as against himself; he creates further problems to add to his unconscious flight from a less bearable anxiety and guilt; he shows a hidden desire to be irresponsible and childlike; and at the same time he reveals a desperate need to have power over his own life, by controlling time and spending it as he chooses. That such simultaneous drives toward and away from power (power over oneself and over others) are mutually self-contradictory does not detract from their psychic logic. For it is the very ambivalence of neurotic drives that makes sense in the conflicted personality.

Jack Kennedy was extremely conscious of time and restlessly impatient to cram as much into his life as he could, as a number of biographers have noted (the frenetic activity of his "first thousand days" as President, when so much seemed to be happening and so little was accomplished, is the prime example). Mrs. Lincoln vividly described Kennedy's constant "stream of words and ideas" as Senator, when he "evidently woke up each morning bursting with new ideas." And yet for all of Kennedy's racing—through letters, dictation, appointments, to airports—his legislative record was largely mediocre and unimpressive. Despite his flow of enthusiasm and ideas, Kennedy was largely an absentee legislator and had a poor voting record. As a Congressman and Senator, he wasted huge amounts of time on trivia and frivolity, and many of the other legislators regarded him as a playboy because of his frequent absences and lack of attention to duty. Here again, Kennedy showed the inner conflicts and contradictions that too often kept him from being really effective.

It is somewhat amusing to note Jack's impatience with his wife, Jackie, who displayed a similar insouciance with regard to the clock. Once when the Senator was awaiting his lackadaisical fiancée at the airport, he called his office, found her there, and gave her a dressing-down that apparently had at least a temporary effect, according to Mrs. Lincoln's observant eye. But Jackie's tardiness continued to irritate the frequently tardy Jack, whose impatient cries of "For God's sake, Jackie!" punctuated many a hurried departure from the Georgetown home of the newly-wedded Kennedys. Jack's own Dagwood Bumstead exits from his Capitol Hill office kept his staff in a perpetual state of nervous exhaustion, fearing that he would never make it alive to Washington National Airport. "The Senator liked to take the wheel and race through the streets, barely missing red lights," wrote his secretary. "Cops would whistle, cars would honk, but he ignored everything other than his objective," barely making the plane each time.

As a child and adolescent, Jack Kennedy's flights from total family domination were probably necessary to maintain a sense of identity under the pressures of being the second oldest Kennedy son. Jack's subtle rebellions against parental overrigidity included the common adolescent failure to fulfill scholastic capabilities. At Canterbury School, the New Milford, Connecticut, prep school which Jack entered in 1930 when he was thirteen, he did poorly in most of his studies, especially spelling and Latin. When his Latin grades dropped below passing, the school told his parents, "He can do better than this." Although Jack procrastinated about his studies and was absentminded with possessions, he loved to read. He wrote his father, "Though I may not be able to remember material things such as tickets, gloves and so on I can remember things like Ivanhoe and the last time we had an exam on it I got a ninety eight." As psychologists well know, people tend to remember what they emotionally wish to remember, and forgetfulness is directly tied to emotional repressions and conflicts (as Freud brilliantly demonstrated in his 1901 pioneering work on this theme, *The Psychopathology of Everyday Life*). "Material things" came from Jack's parents and so were logical targets of his filial hostilities; literary imaginings were alien to the elder Kennedys, who were definitely nonintellectual and non-literary, and thus literature and history could be safely explored and possessed by Jack with a sense of personal ownership and pride. Jack also went out for football at Canterbury, but unlike the stronger and heavier Joe at Choate, he could not make the first team. In the spring of 1931, an emergency appendectomy abruptly ended Jack's stay at Canterbury, his only Catholic school.

Young Joe was doing so well at Episcopal Choate, also in Connecticut, that the Kennedy parents transferred Jack there in the fall of 1931 after a summer of convalescence. Again the boys were brought together in direct sibling rivalry, and again Jack refused—or was emotionally unable—to apply himself seriously to his studies. His housefather wrote the Kennedys, ". . . he is casual and disorderly in almost all of his organization projects. Jack studies at the last minute, keeps appointments late, has little sense of material values, and can seldom locate his possessions." Joseph Kennedy kept after Jack with a barrage of criticism, but this apparently only weakened Jack's already damaged self-confidence. As one Kennedy biographer and admirer described Jack's Choate years, "His letters home were full of defensive, self-belittling remarks about his grades and his athletic skills. He offered excuses for his poor showing, at the same time denying that these were alibis." Jack wrote hopefully to his mother, "Maybe Dad thinks I am alibing but I am not. I have also been doing a little worrying about my studies because what he said about me starting off great and then going down sunk in."

When Jack was a Choate senior, his father offered a specific incentive that had some effect: a trip to Europe. In the Kennedy carrot-stick approach, achievement was rewarded materially with a sailboat, pony, toys, and trips. Jack wrote his father that he had "definitely decided to stop fooling around. I really do realize how important it is that I get a good job done this year, if I want to go to England. I really feel, now that I think it over, that I have been bluffing myself about how much real work I have been doing."

Kennedy Senior (then the new SEC chairman) replied from Washington. His letter is a poignant combination of parental overconcern and moral righteousness, an unwitting form of nagging in which the father denied the very thing he was doing. Joseph Kennedy first expressed "great satisfaction" about Jack's "forthrightness and directness that you are usually lacking." Then he added, "Now Jack, I don't want to give the impression that I am a nagger, for goodness knows I think that is the worst thing any parent can be. After long experience in sizing up people I definitely know you have the goods and you can go a long way. Now aren't you foolish not to get all there is out of what God has given you. . . . After all, I would be lacking even as a friend if I did not urge you to take advantage of the qualities you have. It is very difficult to make up fundamentals that you have neglected when you were very young and that is why I am always urging you to do the best you can. I am not expecting too much and I will not be disappointed if you don't turn out to be a real genius, but I think you can be a really worthwhile citizen with good judgment and good understanding. . . ."

Clearly, Joe Kennedy thought he was expressing confidence in Jack's ability to do well, but in reality he was tearing down Jack's self-respect in a dreadful way. The father's conscious intentions were all for the best, but his unconscious fears drove him again and again to the most rending sort of judgments and obsessive doubts. A parent's persistent lack of confidence in his child creates exactly what he most dreads, a weakening of the child's own self-confidence. As we have seen, Joe Kennedy's compulsive urging of his children to win the best of everything grew out of his own gnawing anxieties and self-doubts. Jack learned to perform for an immediate prize—such as the trip to England—but between such crises of urgent goals his lack of self-created inner direction caused a great deal of aimless drifting. This pattern, which was first set in Jack's early childhood, was to affect seriously his performance as U.S. Congressman, then Senator, and finally as President of the United States. While political goals with specific rewards later gave Jack the impetus to enormous effort, once the goal was won he seemed to lack any clear social aims beyond the resolution of immediate crises. What is important in this chapter is to understand how such emotional patterns developed in Jack Kennedy as a boy, adolescent, and young adult.

Jack's academic foot-dragging, however, did not keep him out of Princeton and then Harvard, for in his last year at Choate he worked hard to follow his father and brother into the Ivy League. Illness took Jack out of Princeton, and his father sent him to Harvard in 1936 where Joe Junior was a sophomore (a curious but understandable repetition of the Canterbury-Choate switch, which suggests Jack's underlying family ambivalences and urges toward independence-submission). Jack's first two college years were relaxed and his grades were mediocre. But after traveling in Europe in the summers of 1938 and 1939, when his father was Ambassador to England, and helping gather diplomatic reports on the approaching war, Jack's political interests deepened. He had also been sent by his father to Glasgow to assist the American victims of a torpedoed British liner. In the spring of 1940, Jack's senior year, the twenty-three-year-old Harvard student finished his honors thesis, which earned him a *magna cum laude*. His professors suggested publication, and Joseph Kennedy's friends helped with the rewriting and publishing. Arthur Krock supplied the title, *Why England Slept* (after Churchill's *While England Slept*), Henry Luce wrote a foreword, and, of course, the Ambassador offered his own expertise. The result was a surprising best-seller which even today makes interesting reading. Jack apparently worked very hard on the book, and he wrote with engaging clarity. His emphasis was on the unwillingness of a democracy to arm for war until the need became unavoidable, an attitude that gives a huge advantage to an aggressive dictatorship.

Jack naturally had to work with the figures and estimates then available, which he set forth with precision. In actual fact, according to at least one prominent British military historian, A. J. P. Taylor, England was not asleep after 1935. Britain's biggest error, according to Taylor's astonishing figures, was to overestimate by far German rearmament and take Hitler's vastly exaggerated boasting at face value. Thus Chamberlain's concessions to Hitler at Munich in September, 1938, were the result of a British illusion that Germany was militarily far more powerful and could have defeated England at that time. But according to Taylor, British airplane production had "almost reached the German level and surpassed it in the course of 1939," while in trained pilots the countries were equal. (His other figures support the same conclusion.) I mention this because John F. Kennedy, understandably conditioned by his experiences in 1939–1941, when these figures were not available, made the same basic mistake when he accepted Nikita Khrushchev's boastings at face value and accelerated the 1961–1963 missile race, in which the United States was actually far ahead. The difference was that intelligence methods had been revolutionized by the time of Kennedy's Administration, and the truth was potentially available; but for political and emotional reasons, Kennedy instituted a policy of military overproduction. *Why England Slept* thus assumes greater significance in the light of Kennedy's own presidency. Jack's experience as a young man seemed to fix in him the idea that a country must always be ready for war with "arms beyond doubt," as he was to put it in his 1961 inaugural address. Unfortunately, this is a historical fallacy in the context of nuclear armaments, one leading to totally different results. World War II, hideous though it was, was also a good deal easier to understand than a potential World War III.

Jack's father, exhilarated by his son's success, wrote approvingly, "You would be surprised how a book that really makes the grade with high-class people stands you in good stead for years to come." It was advice that other Kennedy sons would take to heart. While Jack, like his brother Joe, largely shared his father's isolationist opinions, he also had a young man's desire not to miss out on whatever action might come to America and tended to respond to an immediate stimulus rather than to longer-range possibilities. While his nation veered toward war, Jack studied for a short time at Stanford University's Business School, then traveled restlessly in Latin America. Returning to find Joe planning to join the Navy, Jack tried to enlist in the U.S. Army, but was rejected because of his weak back (injured in Harvard football). After strengthening himself with five months of daily exercises,

Jack was accepted by the Navy in Sepember, 1941, and donned the uniform of an ensign. But before following Jack Kennedy into his famous PT-109 adventure, we must return briefly to trace the second pattern of unconscious rebellion that seemed to grow out of his unconscious resistance to his parents' domination.

This second psychological weapon of self-defense was the self-defeating, as well as ego-preserving, technique of withdrawing from competition because of illness and injury. Jack's unusual number of childhood illnesses strongly suggests an underlying psychosomatic basis. He was not a frail boy. Although slighter in build than his husky older brother, Jack was tall, well built, well coordinated, and, like all the Kennedys, adept at strenuous outdoor sports. Yet he suffered from constant poor health. He was often sick in bed even during the relatively carefree summers at Hyannis Port. Some of his sicknesses seem entirely organic (although doctors are continually making surprising discoveries about the psychic roots of supposedly physiological illnesses). At four, Jack had scarlet fever, and in prep school, as noted, an appendicitis attack took him out of Canterbury. Such diseases as jaundice and influenza, however, are more open to suspicion of psychological influences. In 1935, after a short apprenticeship to Professor Laski, Jack left the London School of Economics with jaundice. The next Christmas, jaundice again took him out of an emotionally difficult situation when he left Princeton, which he had entered rather than follow his father and brother to Harvard. Again, illness brought him back into the dominant family pattern as a Harvard undergraduate. Yet at Harvard Jack continued to suffer both injuries and self-encouraged sicknesses. Flu kept him out of a varsity swimming race. When Jack secretly practiced in the gym while still ill, his exertions kept him sickly the rest of the year.

Earlier in this chapter, I remarked upon some of the physical punishments the Kennedy sons seemed literally to invite in their overstrenuous and often wildly reckless behavior. Regarding Jack specifically, he tallied up a long record of largely unnecessary injuries, all the way from the twenty-eight stitches sewed in him after a head-on collision with brother Joe, down to the facial scratches marking his collision with a rose bush on the eve of his wedding. In between, Jack injured his back so severely both at college and in his wartime disaster that he nearly died in a subsequent operation to relieve the pain and suffered from a weak and often highly painful back—as well as an adrenal insufficiency—for the rest of his life. It may seem farfetched, but in a psychoanalytical context it is not improbable, to view Jack Kennedy's back troubles as at least partially a symbolic revenge and expiation of guilt toward the oppressive parents who, in many ways psychologically never "got off his back." How curious it is in retrospect to find a rocking chair the national symbol for a President who wished, above all, to be remembered as a great and heroic leader. A rocking chair brings to mind images of a mother, an invalid, and an old man, none of which could have consciously appealed to Kennedy, but which together suggest elements of immaturity, mother need, psychic injury, and a death wish. These traits, the evidence suggests, quite definitely existed in Jack Kennedy's characterology and helped to determine his personal and political actions.

Frequent sickness, as noted, can serve several unconscious purposes. It can be a way of withdrawing from both outer and inner conflict and maintaining a sense of personal autonomy, however illusory that feeling may be. Illness can offer at the same time a chance for heroic exertions or endurance which would clear the sufferer of any malingering charges and, at the same time, might incapacitate him even further. Thus a neurotic can have it both ways: while appearing courageous, he effectively, if only temporarily, removes himself from the arena of combat. Yet the personal cost to such an individual is high, not only in conscious physical and emotional suffering, but more seriously in the unconscious strengthening of negative attitudes and behavior, including his already considerable burden of unconscious guilt. In Jack's case, his illnesses could have served two further ends (which are probably present to some degree in all psychosomatic cases): unconscious punishment of his parents; and punishment of himself for all the stored-up hostility he must have felt toward his parents and his domineering, constantly victorious brother Joe.

It is essential to remember that neurotic people always feel guilty. They feel guilty first for the vindictive rage within themselves (which may or may not be totally repressed, although its effects are bound to appear). Secondly, and most basic and damaging, such disturbed individuals feel guilty because of the rejection suffered in childhood. Parents may be hated, but they are also desperately needed by the child. What is so needed cannot possibly be seen as bad, because this would be too threatening. Therefore the child unconsciously feels that the bad must be in himself; *he* must be the cause of his own rejection, not his parents. The very ambivalence of this love-hate dependency increases the rejected child's growing guilt, and thus his inner rage.

Part of the child's rebelliousness is not only outrage and hostility against the parents; it is also a way of making the mysterious rejection feel "justified" and therefore more tolerable. Rejection is not the child's fault, but he must feel it is in order to relieve the terrifying sensation of incomprehensible desertion. He may therefore unconsciously seek punishment to create a "reason" for his rejection. This gives him the hope of ultimate acceptance. Parental rewards that follow the carrot-and-stick philosophy often strengthen the child's belief in an acceptance that can be earned. The inner tragedy, however, is that genuine acceptance can never be earned, as earlier pointed out, but only freely given and received.

Jack Kennedy's frequent illnesses are understandable in light of the constant and exaggerated pressures kept up by the Kennedy parents on their children. Kennedys were never allowed to relax, be themselves, and grow up at their own individual rates and in their own individual ways. As discussed in previous chapters, such parental demands—which are disguised rejections of the natural child as an individual worthy of respect in his own right—will inevitably have harmful repercussions. In the words of one friendly Kennedy biographer, "Wherever he was, at school or at home, Jack was conscious of his father's incessant concern that he do better, especially in his studies." But we must remember, too, that the senior Kennedys *consciously* intended the best for their children. It was not their intentions, but their own unconscious inheritance of emotional conflict that prevented Joe and Rose Kennedy from becoming fully mature adults and genuinely supportive and accepting parents.

Jack's self-punishments soon progressed to a point where he began injuring himself in "accidents" of increasing seriousness, to such an extent that some friends regarded him as accident-prone. As a youngster he had undergone frequent bloodying—as did most of the Kennedys—on the playing fields. In addition, Jack's intense rivalry with Joe Junior included fights, which were later vividly recalled by a terrified Bobby, and the previously mentioned head-on bike duel. During his European travels in the summer of 1939, Jack and his Harvard roommate, Torbert Macdonald, drove from Paris to the Riviera. Jack, "who was driving as fast as he could," according to Macdonald, lost control and the car swerved off the road and turned over, skidding along on its top for about thirty feet before coming to a halt, still upside down. Jack looked at his roommate and said casually, "Well, pal, we didn't make it, did we?" This obscure incident is buried in the Kennedy literature. Later it would be Teddy, not Jack, who became famous for his wild driving, but in actual fact, all four Kennedy sons, including Bobby, often drove recklessly and with little concern for their own safety or that of their passengers and other cars.

Finally on Harvard's football field, Jack achieved what one might call a psychological *pièce de résistance*, a lasting stroke of unconscious resistance to parental pressures and internalized commands. Playing end on the junior varsity, Kennedy was thrown hard on the frozen ground and severely injured his back. The psychological roots of Jack Kennedy's famous back injury become even more apparent when we consider his subsequent history. As a young naval officer in 1941, Kennedy used his father's political pull to transfer from Intelligence work to active sea duty—in PT boats. On the surface, this move would pragmatically utilize Jack's yachting experience. But PT boats are also notorious body-pounders; other than para-chuting, it would have been hard for Jack to choose a service better guar-anteed to worsen a bad back.

As the skipper of PT-109, Kennedy's lack of organization and personal recklessness involved the lives of other men. According to one of his friend-liest biographers, Jack "once received a low rating in military bearing and neatness; and when he took off for his most memorable sea action, the PT base lacked a record of the men aboard because he had neglected to see to it that a muster sheet was turned in to headquarters." Kennedy's checkered seagoing career included a little-known escapade in which, trying to beat another boat home at all costs, he failed to reverse engines in time and rammed the pier. Jack also gave an ensign the worst "chewing out" of his life for tardiness, an example of relieving likely guilt feelings over his own symptomatic weakness. Robert J. Donovan, the careful although un-analytical author of *PT-109*, related the dock incident in vivid detail that implied Kennedy was lucky not to have killed anyone. At their South Pacific base, the PT crews raced to refuel because only then were they allowed breakfast and rest. Here is Donovan's significant version of "Shafty" (Kennedy's nickname) shafting the dock.

". . . From the time he had taken command nearly two months before Kennedy was possessed with a desire to make the boat go faster. He was forever instructing the motormacs, 'Let's get more speed.' He loved to be at the wheel, and he loved speed. On these sprints to the fuel dock he would roar into the cover with a rooster tail arching in his wake and throttles wide open. He would hold his speed to the last second, then order the engines into reverse just in time to brake his momentum in front of the dock. The hairbreadth finishes began to worry the motormacs. The braking at such speed put a heavy strain on the engines. Drawdy cautioned Kennedy that the engines might not always reverse under such pressure. However, they always *had*, and Kennedy liked to win.

"One morning . . . he found himself in a furious race with another boat. . . . Gradually he crept up even with the other PT, and as they raced prow to prow the issue resolved itself into the simple matter of which skipper would have the nerve to hold his speed the longer with the dock rushing in on both of them. In the end Kennedy held just long enough to go in front. Immediately he ordered the engines into reverse. All three conked out, and PT-109 went streaking at the dock like an eighty-foot missile on the loose.

"On the dock, the fueling crew had reported and a work party under a warrant officer had entered the shed to get out the tools when the whole world came crashing down on them. Tools flew in all directions. Wrenches, jacks, screwdrivers and hammers plopped into the water. Some of the men who were still outside toppled off the dock. Those on the inside who weren't too terrified to move clawed their way out. When they burst through the door, however, they beheld not the expected formation of Japanese dive bombers overhead, but a single PT boat sliced into a corner of the dock, her skinny bronzed skipper standing in his motionless cockpit, ruefully surveying the scene. Some of his crew were motionless, too, having been knocked flat by the crash."

Such incidents are amusing only when there are no casualties. Fortunately for Kennedy, several nearby PT boats broke loose from their moorings, and in the diversion Jack idled his boat away and hid up a small stream "until the trouble blew over." Kennedy was lucky to have avoided injury to his crew, serious damage to his boat, and disciplinary action. Young officers often received ten days "under hatches" for far less, as naval men well know. According to Donovan, Kennedy usually won the races, indicating that the other skippers were more sensible about conserving engines, gear boxes, boats, and crews. The conclusion seems obvious that Jack's obsessively competitive spirit, underlined by a deeply repressed drive toward self-punishment, needlessly endangered his crew, boat, and other sailors.

Even before the dramatic dock-ramming, Jack had shown some curious instances of poor seamanship and a strong need to demonstrate his own physical courage and toughness. When his group of PT boats was en route from Rhode Island to the Pacific, one boat ran aground off North Carolina. Jack had gone to her rescue in PT-101 and tossed over a line to tow the stuck boat. But the line was apparently so ineptly thrown or secured that it caught in one of his own propellers. Compounding this error, Jack himself dived overboard to retrieve it, an irresponsible act for a skipper in such circumstances. The icy water gave him such a high fever that he had to go to a Jacksonville hospital for several days. Kennedy's "grandstanding" thus put him temporarily out of command, whatever the exact cause of the accident.

But Jack Kennedy's only popularly known PT adventure came when a Japanese destroyer rammed his boat at night, slicing PT-109 in half and seriously injuring Kennedy's weak back. A close study of the ramming indicates general carelessness and poor judgment under immediate stress. On the night of August 1–2, 1943, Kennedy's PT-109 was part of a fifteen-boat patrol trying to intercept Japanese troop ships reinforcing New Georgia in the Solomon Islands. In Jack's division of four boats, only the leader, PT-159, carried a primitive radar set. The night was inky, with visibility almost zero. Kennedy and his patrol mate, PT-162, became separated from the other two boats. They were not informed that several PT boats had unsuccessfully attacked four Japanese destroyers. Instead, Kennedy and his companion mistook the distant gunfire for shore batteries. The entire American patrol had become scattered and confused through poor leadership and lack of communication. PT-109 and PT-162, joined by PT-169, continued their silent scouting, each moving slowly on only one engine. None of them knew that the Japanese destroyers had safely reached their goal and were returning directly across the path of PT-109.

Jack's boat was moving almost as quietly as a sailboat, but a Japanese lookout sighted it low in the water. At the same time, a PT-109 crewman spotted the destroyer *Amagiri*. Kennedy glanced off his starboard bow, and for a few seconds thought the shadowy form was one of the missing PT boats. Then he and others quickly recognized it was some other craft. "Lenny," Kennedy said matter-of-factly, "look at this." Ensign Thom stood up.

According to Donovan, what followed took place within an estimated forty seconds. The Japanese commander recognized the PT boat and decided to ram it. As the destroyer turned toward PT-109, Kennedy said, "Sound general quarters," then spun his wheel to make a torpedo attack on the *Amagiri*. In the panic of the moment, Jack forgot that the torpedoes were not set to explode at such a short distance. In addition, the sluggishness of his single running engine allowed him no maneuverability. In another instant or so the destroyer's bow crashed at a sharp angle into Kennedy's boat just aft of the cockpit, hurling Jack against a steel brace as the destroyer swept past only a few feet away from him. In a matter of minutes, Kennedy and his struggling crewmen, minus two dead, were left alone with the wreckage of their boat in the flame-lit, then totally dark, night.

The exact circumstances of Kennedy's failure of command on PT-109 will perhaps never be known. But Donovan's research and the opinions of many military men leave the lay reader with considerable doubt about Jack's judgment under severe stress. It is surprising to learn that, until the ramming, his crew was not at general quarters, a standard procedure on a combat operation. We are also left to wonder why Kennedy did not immediately start his other two engines during the thirty to sixty seconds left him after the destroyer was sighted. There apparently had been no consideration of what to do in the event that actually materialized, although the Japanese skipper had thought of such a possibility. As one critical writer commented, "There were those Navy sceptics who wondered how it was possible for Jack, as the skipper of PT-109, to have gotten such a small maneuverable craft into position to be slashed in two by the bow of a Japanese destroyer. . . . No other motor torpedo boat was reported to have suffered such singular misfortune in any of the oceans in World War II."

A further shadow falls over the question of Jack's leadership competence in a seemingly innocent passage in a book by Paul Fay, Jr., the lighthearted

Navy friend whom Jack later appointed as Under Secretary of the Navy. In *The Pleasure of His Company*, Fay quoted Kennedy's political pep talk to the old PT-109 shipmates he gathered in 1960 to help him win the Wisconsin primary. In outlining their television program, the ex-skipper urged each man to introduce himself briefly and to emphasize their common effort in the war. Then Kennedy would carry on. However, he did caution them not to allow Bill Johnston, a motor mechanic on the ill-fated vessel, to say too much — perhaps, Kennedy quipped, he should only be permitted to give his name — for if Johnston were given the chance, he could destroy the senator's heroic war image. Fay and the other crew members followed Jack's instructions. And, in fact, when Johnston did arise to speak, he managed no more than two words before he was cut short and his presentation ended. Thus any potentially damaging remarks were averted. Since the motormacs were precisely those crewmen who knew the truth about the condition of Kennedy's engines, which had been strained in his dock races and failed at least once, we must again wonder what Jack was trying to suppress, under the guise of humor, in the memory of Bill Johnston. Again, I must emphasize that Kennedy's genuine physical courage is not in question. Quite the contrary, at times he seemed to test his physical endurance with reckless abandon.

Back in 1943, having lost his boat and two of his men, and with one crew member helpless from his wounds, Kennedy took direct and brave action. The whole world knows how he rescued this man, despite his own agonizing back injury, and eventually brought the survivors to safety. This was an ordeal that required great endurance and determination, and Jack's character included these highly laudable traits. But again, even during this island rescue, Jack's emotional ambivalence led him to actions containing elements of apparent rashness and irrationality. Trying to signal American PT boats which patrolled a nearby channel at night, Kennedy swam alone into the dangerous passage and was almost carried out to sea by the current. There was no need for such foolhardiness, which endangered not only Jack but the rescue of his crew. He had eight uninjured men with him, plus a plank, lifejackets, and the island growth from which to make some sort of float or raft (as recommended by Navy survival doctrine in the South Pacific at that time) on which Kennedy and another man could have put to sea. Jack's impetuousness raises the question of whether he was secretly hoping to be lost on this brave but ill-planned venture and thus be absolved of his failure in losing his boat and two men, an extreme but far from unknown means of self-redemption.

Kennedy's probable guilt feelings, as well as his acquired patterns of unconscious self-defeat, seem to have guided his behavior after the rescue. Instead of going home to recover from a serious and painful back injury, as his shipmates expected, Jack (as brother Joe would do next year) refused to return. Instead, he concealed the extent of the spinal injury from his commander and asked for another boat and more combat. Donovan described Jack as "brooding" over his experience. Despite his imminent promotion to full lieutenant, his Purple Heart, and his Navy and Marine Corps Medal awarded for gallantry toward his shipwrecked crew, "Kennedy did not feel that his career in the South Pacific was anything to write home about."

Jack was given PT-59, which had been converted into a gunboat to attack offshore enemy barges. His squadron commander commented on Kennedy's recklessness: "Working against Jap barges close to shore with a slow overloaded PT like that was really perilous and terribly exposed fighting, but Jack kept at it. It got so that the crew didn't like to go out with him because he took so many chances. He even wanted to make a run up the Choiseul River, which was loaded with Japanese guns. Finally he began to realize that our experiment with the beautiful little gunboats was less than a complete success, and it was only then that we were able to persuade him to go home and get his back looked at. I'll never forget the way he insisted on staying on the job when he had a legitimate reason for returning to the States that any of us would have jumped at."

Again, in the light of Jack Kennedy's past and future history, we can sense the unconscious ambivalence of his motives. The drive to heroic glorification was deeply implanted in the Kennedy sons to an irrational degree. Paralleling this drive were many elements of unconscious self-defeat arising out of parental pressures, rejection, and self-contempt for not living up to expectations. On a deeper emotional level, self-contempt would also grow out of the very fact of being subjected to such unreasonable—and thus unhuman—demands. Kennedy's wartime experiences seem to illustrate something of his second method of neurotic defense: an irrational physical aggressiveness that could result in his own injury, as well as in injury to others. Hostility toward oneself inevitably produces hostility toward others. However shocking the idea, we can see in all four Kennedy sons the overlap of self-damage into the damage—even though often consciously unintended—of others.

In addition to courting illnesses and physical injuries, Jack Kennedy showed evidence of developing a third method to defend himself against the onslaughts of his parents' and his own emotional imperatives. This third defense was the withdrawal of his emotions from others as well as from himself. Unfortunately, while removing his vulnerable real self from attack, pressure, and humiliation, the threatened person also tends to remove his defended self from his own awareness. Thus he is apt to become increasingly detached from his own genuine feelings and creative potentials as well as from the emotional threats of others. This trend is detectable in Jack Kennedy (and in many of the other Kennedys) from the circumstantial evidence of his known life, attitudes, and behavior.

Kennedy's trait of emotional withdrawal has often been admiringly described as his "ironic detachment," "unemotional objectivity," "restraint," and "cool intellectualism." The quality of detachment or "keeping one's cool" has become excessively admired in America, especially among young people and older intellectuals, who formed a major portion of Kennedy's most ardent and articulate supporters. While the ability to view oneself and others with considerable objectivity and humor is part of a mature personality, such an ability can also be bent to serve neurotic needs. In particular, when a person's attitude and behavior emphasize rigid emotional control and an absence of emotional expression, there is the suggestion of an unconscious taboo against showing emotions, and quite possibly a prohibition against feeling strong emotions. If such a taboo seems present from the evidence, we must ask what purpose it might serve in that person's known personality structure, and what effect it could have on his development toward mature self-realization and healthy relationships with others.

Many observers have commented on Jack Kennedy's striking detachment and lack of emotional display. Although he was generally seen as a warm rather than a cold personality, Kennedy's warmth took the form of a casual friendliness and political responsiveness toward strangers, and a bantering playfulness toward friends. But the spontaneous warmth of a genuinely outgoing political personality such as Hubert Humphrey, for example, was definitely missing. At the beginning of Jack's political career, the famous Kennedy "charisma" was noticeably absent (people often walked out on his dull speeches as a Congressman). While Jack apparently never lacked loyal friends, he carefully kept his friends and associates in separate categories, who never mixed, and saw them according to his own personal needs of the moment—his college pals, Navy "buddies," theater and Hollywood friends, political cohorts, close advisers, and, probably his only real intimates, Kennedy relatives (the Kennedy "clan"—so-named by Joe Junior—was, in fact, extremely clannish).

While Jack maintained a not unfriendly but definitely controlled distance toward others, he also showed hyperactive sexuality. This took the form of an obsessive need to conquer a multitude of women. Although some of the present claimants to membership among "Jack's girls" must be viewed skeptically, the widespread persistence of such reports, as well as the integrity of some of the reporters, present solid evidence that Jack Kennedy was an intensely sex-driven man. Apparently much of this drive grew out of his competition with his older brother (and father) to live up to the Kennedy "masculine mystique." At Harvard, the young Kennedys competed constantly for the best-looking and most famous females among their father's theatrical contacts. This competitive pursuit continued in England, according to various observers, and during the war reached such a pitch that Jack and Joe were regarded as engaged in an international woman-chasing contest. During his Navy years, Jack was known as "Shafty," a nickname that some writers claimed came from his "shafting" of the dock in his PT boat. According to others, Jack was called Shafty in his Rhode Island training days. Although Jack's thin lankiness might have suggested one meaning, his erotic reputation definitely lends a sexual implication to this nickname. Jack's exaggerated sexual activities continued in his congressional and even presidential years, despite his marriage to the glamorous but equally detached Jackie.

Sexuality, however, can have little or nothing to do with a person's real warmth and concern for others, and in fact is often used as a shield against feeling or showing spontaneous tenderness toward another, for such feelings can carry the threat of rejection. Jack's sense of detachment toward himself seems evident in the remark he made to his PT-109 crew as they swam around the sinking hull. "What do you want to do?" asked Kennedy. "I have nothing to lose." Eleven years later, when Jack lay critically ill after an operation, his father was struck by his son's fatalistic attitude. Either he would die or he wouldn't, said Jack. There wasn't much he could do about it.

Kennedy's cool detachment continued in the White House. As William Manchester once described his presidential personality, "Kennedy is bland, wary, polite. The qualities he doesn't have are the qualities the young marrieds in the suburban developments don't want. He lacks emotional fire, and they distrust fire; they associate oratory with hams. The message of his career is clear: the new strength is a muted strength. The new leader must be restrained . . . detachment has run through his forty-five years like a lonely thread." Tom Wicker, the perceptive *New York Times* correspondent, said of JFK, "If that human Kennedy still seems to me to have been altogether too detached and too controlled to have been, as were Nixon and Lord Jim, 'one of us,' with all those fascinating hesitancies and inadequacies and torments . . . nevertheless he was a man 'of few days and full of trouble' . . . ." Wicker, however, failed to see the very real inner "hesitancies and inadequacies and torments" behind the carefully-styled exterior.

Professor James MacGregor Burns wrote in *John Kennedy: A Political Profile* that in his youth Jack "was even less committed than his father or Joe. He seemed even more detached than the rest of the family. Alert, inquisitive, receptive, but somewhat remote, he looked at the world with quizzical gray eyes . . . . One word describes Kennedy more exactly than any other—self-possession. He has never been seen—even by his mother—in raging anger or uncontrollable tears. He does not lose himself in laughter; the only humor he displays, aside from the contrived jokes of a political speech, is a light, needling, slightly ironic banter, such as one often meets in war or in other times of stress. He dislikes emotional scenes, at home or at work. His driving ambition to win out in politics seems to rise less from an emotional compulsion—though emotional drive manifests itself in his restless, hard-working, single-minded will—than from a calm evaluation of what he can do if he puts everything he has into it. He has apparently never lost himself in a passionate, unrestrained love affair; 'I'm not the tragic lover type,' he said once when pressed about whether he had ever gone through youthful agonies of love . . . .

". . . the roots of his dispassionate attitude toward personal and political matters can be traced in part to his background, as can the origin of his competitive will power; in his family the price of acceptance was effort and success. He grew up in a family that was moving from Boston to New York to Palm Beach and Hyannisport, that was rising from lower-middle-class environs to the financial and social pinnacle, that swung away from its lace-curtain Irish ties but did not forge new ones with any social or economic or ideological group. Kennedy, while friendly to all groups, has found a place for himself in none. The fear of making too much of a commitment, of going off the intellectual deep end, is locked in Kennedy's character. To him, to be emotionally or ideologically committed is to be captive. On the few occasions when he has acted immoderately, he later regrets it."

The predominant quality in this insightful description is caution, based on an undertone of fear. Kennedy is pictured as a man for whom control and self-protection by nonemotional detachment are the paramount values, equal only to the need to win. John Kennedy, like his father, never threw himself into desperate or impersonal causes. When he gave his all for something, that effort was always based on a shrewd and careful analysis. And it is noteworthy that all of Kennedy's major efforts were for the entirely personal goal of self-election. Kennedy never made equal efforts for anyone or anything else. As Professor Burns observed, "in his family the price of acceptance was effort and success." While such caution may seem the opposite of physical recklessness, in neurotic individuals a characteristic usually contains its repressed converse. Non-neurotic people also have opposite qualities, but they do not produce extremes of action and reaction. In John Kennedy, physical recklessness and political-emotional caution were parts of the same neurosis: an inability to accept himself wholeheartedly and thus to give himself to ends that could both transcend and reaffirm his own identity.

Norman Mailer once sensed with a novelist's intuition the basic detachment of Kennedy from himself as well as from others. Watching Kennedy at a press conference, Mailer found "there was an elusive detachment to everything he did. One did not have the feeling of a man present in the room with all his weight and all his mind. Kennedy had a dozen faces." Yet in a world where politicians are often seen as overly assertive and self-seeking, Kennedy's air of detachment was a winning quality. To most people, it looked like a charming objectivity and a form of humility which overrode his occasional overt arrogance. Kennedy also had a certain winning gaiety and ability to enjoy life. But his pleasures seem to have grown out of an ironic view of life and the combined hedonism-stoicism that formed part of his basic guard against ever being "caught" unprepared. He could enjoy the pleasures and trappings that go with wealth and power, but one suspects that they never "got to" Kennedy precisely because very little ever got to him in an emotional sense. For emotional detachment can also serve to mask an indifference and basic hostility toward people—and oneself—that can be far deeper and stronger than surface "egotism."

Detachment is also a method of avoiding conflict with others and with oneself. (Excessive dependency is merely the opposite side of the coin. Some repressed dependency is always present in detachment, and vice versa.) While the technique of detachment clearly brought Jack Kennedy a certain sensation of calm strength, he showed multiple signs of repressed tension that belied that calm certainty. Physically, Kennedy's backaches and adrenal insufficiency continued through his presidency, and, according to at least one studious physician, Kennedy was a very sick man. Moreover, Jack's hands often trembled (for example, during a speech in 1963, after he had been in politics seventeen years), he constantly gulped his food, and he had many persistent nervous habits (such as tapping his teeth and fingers and repeatedly brushing back his hair). Kennedy's tension also showed in the awkward way he held and used his hands, clearly visible in photographs.

To return to Jack's chronological history, following his discharge from the Navy in March, 1945, after medical treatment, his life plans were uncertain. His only experience was in writing, and so he first considered becoming a journalist. His father got Jack a job as a special correspondent for Hearst's International News Service, owned by Joe Kennedy's old friend. But after covering the founding of the United Nations in San Francisco and Churchill's fall from power in England, Jack grew tired of the "too-passive" profession, as he saw it. Next he briefly considered teaching; but that would have required studying for an advanced degree, which didn't appeal to him. At one point his father thought about buying a newspaper for Jack to manage, but that again seemed too confining.

Then chance and circumstance provided the ideal solution for both the unfulfilled ambition of Kennedy Senior and the empty life of his next surviving son. Joe Junior was to have been the family's politician before his wartime death. Now the political mantle fell naturally upon Jack's still ailing but otherwise unburdened shoulders. Kennedy confided to his Navy friend "Red" Fay shortly after leaving the service that he was becoming more and more aware of his father's desire that a son should enter politics. Fay felt that while Jack wanted to be a writer, perhaps a political commentator, his thinking was beginning to conform more to his father's. Fay visited Jack often in Florida, and early in 1945 he was given a hint of Jack's future course. Someday, Jack said, he and his father would be concentrating their energies on maneuvering the PT-boat experience and his injured back into political advantage. His father, Jack admitted, was enthusiastic and ready to go and could not understand why his son's zeal did not match his own. Fay himself could see that Jack was unenthusiastic about a career as a politician, yet he sensed that Jack was leaning in that direction. So he was not surprised when Kennedy announced his decision to run for the House of Representatives in 1946.

The opening to run for Congress from Massachusetts' Eleventh Congressional District had been provided, ironically, by Honey Fitz's old political foe, James Michael Curley. In 1942, Curley, Boston's controversial ex-mayor, had won a seat to Congress, but in 1945 he had regained City Hall, his favorite stomping ground. This left Curley's congressional seat vacant. Joe Kennedy, who had rejected a lieutenant-governor candidacy for Jack, decided this was the opportunity the Kennedys needed. The Eleventh District, which included Boston's East, North, and West End, as well as Charlestown, Cambridge, and part of Somerville, was old Kennedy and Fitzgerald political territory, and solidly Democratic. The June primary in effect meant election. The race was wide open, for the district had no single boss or organization. But although ten candidates had announced by April, 1946, none of them ever had a real chance against the Kennedy name, fortune, and power (brainpower as well as manpower). There was truth as well as exaggeration in Curley's comment, "Kennedy! How can he lose? He's got a double-barreled name. . . . He doesn't even need to campaign. He can go to Washington now and forget the primary and election."

On the other hand, Jack Kennedy was a stranger to Boston, an unknown, shy young millionaire. It was Kennedy's war record, inflated into shining heroism and lavishly publicized, that made the stranger fully acceptable. Kennedy had other enormous advantages in addition to his family name and an unlimited money supply. Foremost was the political shrewdness of his influential father, who could summon and weld together a wide array of supporters ranging from old pros to Jack's eager Navy buddies. To these assets, Jack added his own personal determination and drive, which kept him campaigning fourteen hours a day (partly on crutches), as well as the huge energies of the large Kennedy clan.

But most of all, Jack's first victory was achieved by his father. Although Jack and Bobby later developed into astute politicians in their own right, in this initial campaign Joe Kennedy ran the show. It was the father who handled the campaign funds, chose the manager, interviewed key workers, and made the major decisions. The Ambassador later said that he "just called people. I got in touch with people I knew. I have a lot of contacts. I've been in politics in Massachusetts since I was ten." As Richard Whalen pointed out, "the scope of his influence was extraordinary." In addition to calling people and directing the hidden professional part of the campaign, Joe Kennedy also hired a public relations firm to mount "the most elaborate professional advertising effort ever seen in a Massachusetts congressional election. . . . The voters of the district were saturated with Kennedy advertising—billboards, posters, car cards, leaflets, and radio 'spots.' The people, a campaign worker remembered, 'saw Kennedy, heard Kennedy, ate Kennedy, drank Kennedy, slept Kennedy, and Kennedy talked and we talked Kennedy all day long. . . . He was well advertised.' "

As old Joe had promised, he sold young Jack to the voters "like soap flakes." As a politician cousin Joe Kane commented, "It takes three things to win. The first is money and the second is money and the third is money." Actually, of course, it took a great deal more: careful planning, a smoothly efficient organization, thorough attention to detail, and the dogged work of the untested candidate himself. Jack's message was a predictable "bread-and-butter" liberalism on housing, jobs, lower prices and rents, Social Security, and veterans' benefits. "Even on this safe ground," observed Whalen, "he was cautious and noncommittal." When a speaker at the Harvard Liberal Union was asked whether Kennedy would make "the kind of progressive representative we're working for," he replied, "I spoke with Jack for about three hours the other afternoon on some of the issues facing this country—and I don't really think I'm qualified to answer your question." The peak of the Kennedy *tour de force* was a unique Boston tea party, a formal reception which brought forth fifteen hundred women in their best gowns. "That reception was the clincher," said an opponent's manager. "Everybody wanted to be in Society with the Kennedys." The Kennedys themselves were not yet accepted by "Society," but they were on their way.

It was no great surprise to insiders when Jack swept the election, taking more than 40 percent of the votes cast for all ten candidates. Kennedy had won not only an election, but also a safe seat. Two years later, not a single Democrat or Republican opponent challenged him for reelection. In 1950, five contenders appeared in the party primary. Kennedy beat them easily, then defeated the Republican nominee nearly five to one. By 1952, Jack was ready to take on bigger game.

Before proceeding to Jack Kennedy's career in Congress and as President, I want to review briefly what seem to me the salient psychohistorical features of his character evidenced in this period. As a young man of twenty-nine, Kennedy accepted his father's—and, to some extent, society's—ethos of "victory at any price" and "only the top is good enough." Jack had never overtly rebelled against the parental rules that dominated his life. His history instead points to his having internalized these rules and made them part of himself. When Jack Kennedy followed his father's wishes and his dead brother's footsteps into politics, he had already largely identified himself with that father and brother (who had closely patterned himself after the father). And although Jack had a literary bent and a personal remoteness unlike most of his family, he had the same Kennedy drive and determination to wrest personal triumphs at all costs. On the other hand, he also showed strong evidence of repressed revolt, which emerged in frequent illnesses and accidents and disguised hostility to others. His deepest emotional defense, however, seemed to be a polite withdrawal and distance from others, and very likely from himself. In this Jack was much like his mother.

But he was also a man of great physical attractiveness, to men as well as women, and he reciprocated women's interest in him. In fact, Jack seemed a prime example of the Kennedy mystique of sexual aggressiveness and repeated triumph, part of the bravery-in-battle-and-in-bed *machismo* that formed such a large part of the Kennedy potency-virility syndrome. Sentimentality far more than genuine pragmatism seemed the fountain that fed the Kennedy drives for constant action and acclaim. Pride and fearfulness existed together in the Kennedy men, sometimes leading them to reckless activity and sometimes smothering them with self-protective caution. Above all, they could see only short distances beyond themselves.

Thus at the beginning of the political career that brought him to the pinnacle of national power, John F. Kennedy had shown himself to be a mixture of a man who believed greatly in nothing outside of Kennedy glorification, and yet who was coming to feel, more and more, that he himself deserved—or needed—the habiliments of power. For only by achieving status on the outside might he snare the elusive security of status on the inside: inside the family and inside himself. In time, Kennedy came to believe that he could win greatness as well. Yet even while he sought and acquired power, his inner sense of powerlessness seemed to remain. Such an emotional ambivalence would prove strange and problematic for the leader of a great nation.

Chapter 6

STEPPINGSTONE
TO THE WHITE HOUSE:
KENNEDY ON CAPITOL HILL, 1947-1960

After all, I wasn't equipped for the job. I didn't plan to get into it, and when I started out as a Congressman, there were lots of things I didn't know, a lot of mistakes I made, maybe some votes that should have been different.

—John F. Kennedy

His performance in the House of Representatives had been considered by most observers to be largely undistinguished—except for a record of absenteeism which had been heightened by indifference as well as ill health and by unofficial as well as official travels.

John Kennedy was not one of the Senate's great leaders. Few laws of national importance bear his name. And after he graduated in November, 1958, from the traditionally inactive freshman class, his opportunities for major contributions to the Senate—except for his battle for fair labor reform against rackets—were increasingly eroded by the demands of his Presidential campaign.

—Theodore C. Sorensen, *Kennedy*

Just as I went into politics because Joe died, if anything happened to me tomorrow, my brother Bobby would run for my seat in the Senate. And if Bobby died, Teddy would take over for him.

—John F. Kennedy

ᘐᘓ

JOHN F. KENNEDY spent six years in the United States House of Representatives (1947–1952) and eight years in the United States Senate (1953–1960) before his successful bid for the presidency. From a study of those years, one overriding politico-historical fact emerges: Kennedy viewed the U.S.

Congress not primarily as a place in which he could significantly serve his country, but basically as a springboard from which to leap to the White House. True to his emotional and philosophical upbringing, Kennedy saw victory as an end in itself—the glory and vindication of the Kennedys and of himself. Throughout these years, while the image of Kennedy matured and his grasp of national issues broadened, the impression remains that his goals were still essentially opportunistic and narrowly personal. Kennedyism, not a genuine humanism, remained the guiding star of Kennedy's attitudes and actions.

Jack Kennedy entered the U.S. House of Representatives in January, 1947, as a callow, unprepared, and generally reluctant young man of twenty-nine. With his "shy, boyish smile, big shock of hair, and gangly frame," as one biographer described him, Kennedy looked even younger than he was. Congressman Kennedy had little notion of what he might do in Congress, other than offering his constituents the standard fare of bread-and-butter promises. For Kennedy, interests wider than clan and constituents still scarcely seemed to exist. (We will find the same initial narrowness of outlook in both Bobby and Teddy Kennedy as they entered politics.) In view of Jack Kennedy's great interest in history, he had a surprisingly unhistoric attitude toward his new role. Perhaps life seemed somewhat unreal to Kennedy at that time. He had survived the war, while his older brother, the one destined for Congress, had been killed. And despite Jack's apparent real desires, he had given in and fulfilled his father's expectations. It would be understandable if for a time he wanted mainly to relax and start to enjoy a life he had, in several ways, never expected to have. The Navy, the shock of the war, and his injuries were scarcely behind him; his back still hurt and his thin face bore the yellowish hue of recent malaria. Even Kennedys occasionally rested between bouts of ambition.

The new young Congressman moved into a comfortable Georgetown house with the devoted housekeeper of his childhood and a Negro valet (formerly with *New York Times* Bureau Chief Arthur Krock, Joe Kennedy's old friend). Kennedy's mother dropped in from time to time to check up on him, just as she had done in his schoolboy years, and Jack's father called him often on the phone. Part of the time Jack stayed with sister Eunice before she married Sargent Shriver. Other sisters and brothers came by to see him on their frequent trips through Washington. While Jack Kennedy had achieved a status of his own outside the family—with the family's pushing, backing, and helping—this continued close support suggests that he had not truly cut the umbilical cord. And Jack, of course, was now the family's "white hope"—their chance for national immortality.

Although the political life had not been Jack's personal choice, he settled into it with surprising ease. Soon, in addition to his pleasant bachelor life of parties, dating, and travel, Jack was busy organizing his office into an effective service center for his Massachusetts voters. While Kennedy had no particular program to offer, he did provide prompt personalized service for his constituents. This, as many Congressmen have found, can provide the route to political longevity. Jack soon had the help of an unusually able assistant, Ted Reardon (Joe Junior's old Harvard friend), as well as a highly efficient and devoted secretary in Mrs. Evelyn Lincoln. (Ted Sorensen would join his staff in early 1953.) Like his father, Jack had the ability to put together a loyal, hard-working staff to handle routine business for him and the multiple demands that are the lifeblood of every politician. In Sorensen, Kennedy later acquired what he called his "intellectual blood bank," a young man of fluent ideas and words who would help write many of Kennedy's most influential speeches as Senator and President.

But, as yet, Kennedy's ideas and interests did not extend beyond the immediate needs of his predominantly working-class Catholic voters. Jack hated to be labeled in any way, and people who called him a liberal or conservative annoyed him; he finally insisted on the neutral title of "Massachusetts Democrat." Jack's hypersensitivity to labels seemed a sign of his unconscious fear of being controlled, a fear that sprang from inadmissible subservience to his parents and unfulfilled emotional needs. A Harvard interviewer had written of Kennedy during his 1946 campaign, "Kennedy seems to feel honestly that he is not hedging . . . by refusing to offer a positive specific program. He feigns an ignorance of much in the affairs of government and tells you to look at his record in two years to see what he stands for."

Joseph Kennedy's biographer, Richard Whalen, made a knowledgeable assessment of Jack Kennedy's lack of a political program or philosophy: "In two years (or four or six, for that matter), the only accurate label for Kennedy would remain the one he had chosen. He voted the interests of his working class constituency in the Eleventh District of Massachusetts, siding with House liberals on Fair Deal measures appealing to low-income voters, switching to the conservative side on foreign policy issues. His was a voting record calculated to please his poor, predominantly Catholic, strongly anti-Communist electorate. Later, when a more consistently liberal 'image' became necessary to fulfill wider ambitions, he offered excuses and explanations for his early wobbling. One in particular had the ring of truth: 'I'd just come out of my father's house at the time, and these were the things I knew.' "

Jack's voting record and speeches during his congressional years reflected his father's staunch conservatism. Kennedy supported the local welfare his constituents demanded, but otherwise he fully favored government economy and restraint. In a 1950 budget debate, he asked the House, "How long can we continue deficit financing on such a large scale with a national debt of over two hundred and fifty-eight billion dollars?" A dozen years later, when he wished to shoot for the moon—literally—he himself added some $30 billion to that deficit without qualms, a 12 percent increase over 1950's debt. During the Korean War, Kennedy supported a balanced budget and higher taxes, and warned against inflation. Jack also echoed his father's anti-Roosevelt opinions, telling his Massachusetts listeners in a January, 1949, speech, "At the Yalta Conference in 1945, a sick Roosevelt, with the advice of General Marshall . . . gave the Kurile Islands as well as control of various strategic ports . . . to the Soviet Union." Unlike most Democrats, Congressman Kennedy also voted for the Twenty-second Amendment to limit the President to two terms, a measure interpreted by many as a postmortem comment on FDR's multiple terms.

But on foreign aid Jack differed from his father. While asserting that the United States "cannot reform the world" (an opinion later reversed by the New Frontier), Jack supported many foreign aid programs. In early 1951, after a six-week tour of the chief NATO countries, Congressman Kennedy spoke out strongly for stationing American troops in Western Europe, which his father opposed. While Jack no doubt had many genuine intellectual disagreements with his father, we must also remember that by then the Congressman was starting to run hard for the Senate. He needed national issues that would give him greater prominence. As we shall see, Kennedy chose the international field, long his favorite, as the best arena for political jousting. Here he could blend both liberal stands (foreign aid and an international outlook) with a strongly conservative anticommunism that appealed to Massachusetts voters.

Actually, Jack's views on specific issues never seemed very important to his father, except as they might help or hurt the Kennedy image. What always mattered most to Kennedy father and son was the basic goal of winning. As biographer Whalen noted, Joseph Kennedy "railed against expanding government and onrushing socialism, but calmly accepted his son's contrary voting record, for he realized such tactical liberalism was expedient in Jack's district. Joe Kennedy admired well-organized, self-disciplined men who were physically tough and agile of mind; what they thought, or said they thought, could be disregarded. It was more important that his son win elections than that their opinions agree."

One of the most damning appraisals of Kennedy's lackluster congressional career has come from Kennedy's own closest assistant, the man he took with him into the White House, Theodore C. Sorensen. In his two books on JFK, *Kennedy* and *The Kennedy Legacy*, Sorensen made some surprisingly critical observations about Kennedy's period on Capitol Hill. Of Jack's years in the House of Representatives, Sorensen notes that Congressman

Kennedy, as a young man "just come out of [his] father's house," had comparatively little interest in civil rights and civil liberties. Although Jack's reputation as a liberal would grow, Sorensen himself was of the opinion that it was not until the second year in the Senate that Jack began to concern himself with such issues.

In *The Kennedy Legacy*, Sorensen offers more explicit criticism of Jack's years of service in the House of Representatives. The voting record of the young Congressman was inconsistent, he concludes. It was basically conservative on international and fiscal issues, a reflection, in part, of positions taken by the father because Jack had not yet established positions of his own. On domestic economic and social issues, however, it showed a decidedly liberal bent, and this Sorensen attributes to Kennedy's constituency, an East Boston district where such issues as rent and price controls, housing, and social security were real concerns of the voter. Overall, Jack's record was marked by a high rate of absenteeism, with world travels, illnesses, and frequent junkets to Massachusetts in early preparation for a state-wide Senate campaign accounting in part for Jack's poor showing.

Sorensen felt that some of Kennedy's positions as a Congressman showed courage, such as a large tax increase to support the Korean War. But this can be equally seen as a reflection of Kennedy's conservatism, patterned after his father's. Sorensen also cites with approval Kennedy's first steps toward anticolonialism and "a recognition that the United States cannot solve all the world's problems." (Paradoxically, it was Kennedy, with Sorensen as his rhetorical ghost, who as President widened American participation in Vietnam and called for American intervention anywhere in the world in defense of "liberty.") Sorensen, despite limited approval of Kennedy's actions as a Congressman, felt that "far more often his positions, when consistent at all, were contrary to those which with greater experience and responsibility he would later take. He opposed, for example, some foreign-aid and most foreign-trade liberalization; he favored cuts in domestic programs not beneficial to Massachusetts; and he supported limitations on Presidential power."

Let us now return briefly behind the scenes for some revealing glimpses of Jack Kennedy in relationship with the close workers who helped present his image and actions to the public. Evelyn Lincoln, Kennedy's secretary for twelve years (1951–1963), wrote an account of those dozen years which highlights more facets of Kennedy's personality than political assessments by a score of reporters might provide. I have already mentioned her description of Kennedy's office confusion, forgetfulness, and last-minute rushes for planes and appointments. Even more pertinent are her comments on Jack's attitudes toward his staff.

Wrote Mrs. Lincoln, "Soon after I went to work for John Fitzgerald

Kennedy I learned that if he wanted something done, he wanted it done immediately. If he selected you to do it, it was because you were on the job and near him at the time. If you proved up to the task, he called on you again. If you were slow on performance, the next time he asked someone else to do it. If he thought you were taking a little longer than necessary to get the job done, he would ask you about the delay. If you had a logical answer, he was satisfied. But if you said, 'I haven't had time to do it,' once again he would lose confidence in you.

"He always wanted perfection. If I ever said, 'I'm sorry, Senator, I couldn't get the reservation for you,' he would say, 'Why?' It didn't make any difference what the reason might be, he would still say, 'Well, call someone else,' or, 'Let me talk to them.' I soon learned that I could not take 'No' for an answer when trying to fill his requests.

"He liked to have the people around him available at all times. When he called, whether it was ten o'clock in the morning or twelve o'clock at night, he wanted to be able to reach you. If you were at the beach or at a night club and couldn't be reached, he was upset, and once again he would turn to someone else. You had to earn his confidence all over again. . . . If someone he relied upon asked for a few days off, he would say, 'I would like to take a vacation, too.' That was his way of registering his displeasure at not being able to reach them. It was not that he felt they did not merit a vacation, it was only his way of expressing his reliance upon them."

This sketch of Jack Kennedy shows several dominant traits. He is portrayed, first of all, as a compulsive perfectionist, a man who demanded immediate action from himself and others. Secondly, he seems to have felt excessively dependent on other people. He wanted them "available at all times," regardless of how this affected their personal lives. He even resented giving his staff vacations because they would be out of immediate touch. There is a suggested lack of real feeling or concern for other people, despite the friendliness and informality which Mrs. Lincoln points out in another passage, with the comment "He wanted people around him to feel his comradeship." Yet, in view of his excessive demands, this "comradeship" seems suspect. We are all aware of the many uses of friendliness, wit, humor, good manners, and approachability for getting what we want out of others. With Kennedy, there was a repeated impression of skillful techniques of friendly manipulation, combined with emotional remoteness. The people around him often did not seem to mean much in themselves, but were valued only for the functions they served. Most of us exhibit an indifference to others and self-centeredness to some degree, but in Jack the degree often seemed marked. Yet Kennedy's arrogance and indifference were usually muted, and often concealed by his superficial affability and his quality of emotional distance from himself. This impassive "standing apart," coupled with Kennedy's wry wit, looked to many like humility and objective realism. Few realized that the mockery, both of himself and others, concealed a probable inability to make a passionate commitment to any project unconnected with the Kennedy mystique.

Kennedy was portrayed by Mrs. Lincoln as a man who both relied heavily upon people and yet deeply distrusted them. This, again, is understandable in the pattern of Kennedy's general ambivalence toward the world and himself. His staff had to earn his confidence again and again; one slip or moment of unavailability and "you had to earn his confidence all over again." This is hardly a healthy relationship that brings forth the best efforts from both parties. Instead, we can sense Jack's repressed anger at his dependency. Such an unconscious resentment would be a natural reaction, for no human being truly desires excessive dependency. We see in Mrs. Lincoln's description a curious contradiction between Jack Kennedy as the active, independent, aggressive, confident, and emotionally aloof "doer," and Kennedy as the passive, dependent, resentful, distrustful, and emotionally involved "done for." Such contradictory and unreconciled opposites are inevitably found in neurosis.

There was clearly a strong unconscious emotional conflict operating in John F. Kennedy, a conflict to which he reacted but of which he was probably very little aware, if at all. Essentially, it seems to have been the old childhood conflict between parental overdominance and the struggle to assert himself as an individual. And we can detect how the shackles of Jack's childhood were carried into his adult life and political career. Thus Kennedy was not only in close and constant touch with his family, but he also created a new family of staff retainers who seem to have served partly as substitute parent images daily filling the old dual role of nursemaids and slave drivers. Many of these staff members came in turn to resent and distrust each other, although they maintained a discreetly united front for the public. For instance, Sorensen, who was himself accused of submerging his personality in Kennedy's, could contrast Mrs. Lincoln's "unfailing devotion and good nature" against her "sometimes overly possessive attitude." Kenny O'Donnell, later JFK's appointments secretary, was resented by some aides for his "stern protectiveness." Kennedy did come to repose considerable confidence in and delegated authority to his closest male aides, but never his female assistants. As Mrs. Lincoln herself commented, "The White House was a man's world. Franklin Roosevelt had a domineering mother, so he turned to women for advice. But Kennedy had a dominant father, so he turned to men." Jack's attitudes toward women were actually more complex than this. His ties to women seemed much more hostile than his ties to men; like the other Kennedy males, he accepted the sex-role stereotypes of his society and never really liked or appreciated women as individuals in themselves. Kennedy essentially disliked and distrusted women. Therefore his strong emotional need for support and approval led him to follow the counsel of male authority figures. Unfortunately, a large number of these authority figures—such as McNamara, Rusk, Acheson, Taylor, Bundy, and Rostow—were as confused and misguided as Kennedy about national values and priorities. The 1971 publication of the *Pentagon Papers* clearly revealed this about their Vietnam policy.

Returning to Kennedy's early political career, in the late 1940s Jack soon became bored with the slow pace of Congress. Lawmaking is often a dull, routine, and tedious job except for either plodders or dedicated legislators. Jack Kennedy was neither. He was highly intelligent but also intensely impatient, and he was not imaginative enough to view his job as one of intrinsic importance. In addition, making laws may arouse unconscious resistance in the lawmaker who has suffered much in his own life from rigid legalisms. It is perhaps relevant in this connection to note that Kennedy drew back repeatedly as President from formulating or pressing forward his own legislative program.

Jack's boredom in the House was reflected in his high rate of absenteeism, as well as in his vacillating policy stands. In August, 1950, he warned the House, "I think that we are heading for a major disaster in Western Europe." But after a trip around the world in the fall of 1951 (with sister Pat and brother Bob), Kennedy told his fellow Representatives, "Many of us feel that the United States has concentrated its attention too much on Western Europe." Even Professor Burns, a liberal Kennedy supporter (to whom Kennedy opened his files in 1959), noted that Jack's conservatism "showed itself sporadically during his first three years in the House and seemed to increase toward the end." Kennedy, for example, voted against funds for the Interior Department, a library services bill, the Tennessee Valley Authority, and the 1950 aid to education bill (because it didn't include federally-funded parochial school transportation). In general, Kennedy was against inflation and for maintaining wage and price controls, high taxes, and a balanced budget. He would completely reverse this deflationary policy as President when his own dramatic plans called for high expenditures. In a later review of his mentor's congressional career to 1953, Sorensen pointed out that, as a freshman senator, Kennedy was not knowledgeable in agriculture, conservation, and natural resources; was uninformed on basic economic, fiscal, and monetary policies; and was lacking broad experience with the variety and scope of the American land and its people.

Yet despite his mediocre record, by 1952 Kennedy had an assured position in the House and the definite possibility of assuming Democratic leadership. His seat was safe, and his variegated voting record gave him appeal among all party factions. But he had been looking toward the Senate since even his early days in Washington. During his second year in office he launched a statewide campaign to build up his reputation all across Massachusetts. Kennedy simply could not stop running for long. From late Thursday until Sunday night, he dashed from one corner of the state to the other, speaking anywhere he could get an invitation. Frank Morrissey, who ran Kennedy's Boston office, said later, "I'll bet he talked to at least a million people and shook hands with seven hundred and fifty thousand." One of Kennedy's Boston public relations men recalled, "Back there in 1948, Jack had me driving on dark winter nights over those steep, icy roads in the Berkshires to meetings of the Eagles and the Loyal Order of the Moose in places like North Adams and Pittsfield."

Another Boston supporter described the typical hectic pace of Kennedy's Massachusetts campaigning: "You're driving with Jack doing eighty miles an hour, and he keeps asking you to go faster because he's already ten minutes late at the next town. A motorcycle cop starts chasing you, so you stop and get out, and, miraculously, you fast-talk the cop into letting you go on. Naturally, you're feeling rather proud of yourself for accomplishing such a feat. A few miles further on, you come to a railroad crossing where the red light is flashing and the bell is ringing. Jack says, 'Come on, we've got to beat that train.' So you step on it and race to the crossing, but the locomotive gets there a couple of inches ahead of you and you just miss hitting it. Jack grits his teeth in disgust. 'If you hadn't wasted so much time back there talking to that cop, we would have made it,' he says." As one friendly biographer commented, "Jack's keyed-up, almost compulsive, competitiveness is usually concealed by his affable and deceptively casual manner."

Politics gave Jack Kennedy both a fresh impetus and an outlet for his compulsively neurotic drives. From all indications he could appease his inner demons only by unremitting efforts to win, not by efforts to achieve more meaningful but less dramatic legislative results. The effort seemed psychically more important than the victory, for, apparently, no victory brought him real or lasting satisfaction. A new and higher goal had always to be set. At the same time, Jack's need for the trappings of political success and the all-consuming intensity with which he chased that success could also gratify his self-destructive impulses. Political campaigning is hard work for anyone, and Kennedy's campaigns were so long and arduous that they invariably provoked the old back trouble and brought him severe pain. Several times in his political life, he nearly succeeded in killing himself.

Yet Jack Kennedy's often relaxed appearance, youthful charm, and deceptive air of casualness hid from many people the tremendous drive, energy, determination, and professionalism that went into the continual political successes. As an associate remarked, "Jack's success in politics ever since his first campaign for Congress in 1946 has been entirely due to hard work and long hours. I don't think any other politician at any time ever shook so many hands in so many small villages and towns or ever shaved in the men's rooms of so many filling stations and bowling alleys." While hard work alone could not have brought Kennedy his brilliant victories, we should never forget that behind this outwardly calm, casual, debonair, literary young man dwelt another man, an entirely different young man who had been caught on a psychological merry-go-round and apparently no longer knew how nor consciously wished to get off.

By the early 1950s, Jack was running hard, although at first he did not know what office he was running for. "I didn't know whether I would run for the Senate or for Governor," he later said. "I would have liked to have run for Governor in 1948, and then run against Saltonstall four years later." But the governorship was closed to Kennedy in 1948; the state constitution decreed that the governor have seven years of Massachusetts residency. In April, 1952, Jack's opening came, when Governor Paul Dever, a close Kennedy friend, decided not to take on Henry Cabot Lodge for the Senate because he thought Lodge unbeatable. The Kennedys, who had pollsters regularly gathering political intelligence, did not agree. Lodge was absent boosting Eisenhower for President against Taft, and many conservative Republicans preferred Taft. As Joseph Kennedy remarked, "This may be the key to the election."

Jack had already been campaigning hard for years. "The pros wait too long to start," he later observed. "I began running four and a half years ahead of time. My opponent, Henry Cabot Lodge, Jr., didn't go into action until two months before Election Day." By that time the Kennedy political organization had spread over Massachusetts like a vast web. Lodge badly underestimated the professionalism of Jack, his father, and the entire Kennedy family, and he paid for this error with his Senate seat. Once again, Joe Kennedy was a key force in Jack's election. As a speech writer recalled, "The Ambassador worked around the clock. He was always consulting people, getting reports, looking into problems. Should Jack go on TV with this issue? He'd call in experts, get opinions, have ideas worked up. . . ."

On the issues there were no real differences between the young Congressman and the fourteen-year Senate veteran. But the Kennedys worked hard to create an image of Jack as a "young reformer bringing change" and Lodge as a "crusty representative of the Old Guard." In reality, the Kennedy forces were assiduously wooing both Left and Right. The Kennedys' political insight and tireless efforts paid off handsomely. In November, 1952, while Eisenhower swept the country and carried a majority of Republicans into office, young Jack Kennedy edged out Lodge with a plurality of 70,000 votes.

Kennedy's objectives in the Senate seem to have been basically the same as his objectives in the House: to avoid real and dangerous controversy, while projecting himself as a national figure. Even a short survey of Kennedy's Senate record outlines this general pattern. For example, in his first two years, his over-all economic conservatism was reflected in his voting with Virginia Senator Harry Byrd's economy bloc on thirteen out of fifteen issues (including votes against a housing research program, loans for rural electrification, and funds for flood control). Kennedy also wanted high tariffs to protect Massachusetts' basic watch, textile, and fishing industries, although in 1954 he was the only New England Senator to support a liberalized foreign trade program. As one writer observed, Kennedy typically "tried to carry water on both shoulders." Jack's ability to do a political quickstep on both sides of several fences, as well as his outward geniality and good humor, soon made him one of the most popular members of the Senate. He has been described as the only Senator who was angry with no one and friendly with almost everyone.

Yet avoidance of controversy, while it can keep a politician out of trouble, can also turn him into a nonentity. But Kennedy was determined never to be a nonentity. In order to create a national reputation, yet remain acceptable to a wide range of political camps, he followed two strategies, both of which he had already used in winning Massachusetts elections. The first gave him national visibility through an astute wooing and exploitation of the mass media. The second gave him national credibility through the exploitation of national or international "issues" that would give him wide publicity at minimum political risk. The first strategy was easier to implement than the second. As a handsome, young, wealthy, Ivy League, and best-selling-author bachelor Senator, Jack Kennedy was natural news material; there was nobody else around quite like him. Soon the country's popular magazines carried frequent features on the man *The Saturday Evening Post* called "The Senate's Gay Young Bachelor." Kennedy's marriage in 1953 to Jacqueline Bouvier, a society beauty and Vassar girl, increased the publicity. By the time children came along, the American public had had a chance to explore every domestic aspect of "life with the Kennedys," which included Jack's still newsworthy and photogenic parents, as well as his handsome brothers and sisters. Joseph Kennedy's wide publishing contacts and appreciation of the news media were important factors in their "discovery" of Jack, which came into full flood in 1957 after his unsuccessful but widely publicized vice presidential attempt the previous year. While the media wooed the Kennedys, the Kennedys also adroitly wooed the media.

Gore Vidal, a critical observer of politicians at work, summarized the development of Jack's expertly shaped political image: ". . . the image was created early: the high-class book that made the grade; the much publicized heroism at war; the election to the House of Representatives in 1946. From that point on, the publicity was constant and though the Congressman's record of service was unimpressive, he himself was photogenic and appealing. Then came the Senate, the marriage, the illnesses, the second high-class book, and the rest is history . . . most of his life was governed, as Mrs. Lincoln wrote of the year 1959, 'by the public-opinion polls. We were not unlike the people who check their horoscope each day before venturing out.' And when they did venture out, it was always to create an illusion. As Mrs. Lincoln remarks in her guileless way: after Senator Kennedy returned to Washington from a four-week tour of Europe, 'it was obvious that his stature as a Senator had grown, for he came back as an authority on the current situation in Poland.' "

Jack Kennedy's second strategy to attain national stature was not quite so simple and led to occasional pitfalls, although he showed himself to be an increasingly surefooted political climber. Jack had launched his Senate career in May, 1953, with three major speeches on New England. These were mainly an elaboration of his House statements (Kennedy now had Ted Sorensen on hand to expand his research and rhetoric). While the South reacted strongly to Kennedy's criticism of its "lures to industrial migration," which were factually valid, the rest of the country ignored him. Clearly New England affairs would not springboard the ambitious young Senator to national attention. But in his early Senate years, Kennedy's votes remained predictably those of a New Englander, with the exception of his support of the St. Lawrence Seaway. However, after his vice presidential bid catapulted him to national fame, his focus became unwaveringly national.

Kennedy's chance at the Democratic vice presidential nomination grew gradually over the years as he worked hard at his media image. The immediate opening, however, came when Adlai Stevenson unexpectedly threw the nomination open to the convention in August, 1956. Kennedy was a strong Stevenson supporter, and had even considered running as a New England favorite son in the New Hampshire primary to help hold New England for Stevenson. Ted Sorensen made an interesting comment on Kennedy's character as suggested by that incident. Sorensen said that the primary wasn't really important to Kennedy, "But he was a man of action; and, in a remark which revealed much about his activist nature, he was contemplating running for President in New Hampshire, he said, 'because that's where the action is now.' " This remark is reminiscent of Kennedy's later comment about his desire to be President, "because that's where the power is." The overwhelming importance of action and power had been drilled into the Kennedy sons almost from birth. Although Jack Kennedy would claim in his 1960 campaign that he wanted to be President to "get things done" (as Bobby would later cry that he wanted to "turn things around"), the Kennedy philosophy and social aims have always been notably vague and rhetorically more stylish than substantive.

Jack Kennedy's rise to political stardom and consideration as a potential Vice President was summarized by the adulatory Sorensen in a passage that suggests far more than the biographer realizes: "His best-selling book and growing number of speeches had made him more widely known than most Democratic office-holders. His youthful, clean-cut demeanor, his candid, low-key approach and his heroic war record gave him a special appeal to both new and uncommitted voters. His television appearances and Harvard commencement address drew national attention. . . ." Not once, we should note, does Sorensen mention a policy position or a legislative act to account for Kennedy's popular rise. Again, glamor, not solid production, seems to have been the core of Jack's prominence.

Stevenson's unexpected decision to make the nomination a real contest caught the Kennedys off balance (as it did the other contenders), but the brothers hastily rallied their forces and made it a close fight. Joe Kennedy was in Europe, after having advised Jack and Bobby not to try for the slot as Stevenson's running mate. The father was sure that the Democratic ticket would again be defeated and that Kennedy's Catholicism would be blamed. But the brothers, unable to resist the challenge, were lucky: Senator Estes Kefauver won by a narrow margin, Jack bowed out gracefully and gained an enormous boost in national prestige. The Kennedys acquired huge and lasting publicity for their candidate and also learned a valuable lesson: Kefauver's televised Senate crime investigations had raised the once-obscure Tennessean to national prominence. The next year, when Jack Kennedy had a chance to join in the Senate labor-rackets probe, he seized on a similar opportunity to increase his national position, which he probably judged more important than the risk of weakening his labor support. After 1956, according to later accounts, Jack's sights had soared beyond the vice presidency.

Meanwhile, the newly prominent junior Senator from Massachusetts finally landed an important committee assignment from which to project his voice nationally. In 1957, Senate Majority Leader Lyndon Johnson (who had thrown Texas votes to Jack in 1956) gave Kennedy what he had long wanted, a seat on the prestigious Foreign Relations Committee. In July, Kennedy spoke out in favor of Algerian independence, an issue calculated to earn the favor of liberals but one of small concern to his Massachusetts constituents. Kennedy's statement caused some adverse reaction (especially from the Eisenhower Administration and the French), but it gained him further national attention. The Senator and his staff now worked hard on foreign policy articles and speeches. Kennedy's travels around the country and abroad increased in the late 1950's, as did his support of foreign aid programs.

But, too often, Kennedy's pronouncements seemed shallow and more opportunistic than straightforward. For example, both Sorensen and Schlesinger in their laudatory and carefully selective biographies mention Jack's Senate speech of April, 1954, against giving military aid to the French (this was the month before the Dienbienphu surrender) or intervening to save a regime which the "great masses" of Vietnamese did not support. But neither biographer mentions the Kennedy speech of June, 1956, which supported the regime of Ngo Dinh Diem as America's "offspring" whom we must not let fail. Later, as President, Kennedy maintained the despotic Diem in office until almost the end, and his Vietnam policy proved one of his costliest mistakes. As Professor Theodore Draper remarked of Kennedy's often contradictory and rapidly changing positions, "The ease with which Kennedy can be quoted against Kennedy suggests the dangers and difficulties of evaluating a statesman whose style is considered more important than his substance." In 1958, as Kennedy's presidential aim became more intense the Senator began warning against an alleged "missile gap" between the United States and Soviet Russia. This gap, after growing wider and wider as the 1960 election neared, vanished once Kennedy was in office (although McNamara's revelation of the gap's nonexistence would be quickly hushed up as the Kennedy Administration increased the arms race).

In civil rights, Kennedy's dominant psychohistorical pattern of political expediency was also evident. Especially in this emotionally charged and politically dangerous area, we encounter the difficult question of when is the compromise political expediency and when is it a realistic salvaging of half a loaf. Kennedy, quite naturally, always argued that his compromises were political necessities. Yet from the record of his political and social views and actions—or nonactions—it seems apparent that genuine racial equality remained largely an emotional blind spot for the founder of the New Frontier. Kennedy's (and Sorensen's) rationalizations for his lack of commitment to civil rights are not convincing. Whatever the arguments, the facts remain that he did very little to further racial equality as Congressman, Senator, and President.

Let us briefly consider Kennedy's ambiguous position on the 1957 Civil Rights Bill. It is true that the Massachusetts Senator had already supported a number of mild—and politically unventuresome—civil rights reforms, such as a stronger Fair Employment Practices Commission (FEPC), an antilynching law, abolition of the poll tax, and amendment of the filibuster rule. The 1957 bill, however, presented the possibility of open opposition to the Southern Democrats who had supported him in his 1956 vice presidential effort and whom he would badly need for his 1960 presidential race. But Kennedy also had to convince the still suspicious Northern progressives of his liberalism. Normally, the passed House bill would first go to the Senate Judiciary Committee. This committee was chaired by Mississippi Senator James Eastland, a determined foe of racial equality and a master parliamentarian capable of waylaying measures he opposed. To bypass Eastland's committee the Senate's liberals planned to use an obscure Senate rule. Kennedy, however, voted against bypassing the Judiciary Committee on the legalistic ground that this would set a dangerous precedent. According to Professor Burns, Kennedy did promise to vote for a discharge petition if necessary; but the bypass was carried by a slim margin.

Kennedy supported the bill's Section 3, which allowed the Attorney General to use injunctive powers to enforce school integration and other rights by initiating civil rather than slow criminal procedures. But a revealing comment showed he did not expect any strong action. As Kennedy reassured his Southern colleagues, "The Attorney General has recently given his assurance that it will not change in any way the deliberate pace at which this decision is to be implemented in the local courts." "Deliberate pace" has more often than not proved to be a euphemism for nonaction. But the Southerners were not convinced, and a conservative coalition defeated this section. The Senate then considered the question of requiring jury trials for criminal contempt cases involving voting rights. The use of juries, liberal critics objected, could undermine the bill's effectiveness, since Southern jurors were certain to exonerate election officials. Kennedy was subjected to great pressure from both sides. After consulting several progressive Northern law professors, he voted for the jury requirement, which he argued would not seriously damage the bill, declaring that Southern juries, "mindful of the watching eyes of the nation," would convict, and if they didn't, Congress could change the law. Such a hope could hardly be taken seriously in view of recent Southern history. On a more realistic level, Kennedy argued that unless the Southern Senators got the jury trial provision they might kill the bill with a filibuster. Kennedy's vote, plus those of a few liberal Democrats and the solid South, passed the jury amendment, 51 to 42. A few days later, the badly shorn bill passed the Senate.

It is relevant to note again Jack's use of arguments centering on "legalisms" and "political practicalities" to support the position he politically wished to take. In an emotional sense, "legality" and "pragmatism" were his twin inheritances from his legal-minded mother and practical-minded father. But between the hammer and the anvil of these two attitudes, the moral reality of truth and justice is often obliterated. Kennedy's adroit hedgehopping gave him answers to pacify the progressives; yet the net effect of his actions was guaranteed to appease the nonprogressive South. Civil rights had scarcely been advanced a step in the South (or North) by this compromised 1957 Act. Jack Kennedy would repeat this pattern of debatable "political necessity" when, as President, he again compromised on a strong civil rights act. Whether in 1957 a discharge petition would have worked against Eastland is questionable (since the South had the votes to defeat Section 3). But it is also questionable whether the Southern Senators would have tried or succeeded in filibustering a stronger law to death. Most liberal Senators were willing to take the chance. As even Professor Burns, a friendly biographer, noted, Kennedy "showed a profile in caution and moderation. He walked a teetering tightrope; at the same time that he was telling liberals of the effectiveness of a bill that included the O'Mahoney provision [for jury trials], he was assuring worried Southerners that it was a moderate bill that would be enforced by *Southern* courts and *Southern* juries— Kennedy's italics."

Another major area of Kennedy's Senate activity was labor reform.Here, too, brief assessments are difficult. But a fairly close study reveals again the outlines of Kennedy's prevalent "caution and moderation" on domestic issues (a caution and moderation which he would often forsake as President in handling foreign relations). Kennedy served on the labor committees of both House and Senate, and organized labor was one of his most powerful backers. In the House Kennedy had opposed the Taft-Hartley bill of 1947 on the ground that it was too restrictive of labor's legitimate and hard-won rights. For a decade his congressional labor votes reflected the aims of his Massachusetts Teamsters supporters. Then, in 1957, Kennedy's relations with union leaders suddenly became strained.

The cause was the Senate's establishment of a special investigating com- mittee on labor rackets, which grew out of information discovered by Senator John McClellan's Permanent Investigations Subcommittee, with Robert Kennedy as chief counsel. Jack Kennedy was asked to join the special committee. The Senator was already chairman of the Senate Labor Committee's Subcommittee on Labor Legislation. The new job held political dangers, but even greater political opportunities. Most important, as Kennedy must have considered this opening, his involvement in national labor investigations would contribute greatly to his national reputation. Similar investigations had done this for Senator Kefauver in the early 1950s. By 1957, after Jack's 1956 vice presidential try and the subsequent flood of favorable publicity, his increased confidence seems to have fixed firmly his previously tentative presidential ambitions. And Kennedy badly needed a dramatic issue of national importance. The role of a corruptions investigator was ideally attuned to America's desire for a national political hero, as well as the country's fascination with violence and crime. Unlike Joe McCarthy, who had raised himself out of obscurity by hunting Communists, Jack Kennedy's targets would not be respected diplomats and intellectuals, but men who were already typecast in the public mind as "seedy underworld characters." No one can determine whether such conjectures were thus precisely weighed by Kennedy, but certainly by 1957 the once-shy young legislator had become an exceedingly clever political psychologist and manipulator of men and issues. Kennedy, in essence, had developed his father's gift of sensing what the public wanted and how to provide it profitably. The older Kennedy had risen in the world by manipulating money and the younger by manipulating votes, and there does not seem to have been any basically great difference in outlook and morality. The goal, according to the historical evidence, was primarily success for the Kennedys.

Richard Whalen has expressed this view in slightly different terms. In *The Founding Father*, he wrote of Jack and his father, "There was no fundamental clash between his dispassionate liberalism and his father's temperamental conservatism. Each was a political pragmatist, alert to the moment's opportunity, heedless of the philosophical inconsistency between one action and the next. Though he attracted intellectuals, Jack did not share their conviction that ideas are the moving force of politics. . . . Like his father, he was intent on the pursuit of power, and left it to the intellectuals to rationalize his deeds. He was in politics, not to advance an ideology, but to derive personal satisfaction. His politics was as self-centered as his father's fortune-building; the one was the natural successor to the other."

But ambition demands an ideological veneer in every field. The Kennedys found theirs in the old American morality fantasy of "cowboys and Indians" or "good guys and bad guys." In this neurotic game, which the Kennedys learned to play skillfully, brother Bobby began to understudy Jack, although their different temperaments brought forth individual performances. In the Senate labor investigations, Bobby became the grim, even vindictive, pursuer of labor evildoers, while the Senator fell naturally into the dignified role of modern reformer and judicious lawmaker. Many labor leaders were at first furious with Kennedy, until Senator William Knowland, the conservative Republican leader, tried to pass some stringent antilabor measures. Reluctantly, AFL-CIO President George Meany and other top leaders accepted the need for moderate reform in labor's internal management. While Kennedy had to resist a variety of political pressures to tone down his investigations, on balance his labor activities in 1957–1959 were a tremendous political boon. They helped build his national reputation as a moderate liberal; they did not alienate the important labor leaders (most of whom were never investigated); most important, they kept him in the public eye via the televised hearings. In 1958, a Kennedy-Ives bill of mild labor reforms passed the Senate 88 to 1, but was buried in the House. In 1959, a Kennedy-Irvin bill was approved in the Senate, 90 to 1. After readjustments with the House-passed Landrum-Griffin bill, the final Senate-House package became the new national labor law.

Pulitzer-Prize-winning reporter Clark Mollenhoff, who was largely responsible for instigating the Senate investigations, has assessed Kennedy's underlying motives in joining the rackets subcommittee: "This was the investigation that put Senator John F. Kennedy on page one of the newspapers. It made him part of a brother act in a fight against the most sordid types of illegal and brutal corruption of the power of organized labor. Until 1957, the bright young Massachusetts senator was one of the glamour boys in Congress. He was characterized by society columnists as a gay bachelor in the House of Representatives and in his first years in the Senate. If his marriage to pretty Jacqueline Bouvier made him a more serious and more effective legislator, it was not obvious in his legislative record up to 1957."

Referring to Kennedy's failure to stop crime-buster Estes Kefauver for the Democratic vice presidential nomination in 1956, Mollenhoff opined, "Out of that convention loss, Senator Kennedy gained his first exposure on national television. He and his brother Robert learned by direct experience that a crime and racket prober who used television properly could have potent grassroots appeal even five years after the Kefauver crime probe had ended. This was no little factor in the Kennedy decision to take on the politically explosive labor racket investigation. . . . Through their own investigations, Jack and Bob Kennedy made personal contact with reporters and editors on nearly every large newspaper in the country. They did not have to seek television coverage, but were sought for appearances on 'Meet the Press,' 'Face the Nation,' and similar nationwide shows. Both Kennedys became cover boys on national publications which would not have given them space a few months earlier. Through his efforts to pass labor reform legislation, Senator Kennedy compiled his only concrete record as a legislator. . . . The effort on this legislation brought him in working contact with men who were later to play top roles in his political campaign and in the Kennedy Administration."

Even more controversial than civil rights and labor legislation was a public issue that had earlier threatened Kennedy's carefully constructed image of moderate liberalism. This explosive issue was "McCarthyism," Republican Senator Joseph McCarthy's abuses of power in investigating alleged Communists in and out of government. The McCarthy tempest lasted from 1950 until 1954, when the Senate voted to censure the Wisconsin Senator for his insults to other Senators. The McCarthy issue was especially tricky for Kennedy. Most of his conservative Catholic constituency were strong McCarthy supporters, accepting the Senator's wild and unproved charges as evidence of widespread internal subversion. In addition, McCarthy was a friend of Kennedy's father, and brother Bobby was a lawyer investigator on McCarthy's subcommittee. Jack Kennedy himself had mildly supported McCarthy's aims in 1950, when he told Harvard students that "he knew Joe pretty well, and he may have something." In Kennedy's 1952 Senate campaign, he had straddled the fence on McCarthy, while his father had persuaded the Wisconsin Republican not to enter Massachusetts on behalf of Republican incumbent Lodge.

In the Senate, Kennedy was appointed to McCarthy's Government Operations Committee, but he refused to join the subcommittee on investigations. Thus Kennedy was not directly involved in McCarthy's notorious hearings. On issues involving "McCarthyism" rather than the man himself, Jack voted against McCarthy (for example, he supported James B. Conant as Ambassador to Germany and Charles Bohlen as Ambassador to Russia, both of whom were strongly opposed by McCarthy). But Kennedy refused to speak out against McCarthy's inflammatory demagoguery that was dividing America, ruining the careers and reputations of innocent liberals, and intensifying the general Cold War paranoia.

McCarthy's unprincipled extremism brought matters to a head in August, 1954, after the vituperative Army-McCarthy hearings. On July 31, Vermont's Senator Ralph Flanders introduced a censure resolution. Kennedy decided to vote against McCarthy, but on different grounds. In a speech he never gave, Kennedy said that the issue did not involve McCarthy's motives, sincerity, or conduct, which the censuring Senators had not questioned at the time of the hearings; Kennedy would vote against McCarthy only for attacking the honor and dignity of the Senate. Both the vote and Kennedy's speech were postponed by a resolution to set up a committee to consider the charges. When the Senate recessed, Kennedy went to Hyannis Port to rest, and then he entered the hospital. By November, when the censure of McCarthy was voted, Kennedy was critically ill. Sorensen later wrote that he did not record Kennedy's position because the Senator had been too sick to study the resolution. But many liberals were never convinced of this and agreed with Eleanor Roosevelt when she commented later that Kennedy should have shown "less profile and more courage."

In fact, Kennedy's back had been causing him increasing pain. He knew that he suffered from an adrenal lack caused by his wartime injury and subsequent malaria. In addition, by 1954, he was under considerable emotional stress from his late 1953 marriage, when he was thirty-six years old, and from the McCarthy debate. Thus, while Kennedy's back trouble was physical in origin, the psychological strains very likely added to his severe discomfort, as such strains commonly do. By August, 1954, Jack was forced to hobble around on crutches. By September, the young Senator entered a Manhattan hospital for back surgery. Spinal fusion surgery offered the best hope of recovery, but it was also very dangerous. But Kennedy found his physical incapacity unbearable. Kennedys had been taught to be stoical under pain, but not under forced inaction. As Jack told a friend, punching his crutches with his fist, "I'd rather die than spend the rest of my life on these things."

There is one strange aspect to Jack's back operation, and it offers more evidence of neurosis. The critical operation was a double fusion of spinal discs. According to Evelyn Lincoln, "The doctors had recommended that it be done in two separate operations, but he [Kennedy] had insisted on having both operations at one time and thereby increased immeasurably the risk involved. It was a long and difficult operation." Once again Kennedy's deeply buried self-destructive urges seemed to have propelled him into an unnecessary flirtation with death. (Significantly, according to Arthur Schlesinger in *A Thousand Days*, Kennedy's favorite poem was "I Have a Rendezvous with Death.") The operation, in fact, nearly killed him. Twice he was given the last rites and his parents were summoned. But by late December Jack had improved enough to be flown, still under heavy sedation, to Palm Beach for Christmas. His recovery was so slow that he was operated on again in mid-February, and again he nearly died. By the end of the month, however, he was able to return to Florida, where he spent the next five months in bed. During that period, to distract himself from pain and boredom, he turned to reading the political history he loved. Out of that enforced leisure and reading grew *Profiles in Courage*, which, published in 1956, became an immediate bestseller and won the Pulitzer Prize in history in 1957.

Although Kennedy received much help in researching and editing *Profiles*, it seems to be true that he wrote the bulk of the book. *Profiles in Courage* contains very readable and dramatic portraits of eight United States Senators, from John Quincy Adams to Robert Taft, who had the courage to stand by their personal convictions under extreme public attack and abuse. Kennedy did not argue the merits of their decisions, although he believed that "the national interest, rather than private or political gain, furnished the basic motivation" for their actions. But the rightness or wrongness of the Senators' convictions was beyond the scope of the book, which was essentially concerned only with the value of courage. "Bravery under fire" was Kennedy's theme, not the moral and human value of that bravery. Throughout the book courage is held to be among the highest human values, perhaps even the supreme value. Courage, not compassion, love, charity, truth, or justice, obsessed John Kennedy all his life.

People are often obsessed by the values which they most doubt in themselves and which have some neurotic meaning for them. Kennedy's fascination with the limits of human courage, both political and physical, suggests that he doubted these qualities within himself. As I have sought to demonstrate, the self-distrust and never-ending need for self-proof that haunted Kennedy's life and career had been implanted early in his childhood. Yet Kennedy's extreme physical risk-taking was in dramatic contrast to his overriding caution in domestic politics. And it is relevant to note here something I will try to analyze further in the next chapter: Kennedy's risk-taking as Chief Executive mainly involved matters of life and death. Kennedy's presidential gambles were almost always taken within the physical arena, where the Kennedy children had been taught from birth to taste combat, rather than in the more difficult and ambiguous realm of human compassion, justice, and individual worth, where the Kennedys had learned primarily to manipulate others for self-survival and emotional compensation.

Profiles in Courage was, in a sense, an expression of Kennedy's alter ego: his portraits were of men who dared to stand against an outraged majority, something which Kennedy himself would never do. It is interesting, and not a little poignant, that Kennedy was intellectually aware of the psychological basis of genuine courage: love of oneself. In his final chapter, "The Meaning of Courage," Kennedy wrote, ". . . what then caused the statesmen mentioned in the preceding pages to act as they did? It was not because they 'loved the public better than themselves.' On the contrary it was precisely because they did *love themselves*—because each one's need to maintain his own respect for himself was more important to him than his popularity with others—because his desire to win or maintain a reputation for integrity and courage was stronger than his desire to maintain his office —because his conscience, his personal standard of ethics, his integrity or morality, call it what you will—was stronger than the pressures of public disapproval—because his faith that *his* course was the best one, and would ultimately be vindicated, outweighed his fear of public reprisal. . . . It is when the politician loves neither the public good nor himself, or when his love for himself is limited and is satisfied by the trappings of office, that the public interest is badly served. And it is when his regard for himself is so high that his own self-respect demands he follow the path of courage and conscience that all benefit. . . ." (Kennedy's italics.)

This passage, and the book itself, reveals several psychological blind spots. While psychologists generally agree that self-love is the basis of human health and strength, there is a fundamental difference between genuine mature self-love and pseudo immature self-love. Neurotic pride can look very much like real self-respect, but it is at heart entirely different. Both neurotic pride and genuine self-respect (which is another word for true self-identity, really knowing who you are and what you stand for in all seasons) may cause an individual to endure the world's wrath, but the motivations are direct opposites. The first is at bottom a need for self-destruction; the other is an affirmation of self-fulfillment. It may often be impossible to judge the motivation from a single deed or even several deeds. Only the general concrete and emotional patterns of an individual's entire life—the psychohistorical patterns—can reveal in depth whether his motivations were mainly healthy or unhealthy.

Kennedy's definition of courage is prone to the common delusion that people act consciously for their own self-good. But all people to a large degree live life unconsciously, and often to their own self-harm. In the instance of John Quincy Adams, for example (Kennedy's first exemplar of courage), all the historical and psychological evidence points to a man caught in the grip of a serious neurosis and largely bent on his own self-destruction. Kennedy was aware of Adams' peculiarities. ("In spite of a life of extraordinary achievement, he was gnawed constantly by a sense of inadequacy, of frustration, of failure. Though his hard New England conscience and his remarkable talents drove him steadily along a road of un-paralleled success, he had from the beginning an almost morbid sense of constant failure.") The symptoms Kennedy described are familiar in the case histories of numerous neurotic personalities. But it does not seem to have occurred to Kennedy that Adams' extraordinary stand against all of New England (without even considering its historical value) might have been unconsciously taken for the express purpose of causing the factual failure which Adams was already experiencing emotionally. Adams, in short, was his own worst enemy, "the enemy within."

This, it seems to me, was the fatal flaw of both Kennedy's insight and his own life. Neurotic pride can drive a person to the heights of success, but it carries the seed of its own destruction. The neurotic may not topple with the resounding crash of a John Quincy Adams; rather, his downfall may even proceed concurrently with his climb to the top and paradoxically both assist and doom that climb (consider, as extreme psychotic cases, Hitler and Stalin). Measured in the light of history, the mountains that the neurotic leader thought he had climbed may be seen as mere foothills; while the real mountains, the invisible Himalayas within and outside himself, remain tall and unscaled. Thus so many of history's "greats" turn out, even in almost contemporaneous hindsight, to have been only human—and more failures than successes—in their neurotic dilemmas.

There is another book, one of Kennedy's favorites, which may throw some light on John Kennedy's personality and sense of values. This was *Lord M* by David Cecil, a penetrating, learned, and witty account of the later life of Lord Melbourne, Queen Victoria's Prime Minister. The first pages of *Lord M* are so striking a partial portrait of Kennedy himself that much seems worth quoting, though the entire section should be read for its full flavor.

"William Lamb, second son of the first Viscount Melbourne, had arrived at the age of forty-seven without achieving anything of significance in the world. He had been born in 1779 with, it might have seemed, every opportunity for success. Nature had made him handsome, agreeable and intellectually distinguished; fate had placed him in the very centre of the small privileged aristocracy who at that time ruled England; and whilst still in his twenties, he had what the world might consider the additional good fortune to lose his eldest brother. So that he moved among his fellows attended by all the special consequence that adheres to the heir to a rich peerage.

"But bad fairies, as well as good, came to his christening: and at first it looked as if their gifts were to prove more potent. His disposition was fundamentally divided against itself. From his mother, a brilliant and unscrupulous woman of fashion, he had inherited a vigorous animal temperament and a hard commonsense intelligence. But there was another strain in him, a vein of dreamy speculation, a power of warm and sensitive feeling. These two were in conflict. Half eighteenth century man of the world, half romantic philosopher, he found his heart stretching out to an idealism which his reason told him was visionary illusion. And unable to decide which side of his nature to follow, he tended from his early years to relapse into a sceptical uncertainty."

This "sceptical uncertainty," which was Melbourne's emotional and political trademark, also became the dominant personality trait exhibited by John F. Kennedy. It seems likely that Kennedy read this book—and probably these opening passages—several times, in view of its frequent mention in the Kennedy literature. We can sense that Kennedy felt a similar inner conflict in himself and that he could identify closely with Melbourne. And David Cecil's beautifully phrased rationale for Melbourne's emotional division, although psychologically shallow, could have given Kennedy a great deal of personal comfort and a feeling of self-understanding.

The remarkable similarity between Melbourne and Kennedy becomes more and more striking in subsequent descriptions. Professor Cecil, a distinguished Oxford don, captured the essence of the future Prime Minister in unforgettably felicitous phrases, phrases that must have delighted the literarily discriminating Kennedy even as he emotionally identified with Melbourne's personal problems and quirks. Although Melbourne belonged to the Whig party, temperamentally "his cautious spirit felt more in sympathy with the middle way policy of that group on the left of the Tory Party which was led by Canning. However, he did not believe in this strongly enough to feel justified in leaving his friends." Compare this with Richard Whalen's judicious assessment: "What Jack Kennedy thought and did politically arose less from adopted liberal conceptions than from instincts conditioned by inherited wealth and assured social position. Thus, while he agreed intellectually with the liberals that 'McCarthyism' was deplorable, he was more comfortable emotionally with his father's wealthy and conservative friends." As Kennedy himself once said, "I had never known the sort of people who were called before the McCarthy committee. I agree that many of them were seriously manhandled, but they all represented a different world to me. What I mean is, I did not identify with them, and so I did not get as worked up as other liberals did."

But it seems highly likely that Kennedy felt at home with the eighteenth-century outlook of the cultivated political gentleman, supported by inherited wealth and position, and could easily identify with Melbourne. (Kennedy also married a woman who said that the eighteenth century was her favorite period and displayed this preference in her own fastidious and cautious behavior, flavored with a certain veiled eccentricity that Jack probably found piquant when he wasn't too piqued by it.) Lord M, according to Cecil, was "one of the best read men of his time," a model Kennedy followed in certain directions. Melbourne also possessed handsome, youthful, sparkling good looks and a casual air of relaxed good-breeding (other Kennedy hallmarks). We can almost visualize Kennedy savoring some of these passages as examples of excellence to copy. ("Natural talent had united with long experience to make him the perfect man of the world, whose manners, at once unobtrusive and accomplished, could handle the most delicate situation with lighthanded mastery, and shed round every conversation an atmosphere of delightful ease. Yet there was nothing studied about him. On the contrary, the first thing that struck most people meeting him was that he was surprisingly, eccentrically natural. Abrupt and casual, he seemed to saunter through life, swearing when he pleased, laughing when he pleased . . . sprawling about in chairs, taking his meals with unashamed relish, and jerking out anything apparently that came into his head. It was his frankness that, above all, astonished.") Kennedy's "naturalness" has also often been remarked upon, as well as his easy manners and charming good humor. Yet, like Kennedy, Melbourne had idiosyncrasies: he rubbed his hands together (Kennedy rubbed his teeth) and put a finger on his head while talking. Lord M also wore beautifully-cut coats bulging with papers and bank notes; he never knew the time, and would drop off to sleep any time and place (all Kennedy characteristics).

More importantly, Melbourne, behind all his outer good humor and casualness, was "mysterious": ". . . for all his apparent frankness, he was discreet. Persons coming away from an interview with him, in which he had seemed to talk with complete candour, would suddenly realize that he had not given himself away on any point that really mattered. On the contrary, they wondered nervously if they had not given themselves away to him." Many of Kennedy's interviewers carried away a similar impression. Melbourne's ambiguous conversation also often puzzled people, as did Kennedy's; sometimes he was delightfully amusing, the next minute grave and serious. His salient tone was that of "a mischievous, enigmatic irony that played audaciously over the most sacred topics. . . ." Kennedy, too, loved to poke fun at people and institutions as well as at himself. He even once parodied his own inaugural address (at a Gridiron Club meeting); and the famous "Kennedy wit" (some of it spontaneous, some professionally contrived) produced several published collections.

As Schlesinger described his first long talk with Kennedy, "I was struck by the impersonality of his attitudes and his readiness to see the views and interests of others. I was also a little surprised by the animation and humor of his assessment of people and situations. I now began to understand that the easy and casual wit, turned incisively and impartially on himself and his rivals, was one of his most beguiling qualities, as those who had known him longer had understood for years."

Yet the candor, informality, humor, and intelligence of both Melbourne and Kennedy, brilliant and endearing men though they were in so many ways, could not give them that inner maturity and direction which both their social and emotional heritage had largely thwarted and which neither really overcame. In many ways these attractive qualities could help hide the inner weaknesses, for they attracted other people and gave their possessors an exaggerated feeling of strength. But in the great and cruelly difficult decisions faced by such leaders, charm and wit were of no avail, and the feebleness of a clear central core in each personality would prove tragic for individuals and nations.

At heart, Lord M was a disillusioned man, a man who could believe firmly in nothing. Such, too, seems to have been the emotional albatross of Jack Kennedy. Kennedy himself often recognized his own disbelief, but he rationalized it as a strength rather than a weakness, an ability to see all sides of a question. As Kennedy wrote in his notes on Robert A. Taft, "He was partisan in the sense that Harry Truman was—they both had the happy gift of seeing things in bright shades. It is the politicians who see things in similar shades that have a depressing and worrisome time of it." While both Melbourne and Kennedy viewed the world with a basically cynical (though not bitter) "realism" that grew out of their inner lack of faith in an unwavering code of values, Melbourne was indolent, whereas Kennedy was hyperactive. One suspects that indolence and hyperactivity, being opposite aspects of the same need, were similarly used by each to compensate for the occasionally felt inner sense of bewilderment. Melbourne waited for chance to push him into power; Kennedy constantly pushed at chance.

By 1958, chance plus hard work and Kennedy political shrewdness had carried Jack forward into national prominence as an undeclared frontrunner for 1960. But to convince the pros who controlled the nomination of his vote-getting appeal, Kennedy had to rewin election to the Senate by a wide margin. According to Sorensen, Kennedy's 1958 campaign opened "the day after his 1952 campaign ended." Kennedy concentrated on five fundamentals: the nurture of his personal statewide organization; statewide mailings on his actions as Senator; weekend speeches in Massachusetts; cultivation of state newspapers; and the constant wooing of his opponents. To try for the presidential nomination, Jack knew he had to win big in Massachusetts. The Kennedy fortune helped build a large and active organization, with brother Teddy as nominal campaign manager and father Joe in the background. Again, the publicity buildup was enormous. And as always, Jack drove himself furiously; an exhausted Jackie (who disliked politicking) recalled it as "the hardest campaign ever . . . just running, running." An easy victory was undoubted, but the size was what mattered. Again, the Kennedy care and hard work produced results: a huge margin of 874,608 votes, the greatest landslide ever in Massachusetts. Kennedy was also the Senate's biggest victor in 1958. The way had been opened to the presidential nomination.

An adequate description of Jack Kennedy's extraordinary capture of the Democratic nomination and then of the presidency itself would require a full book (in my opinion, no really first-rate account has been written). In this brief section, I will try simply to summarize the main Kennedy strategy so that the factual highlights may be better understood. My purpose is to suggest the existence of a historic commonplace that seems simple and understandable in history books, but staggering and imponderable when it occurs in one's own lifetime and culture: namely, that people who are outstanding successes in some areas of life can become dismal failures in other areas, and that the excellent politician is not necessarily the political leader of excellence. In brief, when the Kennedy campaigns are studied in some detail, it becomes evident that the Kennedy men, father and sons, were masters of the techniques of winning elections in an industrial-technological society. This included a high ability to create public images of private virtues and qualities which were often lacking. Thus, in order to penetrate the intimidating idea that a man must be great—or certainly non-neurotic—even to become President of the United States, we should consider more rationally the means whereby individuals actually do become President in our political era and evolutionary epoch.

Both campaigns—for the nomination and then the election—were carefully wrought and carried out by the highly skilled Kennedy clan. I have already outlined the general Kennedy approach to previous campaigns. We find again the familiar ingredients of long preparation and preplanning; a glamorized, expertly-briefed candidate whose image was projected by mammoth mass media "blitzes"; a tightly-controlled and heavily-financed campaign organization which concentrated on mass participation by volunteers and massive coverage of the immediate election area; the use of modern polls and advertising techniques; the active participation of the socially chic and poised Kennedy family, including all the women and in-laws; and, especially important for the first time in affluent 1960, a skillful concentration on the widespread and immediate impact of television, a medium well-suited to Kennedy's youthful good looks, quick intelligence, and alert nonchalance.

Money was the essential underpinning of all these elaborate operations, and this the Kennedys had in abundance. The Kennedy fortune was especially significant in Jack's defeat of Hubert Humphrey, an experienced and highly articulate politician, but one handicapped by a lack of personal wealth and a tendency to talk more than he calculated. Humphrey's insights and social understandings were far deeper than Kennedy's illusory self-confidence, but they did not project well in the media, nor did Humphrey know how to shape his real qualities into these narrow projections.

The crucial West Virginia Democratic primary in May, 1960, was also the scene of some outrageous Kennedy political practices, including probable large-scale vote-buying (which Theodore White excuses as an old West Virginia custom) and, again, the exploitation of the Catholic issue by the Kennedy team, who kept claiming they wanted to "keep religion out of the campaign." Most of all, however, Humphrey was simply outnumbered, outgunned, outfinanced, and outsmarted by the thoroughly professional Kennedys. One close student of that key primary made the assessment that "the religious issue occupied only the surface level of the campaign, the level of speechmaking and publicity; below that there was another level of campaigning, the obscure realm of machine-style party politics. Kennedy's looks and wit and personal charm worked for him on the first level; on the second he used his good political judgment, his money, and his large and competent team of advisers. West Virginia is a state in which a lot could be done on the second level. On any fair scale of political corruption and election mismanagement in contemporary America it would deserve an extremely high rating, somewhere up there among the most machine-dominated urban areas in the northern states and the comfortable, wheeling-and-dealing rural oligarchies of the South."

After the West Virginia triumph, the Kennedys were ready for the Democratic convention. They had also been busy for months behind the scenes, lining up delegates and promises of support, hinting at future rewards or punishments, maneuvering with the power brokers in an area of life familiar to them since childhood. Los Angeles was basically Boston on a grander scale. By this time, both Jack and Bobby had developed into true political heirs of their grandfathers, and father Kennedy still hovered in the background lending his skills, contacts, and millions to the common effort. While the Kennedys never felt they had the nomination "sewed up," as some have seen it in retrospect, their opposition, including wily Lyndon Johnson, failed to muster enough force against their hard-driving push, which was captained by an indefatigably aggressive Bobby. Jack's surprise choice of Johnson as his running mate deftly pulled enough of the South into his camp to help capture the election.

In the national election, both Nixon and Kennedy were amply financed. The great differences here, as Eric Severeid early saw, were far more those of style than of substance; and in style Kennedy was a more personable man, although the famed Kennedy "style" was more a postelection invention than a 1960 reality, as was evidenced by the unusual closeness of the race. When Severeid commented in print that Kennedy and Nixon were essentially peas from the same pod, the "first completely packaged products" of the managerial revolution, Kennedy was exasperated. "He has no taste," Jack remarked contemptuously of Nixon, who he also felt was ten years behind himself on the issues. Severeid, however, saw both candidates as "sharp, ambitious, opportunistic, devoid of strong convictions and deep passions, with no commitment except to personal advancement."

But it was Kennedy's ability to project a vision of America's future which, in Theodore White's analysis, largely won him the election. White's immensely readable account, *The Making of the President, 1960*, although flawed by some serious political simplicities and most especially by a roseate view of the candidates, contains interesting insights. Nixon, in both White's and Kennedy's opinion, failed to offer the electorate any inspiring view of their future, but instead "talked down" to the country while Kennedy stirred up excitement with a challenge to "move forward." Nixon and his managers also made serious tactical errors, which included poor scheduling of the candidate; a refusal to appeal to the pivotal black vote (as Kennedy did with his timely phone call to Mrs. Martin Luther King when her husband was imprisoned) in hopes of swinging the South; the candidate's isolation from helpful advisers; and the too-late use of Eisenhower's immense popularity. On top of these errors, compounded by Nixon's knee injury and temporary hospitalization, the famous television "debates" reversed the Nixon trend, gave Kennedy sudden public exposure and national stature, and may well have been the campaign's major turning point (as both candidates later thought). As many writers have pointed out,

Nixon looked haggard and worried on the first debate, while the more telegenic Kennedy appeared vigorous, mature, and self-assured. Perhaps even more important, Nixon made the mistake of addressing Kennedy directly like a debater making points (Nixon had been a champion high-school and college debater), while Kennedy talked to the country at large, emphasizing national themes.

Yet those who later saw Kennedy's election as inevitable often forgot how very narrow was the outcome: Kennedy won by a razor-thin one tenth of one percent, or a miniscule 112,000 votes out of a total 68,832,818 cast. Kennedy gained 49.7 percent of the vote to Nixon's 49.6 percent (other candidates divided the small remainder). Although Kennedy won by 303 electoral votes to Nixon's 219 electoral votes, the shift of less than 40,000 voters in key states such as Illinois and Texas could have given Nixon the election. Kennedy himself saw his victory as a "miracle."

Even so, the Kennedy victory, narrow though it was, must be considered a major triumph for a man far less nationally known than Vice President Nixon and with so many apparent handicaps (some of which would prove more apparent than real): his youth, religion, relative inexperience in high public office, and lack of a dramatic record. Kennedy's Catholicism turned out to be perhaps even more of a help than a hindrance. While Catholics did not always support him as he expected (Wisconsin, contrary to White, did not divide wholly along religious lines in the Democratic primary), Kennedy sometimes subtly used the religious issue to fan fear in reverse; i.e., many Protestants were made to feel that opposing Kennedy would be bigotry. There was also occasional unscrupulous use of the Catholic issue by the Kennedy forces, such as the flooding of Wisconsin with anti-Catholic hate literature during the Kennedy-Humphrey contest. This trick would have been familiar to the old Boston "pols" of Honey Fitz's and Grand-father Kennedy's era, when political workers were sent to hammer on doors at ungodly hours crying for the election of the candidate they opposed. In the national election, however, Kennedy met the religious issue openly in a dignified statement that he was the Democratic, not the Catholic, can-didate.

The Kennedys' winning of the United States presidency was totally in keeping with the family history of neurotic success. The victory was, indeed, the culmination and pinnacle of an extraordinary drive to power. Again we must ask, is it necessarily neurotic to want to be President of the United States? The answer, again, is not new. The desire for power and high office is *not necessarily* neurotic; it may be, it may not, or not predominantly. How do we tell the difference? Only, I believe, by studying the historical facts, and by subjecting these facts to the well-established general principles of humanistic psychology.

As I have tried thus far to trace, John F. Kennedy's over-all personal and public history seemed to point toward an unconscious obsessive need for greater and greater confirmation of his personal worth. Circumstance steered Kennedy into politics, and his natural talents helped him develop into a highly astute politician. Neurosis does not primarily affect the mind, but mainly the uses to which the mind is put (it does affect the ability to use basic mental resources). Kennedy put his mind to becoming President of the United States, and this he accomplished. It was when he tried to fulfill the arduous demands of that office that the neurotic base of his power drive brought him to frequent disaster, as I shall attempt to show in the next two chapters. Many neurotics in varying degrees have, of course, become President of the United States, as well as presidents, prime ministers, kings and queens of other nations. Unfortunately, we draw back from observing this common phenomenon close at hand, while acknowledging that history books are filled with troubled, unbalanced, and even insane leaders and rulers.

Yet despite Kennedy's neurotic trends, his drive toward self-assertion certainly had many healthy elements and won out in some respects over his more negative pulls. To become President is undeniably a great and extremely difficult goal, although the goal is not enough in itself. There must also be the ability to use that enormous power for public service and non-self-centered aims. But tragically, the neurotic, despite his best conscious intentions, is emotionally centered on himself. Alienated from his real center of genuine ego strength, he expends many or most of his energies trying to fulfill his fantasized, glorified self, which he takes to be his real being. Thus the neurotic leader is in large degree incapable of the truly meaningful service which he may ardently wish to perform. His aims are obscured, his desires confused, his powers diluted, and his motives made a contradictory tangle by the strength of his unconscious emotional conflicts.

Theodore White described rather neatly the profound difference between becoming President and being President, when he wrote that "a President governing the United States can move events only if he can first persuade. Each Presidency is unique, for each President must face in his own time an area of new unknowns, where both answers and questions are fresh, where only his instinct can produce those initiatives that the nation unknowingly and unwillingly requires, where only his skill can persuade the nation to follow. This art of persuasion is politics—yet entirely different from the kind of politics that brings a man to the White House.

"For the winning of the President's power lies in noise and clangor, the flogging of the emotions and the appeal to all the tribal pasts of America. But the exercise of the President's power must be framed by reason, by the analysis of reality as it can only be seen from the President's desk—and by leading other men to see this reality as he alone perceives it."

The question we shall now pursue is this: Did Kennedy's presidential analysis of America's problems and opportunities lead generally to reality and national progress, or was he prone to delusion and misperceptions which resulted in frequent irrational responses? Was John F. Kennedy, in effect, a Chief Executive whose attitudes and acts were more of a neurotic nature than otherwise?

Chapter 7

CAMELOT REVISITED I:
JFK AND THE AMERICAN CRUSADE

It has been lately urged in a very respectable quarter that it is the mission of this country to spread civil and religious liberty over all the globe . . . even by force, if necessary. It is a sad delusion. . . . To preserve it [liberty], it is indispensable to adopt a course of moderation and justice toward all other countries; to avoid war whenever it can be avoided; to let those great causes which are now at work, and which by the mere operation of time, will raise our country to an elevation and influence which no country has ever heretofore attained, continue to work. By pursuing such a course, we may succeed in combining greatness and liberty . . . and do more to extend liberty by our example over this continent and the world generally, than would be done by a thousand victories.
—John C. Calhoun (1782–1850)

As missionaries of the American experiment, we would offer our assistance to others, who were free to accept or reject it. As crusaders, we would impose it on the rest of the world, with fire and sword if necessary. The actual limits of such a crusade would be the limits of American power, its potential limits would be the limits of the globe. The American example is transformed into a formula of universal salvation by which right-thinking nations would voluntarily abide and to which the others must be compelled to submit.
—Hans J. Morgenthau, *A New Foreign Policy for the United States*

Reflecting and speaking the language of liberal imperialism and American interventionism, the Kennedy circle quite early embraced a global activism. . . . That the roots of present calamities are to be found in Kennedy policy is of course ancient history . . . what John Kennedy did prepared the way for the deterioration that followed him. It is harsh but unavoidable to say that like such less appealing

political leaders as Leonid Brezhnev, Mao Tse-tung, and Gamal Abdel Nasser, President Kennedy directed his people's attention away from the complex and intricate issues which divided them toward the enemies who appeared to threaten their interests. For us, Cubans and North Vietnamese served much the same domestic functions as Israelis for Arabs and Chinese for Russians. The foreign policies of 1961–63 foreshadowed later Vietnam policy and limited the resources available for domestic improvement.
—Robert Lekachman, "Money in America: The End of the Economists' Dream," *Harper's Magazine*

Kennedy began where Dulles had left off, as much because of his conservative Catholic background as the hard-nosed young men he brought from the Charles River to the banks of the Potomac. Dulles, for all his talk of massive retaliation and agonizing reappraisals, helped to involve the country in nothing more serious than the Lebanese landings. Kennedy accepted all the rhetoric and acted upon it. Unlike in domestic affairs, he was aggressive and romantic abroad. After the fiasco of the Cuban invasion, he reaffirmed the Monroe Doctrine as legitimate authority for United States domination over the Americas. This was an extraordinary assertion of imperial power, no less than the doctrine expounded by Leonid Brezhnev after the invasion of Czechoslovakia.
—Louis Heren, *No Hail, No Farewell*

. . . it would be wise to take a clear-sighted view of the Kennedy Administration because it was the first U.S. government in the nuclear age which acted on the belief that it was possible to use war, or the threat of war, as an instrument of politics despite the possibility of annihilation. It was in some ways a warlike administration. . . . The Kennedy Administration, in violation of our own laws and international laws, permitted that invasion from our shores which ended so ingloriously in the Bay of Pigs. It was the Kennedy Administration which met Khrushchev's demands for negotiations on Berlin by a partial mobilization and an alarming invitation to the country to dig backyard shelters against cataclysm.

Finally we come to the October crisis of a year ago. . . . When a whole people is in a state of mind where it is ready to risk extinction—its own and everybody else's—as a means of having its own way in an international dispute, the readiness for murder has become a way of life and a world menace. Since this is the kind of bluff that can easily be played once too often, and that his successors may feel urged to imitate, it would be well to think it over carefully before canonizing Kennedy as an apostle of peace.
—I. F. Stone, "We All Had a Finger on That Trigger," *I. F. Stone's Weekly*

ONE OF THE deepest and most ironic tragedies of the Kennedy history is that while John Kennedy saw himself as particularly fitted to shape and direct American foreign policy—his greatest interest—it was in the international realm that he made his most far-reaching and longest-lasting mistakes. The Kennedy neurosis, as I have tried to trace it, grew not only out of the Kennedy family history but also out of a centuries-old cultural neurosis: America's obsessive drive to material success, belief in national omnipotence, and sense of crusading mission to spread the blessings of the American experiment to alien—and often highly unreceptive—soil.

We can see this national delusion clearly in the exaggerated rhetoric of Kennedy's inaugural address, a speech which, despite the terrible toll taken by poverty and discrimination among Americans, never once mentioned the domestic scene. Kennedy spoke with the voice of a typically grandiose American crusader, calling on the entire globe to unite in an alliance against "tyranny, poverty, disease, and war itself." Kennedy welcomed the role "of defending freedom in its hour of maximum danger," and announced America's willingness to "pay any price, bear any burden, meet any hardship, support any friend, oppose any foe to assure the survival and the success of liberty." This dangerous nonsense went almost totally unnoticed in the outpouring of lavish praise for the bright, young, energetic new President. It also unfortunately set a tone of impossible expectations for Kennedy's Administration, and very likely reinforced Kennedy's unconscious belief in his personal destiny of heroic triumph.

Many of Kennedy's dilemmas and frustrations arose from a simplistic Cold Warrior view of the world, a view that by the early 1960s (and even in the 1950s) had become in many ways obsolete. Much Cold War imagery had always been unreal. The world had never been neatly divided into free and unfree halves, for the so-called Free World contained regimes as oppressive and undemocratic as any Communist system. Many of America's closest allies were authoritarian rulers (such as Korea's Syngman Rhee, Nationalist China's Chiang Kai-shek, South Vietnam's Ngo Dinh Diem, Spain's Francisco Franco, and numerous autocrats in Latin America). The illusory Communist monolith had already begun to fall apart by the time of the Korean War, which was started by the Russian-backed North Koreans and not the harassed and defensive Communist Chinese. Russia's own satellite system was showing revealing cracks of dissidence and unwieldiness. And the Russians, while giving many signs of paranoic hostility, could point to similar reactions by the Americans. For it had also become a fixture of U.S. policy that nationalists who had, or were said to have, any taint of Communism were to be suppressed; whereas even terroristic anti-democrats would be supported in office as long as they were anti-Communist. Nor was the United States hesitant about forcing its views on the rest of the world when opportunity arose, for all intervention could be rationalized as a legitimate defense of the "free world." Thus America's attempted containment of Russia and China was seen in the most moralistic terms, while any similar Communist influence in the Western Hemisphere was viewed through American eyes as an intolerable aggression.

This paradoxical self-justification grew partly out of America's World War II battles with the Axis powers, when simplistic condemnation of the "enemy" was both more useful and more justified, as well as out of a historic American tendency toward "demonology." But the world had changed enormously since 1945. Unfortunately, human outlooks change far more slowly than human events. John F. Kennedy was, by and large, a product both of his father's narrow conservative views and his own philosophically simple wartime experience. Kennedy's father had taught his sons to be "tough," and Kennedy had tried hard in battle to prove his "toughness." Now, as President, he had the chance to become the great man his father had told him he could be. But greatness, in Kennedy eyes, meant above all else the qualities of action, toughness, and never losing.

Some of this dangerously extreme and narrow outlook is seen in JFK's post-Cuba comment in the spring of 1961: "When you look around the world, when you look at the whole vast periphery which we alone guard day and night—we alone stand between the Russians and the free world—Cuba doesn't seem so important." For a President of the United States to believe that the Soviet Union, whatever its own exaggerated ambitions, actually had the capacity, if permitted, to gobble up the world—and that only the United States could prevent this—was an illusion that would lead Kennedy into militaristic stances and even aggrandizements that are as yet far from ended. JFK would also help lead the American people still further along the hazardous course of a Cold War outlook and increase the power of the military-industrial superlobby against which President Eisenhower had warned in his farewell address.

Kennedy's frequent doomsday outlook also had occasional paranoic elements which are strongly reminiscent of Joe Kennedy's personal pessimism and anxiety. "What gets me," JFK told a reporter in the gloomy days after the Cuban disaster, "is that all these people seem to want me to fail. I don't understand that. If I don't succeed, there may not be another president." Kennedy was perpetually describing his Administration as America's last hope, a curiously unreal and arrogant position for a man supposedly so widely read in history, although understandable in the light of Kennedy's neurotic insecurities.

When the thirty-fifth President of the United States delivered his inaugural speech on January 20, 1961, America was about to enter the fifteenth year of its so-called Cold War with the Soviet Union and the other Communist powers. Since the spring of 1947, when the Truman Doctrine and the Marshall Plan were formulated, American foreign policy had concentrated on the "containment" of Russian expansionary trends, which were seen primarily as the inevitable outgrowth of Communist doctrine. By building a strong bulwark of anti-Communist nations in wartorn Western Europe and a global network of miltary alliances, the United States hoped to prevent Communists from taking over the governments of countries outside the Soviet sphere. The Chinese Communists, who came to power in late 1949, were viewed as part of a monolithic Communist conspiracy. The 1950 Korean War was falsely interpreted by America as a basically Chinese aggression, as was the second Vietnam war, which began about 1958.

Kennedy, like his predecessors, largely failed to understand the great divergencies among the many different Communist nationalists, and that the radical reforming appeal of Communist ideology cannot be fenced off by bayonets. Verbally, and as a member of Congress, Kennedy sometimes showed a sophisticated understanding of international realities. But as President, his deeds seemed to be a direct outgrowth of the Truman-Eisenhower security policies which relied on armaments and alliances (even with dictators as long as they were anti-Communist) rather than on a humanistic understanding of people's needs and aspirations. Kennedy actually went beyond Eisenhower's more self-confident restraint and added a greatly heightened bellicosity to America's attitudes in world affairs. In brief, the dogma of an implacable Communist menace seemed to grip the deepest emotions of the men who ran the Kennedy Administration, including the President himself, imbuing their policies with an ignorance and arrogance appalling in their dimensions and devastating in their consequences.

Communism, one can only suspect, was the rationalized devil and symbol of far deeper fears growing out of these men's individual and national experiences. In this sense, the psychohistorical evidence points to a continuous undercurrent of neuroticism which helped propel Kennedy and his advisers into so many conflicted and self-defeating avenues. I will explore this thesis more specifically regarding Kennedy's policies on Castro's Cuba, the arms race, the space effort, the Berlin crisis (of 1961), the Cuban missile crisis, and Vietnam. In the last short section of this chapter, I will briefly suggest how Kennedy may have been driven by an unconscious need for constant crisis into many of these national predicaments. For it seems to me that Kennedy's unconscious emotional "balance of power" between his genuine individual needs and constant parental-social pressures was projected upon his reactions to international realities.

As one political scientist put it, "The idea that the power of the West and the Communist bloc were in a balance that required constant vigilance to be preserved drove Kennedy not only to look on insurgencies as suitable for

American military involvement, but also led him to invest every direct Soviet-American problem with a high degree of passion. The passion was of a special sort: an intense desire to avoid giving the impression of weakness. Let it be noted that this desire is not the same as the desire to give the impression of overbearing strength. No one could ever accuse Kennedy of enjoying the role of bully. The matter is more sad, more complicated. In his early book, *Why England Slept*, he expressed the belief that democracies were inherently pacific and self-absorbed, and that they had to have 'shocks' to keep them alert to the dangers surrounding them. Being alert, they would not give the appearance of weakness; they would thereby dissuade aggressors from rashness. In line with this aim, Kennedy wanted to raise taxes in 1961 in order to enhance a sense of sacrifice and impress on Americans the gravity of world affairs. His ill-considered support of fallout shelters was part of the same purpose. More than that, all one can briefly say is that Kennedy seems to have had a naturally agonistic conception of world politics. He did not look for fights; rather he thought that they were inevitable, that crisis was the normality of international relations, even in the nuclear age. (He shocked Stevenson by referring to disarmament proposals as 'propaganda.') Beyond the conflict of aims that always exists between nations, Kennedy saw a contest of wills, an almost formal antagonism in which the prize was pride at least as much as any substantive outcome."

Surely JFK's peculiar "passion" (especially suspect in so dispassionate a man) for U.S.-Soviet confrontations is most understandable in light of his conflicted boyhood. Kennedy's adolescence was largely dominated by "confrontations" and fights with his older brother, Joe Junior, each impelled by a need to prove himself a worthy son in the eyes of an excessively demanding father. The matter of presidential compulsions is indeed "more sad, more complicated" than history books would have us believe. Let us then first examine the broad aspects of Kennedy's most crucial international decisions before returning to the underlying question of why he chose certain policy directions rather than others.

I. The Bay of Pigs: The Aborted Crusade

The folly of the American Government in believing that 1,400 Cuban exiles, armed, trained, supported and guided by the United States, could have held a beachhead in Cuba against the Castro forces was beyond belief at the time. This is not wisdom after the event. Those who knew anything about Fidel Castro and the internal situation in Cuba were saying before the invasion started that it was certainly doomed to failure if President Kennedy carried out his public pledge not to use American armed forces to support the attack.

—Herbert L. Matthews, *Fidel Castro*

. . . the incident on the Bay of Pigs earned its place in the annals of modern history as one of the great fiascos in military leadership, intelligence gathering, and psychological preparation and execution. Invasions had failed before, but seldom had a great power like the United States allowed itself to be caught in so embarrassing a predicament as in the attack on Cuba, mounted, financed and executed by the Central Intelligence Agency. The military implications of the disaster were obvious: an operation bearing the stamp of approval of the Joint Chiefs of Staff of the world's most powerful nation was destroyed in less than three days by half-trained, part-time militia troops of a disorganized, revolutionary state led by a bearded guerrilla leader who had somehow taught his men to use with devastating effect the most modern Czech and Soviet weapons.

But the political repercussions were even more humiliating. As the invasion approached its tragic denouement, the United States buried itself deeper into the white lies, contradictions, and deceptions stemming from its own confusion and uncertainty. . . . It is our contention that the invasion was not only wrongly executed but wrongly conceived. It was based on a grievous misreading of the Cuban revolution and an ignorance of the internal forces at work on the island. It put the United States in the distressing position of breaking the same treaties that Dr. Castro had been exhorted to respect, and it raised grave questions about compromising the institutions on which a free society rests.

—Tad Szulc and Karl E. Meyer, *The Cuban Invasion: The Chronicle of a Disaster*

The ill-fated invasion of Cuba in April, 1961, was one of those rare politico-military events—a perfect failure.

—Theodore Draper, *Castro's Revolution: Myths and Realities*

Thank God the Bay of Pigs happened when it did. Otherwise we'd be in Laos by now—and that would be a hundred times worse.

—President John F. Kennedy to Theodore Sorensen

. . . in Western Europe I found widespread disenchantment. In the brief time from the Inaugural to the Bay of Pigs, Kennedy had come to seem the last hope of the west—a brilliant and exciting hope. He had conveyed an impression of United States foreign policy as mature, controlled, responsible and, above all, intelligent. Western Europe in return had made a heavy political and emotional investment in him. Now he suddenly seemed revealed as a mere continuator of the Eisenhower-Dulles past. The New Frontier looked like a collection not only of imperialists but of ineffectual imperialists—and, what was worst of all, of stupid, ineffectual imperialists. . . .

When I returned on May 3, Kennedy commented wryly on the discrepancy between the European and American reactions. If he had been a British prime minister, he remarked, he would have been thrown out of office; but in the United States failure had increased his charm; "if I had gone further, they would have liked me even more." At this point, Evelyn Lincoln brought in an advance on the new Gallup poll showing an unprecedented 82 per cent behind the administration. Kennedy tossed it aside and said, "It's just like Eisenhower. The worse I do, the more popular I get."
—Arthur Schlesinger, Jr., *A Thousand Days*

ꙩꙨ

ONLY IN RETROSPECT, and in the perspective of Kennedy's entire Administration, can the psychohistorical meaning of the disastrous Cuban invasion be seen as a logical extension of the general emotional pattern which I have called the "Kennedy neurosis." This recognizable pattern, to resummarize, appeared to grow out of a deep-seated and unconscious feeling of social and parental rejection suffered by the Kennedy parents and then their children in varying degrees. For the sons, the compensatory defense trends seemed to take the form of a drive toward heroic vindication and virile independence, which was directly tied to an unconscious inner sense of powerlessness. In this context, we can begin to see more clearly how the Bay of Pigs venture appealed to John Kennedy's need for glory and omnipotence and at the same time aroused his secret feelings of helplessness. Irresistible power and immovable powerlessness were the ambivalent dynamics that helped trigger both his rashness in authorizing the invasion and then his inability to closely and rationally supervise the plan. For Kennedy to have supported the feeble invasion with American military force would have compounded the rashness. But not to assure beforehand that the mission had some minimal chance of success, including secrecy, competence, and, above all, a link with the opposition to Castro within Cuba, was an error for which the President as well as his subordinates was responsible.

Far more serious than the staggering lack of realism was the lack of morality. Few writers (with notable exceptions) have commented on the essential immorality of the United States having backed and launched the invasion of a sovereign state with which we were not at war and which was not threatening our national security. For the United States to claim it has a special possessive interest in the Caribbean and Latin America, as the Monroe Doctrine states, while at the same time denying the Soviet Union similar geographic buffers, is irrational and unconvincing. In the context of human morality (which should be the context for all political acts) both powers err in their paranoic obsession with self-defense via the overcontrol of other countries. It is true that the line cannot always be clearly drawn between legitimate assistance to nations struggling to survive and an unwarranted and undemocratic interference in other nations' affairs (the Marshall Plan exemplifies the former, Vietnam the latter). But in general we should seek to communicate with, rather than to contain, powers which we feel to be hostile and threatening.

It begs the point to claim that America was trying to establish a Cuban democracy whereas the Russians were maintaining an imperialistic and undemocratic rule in their satellites and encouraging Communist dictatorships elsewhere. Prior to Castro, the United States for years supported Batista's bloody regime in Cuba (and continues to support other bloody-minded Latin American dictatorships). Though the force was ostensibly Cuban, Kennedy's claim that this was a liberating invasion was hardly more justifiable than Khruschev's claim that he was merely supporting wars of national liberation in Asia and elsewhere. The fact remains that America had no internationally legal or moral right—according to the tenets of self-determinism which the United States officially supports—to try to overthrow the government of another country that could not rationally be regarded as threatening the existence or stability of the United States.

As to Castro's own announced "wars of liberation," which were so vastly exaggerated in the American mind, the knowledgeable *New York Times* editor Herbert L. Matthews commented, "Of the so-called-invasions from Cuba in 1959, only one—the two groups that entered the Dominican Republic in June—had official Cuban backing. Fidel told me about the Dominican involvement and it was a shock to him that it failed so quickly and disastrously. The other 'invasions' were made either by adventurers and mercenaries, like the landings in Panama in April and Haiti in August, or by groups that evaded Cuban vigilance. The State Department must have known these facts but chose to make a big propaganda issue against Fidel Castro for policy reasons."

Kennedy's Cuban policy was to some extent the result of his politically expedient responses to Republican charges during the 1960 presidential campaign. In general, Kennedy sought to portray himself as a fighter and man of action, although he also called for the peaceful spread of democratic ideals. But to a considerable degree, Kennedy as President seems to have become a victim of his own extreme campaign oratory. From early October, 1960, candidate Kennedy had hammered ceaselessly on the theme that Cuba had become "communism's first Caribbean base" because of Republican blunders. Vice President Nixon retorted by calling (on October 18) for a quarantine of Cuba, and Eisenhower backed him up the next day with a sweeping trade embargo. Senator Kennedy sharply criticized the embargo as "too little and too late" after "an incredible history of blunder, inaction, retreat and failure." Said Kennedy, "For six years before Castro came to power the Republicans did absolutely nothing to stop the rise of communism in Cuba. Our Ambassadors repeatedly warned the Republicans of mounting danger. But the warning was ignored. . . . " The Democratic candidate urged stronger sanctions and an American effort "to strengthen the non-Batista Democratic forces in exile and in Cuba itself. . . ." Nixon struck back by accusing Kennedy of advocating a "shockingly reckless" proposal that would be "a direct invitation for the Soviet Union to intervene militarily on the side of Cuba." (It later came to light that Nixon at that time was privately approving the CIA support of anti-Castro groups in Miami.)

In the October 21 television "debate" between Kennedy and Nixon, the two Cold Warrior candidates (who differed very little in their basic assessment of the international Communist peril) jousted over Cuba in words that two veteran reporters (Karl E. Meyer and Tad Szulc) called "the campaign's low in political humbug." By then, Castro had nationalized the Cuban sugar industry, and invasion rumors grew to the point where the Cuban delegation to the United Nations in November brought a formal charge of such planning against the United States. In fact, President Eisenhower had directed the CIA to recruit and train Cuban exiles as early as March 17, 1960, although at that time only guerrilla action was contemplated. But such projects have an inner momentum, and the CIA plan grew steadily in size and irrationality. From the initial concept of small groups slipping into Cuba to form centers of resistance, the idea grew to include a direct beachhead assault in multiple landings. Kennedy, however, knew nothing of this project until after his election, when CIA chief Allen Dulles briefed him on November 17, 1960. Kennedy decided to continue the project, but as an option rather than as a definite decision. At that time the President-elect was too busy forming his new Administration to think much about Cuba. Thus the CIA went ahead in its secret planning and training of the Cubans in Guatemala. In December, the multiple-landings strategy evolved into a single invasion force which would hold a beach-

head long enough to attract activists and defectors from Castro and set off
a general uprising. Later the idea was added that an exile government
would be flown in which could then call for U.S. support. In case of failure, the invaders could retreat to the mountains. But the ground rule held:
no American forces would participate in the initial invasion. The CIA hoped
to repeat its 1954 Guatemala coup, although it conveniently overlooked the
vastly different conditions in Cuba.

In January, 1961, as Kennedy took office, the Joint Chiefs of Staff for
the first time began to consider possible levels of U.S. military involvement
in the CIA plan. Meanwhile, recruitment of Cuban exiles was stepped up,
and the CIA consolidated its control of the invasion leadership. Castro
could follow almost every detail of these machinations, for CIA and Cuban
security was unbelievably lax—and Castro's agents were everywhere
among the politically divergent groups in Florida. Equally crucial, the
initial inclusion of the Cuban underground in the planning was largely
dropped as an Anzio-type landing became the CIA objective. On January
22, leading Kennedy advisers, including Secretary of State Rusk, Defense
Secretary McNamara, and Robert Kennedy, reviewed the plan. On January 28, President Kennedy held his first White House review. Schlesinger
describes Kennedy as "wary and reserved in his reaction." The President
ordered Defense to review the CIA military plans and the State Department to prepare a program for isolating Cuba through the Organization of
American States (OAS). Overt U.S. participation in an invasion was still
ruled out. The JCS produced an ambiguous evaluation, but finally concluded in early March that internal resistance was indispensable to success.

Other events combined to confront Kennedy with what Schlesinger called
"a now-or-never choice" in mid-March: Guatemala asked for the departure
of the invasion force from its soil by the end of April; the Cuban fighters
were demanding action and they might be demoralized by further postponement; the rainy season would soon begin; and, perhaps most pressing,
Castro would shortly receive jet airplanes from Russia and Cuban pilots
trained in Czechoslovakia. According to Schlesinger, "After June 1, it
would take the United States Marines and Air Force to overthrow Castro.
If a purely Cuban invasion were ever to take place, it had to take place in
the next few weeks." All at once, it seemed, Kennedy's presumed planning
contingency had turned into an urgent reality.

On March 11, 1961, the President held a decisive conference, which
included Rusk, McNamara, Allen Dulles, the three Joint Chiefs, and
officials responsible for Latin American affairs. Schlesinger was also there,
having earlier sent Kennedy a memorandum opposing the operation. In
A Thousand Days he quotes himself as having told Kennedy, "This would be
your first dramatic foreign policy initiative. At one stroke you would dis-

sipate all the extraordinary good will which has been rising toward the new Administration through the world. It would fix a malevolent image of the new Administration in the minds of millions." Dulles and his assistant, Richard M. Bissell, Jr., made the final presentation for their project, and both were highly persuasive. Dulles emphasized that disbanding the Cuban Brigade could only embarrass the United States in the eyes of the world, for the disappointed Cubans would be certain to spread their resentments, and Castro would be encouraged to stir up revolutions throughout the Caribbean.

In the face of such forcefully presented arguments, "Kennedy tentatively agreed that the simplest thing, after all, might be to let the Cubans go where they yearned to go—to Cuba." But he was very concerned about the political risk, and wanted a quiet night landing. Again, Kennedy insisted there would be no U.S. military intervention. No one at the time objected, although in the light of events it seems clear that many people both inside and outside the government expected Kennedy to intervene if necessary. *New York Times* editor Herbert Matthews, for example, assumed that, if necessary, Kennedy would support the invasion with American force, using anti-Communist arguments to justify the intervention. Reportedly Kennedy told a *Times* editor the day before the landing that he thought the invasion had a "fifty-fifty chance." One can only wonder what contradictory feelings of success and failure were passing through the President at this time.

Kennedy and his counsellors met again on March 15, when "the President, listening somberly, suggested some changes, mostly intended to 'reduce the noise level'—such as making sure that the invasion ships would be unloaded before dawn." Then Kennedy authorized the planners to proceed, but in a way that would allow him to call off the invasion as late as twenty-four hours ahead. Kennedy also repeated his decision against any form of U.S. military intervention. (As it turned out, the first frogmen ashore were Americans; and at least four Americans were killed piloting B-26's over Cuba. Also when defeat loomed, Kennedy allowed a two-hour fighter cover from nearby carriers, but because of a mix-up the jets arrived too late to save the B-26's. Thus some overt intervention did occur, although it was petty compared with the overriding fact that the United States had planned, directed, organized, financed, and transported the entire operation.) At this March 15 meeting, Kennedy stated that he was still reserving final judgment.

We can see in Kennedy's hesitancies his ingrained sense of caution, which repeatedly conflicted with his emotional need for action and an appearance of strength. Kennedy's apparent dual feelings of aggressive power and predestined helplessness, which Dr. Karen Horney found present in all neuroses, are suggested in an episode described by Ted Sorensen. When this aide, who had been left out of the planning for the invasion, asked Kennedy about a hint that he had gleaned from another meeting, Kennedy answered with an earthy expletive. Too many counsellors, the President said, seemed frightened by the idea of a fight, but he stressed that he had no alternative. Yet Kennedy, as we have seen, had ordered the operation set up so that it could be cancelled within twenty-four hours. The alternative to cancel existed until the final hours, although the thought of consequent problems must have added impetus to Kennedy's desire for a "fight." Here again is Kennedy's emotional conflict of impulse-caution, an unresolved conflict which seemed basic to his deeply repressed desire for both independence and dependency.

In addition, both Kennedy and his advisers suffered from a neurotic form of wishful thinking that was to lead them from the deadly swamps of Cuba to the rice-paddy quagmire of Vietnam. The euphoria of the Kennedy Administration after Kennedy's astonishing winning of the presidency was evident to Schlesinger, who in many ways was the most realistic and candid of the Kennedy counsellors (but, unfortunately, one of the least influential). The following passage from *A Thousand Days* sheds much psychological light on the Bay of Pigs: "The President knew better than anyone how hard his life was to be. Though he incited the euphoria, he did so involuntarily, for he did not share it himself. I never heard him now use the phrase 'New Frontier'; I think he regarded it with some embarrassment as a temporary capitulation to rhetoric. Still even Kennedy, the ironist and skeptic, had an embarrassed confidence in his luck and in these weeks may have permitted himself moments of optimism. In any case, he knew the supreme importance of a first impression and was determined to create a picture of drive, purpose and hope." Here again is Kennedy's obsession with appearances rather than actualities. In discussing the President's final decision to go ahead, Schlesinger noted Kennedy's "enormous confidence in his own luck. . . . Everything had broken right for him since 1956. . . . Everyone around him thought he had the Midas touch and could not lose. Despite himself, even this dispassionate and skeptical man may have been affected by the soaring euphoria of the new day."

In truth, Kennedy was not nearly as "dispassionate" and "skeptical" as his eulogizers have portrayed him. The Kennedy sons frequently exhibited a strong sense of personal luck, intermingled with a fatalistic feeling of personal doom. JFK fully shared this emotional duality. From the psychological view, a belief in either luck or fatalism is often a rationalization for darker, unconscious influences at work in one's personality. Indeed, Kennedy's confidence, while sometimes warranted by careful planning (as in his campaigns), led him to take extraordinary risks and deal in illusions uncorrected by hard questions and close study (as, again, exemplified by Cuba and Vietnam). In the international realm, where Kennedy's hopes of glory essentially lay, his deep caution and skepticism led him to take superficial safeguards; but again and again, his deeply repressed contradictory drive toward neurotic self-glorification and self-defeat seemed to be stronger.

Thus, in the spring of 1961, the important questions that would have dissolved the veil of illusion which Kennedy and his top advisers had woven for themselves remained too little asked and too little answered. Kennedy still had serious reservations, but he had been misled into believing that the operation had been coordinated with the Cuban underground. In fact, the CIA intended to invade without depending on sabotage and insurrection from within. It was one of several crucial mistakes, for Castro's men temporarily imprisoned almost the entire underground among the 200,000 suspects they arrested.

In the light of what we know today, the intelligence failures of Kennedy's responsible advisers in this episode are quite extraordinary. Schlesinger reported in his history that British Ambassador David Ormsby Gore later told him that British intelligence estimates, which had been given to the CIA, "showed that the Cuban people were still predominantly behind Castro and that there was no likelihood at this point of mass defections or insurrections." A 1969 study of U.S. interventions, *By Weight of Arms: America's Overseas Military Policy*, confirmed that this fact was well known even outside the military and intelligence establishment. As the authors noted, "The primary cause of the failure was the lack of popular support in Cuba, the key assumption in the planning of the invasion. The Cuban people, especially the peasantry, which comprised most of the population, were thoroughly satisfied with the Castro regime. American sociologists had verified this conclusion some three months before the invasion but the information had not been made available to the Washington officials in control." But as Schlesinger makes clear, the top proponents of the invasion, such as CIA chiefs Allen Dulles and Richard Bissell, did not ask for assessments from their subordinates (who might be expected to know what outside experts, such as sociologists, were thinking). Dulles's excuse, offered in *The Craft of Intelligence*, that the landing was not expected to ignite an armed uprising is patently bogus. The entire invasion was predicated on an internal uprising, for the military force involved was vastly inferior to Castro's armed strength. While it is true that Kennedy was greatly misguided by his intelligence men, this does not exonerate the President from a personal naiveté and romantic wishful thinking in two areas where he had direct experience, war and politics—a naiveté, we might note, that was not shared by a mere history professor, Arthur

Schlesinger, Jr. (Kennedy was also supposed to be a historian of some stature.)

The White House meetings continued through March with little opposition. The strongest objector to the invasion was Senator William Fulbright, chairman of the Senate Foreign Relations Committee. He wrote Kennedy to argue against the forceful overthrow of Castro, saying that such a policy would violate the OAS charter, hemisphere treaties, and U.S. legislation. If the invasion succeeded, it "would be denounced from the Rio Grande to Patagonia as an example of imperialism." If we used our own arms, the United States "would have undone the work of thirty years in trying to live down earlier interventions." And we might be left with an onerous responsibility for post-Castro Cuba. "To give this activity even covert support," wrote Fulbright, "is of a piece with the hypocrisy and cynicism for which the United States is constantly denouncing the Soviet Union in the United Nations and elsewhere. This point will not be lost on the rest of the world—nor on our own consciences." Fulbright urged containment instead through the Alliance for Progress.

Senator Fulbright gave the President this memo to read over Easter weekend, which Kennedy was spending with his parents in Florida. Schlesinger notes that "it was a brilliant memorandum. Yet the President returned from Palm Beach more militant than when he had left." One can only guess, but it seems not improbable that Joseph P. Kennedy was partly responsible for this new zest in his son's fighting spirit. As earlier discussed, Kennedy's father was a simplistic American crusader typical of the Wilsonian generation. Good and evil to him seemed entities best faced in the manner of a hard-swinging American businessman. Might, in Joe Kennedy's outlook, generally did make right.

Whatever the exact source of John F. Kennedy's new determination, the climactic meeting took place on April 4 after his return. The President asked each adviser in turn to give his opinion. Only Fulbright denounced the operation as, according to Schlesinger, "wildly out of proportion to the threat. It would compromise our moral position in the world and make it impossible for us to protest treaty violations by the Communists." After the meeting, Schlesinger wrote a full explanation of his opposition, which was based on "the implausibility of its two political premises" rather than a rigid opposition to intervention. As the Harvard historian logically pointed out, "No matter how 'Cuban' the equipment and personnel, the U.S. will be held accountable for the operation, and our prestige will be committed to its success." Secondly, since evidence for a mass insurrection was lacking, the operation might turn into a prolonged civil conflict that would bring strong political pressure on Kennedy to intervene. What was lacking was a direct and demonstrable threat to U.S. security. Without it, such an action could only seem like a "calculated aggression" to much of the world. Schlesinger feared that an invasion would destroy the international credibility of Kennedy himself, which he saw as one of America's greatest assets.

Yet despite the profound doubts and clear counterarguments of Fulbright and Schlesinger, Kennedy's misgivings were overcome by the arguments of more prestigious and more powerful advisers, notably Allen Dulles and Rusk, with the Joint Chiefs and McNamara acquiescing in the military plans. Later Sorensen, the President's chief personal aide, would claim that Kennedy approved the operation on the mistaken impression that it was to be a basically quiet, though large-scale, reinfiltration of patriot rebels into Cuba; that, in the event of failure, the rebels could become guerrillas in the mountains; that the exiles had been informed there would be no American armed support; that the operation was coordinated with the Cuban underground; and that Castro would shortly acquire decisive military strength (the jet fighters). In fact, according to Sorensen, the operation was planned and widely publicized by the CIA as a large-scale invasion; there were no plans for a mountain retreat, which was unrealistic in any event (eighty miles distant across well-guarded swamps); the exiles believed and had even been told by the CIA field operatives that the United States would openly assist them if necessary; there was no genuine coordination with the underground; and Castro already possessed the capability to devastate the invasion—four jet trainers that had been overlooked. These jets would, in fact, wreck the invasion and speed the surrender of a basically hopeless operation.

Schlesinger generally supports this impression that Kennedy was a prisoner of basic misconceptions as well as momentum. By Saturday, April 8, the President seemed to have made up his mind. According to Schlesinger, Kennedy said he had successfully reduced the operation "from a grandiose amphibious assault to a mass infiltration." The President accepted CIA assurances about the contingency escape and felt that failure, if it came, could now be tolerated. "If we have to get rid of these 800 men," JFK told Schlesinger, "it is much better to dump them in Cuba than in the United States, especially if that is where they want to go." The historian felt that Kennedy's decision also resulted from his newness in office, and believed that the opposition of one senior adviser would have led to cancellation. Yet this opinion seems dubious in light of the compelling counterarguments offered by Senator Fulbright and Schlesinger himself. (We must always remember that both Schlesinger and Sorensen had a vested interest in building Kennedy's reputation as a great leader.)

Yet Sorensen has sharply criticized Kennedy's handling of the Bay of Pigs incident, and his comments are psychologically significant. According to Sorensen, the President made "many and serious" mistakes. The President should have had, despite his recent arrival in the Oval Office, the confidence to cancel the plans of the experts and the exiles, but he did not because he feared he would be thought arrogant and presumptuous. Kennedy should have known his advisers better and should never have proceeded, so early in his Administration, with a project about which he had deep misgivings. Sorensen's litany continues: Kennedy let his deep personal antipathy to Castro interfere with his better judgment; he was overconcerned with public opinion and what the reaction might be if it was learned that he had abandoned a plan to dispose of Castro; he should have moved the brigade from Guatemala to another camp and given more thought to its future; and if he had disbanded the brigade, the consequences would have been milder than the course he chose.

While all of these elements very likely had some effect, it also seems probable in view of John F. Kennedy's psychological history that his unconscious emotional need to be a hero played an important part in his decision. Both Schlesinger and Sorensen touch indirectly on this psychological need, but they see it as Kennedy's belief in his own luck and his sensitivity to public criticism. Actually both a personal sense of omnipotence (commonly thought of as "luck") and a hypersensitivity to others' opinions are parts of a neurotic whole and present in most neuroses. The most telling argument against Schlesinger's and Sorensen's overrationalized simplicities is Kennedy's subsequent pattern of behavior in the international realm of danger and high-drama action.

Regarding Kennedy's unusual "deep feeling" against Castro, it is interesting to consider the comparison of Castro and Kennedy offered by Tad Szulc and Karl Meyer: "Both had in common a background of family wealth, both attended respectable schools, both were fiercely ambitious, and both were men who could coolly estimate the odds and take a chance. But Castro was a rebel and Kennedy was not. In whatever environment, Castro surely would have wound up with a sword in his hand as an avenging revolutionary. Fidel had little respect for the wisdom of his elders or the mysteries of traditional society. In contrast, Kennedy was a seeker of advice, a heeder of expert opinion. He came to the White House not as an innovator but as a specialist in effective political management. Whereas Castro cared little for the counsel of men of rank (especially if they wore a uniform), Kennedy at that time gave considerable weight to the words of the Establishment hierarchy." Kennedy, in these reporters' view, was "palpably aching for greatness. After his narrow win over Mr. Nixon, the President was especially anxious to bring off a victory in the first months, to certify his title to office by popular acclaim." This seems a shrewd assessment, and one that helps explain the logic of Kennedy's unusual resentment of Castro. As I explore further in another section (in suggesting reasons for Kennedy's admiration of mandarin-dictator Ngo Dinh Diem), Castro seems in many ways Kennedy's alter ego: the bold leader Kennedy longed to be but could not bring himself to become. Kennedy's "obsession" (as one political analyst called it) with Castro became so intense that JFK even discussed Castro's possible assassination with his old friend Senator George Smathers, though how seriously we do not know. But that Kennedy even toyed with the idea surely indicates an emotional fixation on Castro, the glamorous, fiery, bearded rebel and fighter who was so much the superficial antithesis of Kennedy, the frustrated man of action. Castro's *machismo* was obvious; Kennedy's Harvard-bred version was subtle and disguised.

There is no need to go into the military details of the Bay of Pigs catastrophe. Two days before the landing, Cuban-piloted B-26's made dawn attacks in an unsuccessful attempt to destroy Castro's air force. The raid's results were exaggerated to Kennedy, and as a result he cancelled a second strike. The effects of this cancellation were later vastly distorted by the press; in reality, the second raid, even if successful, could only have postponed the Brigade's defeat. The clumsy CIA plot, which included the wrong type of B-26's as alleged Cuban planes seized by defectors, merely alerted Castro further. Even worse, it severely embarrassed Adlai Stevenson, the U.S. Ambassador to the U.N., who had not been informed of this secret plan and publicly claimed American innocence. The entire invasion was carried out with this same ill-fated lack of care and overoptimistic bungling. In addition, Castro and his forces were unexpectedly efficient and well organized. There was no revolt in the 250,000-member Cuban army and militia; Castro's patrols and planes reacted vigorously; his soldiers fought hard, while his police rounded up potential resisters; and Castro himself led his forces with skill. The Cuban Brigade landed in the early hours of Monday, April 17; on Wednesday they were forced to surrender to overwhelming forces.

Kennedy himself took the stunning fiasco with outer calm, for he was a man of great composure in times of crisis. Emotional detachment, as we have seen, was one of Kennedy's chief psychological defenses, and in defeat it could be a useful protection. Yet while Kennedy assumed full public responsibility for the Bay of Pigs, he also subtly disclosed to friends among the press some of the inside story, an indirect way of sharing blame. In addition, his White House staff held "backgrounders" for the press which revealed CIA and JCS ineptitudes. Schlesinger recounts that on that tragic Wednesday, the President invited him and James Reston, *The New York Times* Washington Bureau Chief, to lunch. "In spite of the news, Kennedy was free, calm and candid; I had rarely seen him more effectively in control. Saying frankly that reports from the beaches were discouraging, he spoke with detachment about the problems he would now face. 'I probably made a mistake in keeping Allen Dulles on,' he said. 'It's not that Dulles is not a man of great ability. He is. But I have never worked with him, and therefore I can't estimate his meaning when he tells me things. . . . Dulles is a legendary figure, and it's hard to operate with legendary figures. . . . It is a hell of a way to learn things, but I have learned one thing from this business—that is, that we will have to deal with CIA.' " But Kennedy kept Dulles in office for many months to divert Republican criticism, as Schlesinger candidly reports. He also appointed an investigative panel. Since two of the four members had helped plan the abortive operation (Dulles and Admiral Arleigh Burke), it is hardly surprising that no fundamental changes were proposed other than a new emphasis on counterinsurgency rather than conventional warfare in such anti-Communist projects.

Another aide later disclosed Kennedy's unpublicized reaction: "When it happened, the President was hit hard. He showed his fatigue for the first time. He looked sad. The exhilaration of the job was gone. He was no longer the young conquering hero, the first forty-three-year-old president, the first Catholic president, the young man smoking his cigar with his friends and telling them how much fun it was. All that was gone. Suddenly it became one hell of a job."

On April 20, a day after the surrender, Kennedy delivered a scheduled speech before the American Society of Newspaper Editors in Washington. (Ironically, Castro had addressed them at the same place exactly two years earlier.) The President's address was a rather typical example of obscure but vigorous Kennedy rhetoric; it made him appear as a fighter without committing him to any specific action. "Let the record show," he stated, "that our restraint is not inexhaustible. Should it ever appear that the inter-American doctrine of non-interference merely conceals or excuses a policy of non-action—if the nations of the Hemisphere should fail to meet their commitments against outside Communist penetration—then I want it clearly understood that the Government will not hesitate in meeting its primary obligations which are to the security of our Nation." "Having uttered this obscure but emphatic warning," Schlesinger commented, Kennedy then warned against Communist aggression by "subversion, infiltration, and a host of other tactics. . . . Too long we have fixed our eyes on traditional military needs. . . . Now it should be clear that this is no longer enough—that our security may be lost piece by piece, country by country, without the firing of a single missile or the crossing of a single border." Kennedy concluded his bellicose address by calling for a reorientation of America's military forces. Subsequently, General Maxwell Taylor, who helped investigate the Bay of Pigs operation, would advance the counterinsurgency proposals that seized so strongly on the imaginations of John Kennedy and his brother Bobby and that beckoned the United States into the bottomless Vietnam quicksand. But as in Cuba, it would prove to be the natives, not the alien Americans, who truly understood the realities of their own country.

In discussing Kennedy's failure to comprehend Cuban realities, as well as the possible psychic dynamics behind his ill-advised decision, I have gone into some detail to suggest the intricate complex of overt pressures and unconscious motivations that largely determine presidential actions. The twin ingredients of defeat seem to me to have been a typically American overconfidence and a typically American indifference toward the responses of the enemy, especially when the enemy is from an economically and racially "inferior" country. This pattern would soon be repeated by the Kennedy Administration in Vietnam.

Richard J. Walton, in his insightful interpretation of Kennedy's foreign policies, *Cold War and Counterrevolution*, points out how Kennedy's apologists such as Roger Hilsman, Theodore Sorensen, and Pierre Salinger claimed that JFK learned a valuable lesson from the Bay of Pigs. Walton shows the falseness of this claim, for if we are to judge by the evidence, Kennedy and his advisers learned nothing. The Cuban invasion led eventually to the missile crisis, when Khrushchev recklessly tried to protect his protégé from further invasion, and before that the Kennedy Administration approached the brink in Berlin and edged into Vietnam.

But Walton also unequivocally states the deeper meaning of the Bay of Pigs, a lesson which is the underlying meaning of emotional neurotic conflict: the inevitable link between irrationality and immorality. Neurosis is a human sickness which prevents the victim from achieving his own humanity and thus from fulfilling his capacity for ethical living. The result, in the case of Kennedy and his advisers, was the passion for power and intellectual arrogance which brought about the inhumanities of such militaristic "adventures." As Walton wisely wrote, "Although it seemed a transient episode during Kennedy's administration, the Bay of Pigs was profoundly revealing. It demonstrated that Kennedy, like his predecessors, like his society, was excessively preoccupied with communism, that he was an interventionist prepared to violate national sovereignty in an attempt to strike it down. It demonstrated that Kennedy lacked prudence, an essential quality in the nuclear age. . . . But even if the planning had not been an exercise in gross incompetence, even if it had not demonstrated a profound ignorance of revolution, even if it had not revealed a political attitude that would lead to more dangerous adventures, even if it had not led directly to the Cuban missile crisis, the Bay of Pigs would have still left an indelible stain on Kennedy's record. It was wrong."

In my last chapter, I will suggest some roots of this immorality so evident in both the Kennedys and American society.

II. The Arms Race:
The Nuclear Crusade

In the area of defense politics Kennedy's political nose sensed an issue that might get votes, and in 1958 he began to emphasize the significance of "the missile gap." He warned: "The deterrent ratio during 1960–1964 will in all likelihood be weighted against us." Presumably the 41-year-old Senator was taking his cue from a close friend, columnist Joseph Alsop, who had published . . . [a] projection of intercontinental ballistic missiles. Some of Kennedy's associates in the Senate regarded these figures as "authoritative" and used them to dramatize the missile gap. . . .

"For many years, now, we have been living on the edge of the crater," Kennedy intoned, and added: "In the years of the gap, our exercises in brink-of-war diplomacy will be infinitely less successful." The irony of the situation was that since 1956 President Eisenhower had authorized U-2 reconnaissance aircraft to overfly the territory of the Soviet Union, and no evidence had been found to verify deployment of a single Soviet ICBM.

—Ralph E. Lapp, *The Weapons Culture*

In the opinion of many knowledgeable observers within the government and without, there was in early 1961 an opportunity to halt the arms race with the Soviet Union. . . . There seemed to be a suggestion that the Soviets were seeking a reduction of tensions and a respite from the arms race. Further gestures were forthcoming and they reinforced that original impression. . . . For various reasons, President Kennedy chose not to take the Soviet overtures seriously. He moved early in his administration to increase significantly the American strategic arsenal—a decision that doomed any immediate chance for agreement on a nuclear test ban and led directly to the Soviet decision to resume testing in the fall of 1961.

—Louise FitzSimons, *The Kennedy Doctrine*

Some observers have speculated that, after the Bay of Pigs debacle, Kennedy felt he had to show strength and thus could not afford to oppose the development of additional missiles. Foster sought in mid-1961 to win the President's approval for a proposal to Moscow calling for a mutual percentage of cuts in missiles, bombers, and naval vessels, but Kennedy replied that it was much too soon for such a move. Six years later, McNamara said that the 1961 buildup of the two missile systems "was necessitated by a lack of accurate information," and he acknowledged that "clearly the Soviet buildup" after the 1964 ouster of Khrushchev was "in part a reaction to our own buildup since the beginning of this decade."

Thus, although Kennedy came to office determined to control and slow the arms race, he actually fueled it with the rapid buildup of new weapons systems. But the atmosphere of the early Kennedy years was not one to suggest a cut-back in strategic weapons. Furthermore, a meeting in June, 1961, with Khrushchev in Vienna raised alarms about a new Soviet-American confrontation over Berlin and confirmed the view of the fearful that a fuller complement of missiles was essential.

—Chalmers M. Roberts, *The Nuclear Years*

This deterrent concept assumes rational calculations by rational men, and the history of this planet is sufficient to remind us of the possibilities of an irrational attack, a miscalculation, an accidental war which cannot be either foreseen or deterred. The nature of modern warfare heightens these possibilities.

—President John F. Kennedy to a joint session of Congress, May, 1961

꙼

KENNEDY'S POSTHUMOUS DEIFICATION as an "apostle of peace" has obscured the fact that his Administration actually did much to heighten Cold War tensions and dangers and that Kennedy showed no sign of slackening the arms race he had greatly increased. Two actions of JFK's last six months, his outstanding June, 1963, speech on international conciliation and his October, 1963, Nuclear Test Ban Treaty, added much luster to Kennedy's reputation. Yet despite his public rhetoric on peace, the record shows that JFK was going full steam ahead on a vast expansion of armaments which could only result in the Russians speeding up their own lagging nuclear stockpiling and delivery. Even the much-heralded Test Ban Treaty did not rule out underground tests, and later evidence indicates that both the United States and the Soviet Union used such tests to increase their nuclear bomb knowledge. In addition, the treaty had no effect at all on the acceleration of missile sophistication, which has now produced the hydra-headed monster of multiple independently-targeted reentry vehicles (MIRVs), thus blowing the lid off missile counting and control (the number of warheads is concealed in each missile cone).

As in so much else, Kennedy said one thing and did another in the increasingly dangerous area of nuclear survival. While making pronouncements on the need for peaceful international cooperation, Kennedy's actions made that cooperation constantly difficult, if not impossible. Unless the United States, which held a large nuclear lead over the Soviet Union, slowed down its vast accumulation of overkill weaponry, the Communists could only conclude that they must arm more and more to catch up with the United States. Thus while Kennedy's conscious intentions were undoubtedly pacific, he showed every sign of accepting the Cold War ideology which led him to invade Cuba, escalate in Vietnam, brandish nuclear bombs over Berlin and Cuba, and step up the thermonuclear juggernaut. Nuclear "superiority" was still the watchword of Kennedy and his Cold Warriors. The idea of "parity" lay years in the future, while "sufficiency" as a genuine American policy was a decade or more away.

One can only speculate on JFK's personal emotional need for being a strong and heroic President. However, the victory-at-all-costs values of his narrow upbringing and the probable deep-seated insecurities instilled in his childhood, as well as the narrow conservatism of his parents which he never truly outgrew, give ample grounds for concluding that Kennedy's own psychological needs were a large part of his reliance on superweapons and an old-fashioned use of force or threatened force against the "enemy." In addition, Kennedy clearly felt at home with generals, admirals, and important men of business and science. He had grown up with material power and wealth and was emotionally attuned to dealing with concrete power, as well as to seeking the advice of those who controlled it. When Kennedy entered the White House, the Pentagon was entrenched as a major power in government. For years hardly anyone—except radicals, pacifists, and Eisenhower in his parting moments—had questioned the need and purpose of new and more expensive weapons technology every year. While Kennedy was often skeptical of people (although not skeptical enough of people he wanted to depend on), he had faith in technology. Like his father, John Kennedy seemed to believe in the dependability of things more than people. Things could be bought, produced, and controlled; people were more difficult (and dangerous). Thus JFK's nuclear stockpiling bore an emotional affinity to Joe Kennedy's financial stockpiling. Both collections could serve as unconscious emotional defenses against feared attack.

In a sense, Kennedy was too old for the Presidency, at least in his antiquated thinking. He had been reared in an outmoded school of winning, but he became President in the new era when military victory as a viable goal had all but vanished. Certainly in any nuclear war there would be no "victors." As Dr. Ralph Lapp, the noted physicist and weapons authority, wrote in *Arms Beyond Doubt*, "We arm not just beyond doubt, but beyond belief. We arm for a weapon war in which all men are victims. No poets can sing of arms, as Virgil once did. Our science has petrified the poets."

But Kennedy still heard the trumpet's tantalizing strains. The over-all impression of Kennedy's campaign oratory, his inaugural address on January 20, 1961, and his first State of the Union message ten days later is that the new young President felt himself cast as a Churchillian leader of the

"Free World," a dramatically heroic figure eloquently exhorting and bravely leading the forces of democracy against the forces of tyranny—in effect, the romantic author of *Why England Slept* now grown up and in command to meet the coming crisis. The man who most probably suffered, consciously or not, from inner fears of being exposed as a pseudo-hero (for the sinking of PT-109, as Kennedy had wryly admitted on several occasions, was not exactly an achievement), and the man who had been raised to feel that being a hero was all-important, now stood ready at the helm of his nation to prove himself a genuine hero for all time. These psychological elements, as well as the inbuilt momentum of the arms race and the arguments of the powerful weapons lobbyists and Kennedy's military advisers, seem logically to have been a crucial part of President Kennedy's decision to increase enormously America's already decisive missile arsenal. For by the beginning of JFK's term, the United States possessed more than 2,000 nuclear delivery vehicles (missiles and strategic bombers), enough to destroy the Soviet Union ten times, as compared to reliable estimates of some 235 Russian nuclear weapons vehicles.

Yet Kennedy, like many neurotics, wanted to have it both ways: to be the bold, unflinching general as well as the prophet and bringer of peace. Consider the astonishingly contradictory words of his inaugural speech: "We dare not tempt them with weakness. For only when our arms are sufficient beyond doubt can we be certain beyond doubt that they will never be employed." In the very next paragraph, Kennedy stated the opposite view: "But neither can two great and powerful groups of nations take comfort from our present course—both sides overburdened by the cost of modern weapons, both rightly alarmed by the steady spread of the deadly atom, yet both racing to alter the uncertain balance of terror that stays the hand of mankind's final war."

I. F. Stone cannily saw Kennedy's essential flaw, though he attributed it to Machiavellian politics: "Basically the opportunity [for curbing the arms race] was missed because Kennedy as President, like Kennedy as Senator and as candidate, tried to ride two horses at once in two opposite directions, rearmament *and* disarmament. In the Senate I can recall an occasion when in the short space of one week he made two speeches, one, idealistic and eloquent, on the need to end the arms race, the other, alarmist, on the need to fill that nonexistent 'missile gap.' This might have been fallacious logic but it was—as they say—practical politics. It served to keep his lines open to two antagonistic constituencies, the powerful armament makers with their allies in the military bureaucracy, and a public increasingly anxious about the mounting cost and danger."

Kennedy entered the presidency determined to be one of the strongest and most forceful Chief Executives in American history, and one able to meet any military or other challenge. Eisenhower's reliance on massive retaliation had, he believed, prevented a flexible response in limited-war situations. Kennedy wanted both the strategic deterrent and the conventional forces able to deal with Russia's announced "wars of national liberation." Although Khrushchev's actions had been far more conciliatory than his words, Kennedy responded to the words—a strong clue to the direction in which his "Churchill complex" of needful emotions was propelling him. Hence, the new President swiftly played upon the public's fears of attack and enlarged them. In his January 30 State of the Union message, Kennedy told the nation that domestic problems "pale when placed beside those which confront us around the world. No man entering upon this office . . . could fail to be staggered upon learning—even in this brief 10-day period— the harsh enormity of the trials through which we must pass in the next four years. Each day the crises multiply. Each day their solution grows more difficult. Each day we draw nearer the hour of maximum danger. . . ." Kennedy revealed that he had already increased the missile program, accelerated the Polaris submarine program, and ordered an enlarged airlift capacity to enable U.S. conventional forces to respond "to any problem at any spot on the globe at any moment's notice."

Soon Kennedy was asking Congress (on March 28) for more defense funds since "It has been publicly acknowledged for several years that this nation has not led the world in missile strength," an outright lie, as Kennedy knew. Despite revelations by journalists and the authoritative British Institute of Strategic Studies that the United States vastly outdistanced the Soviet Union in nuclear striking power (as it turned out, by ten times as much), Kennedy asked for nineteen more Polaris subs, each armed with sixteen missiles, a doubling of Minuteman production, development of the Skybolt bomber-launched missile, and other boosts.

In McNamara's candid retrospection of September 18, 1967, the Defense Secretary recalled, "In 1961, when I became Secretary of Defense, the Soviet Union possessed a very small operational arsenal of intercontinental missiles." McNamara justified the U.S. buildup as a hedge against possible future Soviet production, but added that the "decision in itself—as justified as it was—in the end, could not possibly have left unaffected the Soviet Union's future nuclear plans. . . . Clearly, the Soviet build-up is in part a reaction to our own build-up since the beginning of this decade." On November 2, 1961, after the Russians had exploded a huge superbomb, Kennedy himself said, "In terms of total military strength, the United States would not trade places with any nation on earth."

The dark picture of the world drawn by President Kennedy in early 1961 was so different from the reality of a vastly stronger United States vis-à-vis Russia and a newly conciliatory Soviet attitude that we must look beyond surface political motives, military misapprehensions, and military-industrial pressures for an explanation. There is no question that Kennedy was a highly intelligent man, and his statements frequently showed a sophisticated understanding of international complexities. Political guile and even deceit were certainly repeatedly used by Kennedy, as they have been by other Presidents. But his crisis rhetoric was so frequent and so extreme, and was followed by such rash actions, that we must infer he genuinely believed in much of what he said. What Kennedy had really learned in his first ten days in office was the preponderant military might of the United States. Yet the existence of this power did not fit into his need to assume the Churchill-crusader role. His internal emotional drama and desire for vindication demanded crisis, and so he both saw and created crisis.

Kennedy's chief science adviser, Jerome B. Wiesner (now president of MIT), described the alternative course of action which he urged on Kennedy: "In 1961 at the start of the Kennedy administration, we had the opportunity to attempt to freeze the ballistic missile forces at the relatively low levels established by President Eisenhower. Soon after President Kennedy took office, we learned that the Soviet missile force was substantially smaller than earlier estimates which provided the basis for the so-called missile gap. We learned, in fact, that the United States probably had more missiles than the Soviet Union, a somewhat surprising and reassuring fact. At the time some persons, including me, proposed holding down the U.S. missile levels in the expectation that if the United States showed restraint, the Soviet Union could be persuaded to do the same and that in any event a force of 200–400 missiles . . . would be a mighty deterrent against any likely Soviet strategic force."

Although newly sophisticated cameras constantly revealed the relative smallness of the Russian deterrent, the Kennedy Administration continued its missile increases. In 1962, fiscal appropriations totaled 600 intercontinental ballistic missiles (ICBM's), which were raised to 800 in 1963 and then to 1,000 missiles. Authorizations to enlarge the Polaris fleet went from 29 craft in fiscal 1962 to 35 the next year and then to 41 in fiscal 1964, making a total of 656 missiles. By late 1963, Kennedy was spending $50 billion a year on arms, a staggering allocation of national resources to the military-industrial complex. In Kennedy's speech scheduled for delivery on November 22, 1963, in Dallas, the President listed figures that revealed the enormous growth of the military establishment during his Administration. It is indicative of Kennedy's conventional and stereotyped thinking that this irrational growth is recited with pride. Like his father, John Kennedy constantly displayed "big business" mentality and emotionality that finds security primarily in material objects and the amassing of endless concrete "weapons" (money or actual guns) against the world's potential and overt hostility.

As Kennedy would have told us in his undelivered speech that November, "The strategic nuclear power of the United States has been so greatly modernized and expanded in the last 1,000 days, by the rapid production and deployment of the most modern missile systems, that any and all potential aggressors are clearly confronted now with the impossibility of strategic victory—and the certainty of total destruction—if by reckless attack they should ever force upon us the necessity of a strategic reply. In less than three years, we have increased by 50 percent the number of Polaris submarines scheduled to be in force by the next fiscal year—increased by more than 70 percent our total Polaris purchase program—increased by more than 75 percent our Minuteman purchase program—increased by 50 percent the portion of our strategic bombers on 15-minute alert—and increased by 100 percent the total number of nuclear weapons available in our strategic alert forces. . . .

"But the lessons of the last decade have taught us that freedom cannot be defended by strategic nuclear power alone. We have, therefore, in the last three years accelerated the development and deployment of tactical nuclear weapons—and increased by 60 percent the tactical nuclear forces deployed in Western Europe. Nor can Europe or any other continent rely on nuclear forces alone, whether they are strategic or tactical. We have radically improved the readiness of our conventional forces—increased by 45 percent the number of combat-ready army divisions—increased by 100 percent the procurement of modern army weapons and equipment—increased by 100 percent our ship construction, conversion and modernization program—increased by 100 percent our procurement of tactical aircraft—increased by 30 percent the number of tactical air squadrons—and increased the strength of the Marines. . . . We have increased by 175 percent the procurement of airlift aircraft—and we have already achieved a 75 percent increase in our existing strategic airlift capability. Finally, moving beyond the traditional roles of our military forces, we have achieved an increase of nearly 600 percent in our special forces—those forces that are prepared to work with our Allies and friends against the guerrillas, saboteurs, insurgents and assassins who threaten freedom in a less direct but equally dangerous manner."

There is a sort of semi-insanity to this seemingly endless progression of force when weighed in the scales of the forces already possessed by the United States at the start of Kennedy's term. While it is true that under Eisenhower the Dulles doctrine of "massive retaliation" had seriously reduced conventional forces, there was no rational need for such a mammoth increase in the military services unless Kennedy genuinely wished

America to become involved in counteracting "wars of liberation" around the globe. Such military increases contain a built-in momentum (as all nations have seen too often, and as Kennedy learned directly from the Bay of Pigs debacle but did not sufficiently appreciate). Kennedy's more cautious buildup in Vietnam had already involved Americans in combat by the time of his death, and was to prove the thin edge of a fantastically escalated wedge under Johnson.

Yet despite the psychohistorical imperatives that constantly propelled Kennedy toward greater armaments, he also believed that he genuinely wished to halt the suicidal arms race. In the aftermath of the October, 1962, missile crisis, when both Kennedy and Khrushchev had brought the world to the brink of thermonuclear disaster, the leader of each superpower turned with relief and renewed urgency toward test ban negotiations. On June 10, 1963, Kennedy gave a major peace speech, and on July 2 Khrushchev responded by finally accepting the banning of tests in the atmosphere and outer space. The remaining details were soon negotiated, and on July 25, 1963, Russia and the United States signed the Limited Nuclear Test Ban Treaty which limited testing to underground sites. On September 24, the U.S. Senate ratified the treaty, after an intensive campaign by Kennedy. Subsequently, this treaty has been hailed as the greatest achievement of the Kennedy Administration.

Unfortunately, the truth falls far short of the praise. For, as I. F. Stone discovered, nuclear testing did not diminish after this treaty, but actually increased. Underground testing swiftly became the sophisticated substitute for previous atmospheric blasts. Despite Kennedy's stirring television address to the world after the signing, his hopeful words were, as Stone put it, "all delusion, a dream which bore little resemblance . . . to the Kennedy Administration's waking and working plans for the aftermath of the treaty." In reality, the 1963 Test Ban Treaty was a victory for American militarists and a considerable defeat for the Russians. Already far behind the United States in the arms race, the Soviets were now limited to underground testing in which they lacked the skill and resources of the Americans. In addition, the price of Pentagon support was a deal between Kennedy and the Joint Chiefs of Staff that the gap would be still further widened by intensified underground testing. McNamara, even while selling the treaty to the Senate, outlined steps for a sharp increase in the arms race. With more than 500 missiles, the United States planned to more than triple that number "to over 1,700 by 1966," despite the estimate that the Soviets had "only a fraction as many ICBM missiles." While Khrushchev had hoped that the treaty would lighten Russia's burden and danger in the accelerating arms race, the Americans dashed his hopes and added another clause to his subsequent dismissal notice (which came in October, 1964).

Thus even as Kennedy struck a dramatic pose as savior of the nation's peace and security, the "safeguards" he had promised to his military chiefs actually assured an intensified arms race and the increased fragility of the thermonuclear peace. As Senator George McGovern, a strong supporter of the treaty, pointed out to his colleagues at the time, "Indeed, Mr. President, the Administration has been called upon to give so many assurances of our continued nuclear efforts after treaty ratification that a casual observer might assume that we are approving this treaty so that we can accelerate the arms race and beef up the war-making facilities of our country!" In retrospect, as journalist Stone has pointed out, "that appears to be exactly what the treaty did." Kennedy and his escalation-minded Defense chief lost the historic opportunity to reduce or at least freeze nuclear inventories on both sides of the so-called Iron Curtain. The lid of Pandora's death-dealing atomic box had been lifted another terrifying notch.

Kennedy has often been described as a pragmatist who compromised with various special interests, and certainly each armed service was lobbying hard for its own weapons systems (the Air Force received 1,000 instead of 3,000 missiles, the Navy got 41 instead of 45 Polaris submarines, and Kennedy gave the Army strong conventional forces instead of the ABM system). It is also argued that Kennedy was trapped by his own campaign rhetoric, and to a degree each of these reasons is true. But both the style and reality of Kennedy's missile decision must be weighed within the context of *all* his actions. From this perspective, Kennedy's acceleration of the arms race can be seen as a logical piece in a general pattern of behavior that can be called irrational to a neurotic degree.

John Kennedy usually appeared supremely confident to his country and to most of the world. He was well schooled in masking his real emotions. But a truly confident person of such evident intelligence does not react in so many negative and essentially stupid ways unless he has serious emotional conflicts. Kennedy was unable to face the Bay of Pigs decision in a mature way and see it clearly. He was unable to judge the inescapable outcome of his arms increase. And when the Russians launched a man into space, Kennedy once again reacted blindly, with the conditioned reflex of a man bred to intense competition and self-defense, not with a cool and critical appraisal of what would be best for his country and thus, ultimately, for himself.

III. The Moon Project: Crusade in Space

A Soviet success and a U.S. failure were forerunners of Kennedy's venture into space during the spring of 1961. On April 12 Maj. Yuri Gagarin was launched into orbit aboard Vostok I to become the first human to travel round the world in ninety minutes. It was depressing news for the young President. On April 17 the ill-fated invasion of Cuba occurred. . . . The restless Kennedy mind was occupied with a message to the Congress on urgent national needs. In the course of work on this message, he conferred with a small group of advisers, predominantly military, who proposed that he take the initiative and announce a dramatic plan to send men to the moon. It was a weekend decision for Kennedy. Had he tarried in talking it over at length, Project Apollo might have died aborning. Most of his White House science advisers (including the members of his Science Advisory Committee) were known to have little sympathy for such a project.

—Ralph E. Lapp, *The Weapons Culture*

Kennedy, who had promised to "get the country moving again," soon discovered the difficulty of moving the Congress toward his economic theories and social programs. After six months as chief executive he declared the moon to be a national objective (against the recommendation of most scientists), almost a substitute avenue of action. Congress was holding his program in abeyance, the economy was sluggish, a recession was beckoning, and new Soviet space achievements seemed to dramatize America's growing discredit. The first manned flight of Gagarin came in April 1961, followed a week later by the Bay of Pigs—two sharp blows for the ambitious young man who seemed to be a helpless captive in the White House. Vice President Johnson, head of the National Space Council, was pushing hard for an augmented space effort. Key congressmen, all the aerospace industry, lobbyists, and promoters of the Air Force and NASA pushed. Perhaps here was the way. Perhaps on this issue the country could be unified and make the breakthrough Kennedy desired into a positive concept of government responsibility and social reform. The moon program was hatched during a hectic weekend in May.

—H. L. Nieburg, *In the Name of Science*

The need to triumph over each other and the tendency to prostrate ourselves before technology are in fact closely related. We turn continually to technology to save us from having to cooperate with each other. Technology, meanwhile, serves to preserve and

maintain the competitive pattern and render it ever more frantic,
thus making cooperation at once more urgent and more difficult.
—Philip Slater, *The Pursuit of Loneliness*

    Some sociologists agree with Science Administrator Killian that
a race to put a man on the moon was carrying America's propensity
of "keeping up with the Joneses" a little too far. . . . Humanists
revive visions of the Greek heroes who had to strike out from home
although they forgot just why—whatever the risk and no matter
the cost. . . . Pork-chop liberals complain that rats are still nibbling
on children in Harlem apartments, a fact which solid-fuel boosters
seem unlikely to alter. The first man in space, Major Yuri Gagarin,
liberals point out symbolically enough, is living on earth in a *two-
room apartment* with his wife and child, and his parents. Is this
allocation of resources a symbol we wish to emulate?
—James Tracy Crown and George P. Penty, *Kennedy in Power*

ᑐᏋ

JOHN F. KENNEDY's determination to set the United States on an enormously expensive "race" to the moon was an apt psychohistorical symbol
of his inflated personal needs for affirmation and achievement. The moon
race also exemplified Kennedy's remoteness from people, for nothing could
be more distant from the needs of earthlings than that uninhabited, cold
planetary body. Psychically, the moon offered an ideal neurotic goal for a
man of Kennedy's inner drives: to reach it required fabulous expenditures
of wealth and talent, a suitable assuagement of guilt; yet the effort was
completely detached from most people. Both triumph and futility were
paradoxically embodied in the eventual attainment (two Administrations
later) of heroic man walking on the moon and bringing back to earth a
handful of lifeless rocks. In this sense, the moon shot was a striking paradigm
of Kennedy's own life: the glory of execution, the emptiness of result.
    At the time of Kennedy's decision, the moon venture was made to appear
an eminently practical project, for the Kennedyites saw themselves as
immensely pragmatic men. In reality, the pressures of international and
domestic politics catapulted the costly project. In the spring of 1961, the
other great Cold Warrior, the Soviet Union, seemed to be forging ahead in
the eyes of the world. Gagarin had soared into space; Kennedy had slipped
on the banana peel of Cuba. Laos was seething, Vietnam was perplexing,
and the Congo was filled with the menacing muddles of "darkest Africa."
The Kennedy Administration clearly needed a public shot in the arm, and
that shot was to cost the American people more than $30 billion. If the man
in the White House no longer quite embodied a change in the tides of

human history, a man on the moon might serve as a temporary substitute.

As a Congressman and Senator, Kennedy had shown no interest in space other than a few routine statements prepared by others. But four months after he became President, the goal of reaching the moon ahead of the Russians suddenly assumed top priority within the Administration. The real goal, as we can see now, was to rescue Kennedy's image, not to save America from any threat, real or imagined. Politics and self-interest, not science or national interest, were the impetus.

As three British journalists pointed out in their careful study of the U.S. space effort, *Journey to Tranquility*, "In one extraordinary convulsion of statesmanship, the scene in space was utterly transformed. . . . Whereas to Eisenhower science was the oracle whose message proved consistently too ambiguous to justify so vast a venture, now, under Kennedy, it was consulted only to be ignored. To him, the intrinsic properties of the moon were of no interest. As a symbol, on the other hand, the moon had everything. It was a symbol, first of all, of himself. . . . Kennedy represented himself as the man of action and drama, of new ideas and new frontiers. . . . It was a theme applied without discrimination to every issue, but to none did it relate more aptly than to space."

For Kennedy, the moon was also a symbol of America and of the nation's strength in relation to Russia. Unlike Eisenhower, JFK believed in prestige with a passion. Although prestige is hard to define, for an individual or a nation, Kennedy pursued it with the compulsiveness with which his father had pursued money and status. Wealth gave the Kennedys power and position; prestige would help keep the family on top and affirm their cravings for a self-image of widespread admiration and respect. Thus the space race had a deeply personal emotional meaning for Kennedy as President: American strength and Kennedy strength had become indissolubly linked. Unfortunately, Kennedy's definitions of strength were often both simplistic and irrational. Had he seen strength in more humanistic, non-*machismo* terms, the country could have benefited enormously from his drive and energy. But Kennedy's view was narrow, and in this self-defeating focus he was aided by men of similar neurotic power needs and directions, such as Vice President Lyndon Johnson, an ardent superpatriot whom Kennedy appointed as chairman of the National Aeronautical and Space Council.

The U.S. Air Force had also mobilized itself to persuade the new Administration that the military belonged in space. The Air Force alerted the space industry and congressional friends to support its campaign. And the National Aeronautics and Space Administration (NASA) was equally prepared to present a new space frontier to the new regime. NASA, despite Eisenhower's refusal to launch a moon program and its own well-known launch failures, had quietly gone ahead with plans and feasibility contracts.

JFK first set up task forces to study the space question. MIT's Jerome Wiesner, his top science and space adviser, cautioned against manned space flights, as did other scientists. Meanwhile the new President was deeply involved in the Laos crisis and had not yet formulated his space policy, despite his flamboyant and jingoistic campaign rhetoric. April 25, 1961, was set by space scientists as the date of America's first manned launch. But then, on April 12, came the Russians' fateful launching of Gagarin into orbit. As a friend of Kennedy's, journalist Hugh Sidey, later wrote, "The pressure on Kennedy to finally come to hard grips with the problem of space mounted after Yuri's orbiting. Only hours after the Soviet success, congressmen and senators cried for more action. . . . 'Kennedy could lose the 1964 election over this,' added another space administrator who had suffered through American missile politics for years."

Kennedy, with his highly-tuned political sensitivities, reacted immediately. On April 12, he held a meeting with Sorensen, Wiesner, Budget Director David Bell, NASA's top officials, and, strangely, journalist Sidey. NASA head James Webb thought the President wanted to impress Sidey with his space knowledge, but instead, as the authors of *Journey to Tranquility* noted, JFK "manifested an almost bottomless ignorance of the matter," as well as a competitive obsession with the Russians. Kennedy tensely asked his science advisers, "Is there any place where we can catch them? What can we do? Can we go around the moon before them? What about Nova and Rover? When will Saturn be ready? Can we leapfrog?" His advisers pointed out the enormous cost of a crash program. Kennedy tapped his teeth, then replied, "When we know more, I can decide if it's worth it or not. If somebody can just tell me how to catch up. Let's find somebody — anybody, I don't care if it's the janitor over there, if he knows how." As the British journalists observed, "What this meeting disclosed more than anything was the sight of a man obsessed with failure. Gagarin's triumph mocked the image of dynamism which Kennedy had offered the American people. It had, one senses, to be avenged almost as much for his own sake as for the nation's."

Only three days after this meeting came the humiliation at the Bay of Pigs. For a man of Kennedy's characterology, the result of these two blows to his personal pride was predictable. On April 19, as Castro captured the remaining Cuban invaders, Kennedy met alone with LBJ. After the meeting, Johnson's chief space aide, Edward Welsh, commented that America "was already halfway to the moon." The next day Kennedy sent the Vice President a directive "whose tone was that of a man willing to pay any price to avoid further disgrace," as the British journalists accurately saw it. This important Kennedy directive deserves to be quoted in full:

"In accordance with our conversation I would like for you as Chairman of the Space Council to be in charge of making an over-all survey of where we stand in space.

"1. Do we have a chance of beating the Soviets by putting a laboratory in space, or by a trip around the moon, or by a rocket to land on the moon, or by a rocket to go to the moon and back with a man? Is there any other space program which promises dramatic results in which we could win?

"2. How much additional would it cost?

"3. Are we working 24 hours a day on existing programs? If not, why not? If not, will you make recommendations to me as to how work can be speeded up.

"4. In building large boosters should we put our emphasis on nuclear, chemical or liquid fuel, or a combination of those three?

"5. Are we making maximum effort? Are we achieving necessary results?

"I have asked Jim Webb, Dr. Wiesner, Secretary McNamara and other responsible officials to cooperate with you fully. I would appreciate a report on this at the earliest possible moment."

Johnson responded to this welcome stimulus with alacrity. Marshaling experts from NASA, the Pentagon, and big business, Johnson gave Kennedy an enthusiastic recommendation for beating the Russians to the moon. The general public was not, of course, consulted, for there was widespread uncertainty: immediately after Kennedy announced his decision, the Gallup poll showed an opposition of 58 percent. Nor were opposing scientists consulted. As Welsh later revealed, "If scientists had had any influence, the space program would have been about one-third the size it has been." The disillusioned Wiesner asked Kennedy "never to refer publicly to the moon landing as a scientific enterprise. And after he had announced the decision, he never did so."

Despite Kennedy's public assertions of peaceful motives, the space program was coupled in the minds of its originators with military power. As NASA head James Webb and Defense Secretary McNamara wrote in their report to the President, "Our attainments are a major element in the international competition between the Soviet system and our own. The non-military, non-commercial, non-scientific, but 'civilian' projects such as lunar and planetary exploration are, in this sense, part of the battle along the fluid front of the cold war." Prestige alone justified the cost: "Major successes, such as orbiting a man as the Soviets have just done, lend national prestige even though the scientific, commercial or military value of the undertaking may by ordinary standards be marginal or economically unjustified."

This militaristic and supercompetitive philosophy fitted with Kennedy's own. On May 25, 1961, the President announced the projected conquest of the moon to Congress. He did not ask for debate, and there was surprisingly little. Rather, Kennedy struck his typical pose as a national supersalesman who regularly told the nation what it needed in the exaggerated terms of today's newest "miracle" soap, rather than using the factual objectivity of a true educator. Despite public hesitancy, the political atmosphere was ripe for a major leap in technological production. Russia's development of larger booster rockets was partly responsible for the general fear of potential Soviet superiority among the men who most influenced U.S. national policy. Also, American industry needed a boost itself. Thus the moon program seemed to offer something for many among Kennedy's chief political backers. The underlying reality was that a policy of "Fly now, pay later" would cost the country far more than it produced in jobs and economic prosperity. Most of the wealth so cavalierly spent by Kennedy and his Administration went either into private pockets or into the emptiness of space itself, with little return—except a dubious chauvinistic thrill—for the American public.

Kennedy phrased his May, 1961, call for an all-out space program in typically grandiose, pseudo-romantic, and mock-heroic terms. "Why, some say, the moon?" asked the President. "Why choose this as our goal? They may well ask why climb the highest mountain? Why thirty-five years ago fly the Atlantic? Why does Rice play Texas?" (Kennedy gave this speech at Rice University in Houston.) As I. F. Stone commented with his usual accurate asperity, this reasoning seemed "to reflect a family characteristic [which] might be called the touch-football-after-lunch explanation; the Kennedys love activity and competition for their own sake. . . . The race to the moon, from this vantage point, is a way to work off excess energy, a cosmic sporting event." To his theme of high (literally!) adventure Kennedy added the nationalistic pitch. "We have vowed that we shall not see it [space] governed by a hostile flag of conquest, but by a banner of freedom and peace." Yet such a chauvinistic appeal invited the very animosity Kennedy pretended to exclude when he added, "there is no strife, no prejudice, no national conflict in outer space."

The Camelot Administration presented the moon to the American people as an object worthy of their dedicated quest. "No single space project in this period," Kennedy told Congress, "will be more impressive to mankind or more important [or] so difficult or expensive to accomplish." But the importance of reaching the moon was never spelled out. Instead, Kennedy tried to carry his audience along on a vicarious and allegedly exciting experience. "In a very real sense, it will not be one man going to the moon . . . it will be an entire nation. For all of us must work to put him there." But as Stone pointed out, "For industry, this is a lush cost plus operation. For the leadership, it provides glamorous politics to be photographed with the heroes. For the rest of us it is only another, though fantastically expensive, form of spectator sports."

In the speech prepared for delivery in Dallas on the day of his death, Kennedy included the customary moonshine that his huge space project was a valuable effort and an important part of the Cold War struggle with the Communists, despite his 1961 assertion that "there is no strife . . . no national conflict in outer space." On November 22, 1963, Kennedy would have told us that "the success of our leadership is dependent upon respect for our mission in the world as well as our missiles—on a clearer recognition of the virtues of freedom as well as the evils of tyranny. And that is also why we have regained the initiative in the exploration of outer space—making an annual effort greater than the combined total of all space activities undertaken during the Fifties—launching more than 130 vehicles into earth orbit—putting into actual operation valuable weather and communications satellites—and making it clear to all that the United States of America has no intention of finishing second in space.

"There is no longer any fear in the free world that a Communist lead in space will become a permanent assertion of supremacy and the basis of military superiority. There is no longer any doubt about the strength and skill of American science, American industry, American education and the American free enterprise system. . . . In short, our national space effort represents a great gain in, and a great resource of, our national strength. . . ."

Exactly how this national space effort could be put to work to solve America's more mundane but far more pressing social problems, however, was a theme Kennedy showed no intention of developing. The Wilsonian crusade had been extended into outer space.

Despite the dramatic success of Project Apollo in July, 1969 (ironically, under the "nonstylish" Nixon whom Kennedy disliked), many Americans have come to feel that the billions of dollars poured into the moon effort could have been far better spent in improving our shoddy social environment and relationships. As a distinguished urban expert expressed these doubts to a U.S. Senate committee in 1970, "Even in our space program, as great as that is, and I admit that it is, it has had relatively little, if any, fallout, so to speak, on the domestic side of our ledger. We have spent just billions of dollars in this effort, some of which I am sure is very legitimate, to attempt to put a man on the moon. We have been successful. I know it sounds trite, but it is true. I don't really see much purpose in putting men on the moon if, for example, you can't walk down Pennsylvania Avenue in this city or Woodward Avenue in Detroit or any other street in any other city and not be fearful of your life and that is what has happened in this country."

The great global prestige that Apollo was supposed to confer on the United States was short-lived. As several foreign critics viewed America's allocation of resources, "If space has produced an image of strength, Vietnam, assassination, ghetto violence and economic injustice have created one of uncertainty and social incompetence. In the terms which men can understand as relating to their own lives, American capitalism of the Sixties does not have an enviable record. It has created great wealth, and it has sent Americans to the moon. But around the world, the United States is despised as much as she is feared, its citizens pitied as much as they are envied. . . . Apollo is the product of a society prepared to devote greater national effort to reaching the stars than to rebuilding its decaying cities. This choice of values is noted by the world, and makes its mark on the American reputation."

It was not, of course, American society as a whole that was to blame, but a failure in national leadership. One of the more invidious problems of an already overly competitive country being led by a hypercompetitive personality such as John Kennedy's is that the all-important question of "Why?" hardly ever gets asked in a way that reaches the general public. In the field of outer space, Kennedy's deep need for personal triumph—the driving force of his family-bred competitiveness, insecurity, and anxiety—led him directly into the initiation of a program to "win" in space by outstripping the Russians. Thus Kennedy's narrow emotional focus precluded considering whether America had far more urgent, though less glamorous, priorities at home. Instead, JFK's emotional inability to weigh possible alternatives objectively, which might have included a more modest level of effort, flung the nation into a "race" that has proved exorbitantly costly in terms of money and talents vitally needed in domestic areas, and in terms of still another lost opportunity to attract the Russians into a cooperative rather than competitive stance. By this irrational decision, Kennedy once again helped make both domestic and international cooperation "at once more urgent and more difficult" (in Professor Slater's words) by ignoring explosive domestic urgencies and by intensifying a dangerously competitive and mutually paranoic relationship with the Soviet Union.

IV. The Berlin Crisis:
Crusade in Europe

The admirers recorded the Berlin crisis as another Kennedy triumph and another step in the ongoing education that prepared him for his supreme triumph: the Cuban missile crisis. There is a mad logic here. The Bay of Pigs, although it could be called a disaster, prepared him for triumph. The Berlin "crisis," in which Kennedy approached the brink, could, by skillful presentation, be made into a triumph. And the Cuban missile crisis, in which Kennedy stood on the very edge of the brink, could be constructed as the greatest triumph of all. There is, to be sure, a consistency here, but it is possible that future historians will see that consistency in a different way from Kennedy's admirers.

—Richard J. Walton, *Cold War and Counterrevolution*

President Kennedy's resolves in the summer of 1961, amid the synthetic Berlin "war crisis," to increase arms spending, call up reserves, and inaugurate a nation-wide network of "fall-out shelters" in preparation for thermonuclear combat, exemplied anew the American delusion that the Communist challenge is a military challenge to be met by military means. The same delusion found new expression in American intervention in South Vietnam in 1961–1962. Since the challenge is of a wholly different character, it must be met by wholly different means. If different means prove politically possible, the future we face may not be one of atomic coannihilation but one of bright promise for better days to come.

—Frederick L. Schuman, *The Cold War: Retrospect and Prospect*

That same year, 1961, there was a crisis over Berlin and the lights were burning low both at the White House and the Pentagon to work out a strategy to meet it. Everyone agreed, Arthur Schlesinger, Jr. tells us, "that a Soviet blockade of West Berlin would have to be countered first by a Western thrust along the Autobahn." General Lauris Norstad, the supreme commander of NATO, and others, however, insisted that the probe be undertaken solely "to create a situation where the West could use nuclear weapons." Conventional weapons and armies, said Norstad, were too expensive and might not result in victory anyway. Hydrogen bombs were a much better response.

—Sidney Lens, *The Military-Industrial Complex*

. . . how tenuous a relation there is between a man's intentions and the consequences of his acts. There is no presumption more terrifying than that of those who would blow up the world on the basis of their personal judgment of a transient situation. I do not propose to let the future of mankind be settled, or ended, by a group of men operating on the basis of limited perspectives and short-run calculations. I figure that the only thing I have left in life is to do everything I can to stop the war.

—George F. Kennan, August, 1961

ℭ

THE BERLIN "CRISIS" of 1961, in the perspective of a decade, seems to have been primarily another example of Kennedy's dangerous tendency to view each Communist probe as a personal affront, a challenge to his prestige and image, and a profoundly important test of Kennedy's and the national will (apparently identical in his mind). As in so many instances, Kennedy's unconscious need for heroic vindication through crisis, confrontations, and reassuring tests of strength—or at least the appearance of deadly duels—led him to misperceive the causes of Russian pressures and to exaggerate their seriousness.

Kennedy had gone to meet Soviet Premier Khrushchev in Vienna in June, 1961, apparently to prevent further worsening of U.S.-Soviet relations by taking a hard-line position, rather than by finding new alternatives to old Cold War attitudes. As Louise FitzSimons wrote in her careful and highly critical study of Kennedy's foreign policy, *The Kennedy Doctrine*, "President Kennedy had assumed in preparing for the summit that to fail to adhere firmly to the Western powers' occupation rights in Berlin would be to show weakness. Crisis planning in Washington was already under way and a series of military steps were under consideration to demonstrate the American will to risk war over Berlin. The President seemed to be expecting the worst."

On the eve of his departure, President Kennedy made two bellicose speeches in May, which, as FitzSimons put it, "suggested the messianic nature of American foreign policy that was to characterize his administration—a prescription for a new kind of American ideological imperialism." Evidently Kennedy's main aim at Vienna was to impress the Soviet chieftain with his determination to use American strength, if necessary, to check what the Administration saw as "encroachments" on the Free World. Any Russian requests at this time seemed to be viewed as encroachments by Kennedy and his most influential advisers.

Berlin remained the unsettled bone of contention left over from World War II, basically because of Western refusals to give up occupation rights and sign a peace treaty sixteen years after the war's end. Eisenhower was moving cautiously toward negotiations when the U-2 affair cut off the

Paris summit meeting. Kennedy, before Vienna, had already decided that any discussions over Berlin would be considered a surrender to Russian demands and a sign of weakness on his part.

Khrushchev, rather understandably after Kennedy's Bay of Pigs fiasco, very likely regarded the new young President as immature and susceptible to demands and threatening gestures. Each leader misread the other both as a person and a national representative. Khrushchev also could hardly have guessed the extent to which Kennedy's obsession with appearances could lead him, especially after Kennedy's back-off in Cuba. In addition, the Soviets were under strong pressure to neutralize West Berlin as a trouble spot in East Germany. Great numbers of East Germans were fleeing through this single small exit to the West, some 200,000 valuable technicians, professionals, and young people each year. Unless Khrushchev closed the escape, East Germany would lose much of its national lifeblood, a drainage that had totaled some 3.5 million people by the summer of 1961.

At the Vienna summit conference, Khrushchev told Kennedy that the Soviet Union would sign a separate peace treaty with East Germany in six months if the United States refused to negotiate. This would give East Germans jurisdiction over Berlin, and further Western access rights to Berlin would have to be arranged with East Germany. The Soviet Union would back up this treaty with force. Essentially, Khrushchev wanted an immediate peace conference to legalize the existing German borders and transform West Berlin into a demilitarized free city. This can be most logically seen as a defensive desire of the Soviets to have Western recognition of the division of Germany and normalization of the post-World War II de facto partition of Central Europe. Since 1958 Khrushchev had been making similar demands without success. The Vienna meeting ended on a note of bitter disagreement, and Kennedy returned home determined to show his inflexible resolve.

On June 6, President Kennedy made a television report to the nation which was seriously misleading in several respects. He stated, "Our most somber talks were on the subject of Germany and Berlin. I made it clear to Mr. Khrushchev that the security of Western Europe and therefore our own security are deeply involved in our presence and our access rights to West Berlin, that we are determined to maintain these rights at any risk, and thus meet our obligation to the people of West Berlin, and their right to choose their own future. Mr. Khrushchev, in turn, presented his views in detail, and his presentation will be the subject of further communications. But we are not seeking to change the present situation. A binding German peace treaty is a matter for all who were at war with Germany, and we and our allies cannot abandon our obligations to the people of West Berlin." Kennedy implied that Russia was wrong to ask for a general peace treaty and that the Allies were being excluded. But Khrushchev wanted all the Western powers to participate and threatened a separate treaty only if there were no meeting. He also asked Kennedy to make counterproposals. But Kennedy refused to make any conciliatory gestures, despite domestic and foreign pressures, especially from Britain, to negotiate.

Meanwhile Kennedy's staff studied the Berlin situation with widely divided opinions. The militaristic hardliners, led by Dean Acheson, whom Kennedy had delegated to study the problem, wanted to respond to any Soviet demands with an immediate show of force. Indeed, as Schlesinger reported, Acheson "startled the British" when Macmillan came to Washington in April, 1961, by his "formidable catalogue of military countermeasures" which ignored diplomatic or economic responses. Acheson saw Khrushchev's object as a test of the general American will to resist, which in reality had nothing to do with Berlin, Germany, or Europe: "This was a simple conflict of wills. . . ." As Schlesinger critically observed, "For Acheson the test of will seemed almost an end in itself rather than a means to a political end." The bellicose former Secretary of State was convinced that Russia had unlimited objectives in the Berlin issues. But experts on Russia, such as Ambassador to Russia Lewellyn Thompson and former Ambassador Averell Harriman, disagreed. They saw Soviet aims primarily as the improvement of the Communist position in Eastern Europe.

Kennedy tended far more toward the extremism of Acheson and the militaristic advisers than the realistic perspectives of those who viewed Russian moves as an attempt to consolidate defenses rather than a preliminary to the aggressive takeover of Europe. Kennedy also feared that Soviet conventional forces might nibble away at Berlin in the face of weaker NATO ground forces and divergent Allied outlooks, with no single step enough to provoke an all-out U.S. nuclear response. It is difficult to see how this could happen, for it would require a major Soviet move to occupy West Berlin and Khrushchev was not so stupid as to risk all-out war over Berlin. Also, it was questionable whether Khrushchev would actually sign the separate peace treaty with East Germany, which he had threatened to do before. Even if he did, there was no certainty that the East Germans would interfere with West Berlin. And if such blockage of the autobahn occurred as had happened in 1947, there remained a wide variety of diplomatic and economic actions that could be taken before overt military pressure was applied. Kennedy, in effect, although less extreme than Acheson, who was ready to leap to the brink at once, reacted several degrees ahead of reality. It was Washington, not Moscow, that was most responsible for transforming the Berlin question into a thermonuclear crisis.

Since taking office, Kennedy, as we have seen, had several times increased defense spending and enlarged the nuclear deterrent. Now the Soviets took alarm. Khrushchev announced on June 21 that "a peaceful settlement in Europe must be achieved this year," and declared an increase in Soviet military spending. But the Russians continued to make conciliatory gestures. Kennedy's response was a June 28 press conference in which he saw Berlin as involving "the peace and security of the Western world" rather than local, limited issues. On July 19, Kennedy repeated his tough position, and on the 25th he gave an apocalyptic speech which spread fear through America and abroad.

As the President of the United States saw the issue of Berlin, "West Berlin . . . above all, had now become—as never before—the great testing place of Western courage and will, a focal point where our solemn commitments stretching back over the years since 1945, and Soviet ambitions now meet in basic confrontation. . . .

"We do not want to fight—but we have fought before. . . . We cannot and will not permit the communists to drive us out of Berlin, either gradually or by force. For the fulfillment of our pledge to that city is essential to the morale and security of Western Germany, to the unity of Western Europe, and to the faith of the entire Free World. Soviet strategy has long been aimed, not merely at Berlin, but at dividing and neutralizing all of Europe, forcing us back on our own shores. We must meet our oft-stated pledge to the free peoples of West Berlin—and maintain our rights and their safety, even in the face of force—in order to maintain the confidence of other free peoples in our word and our resolve. The strength of the alliance on which our security depends is dependent in turn on our willingness to meet our commitments to them."

Kennedy followed his alarming words with even more alarming actions. He announced a request for $3.25 billion more in defense funds, for large increases in the armed forces, for a doubling, then tripling, of the draft, and for authority to call up 150,000 reservists. Most appalling of all was Kennedy's announcement of an enlarged civil-defense program:

"Tomorrow, I am requesting of the Congress new funds for the following immediate objectives: to identify and mark space in existing structures—public and private—that could be used for fallout shelters in case of attack; to stock these shelters with food, water, first-aid kits and other minimum essentials for survival; to increase their capacity; to improve our air-raid warning and failout detection systems, including a new household warning system which is now under development; and to take other measures that will be effective at an early date to save millions of lives if needed. In the event of an attack, the lives of those families which are not hit in a nuclear blast and fire can still be saved—*if* they can be warned to take shelter and *if* that shelter is available. We owe that kind of assurance to our families—and to our country. In contrast to our friends in Europe, the need for this kind of protection is new to our shores. But the time to start is now. In the coming months, I hope to let every citizen know what steps he can take without delay to protect his family in case of attack. I know that you will want me to do no less."

The dread of nuclear war rose in the United States and over much of Europe. Yet this dread was almost entirely caused by John F. Kennedy. As Walton points out, "For whatever reason, he had chosen to alarm the nation in a speech that was moralistic, specious, and jingoistic. *It had absolutely no basis in fact.* No assessment of Kennedy as President and man can ignore that speech and what resulted from it." (Walton's italics.) Kennedy's private remarks were equally irrational. He told James Wechsler of the *New York Post* that "If Khrushchev wants to rub my nose in the dirt, it's all over." But Khrushchev was doing no such thing. He was not threatening war, but only asking for negotiations. On August 7, in the midst of Washington's war hysteria, the Soviet Premier said on television, "We do not intend to infringe upon any lawful interests of the Western powers. Barring of access to Berlin, blockade of West Berlin, is entirely out of the question."

While Khrushchev pondered how to normalize Berlin, Kennedy pondered the approach of nuclear war. As Hugh Sidey later wrote, "It had been Bob who sat one night late in the White House with his brother and talked about Berlin. The two Kennedys had discussed all the details, all the possibilities. John Kennedy had been more somber than ever. All his days had been spent planning the steps up to and into nuclear war, should it be required of this country. On that night as they talked, there was the eerie realization that war could be the product of a whim, a misunderstanding, a human mistake." This atmosphere of nightmarish insanity would be repeated, as we will see, in the next Kennedy confrontation, the Cuban missile crisis.

Fortunately for world peace, the Russians were thinking in more realistic terms. On August 13, the Soviets stopped the flood of refugees by swiftly building the Berlin Wall. Although the West reacted with shock, the move actually contributed to the deflation of crisis emotions, for the Russians had partially solved their own localized crisis. Kennedy sent 1,500 American troops and Vice President Johnson to show the flag in West Berlin and reassure the frightened Berliners that their protectors were steadfast. But, in effect, the status quo had been stabilized by the Wall, tragic though it was for the trapped East Germans. More reasonable minds were also gradually prevailing in Congress, the American press, and the Kennedy Administration itself. On August 21, the President told Secretary of State Rusk that the United States would invite Russia to negotiations before September, and to so inform the Allies. In mid-September, the talks began, and on October 17 Khrushchev announced that the Western powers showed signs of seeking a settlement and therefore Russia would not insist on signing a separate peace treaty in December.

The Berlin "crisis" of 1961 was over, but its repercussions continued. Despite an uneasy truce and intermittent border incidents in 1962 and 1963, the threat of direct confrontation over Berlin receded. It was, in retrospect, a confrontation basically created by Kennedy and his equally fixated coterie of dangerously obsessed—and, one must add, equally neurotic—advisers. While their neurosis had stopped short of war, the potential for war had been tragically heightened—in increased armaments and mobilization by both sides, in greater East-West tensions, in the forthcoming testing of new superbombs, and in the increase of Cold War suspicions and attitudes that could well lead to renewed crisis.

V. The Missile Crisis: Charging to the Brink

It has been widely accepted that the Cuban missile crisis was the occasion of John Kennedy's greatest triumph. I disagree. I believe that his decision to go to the brink of nuclear war was irresponsible and reckless to a supreme degree, that it risked the kind of terrible miscalculation that Kennedy was always warning Khrushchev about, that it was unnecessary, and that, if one assumes minimum competence, the Kennedy administration knew it was not necessary. I argue, in short, that Kennedy, without sufficient reason, consciously risked nuclear catastrophe, with all that implied for the people not only of the United States and Russia but of the entire world.
—Richard J. Walton, *Cold War and Counterrevolution*

The world was taken to the nuclear brink although Khrushchev was prepared to remove the missiles from Cuba if Kennedy took American missiles out of Turkey. It was an obvious solution, but one of Kennedy's biographers, Arthur Schlesinger, Jr., wrote of Kennedy's consternation when Radio Moscow broadcast the text of Khrushchev's letter. The offer was rejected, but the reason was never explained. The crisis took place just before the midterm elections, and another biographer, Theodore Sorensen, indicated that they were much in Kennedy's thoughts when he demanded what amounted almost to unconditional surrender.
—Louis Heren, *No Hail, No Farewell*

In October of 1962, in order to force Soviet missiles off the island of Cuba, John F. Kennedy risked a nuclear war that might have meant the destruction of all life on earth. . . . many have forgotten, in the flush of success and relief from danger, that Kennedy was

determined to force Khrushchev's total capitulation—no matter
the cost. . . . By all accounts, President Kennedy never considered
any course other than military confrontation. When he learned of
the missiles on the morning of October 16, his immediate reaction
was that they must be removed. From the first, he sought unconditional surrender and he never deviated from that objective. . . .
                              —Louise FitzSimons, *The Kennedy Doctrine*

The Cuban missile crisis of October 1962, of course, brought the
nation as close to an all-out nuclear war as it ever has been. Had it
broken out, Kennedy said, there would have been 80 million dead
Americans within a few hours no matter who pressed the button
first. . . . The Kennedy brothers evidently were the moderates
during the missile crisis, compared to those who were ready to
start dropping nuclear bombs without ceremony. But it is a testament to the fragile logic of a militarist era that John Kennedy could
say at the height of the crisis that if war were to break out "even the
fruits of victory would be ashes in our mouth"—and then add:
"but neither will we shrink from that risk at any time it must be
faced."
The willingness to gamble with the idea of nuclear war, even
when "victory" would simply mean "ashes," indicates a loss of
touch with reality, almost a suicidal impulse.
                              —Sidney Lens, *The Military-Industrial Complex*

Through thirteen beautiful October days in 1962, the young
President of the United States played nuclear poker with Nikita
Khrushchev and won. How close we came to Armageddon I did
not fully realize until I started researching this book.
                              —Elie Abel, *The Missile Crisis*

ℑℭ

THE OCTOBER, 1962, missile crisis has often been portrayed by the popular
press and Kennedy iconographers as JFK's finest hour; but there is good
reason to believe that in fact President Kennedy brought the United States
perilously near to a nuclear holocaust without rational need. Let us examine more closely the historical facts that support such a harsh accusation.
The general circumstances of the crisis are well known. On October 16,
1962, from U-2 photos taken on the 14th and analyzed on the 15th, Kennedy learned for the first time that the Russians had secretly installed
nuclear missiles in Cuba in the course of their military buildup of Castro's
regime. This was the first genuine evidence of such installations, which
Cuban refugees had been reporting for years (reports repeated and elab-

orated upon by Senator Kenneth Keating and others without factual
support). Kennedy was shocked and angered by Khrushchev's action, for
the Soviet Union had denied any intention of installing missiles outside of
Russia, and Khrushchev had told Kennedy he would do nothing to upset
the imminent congressional elections of November, 1962. Now, despite
these reassurances, the Russians had suddenly faced Kennedy with a dual
blow to his prestige: as leader of the Western Hemisphere and defender of
Latin America; and as Democratic leader of the party which was now certain to lose the November elections and control of Congress unless the
missiles were removed in time.

The general American public, however, nurtured on years of Cold War
rhetoric, would be led to see the Cuban missiles more starkly as a terrifying
threat to U.S. cities and a change in the nuclear balance of power. Some
observers have contended that Khrushchev's real goal in his risky gamble
was to narrow the missile gap between the United States and the Soviet
Union, a gap that Kennedy had widened in his escalation of the arms race.
While the Cuban missiles would not change the basic fact that the nuclear
giants could largely destroy each other should one or the other launch an
attack, these missiles would raise Khrushchev's international prestige, give
him a closer striking position, and ease some of the pressure in Russia's race
to catch up with America. As Sorensen pointed out, the Cuban missiles,
in themselves, did not affect the strategic balance of power "in fact,"
since the Soviet Union was capable of directing massive megatonnage at
the United States without them; but permitting the missiles to remain
would alter the balance "in appearance." And, as Kennedy later said,
"such appearances contribute to reality" in matters affecting the national
will and world leadership.

Indeed, as I. F. Stone so clearly saw, "The real stake was prestige. The
question was whether, with the whole world looking on, Kennedy would let
Khrushchev get away with it. The world's first thermonuclear confrontation
turned out to be a kind of ordeal by combat between two men to see which
one would back down first." In the Kennedy lexicon of manliness, not
being "chicken" was a primary value. The Bay of Pigs had shaken his
confidence and reputation for toughness. In the subsequent Berlin crisis, he
had overreacted to Khrushchev's demands. Now it apparently seemed to
Kennedy that Khrushchev was daring to rattle rockets directly in his face,
although U.S. rockets had faced the U.S.S.R. for years in adjacent Turkey
and in Italy. In essence, the Cuban missiles were taken as a personal
challenge to Kennedy's courage and status, since it was questionable whether they significantly altered the balance of nuclear power between the
two nations. As Defense Secretary McNamara pointed out, a few missiles
in Cuba did not matter much: "A missile is a missile. It makes no great

difference whether you are killed by a missile fired from the Soviet Union or from Cuba." America's European allies had long since learned to live next door to Soviet missiles. Thus for many Europeans, the American reaction to Cuba seemed to border on the hysterical.

Kennedy had already warned Russia (on September 14) against carrying its arming of Cuba too far: "If at any time the Communist buildup in Cuba were to endanger or interfere with our security in any way . . . or if Cuba should ever . . . become an offensive military base of significant capacity for the Soviet Union, then this country will do whatever must be done to protect our own security and that of its allies." The moment had now come for determining what action the new situation required.

Kennedy immediately summoned his top advisers for the start of what would be a thirteen-day series of continuous daily meetings to determine policy. The main participants included Rusk, McNamara, the new CIA Director John McCone, Robert Kennedy, Maxwell Taylor, Under Secretary of State George Ball, Deputy Defense Secretary Roswell Gilpatric, White House aides McGeorge Bundy and Theodore Sorensen, and, from time to time, others such as Dean Acheson and Adlai Stevenson. Alternatives were explored and reexplored, and each participant found his first position shifting as he realized the complexities, advantages, and disadvantages of each possible action. The over-all options were to do nothing, take diplomatic action, destroy the missiles in an air strike, or follow some combination of diplomatic and military action. Meanwhile U.S. forces were ordered to prepare for possible action in a week, and U-2 surveillance of Cuba was stepped up. The President and his officials continued to fulfill their normal round of duties and meet in extreme secrecy so that the outside world would not yet suspect their discovery.

In a key passage in *Kennedy*, Theodore Sorensen has revealed Kennedy's state of mind at the time and, inadvertently, supports my contention that JFK's emotional needs rather than the security needs of the nation underlay the decision to force Khrushchev into a public showdown. Sorensen, unlike Schlesinger an actual participant in the debates, notes that two options were available: to do nothing in the first instance, or to restrict the American response to diplomatic action, in the second. Some Pentagon officials reminded Kennedy that Americans had learned to live within range of Soviet missiles, that we expected Khrushchev had resigned himself to living with ours nearby, and that if we did not get excited about the Cuban missiles, Khrushchev would be prevented from inflating their importance. The second option was considered again and again as the risks of other courses of action became apparent. At the crucial Thursday night meeting, a regular member of the group advocated it as a preferable alternative to a blockade. But, Sorensen adds, *"the President had rejected this course from the outset."* (Italics added.)

According to Sorensen, the military implications of the missiles bothered Kennedy less than the effect on the global political balance. Missiles in the Western Hemisphere, with their psychological and political effect on Latin America, were very different from missiles on Soviet territory, and history showed that Russian intentions toward smaller countries differed from our own. If we accepted this move in Cuba, more would follow. And Kennedy's pledges of action, only a month before, had called this move unacceptable. Though Kennedy wanted to combine diplomatic maneuvers with military action, he was not going to permit debate and equivocation to continue while the missiles were made operational.

There is a great deal of untrue assumption in this fine smokescreening. From the point of view of many Latin American people—as separate from their often repressive and exploitative governments—Soviet missiles on Cuban soil might be welcomed as cutting the American giant down to size; and the history of American intentions in Latin America seemed to many as suspect as Soviet intentions elsewhere. More important in the immediate situation, Kennedy had earlier said that if Cuba became an offensive military base, the United States would do "whatever must be done to protect its own security and that of its allies"; the nature of such action— which could be limited to diplomacy—had not been defined. Whether or not the missiles were operational was largely irrelevant to the confrontation: the nuclear superpowers, with or without the Cuban missiles, still faced each other with the potential of enormous destruction.

While Kennedy did indeed feel an urgency of time, this pressure was more political than military. Neither Sorensen nor Schlesinger directly mentions the domestic American political context within which the missile crisis occurred, but Roger Hilsman is less circumspect. Although Hilsman, then head of State Department intelligence, fully supports the Kennedy Administration position (in his 1967 book, *To Move a Nation*), he admits the importance of domestic political pressures: "The fact of the matter was that President Kennedy and his administration were peculiarly vulnerable on Cuba. He had used it in his own campaign against Nixon to great effect, asking over and over why a Communist regime had been permitted to come to power just ninety miles off our coast. Then came the Bay of Pigs, and now the Soviets were turning Cuba into an offensive military base." In October, 1962, as Hilsman guilelessly says, while "the United States might not be in mortal danger . . . the administration most certainly was."

I. F. Stone states the case more explicitly: "There might have been dispute as to whether those missiles in Cuba really represented any change in the balance of terror, any substantial new threat to the United States. There could have been no dispute that to face the November elections with these missiles intact would have been disastrous for Kennedy and the

Democrats. . . . The election was only three weeks off when the presence of nuclear missiles on the island was confirmed. . . . There was no time for prolonged negotiations, summit conferences, or UN debates if the damage was to be undone before the election." Politically, "Kennedy could not wait. But the country and the world could. Negotiations, however prolonged, would have been better than the risk of World War III. This is how the survivors would have felt. Here Kennedy's political interests and the country's safety diverged."

A conversation related by Robert Kennedy in *Thirteen Days* strikingly indicates the deep insecurities of the two brothers. At the height of the crisis President Kennedy said to his brother, "It looks really mean, doesn't it? But then, really there was no other choice. If they get this mean on this one in our part of the world, what will they do on the next?" Bobby replied, "I just don't think there was any choice . . . and not only that, if you hadn't acted, you would have been impeached." According to Bobby, "The President thought for a moment and said, 'That's what I think — I would have been impeached.' " That such an incredible idea as impeachment crossed the minds of the Kennedy brothers strongly suggests the ramifications of their inward guilts and anxieties. Better to risk annihilation, they seemed to feel, than the threat of personal punishment and shame.

There are two specific aspects of the missile crisis which strongly support the view that Kennedy's unconscious emotional drives and his conscious political needs took precedence over his country's safety. The first is his refusal to trade the American missiles in Turkey and Italy for the Soviet Cuban missiles. The second is the unnecessary—and extremely dangerous— time limit Kennedy set on Soviet acquiescence. Although the Kennedy brothers did reject the idea of an air strike, which was repeatedly advanced by their military-minded advisers, and Robert Kennedy spoke out persuasively against the morality of a surprise attack, the Kennedys' caution and moderation did not hold up in the final analysis. Let us consider these two essential aspects in some detail.

Even from the first discussions, one obvious solution was to trade the American missiles in Turkey for the Russian missiles in Cuba. Such a move, however, would not have portrayed Kennedy in a heroic light, but could have been presented by his critics as an American "surrender." Kennedy's realization that his image would suffer (although his country might be saved from a thermonuclear war) is suggested by his anger, rather than his relief, at learning that the missiles in Turkey and Italy had not yet been removed, despite his explicit orders to do so earlier in the year. The ironic fact is that these missiles were, in Hilsman's words, "obsolete, unreliable, inaccurate, and very vulnerable—they could be knocked out by a sniper with a rifle and telescopic sights." Kennedy had wisely seen their existence as unnecessarily provocative and had ordered them removed in August. But bureaucracy moves slowly, and in October the missiles were still in place. The fact that Kennedy could have traded these militarily worthless missiles—which he wanted removed anyway—for the provocative Soviet missiles in Cuba, but refused to consider such a quid pro quo, is a strong indication of his profound emotional insecurity and confusion. The Russians themselves, under pressure of the subsequent blockade, proposed exactly such a swap (on October 21); but, again, Kennedy refused to listen. His personal needs demanded a Russian surrender, not an exchange of missiles that would look like a mutual compromise (though in fact it was not).

The second critical decision came in the final days of the crisis. On October 22, Kennedy had publicly announced the discovery of the Soviet missiles, demanded their removal, and inaugurated a "quarantine" (actually a blockade, in international law an act of war) around Cuba to intercept future missiles. The imposition of this blockade, although risky, was skillfully managed by Kennedy and his aides, with gradually increasing degrees of pressure rather than immediate general force. Moscow, in turn, reacted cautiously in deed, if not in denunciation. The showdown came on October 26 and 27. The U.S. Navy had prevented further imports, but work on the still nonoperational missiles in Cuba was nearing completion. Unless this work stopped, Kennedy felt that he would soon have to take more definite action. As Hilsman phrased it, the message was communicated to the Soviets "that the United States could hold off its next step for no more than one or two days."

Signals now came from Moscow—both indirectly and directly—that the Soviets wanted to negotiate. While an informal source (a Russian Embassy official) indicated a willingness to trade the missiles for a noninvasion promise, a letter from Khrushchev to Kennedy strongly indicated the need for agreement, although this letter made no specific proposals. Kennedy and his advisers decided that an immediate halt of work on the missiles must precede any negotiations.

Then, as they met on Saturday morning (the 27th) in an optimistic mood, a new Soviet note broadcast from Moscow offered to trade the missiles for the American missiles in Turkey. The earlier apparent Russian proposal to trade the missiles merely for a pledge not to invade Cuba was entirely unofficial and was actually communicated to the Kennedy Administration via a television newsman. The reaction of Kennedy's men to this dashing of their hopes of a total Russian capitulation is indicated by Hilsman's statement that "If the Soviets were bargaining, it was a highly dangerous form . . . an actual invasion of Cuba might be no later than forty-eight hours away."

Robert Kennedy now suggested that the Americans ignore the latest

Soviet note and reply only to the indirect proposals. President Kennedy therefore sent a message to Moscow stating that if work on the missiles were halted at once, they could then proceed to negotiate for removal of the missiles in return for a noninvasion pledge. There was no mention of the American missiles in Turkey. This suggestion by Robert Kennedy has been presented to the American public (in his own book, *Thirteen Days*, and the books of the Kennedy in-house historians) as a brilliant diplomatic move. What is generally overlooked is the ultimatum that accompanied this proposal. As Hilsman put it, "The President then personally dispatched Robert Kennedy to make crystal clear to Dobrynin [the Russian Ambassador] the full sense of urgency and seriousness felt in Washington, the fact that the United States would wait no longer but would have to proceed toward an agreement and peace if the missiles were withdrawn or toward 'strong and overwhelming retaliatory action.' What the United States could not do, the Attorney General made clear, was remain any longer on dead center."

"Strong and overwhelming retaliatory action" could mean no less than an attack on the missile sites, probably accompanied by an invasion of Cuba (which the Joint Chiefs had said was necessary to remove all the missiles). This, in turn, could easily force Russia into retaliatory action and thus trigger World War III. In effect, the Kennedy brothers were rattling their own nuclear rockets directly in the face of Khrushchev. This direct threat was omitted from the public version, which was released at the time of transmission to Moscow and stated that "The continuation of this threat . . . would surely lead to an intensification of the Cuban crisis and a grave risk to the peace of the world." But as Sorensen, like Hilsman, wrote, Robert Kennedy delivered this letter "with a strong verbal message: The point of escalation was at hand; the United States could proceed toward peace and disarmament, or, as the Attorney General later described it, we could take 'strong and overwhelming retaliatory action' . . . unless the President received immediate notice that the missiles would be withdrawn."

As we now know—since we are alive to write and read this—Khrushchev had the sense to back down. Capitulation came almost immediately, at nine o'clock the next morning, October 28. Had Khrushchev not done so, there might well have been no later historians either to exalt Kennedy, or, as this historian is attempting to do, to record the perilous path of the "Kennedy neurosis." Just how virulent that neurosis was is suggested by Robert Kennedy's later comment, recorded by Schlesinger, after Bobby had delivered the ultimatum with a twenty-four-hour deadline: "We all agreed in the end that if the Russians were ready to go to nuclear war over Cuba, they were ready to go to nuclear war, and that was that. So we might as well have the showdown then as six months later." The truth seemed to be that the Kennedys, not the Russians, were ready to go to nuclear war over Cuba. As the President himself commented after he had sent Khrushchev his ultimatum, "Now it can go either way." Also according to Schlesinger, JFK said a few weeks later, "If we had invaded Cuba . . . I am sure the Soviets would have acted. They would have to, just as we would have to. I think there are certain compulsions on any major power." The compulsions, however, in light of the psychohistorical evidence, were more within the leaders than upon their nations.

Kennedy himself seems to have sensed the frightful possible consequences of his nuclear adventure. In a more clearheaded mood that suggests a latent sense of guilt, Kennedy gave a speech on June 10, 1963, calling for greater international understanding: "And above all, while defending our own vital interests, nuclear powers must avert those confrontations which bring an adversary to a choice of either a humiliating retreat or a nuclear war. To adopt that kind of course in the nuclear age would be evidence only of the bankruptcy of our policy—or of a collective death-wish for the world." Yet Kennedy had already forced Khrushchev into just such a "humiliating retreat," with only the merest sop to save face (Kennedy's pledge not to invade Cuba).

JFK's subsequent intellectual realization of the mortal perils of nuclear brinkmanship was no guarantee that his emotional immaturities would not again lead him to risk national annihilation in the testing of his personal courage and resolve. Louise FitzSimons has clearly expressed the basic political meaning of Kennedy's mistaken insistence on removal of the missiles at all costs: "The only conceivable time when national leadership can be justified in risking a nuclear holocaust is in the face of an immediate and overwhelming threat to the very existence of the nation. Even then, a strong argument can be made by those who believe that such a risk is never justified. . . . If all other threats are less than mortal, then the means to counter them must be primarily political; they should be removed by negotiation. This is not to say that one need immediately make concessions. But the primary emphasis should be on willingness to talk rather than insistence on unconditional surrender of the enemy."

A psychohistorian must ask the further question of why a particular President should insist on unconditional surrender, and why he staged this surrender for the utmost dramatic effect in the eyes of the world at whatever hazard to his own nation and the future of the human race. While political scientists differ in their opinions of why Khrushchev put missiles into Cuba, they agree that Kennedy saw the move mostly as a challenge to his prestige. In effect, a Kennedy was being called "too soft to fight." We must recall

Kennedy's earlier revealing interview with *New York Post* editor James
Wechsler. According to Arthur Schlesinger:

". . . What worried him was that Khrushchev might interpret his reluctance to wage nuclear war as a symptom of an American loss of nerve. Some
day, he said, the time might come when he would have to run the supreme
risk to convince Khrushchev that conciliation did not mean humiliation.
'If Khrushchev wants to rub my nose in the dirt,' he told Wechsler, 'it's
all over.' But how to convince Khrushchev short of a showdown? 'That
son of a bitch won't pay any attention to words,' the President said bitterly
on another occasion. 'He has to see you move.' "

Fortunately for us all, Khrushchev was not so imbued with the neuroticism of Kennedy's *machismo*, and suffered humiliation rather than wreak
destruction. We are left to wonder, had their roles been reversed, whether
Kennedy would have done the same.

VI. Vietnam: The Lost Crusade

The Pentagon's study of the Vietnam war concludes that President John F. Kennedy transformed the "limited-risk gamble"
of the Eisenhower Administration into a "broad commitment" to
prevent Communist domination of South Vietnam.

Although Mr. Kennedy resisted pressures for putting American
ground-combat units into South Vietnam, the Pentagon analysts
say, he took a series of actions that significantly expanded the
American military and political involvement in Vietnam but
nonetheless left President Lyndon B. Johnson with as bad a situation as Mr. Kennedy inherited.

"The dilemma of the U.S. involvement dating from the Kennedy
era," the Pentagon study observes, was to use "only limited means
to achieve excessive ends."

Moreover, according to the study, prepared in 1967–68 by
Government analysts, the Kennedy tactics deepened the American
involvement in Vietnam piecemeal, with each step minimizing
public recognition that the American role was growing.

> —Hedrick Smith, "The Kennedy Years: 1961–1963,"
> in *The Pentagon Papers*

Characteristically, the world at large believes that if J.F.K. were
alive there would be no war in Vietnam. The mythmakers have
obscured the fact that it was J.F.K. who began our active participation in the war when, in 1961, he added to the six hundred
American observers the first of a gradual buildup of American
troops, which reached twenty thousand at the time of his assassination. And there is no evidence that he would not have persisted

in that war for, as he said to a friend shortly before he died, "I have to go all the way with this one." He could not suffer a second Cuba and hope to maintain the appearance of Defender of the Free World at the ballot box in 1964.

—Gore Vidal, "The Holy Family," *Esquire*

As early as 1956 John F. Kennedy declared that "Vietnam represents the cornerstone of the free world in Southeast Asia, the keystone to the arch, the finger in the dike." It was Kennedy who first sent troops to Vietnam, who was infatuated with counter-insurgency and wanted to prove that "wars of national liberation" could be defeated by his Green Berets, and who in July, 1963, declared, "We are not going to withdraw. . . for us to withdraw . . . would mean a collapse not only of South Vietnam but Southeast Asia."

Cooper is right in pointing out that Lyndon Johnson inherited "more than 'the dirty little war' in Vietnam. He inherited Kennedy's principal advisers on foreign affairs. . . . "

But it is idle to assume that Kennedy, confronted as Johnson was with the imminent collapse of the Saigon regime, would have behaved differently. They were both soldiers in what Cooper calls the "American crusade to save the world from Communism," and they both believed that American power had to be used to prevent the postwar ideological boundaries from shifting—even in areas where no threat to American security could be discerned. They were guardians of an informal empire of dependencies and client states.

—Ronald Steel, reviewing *The Lost Crusade* by Chester L. Cooper
New York Times Book Review

Kennedy assumed that the war was going well in 1961 and 1962, but at the end of 1962, in a conversation with Roswell Gilpatric, he talked in a restless and impatient way about how the U.S. had been sucked into Vietnam little by little. By the autumn of 1963 he seemed sick of it, and frequently asked how to be rid of the commitment. . . . But he also knew that he could not get out of Vietnam before the elections in November, 1964, without inviting his own political eclipse. In a way, the Green Beret that lies on his grave in Arlington Cemetery is the symbol not only of individual heroism but also of a major miscalculation in war and politics.

—Henry Brandon, *Anatomy of Error*

ᕙᕗ

KENNEDY'S REACTIONS AND policies toward the complex situations in the Southeast Asian countries of Laos and South Vietnam demonstrate two major attitudes, both of which rested on historical and psychological fallacies. The first was Kennedy's belief in the essential Eisenhower-Dulles definition of the Cold War as a struggle between the "Free World" and the "non-Free World," or the good guys and the bad guys. The second was Kennedy's own need to be a strong man and the hero-leader of the Free World. Neither concept, of course, was presented in such crude terms. But if one looks closely behind the appealing rhetoric in which Kennedy typically clothed his attitudes, these two basic lines of approach remained quite unmistakable for at least the first two years of his not-quite three-year term in office. Only toward mid-1963, with his June, 1963, speech on foreign policy at American University, did Kennedy demonstrate a far more realistic grasp of international and moral complexities and the need for American restraint rather than moralistic "big-stick" waving.

Yet even then, Kennedy's continuation of the South Vietnam intervention, which was to lead directly into Johnson's disastrous widening of that war, casts serious doubt on Kennedy's actual ability, despite his intellectual insights, to change the negative directions of his basic approach. (The American speed-up of the arms race cast further doubt, as we have seen.) In effect, the signs were that the Free World and Great Hero mystiques were still guiding Kennedy's preponderant behavior, although he would probably not have repeated the initial display of raw power in Cuba. Yet the evidence strongly suggests, despite posthumous disclaimers by Kennedy's staff, that JFK would have continued a gradual escalation of the Vietnam war. He would probably have proceeded far more cautiously than Johnson, however, who saw Vietnam as his own personal chance to become an Alamo-like hero in the full American mythic tradition (ignoring the lesson learned by Kennedy in April, 1961). I will now examine in somewhat more detail the two major areas of Southeast Asian conflict in which Kennedy pursued his twin and closely-related desires for meaningful East-West confrontations and an affirmation of himself as a Wilsonian-type hero.

When Kennedy became President in January, 1961, America's direct involvement in Vietnam was six years old and its indirect involvement went back another decade. During World War II, President Roosevelt's Atlantic Charter had declared the principle of self-determination for all peoples, and Ho Chi Minh's nationalists had cooperated with the American OSS against Japanese forces in Indochina. But after the war, President Truman began underwriting the return of French imperialism in Southeast Asia by economic and military aid to the French. In this antidemocratic policy, Truman and his Secretary of State, Dean Acheson, were guided by their primary desire to strengthen France as a bulwark in Europe against Russian expansion and by their Cold War policy of containing communism in all areas. The French army, aided by a British commander's trickery, reasserted their control over Vietnam, and Ho Chi Minh and his supporters retreated into a protracted guerrilla war.

President Eisenhower continued and increased Truman's support of the French, until the United States was largely subsidizing the first Vietnam war, which lasted from 1946 to 1954 and cost America some $2 billion. In May, 1954, the Communist-led Vietminh defeated a large French force at Dienbienphu. Eisenhower refused to intervene without British backing, despite the urgings of Secretary of State John Foster Dulles, Vice President Nixon, and Admiral Radford. Paradoxically, Senators Kennedy and Johnson supported Eisenhower's decision. Kennedy stated at the time, "I am frankly of the belief that no amount of American military assistance in Indo-China can conquer . . . 'an enemy of the people' which has the sympathy and covert support of the people. . . . For the United States to intervene unilaterally and to send troops into the most difficult terrain in the world, with the Chinese able to pour in unlimited manpower, would mean that we would face a situation which would be far more difficult than even that we encountered in Korea." Yet seven years later, Kennedy himself opened the door to such a disastrous policy.

The French liquidated their immensely costly war by the Geneva Treaty of 1954 (which the United States verbally supported). A temporary line was drawn between North and South Vietnam until elections could be held in 1956. Meanwhile, the United States brought in a caretaker government for the South headed by Ngo Dinh Diem, a Catholic nationalist living in America. Soon American support of Diem hardened into a firm policy, and Diem—contrary to the Geneva Treaty—refused to hold elections to unify the country in 1956 (elections in which, Eisenhower commented, 80 percent of the votes might have gone to the country's most venerated patriot, albeit a Communist, Ho Chi Minh). President Diem proved unexpectedly forceful in suppressing all political opposition as, with American aid, he built up his own internal police and military forces. Although Eisenhower had made American assistance conditional on South Vietnam's democratic performance, this condition was never enforced. As Diem's regime grew increasingly dictatorial and repressive, American help continued to bail him out of intermittent crises. Thus it was actually the United States which created and maintained the government of South Vietnam in direct violation of the Geneva Treaty. Meanwhile Ho Chi Minh consolidated his equally harsh Northern rule and armed to defend himself and regain the Southern half of Vietnam.

South Vietnamese resistance to the oppressive Diem and his ruling family gradually developed into the Communist-led Vietcong, who little by little seized control of the countryside from Diem's corrupt administrators and army "warlords." It is an American myth that North Vietnam first invaded

South Vietnam to overthrow Diem. There was no initial "external aggression" and no infiltration from the North for the first few years. According to U.S. government figures, the North had contributed only some 56,000 soldiers out of a total of 415,000 to 445,000 Vietcong troops as of late 1965. The Pentagon has confirmed that as of late 1964, when the Johnson Administration was considering a major intervention, there were only 400 North Vietnamese troops in the South. The "aggression" charge was based on the infiltration of Hanoi-trained guerrillas—most of them Southerners— and the charge that Hanoi was directing the war. But only after President Johnson's massive increase in American soldiers did North Vietnamese regulars come South in considerable numbers. The truth is that the Vietcong was largely formed of Southern patriots, both Communist and non-Communist, who saw the Americans as invaders of their artificially split country. From Truman to Nixon, the overriding existence of unquenchable Vietnamese nationalism has been the driving force behind what is in reality a combined civil and anticolonial war. This truth has been hidden from the American people until recently by the Cold War rhetoric of all five post-World War II U.S. Administrations, whose fears of Russia were translated into an obsessive fear of any sort of Communist regime anywhere in the world. It is also false to view the Vietnam war as a Chinese-instigated rebellion. All Vietnamese have an ancient mistrust and fear of China, their hereditary foe. The acceptance of both Chinese and Russian aid was forced on North Vietnam by necessity, not by design. Ho's nationalism, in the view of many Asian authorities, always took precedence over his communism.

Jack Kennedy, who was a son of the war against Hitler and came to national prominence at the peak of Cold War hysteria (as exemplified by his family's friend, Senator Joseph McCarthy), saw the world in simplistic patterns basically similar to those perceived by Presidents Truman and Eisenhower. Kennedy's Secretary of State, Dean Rusk, while devoid of the overt missionary personality of his predecessor, John Foster Dulles, was equally convinced of America's righteousness and its duty to lead the world. As former Air Force Under Secretary Townsend Hoopes recently wrote about Rusk in *The Limits of Intervention*, "Of the close advisers on Vietnam, Dean Rusk seemed the very embodiment of the embattled Cold Warrior, with convictions rooted in the Stalinist period." British journalist Henry Brandon described Rusk as "an extraordinarily tolerant man, except on Vietnam. This was his field of honor, and on it he staked all he had. It was his passion to the extent of being an affliction. It was to him the supreme test of the American will."

In Kennedy's first months in office, the Asian situation was complicated by the internal struggle in Laos (formerly part of French Indochina), where the Communist-led guerrillas under Prince Souphanouvong had seized the eastern half of the country by early 1961. Under Eisenhower, the CIA had clumsily imported a conservative Lao army officer, Phoumi Nosavan (against the State Department's candidate!), which resulted in a coup to restore neutralist Prince Souvanna Phouma. Phoumi, armed by the United States, marched on the capital and overthrew Souvanna Phouma's government. When Kennedy entered the presidency, the United States had already recognized and backed one Lao government (the conservatives), the Soviet Union had recognized and backed the neutralist, Communist-supported government led by Souvanna Phouma, and a civil war raged in much of Laos. In violation of the 1954 Geneva agreement, Eisenhower sent Phoumi a few advisers and planes in January, 1961. But the combined neutralist and Communist Lao armies were far more effective, and by February, 1961, they were threatening the capital of Laos. Kennedy's brand-new Administration held agonizing meetings over alternative American actions, including air-dropping U.S. marines (an idea Kennedy wisely killed). The Joint Chiefs were reluctant about a limited intervention, and forces were lacking for a large effort without denuding Europe, where the Berlin crisis threatened.

Kennedy, seeking a political solution, held a press conference on March 23 in which he warned that if "armed attacks by externally supported Communists" did not stop, then "those who support a truly neutral Laos will have to consider their response." This statement, of course, ignored the fact that externally supported conservatives had been attacking the Lao neutralists. To back up his veiled military threat, JFK, at the urging of Walt Rostow, sent marines into neighboring Thailand, where the United States had bases, and the Seventh Fleet into the China Sea. Troops were alerted to carry out Kennedy's warning if necessary, but no aggressive moves were made, and the President enlisted British and Indian support for a cease-fire as a precondition for negotiations. Kennedy was condemned by American conservatives for now supporting a coalition government headed by Souvanna Phouma that would include Communists; yet few Americans wanted to commit U.S. troops. The Russians, heavily committed elsewhere, did not wish to engage in war over tiny, though strategic, Laos, which they believed would ultimately go Communist anyway. In early May, the cease-fire was agreed upon, and a new Geneva conference opened on May 16, 1961. Kennedy had shown far greater restraint in distant Laos than in nearby Cuba—influenced, as he himself admitted to Sorensen, by the Bay of Pigs fiasco. Intermittent fighting continued in Laos as the negotiators met, but the two superpowers held to their positions that they did not wish war over Laos.

The neutralist, Communist, and conservative Lao factions continued to bicker into the fall of 1961, with conservative Phoumi refusing to compromise. Finally, at the urging of Averell Harriman (in many ways the most able of Kennedy's advisers), payments to the conservatives were stopped. An uneasy truce was at last reached, but only after intermittent crises and limited Communist attacks. Inevitably, in view of the U.S. policy toward containing communism in Southeast Asia, Laos has been drawn deeper and deeper into the Vietnam maelstrom. CIA operatives and mufti-clad Pentagon advisers continued to work behind the scenes in the secret war that today goes on in Laos. Johnson's bombing of North Vietnam in 1965 was soon followed by continual heavy bombing raids on the supply routes which cross Laos to South Vietnam. Soon villages and populated areas were added and the bombing of Laos has increased under the Nixon Administration. To the peaceful Lao people, these cruel American depredations must seem as senseless as the Communist intrusions, as each side seeks to "contain" the other in regional wars that are essentially struggles between different kinds of nationalists. The Laos dispute had not been settled in 1961, but merely postponed.

While Kennedy wrestled with Laos, he was also digesting the new counterinsurgency doctrine being developed by such enthusiasts as General Maxwell Taylor, Kennedy's special military adviser and later JCS chairman, and ex-OSS agent Roger Hilsman, director of State Department Intelligence and subsequently Assistant Secretary of State for Far Eastern Affairs. Robert Kennedy was also an early convert to the idea of fighting guerrillas with guerrilla techniques. Although this doctrine theoretically has much to commend it, the American counterinsurgency idea has rested on one basic and fatal flaw: a superficial understanding of the absolute necessity of popular support in the country where operations are carried out. In Vietnam, the Vietcong retained wide popular support, as evidenced by their long-range success against overwhelming forces. The American Green Berets were not only white aliens, but were supporting oppressive regimes which exploited the Vietnamese peasants rather than aided them. The lack of American insistence upon real reforms in the South Vietnam government doomed the counterinsurgency effort from the start.

But back in 1961, the new antiguerrilla warfare struck the Kennedy brothers as something bold, bright, tough, and practical, "a whole new kind of strategy," as JFK called it in June, 1962. It appealed to their love of the heroic as well as their desire for immediate action. As Stanley Karnow, a veteran reporter of the Vietnam war, recollected a decade later, "The name of the game was 'counterinsurgency,' and it captured the imagination of the Kennedy administration. Suspicious of the Pentagon, which was still clinging to the 'massive retaliation' doctrine of the Eisenhower era, the Kennedyites believed that they could spawn a new breed of American soldier capable of coping with 'brushfire wars.' Hence the fanfare that heralded the 'Green Berets,' those romantic figures destined to use Communist tactics against the Communists in jungle conflicts from Laos to Venezuela." Yet the counterguerrilla Special Forces created by Kennedy remained a small part of the Vietnam war, because the conservative Pentagon leadership believed mainly in conventional warfare. But this does not lessen the probability that in the long run the effect of the Green Berets would have been marginal even if the military hierarchy had been as enthusiastic about them as the Administration. For the problem in Vietnam, as Kennedy sometimes saw but failed to act on decisively, was political, not military. And the basic political problem was South Vietnam's President. Ngo Dinh Diem was a mandarin-type autocratic ruler who did not believe in democracy or popular self-government and actually destroyed (in 1956) the grass-roots democracy that had tradtiionally existed in the villages. Diem and his half-lunatic brother, Ngo Dinh Nhu, together with Nhu's fanatical wife, in time came to be as repressive as any Communist regime in their cruel efforts to destroy all opposition.

As David Halberstam, who won a Pulitzer Prize for his Vietnam reporting, wrote of Diem's regime, "Eventually South Vietnam became, for all intents and purposes, a Communist-type country without Communism. It had all the controls, all the oppressions and all the frustrating, grim aspects of the modern totalitarian state—without the dynamism, efficiency and motivation that Communism had brought to the North. It was a police state, but it was unique in that its priorities were so haphazard; as a result, it was hopelessly inefficient."

Senator Ernest Gruening summarized Kennedy's failure to understand Vietnamese realities in *Vietnam Folly:* "The Kennedy Administration's view of the situation in Vietnam apparently was that nothing had changed there since 1950. It was as though nothing had happened in the intervening years except the banishment of the communist Ho Chi Minh north of the 17th parallel. The broken pledge of holding reunification elections in all of Vietnam in 1956 was forgotten. The repressive measures of Diem against his own people were overlooked. Just as the strong nationalist motivation of the Vietnamese people was discounted when the United States went to the aid of France in 1950 so, in 1961, the resistance of the South Vietnamese to the oppressions of Diem was laid at the doorstep of Ho Chi Minh, who was being told what to do by Peking and Moscow. The facts were made to fit the theory. Those that did not fit were not mentioned."

Arthur Schlesinger, Jr., later came to see this same fatal flaw in the Kennedy policy. In *The Bitter Heritage: Vietnam and American Democracy, 1941–1966*, Schlesinger wrote, "Kennedy, who had long believed that the main communist reliance in the coming period would be on neither nuclear

nor conventional but guerrilla war, saw the answer to the Viet Cong in-
surgency in counterinsurgency. . . . Guerrilla warfare, he well understood,
was essentially political warfare. Effective counter-insurgency, for example,
depended on swift and accurate intelligence from the countryside. The
Viet Cong could never be defeated unless the Saigon regime could enlist the
support of the peasants. . . .

"The first effort of the Kennedy years was to persuade the Diem regime
to move along these lines. Success in this effort would have been unlikely in
any case, given Diem's conviction that the Americans were impatient,
naive and childlike, to be humored but never to be heeded. And it became
all the more unlikely when the senior American diplomatic and military
officials in Saigon decided that Diem was the key to stability and that the
only policy was to win Diem's confidence by assuring him of Washington's
unconditional support."

In his first weeks in office, Kennedy created a task force of experts from
State, Defense, CIA, USIA, and his White House staff to recommend policy
on Vietnam. In late April and early May, 1961, he considered the recommendations, which called for a commitment of American combat troops.
Burned by the Bay of Pigs, Kennedy demanded more alternatives. In
May, Vice President Johnson (accompanied by Jean Kennedy Smith and
her husband) visited Saigon and urged a major buildup of Vietnam, including American advisers but no troops. An American economic mission
followed, but the situation in Vietnam continued to deteriorate. By September, 1961, the Vietcong were plainly winning the war.

Early in October, Kennedy sent General Maxwell Taylor and Walt
Rostow on a fact-finding mission to Saigon. This mission was to prove
crucial to Kennedy's decision to back a largely military approach to the
Vietnam problem. Both Taylor and Rostow were hard-line militarists and
staunch supporters of counterinsurgency. The mission included no counter-
vailing State Department official, for, according to Schlesinger, "It expressed a conscious decision by the Secretary of State to turn the Vietnam
problem over to the Secretary of Defense. Rusk doubtless decided to do this
because the military aspects seemed to him the most urgent, and Kennedy
doubtless acquiesced because he had more confidence in McNamara and
Taylor than in State." Thus from the very beginning the Administration's
outlook on Vietnam was heavily weighted by military rather than political
thinking. This was the point of view which would lead America constantly
deeper into the Vietnam quagmire.

While Kennedy was attracted by the subsequent Taylor-Rostow recommendation of American advisers to stiffen the Vietnam army, he cautiously
held off any direct military commitment. He also asked for the opinion of
his Ambassador to India, John Kenneth Galbraith, who reported that

Ngo Dinh Diem was totally ineffectual and the war would be lost unless he were removed. In the Taylor-Rostow view, the crisis was military; in Galbraith's view, it was political. The military view was backed up by the American ambassador, Frederick Nolting, and the U.S. military commander in Vietnam, General Paul Harkins, who "saw Diem as the key to success." Thus, "reposing particular confidence in McNamara and Taylor, Kennedy prepared to go ahead."

As with so many of his actions, Kennedy tried to take the easy way out by emphasizing the concrete, material aspects of the problem (more guns, helicopters, advisers) but without committing himself entirely in one direction. Sorensen, one of his closet aides, has written that Kennedy never actually made a final decision against sending troops, and in a typical Kennedy ploy, maneuvered so that it would be difficult for any of the pro-interventionists to accuse him of weakness. He instructed the service departments to be ready for the introduction of combat troops if needed, and he expanded the military assistance mission gradually. By dispatching combat support units, air combat and helicopter teams, more military advisers and instructors, and 600 Green Berets to train and lead the South Vietnamese in antiguerrilla tactics, the American involvement grew from 2,000 men at the end of 1961 to 15,500 by the end of 1963.

Kennedy sealed his new policy in an exchange of letters with Diem on December 15, 1961. Though Diem shied away from needed reforms, Kennedy put no limit on the amount or duration of American support, commenting only that the assistance would not be necessary when North Vietnamese aggression ceased. He did underline the fact that the South Vietnamese would still have primary responsibility to manage the conflict, and he expressed confidence that they would retain their independence. This sophistry, so reminiscent of all Cold War pronouncements from Truman through Nixon, ignored the fact that the South Vietnamese had no genuine independence to preserve. Again, the convenient but false argument of North Vietnamese aggression as the sole cause of the war was repeated. Although Kennedy paid lip service to social reform, his repeated inability to follow through on the far more difficult and publicly unpopular aspects of problems doomed his policies to failure. In the ultimately inescapable realm of political values and human judgments, John F. Kennedy, from the evidence of his actions, was neither emotionally nor philosophically equipped to make correct long-range judgments. He felt too keenly the pressures of events as affecting his personal image far more than his nation's well-being. As Stanley Karnow mentioned in his article, "In a brilliant analysis of the American commitment to Vietnam published a couple of years ago, James C. Thomson, Jr., a onetime White House aide, contended that the Bay of Pigs fiasco, Khrushchev's truculence at Vienna and the Berlin crisis all combined in 1961 to create an atmosphere in which President Kennedy felt compelled to demonstrate America's mettle. The arena for that demonstration was Vietnam. Accordingly Diem was our man."

Thus in 1962, America's Vietnam policy concentrated on the military effort. Although a program of social and economic reform had been developed in Washington in 1961, it was never adequately pushed in Saigon, and was soon dropped in the face of Diem's evasions and recalcitrance. Schlesinger admitted, "In place of a serious attack on the central problems of land and taxation, the regime announced a number of marginal and largely meaningless reforms to placate the Americans and did very little to put even these into effect." The result of continued government oppression and confusion was inevitable: some 15,000 Vietcong guerrillas operated in widespread hit-and-run attacks and increased their control of the villages, which 250,000 of Diem's soldiers were unable to stop.

Yet at first the large injection of U.S. military aid and advisers seemed to promise the solution to the war. The helicopters in particular had an initially devastating effect on the Vietcong. American and diplomatic officials took the decline of Vietcong activity at face value. In early 1962, McNamara went to Vietnam and announced, "Every quantitative measurement we have shows we're winning this war." Kennedy, besieged by a multitude of apparently more urgent problems, accepted the cheerful opinions of the military-minded men he trusted far more than his political doubters (such as Galbraith and Harriman). In early 1963, Kennedy announced in his State of the Union message, "The spearpoint of aggression has been blunted in South Vietnam."

The reality was quite different. Although the 1962 influx of American military equipment, helicopter pilots, and advisers had temporarily pushed back the Communist control of much of Vietnam, the Vietcong swiftly began retaliating for their military defeats by a large-scale campaign of political kidnappings and assassinations. Even more basic, President Diem's repressive rule increased, and his political support narrowed as villagers were forced into "strategic hamlets" which generally lacked both genuine self-defense and the social services that could win the farmers over to their government. In addition, Diem's distrust and fear of his own generals— fueled by an abortive November, 1960, coup and the strafing of his palace in early 1962—led him into the self-defeating policy of dividing his officers against each other. Diem's tight control of his cautious, inept military operations and the corruption of many officers further demoralized the Vietnamese army.

Diem's brother, Ngo Dinh Nhu, became increasingly powerful as his secret police arrested suspected political opponents, harassed the Buddhist majority in favor of the Catholic minority (about one million out of a population of sixteen million), suppressed the opposition press, and controlled elections. American journalists in Vietnam saw and reported these ominous developments in increasingly outspoken language, but Kennedy and his most influential advisers refused to listen to any opinions that contradicted their illusions. The President even exerted pressure (unsuccessfully) for the removal of one of the most persistent journalist gadflies, David Halberstam of *The New York Times*.

The political pressures in South Vietnam blew up in May, 1963, when Diem's soldiers fired on a Buddhist religious demonstration in Hue. Diem rigidly turned his back on any compromises or reforms, and the demonstrations spread to Saigon. In early June, a monk burned himself to death, starting a series of self-immolations which were highly effective political symbols in Vietnam. On August 21, Diem allowed Nhu to attack Saigon's Buddhist temples with Diem's own Special Forces, an act that enraged the general populace. Thousands of students joined the Buddhists in demonstrations lasting into September. Diem closed Saigon's universities and secondary schools and arrested 4,000 students, including many sons and daughters of military officers and government officials.

On September 2, President Kennedy in a television interview stated that Diem's government had "gotten out of touch with the people," and called for "changes in policy and perhaps with personnel." Kennedy also commented, "I don't think the war can be won unless the people support the effort. . . . In the final analysis, it is their war. They are the ones who have to win it or lose it. We can help them, we can give them equipment, we can send our men out there as advisers, but they have to win it, the people of Vietnam, against the Communists." And, revealingly, he added what his supporters delete: "All we can do is help, and we are making it very clear, but *I don't agree with those who say we should withdraw. That would be a mistake.*" (Italics added.) Kennedy's lack of understanding of the Vietnamese realities is also reflected in his comment that "in the last two months the government has gotten out of touch with the people." The truth was that Diem had never been *in* touch with his people and that the ostensibly democratic government Kennedy was trying to prop up was rotten at the core and as dictatorial as any Communist regime.

The time was long past for reform, but Kennedy's hopeful advisers (now joined by McNamara and newly appointed Ambassador Henry Cabot Lodge) urged pressure on Diem for political changes. Accordingly, U.S. payments for Vietnamese imports and Diem's Special Forces were suspended. Inside Kennedy's Administration, bitter disputes raged. The President was given sharply differing recommendations, ranging all the way from the military-CIA view that Diem was the only able leader available to the belief of those who felt the war could never be won with Diem in office. Diem's own generals read the American disapproval of Diem as a signal that a coup would not be blocked, and finally Kennedy gave his secret approval (as *The Pentagon Papers* revealed). On November 1, a military junta seized control in Saigon. Diem and Ngo Dinh Nhu were shot shortly after their capture.

Kennedy was shocked by this murder of the American protégé, despite his knowledge of the impending coup and Diem's deficiencies. Here again, we can see Kennedy's failure to understand or sympathize with the profound grievances of a people exploited and brutalized for many years. Diem was well educated, articulate (to the point of neurotic verbosity), personally honest, a scholar, a gentleman, and a fellow Catholic. These qualities appealed to Kennedy's social and intellectual snobbishness and seemed to keep him from realizing that great evil can be as easily committed by an aristocrat as by a rough-hewn (though upper-class) militant such as Castro, a genuinely bohemian rebel and radical intellectual. While Castro personified the heroic but threatening adventurism that attracted and frightened Kennedy, Diem appeared to be the familiar mandarin-priest figure of personal rectitude and iron authority with whom Kennedy could feel comfortable. The potential rebel and conformist struggled to some degree within John Kennedy, but the conformist inevitably prevailed. Three weeks after Diem's death, Kennedy himself was assassinated, an event that has drawn a murky veil over our ability to assess his attitudes toward Vietnam.

Before considering what Kennedy might have done had he lived, let us weigh the psychological and moral dynamics of what he actually did in Southeast Asia. Vietnam might have taught him that in some places and situations "toughness" per se was not relevant, and even highly destructive. Kennedy's toughness, like that of his successors, turned out to have disastrous components of Hemingwayesque sentimentalism in which manhood could only be proved at a tragic cost in human lives and human values. The historical and immediate facts about Vietnam were available from many sources, including a dozen on-the-spot and highly able reporters and informed, perceptive historians such as the late Bernard Fall. The French had already provided America with an eight-year-long example of arrogance and illusion in Vietnam. The truth seems to be that Kennedy and his men had emotional and political investments in hanging on to South Vietnam at all costs. Halberstam, in a 1968 book on Robert Kennedy, indirectly referred to JFK's personal insecurity when he noted that Eisenhower "had never felt the political pressure to be a hero or to prove his anti-communism that his two successors might feel." But John Kennedy had returned from World War II a decorated hero, if hardly on Eisenhower's level. One wonders if he really believed in his own heroic qualities, knowing as he did how they had been exaggerated by political publicity. For a man who is sure of his own courage is not obsessed with valor and death as was John Kennedy.

The falsity and hazards of Kennedy's Vietnam policy were also often pointed out by that shrewd and skeptical critic of American journalism, I. F. Stone. In a prophetic piece published barely a month before Kennedy's assassination and less than a week before Diem's murder, Stone wrote that Washington was the "primary obstacle" to negotiations to end the war. "Kennedy cannot afford to go into the campaign next year and face a Republican cry that under the Democrats we 'lost' Vietnam, whether by withdrawal or negotiation. The politically safest course is to 'stand firm,' i.e. to follow the line of least resistance, though this means continuation of a war that most observers agree cannot be won, and could at any time expand dangerously. As in France, the national interest is to be subordinated to the convenience of the political leadership; we will go on pouring out blood and treasure. . . ."

Stone also condemned the basic immorality of Kennedy's opportunistic policy: "The outcry about Diem diverts attention from the policies of Kennedy. The inhumanity which has made a world scandal of South Vietnam has its origin as much in Washington as in Saigon. The uprooting of the rural population and its incarceration in stockaded villages, the spraying of poisons from the air on crops and cattle in violation of the Geneva convention, the use of napalm for attack on villages suspected of harboring rebels—these policies were all formulated and directed out of Washington. The familiar belief that the end justifies the means in any conflict with communism was enough to wipe out qualms, if any, about the mistreatment of the Vietnamese. . . . Mr. Kennedy condemned the repression of the Buddhists but again his choice of words was tepid; he called it 'very unwise.' The words reflect neither moral revulsion nor human sympathy but only cool calculation. At a press conference a week later he summed up his policy. The test of official action in our government or Diem's was to be whether it might 'handicap the winning of the war.' This, and not justice for the people of South Vietnam or the establishment of a decent regime there, is our No. 1 aim."

The final question remains: Would Kennedy have maintained the U.S. involvement and escalated it to the point of final futility subsequently faced by President Johnson? The evidence of known facts and Kennedy's attitudes strongly suggests that he would have continued and escalated the Vietnam war, though perhaps never to the enormous extent that Johnson did. We must weigh Kennedy's obvious dismay, irritation, and disgust with Vietnam against his basic Cold War outlook; his extreme sensitivity to American political reactions about a "pullout," coupled with the impending 1964 presidential election; his personal emotional image as a winner, fighter, and tough leader; his belief in the new counter-insurgency methods; the preponderance of his advisers who believed in the counterinsurgency-military hard line; and the extent of the American effort up to November, 1963. Once before Kennedy had blamed "the people" for not defeating the Communists (the Cuban people in April, 1961). Could he politically have afforded to give up on another supposedly dilatory populace and let the Communists have a second great victory? In view of Kennedy's three-year-old commitment to Vietnam, it is hard to feel that he would have withdrawn, especially with the difficult Diem gone and a new group of presumably more enlightened generals to support in "their" war.

American "know-how" also remained, and Kennedy's huge arrogance as a political manager and technocrat is revealed nowhere more pathetically—and frighteningly—than in his presumptions about Vietnam. How could the South Vietnamese lose with the American superpower and its brilliant bureaucrats on their side? This irrationality is expressed in *The Pentagon Papers:* "The study also observes that the pervasive assumption in the Kennedy Administration was that 'the Diem regime's own evident weaknesses—from the "famous problem of Diem as administrator" to the Army's lack of offensive spirit—could be cured if enough dedicated Americans, civilians and military, became involved in South Vietnam to show the South Vietnamese, at all levels, how to get on and win the war.' President Kennedy and his senior advisers are described in the study as considering defeat unthinkable and assuming that the mere introduction of Americans would provide the South Vietnamese with what the authors call 'the elan and style needed to win.' "

Two other indications support the opinion that Kennedy would not have withdrawn from Vietnam. One is his July, 1963, statement at a press conference that America's goal in Vietnam was "a stable government there, carrying on a struggle to maintain its national independence. We believe strongly in that. . . . In my opinion, for us to withdraw from that effort would mean a collapse not only of South Vietnam but Southeast Asia. So we are going to stay there."

The second was inadvertently revealed in 1970 by one of Kennedy's closest political advisers, Kenneth O'Donnell. In a *Life* article, O'Donnell said that President Kennedy told Senate Majority Leader Mike Mansfield in the spring of 1963 that he agreed with Mansfield's desire for a complete withdrawal from Vietnam. But, according to O'Donnell, Kennedy also told Mansfield that "I can't do it until 1965—after I'm re-elected."

Yet by 1965 Kennedy would have faced the same internal crisis in South Vietnam's succession of tottering and totally inept governments that Johnson faced. Kennedy's "It's their war" line was similar to Roosevelt's "I will

CAMELOT REVISITED I   221

never send our boys to fight in foreign wars" and Johnson's "We don't want our American boys to do the fighting for Asian boys," both of which preceded a large American war. In addition, JFK would probably have wished to safeguard the presidential chances of his brother, Robert, for the Kennedy family believed firmly in the right of political dynasty. Thus the political dangers of a Kennedy withdrawal would have continued. And Kennedy had already ordered the service departments to be ready for the introduction of combat troops if they should be needed. The weapons were ready and loaded for further escalation. It is hard to believe that John Kennedy, with his dual load of psychic difficulties and political vulnerabilities, would have avoided using them.

VII. A Crisis-Oriented President?

HAVING REVIEWED THE major presidential decisions of John F. Kennedy in the vital area of international relations, we can ask if there is any general behavioral pattern that emerges from his policies. To my mind, there is one striking pattern above all in the six important decisions discussed: the prevalence of crisis. It is not enough to say that Kennedy presided over our national destiny in a crisis-ridden age. In many senses, all ages are crisis-ridden. In addition, an examination of his policies has revealed one outstanding trend: the crises faced by Kennedy were repeatedly either (1) self-generated, or (2) greatly exacerbated by Kennedy himself. Twice Kennedy seemed ready to resort to nuclear war in order to force his opponent into total capitulation: in the Berlin crisis of July–August, 1961, when Kennedy overreacted to fairly routine Russian pressures; and in the October, 1962, missile confrontation, when Kennedy demanded—and got—a nearly total Soviet surrender of position and prestige.

Two other Kennedy crises were largely self-created. One was the abortive Bay of Pigs invasion in April, 1961; the second was his decision to intervene militarily in South Vietnam, where the results are now all too tragically evident. A fifth and continuing crisis, the mad momentum of the nuclear arms race, was severely heightened by Kennedy's extreme insecurities and dread of ever appearing weak. As we shall see in the next chapter, Kennedy's domestic crises came about partly because of his obsessive focus on foreign affairs. This focus, part of Kennedy's protective emotional distance from himself and others, was exemplified in his unnecessary and extravagant space program which absorbed badly needed resources and talents and distracted public attention from the desperate plight of the poor and despised in America.

As critics such as Richard Walton saw Kennedy's foreign absorption and neglect of domestic problems, "Kennedy spent so much time on foreign affairs, often dealing with crises of his own making, that he devoted insufficient time to domestic matters. In fact he, like his predecessors, seemed largely unaware of the enormous problems festering just beneath the surface of American life. If he had devoted adequate time, energy, and resources to domestic problems, some of them might not have erupted after his death in such virulent form. His neglect of them was a major failing."

It seems evident that Kennedy as President was a man who felt an unconscious inner need for recurrent outer crises which would drive him into action and heroic vindication. This pattern was a continuation of his boyhood and young-adult tendency to get himself into tight situations—such as bad schoolmarks and a wartime wreck—so he would then have to respond with great determination and courage. One of Kennedy's major weaknesses was his real lack of boldness. It seems likely that he sensed strongly—if unconsciously—this lack in himself and tried to rectify it by driving himself into desperate situations where boldness would be required to avert disaster. That such boldness might also court total disaster merely heightened Kennedy's inner tensions and conflicts between his self-defeating, self-annihilating trends and his drives to achieve, perform, and succeed. But, as we have seen, while this inner confusion may drive a person toward outer success, if that person is president of a nation, he will inevitably sow seeds of future calamities—granting that present ones are averted—for his unlucky successors.

The great irony of Kennedy's crisis-created—and crisis-ruined—presidency is suggested, though never understood, in this passage from Theodore White's *The Making of the President, 1960*: "But John F. Kennedy was inaugurated in 1961, to preside over a nation to which no crisis was clear. The nation recognized, or at least it so indicated by its voting for him, that it sensed crisis—but crisis locked in the womb of time, swelling uncomfortably in embryo, crisis whose countenance was still unclear. If there were any mandate in the election of 1960, it was that the new President prepare for such obscure crises." But the embryos of "obscure crises," as it turned out, were as much locked in the psyche of John F. Kennedy as in the womb of time.

For as former White House assistant George Reedy has pointed out, "A president, in a peculiar sense that does not apply to other people, is the master of his own fate and the captain of his own soul. . . . There was no categorical imperative which required McKinley to declare war on Spain, Woodrow Wilson to serve an ultimatum on Germany, John F. Kennedy to order the invasion of the Bay of Pigs, or Lyndon Johnson to increase American forces in Vietnam from 20,000 to 500,000. These were all decisions made by human beings who had other options. Whether they were right or wrong is another matter which will not be discussed here. The only truly relevant point is that *none of these presidents was a prisoner of history at the crucial moment of truth.* They may have been prisoners of psychological forces in their childhood, of racial and ethnic memories, of environments which molded their thinking and conditioned their reflexes. But whatever psychic forces may have been playing upon them, they could all have said 'no.'

"This is a point well worth bearing in mind. The essence of the presidency is the responsibility for making decisions and the necessity for making them without peers—with advice and counsel, yes; but also in the sure knowledge that the president alone bears the full and complete burden." (Italics added.)

In conclusion, what are some of the possible psychic dynamics behind a crisis-oriented personality? I have already touched on many of these in this and preceding chapters. To put it in capsule form, recurrent crisis in life can serve as a constant prod, challenge, distraction, excuse, punishment, and, paradoxically, a goad both to real achievement and repeated self-defeat. Success and failure are often inextricably mixed in our lives, and a certain portion of each is almost unavoidable. But when the portions reach explosive proportions, and these personal equations in turn help formulate the calculus of a country's future, then the inner unbalance of personality can become as dangerously unstable as the ingredients of a nuclear bomb. Put most simply, for a President of the United States not to understand the dimensions of his own personality, and for these dimensions to be in constant flux, conflict, and contradiction with each other, is a highly volatile condition for the citizenry he attempts to lead.

Chapter 8

CAMELOT REVISITED II:
JFK AND THE AMERICAN DREAM

As Mr. Kennedy defined American foreign policy, large increases in military spending were essential. This central evaluation had important budgetary consequences. To the general reluctance of Americans to pay higher taxes for social purposes was added the beginnings of that military preemption of available funds from present taxes which has reached fruition in Richard Nixon's Washington.

There is a further point. Any President has a limited stock of political capital and a limited access to the ear of his constituents. If he asks for some things, he cannot feasibly ask for others. In his three years, what John Kennedy asked for had rather little to do with social improvement. The better part of a year was devoted to passage of the Trade Expansion Act, a much oversold piece of legislation fueled as much by the calculations of NATO strategists as by economic evaluations of American commercial interest. And then there was the moon race, the mobilization of American technology and science in the interests of winning the big game with the Russians. In short, President Kennedy, motivated by the successful politician's blend of personal preference and electoral calculation, took the easier of the available courses. He appealed to American pride, competitiveness, distrust of Communists, and affection for technology.

—Robert Lekachman, "Money in America: The End
of the Economists' Dream," *Harper's Magazine*

Presidents are supposed to be made in their first 18 months. That's when they're able to push through their programs. Kennedy's first 18 months were a blank. Nothing happened. And by his third summer, it was plain even to him that he was botching the job. In private, he was full of complaints and excuses. He felt that he could do nothing with the Congress, and so he did nothing with

224

the Congress. Re-elected in 1964 with a proper majority, however, he thought he would do great things. But, again, I doubt it. For one thing, he would have been holding the franchises for his brother and that would have meant a second Administration as cautious as the first. More to the point, the quality that gave him his great charm was not of much use to him as Chief Executive: an ironic detachment about himself and others.

—Gore Vidal, *Playboy*

. . . as Congress saw things, Kennedy had not only failed in his first big tests; he had botched the job. The minimum wage bill might have been passed at smaller political cost; the education bill might have been steered or slipped through if the President had not at first stood so firm, only to retreat so swiftly. The intellectual playboy was not, after all, another F.D.R.; it was not necessary to fear him and it might be risky to follow him. Since a leader requires, above all, the respect of his followers, in losing at the outset the essential respect of the Eighty-Seventh Congress, John Kennedy had lost whatever chance he had had to remake his country.

—Tom Wicker, *JFK and LBJ: The Influence of Personality upon Politics*

Just as the road to hell is paved with good intentions, the pages of history are studded with countries that disappeared because they couldn't turn their good ideas into action.

—John F. Kennedy

☰

THE EIGHT-INCH SNOWFALL that blanketed John F. Kennedy's inauguration on January 20, 1961, was something of an omen, although at the time it was scarcely seen as such. Like the three years of Kennedy's Administration, the snow was dazzling bright on that sunny January day. But, despite its surface brilliance, the snowfall, like the Kennedy years, stalled significant movement. The great irony of Kennedy's presidency was that, while elected on a clarion call to "get the country moving again," Kennedy's basic conservatism and personal caution kept the country going in circles. Yet the ceaseless whirl of activity around the White House concealed the lack of real progress, and the incessant Kennedy voices drowned out the soft ticking of the double time-bombs which would explode two years after Kennedy's death in the jungles of Watts and Vietnam.

But none of this was suspected in that silvery inaugural winter of 1960–1961. The Cold War was still uppermost in the minds of most Establishmentarians, Democrat and Republican alike. Thus it was that Kennedy had stepped into the White House across an illusory—as we have seen—

missile "gap." And thus it was that he devoted nearly his entire inaugural address to foreign affairs. As an inbred Cold Warrior, John Kennedy did not see the discontent and pressing needs at home. For Kennedy's vision, like his repressed emotions, seemed to remain largely distant from human beings. Foreign affairs—and history—were safely remote and impersonal. Instead of hearing the cries in the streets, Kennedy flung out empty challenges to the moon and to alien Asian lands. By the time the cries had turned to roars of fury, Kennedy himself would be gone.

From the psychohistorical point of view, there are two major questions to ask about the Kennedy Administration of two years, ten months, and two days. Psychologically, did the White House change Kennedy in any basic sense? And, historically, did Kennedy change the direction of his country as he had so ardently promised? In the international realm, we have seen, Kennedy's obsessions and blindnesses actually heightened the perils of the thermonuclear-threatened rivalry between the United States and Soviet Russia. Rather than calming the climate of mutual paranoia, Kennedy's tendency toward international confrontation, underlaid by a constant need for self-vindication, repeatedly contradicted his conscious desire for peaceful accommodation. In addition, Kennedy's foreign fixations drained off much of America's economic strength for nonproductive and nonhuman purposes and repeatedly distracted the President's attention from the urgent problems at home.

The domestic scene had never attracted Kennedy's interest as did the foreign arena, for it lacked the elements of grand drama and clear-cut rivalry that made international jousting so colorful and ego-gratifying. There were, in a word, no discernible villains on the domestic scene. On the contrary, domestic affairs seemed continually bogged down in an unappealing and complicated muddle of business and labor interests, with a less visible miasma of poverty and racial and sexual discrimination hovering over all. Yet national housekeeping continually forced its attention on a distracted Kennedy, and in time he mastered the superficialities, moving with studied caution and responding only when crisis was forced upon him, and then only with temporizing and appeasing gestures.

Both the inbred caution and the curious sense of powerlessness (a common trait in neurosis) evinced by Kennedy were noticed. Tom Wicker, at the time *New York Times* Washington Bureau Chief, wrote of JFK's domestic legislative proposals, "Whether as a result of the Southern menace or not, Kennedy was not even demanding much in the way of innovation. Every one of his five priority bills—minimum wage, education, area redevelopment, housing, medical care for the aged—was as familiar in Congress as Sam Rayburn's bald head. Democratic liberals were for these programs, had been for them for a decade or more; but did the new young liberal

President, elected in the image of F.D.R., have nothing more to offer than the same old programs that had been fought over throughout the Fifties? Between the apparent paucity of his ideas and his obvious conciliation of the South, Kennedy was diluting the enthusiasm and loyalty he needed from the urban liberals who made up his power base."

Of JFK's Administration, Paul Goodman observed, "During the activist Kennedy regime, frustration was continually expressed because, somehow, the Cabinet and the President himself were powerless . . . . When people feel powerless, they no longer think there is practicable history. 'Pragmatic,' as used for instance by the Kennedy regime, comes to mean keeping the works going, without a goal outside itself, and finally without information outside itself. So, in both domestic and foreign affairs, history and policy consist of coping with unanticipated events, almost on a day-to-day basis."

I have already analyzed how Kennedy's foreign policies rapidly fell into a prevalent pattern of crisis-reaction that seemed, in many ways, to reflect the activist reactions of his pressurized childhood. In the international realm, as also suggested, the challenge assumed the nature of physical threat and combat, even annihilation (in the form of thermonuclear war). Kennedy's "tough-guy" stance in foreign affairs mirrored the Kennedy mystique of masculine assertiveness and physical dominance. In the domestic area, on the other hand, Kennedy seemed to revert to his parallel childhood pattern of pacifying and conciliating the threatening parents, who could well have been unconsciously embodied in the generally conservative businessmen he appointed to run the economic-military part of his Administration (such as ex-Ford president McNamara as Defense Secretary and Republican Wall Street financier C. Douglas Dillon as Treasury Secretary). As we will see, Kennedy's domestic policies were largely calculated to appease and profit the industrial giants of America. As a political manager, Kennedy paralleled and mirrored the essentially status-quo outlook of the industrial and military managers who dominated the established order. Profit was the order of the day: for Kennedy, profit in votes, power, and personal prestige (since he didn't need money); for the others, profit in status and wealth.

While Kennedy's rhetoric on civil rights, poverty, and tax reform was liberal and progressive, his performance, as several sociologists and economists have noted, fell well within the range of Republican-conservative ideology. John F. Kennedy, in effect, was a true son of his socially conservative father. Both believed essentially in the maintenance of the economic status quo rather than in the humanitarian goals of a decent standard of living and economic opportunity for all at the cost of making basis changes in that status quo. The root of economic injustice in America is not the unequal distribution of scarce wealth, but the inequitable, often inhuman distribution of abundance. The United States is so extraordinarily rich that few citizens can comprehend it or grasp the vast differences in opportunity and wealth that divide the majority and the minority.

The majority of Americans are female (52 percent) and thus lack the social-economic acceptance, the necessary skills and education, and the psychological motivation to attain equitable jobs and pay. (A 1970 report by U.S. Representative Edith Green's subcommittee reveals clearly the widespread extent of such discriminations, which result in women's average income being well below that of men's, black as well as white.) The number of American poor have been variously computed as between one fifth and one third of the population. These include most American Negroes, who are a tenth of the population, and many women, both white and black. The great irony is that the United States has both the wealth and the techniques to raise every citizen to a life of decency and self-respect—if national priorities are reordered.

Kennedy called ringingly for a $30 billion trip into outer space, playing on the most juvenile fears and desires of America's longing for heroics. He also called repeatedly for "sacrifice," although no sacrifice was really elicited from affluent America. The only genuine sacrifices in view were those being made unwillingly by the callously ignored unaffluent Americans, who could have been given a way out of degraded and hopeless lives by a mere $10 billion trip into inner America. But John F. Kennedy failed the desperate dreams of the black and impoverished in America and, in the end, failed his own dream of becoming a great activist President.

I. Black America: The Dream Postponed

At the time [1961] . . . it seemed shrewd politics for Kennedy to have omitted a civil rights bill from his program, while Administration leaks discussed at every opportunity the "executive action" that was planned in this field. Two rights bills had been passed in the late Fifties, and the need seemed less pressing than once it had; in the Senate, a civil rights bill was sure to provoke a long filibuster, delaying other legislation. . . .

In retrospect, this analysis is questionable. Fighting for a strong civil rights bill, whether it could pass or not, would have done a great deal to shore up the notion of Kennedy as a vigorous liberal and to hold his supporters together in loyalty and enthusiasm. The measure might even have passed, because it would have been hard for the Republicans to refrain from supporting it; and the Southerners were alienated anyway. . . . It may be hindsight, moreover, but it is nonetheless true that Kennedy's failure to send up a strong rights bill was another link in a long chain of cynical or blind

American refusals to act either swiftly or adequately in correcting a century of injustice to Negro citizens. And even in Kennedy's brief term, the nation would begin to suffer the consequences of that shameful neglect.
—Tom Wicker, *JFK and LBJ: The Influence of Personality upon Politics*

The forlorn Mississippi engagement of 1961 and 1962, after the experience of the Freedom Rides, fired in the thinking of SNCC a train of disillusionment with the character of democracy in America. Kennedy's speech-writers rang increasingly hollow. A President who risked war to acquire Cuba for capitalism, but not even a skirmish to acquire the Deep South for democracy; who visited Berlin to proclaim "I am a Berliner," but not Mississippi to proclaim "I am a Negro"; who partly settled his new frontiers by appointing to the federal bench in the Deep South several champions of white supremacy, called into question the genuineness of his liberal commitment. . . .
—Ronald Segal, *The Americans: A Conflict of Creed and Reality*

Only a President willing to use all the resources of his office can provide the leadership, the determination and the direction . . . to eliminate racial and religious discrimination from American society.
—Senator John F. Kennedy

In the decade that lies ahead, the challenging, revolutionary Sixties, the American Presidency will demand more than ringing manifestos issued from the rear of the battle. It will demand that the President place himself in the very thick of the fight, that he care passionately about the fate of the people he leads, that he be willing to serve them at the risk of incurring their momentary displeasure.
—President John F. Kennedy

$\mathcal{SC}$

PRESIDENT KENNEDY HAD barely recovered from the Bay of Pigs fiasco on April 17, 1961, when his attention was diverted to the domestic scene of civil rights activity. On April 28, the Congress of Racial Equality (CORE), under the militant directorship of ex-NAACP program director James Farmer, wrote Kennedy that its announced program of Freedom Rides through the South would soon be launched. CORE asked for federal protection. On May 4, without such protection, the rides began. This action was the first in a series that would eventually propel Kennedy reluctantly into the politically hazardous field of civil rights legislation. The Freedom

Rides lasted from May 4 through May 28, and involved over a thousand persons from four major organizations (CORE, the Nashville Student Movement, the Student Nonviolent Coordinating Committee or SNCC, and Martin Luther King's Southern Christian Leadership Conference). Dozens were arrested, riders were savagely beaten, a bus was burned, and some riders were sent to prison farms.

The reactions of the Kennedy brothers hardly accorded with the Kennedy mythology of bold, direct action. Instead, they acted throughout with a feeble caution that did not augur well for future Kennedy programs. Failing to supply any federal protection to the Freedom Riders, the President and the Attorney General responded to the first attacks and arrests with futile phone calls to the local state authorities and Alabama's Governor John Patterson. Not until Robert Kennedy's administrative assistant, John Seigenthaler, was knocked unconscious in Montgomery did the Attorney General order federal marshals to Alabama on May 20. Four days later, Robert Kennedy called on the Negroes for a "cooling-off period," but Martin Luther King refused to halt the rides. Finally, on May 29, under the pressure of continuing arrests and national publicity, the Attorney General asked the Interstate Commerce Commission to ban segregation in interstate bus terminals. Inexplicably, it took the ICC four months to issue this order (on September 22) and more than another month to make it effective (November 1). But CORE and its supporters, not the Kennedys, had opened the way to an irrepressible black revolution for genuine equal rights. Throughout the Kennedy Administration, it would be the President and his brother who raced hard to catch up with black demands and actions, trying all the time to slow the momentum of justifiable rage with the political brakes of tokenism, legalism, and tactical justification. The Kennedys genuinely supported racial equality, but their personal fears and ingrown opportunism nearly always weighted their actions in the direction of caution and expediency.

The Kennedys' prevalent pattern of excessive political caution and weak gestures in domestic crises rather than genuine moral courage and strength was further revealed in the black nonviolent campaign of 1962 to break segregation in rigidly racist Albany, Georgia. (Details of this significant and generally unpublicized campaign are included in William Robert Miller's excellent biography of Martin Luther King, Jr.) From late 1961 into the spring of 1962, King and other members of the Albany Movement participated in sit-ins, marches, and bus and buying boycotts to force a change. On May 17, 1962, King presented President Kennedy with a petition appealing for "national rededication to the principles of the Emancipation Proclamation and for an executive order prohibiting segregation." The carefully prepared document pointed out Southern failures to obey federal laws and court rulings against segregation and included "a discussion of the President's power and duty to secure the rights of citizens ... including an analysis of the President's power to enforce judicial decrees and the 1957 Civil Rights Act."

The concluding paragraphs declared, "In short, Mr. President, we are firmly convinced that there exist sufficient constitutional and statutory sources of power to enable you to use creatively the authority and moral prestige of your office to dramatically advance human rights in America." Kennedy's response, as the Albany demonstrations and arrests continued, was to say publicly (on August 1) that he could not understand the refusal of Albany officials to negotiate with the black leaders. Georgia's white supremacists replied by blowing up rural black churches and terrorizing the countryside. The Albany Movement was not a factual success (no real changes were made until 1964), but it had great moral and psychological repercussions and should have alerted Kennedy to the increasingly determined and activist mood of black Americans, as well as to the ruthless refusal of many racists to accord human rights to others.

Yet the next peak of black activity, James Meredith's attempt to register at the University of Mississippi, again caught the Kennedys unprepared. Meredith, a nine-year Air Force veteran and a black Mississippian, had written for an application to "Ole Miss" on January 20, 1961 (prophetically, the day of Kennedy's inauguration). Refused admission, he took his case to court. Denied again, but now represented by the NAACP, Meredith had secured a reversal of the court that supported his rejection, a reversal that was affirmed subsequently by the Supreme Court. On September 20, 1962, Meredith, accompanied by federal marshals, went to the University to register. Meanwhile Governor Ross Barnett had whipped the bigots into a frenzy of hatred. Barnett issued a proclamation refusing Meredith's application. Behind the scenes, the governor hedged on all overtures by the President and his Attorney General for Meredith's peaceful entry.

Although the Kennedys prepared to move troops to Mississippi, they continued to hope that civil force would suffice despite the mounting evidence of Mississippi fanaticism. It is curious to find the Kennedy brothers, who prided themselves on their toughness and hardheaded pragmaticism, finally accepting the word of a diehard racist governor that he would provide ample state police protection if Meredith were secretly registered in another town. The naiveté of such misplaced trust should have been revealed to the Kennedys by their sorry experiences during the 1961 Freedom Rides, when state police failed to protect the riders from violent mobs. Yet at seven o'clock on the night of September 30, the President reluctantly accepted Barnett's proposal to register Meredith secretly in Jackson. But three hours later, as Kennedy was going on national television to call for acceptance of the law, the Mississippi governor phoned Robert Kennedy and canceled the deal.

Even as President Kennedy fervently pleaded on television with the students and Mississippians to honor their traditions (pleas which brought widespread scorn from skeptical liberals and blacks), a wild mob was attacking the federal marshalls guarding Meredith at Ole Miss. For nearly two hours, from the President's broadcast until midnight, the Kennedys listened to the worsening reports from the riot scene. Finally at midnight, Deputy Attorney General Nicholas Katzenbach, directing the federal forces in Oxford, Mississippi, asked the President to send in the Army. Kennedy's delay nearly cost the lives of far more than the two bystanders (one a newsman) killed in the clash. Dozens of marshals were wounded and their tear gas had run out before the troops finally reached the campus from Memphis, an incredible three and a half hours after the order was given. The President himself sent an anguished message directly to the Army commander who was assembling his troops at the Oxford airport: "People are dying in Oxford," said Kennedy. "This is the worst thing I've seen in forty-five years. I want the military police battalion to enter the action. I want General Billingslea to see that this is done." Fortunately, despite the nearly disastrous delay and mixup, the soldiers arrived in time to rescue the besieged federal marshals. In August, 1963, the valiant Meredith was graduated from Ole Miss, having finished his courses under a constant guard of troops and marshals. The Kennedys had acted in time, but barely.

Yet the world saw and remembered the over-all result, and either forgot or never knew of Kennedy's foot-dragging. Kennedy compounded this narrow victory by finally issuing an executive order to desegregate federal housing a month later (on November 20). In his presidential campaign, he had promised to issue this order by "a stroke of the pen" the minute he was elected. Disappointed Negroes had subsequently sent him dozens of pens to end the long delay. But Kennedy did not abandon his "Southern strategy" with this housing order, for it actually covered only 15 percent of residential mortgage holdings. Yet once again, the limitations of Kennedy's action were largely overlooked by the majority of citizens. In mid-1963, a Louis Harris poll of Negroes put Kennedy in the triumvirate of those who had done most for black rights. (The others were the NAACP and Martin Luther King, Jr.)

King, however, was well aware of Kennedy's shortcomings. According to his biographer, "King was highly critical of the Kennedy Administration's handling of the disorders there [in Oxford], and of the general inadequacy of the White House's response. On October 16, he spent an hour with Kennedy, seeking presidential action on SCLC's May 17 appeal, and he found him affable but evasive. 'The President,' he later said, 'must change the trend from that of saying, "Something must be done," to coming up with a strong, specific program. It does no good to apply Vaseline to a cancer.' " Later King wrote, "If tokenism were our goal, this Administration has adroitly moved us toward its accomplishment. But tokenism can now be seen not only as a useless goal, but as a genuine menace. It is a palliative which relieves emotional distress, but leaves the disease and its ravages unaffected. It tends to demobilize and relax the militant spirit which alone drives us forward to real change."

Kennedy's tokenism had included the appointment of more Negroes to high-visibility federal posts, ambassadorships, and judgeships. The core of Kennedy's civil rights strategy was to provide the appearance of adequate forward movement by focusing on the Justice Department, where Kennedy counted on his energetic brother to carry out a widespread campaign of black voter registration in the South. Robert Kennedy and his assistants also brought about the peaceful desegregation of a number of Southern schools. Yet despite the liberal acclaim that greeted these efforts (helped by the Kennedy talent for public relations), it is hard to escape the conclusion that the Justice Department efforts were only a few drops in the bucket of racial drought. Even Arthur Schlesinger, who goes out of his way to praise his patron, occasionally lets slip revealing historical contradictions. For example, Schlesinger noted that by mid-1963 the Justice Department had filed forty-two suits, eight of them in Mississippi. But the Harvard historian had already mentioned that "in at least 193 counties fewer than 15 per cent of eligible Negroes were permitted to register; in Mississippi this was true in seventy-four out of eighty-two counties. In thirteen southern counties not one Negro was on the rolls." By Schlesinger's own figures, the much-vaunted efforts of the Attorney General had affected little more than 10 percent of the most repressive counties in Mississippi alone.

Meanwhile, the President's determined refusal to press for new civil rights legislation in the face of what he claimed was hopeless Republican-Southern opposition in Congress brought increasing disillusionment to the Negro leadership. Martin Luther King described 1962 as "the year that civil rights was displaced as the dominant issue in domestic politics. . . . The issue no longer commanded the conscience of the nation." Certainly Kennedy was doing his best to ignore politely the politically threatening issue. The President's legalistic and administrative tokenism seemed to have succeeded in constricting the movement; as King lamented, "A sweeping revolutionary force is pressed into a narrow tunnel."

If the black intellectuals and leaders were disenchanted with Kennedy's feeble performance, the general black masses revered the young President as the liberal leader who would bring them genuine equality. When a black leader such as the NAACP's Roy Wilkins tried to dispel the Kennedy folklore of aggressive liberalism, the Negro audience, as Wilkins reported to his fellow civil rights leaders, was unresponsive. "I attacked John Kennedy for ten minutes and everyone sat on their hands," Wilkins said in January, 1963, when the black leadership was considering a statement condemning the President. "Then I said a few favorable words about the things he had done, and they clapped and clapped." Much of this goodwill went back to Kennedy's 1960 election-eve telephone call to Coretta King when Martin was imprisoned. In comparison with past Presidents, Kennedy looked good, and he sounded even better. The black population as a whole took his gestures and words at face value, not understanding how his tokenism could dampen the ardor for meaningful change and restrict the latent black revolution to narrow legalistic channels. The pathetic truth was that to the downtrodden and despised mass of black Americans, even the weak gestures of a politically opportunistic President aroused long-repressed hopes for a better world. To the average Negro, unsophisticated in political manipulation, Kennedy seemed to be doing his best.

Some members of Kennedy's own Administration, however, were far less delighted, including his Civil Rights Commission. In March, 1963, the Commission, which had been repeatedly delayed from holding hearings in Mississippi by Attorney General Robert Kennedy, issued an angry interim report. One of its members, Dean Erwin Griswold of the Harvard Law School, told an interviewer that "a great many very bad things were happening in Mississippi and the government was not doing anything appreciable about it. People were being shot at, the home of one of our state advisory committee members was bombed, another member had been jailed, and so on." The interim report stated bluntly that constitutional rights of Mississippi citizens were being denied: "Citizens of the United States have been shot, set upon by vicious dogs, beaten, and otherwise terrorized because they sought to vote. Since October, students have been fired upon, ministers have been assaulted . . . children, at the brink of starvation, have been deprived of assistance by the callous and discriminatory acts of Mississippi officials administering Federal funds." The Commission concluded unanimously that "only further steps by the Federal Government can arrest the subversion of the Constitution in Mississippi." The members asked the President to explore his legal authority "to withhold Federal funds from the State of Mississippi until the State of Mississippi demonstrates its compliance with the Constitution."

Yet Kennedy, when presented with this document, gave a variety of rationalizations why he could not take strong action. The man who was ready to take his country to the brink of war over Cuba and the rights of Berliners was not ready to consider cutting off government funds to an American state to protect the rights of American citizens. Such a step,

said Kennedy, was "subject to misunderstanding. I am not sure it is constructive . . . . I know some of the agencies have been dragging [their feet].
I am doing everything I can to see that they get in line. Your Commission
doesn't understand I can't do it alone. The Commission report would be
better directed at the Congress. That is where the trouble is—appropriations, etc. As the report reads now, you make it appear that I have the
power to do all these things, and I don't. Such power might be dangerous.
Even if it existed, it would not be understood." We see here Kennedy's
recurrent ambivalence and deep inner contradiction between a sense of
power and of powerlessness. What a contrast there is between this fearful
reaction and Kennedy's preelection assertions that the presidency was as
strong as the President.

Black leaders, who faced brutality, imprisonment, and even death
without flinching, were proving themselves far stronger than white leaders,
who knew none of these everyday realities. A complacent nation was about
to be stirred into at least momentary awareness of the racial crimes it
harbored. In the fall of 1962, the black Christian leaders made secret plans
for a well-organized and sustained campaign in the toughest city in the
South, Birmingham, Alabama. Martin Luther King was determined that
the validity of his nonviolent militancy to force revolutionary social changes
would be truly tested in a direct confrontation. After many meetings and
training sessions for volunteers, the Birmingham campaign opened on April
3, 1963. For a tumultuous month, thousands of Negro men, women, and
children braved police threats and clubs, high-pressure fire hoses, police
dogs, and the hardships of jail by marching through the streets of Birmingham to demand an end to racial segregation.

As a shocked nation and world watched the police brutalities on television
and in the press, criticism mounted against the Kennedy Administration for
its inaction. Sharp rebukes came from Senators Wayne Morse and John
Sherman Cooper and the president of Morehouse College, who said that if
protesting Catholics or Jews had been treated the same, "the Federal
Government would have found a way to step in." One obvious way seemed
to invoke the Fourteenth Amendment, which promises "equal protection
under the law" to all American citizens. But the Kennedy Administration
timidly limited itself to sending observers to the scene and bringing pressure
to bear on influential Birmingham businessmen. Finally, on May 9, a
limited agreement was worked out between King's group and the Birmingham citizens' committee.

Violence broke the truce on May 11, when racist hoodlums bombed the
home of Dr. King's brother and the motel where King and his co-leaders
had been staying. State troopers arrived spoiling for a fight, but were largely
restrained by the Birmingham police and black civil rights workers. Finally

alarmed at the potential for bloody riots, President Kennedy dispatched federal troops and took preliminary steps to federalize the Alabama National Guard. By May 13, some 3,000 federal troops were stationed in and around Birmingham. When these actions were challenged by Governor Wallace, the President replied that the authority to act came from Title 10, Section 33, Paragraph 1 of the U.S. Code which entrusts to the Chief Executive "all determinations as to (1) the necessity for action; (2) the means to be employed; and (3) the adequacy or inadequacy of the protection afforded by state authorities to the citizens of that state." Clearly, then, Kennedy's earlier refusal to act to protect Negroes had been political rather than legal.

Continuing desegregation drives and court suits in both South and North throughout the summer and fall of 1963 were marked by sporadic violence and atrocities, including the inhuman murder of four Negro children when their Sunday School was bombed. Journalist I. F. Stone, who has one of America's finest senses for moral hypocrisy, commented bitterly, "Despite the formal expressions of regret, the sermons, the editorials and the marches, neither white America nor its leadership was really moved. When Martin Luther King and six other Negro leaders finally saw the President four days after the bombing, it was to find that he had already appointed a two-man committee to represent him 'personally' in Birmingham, but that both men were white. This hardly set a precedent for bi-racial action. If Mr. Kennedy could take a judge off the Supreme Court to settle a labor dispute, he could have taken one of the country's two Negro judges off the Court of Appeals to dignify a mission of mediation. He might have insisted, for once, after so terrible a crime, on seeing white and Negro leaders together, instead of giving a separate audience four days later to a white delegation from Birmingham. It is as if, even in the White House, there are equal but separate facilities."

By the early summer of 1963, pressure had been built up throughout the country by the three years of Negro demonstrations for new national legislation. America's conscience was aroused, and Northern liberals called for action. "The cause of desegregation must cease to be a Negro movement, blessed by white politicians from the Northern states," wrote Walter Lippmann. "It must become a national movement to enforce national laws, led and directed by the National Government." Said *The Washington Post*, "The great need now is for dynamic national leadership to tell the country of its crisis and to win public opinion to support the dramatic changes that must take place." On June 11, Governor Wallace tried to prevent two Negroes from enrolling at the University of Alabama; Kennedy ordered the state's National Guard into federal service and Wallace stepped aside. In a speech on the crisis, Kennedy finally announced his decision to ask for a new civil rights act (actually reached May 31). On June 19, his proposal was sent to Congress.

Kennedy's bill, while better than previous legislation, was still a highly cautious compromise between black needs and conservative counsels. Civil rights groups and the Democratic liberal leadership had worked hard to convince the White House of the desperate need for more progressive measures. As James L. Sundquist, a former executive in the Kennedy Administration, viewed the program in his 1968 study, *Politics and Policy: The Eisenhower, Kennedy, and Johnson Years*, "It was clear that counsels of caution had, on the whole, prevailed." Kennedy proposed cutting off federal aid to discriminating firms, but made this action optional on the executive branch rather than mandatory. Instead of including provisions for fair employment practices, he endorsed pending legislation. Public accommodation clauses were limited to businesses having a "substantial" effect on interstate commerce. School suits put the burden of proof on the aggrieved citizen. The bill lacked any new voting rights provision. Typically, Ted Sorensen explained that the President "was looking for a law, not an issue," a justification applicable to any bill when the President feared to attempt profound changes.

While easily satisfied or cynical liberals hailed Kennedy's "achievement," many activists in the civil rights movement were sharply critical. During the August 28, 1963, civil rights March on Washington, the disillusionment of black militants with Kennedy's politically expedient do-little policy was expressed by John Lewis, chairman of the Student Nonviolent Coordinating Committee (SNCC). In his original speech, which was softened to placate some of the march's co-sponsors, Lewis stated, "In good conscience, we cannot support the Administration's civil rights bill, for it is too little, and too late. There's not one thing in the bill that will protect our people from police brutality. The voting section of this bill will not help the thousands of citizens who want to vote; will not help the citizens of Mississippi, of Alabama, and Georgia who are qualified to vote, who are without a 6th grade education. 'One Man, One Vote,' is the African cry—it is ours, too.

"People have been forced to move for they have exercised their right to register to vote. What is in the bill that will protect the homeless and starving people of this nation? What is there in this bill to insure the equality of a maid who earns $5.00 a week in the house of a family whose income is $100,000 a year? This bill will not protect young children and old women from police dogs and fire hoses for engaging in peaceful demonstrations. This bill will not protect the citizens in Danville, Virginia, who must live in constant fear in a police state. This bill will not protect the hundreds of people who have been arrested on trumped-up charges, like those in Americus, Georgia, where four young men are in jail, facing a death penalty, for engaging in peaceful protest."

Lewis asked, as thousands had been asking, out loud or in their hearts, "Which side is the federal government on?" As a leader of the new, nonviolent revolution, he asserted the Negroes' right to freedom now, without any more waiting. Time and patience had run out. The time for change had come, and the masses would create the power for change. "The revolution is a serious one. Mr. Kennedy is trying to take the revolution out of the streets and put it in the courts. Listen, Mr. Kennedy, listen, Mr. Congressman, listen, fellow citizens—the black masses are on the march for jobs and freedom, and we must say to the politicians that there won't be a 'cooling-off period.' "

Kennedy died three months after these prophetic words, leaving to his successor the task of passing the Civil Rights Act of 1964 and of coping with the racial explosions that began to rip the country apart in the long hot summer of 1965. Kennedy's "finger in the dike" attitude to the latent black revolution had merely delayed it. The bright, highly-gifted, energetic President who had promised to "get the country moving again" had stalled repeatedly; he had not prepared a dynamic strategy to lead the way. For behind the façade of presidential concern fluttered the pulse of a conventional politician and an emotionally conflicted personality. Kennedy, I believe, was unable either to care or dare enough because his inner strength was insufficient for the needs of his time.

II. Kennedy and the Economy: The Failure of Human Priorities

Of all the myths in current political and economic literature, one of the most imaginative and furthest removed from reality portrayed President Kennedy as anti-business. In fact, in every significant area—wage policy, tax policy, international trade and finance, federal spending—the President showed a keen understanding and ready response to the essential corporate program. It is doubtful that a Republican president, historically vulnerable to the charge of "business tool," could have done as much. Indeed, Eisenhower didn't. . . .
—Bernard D. Nossiter, *The Mythmakers: An Essay on Power and Wealth*

As of mid-1959 the poorest one-third of Americans own 1% of the wealth of the United States. The next 23% up the scale owns 5%. Thus, well over half the population owns 6% of the wealth of the United States. The richest 1.6% own nearly one-third of the country's material assets.
—W. H. Ferry of the Fund for the Republic

By proper application of the old-school criteria, Kennedy was, on balance, conservative. Most of his programs belong to the right of center . . . and he did an amazing number of things that showed a preference for private-sector activity. . . . Examples include his "actuarially sound" Medicare, his investment tax credit and tax cut proposals, his preference for expansion of housing through investment incentives, his reluctance to ask for new civil rights legislation, his appreciation for governmental contracting and other executive powers to deal with civil rights, his opposition to "Powell Amendments" and parochial school aid in federal education legislation, his concerted effort to make agriculture controls work, his support for very permissive depressed-areas legislation that would bail out needy businesses and industries while reducing needs of or pressures on entrepreneurs to move to some other section of the country.

—Theodore J. Lowi, *The End of Liberalism*

In a country of such opulence, it is a morally revolting spectacle to behold the low and even dangerous standards of life of the big minority of citizens at the economic bottom. After the Negro rights issue, this is the great shame of our exceptional nation. Both of these configurations are derived from prejudice and stupidity— there is no real hard necessity of any kind involved in their continuance. They are that rare thing—stupidly willed evil. . . . Just about everything the poor need is in surplus supply either as existing inventory or productive capacity.

—David T. Bazelon, *The Paper Economy*

꩜

ALONG WITH HIS international, space, and civil rights promises, John Kennedy also made lavish economic promises to spread prosperity and opportunity throughout the country, especially among underprivileged Americans. As with his other promises, JFK failed to deliver the economic goods.

In order to weigh the fairness of this appraisal, we must consider the following questions: What was the general state of the national economy during Kennedy's term in office? What general economic directions did he follow? What programs did he consider worth large expenditures? What potential programs did he ignore or fail to press?

When Kennedy was elected President, the United States as a whole had reached a stage of unparalleled prosperity, despite its third recession in less than eight years. Yet along with general affluence, the disturbing fact of increasing unemployment and vast areas of poverty in the midst of abundance raised doubts about the ability of the entire economic, social and political structure to fairly distribute opportunity and well-being to all

American citizens. The fact seemed to be that while America was physically capable of providing amply for all its people, the country's leadership was psychically unable to make radical changes in the entirely inadequate means of distribution. And as some observers (such as reporter Edgar May and economists John Kenneth Galbraith and David T. Bazelon) noted, a destructive psychology of poverty ("The poor are always with us," a misunderstanding of the New Testament) continued to grip the minds and emotions of those in positions to effect changes. The old Calvinist morality and closely-related nineteenth century Social Darwinism of "Go to the ant, thou sluggard, consider her ways and be wise" (Proverbs, 6:6)—a guiding Kennedy precept—continued to take precedence over the humanistic idea of "And if thy brother be waxen poor and fallen in decay with thee, then thou shalt relieve him. Yea, though he be a stranger or a sojourner, that he may live with thee" (Leviticus, 25:35).

The level of national unemployment had risen with each postwar business cycle. From 1958 through the first half of 1963, the jobless rate averaged 5 percent or more. In the period which largely encompassed Kennedy's Administration, from May, 1960, through the second quarter of 1963, unemployment averaged 6 percent. During Kennedy's first year in office, the President took the "structural" approach to unemployment; namely, that rapid technological change required the training of displaced unskilled workers. Although Walter Heller, Kennedy's head of the Council of Economic Advisers, and Arthur Goldberg, his Labor Secretary, urged a public works measure to pump $1 billion into the sagging economy, Kennedy felt bigger deficits would be inflationary. In addition, the defeat at the Bay of Pigs, the mess in Southeast Asia, and the Russian orbital triumph made Kennedy unduly wary of changes on the home front.

This interpretation is ably presented by Arnold Schuchter, author of the scholarly study, *White Power/Black Freedom:* "With this single concession to Keynesian theory—a 7 per cent investment tax credit for business purchases of machines, equipment, and facilities—President Kennedy, in effect, adopted a 'structural' approach with the Area Redevelopment Act (ARA), the Manpower Development and Training Act (MDTA) of 1961, and other social welfare legislation. These formed an important part of the New Frontier image. However, the image of progress for the disadvantaged under New Frontier legislation far outdistanced actual payoffs for the poor and Negroes. The failure of human resources planning under Kennedy's New Frontier was probably its most significant legacy to Johnson's Great Society program. The latter simply has managed to increase the scope and variety of that failure."

In 1962, however, Kennedy became a recruit to the "New Economics" proposed by Heller, Goldberg, Galbraith, and others, who felt that only a rapidly expanding economy would reduce serious unemployment. To expand the economy, Kennedy had two basic choices: significant social welfare spending or a major tax reduction. True to his conservative upbringing, Kennedy took the easy and politically expedient course of reducing taxes by some $10 billion, a policy which did indeed bring about large economic growth under Lyndon Johnson. Measured in terms of Gross National Product, Kennedy had wrought a great change in stimulating economic expansion. But measured in human lives and hopes, Kennedy had largely made the wealthy wealthier and the prosperous middle classes more prosperous, without affecting the lives of millions hopelessly trapped in poverty and the black ghettos that are America's invisible concentration camps.

As Mr. Schuchter clearly spelled out, economic expansion took place "by enabling the prosperous majority of Americans to save over $23 billion in taxes since 1963." But "in terms of public-policy alternatives available to the President, Kennedy could have chosen the politically less popular approach: a sharp increase in federal spending for social welfare—the Galbraith emphasis which, like that of Keyserling, Lekachman, Gass, Tobin, and others, failed to influence a President who understood the problems of business better than the problems of the masses outside the affluent society." And as economists also noted, the Kennedy Administration could have largely solved the problem of meeting social needs by plugging the manifold loopholes in the tax laws.

Despite the gradual reduction of unemployment through a rapidly expanding economy (down to 5.6 percent by early 1963), there were still vast discrepancies between Administration claims and tragic realities. Much unemployment among the unskilled went unreported as thousands lost heart and stopped looking for work. And in the ghettos, conditions actually grew worse. As Schuchter reports, "Negroes have shown no signs of catching up; indeed, Negro children in large families were deeper in the cycle of poverty. In 1964, 76 per cent of all Negro families with five or more children were poor, compared with 71 per cent in 1959. About one in three of these families had a woman at the head; another third, however, were headed by a man with a full-time job throughout the year." As anthropologist Thomas Gladwin clearly described in *Poverty, U.S.A.*, the very fact of poverty creates both economic and psychological reasons that make it impossible for the majority of the impoverished to raise themselves out of the trap of poverty without considerable outside help of various kinds. "If, to borrow from Paul Jacobs' phrase, the poor are kept poor not simply because of deliberate exploitation and discrimination, but also because being poor is economically so inefficient that people are usually unable to escape from poverty by their own efforts no matter what they do, what does this suggest with respect to planning programs to help poor people? One conclusion which emerges compellingly is that even complete elimination of discrimination against members of any minority group will not substantially improve their life circumstances if they are genuinely poor . . . . it seems inescapable that if you are born in the mid-twentieth century of really poor parents in an urban slum (or on a sharecropper's farm) the purely economic dice are loaded so heavily against you that the likelihood of your achieving a position of real dignity or security is almost precluded. Put in another way, if only *equal* opportunities are extended to the minority poor and they are therefore subject to the same rules of business which govern middle-class people their limited cash resources will prevent them from deriving any lasting advantage from this 'equality.' Thus many of the demands which are currently being made by civil rights leaders in northern as well as southern cities appear impossible of fulfillment within our economic system as it presently operates." Both Gladwin and Schuchter, among others, strongly recommended a minimum guaranteed income as the indispensable basis on which very poor people can begin to build new lives.

Many economists have criticized the Social Security Administration's narrow poverty criteria, based on the Agriculture Department's *emergency* food plan (which is nutritionally totally inadequate) by which the poor are statistically reduced by the federal government while actual malnutrition and starvation continue. According to Schuchter, "In the five-year period between 1959 and 1964, the number of poor, by the stringent SSA definition of poverty, decreased by almost 5 million households. However, the gap between the poor and the mainstream of America increased: the median income of four-person families in 1964 was nearly two-and-one-half times the poverty non-farm income level of $3,130 as compared with just twice the poverty index in 1959. The number of near-poor in 1964 (just above the poverty line), about fifteen and three-quarter million persons, remained unchanged, despite the reduction of 'official' poverty. Poverty statistics, like unemployment data, can be disturbingly deceptive."

Could Kennedy have changed this appalling situation? He and his supporters claimed that Congress would only pass a tax reduction and not large social welfare funds. This leaps over the question of what a determined President might accomplish with the potent weapons of an aroused public opinion and legislative skills. It also conveniently ignores the many other tools by which a strong President can significantly reshape the national economy. For, Schuchter pointed out, "The arsenal of tools at the disposal of the federal government for achieving and maintaining full employment and economic stability is formidable: credit controls administered by the Federal Reserve System; debt management policies of the Treasury;

authority of the President to vary the terms of mortgages carrying federal insurance; flexibility in administration of the budget; agricultural supports; modification of the tax structure; and public works. The federal government is also empowered to develop and administer a vast array of programs in the areas of health, education, welfare, manpower development, housing, and community redevelopment, all of which potentially can serve the full-employment goal. However, the 'decision mix' of fiscal, monetary, and program elements in the postwar period failed to directly confront the enormous economic and employment problems of the impoverished Negroes within, and heading for, growing slum ghettos."

The millions of black Americans were actually a minority of those who suffered from the Kennedy Administration's shortsighted and cowardly policies, for poor whites outnumber poor blacks. No one knows the exact number of impoverished Americans, since poverty standards vary widely. But in 1960, the year of John F. Kennedy's election to the presidency, one of the most respected reports (Leon H. Keyserling's *Poverty and Deprivation in the United States*) estimated that a total of 38 million Americans, or more than one fifth of the nation, lived in poverty. These impoverished included almost 10.5 million multiple-person families with annual incomes under $4,000 and almost 4 million unattached persons with incomes under $2,000. Thus Kennedy's campaign statement that 17 million Americans go to bed hungry at night was hardly an exaggeration. The question in 1961 was exactly what the new young multimillionaire President could and would do about it.

The claims of Kennedy's awakening to the reality of poverty are highly suspect. First of all, Kennedy had John Kenneth Galbraith's graphic and powerful study, *The Affluent Society*, to open his mind; yet the new President sent Galbraith off to distant India as U.S. Ambassador rather than retaining his innovative brilliant mind close at hand. Many writers claim that the grinding poverty of West Virginia, first viewed by Kennedy during his 1960 primary campaign there, shocked him into sudden awareness. Yet others attribute his "awakening" to Michael Harrington's book, *The Other America*, which Kennedy reportedly read in December, 1962. The truth seems to be that, despite moments of genuine concern, Kennedy never really woke up to the dimensions of poverty, hunger, and disease in America.

Consider this passage from Nick Kotz's careful study of slow starvation among the American poor, *Let Them Eat Promises: The Politics of Hunger in America:* "Moved by the poverty he saw during the West Virginia primary, President Kennedy, on his first day in office, doubled the existing commodity aid program, and during the following years the quantity of food aid was expanded greatly. Compared to existing programs, these reforms were impressive; compared to the need, they were minimal. The fact that millions of Americans had too little to eat still made no strong impression on government or the public, and there still was no national commitment." And as Harry Caudill made clear in his moving book, *Night Comes to the Cumberlands*, years after Kennedy's committee had studied West Virginia's problems, no real changes had been made.

Kennedy's general failure in both concept and activity in the poverty area was so apparent that it provoked criticism from even such a mild analyst as James Sundquist, who generally idealizes Kennedy. Sundquist describes the "attitude that had become pervasive in Washington as the Kennedy administration entered its third year—a feeling that the 'New Frontier' was made up mainly of old frontiers already crossed, and that all of those old frontiers, all of the innovations conceived over the course of a generation and written into law would not, singly or collectively, change the gray face of the 'other America.' The Kennedy piecemeal programs, built upon those of his predecessors, were reaching toward the substratum of the population where all of the problems were concentrated, but the programs were somehow not making contact, not on a scale and with an impact that measured up to the bright promise of a 'New Frontier' or to the specific pledges made by a presidential candidate in West Virginia. The measures enacted, and those proposed, were dealing separately with such problems as slum housing, juvenile delinquency, dependency, unemployment, illiteracy, but they were separately inadequate because they were striking only at surface aspects of what seemed to be some kind of bedrock problem, and it was the bedrock problem that had to be identified so that it could be attacked in a concerted, unified, and innovative way. Perhaps it was Harrington's book that defined the target for Kennedy and supplied the coordinating concept—the bedrock problem, in a word, was 'poverty.' "

The vast tragedy of American poverty is that only a partial shift of priorities and resources could virtually wipe out human need in this country. Several economists have set $10 billion a year as the amount needed to eliminate poverty over ten years. Professor Ben B. Seligman calculated that "to bring six million poor families and three million poor individuals just over a $3,000-a-year poverty line would cost about $10 billion." British economist Norman Macrae wrote, ". . . by 1967 a transfer of only $9.7 billion a year to the poor would have been needed to lift every American above this generously defined poverty line [of $3,335 for a four-person non-farm family]. This amounts to only about a quarter of a single year's normal increase in real GNP [Gross National Product]. It is rather less than the yield of the 1968 surcharge on income tax. . . ." While $3,335 for four people can hardly be described as a "generously defined poverty line," closing the poverty gap does seem well within America's financial means.

The gap in understanding by Kennedy's New Economists has been clearly spelled out by Robert Lekachman: "The New Economists' growth preoccupations left little room for analysis of the inequities of the distribution of income and wealth. At an inflationary time like this one [1970], it would make excellent sense to raise higher-bracket tax rates, impose punitive inheritance levies, and really plug the tax loopholes. An awful lot of money would be collected, enough both to repress inflation and to do something for the cities, the poor, and the unemployed."

Unhappily for the other America of hunger, poverty, illiteracy, and unemployment, Kennedy was not a genuinely innovative President. Nor, despite his posthumous idealization, does he appear to have been a man of acute sensitivity to the desperate plight of millions of Americans less fortunate than himself. Much has been made of Kennedy's shock and concern over the poor Americans he confronted personally for the first time in his life during his 1960 West Virginia primary contest. Yet, if it was Harrington's book that aroused the President in late 1962 (according to Schlesinger and Sundquist), then apparently the West Virginians and all their condition suggested had been largely forgotten in the intervening two years. I. F. Stone, as we have seen, bitterly criticized Kennedy for his lack of human concern over the atrocities of the Vietnam war and the South Vietnam dictators. Similarly, Kennedy showed a cold-blooded detachment from the cruel entrapment of black America in terror and repression. Again, in the even wider realm of national poverty, Kennedy made small and limited gestures of concern, but he clearly lacked the sense of moral outrage and deep commitment that could have changed the paradox of poverty in the midst of plenty. Kennedy was neither a heartless nor a stupid man. But he was, as I have tried to show, a man of severe limitations in both philosophical outlook and emotional capacity. That even the presidency produced little growth in Kennedy is amply demonstrated by his repeated failures in both domestic and international policies.

Thus we have seen that Kennedy's over-all policies followed what we have come to think of as generally conservative lines. That is, he made no significant changes in the economic structure, which continued to be oriented toward the private sector, and he spent the greatest sums to maintain America's international prestige, primarily by military means, rather than to ameliorate our domestic ills. In this pattern he largely copied his predecessor, despite the influx of "bright young men" to the Kennedy Administration and their rather arrogant assumption of infallibility. In some ways Kennedy was even more pro-business than Eisenhower, for he expanded the defense establishment far beyond Eisenhower's program and beyond all rational need, and at the same time launched an enormously expensive and even less justifiable moon project.

But domestically, although Kennedy made progressive sounds, he spent meager amounts to bring a long-delayed cure to the deep cancers of poverty, pollution, and discrimination of many types in the social body. Thus, in the traditional manner of American conservatives, Kennedy spent where there were great corporate pressures urging him to spend and failed to spend where the cries for help were weak because powerless, where results would have been slower and undramatic. The need was real rather than illusory, yet far more difficult to demonstrate to the traditionally attuned public opinion.

The billions consumed by irrelevant (and dangerous) missiles and un-necessary space exploration could induce temporary prosperity in certain large industrial segments of the economy, but by and large this money only benefited the corporate, military, and technological directors and their legions of workers. Meanwhile the untrained poor remained poor, or grew poorer; increasing technology and computerization threw more millions into the pool of unskilled or underskilled unemployables; city decay and pollution continued rampant; and disease and hunger spread among the millions untouched by the affluence of the new technologies. The overstockpiling of sophisticated weaponry and the development of space rocketry did not add real wealth to the economy in comparison with what they took away. While some workers prospered and thus added to tax revenue, the trickle of money going back into the social base—housing, schools, hospitals, libraries, parks, roads, clinics, and community centers— was tiny compared with the flood of money rushing away from it.

In essence, if all the overkill weapons and all the space rockets had been dumped into the Atlantic Ocean, America would have been none the poorer, and in many ways far richer. For then our huge talents and human-power could have been used for life-giving purposes, rather than drained away into tasks that were not only by and large meaningless, but actually harmful to human health. The harm has gone far deeper than the waste of human lives and material resources. Psychologically, too many Americans have been drawn close to machines and away from other human beings. One can see this often in engineers and computer technologists, who feel vastly more comfortable in "interface" relationships with their technical equipment than in "face-to-face" genuine emotional relationships with other people. Were American technology turned away from war (killing people) and the emptiness of outer space (ignoring people) and focused primarily on helping and knowing people, then perhaps the technologists could find a truly human balance between our material inventions and our emotional needs. We could, in short, have happy relationships both with people and with machines, because the people would always come first.

An understanding of a society's economic values is basic to an under-standing of a society's human and psychological values. Thus it is quite useless for psychiatrists, as they often do, to try to "adjust" their patients' emotions to conform with social patterns without considering what these social patterns may be. Surely the lessons of even the recent past (Hitler's Germany) and the current present (Communist Russia and China) should have taught us this much. And this great question, I think, is precisely what is behind the enormous agitation of today's educated and affluent young. They are demanding values rather than statistics, and in this lies the hope of our nation.

If I have seemed to wander polemically astray from a psychohistorical consideration of the Kennedy Administration, I hope the reader will be induced to think through his own interpretation of the social setting for JFK's economics. Kennedy, like all of us, was a product of both his personal and his social past. Thus Kennedy's irrationalities were not singular, but were shared by most Americans. A country that spends more on cosmetics than on education could hardly be expected to denounce a President who spent more on saving "face" than on salvaging human lives. So as we come to question the wisdom of the Kennedys and the meaning of their values, we must also face the personal pain of questioning our own wisdom and values. The Kennedys were, in essence, what most of us wanted and most of us permitted. Although half the nation voted against JFK for President in 1960, we can see now, a decade later, how little difference in fact existed between the candidates in substance rather than style. Style helped Kennedy gain the White House, but style, even coupled with intelligence and good intentions, would not feed the bodies or souls of millions of hungry, dehumanized, desperate citizens whom the President alone could help.

I have already reviewed Kennedy's major inadequacies in bringing genuine justice to race relations and real human concern to the poor. In the next short sections, I will try to highlight JFK's attitudes by a brief consideration of two claimed triumphs of Kennedy economics: the bill to reduce taxes and his ostensible battle with Big Steel in 1962. In both these areas, it seems evident that Kennedy was thoroughly grounded in the cautious conservatism of his father, a conservatism that was heightened by the demands of his inner psychology.

III. Kennedy's Tax Bill:
Helping the Rich Get Richer

The President . . . made reduction of tax rates his chief legislative goal for 1963. . . . The heart of the plan was the cut in rates—not reforms—and the suggested rates paralleled to a remarkable extent those urged by the United States Chamber of Commerce. . . . The simple fact is that the Kennedy proposals offered gains of substance to those in the upper brackets. . . . To be sure, all these disparities would be narrowed by passage of the Kennedy reforms. But the President himself had made clear that he would be well satisfied with limited change in this area. Indeed, the Administration embraced another version of the bill in the summer of 1963 that abandoned most of the reforms and provided even greater maldistribution of rewards.

—Bernard D. Nossiter, *The Mythmakers: An Essay on Power and Wealth*

The legacy of the New Economics to the 1970s is an enlargement of the American appetite for tax reduction, a taste already much too ravenous for the national good. The great failure of the New Economics was its sunny confidence in growth as the universal solvent of social ills. It is, of course, true that political choices are easier when they concentrate upon redistribution of increments to national income rather than upon a static national income itself. It is easier to divide something new than to take something away from one group and give it to another. And it is only fair to add that the New Economics accomplished something of value in shoving the economy to higher levels of employment than had been customary during the 1950s. Unhappily, although wise decision was made somewhat easier, the terms of the discussion during the early 1960s did not convert opportunity very frequently into adequate policy. When economic growth occurs in the context of military and space programs and tax reductions, all that the exercise of creating the growth may do is enlarge the taste for more tax cuts and increase general indulgence for military and space spending.

—Robert Lekachman, "Money in America: The End of the Economists' Dream," *Harper's Magazine*

Economic growth as an all-embracing goal has a more serious shortcoming. Though it is a condition precedent for solving most social problems, there are many it doesn't solve. And it creates new ones. To be specific, economic growth does not provide the new and improved public services that are required by a higher level of private consumption or which mark our progress towards a more civilized existence. Nor does economic growth solve the problems of environment and especially of urban environment. On the contrary, it makes these problems infinitely more urgent. And, thirdly, economic growth does not help those who, for reasons of race, educational deprivation, early environment, location, health, age, family situation, mental retardation, are unable to participate fully in the economy and its gains.

—John Kenneth Galbraith, "An Agenda for American Liberals," *Commentary*

꩜

A STANDARD REFRAIN in the Kennedy literature has it that John Kennedy's great contribution to the New Economics was his tax cut of some $10 billion (actually passed in 1964), which triumphantly proved the theory that only a rapidly expanding economy can provide jobs, prosperity, and happiness for all Americans. It is true that this major tax cut did produce significant economic growth. It is also true that such growth stimulates the job market and increases prosperity for many segments of American society. But imbedded in the folklore of Kennedy's economic "miracle" are two cruel facts: economic expansion per se does not touch vast segments of the American poor and may actually serve to conceal even further their desperate plight; and Kennedy's tax cut primarily benefited those who were already affluent.

Kennedy's first tax proposal of April, 1961, did contain significant tax reforms, but it was soon changed under the impetus of the powerful corporate lobbyists. Eighteen months later, the bill not only followed business community desires, but contained an additional investment credit. There was no provision for withholding tax on dividends and interest to prevent evasion (only wage earners suffer withholdng taxes); nor had the bill plugged other loopholes, which annually cost the U.S. Treasury billions of dollars in lost revenue. To those who argue that Kennedy's earlier bill indicated his real intentions, critics such as *Washington Post* economist Bernard Nossiter have countered that Kennedy could have vetoed the bill as enacted. But, in fact, the President and his aides worked hard to secure passage of the final version.

Senator Joseph Clark of Pennsylvania called the bill a "tax dodger's delight," but Treasury Secretary Dillon declared, "The bill . . . represents a major advance toward our national goal of a revised and modernized tax system. In its tax reform provisions, the bill makes substantial headway in eliminating many long recognized abuses. The investment credit provides a significant stimulus both to economic growth and America's competitive position in the world . . . . The bill . . . is a significant first step toward the reform of our present outmoded tax laws." Kennedy himself stated, when signing the bill in 1962, "This is an important bill—one possessing many desirable features which will stimulate the economy and provide a greater measure of fairness in our tax system."

In 1963, Kennedy made the reduction of tax rates his chief legislative goal. Even a brief survey induces considerable skepticism about Kennedy's notion of "fairness." As Nossiter noted, "the suggested rates paralleled to a remarkable extent those urged by the United States Chamber of Commerce. The President proposed cutting the rate in the top income bracket from 91 percent to 65 percent. At the bottom, he suggested that Congress replace the 20 percent rate with 14 percent on the first $1000 of taxable income and 16 percent on the next. The Chamber had urged the very same cut at the top; it would be less generous to the bottom, however, lowering only the take from the initial $1000 and setting that rate at 15 percent. Going up the income scale, the Chamber proposed somewhat smaller reductions than the President. But at the $38,000 bracket and higher, the two plans were identical. Similarly in the corporate sphere, Kennedy and the Chamber were at one. Both urged dropping the corporate income tax from 52 percent to 47 percent." The business community, however, objected loudly to Kennedy's proposed tax reforms. To assuage their fears, the President went before a group of bankers and five times promised them that reforms would not get in the way of tax cuts. He was right.

As both Bernard Nossiter and Arnold Schuchter analyzed Kennedy's tax reductions, the 2.4 percent of taxpayers with taxable incomes of $20,000 or more (the 200,000 richest taxpayers) would gain $2.3 billion, an average of $4,600 each. But the 40 percent of taxpayers with taxable incomes of $5,000 or less (the 20 million poorest taxpayers) would gain a total of only about $1.5 billion, or some $75 each. The total corporate gain amounted to another $2.6 billion (on top of the 1962 tax savings of $1.5 billion from the new depreciation allowance and $1.3 billion from the new investment credit). As Schuchter later summarized the result, "The projected economic expansion has indeed taken place, by enabling the prosperous majority of Americans to save over $23 billion in taxes since 1963." (These figures were published in 1968.) We have already seen how little of the largess of an expanded economy trickled down to the poor and the powerless.

In addition to funneling increased incomes to the affluent by major tax reductions, Kennedy also failed to close the vast tax gaps which could have provided him with the funds to end poverty in America. As Schuchter reported, "The Kennedy Administration conceded that tax laws were riddled with loopholes. For example, twenty people with annual incomes of over a half-million dollars, five of whom had incomes of over $5 million each, paid no federal income tax whatsoever. Taxpayers with annual incomes of between $1 and $5 million paid at an effective rate of about 24 per cent." By 1971, according to columnist Jack Anderson, the U.S. Treasury was losing a staggering $50 billion a year through tax loopholes to privileged taxpayers and tax evaders. The New Frontier and its New Economics had, after all, proved to be only another familiar stage in the expansion of America's affluent conservatism rather than a marker of genuine social reform. Under Kennedy, as under Nixon, the rich grew richer, the poor poorer, and the country less certain of a united and progressive future.

IV. The Steel Crisis:
Demythologizing the Dragon-Slayer

While Kennedy's treatment of the Business Council, anti-recession measures, balance of payments and trade bill all comported with the standard doctrine of important segments of business, his angry quarrel with Chairman Blough of Big Steel appeared to break the pattern. Indeed, after the famous clash, some sophisticated observers spoke of a new Kennedy "opening to the left" and predicted that the President's anchor on the right, Treasury Secretary C. Douglas Dillon, would lose his role as the Cabinet's economic strong man.

Perhaps no domestic incident of the Administration's first three years has been so misunderstood. The confusion has arisen because conventional wisdom attributed political motives to the President and economic concerns to Blough; in fact, the very reverse better explains what happened.
> —Bernard D. Nossiter, *The Mythmakers: An Essay on Power and Wealth*

Rather than being anti-business, this Administration, except for its actions during the steel price incident, has exhibited a sympathetic and constructive attitude towards the business and financial community.
> —Charles Walker, Executive Vice President of the American Bankers
> Association

ᔥ

PROBABLY NO SINGLE action of John Kennedy's aroused such ecstasies of reportorial prose as his April, 1962, battle to force U.S. Steel and its followers to rescind their price increases. The fight, which resulted in Big Steel's rapid surrender, seemed at a stroke to demolish liberal doubts about Kennedy and raise him to the position of champion of American workers and consumers.

A closer look at the facts, such as that offered by Bernard Nossiter, shows a somewhat different aspect of the commonly accepted picture. According to Nossiter, Kennedy had worked hard to hold down steel prices in order to keep the steel unions from demanding a significant wage increase. By preventing a wage hike in the key steel industry, Kennedy hoped to prevent a renewed wage-price inflationary spiral. In October, 1961, the President had persuaded the steel leaders not to raise prices, and in return he had used his influence to keep the United Steelworkers from demanding a sizable wage increase in March, 1962.

Then, ten days after the new contract was signed, Roger Blough, president of U.S. Steel, announced a price rise of about $6 a ton. This sudden switch by industry, if allowed to stand, would have angered the unions into demanding higher wages and encouraged other corporations to raise their prices. Kennedy himself explained his actions against Big Steel in just such terms in a later interview: "The steel union had accepted the most limited settlement that they had had since the end of the second war, they had accepted it . . . in part, I think, because I said that we could not afford another inflationary spiral . . . if I had not attempted to use my influence to have the companies hold their prices stable, I think the union could have rightfully felt that they had been misled. In my opinion, it would have . . . made it impossible for us to exert any influence from the public point of view in the future on these great labor-managment disputes . . . ."

Kennedy took immediate steps to pressure the steel industry into line on steel prices. Attorney General Robert Kennedy announced an immediate price probe by the Justice Department. Senator Kefauver's subcommittee launched an investigation. Administration supporters publicly denounced the increase, and private steps were taken to persuade other steel companies not to follow U.S. Steel. The President made a strong televised statement against the price rise. Solicitor General Archibald Cox began drafting new antitrust legislation, the FBI subpoenaed steel mills for data, and Administration officials continued informal contacts with the steel industry. Two days after the announced rise, Roger Blough went on televison to defend his position. But the break had already come: Inland Steel announced on April 13 that it had decided not to raise prices. Other firms sat tight, and in the afternoon Bethlehem Steel rescinded its increase. Two hours later, U.S. Steel surrendered, and the rest quickly followed.

Why had the crisis occurred? Bernard Nossiter felt that Blough's move was basically ideological rather than economic, and that he had acted to reestablish the primacy of industry's right to set its own prices rather than having to follow government guidelines. If Blough had moved more adroitly, he might well have accomplished his aim. As Nossiter pointed out, "Had U.S. Steel nibbled away at the lid on prices, raising one steel product here, lowering another less important one there and stretching the whole process out over several months, public opinion could not have been mobilized and Presidential wrath would probably not have been incited." Kennedy's aim, on the other hand, was economic, not ideological: a desire to avoid politically embarrassing inflationary leaps, rather than a belief in giving labor or the deprived a greater slice of the economic pie.

In fact, 364 days after Kennedy's widely acclaimed victory, a trial scattering of steel price rises was announced. The President stated that selective price rises "are not incompatible with a framework of general stability," and hailed the over-all rise of about 1 percent as "restraint." Although Kennedy probably could not have prevented this increase, he could definitely have proposed new procedures to deal with corporate pricing power. But when Kennedy's Solicitor General, Archibald Cox, actually suggested some badly needed mechanisms, his advice was ignored. Once again, the Kennedy Administration fell into line with business wishes, and the dragon-slayer sat down to dine with the dragon.

V. The High Cost of Neurosis

IN ALL THE domestic areas of major concern, it seems to me that Kennedy suffered—and the country suffered geometrically—from two basic flaws: a failure of imagination resulting primarily from his neurotically-conditioned self-centeredness; and a fear of confronting entrenched national authority figures with the critical need for social change in America. John F. Kennedy, the man who as a youth had written so eloquently against England's appeasement of Hitler, gave strong evidence of being, in fact, a person who steered a cautious course through life by the main psychic tools of placation, passive resistance, and avoidance of direct conflict with personalized authority figures.

I am aware that this interpretation seems to conflict with my analysis of Kennedy's need for international confrontations and heroic vindication. But in fact it does not. To understand this subtlety, we should consider the essential difference between the figures faced internationally and the figures avoided domestically. Nikita Khrushchev was not only an alien chieftain, but, in the American Cold War and puritanically classical view, an incarnation of Satan himself. (Of course, the devils seen outside largely reflect the devils within—the guilt and anxiety present in all neurotic conflict.) Communism had been so mythologized by the time Kennedy came to power (and Kennedy himself had been thoroughly imbued with that mythology) that it had become to most Americans the modern version of the seventeenth-, eighteenth-, and nineteenth-century devil. Communist leaders, in such a pathological world view, were of necessity devils themselves.

This national psychohistorical dehumanization of foreign foes was reinforced in Kennedy's case by his own personal history, which put such excessive emphasis upon the need for personal victory over competitive opponents. Thus one would guess that Khrushchev and Castro were deeply felt by Kennedy, if not consciously seen, as internalized devil figures. On the other hand, the American financial, industrial, and political leaders whom Kennedy encountered at home would be easily identifiable with his authoritarian father. Kennedy's outburst against businessmen—"My father always told me that all businessmen were sons-of-bitches"—seems to have been more a momentary pique than a significant belief; for Joseph P. Kennedy himself was, above all else, one of the world's shrewdest businessmen. And regarding JFK's inability to face down entrenched political leaders, it should be recalled that both of his grandfathers were successful politicians with whom he had identified from childhood.

We must also remember how Jack Kennedy's emotional distance from people was part of his defense system, an avoidance of too-close and potentially threatening relationships. Just as Kennedy compartmentalized his relationships, so, too, it strikes one as likely that he unconsciously compartmentalized his feelings about people, so that everyone was seen only in part and never as a full human being (a trait commonly exhibited, in varying degrees, by most neurotics). This tendency would also help to explain why Kennedy might have regarded Communist leaders as alien menaces requiring direct and strong responses, while he tended to conciliate and appease the father figures in the American political and business establishments. Both Kennedy's anticommunism and economic conservatism were deeply internalized in his psychic responses. Therefore it would be no real contradiction, in psychological terms, for him to have sought heroic confrontations in the foreign field and avoided direct conflict whenever possible at home.

It is important, though, to note Kennedy's predilection for crisis situations both internationally and domestically. While some of these were beyond his control, more show evidence of being either self-created or greatly worsened by Kennedy's reactions. Psychohistorically, Kennedy's inner pull toward self-defeat and self-punishment seems to have unconsciously motivated him to commit multiple errors of commission and omission. In repeatedly punishing himself, unfortunately, he also—quite unconsciously but inevitably—punished his country. Perhaps this is one reason Kennedy's death produced such an irrational flood of guilt and sense of loss: not because he was a great leader, which he demonstrably was not, but because he was a leader who mirrored so many of our own conflicts and fantasies.

Bobby Kennedy's first reported words on learning of Jack's death were, "He had the most wonderful life." Since much of this book's validity rests on the thesis that Jack's life was not nearly so wonderful as it seemed, let us briefly reconsider that assessment. On the obvious, positive side, we can only agree: JFK was a young, handsome, vigorous, rich, intelligent, and generally popular President of the United States; he had a beautiful, talented, immensely popular wife and two lovely children whom he adored. Although much of his administrative program had not been achieved and he had suffered inevitable setbacks, he had great plans for the future, and several of his accomplishments seemed to fall within the realm of genuine statesmanship. His reelection the next year was practically assured, and in his second term it seemed probable to both Kennedy and his hard-working, extremely loyal staff that important things would be accomplished.

Now we must look at the less visible realities. In his personal life, President Kennedy suffered continuous back pain, which seemed to come and go to a considerable degree with the tensions of his work. His marriage was also undergoing considerable strain, and there is strong evidence that JFK was frequently faithless to his wife and that she knew it. But both Jack and Jackie were intensely ambitious, and both were willing to maintain harmonious appearances and conceal inner unhappiness for the sake of their ambitions. On the public side, Kennedy was capable of committing both impetuous and immoral presidential acts, as evidenced by the Bay of Pigs invasion; he seemed to consider personal vindication more important than national survival, as evidenced by the 1962 missile crisis; he was apparently often incapable of judging historical and social realities, as evidenced by his expansion of the Vietnam war and support of the unpopular dictator, Ngo Dinh Diem; and, domestically, he had little insight into the realities of widespread poverty, lack of opportunities, inequalities, and discrimination against major "minorities" of the American public (notably the poor, black, and female).

Thus when Kennedy died, he did not leave the shining legacy that his election seemed to promise; rather, he left great stores of international and social high explosives. In the arms race, which Kennedy had speeded up, the United States and Russia, while ostensibly leveling off their stockpiles of nuclear overkill weaponry in accordance with the Test Ban Treaty (limiting all but underground tests of nuclear weapons), were actually racing ahead more irrationally than ever to "keep up" with each other. In Vietnam, Kennedy's escalation from 600 to 16,000 American forces would propel Lyndon Johnson into the gigantic error of outdoing Kennedy by continuing and then enormously enlarging the Kennedy stance of "peace through strength." In Detroit and Watts and Chicago and New York and Newark and Baltimore and Washington, D.C., to venture no further south, black people were still living warped human lives in veritable hellholes of physical torment, hellholes which had not been cooled or opened far by Kennedy's glowing rhetoric, although more Negroes in the South could vote and a handful of blacks could attend state universities. American working women still earned only about half the wages of American working men, and the gap was widening. And there were still millions of Americans, men, women and children, who went to bed hungry and nearly hopeless every night.

Kennedy, of course, did not create much of this shocking situation, especially the domestic chaos. But he did very little to change it. The times demanded a national leader capable of a revolutionary approach, a person who felt the terrible need for enormous change in his heart and bones and was not content with forming the words with his lips. Kennedy was emotionally incapable of such a response, for his best emotions seemed to be locked tightly within himself. He had insulated himself too successfully from his own feelings. Thus his undoubted natural and cultivated intelligence could only function at half-power, for intelligence is largely motivated and broadened by feelings. Kennedy could not see clearly because he could not feel clearly. Although verbally articulate, he was psychologically separated from the agonies of the nation he wished quite genuinely to lead and help. We can only help others to the extent to which we have helped and been helped ourselves. A man who had been in a large sense emotionally stunted by his parents and his upbringing had too little psychic strength to assume the tremendous burdens of the even more stunted people who looked to him for support. If this seems a harsh assessment, the reality of America for the majority of Americans is harsh. While we may understand and forgive the Kennedys, just as we should understand and forgive ourselves and each other, we should not turn aside from or sentimentalize the truth; and we should not forget.

Regarding Kennedy's prospective second term, it seems extremely doubtful that he would have made any great changes after his reelection. Even leaving aside his own characterology, the double facts remain that, historically, Presidents grow politically weaker rather than stronger in their second terms; and neither Kennedy nor the recalcitrant and often narrow-visioned Congress which repeatedly rejected his measures had shown much interest, inclination, or ability to effect a working rapprochement. Put briefly, if Kennedy had not changed his basic outlook (which seemed little enlarged by late 1963); if his second term had been influenced by maintaining support for the next Kennedy "heir"; if Congress continued to be uncooperative (and why should it essentially change?); and if Kennedy could not vastly improve his influence over that Congress; then how could the marvelous deeds supposedly envisioned by Kennedy and his staff ever be enacted? In addition, the fighting continued in Vietnam, and I have shown why I think Kennedy would inevitably have continued and gradually enlarged the war; the ghettos waited for the sparks of summer; the cities were decaying and the air filling with pollution (although few people smelled it as yet); the students were beginning to grow restless. And America still awaited a leader of sufficient vision and inner strength to realize its magnificent dream.

Arnold Schuchter admirably expressed this idea of the still unfulfilled presidential potential in America when he wrote, in *White Power/Black*

Freedom, "A President is limited by national fiscal resources; yet, there exist latent national resources—capital, manpower, talents, energies, and youth —that have barely been tapped, through leadership default and ineptitude. A President is constrained by the workings of party politics; but presidents have been known to rise above party politics, especially during periods of national crisis. In an age seemingly captured by mammoth organizations and bureaucracy, the shape of the future will still depend greatly on individuals, especially those struggling to govern the basic institutions which exercise power in this nation—and, above all, the Presidency."

John F. Kennedy became an expert in building political power to shape his own narrow personal ends. But his emotional obstacles prevented him from ever using his intelligence and great political expertise to build political power for the shaping of answers to urgent human needs within the society he tried to govern. Therein lay the great tragedy of Kennedy himself and of the country he failed to change.

In summation, Kennedy as President was generally a mediocre Chief Executive and occasionally a dangerous one (mediocrity is also a danger in times of pressing need and high nuclear risk). As an individual, Kennedy was a man of great intelligence, high personal integrity, enormous physical courage, and considerable personal charm. The tragedy is that his very large talents and character strengths were so largely offset and undermined by unconscious emotional conflicts and uncertainties. Thus Kennedy constantly exhibited a surprising caution and sense of powerlessness in coping with the urgent domestic needs of poverty and race relations, whereas in the international realm he often plunged heedlessly ahead from an apparent feeling of omnipotence. As mentioned, these diametric characteristics—concurrent feelings of impotence and omnipotence—are usually found to some degree in all neurotic personalities.

Thus in both the domestic and international arenas, Kennedy failed to come to grips with reality. At home, he retreated from confronting a supposedly intractable Congress; abroad, he advanced to bridge a nonexistent missile gap, thus intensifying the highly dangerous arms race, and in Southeast Asia, plunged into a foreign civil war which fifteen years of history had already proved was unwinnable by a Western power as well as immoral by the standards of America's own ideology. Kennedy's legacy to the American people was not a happy one: racial turmoil at home, an expanding war overseas, and a terrifying acceleration of the U.S.-U.S.S.R. arms race. The fact that his successor, Lyndon Johnson, generally acted like an arsonist rather than a fire department in coping with these tragic conflagrations should not hide the fact that it was Kennedy who either scattered the sparks or failed to dampen them. Kennedy's extraordinarily exaggerated "style" has all but belied the evidence of events. It is time we learned to judge our Presidents less by their looks, personalities, and words than by their achievements.

In a sense, as I. F. Stone realized, Kennedy died just in time to retain his inflated prestige. Had he faced the Watts and post-Watts riots with his customary wavering, and had he further enlarged the Vietnam war, as appeared all too likely, he might well have left his second term with a blasted reputation that would have ended all hopes of a Kennedy successor. That a potential Kennedy successor is still with us nine years after John Kennedy's death is ample testimony both of Kennedy determination and of America's predisposition to overlook delivery when the promises are hypnotic. For if Prince Charming needed his throne, it seems equally true that much of America has needed a Prince Charming.

VI. JFK's Health:
Did Kennedy Have Addison's Disease?

A MAJOR THEME of this book is that President Kennedy's shortcomings in policy and performance stemmed largely from neurotic patterns of outlook and behavior typical of the entire Kennedy family. But we must also consider the question of Kennedy's physical health and whether his physical problems had an equal—or greater—effect on his presidency.

It is now well established that Jack Kennedy suffered from a form of Addison's disease, which is a deficiency of the adrenal glands. Several physicians, including Dr. Hugh L'Etang in his book *The Pathology of Leadership*, have stated this fact. Dr. L'Etang wrote of Kennedy's condition in his study of the effects of disease on twentieth-century national leaders:

"Shortly before polling day in November 1960, Walter H. Judd, a Republican Congressman and a former medical missionary, demanded that Kennedy should confirm or deny whether he had Addison's disease as he had been identified as the patient, with Addison's disease and spinal trouble, whose case history appeared in a surgical journal in 1955. Painstaking research work in 1967 clearly identified Kennedy as this patient and the article clearly defines the state of his adrenals and his need for steroids such as cortisone.

"At the time of the operation in 1954 Kennedy was receiving 25 mg. cortisone daily and one 150 mg. implant of desoxycorticosterone acetate every three months. The dose of cortisone was increased in 1961 and the White House correspondents, soon aware that steroids can cause facial oedema, became experts at assessing the puffiness of his cheeks. Even Kennedy had to admit to Schlesinger, 'The doctors say I've got a sort of slow-motion leukemia, but they tell me I'll probably last until I'm forty-five.' "

Dr. L'Etang noted that a well-advanced case of Addison's disease can lead to debility, susceptibility to fatigue, nervous irritability, emotional instability, periods of depression and negativistic conduct. But cortisone "in the dose range administered to Kennedy in 1954, works wonders." The patient is restored to an active, interested and alert personality, although some euphoria may occur.

In analyzing Kennedy's presidential behavior, Dr. L'Etang suggests the possibility of "elements of imprudent overconfidence and unfounded optimism" that influenced Kennedy's decision to go to Dallas against the advice of many. As further possible evidence of euphoria caused by cortisone, L'Etang also mentions JFK's defective judgment and poor leadership during the Bay of Pigs as "not necessarily attributable to his own inexperience and to the failures of his advisers. Nor is his brilliant statesmanship during the Cuban missile crisis one year later entirely explained by added experience and better advisers." Without any detailed analysis, Dr. L'Etang found in JFK's Administration "certain inconsistencies of behavior that have not been admitted, investigated or explained."

In this book I have considered an alternate explanation for Kennedy's "inconsistencies of behavior"—one that is largely psychological rather than physiological. A close examination of the record supports this view rather than the thesis that Kennedy suffered bouts of emotional instability because of cortisone injections. The Bay of Pigs was not a snap "euphoric" decision, but one that was studied and agonized over for months, and eventually resolved in a direction consistent with the Kennedy belief in personal and national omnipotence and superiority over "backward" peoples. His Vietnam intervention revealed this same underlying blindness, an emotional shortcoming shared by most of Kennedy's top advisers (who were not taking cortisone), as well as by his presidential successor. Similarly, I would not agree with Dr. L'Etang that the Cuban missile crisis showed "brilliant statesmanship," but, rather, once again a partially irrational overboldness that this time turned out luckily. Again, Kennedy's Dallas trip was entirely in line with his familial pride in personal physical courage and his deep-seated sense of fatalism.

Thus, despite evidence that Kennedy was an ailing President and under heavy cortisone treatment, the fluctuations in his psyche seem to have been more the result of his childhood experiences and his personal and social psychohistory than of his medical history. In short, I believe that neurosis, not steroids, essentially caused the Kennedy Administration to fail in its great promise to the American people.

Chapter 9

ROBERT FRANCIS KENNEDY: THE RUNT OF THE LITTER, 1925-1963

He was the smallest and thinnest, and we feared he might grow up puny and girlish. We soon realized there was no fear of that.

Bobby has been a great joy and blessing to me and my husband always. He has taken his religion seriously and still does. We never had any worries about him.

—Rose Fitzgerald Kennedy

If one of you guys writes one more time about his looking like a choirboy, I'll kill you. A choirboy is sweet, soft, cherubic. Take a look at that bony little face, those hard, opaque eyes, and then listen to him bawl somebody out. Some choirboy!

—State Department official to a reporter

I was the seventh of nine children. And when you come from that far down, you have to struggle to survive.

—Robert Francis Kennedy

Once he identifies an injustice, Kennedy loathes it with rare intensity and works relentlessly against it. A moralistic, judgmental viewpoint can often though not inevitably lead to arrogance, self-righteousness, and oversimplification of what is complex. Kennedy has been guilty of these failings at times but less so of late than in the early years of his career. Notwithstanding these offsetting weaknesses, Kennedy's moral force remains one of his major sources of strength. It gives purpose to his other qualities such as courage, loyalty, and intelligence. It is what makes Kennedy a solid man to rely upon in a crisis.

—William V. Shannon, *The Heir Apparent*

It is the conjunction of moral certainty about right and wrong with calculated opportunism which accounts for Kennedy's reputation for ruthlessness. He gives the impression that personal success and the triumph of right are interchangeable.

—Hans J. Morgenthau

꙳

EVERY MAN'S CHILDHOOD is different, no matter how close-knit the family into which he is born, nor how determining that family's influence and values; and every person's temperament and personality are wholly his own, shaped out of his unique life patterns and responses, no matter how nearly his childhood experiences resemble those of his brothers.

Robert Francis Kennedy, the third son and seventh child of Joseph and Rose Kennedy, was no exception to this rule of psychology. While in many ways he was shaped by the powerful ambitions and demands of his strong-willed parents, Bobby Kennedy also developed his own personal reactions and answers to those demands. Unlike brother Joe, and later brother Teddy, Bobby did not generally move warmly toward people outside his immediate family, except in his earliest years and, in certain ways, in his later years. Nor did he emotionally withdraw himself from direct conflict, as did brother Jack. More and more, Bobby seemed to turn toward overt expressions of his inner drives, expressions that often changed with bewildering rapidity. By his twenties he had become a young man who alternated frequently between open anger and moody coldness; a man both shy and silent, harsh and outspoken in his judgments of others; sometimes vindictive, and sometimes surprisingly thoughtful, humorous, warm, even tender.

Most of all, it could be said that Robert Kennedy was a person of intense emotions who revealed much inner unhappiness and disequilibrium, yet who was apparently motored by strong forces directing him steadily onward toward the achievement of high position and power. In a very real and important sense, the volatile Bobby was probably the most emotionally reachable of all the Kennedys, as well as the most controversial. Bobby's emotional vulnerability became, in many respects, his greatest strength. He could often directly empathize with people as the other Kennedys could not; and being able to feel more spontaneously than the others, he was also more emotionally responsive to the urgent needs of his troubled nation, although even in his last years he continued to show a deep ambivalence between personal ambition and genuine concern.

As a sympathetic associate wrote after Bobby's death, "Kennedy's emotionalism was one of the crucial differences between him and his brothers. It was the quality that made him so vulnerable to actual experience. For example, it was Michael Harrington's book, *The Other America,* that opened the more intellectual John Kennedy's eyes to poverty. But for Robert Kennedy, it was his walks through the ghettos, his visits to the Mississippi Delta and Latin America, that made him feel the question of poverty so personally and deeply. For Robert Kennedy, the sight of one hungry black child in Greenwood, Mississippi, had a greater impact than a million words or statistics."

An English observer saw the same quality and wrote, "Humanity remains his strongest asset—and one that is least recognized and valued both by himself and some of those around him, except in purely personal terms. While he lacks the imagination to project himself into distant situations he does identify wholeheartedly and at once with the underprivileged who are close to him: hence, the real need for constant trips to go and see for himself. At short range, his energy goes full speed ahead; the results are likely to be pithy, pungent, and sometimes not far short of pugilistic."

There were also potential dangers in Bobby's intense emotionalism. At times, as even supporters noticed, his emotions were too intense for him to handle, as, for example, in his clashes with professional politicians whom he distrusted and disliked. Strong and spontaneous emotional responses can bring a person close to people and problems; but when poorly used, they can also create barriers to understanding and arouse deeply repressed conflicts and fears within oneself (or serve to cover up these fears and repress them still deeper). I will try to clarify both the advantages and drawbacks of RFK's emotionalism in developing the history of his life and times.

Robert Francis Kennedy was born on November 20, 1925, when Joe Junior was ten and Jack eight. Bobby lived only six months in the Brookline, Massachusetts, neighborhood that had been home for Joseph and Rose Kennedy since their marriage in October, 1914 (they had moved once to a larger house a few blocks away). Then, early in 1926, Joseph Kennedy took his family to the fashionable Riverdale section of New York City. This move was only the first of many for Bobby, who, of all the children, was probably shifted around most often in his formative years. In 1929, when Bobby was three, the Kennedys bought an even more imposing house in Bronxville. But a degree of stability had been added the prior year by the purchase of the Hyannis Port summer home, which would remain everyone's favorite.

In Bobby's earliest years of childhood and adolescence, he could show a touching gentleness and sweetness that his later embittered opponents would have considered extraordinary, although close friends found these qualities as typical of Kennedy as his aggressiveness and frequent rudeness. His nurse, Luella Hennessey, thought Bobby "the most thoughtful and considerate of all the Kennedy children." A primary schoolteacher remembered him as "a nice freckle-faced little kid, his hair some shade of brown, a regular boy. He needed no special handling. It seemed hard for him to finish his work sometimes, but he was only ten after all." Journalist Arthur Krock noticed Bobby's affectionate nature, especially with his mother. "He was very gentle to his mother—like a ewe lamb," said Krock. According to Lem Billings, a Choate roommate of Jack's, "Bobby was a hell of a nice little boy, one of the nicest I ever met. He always was responsible, friendly, and thoughtful."

Yet from his earliest years, Bobby was also seen by others as a shy, quiet boy who didn't make friends easily. The frequent changes of schools must have discouraged close friendships. In addition, Bobby had the emotional handicap of being a seventh child in a highly competitive family, with four bigger sisters between himself and his older brothers. As Bobby later commented on his own feelings of inferiority and sibling rivalry, ". . . when you come from that far down, you have to struggle to survive." A family friend echoes this observation: "He's feisty and strong-tempered. But remember, he was the runt of a pretty competitive family. It's a matter of a couple of inches in the tibia."

Bobby's relative smallness—not quite five-feet-ten compared to three brothers all six feet tall or over—probably did add to his general insecurity. At first his size worried his mother, who once said, "He grew up in the shadow of Joe, the oldest, and of Jack, with his sisters and Ted, the baby." Bobby later recalled his own boyhood shyness and lack of physical coordination: "What I remember most vividly about growing up was going to a lot of different schools, always having to make new friends, and that I was very awkward. I dropped things and fell down all the time. I had to go to the hospital a few times for stitches in my head and my leg. And I was pretty quiet most of the time. And I didn't mind being alone." Frequent accidents are often an unconscious way of asking for attention and affection, which in Bobby's case would not be surprising. Many observed the continuance of these characteristics in the grown-up Bobby. Jack Newfield wrote, "As an adult he was the least poised, the least articulate, and the least extroverted of the Kennedy brothers. He was also the most physical, the most passionate, and the most politically unorthodox."

Bobby's "struggle to survive" began young. From an early age he exhibited an unusual physical assertiveness and tenacity. At four, he infuriated Joe Junior and Jack one day by repeatedly jumping off their sailboat in Nantucket Sound in a memorable swim-or-sink effort. As JFK wryly recalled, Bobby's determination showed "either a lot of guts or no sense at all, depending on how you looked at it." Bobby's intense need to test and prove his physical courage would be displayed often in his adult years in dangerous exploits of skiing, rapids-shooting, mountain-climbing, and jungle exploration. As with the other Kennedy boys, Bobby's obsession with valor suggested mixed elements of a zest for adventure and a desire for heroic vindication, along with undertones of self-punishment and self-destruction. But Bobby could also be reasonably cautious when his judgment overcame his desire for glory. As a boy he and the chauffeur's son once made parachutes out of sheets for jumping off the roof. The other boy jumped first and broke a leg; Bobby didn't jump.

Years later, a close friend of Bobby's commented, "He was the little brother, the one who got beaten up by his big brothers. It's on his mind and he often says now that he's going to bring up his children differently. When he was little, it was always, 'Robert, go fetch the ice cream.' And he was always fighting with Jack over the radio—the Senator liked jazz, even when it was Benny Goodman, and Jack didn't." Arthur Krock, who remarked upon Bobby's gentleness with his mother, also noticed his ability to fight back and later wrote, "[he] became heir apparent to the political dynasty, bullied by his elder brothers but still managing to keep a kind of savage individuality. At whatever sport it was, this boy of fifteen was always trying to beat one of the older boys to overcome the age handicap."

In Bronxville, Bobby attended a nursery school, a private school for the first and second grades, and a public school for the next three grades. In March, 1938, when he was twelve, Bobby was taken out of another exclusive school he had only recently started and sailed with his family to England. The previous month, Joseph Kennedy had arrived in London as FDR's new U.S. Ambassador. An Englishman, David Ormsby Gore (later Lord Harlech and British Ambassador to Washington), remembered Bobby at that time: "When I first knew Bobby I was about nineteen and he was eleven—so I didn't speak to him much except to say 'Hello, Bobby,' and ask him how school was. I think he loathed his English school. They made him wear one of those things worse than a cap, you know, they look as if they're made of cloth." England never appealed to the younger Bobby as it did to brothers Joe and Jack, who enjoyed the social whirl, nor did cricket, which he learned to play at his aristocratic prep school.

Like so many children who need some feeling of distinction, Bobby loved to dress up in various uniforms. This may have been one reason he decided to become a Boy Scout at twelve. But Bobby refused to join the English Scouts, who required a pledge of allegiance to the Crown; instead, his father went to considerable trouble to enroll him as a long-range American Scout. Perhaps, too, Bobby was influenced by the growing war fears that were enveloping Europe and America. On September 1, 1939, Hitler's troops marched into Poland; two days later, England and France declared war on Germany. Later that month, the Ambassador shipped his family back to Bronxville, while he remained in England for another lonely year.

During his teens and college years, the third son continued to show the shyness and diffidence that often marked his adult years and puzzled those who knew his strain of arrogance. Unlike his more worldly brothers, Bobby was also intensely religious, a devoutness he shared with his mother and sister Eunice. For a short time he went to St. Paul's School, an Episcopal preparatory school in Concord, New Hampshire, but after he complained to his mother about the required daily Protestant chapel, he was withdrawn. For the next three years, Bobby attended a very strict and competitive Catholic school, the Portsmouth Priory School in Rhode Island, run by the famous Order of St. Benedict. At about this time, he briefly considered becoming a priest. Although scholastically he plodded along in the lower half of his class, Bobby did well in sports, which apparently interested him more.

But the Ambassador wanted all his sons to have a secular and practical education at an Ivy League college, preferably his own. Worried about Bobby's low grades, his father sent him to Milton Academy in Milton, Massachusetts, which specifically trained its students to enter Harvard. Bobby's Milton housemaster remembered him as a dogged worker rather than an outstanding student or leader. "He was not outstandingly brilliant; he got good grades and graduated. He was not a naturally brilliant student, who just flicked off the grades. He had to work and he's always worked hard. He's always been full of industry and has worked for whatever he's gotten. And I remember him mostly on the football field, really, because I didn't have him in class. On the football field you knew he was around. He was pretty active—he'd win at anything."

Milton classmates noticed the young man's difficulty in making friends. When one suggested of Bobby "probably he would have been happier if he'd had more friends of his own age," a schoolmate who had known him on the playing fields snapped back, "He'd have been happier if he'd had more friends." Bobby did make one lasting close friend at Milton, David Hackett, who later wrote an amusing satire of Kennedy competitiveness. A less fond classmate characterized Bobby tersely: "He was no good at small talk, he was no good at social amenities, he was no great lover."

When Bobby was graduated from Milton in 1943, Joe Junior and Jack were in the midst of the Second World War—Jack in South Pacific PT boats, Joe flying patrol missions over the English Channel. Bobby longed to get into the action; at eighteen he followed his brothers into the Navy and signed up for officer candidate classes at Harvard, which he entered that fall. The shocking death of young Joe the following August propelled Bobby into more immediate service. At nineteen, he resigned from officer training and left Harvard to serve as an enlisted man aboard the U.S.S. *Joseph P. Kennedy, Jr.*, the destroyer named posthumously for his brother. But the war ended just too soon for Bobby to see combat. His sea duty was spent peacefully in the Carribbean.

Bobby returned to Harvard in 1946 for his last two years. During college, he again showed much more interest in athletics than in studies. As he said later, "To tell you the truth, I didn't go to class very much. I used to talk and argue a lot, mostly about sports and politics." Football gave Bobby a chance both to prove himself and vent his aggressive energies. Although he was smaller, lighter (only 150 pounds), and slower than most of the players, Bobby made himself into a varsity end through sheer combativeness. Kenneth O'Donnell, the Harvard football captain who later became a trusted aide to both JFK and RFK, commented on Bobby's surplus of perseverance and lack of brawn: "I can't think of anyone who had less right to make the varsity squad than Bobby, when he first came out for practice. The war was over and we had plenty of manpower, all of it bigger, faster, and more experienced than he was. But every afternoon he would be down on that field an hour early and he always stayed an hour later. He just *made* himself better."

Throughout his life, Robert Kennedy displayed the same fierce determination to win an immediate goal, no matter what the handicaps. It was a quality that could lead both to success and to obsessive fixations on objects not always worth such intense efforts. Bobby's intensity exacted a noticeable physical and emotional price; by his early forties he was a frequently tired person.

At Harvard, Bobby's gritty self-discipline at football brought him a triumph that had eluded his two taller and faster older brothers—the prized Harvard letter. For some reason, perhaps simple admiration of the battered Bobby's unflinching toughness, the same coach who had kept Joe Junior out of the essential Harvard-Yale game gave Bobby his chance. Bobby limped painfully onto the field for the final pile-up, one leg taped from a scrimmage injury. Harvard lost, but Bobby, for the first time in his life, had really won. Football always remained important to Bobby, and he enjoyed impromptu touch football games all his life. As Attorney General, he even once told a meeting of college coaches, "Except for war, there is nothing in American life—nothing—which trains a boy better for life than football." (Bobby later changed his mind about war.) Here we can see a belief in the masculine mystique of physical toughness, and also a probable need for reassurance and affection through physical contact with other males that was more difficult to express directly. Football for the Kennedy sons—and especially Robert, who even kept a football in his Attorney General's office and often tossed it around with his staff—carried deep psychological undertones of emotional need and gratification.

Bobby's shyness and unsocial tendencies continued to be evident at college. A contemporary saw him as "very shy—not at all pushy." Bobby joined his father's old club, Hasty Pudding, Jack's Spee Club, and the Varsity Club, but he seemed to feel more at ease with socially obscure and unaffluent Harvard men. This is understandable in view of his "underdog" position in the family and the emotional insecurity he never lost. Kenny O'Donnell said of Bobby, "In college in those years most of the guys were older than Bob and he was less sure of himself. Bob didn't go to social affairs or dances. He went with the common herd. His friends were persons who couldn't scrape twenty-five cents together. Bob was like the rest of us— finding himself."

Bobby's puritanism provided a rationale for his emotional reluctance to assert himself socially and his feelings of being an outsider. Until his thirties, he was rigid in his own habits, not smoking or drinking and dis- approving of those who did. Of party-goers, Bobby once commented, "Nobody who ever went to them made any real contribution. What's the good of going to those things and drinking? I'd rather do something else." Bobby's parents contributed strongly to this moralistic outlook. Neither Joe nor Rose approved of drinking or smoking; the Ambassador even offered a thousand dollars to any son who finished college without using alcohol or tobacco. Bobby, unlike Jack, collected. Another contemporary's description showed Bobby's typical out-of-pockets financial condition and his generous streak: "He was different from some of the fellows with a lot of money, I can tell you. There were times when I had more money in my pocket than he did. There were times when we had to treat him to a hot dog or soda. A couple of times he helped friends of ours—financially—and I found out about it later. He would give you the shirt off his back." Joe and Rose kept the boys on small allowances, with both positive and negative results. The Kennedys were not "spoiled" in the usual sense of rich, over- indulged children; on the other hand, they had little understanding of the meaning of money for ordinary people, were not generous with their own employees, and often borrowed small amounts without repaying.

When Bobby received his Harvard diploma in June, 1948, he decided to follow Jack's example and do a stint as an overseas journalist. His father's connections gave each boy a chance for a short, adventurous tryout in the newspaper world. The experience also offered Bobby his first look at war. In 1948, the Israelis were fighting a desperate, bitter battle for survival against the Arabs; Bobby was sent to the Middle East by the *Boston Post*, a paper indebted to Joseph Kennedy. Here Bobby had his first personal brush with death. By chance, he met an Israeli tank captain who had known his sister Kathleen in England. The Israeli offered Bobby a ride from Tel Aviv to Jerusalem in his tank; the convoy Bobby would otherwise have taken was wiped out. Although Bobby was a neophyte correspondent, he showed a keen judgment of directly experienced reality when he reported that Israel would win because the Jews had "more, much more spirit . . . were tougher than the Arabs." (Spirit and toughness were qualities Robert Kennedy always admired.) He also went to West Berlin to observe the airlift, but was unable to travel to Communist East Europe.

Back home from his successful brief tour as war correspondent, Bobby entered the University of Virginia Law School in the fall of 1948 (Harvard Law had rejected him) and was graduated in June, 1950. Although he ranked only fifty-sixth in a class of 125 law students, his interest was aroused by several projects where he revealed genuine ability. He was never a bookish intellectual like Jack; yet there are indications that his mind was equally responsive in different ways. Bobby was far more physical than his brothers; the senses, rather than words or ideas, fed and excited his mind. While many judged Bobby to be not as basically intelligent as the others, this seems questionable. As an adult, he received challenges often lacking in his prosaic school years (as witness the insight of his Israeli war reports), and faced with concrete problems, Bobby could show as much judgment and perception as Jack—and sometimes more.

At the University of Virginia, Bobby wrote a paper on the Yalta Conference which, although following his father's views, showed some scholarship. More significant for demonstrating his real potential were his extracurricular activities as president of the moribund Law School Forum. Bobby used his managerial ability and his father's influence to bring famous speakers to the school, including Supreme Court Justice William O. Douglas, Senator Joseph McCarthy, and the former Ambassador himself. When Bobby invited Ralph Bunche to speak in segregated Charlottesville, many university members protested; but Bobby refused to compromise on his mixed-seating plans, Bunche came, and there were no incidents.

June, 1950, brought Robert Kennedy more than a useful LL.B. degree. Far more important to the substance of his entire life, he received an emotional support that never failed him. On June 17, Bobby married Ethel Skakel, who came from an extremely wealthy family in Greenwich, Connecticut. He had met her several years earlier on a ski trip and had first dated one of her sisters. Ethel liked Bobby immediately, and she visited him often in Charlottesville. In his wife, Bobby found a person who reflected many of his own deepest drives (his passion for physical sports, strong religious beliefs, and desire for a large family to give him paternal status).

Most essential, Ethel's own emotional pattern ideally suited her to a person inwardly troubled and torn by self-doubt, a person who could never fully believe that he was genuinely accepted and acceptable. Ethel accepted Bobby wholly, with all of his faults and weaknesses. Supporting

Bobby, in fact, became the chief object of her life. She devoted herself entirely to him, not even putting their many children first, although she was a loving mother. Ethel's temperament was in many ways the opposite of Bobby's: warm, friendly, zestful, optimistic, spontaneous, enthusiastic. If Ethel had doubts, she firmly refused to look at them; and her supply of natural energy seemed even greater than Bobby's. In multiple ways, Ethel fed and supported Bobby's ego needs (as his own parents had not been able to do). However far he journeyed or to whatever depths he descended, Bobby Kennedy could always count on Ethel's unquenchable cheerfulness and understanding to rest and encourage him at home. Ethel, it seems amply evident, gave Bobby the all-consoling, all-accepting mother figure he longed for. Yet there was a less fortunate side to this relationship. Continued emotional dependence on another person carries a considerable penalty. At the end of this chapter, I will examine further Bobby's apparent relationship with his wife and his general attitudes toward women.

In the decade between Bobby's 1950 graduation from the University of Virginia Law School and his swearing-in as the second youngest United States Attorney General in American history in January, 1961, the third Kennedy son developed two distinct careers and professional identities: as a political manager, and as a legal investigator-prosecutor. The first experience channeled his executive and power drives; the second outlet gave him release for his strong puritanism and simplistic moral imperatives (which were probably invigorated by considerable unconscious guilt feelings arising out of a childhood sense of inadequacy).

Bobby's political education had actually begun earlier, when he was a shy sailor waiting to reenter Harvard in 1946. That fall, brother Jack began his first congressional race in Massachusetts. True to form, all the Kennedys rallied to campaign for Jack, including serious and socially awkward twenty-year-old Bobby. A vivid picture of Bobby's painful inarticulateness at that stage has been given by the exuberant Red Fay, Jack's Navy comrade. Fay, who had met Bobby at Palm Beach, remembered him as "a small, very quiet boy." When word came that Bobby was taking leave to help campaign, Jack commented wryly, "It's damn nice of Bobby wanting to help but I can't see that sober, silent face breathing new vigor into the ranks. The best plan is to make it known to the press. One picture of the two brothers together will show that we're all in this for Jack. Then you take Bobby out to the movies or whatever you two want to do."

Fay decided to take Bobby to a Boston movie-vaudeville theater. When Bobby arrived, according to Fay, his physical being was the only proof of his presence. He spoke very few words and, in a manner that implied a complete inarticulateness, tersely agreed to Fay's suggestion. En route to the theater Fay found himself awkwardly trying to carry on a one-way conversation, Bobby's only contribution being an occasional "yes" or "no." To Fay the movie was a welcome relief from the arduous task of trying to communicate with the uncommunicative young man. Then the tumbling and juggling acts came on, followed by a comedian whom Fay found extremely funny. Certain that his young charge was enjoying himself, he glanced in Bobby's direction — and immediately knew from his facial expression that he was wrong. When a string of hilarious jokes did not get a rise from Bobby, Fay could feel his own enjoyment disappearing. Another ten minutes was all that Fay could stand, and he asked Bobby whether he wanted to leave. Without the slighest pause, Bobby arose, and the two departed in silence. Fay, describing the incident in *The Pleasure of His Company*, later wrote, "As we came out of the theater that day, I would have cheerfully taken bets against the possibility that I would ever volunteer to spend an hour with Bobby Kennedy again. But I would have lost. In the years since, I've spent hours, evenings, weekends and entire vacations with him — and enjoyed them all."

Despite this somber personality with the older Fay, Bobby made a definite mark on Jack's campaign. Assigned to run an office in a tough East Cambridge neighborhood, Bobby was expected only to cut the anti-Kennedy vote from five-to-one to four-to-one. Instead, he shook hands and ate spaghetti with the Italian voters and played softball with children in a park across the street from his office, and Jack ended up running neck and neck in Cambridge with the local favorite, the mayor. Bobby seemed able to relax much more when he was away from his family's critical eye, especially with children and social inferiors, who accepted him for himself and did not sit in judgment. (This characteristic lasted into his own political campaigns in 1964 and 1968, when he emotionally identified with the poor, the young, and children, but tended to freeze with intellectuals and professional politicians.) Bobby's success in Jack's 1946 campaign increased his standing with the other Kennedys, who began to take him more seriously. It must also have given Bobby considerable personal satisfaction. His first venture into politics had been a gratifying experience.

In late 1951, Bobby became a Justice Department attorney in Brooklyn, New York. His legal career now progressed parallel to his political development. As a federal lawyer, Bobby worked for the Criminal Division uncovering evidence against grafters and tax evaders. It was his first glimpse into the underworld that he later explored as chief counsel for the Senate McClellan Committee on labor racketeering. Many people have speculated why investigative work fascinated Bobby, as it never did his brothers. This early obsession has been attributed to Bobby's severe puritanism and strong desire to hunt down evil. There is probably a good deal of truth in this interpretation, for at that time Robert Kennedy was strikingly conservative, authoritarian, and simplistic in his moral view of the world. As Ethel Kennedy once characterized her husband, "With Bobby, it's always the white hats and the black hats, the good guys versus the bad guys." Probably, too, Joseph Kennedy's frequent exhortations to his sons on the value of public service had a definite influence on Bobby's career choice. In addition, at that time government investigation offered the excitement of taking a direct part in challenging issues. The Korean War was raging, and congressional investigations of alleged Communists and Communist influence were popular and had not yet provoked revulsion against their most extreme practitioner, Wisconsin's Senator Joseph McCarthy.

But Bobby's investigative career was soon interrupted by the demands of family politics. This time, in 1952, Jack was running on a higher level, for the U.S. Senate. While the 1946 campaign had given young Bobby a preliminary taste of political combat, the 1952 campaign engaged his energies and ambitions far more intensely: 1952 launched Bobby on his rapid transformation from a "wet-behind-the-ears" kid brother into the tough, skillful, effective, and tremendously hard-driving politician who managed the campaign that eight years later put his older brother in the White House. But in 1952 Bobby was just learning the political ropes. The second vital Kennedy campaign was again largely directed by the "founding father" from behind the scenes, as described in earlier chapters. This time, however, Bobby was given a much more important though largely titular role. When the Ambassador fired the genial, low-pressure lawyer who had managed Jack's 1946 campaign, to everyone's surprise he named twenty-six-year-old Bobby as the replacement.

Bobby's unfamiliarity with Boston politics and his tendency toward arrogance, which probably was overcompensation for self-doubt, antagonized the old pros. When he berated Governor Dever for a supposed mistake in strategy, Dever angrily ordered him out of his office, then called the elder Kennedy and told him to "keep that fresh kid of yours out of my sight from here on in." While Bobby was still not ready for leadership, he worked hard with the rest of the clan ringing doorbells, giving speeches, attending parties, and accompanying Jack in his forays throughout the state. Bobby's best-known "speech" in this campaign was the shortest of his career. Still shy and tongue-tied in public, he told one group of voters whom he had to address on short notice: "My brother Jack couldn't be here. My mother couldn't be here. My sister Eunice couldn't be here. My sister Patricia couldn't be here. My sister Jean couldn't be here. But if my brother Jack were here, he'd tell you Lodge has a very bad voting record. Thank you."

While Bobby's managerial responsibilities were limited, he worked hard at the routine but essential chores of promotion and office organization. Jack later said, "Bobby works at high tempo. I remember when some politicians came into our headquarters and stood around gabbing. Finally Bobby told them: 'Here are some envelopes. You want to address them? Fine. Otherwise, wait outside.' They addressed the envelopes. Every politician in Massachusetts was mad at Bobby, but we had the best organization in history. You can't make an omelet without breaking the eggs." Commented Bobby, "Those politicians just wanted to sit around and talk about it and have their pictures taken at rallies." Bobby's disgust for most professional politicians, whom he considered lazy and venal, never changed.

If Bobby's 1952 political contribution was far from the masterly direction which writers later portrayed, it made a lasting impression on his ambitions. He had started absorbing political realities in the best possible school, multilevel experience, with the great added advantage of his father's shrewd teaching. Equally important, Bobby and Jack were now drawing closer together both privately and publicly. In a few short years, the famous Kennedy "team" would be projected into millions of American living rooms via the televised McClellan Committee hearings.

But in late 1952, with brother Jack shifting his Capitol Hill office to the Senate, the family's young lawyer was out of a job. Bobby now had to decide on a direction for his own career. The Ambassador's wide-ranging and high-level connections in government and business gave Bobby a variety of good choices. In 1953, he worked briefly for the Hoover Commission, headed by the former President and Joe Kennedy's old friend; but reorganizing the government was too tame for the restless Bobby, who always seemed to need action to feel really alive. Then Bobby learned that the Senate's Permanent Subcommittee on Investigations, under Senator Joseph McCarthy, wanted an assistant counsel. Bobby felt that McCarthy's investigation of Communists in government was "work that needed to be done then," as he later put it. Uncovering conspiracies and corruption appealed to his moralistic side and to his love of adventure. Against the advice of Jack, who sensed dangerous controversy, but with his father's encouragement, Bobby joined McCarthy's staff.

Bobby Kennedy's investigative period in the Senate fell into three periods: first, as assistant counsel to McCarthy's subcommittee, which he left after six months when Roy Cohn, a detested competitor, was given charge of the staff; then, returning in January, 1954, as counsel for the minority Democrats, who had also withdrawn in disapproval of Cohn; and, most important, his five years as chief counsel after the 1954 elections gave the committee chairmanship to Democrat John McClellan. As an investigator, Bobby first made headlines in May, 1953, when he testified on Allied trading with Communist China while the Korean War was still underway.

Although Kennedy was present as minority counsel during McCarthy's final semi-psychotic attacks on the Army in the summer of 1954, he was not actively involved. Yet Bobby's close association with McCarthy haunted him politically all his life and added to liberal doubts about his concern for the constitutional rights of others.

But it was Bobby's pursuit of Teamster leader James Riddle Hoffa that made him famous. In 1955, McClellan's subcommittee began hearings on conflict-of-interest cases (one caused the resignation of Eisenhower's Air Force Secretary). Then, in 1956, a determined labor reporter, Clark Mollenhoff, convinced Bobby that corruption in the powerful Teamsters Union badly needed investigating. For much of 1956, Bobby was engrossed in the clothing procurement scandal, followed by his brief attempt to win the Democratic vice presidential nomination for Jack in July, 1956. That August, Mollenhoff finally persuaded Bobby, who in turn won over Chairman McClellan. In mid-September, the Government Operations Subcommittee (soon known nationally as the Rackets Committee) had its first look at Teamster records, and a long investigation began.

Mollenhoff, who received a 1958 Pulitzer Prize for his reporting, has described Bobby at that time: "Kennedy had shown that he knew how to dramatize hearings during the clothing procurement investigation, but he also had shown signs of unsteadiness. He sometimes lost his temper, and occasionally a little-boy impetuousness marred his performance. Members of the press were inclined to give a major part of the credit for those successful investigations to Carmine Bellino, Jerome Adlerman, Alphonse Calabrese, and other older, more experienced members of the staff. To the press, 'Bobby' was just the little brother of Senator John Kennedy. . . . He did not have to work for a living. He was likeable, but he was not a politician. He had a tendency to use acid sarcasm, and he was inclined to be irritable or rudely blunt when he was crossed."

Despite the handicaps of youth, inexperience, and temperament, Bobby soon became the main force behind the labor investigations. After a month's absence traveling with Adlai Stevenson's campaign in the fall, Bobby speeded up the committee work in mid-November. He and his staff flew back and forth across the country investigating Teamster activities. In January, 1957, the Senate expanded the special McClellan Committee; Senator John F. Kennedy, who was on the parent Government Operations Committee, joined the eight-member subcommittee as one of four Democrats. Labor probing offered both risk and opportunity to the fast-rising young Senator, whose ambitions had been encouraged by his vice presidential near-miss. Jack risked alienating labor and liberal support; but participation made him part of an important investigation that could lead to national publicity and major legislation. There was also the element of family loyalty deeply ingrained in all Kennedys. As Jack told Mollenhoff in 1957, "The Labor Committee seems to have the best claim on jurisdiction, but Bobby has worked terribly hard on this investigation, he believes it is important, and he wants to do it."

The labor hearings dominated Bobby's life for the next three years, until he resigned in the fall of 1959 to head Jack's campaign for the presidency. During that time, Bobby's investigation of Jimmy Hoffa, who soon succeeded embezzler Dave Beck as Teamsters president, took on the quality of a personal vendetta. This word does not seem too strong in light of the many similar accounts by observers of different political backgrounds. Hoffa held an undeniable fascination for Bobby. Indeed, in many ways they closely resembled each other. Both men were intensely ambitious, hard-working, intelligent, and hot-tempered. Both were also puritanical in their personal habits, devoted to physical fitness, filled with excessive energy and nervous tension, outwardly tough but often secretly generous, devoted to their families, loyal to their friends, and surprisingly open in person. Each was also relatively small physically.

Yet Robert Kennedy believed that Hoffa was the personification of evil, and he spent a significant part of his life trying to prove it and inflict punishment on Hoffa. The question here is not Hoffa's personal morality, except as it sheds light on Kennedy, but rather why Bobby was so obsessed with Hoffa. Here is a partial description of Hoffa's ethics by two economists who accepted an extraordinary invitation by the union leader to spend several months with him on a nearly round-the-clock basis, question his associates, attend his meetings, and examine his papers and Teamster records going back decades. In their dispassionate account, *Hoffa and the Teamsters: A Study of Union Power*, Ralph and Estelle James wrote, "Hoffa's personal morality is pragmatic. Behavior which, in his opinion, improves his performance is sanctioned, and that which is likely to impair his effectiveness is prohibited: thus, his no sexual promiscuity, no alcohol, no tobacco rule. Loyalty to family and close friends is also part of this code, as is his reputation for honoring his word. In contrast, he is a master of deceit and subterfuge before reaching an agreement, when he finds this helpful in imposing his will on others. Hoffa rationalizes his 'anything goes' philosophy on grounds that 'life is a jungle' where one must constantly fight to survive. People who think primarily in terms of right and wrong are 'naive'—Hoffa's favorite characterization of those with an approach to life different from his own."

In many ways, Hoffa also resembled Bobby's father. Joseph Kennedy also saw life as a jungle in which winning was more important than following rules. Despite his religion, Kennedy Senior seemed to have few firm ideas of right and wrong other than in relation to his family. The Ambassador, according to many past associates, did not scruple to use subterfuge in business dealings; nor did he hesitate to deceive the public during his profitable stock-market period, although Joe Kennedy, unlike Hoffa, may have stopped short of actually breaking the law (at that time there were few laws controlling stock-market operations). This is not to say that the Kennedy patriarch was a "white-collar Hoffa" or had ties with gangsters (which has been well documented in Hoffa's case). But the evidence does suggest that the black-and-white picture generally drawn of Hoffa as a monster (including the pejorative account by reporter Mollenhoff) is an oversimplification, just as the laudatory praise of the Kennedys has often been an oversimplification (as have the diatribes). One must look further and probe deeper, beyond the magical devils and gods.

The psychological meaning of James Hoffa for Robert Kennedy can only be guessed. Let us first examine the question of whether Kennedy violated Hoffa's constitutional rights in his hearings, and whether Kennedy's investigations and actions went beyond the limits set by Congress. At least several informed observers felt Bobby did both. Yale law professor Alexander Bickel (who campaigned for the newly liberal RFK in 1968) wrote that the committee, "With Mr. Kennedy in the lead . . . embarked on a number of purely punitive expeditions [involving] relentless, vindictive battering [of witnesses]. . . . Mr. Kennedy appears to find congenial the role of prosecutor, judge and jury, all consolidated in his one efficient person."

Liberal journalist Paul Jacobs, who analyzed Kennedy's role in his book *The State of the Unions*, felt that Bobby from the start of his Teamsters investigation saw the union under Hoffa as a "conspiracy of evil." The country's good, in Kennedy's view, required Hoffa's jailing, or at least his ousting as the Teamsters' president. Jacobs pointed out that as congressional committee counsel RFK used his legal power and staff to help a group of anti-Hoffa Teamsters who were privately suing to prevent the union's 1957 convention. While Bobby believed the convention had been rigged to reelect Hoffa, the Kennedy Administration's own Solicitor General, Archibald Cox, commented two years later that "no one seriously believes that the majority of the members desired a different president." After this effort failed, because, as Chief Justice Warren said, "It called for an extraordinary exercise of judicial power," the court assumed supervision of the union through a board of monitors. Again, Kennedy's Justice Department helped the anti-Hoffa monitors try to oust Hoffa and block a Teamsters convention. And again the courts overruled these extralegal methods.

Paul Jacobs strongly criticized Kennedy's authoritarianism as an investigator and his willingness to trespass on the civil rights of citizens he judged guilty of criminality. Jacobs disapproved of Hoffa, but equally of Bobby's methods: "Jimmy Hoffa and the Teamsters Union are the antithesis of what I believe a union leader and a union ought to be. But my feelings about Hoffa are only important insofar as they affect what I write about him. Robert Kennedy's behavior toward Hoffa is of far greater significance, for Kennedy is not a private citizen. . . . As staff counsel for the McClellan Committee and as Attorney General, he acts in a public capacity in the name of every citizen. For this reason he is open to judgment about *how* he exercises that responsibility. . . . The evidence demonstrates to me that the committee and its staff, under Robert Kennedy's direction, trespassed heavily upon the rights of Hoffa and the union. It is a cliché and a truism that the most important civil rights are those of our enemies—of the people with whom we disagree. And so, although I have nothing in common with Hoffa, the union leader, Hoffa, the citizen, is me. His rights are the same as mine and require the same protection."

Kennedy's obsession with Hoffa would continue into his term as Attorney General. As Professor Monroe Freedman later wrote in the *Georgetown Law Journal*, "From the day that James Hoffa told Robert Kennedy that he was nothing but a rich man's kid who never had to earn a nickel in his life, Hoffa was a marked man. When Kennedy became Attorney General, satisfying this grudge became the public policy of the United States, and Hoffa, along with Roy Cohn and perhaps other enemies from Kennedy's past, was singled out for special attention by United States Attorneys. This is, of course, the very antithesis of the rule of law, and serves to bring into sharp focus the ethical obligation of the prosecutor to refrain from abusing his power by prosecutions that are directed at individuals rather than at crimes."

Weighing such evidence, we can sense that Bobby's pursuit of Hoffa had unconscious elements underlying a conscious dedication to justice and the elimination of union corruption. As newsman Dick Schaap saw Bobby, "Two men pervaded his life as an investigator, and their impact was so great that even now, with one of them dead and the other in prison, they exert an influence upon his image and his ambitions. One was Senator Joseph R. McCarthy of Wisconsin, the other James Riddle Hoffa of Detroit, and they shared, besides a gruff personableness and a hunger for power, a glaring disregard for principle." Joseph Kennedy shared these same traits, as, on occasion, did Robert Kennedy himself.

What are we to make of these similarities? That Bobby was hunting not only Hoffa, but, on unconscious levels, both his father and himself? Bobby, as earlier noted, was the son most like his father. The Ambassador himself had pointed this out: "Bobby is more direct than Jack. Jack has always been one to persuade people to do things. Bobby tends to tell people what to do. He resembles me much more than any of the other children. I make up my mind quickly and go ahead and get it done. Bobby is the same way."

Hoffa could well have served an unconscious need of Bobby's for an alter ego on which to project his hostilities. This is a common neurotic compulsion suffered by many people (and even nations) in varying degrees. It is not fanciful or implausible to see Hoffa primarily as a figure representing Bobby Kennedy's deepest fears about himself—Hoffa seems to have embodied the destructive and hostile impulses that Kennedy sensed and feared in himself. All human beings share a potential for evil. Neurotic people tend to feel and fear this capacity more strongly than others. Bobby struggled hard all his life to be not only good, but perfect. Hoffa personified evil, the opposite of the Christian ideal. In his excessive efforts to destroy Hoffa, efforts that carried him beyond legal and ethical boundaries, Bobby may well have been unconsciously trying to destroy the guilt and furies within himself. It was ironic that by the time Bobby finally "got" Jimmy, in early 1964 when Hoffa was convicted of attempted jury bribery (though he stayed out of jail three more years on appeals), Bobby no longer cared. By then the most devastating blow of RFK's life had fallen, his brother's murder, and his psychic energies were fully concentrated on psychological survival.

Bobby left the McClellan Committee in the summer of 1959 to write his first book, *The Enemy Within*, and then to direct Jack's presidential campaign which quietly opened that fall. Bobby's first book was an interesting account of his crusading days against corruption in national labor unions, although the tone was intensely moralistic ("good guys versus bad buys") and the style hackneyed. His central message was the familiar one of good versus evil, with Hoffa and his cohorts portrayed as a "conspiracy of evil." Bobby was unmistakably self-righteous; as, for example, when he castigated witnesses who took the Fifth Amendment. But *The Enemy Within* (a curiously apt title) is also filled with solid information on concrete methods and examples of labor-leader gougings of powerless union members. Kennedy's own emotions were clearly involved in his account. For Bobby, crime and corruption were the most satisfactory and clear-cut targets he ever had. Subsequent evildoers would prove far more elusive and unbeatable (such as, for a while, the Vietcong).

The Rackets Committee had made the Kennedy brothers into national heroes. Perhaps more than anything, the dramatic duel of wits and nerves between Bobby and Hoffa riveted the public's gaze. As Mollenhoff put it, "This was the investigation that put Senator John F. Kennedy on page one of the newspapers. It made him part of a brother act in a fight against the most sordid types of illegal and brutal corruption of the power of organized labor."

But if the investigation brought the necessary attention to John F. Kennedy, it was the 1956 grab for the Democratic vice presidential spot, capitalizing on a Southern surge to "stop Kefauver," that had given Jack and

Bobby reason to try for more. Bobby's experiences in Chicago that summer were to have a definite shaping effect on his future. It was he who led the impromptu floor fight in August when Adlai Stevenson unexpectedly opened the selection of a running mate to the delegates. Working with his usual cool intensity under pressure, Bobby helped produce overnight campaign materials, gather workers, and see key state leaders and caucuses. But the Kennedys had no time to organize. At the last minute, Bobby was pleading frantically with delegates on the convention floor. A North Dakota delegate said, "I'll never forget Bobby Kennedy during the balloting. Standing in front of our delegation with tears in his eyes he pleaded for our support. It didn't do any good. Jack had voted for sliding-scale supports and they don't like sliding-scale supports in our country." The race was close, but Kennedy could not carry the Western Protestant farm and ranch areas.

Jack remained outwardly calm through the fight and the defeat, but Bobby was furious at political friends who he felt had let them down. The experience also held valuable political lessons. Bobby later said, "It really struck me that it wasn't the issues that matter. It was the friendships. So many people said to me they would rather vote for Jack, but that they were going to vote for Estes Kefauver because he had sent them a card or gone to their home. I said right there that we should forget the issues and send Christmas cards and go to their homes next time."

Kefauver's victory at the 1956 convention also showed the Kennedys the political uses of well-publicized Senate crime investigations. As Mollenhoff pointed out, Jack and Bobby "learned by direct experience that a crime and racket prober who used television properly could have potent grass-roots appeal even five years after the Kefauver crime probe had ended. This was no little factor in the Kennedy decision to take on the politically explosive labor racket investigation—an investigation that had been killed more than a half-dozen times between 1953 and 1956 by the tremendous political power of organized labor within both parties in Congress."

By late 1959, the Kennedys had turned a politically dangerous investigation into a personal triumph. The probe brought them into touch with reporters and editors from the nation's largest newspapers. Television networks sought them out for *Meet the Press, Face the Nation*, and other nationwide shows. Bobby and Jack were featured on the covers of national publications which had ignored them a few months earlier.

As campaign manager for Jack's presidential race in 1959–1960, Bobby's political and managerial talents came to fruition. His election experiences of 1946, 1952, and 1956 had taught him the realities of campaigning. In addition, he had shrewdly traveled in Adlai Stevenson's 1956 presidential party as an observer, taking notes on how *not* to run a campaign. Unlike Stevenson and Humphrey, the Kennedys were intensely aware of the need for efficient and highly detailed organization and the importance of the mass media, especially television, to project the desired image. The Kennedys, of course, had the money to do these things thoroughly, which their opponents often sorely lacked (Humphrey's 1960 primary campaign was run on a comparative shoestring). But we should not underestimate the keenness of the Kennedys' political imaginations. As political salesmen and manipulators of mass emotions, the Kennedy clan has ranked among the century's greatest.

The all-important 1960 effort also brought out several of Bobby's deepest emotional ambivalences. His two most neurotic characteristics at this time seemed to be, first, his arrogance and anger when directing others, which suggest his insecurity and fear of people rejecting his orders (and hence himself); and, second, his readiness to use unethical methods and make flagrantly untrue charges against opponents (the anything-to-win attitude taught by his father). The widely-held picture of Bobby as a ruthless opportunist derived in large part from his conduct of the 1960 campaign. As Jack Newfield, a later Kennedy convert, observed, "He directed his brother's 1960 Presidential drive with a single-minded intensity. Delegates and rivals were threatened, and Kennedy seemed indifferent to substantive issues of policy. The tactics used to win the West Virginia primary were ugly and foul. At one meeting of campaign workers Kennedy said, 'It doesn't matter if I hurt your feelings. It doesn't matter if you hurt mine. The important thing is to get the job done!'"

Another convert to the "new" Robert Kennedy of 1967–1968, David Halberstam, saw similar characteristics: "Robert Kennedy had been the tough guy, ramrodding through his brother's nomination and election. . . . The reformers were too soft; too issue-prone; too—and this was the worst word yet—predictable. In 1960 Kennedy had exploded before New York's finest and purest reformers, saying, 'Gentlemen, I don't give a damn if the state and county organizations survive after November and I don't give a damn if you survive. I want to elect John F. Kennedy President.' And they loved that, though in later years when they thought warm thoughts about the Kennedy Presidency they would not remember Robert Kennedy's hard work and vital contribution to that end, but rather the harshness of his words." While Bobby was, from many accounts, undeniably harsh in 1960, no one has questioned his general effectiveness. He drove himself even harder than he drove his campaign workers. His father commented with typical overstatement: "Jack works harder than any mortal man. Bobby goes a little further." After Jack's nomination, the Ambassador told an exhausted Bobby, "It's the best organization job I've ever seen in politics."

The Kennedys had hoped the Wisconsin primary would finish Humphrey. To their disgust, their first victory was widely interpreted as a failure.

Jack, whose state staffing far outnumbered Humphrey's, although Humphrey was operating in his own backyard, won 56 percent of the popular vote, an apparently indecisive amount since it was mainly Catholic. West Virginia, 95 percent Protestant, seemed to offer a real test, although most West Virginians were actually indifferent to religion, being absorbed in a grim struggle for daily survival. The Kennedys headed immediately for West Virginia, where Bobby and his team mounted the attack like a blitzkrieg. As Theodore White analyzed the Kennedy mood, "at the moment they were furious. They had fought a clean and elevated campaign in Wisconsin. Now Humphrey refused to accept the decision. He was preparing to frustrate them in West Virginia—not, it seemed to them, out of any hope in his own eventual triumph at the Convention, but only to deny it vengefully to John F. Kennedy in the name of shadowy third persons who disdained the ardor of field combat in the primaries. Whatever Humphrey's personal reading of his chances in West Virginia, the Kennedy reading was that Humphrey faced them chiefly as a spoiler. In the Kennedys too the combat venom rose. They had played by Wisconsin rules in Wisconsin; they would play by West Virginia rules in West Virginia. And they meant to win."

White's assessment of Bobby's Wisconsin tactics as "clean and elevated" seems exaggerated. In Wisconsin, Bobby had made speeches implying that Hoffa was backing Humphrey. Humphrey denied the smear, saying that whoever was responsible "deserves to be spanked—I said spanked because it applies to juveniles." But Bobby went right ahead, and later in West Virginia tried again to connect Humphrey with the discredited Hoffa. There, in addition to almost unlimited money and manpower, the Kennedys had the religious issue, which they adroitly reversed against Humphrey. With the advantage of constant press publicity and support, Jack and Bobby proclaimed repeatedly that they wanted religion kept out of the campaign. As White more sagely remarked, "Once the issue could be made one of tolerance or intolerance, Hubert Humphrey was hung . . . any man, indecisive in mind on the Presidency, could prove that he was at least tolerant by voting for Jack Kennedy." In addition, the art of buying votes was a time-honored tradition in West Virginia and, as students have suggested, was doubtlessly well explored in the 1960 campaign.

Two journalists, William Johnson and Nick Thimmesch, saw the West Virginia race as "angry and high-strung, loaded with sinister innuendoes. Humphrey hinted that the Kennedys were scurrying about the state with a 'little black bag and a checkbook' buying votes. In turn, Franklin Delano Roosevelt, Jr., lent his booming voice to the Kennedy campaign by implying that Humphrey might have been a draft-dodger. 'He is a good Democrat,' said FDR, Jr., 'but I don't know where he was during World

War II.' (Humphrey was 4-F.) Bobby didn't stay completely out of the fireworks either. At one point he snapped that Humphrey had 'played fast and loose with smears and innuendoes,' adding that 'I do not intend to take this kind of abuse indefinitely.' Mildly amused at Bobby's youthful show of temper, Hubert cracked back, 'Politics is a serious business, it's not a boy's game where you can pick up your ball and run home if things don't go according to your idea of who should win. Bobby's statement indicates they're pushing the panic button.' "

Actually, it was Humphrey, not the Kennedys, who had reason to panic in West Virginia, although he fought gamely to the end. There the Kennedys' well-developed machinery—ready money, political expertise, and superb organization—brought its full weight to bear, sweeping all but seven of the state's fifty-five counties. The West Virginia triumph knocked Humphrey out of the race and gave Kennedy the momentum to win the seven state primaries that he had entered. The Kennedy fortune gave Jack the punch of multiple political techniques—polling, television, direct mailings, newspaper advertising, contributions—in a word, the works. Bobby Kennedy and his new breed of "young pros" were using every technological device available to make exact measurements of the political process. Television, "in-depth" polling, electronic analysis, and rapid communications and transportation gave the Kennedys the weapons they knew how to use. The political revolution ushered in by the Kennedy organization men was a revolution of technique, not of substance. By the eve of the Democratic convention, Jack Kennedy had been promised at least 600 of the 761 votes needed to win the nomination.

Bobby Kennedy knew the first ballot was crucial. He kept up a grueling pace for himself and his staff. In Los Angeles, just before the convention opened, he told the workers, "We're not out here to go to Disneyland. We're not out here to go to nightclubs. We're out here to work. If you're not, you can turn in your staff badges right now—we've got a lot of people who would like to have them." While Bobby was an effective Patton-like commander, he was not a diplomat (also like Patton). At one point he demanded of Humphrey, "Hubert, we want your announcement and the pledge of your delegation today—or else." Humphrey reportedly turned red and snapped, "Bobby, you go to hell." Bobby's superb communications network of telephones and walkie-talkies covered the convention floor's key points, which he commanded from a rented cottage outside. By phone, Bobby directed his chief aides, with a man assigned to each state delegation. Right before the balloting, Bobby phoned Larry O'Brien and said, "This is it. We're going to win." Bobby predicted a victory of 803 votes; on the first ballot, Jack received 806.

The battle was only half won. With the nomination secured, the general election still lay ahead. Bobby's presidential campaign organization was enormous, but he kept a tight grip on every detail. For example, when an assistant said that the campaigning was going "pretty good" in a section of New York State, Bobby shot back, "You know damned well they aren't going 'pretty good.' I was there yesterday." Setting out to register 10 million new voters, Bobby told Jack, "If I were running the party, I sometimes think I'd scrap everything, close up national headquarters, and spend every nickel we had on registration." Bobby carefully directed his brother's television appearances—"Bread-and-butter, peace, get Jackie . . . that religious thing, say it again." Before the first decisive television debate, Bobby studied Nixon's appearance with inner glee, noting his paleness, sunken cheeks, and shadowed eyes. When a Nixon aide naively asked his impression of the makeup, Bobby coolly answered, "Terrific. Terrific. I wouldn't change a thing."

Bobby ruled his political army like a wartime general, coordinating local groups and reducing friction. "It's like the Gaza Strip," he once said. "You have to watch it all the time and make sure the little fights don't become wars." Jack appreciated Bobby's hard work: "I don't even have to think about organization. I just show up. He's the hardest worker. He's the greatest organizer. He's taken no time off. He's fantastic. He's living on nerves." If Bobby often angered people, he felt it was unavoidable. "I'm not running a popularity contest," said the abrasive campaign manager. "It doesn't matter if people like me or not. Jack can be nice to them. I don't try to antagonize people, but somebody has to be able to say no. If people are not getting off their behinds, how do you say that nicely?" On election night at the Kennedy command post in Bobby's Hyannis Port home, a hoped-for landslide turned into a razor-thin margin. Only Bobby stayed up all night to learn in the early morning that Jack had won by a miniscule 112,000 votes out of 68,000,000 cast. Bobby said later, "If we'd done one bit less of anything, we might have lost."

In December, 1960, the new President-elect chose thirty-five-year-old Bobby as his Attorney General, and a brief national uproar ensued. Joseph Kennedy was irritated at the criticism. "Nepotism, my foot!" he cried. "Why would anybody think that Bobby needs a job? He fought this nomination, fought it until he drove Jack and me crazy. A lot of people in our own camp fought it, too, and agreed with him. They wanted to see him go back to Boston and become Senator. Not me!" Actually, both Bobby and Jack at first opposed the nomination, but their father's desire was decisive. Kennedys needed Kennedys, ruled the patriarch. No other adviser could be as trustworthy.

In a detailed and well-researched study of Robert Kennedy as Attorney General, *Kennedy Justice*, Victor S. Navasky writes that he is convinced there was a Kennedy Code of genuine liberalism, devotion to justice, and "dedication to excellence." (I am not.) But he is also careful to point out the considerable failures of the Justice Department under Kennedy—his approval of wiretapping and his lax approach to electronic surveillance of all kinds; the excessive allocation of resources to "getting Hoffa"; the refusal to protect civil rights workers for political reasons; and the appointment of racist judges in the South (five out of twenty lifetime appointments). As Navasky commented, "No aspect of Robert Kennedy's Attorney Generalship is more vulnerable to criticism than these appointments. For it was a blatant contradiction for the Kennedys to forgo civil rights legislation and executive action in favor of litigation and at the same time to appoint as lifetime litigation-overseers men dedicated to frustrating that litigation. It was also a comedown from the characteristically lofty JFK oratory of May 20, 1961, the day he signed the Omnibus Judgeship Bill. . . .

". . . at a period in our history when men, money and time were in short supply, when the Civil Rights Division's 1961 budget was one of the Department's smallest, when *ad hoc* crises requiring the government's legal attention were erupting daily, the Kennedy Justice Department was forced to devote thousands of man hours, hundreds of thousands of dollars, untold energy, imagination and brilliance, all to counter the obstructionist tactics of its own appointees, five of whom decided over one hundred cases against the Negro, the Civil Rights Division and the Constitution while Robert Kennedy was Attorney General. In the process they contributed— to what degree we can never know—to the alienation of the black American from law as an effective problem-solving instrument. They solidified Southern resistance to desegregation at a time when it had a chance of cracking. They undermined the effective administration of justice. They undermined respect for law. They appeared to make a mockery of the Kennedy's pledge of equal justice for all."

In this vital area of civil rights, Bobby initially revealed a narrow understanding of Negro grievances. Jack Newfield, the liberal who later backed Bobby for President, was bitterly critical of him at that time: "As civil rights activists in 1963, we liked Kennedy as little as the Southern governors did. We saw him recommend Harold Cox, James Eastland's college roommate, to be a judge in the Fifth District Court, where he was to call Negro defendants 'chimpanzees' from the bench. We saw him indict nine civil rights workers in Albany, Georgia, on conspiracy charges, while white men who burned down Negro churches, and shot at civil rights activists, went unpunished. We saw Negroes trying to register to vote in Greenwood, Mississippi, urinated upon by a white farmer, while lawyers from the Justice Department calmly took notes destined to be filed and forgotten. We agreed with James Baldwin, who pronounced Kennedy, after their stormy confrontation, 'insensitive and unresponsive to the Negro's torment.' " Although five years later Newfield and millions of others would see Robert Kennedy as black America's best hope, during 1961–1963 the young Attorney General took only the first steps along his long and painful road to a more compassionate awareness.

As we have seen, the much-publicized "restraint" of the Kennedy Administration was largely a restraint that allowed mobs and police to brutalize civil rights demonstrators and black citizens courageously asserting their basic freedoms. At that time Bobby understood neither the depth of white fear and hatred nor the new black anger and determination to achieve equality. In the most famous episode of his Attorney Generalship, the registration of Negro James Meredith at the University of Mississippi in October, 1962, Bobby misread the situation and sent less than two hundred federal marshals to protect Meredith. Thousands of enraged segregationists nearly overwhelmed this small force, who desperately fought back with tear gas until the President sent in federalized Mississippi National Guardsmen. State Governor Ross Barnett had broken his promise to provide protection; two men were killed and hundreds wounded. Reality had confronted the naive optimism Bobby had expressed early in 1961 when asked what he would do if faced with another Little Rock. At that early date of inexperience and overconfidence, the Attorney General had replied, "I don't think we would ever come to the point of sending troops to any part of the country on a matter like that. I cannot conceive of this Administration's letting such a situation deteriorate to that level."

Even after such incidents, including the violence against the Freedom Riders in May, 1961, both Kennedys continued to share the illusion that progress could be made through the slow processes of law, and that black Americans would continue to wait patiently. When Bobby asked Martin Luther King to postpone his planned marches, King replied, "This 'Wait' has always meant 'Never.' " In April, 1963, King opened his massive campaign of nonviolent demonstrations, which included hundreds of children. The unleashing of police dogs in Birmingham finally aroused Bob Kennedy's latent sense of moral outrage. At last, in June, 1963, the Kennedy Administration sent its long-delayed civil rights bill to Congress. Despite the bill's inadequacies, at least it was a first step. Meanwhile Bobby had worked hard to take political pressure off Jack by forwarding Southern registration of black voters, peaceful school desegregation, and integration of travel stations.

Bobby's greatest interest as Attorney General, however, continued to be his fight against organized crime. He greatly expanded investigations and brought the Internal Revenue Service and the previously aloof FBI into his anticrime war, although the price paid was a dangerous enlargement of

FBI influence. Kennedy also had not forgotten his old arch-enemy, Jimmy Hoffa. Armed with the full power of government, Bobby was almost certain someday to make a charge stick. As one reporter described this intensive manhunt, "The crusade to get Hoffa was indeed ruthless, justifiably ruthless by Kennedy's measurement. The Justice Department employed walkie-talkies, electronic recording devices, cameras, informers, pressure, harassment, every conceivable tactic to pin a criminal charge upon Hoffa. Finally, the Justice Department scored—with a spy . . . hidden among Hoffa's entourage." Hoffa was finally convicted in two major trials, along with 115 other Teamster officials and associates by the time Bobby left the Department. It was, in Navasky's view, "an extraordinary administrative accomplishment." But Navasky also saw the hazards: that Kennedy's Get-Hoffa Squad had set a dangerous precedent for other "assassination bureaus"; that the focus on Hoffa had resulted in a "disproportionate allocation of men, money and time" which could subtly change a case from prosecution to persecution; that the chase of Hoffa illustrated the danger "that a prosecutor will pick people he thinks he should get instead of crimes that need to be prosecuted"; that "whatever his motives . . . Robert Kennedy allowed the pursuit of justice to look like the pursuit of Hoffa"; and that "the Hoffa thing" resulted in poor morale elsewhere in the Justice Department and depleted valuable manpower. As some Justice lawyers saw it, "Too many brilliant young men who might have been bringing Southern sheriffs or Eastern conglomerates to justice were out chasing Hoffa."

But most important to JFK was Bobby's position as his closest adviser. After the disastrous Cuban invasion in April, 1961, Bobby's advice became even more crucial on foreign policy. Arthur Schlesinger wrote, "When he first decided to appoint his brother to the cabinet, I do not know how much John Kennedy expected Robert to do besides run the Department of Justice and be available for private advice and commiseration. The Bay of Pigs, however, changed all that. Thereafter the President wanted Bobby at every crucial meeting. He did not necessarily agree with his younger brother; the Attorney General was one more prism which he read like the others. But the President trusted him more than anyone else to get to the bottom of an idea or project, to distinguish what was operational from what was literary, to anticipate consequences, to ride herd on execution, to protect the presidential interest and, above all, to be candid. Within the cabinet, Robert Kennedy became a constant and steady liberal force, no matter how much it irritated him to have this pointed out. Whatever the issue, one could expect a reaction on the merits, without regard to vested intellectual or administrative interests. One could expect a reaction on political feasibility also; but the two were kept carefully separate. . . ."

While one may question the depth of Bobby's liberal beliefs, some real changes and maturing did seem to be occurring in his personality. There was no sudden transformation of the old "Bad Bobby" into the new "Good Bobby" before or after his brother's death, as much Kennedy hagiography would have us believe. But the wide responsibilities of Bobby's dual role as Attorney General and intimate presidential adviser offered the direct experiences that always made the deepest impressions on his responsive personality. Bobby's tendencies toward authoritarianism and moral rigidity continued, especially in his attitude toward the civil rights of accused criminals. And his understanding of Negro outrage was still limited. But Robert Kennedy was plainly growing. In foreign affairs, Bobby made several important contributions with both positive and negative elements. One was his lesser-known role in the missile crisis of October, 1962, as a strong adviser against an air strike on the Cuban missiles. Schlesinger, Sorensen, Robert McNamara (then Defense Secretary), and others have all praised the Attorney General's important—perhaps decisive—counsel of moderation and morality. Many advisers urged immediate bombings before the still incomplete missile sites could be made operative. Listening to the discussion, Bob Kennedy scribbled a note to his brother, "I now know how Tojo felt when he was planning Pearl Harbor." Then he argued for a consideration of more alternatives, such as counterpressuring the Russians by putting nuclear missiles in Berlin. Three days later, after JFK had decided on a blockade as an initial step, strong support again arose for an air strike. But Bobby spoke out eloquently against a surprise blow on a small nation as totally contradicting American traditions.

In the fall of 1967, Robert Kennedy wrote a short memoir of the missile crisis, which he never had time to finish or revise. In this essay, published posthumously as *Thirteen Days: A Memoir of the Cuban Missile Crisis*, Bobby analyzed his own attitude: "I supported McNamara's position in favor of a blockade. This was not from a deep conviction that it would be a successful course of action, but a feeling that it had more flexibility and fewer liabilities than a military attack. Most importantly, like others, I could not accept the idea that the United States would rain bombs on Cuba, killing thousands and thousands of civilians in a surprise attack. Maybe the alternatives were not very palatable, but I simply did not see how we could accept that course of action for our country." Kennedy then related how former Secretary of State Dean Acheson strongly favored an air attack. Although a great admirer of Acheson's intelligence and forcefulness, Bobby opposed his position. "With some trepidation, I argued that, whatever validity the military and political arguments were for an attack in preference to a blockade, American traditions and history would not permit such a course of action. Whatever military reasons he and others could marshal, they were nevertheless, in the last analysis, advocating a surprise attack by a very large nation against a very small one. This, I said, could not be undertaken by the U.S. if we were to maintain our moral position at home and around the globe. Our struggle against Communism throughout the world was far more than physical survival—it had as its essence our heritage and our ideals, and these we must not destroy. We spent more time on this moral question during the first five days than on any other single matter."

Yet despite this initial display of mature judgment, Bobby Kennedy's deep streak of irrationality came out later in the crisis. Rather than agreeing to the Kremlin's offer to trade Cuban missiles for U.S. missiles in Turkey (which JFK wanted removed anyway), Bobby advised the President to ignore this communication and focus on an earlier vague but conciliatory message from Khrushchev. The Kennedy brothers issued a semi-ultimatum for the removal of the Cuban missiles in return for a U.S. pledge not to invade Cuba. By putting a brief time limit on their demand, the Kennedys considerably shortened the fuse leading toward a nuclear holocaust. Fortunately for both the Kennedys and the world, Khruschev's fears overcame his pride, and he gave in. A later remark by Bobby suggests the depth of neurotic unreality through which he intermittently viewed the crisis: "We all agreed in the end that if the Russians were ready to go to nuclear war over Cuba, they were ready to go to nuclear war, and that was that. So we might as well have the showdown then as six months later." Fortunately, the Russians did not share this extraordinarily destructive attitude.

On the other hand, we must bear in mind that it is questionable whether the Kennedys would actually have gone to war over Cuba at that point, or whether they would have made strong diplomatic efforts before taking concrete action. We will never know how far Jack and Bobby might have pressed their power if the Russians hadn't backed down; whether, in fact, the Kennedys would have been willing to bring on World War III rather than "lose face" over Cuba. It was not really a question of a nuclear threat to America, since that threat already existed. What was chiefly at stake was U.S.—and Kennedy—prestige at home and around the world, particularly important just then in view of the imminent congressional elections. Because Khrushchev did give in quickly, the missile crisis is often simplistically seen as a matter of bravely standing up to challenge; in fact, it was a far more complex and dangerous affair.

The Vietnam issue was the most important question touching directly upon Bobby Kennedy's unresolved inner conflicts. The growing conflict aroused his strong tendencies toward dramatic heroics, produced on the Kennedy playing fields and in reaction to his father's barrage of criticism and exhortation. These drives were to find outlet in his espousing of counter-insurgency or guerrilla tactics, symbolized by the Green Berets. Schlesinger later claimed that as Attorney General, Bobby "freely attacked the policy of association 'with tyrannical and unpopular regimes that had no following and no future.' " Yet in the complicated and alien Vietnam situation, Bobby helped his brother follow just such a policy.

In the Kennedys' attitude toward the Communist nationalists of Vietnam perhaps more than anywhere else, we can see the results of their upbringing by rigidly conservative, self-righteous, and moralistic parents in a society historically more attuned to irrational black-and-white values than to a humanistic and rational sense of moderation and flexible understanding. Bobby and Jack, despite their caution, were not essentially moderate or humble men. Despite their superficial pragmatism, they both seemed often to feel typically American impulses of omnipotence and grandiosity. All of these personal and socio-pathological chickens would come to roost tragically in the Vietnam barnyard.

During the Kennedy Administration, Robert Kennedy fully accepted the American ideology that led President Kennedy to commit American troops to an Asian land war in 1962 (JFK enlarged the U.S. military in Vietnam from Eisenhower's 800 advisers in early 1961 to more than 16,000 men by late 1963). In addition, Bobby became one of the Administration's most ardent advocates of counterinsurgency. Indeed, so great was Bobby's enthusiasm that he became known in Washington as "Mr. Counterinsurgency," a term that must have flattered the warrior part of his self-image. In February, 1962, three months after JFK's decision to send more American advisers, the Attorney General visited the Far East. In Hong Kong he said, "The solution there [in Vietnam] lies in our winning it. This is what the President intends to do." Shortly after, in Saigon, Bobby told a press conference, "We will win in Vietnam and we shall remain here until we do." Not until 1965 and 1966, under the outer pressures of political necessity and the inner prodding of his own doubts, did RFK begin to reassess his Vietnam position. This reconsideration finally led to his complete denunciation of the war—which had become the despised Johnson's war.

The ambiguities that helped shape and constantly perplexed Bobby in his public life also had inevitable repercussions in his private life. I have mentioned both Bobby's intense Catholicism and the personal devotion of his equally religious wife. Catholicism puts an extreme priority on sexual chastity, particularly for females, while at the same time arousing latent sexual fears and desires among its practitioners. And, as previously discussed, the Kennedy family's *machismo* of male sexual prowess implanted further conflicted attitudes in the Kennedys regarding male-female relationships and sexual behavior. The result, as to be expected from the neurotic trio of these unhealthy religious, family, and social pressures (exerted by a sexist male-dominated society), was a pattern of active masculinity by the Kennedy men and passive loyalty by the Kennedy women. The women knew, of course, that it was extremely unlikely any husband would stray in public, no matter how selfish and self-indulgent his behavior in private. The strictures of both Catholicism and political necessity ruled out much overt wandering. Private lusting, however, was another matter, and here the evidence is strong that the Kennedy father and all four sons sought repeated solaces and affirmations of manhood from women other than their wives.

Bobby Kennedy's general attitudes toward women mirrored those of his father and older brothers. Women were sought for their beauty and companionship, and wives were valued as loyal and necessary supporters. But to be "womanly" was considered a deadly insult by Kennedy men, particularly Bobby. The Kennedy males were socialized by both society and their religion to consider females their natural inferiors. We can see this most obviously in the fact that only the sons, no matter how apparently unpromising, were groomed for political careers, while the daughters who shared equal or even superior political talents (such as Eunice) were never considered for overt political roles in their own right.

The Kennedy virility cult was bound to carry over into child-raising practices. In Bobby especially, we can see how his own need for personal heroics made him into a father who perpetually pushed competition, the need to win, and toughness on his children. As a journalist recently wrote, "Being number one is still uppermost with the Kennedy kids, but their fierce competitive drive has not always won them praise. When the Kennedys held their pet show [at Hickory Hill], two protesters, seven and eight years old, arrived carrying a sign which read, 'Canine-Feline Protest For Equal Opportunity: Is that fair judging?' They then unrolled a scroll saying, 'Why do the Kennedys win all the prizes?' " Apparently typical of Bobby's attitude was his exhortation one day to some of his swinging children to "swing higher and try for a new record. A Kennedy shouldn't be scared." Bobby's children were told that "Kennedys don't cry," and urged into constant games of competitive sports, just as Bobby and his brothers and sisters had been. But Bobby discouraged one of his sons from flower collecting by scorning it as "sissy stuff."

It is interesting to imagine how a male rebel or nonbeliever in the masculine mystique would have been treated by Bobby Kennedy, and the sort of Eugene O'Neill drama that could have emerged between father and son. But none of Bobby's children apparently reacted openly, although manifestations of hidden conflict later emerged in the two oldest boys. Young Joe (Joseph Kennedy III) reportedly got into trouble one summer in a Chappaquiddick brawl. And in the summer of 1970, the next son, Bobby

Junior, then sixteen, was charged with possessing marijuana along with other juveniles, including his cousin Sargent Shriver III (Eunice Kennedy's son), and placed on a year's probation. It is too early yet, and too little information is available, to assess the reemergence of the "Kennedy neurosis" in this third generation. But it is highly likely that considerable unconscious ambivalence has been woven into the personalities of many of these grandchildren.

Chapter 10

THE IMPORTANCE
OF BEING PRESIDENT:
WHAT MADE BOBBY RUN? 1963-1968

Robert Francis Kennedy was the most intense of the male members of his remarkable family. In this he more nearly resembled his father than any of his brothers—he had the same capacity for likes and dislikes, for love and hate, for compassion toward the denied and the oppressed but with a simultaneous concentration on serving personal ambition.

Like others who are driven by a thirst for power, he unquestionably sought it in the conviction that among his rivals he was best qualified to make an effective attack on the injustices and kindred evils that afflict the United States and human society as a whole. Into this pattern perfectly fits the desire to become President. Hence the bitterness with which so many sought to stop him on the way can be accounted for only by the provocations he especially engendered: the obvious passion of his pursuit; the widespread feeling the Kennedys had come to think of the Presidency as a family fief; and the advantage over competitors inherent in huge financial resources that obviate the need of contracting the obligations that go with campaign contributions.

—Arthur Krock, *Memoirs: Sixty Years on the Firing Line*

There is a mysterious, provocative, exciting element in Kennedy's personality. It inspires many and alarms others. He is "a swinger" who brings to public affairs a hint of danger and unpredictability: he is not a man whose line of development can easily be forecast; what he does or what positions on public issues he adopts may be considerably different ten years from now. In his compulsive athleticism, his reckless risk-taking, his aggressiveness, he seems to be driven by something not accounted for by the realities which engage him and not compatible with the high seriousness of his public ambitions.

—William V. Shannon, *The Heir Apparent*

291

Fresh challenges are always needed to stimulate him. New physical experiences even seem to be needed to complete mental changes in him. He did not fully realize what poverty could be until he saw the people in West Virginia living on lard and flour. His emotional conversion to civil rights was not complete until he saw Bull Connor's dogs leaping at the Negroes. There is one outstanding danger in a development that depends so much on close contact with reality: the man of imagination is nearly always there first. The cautious prognosticator also asks: How many new and shocking experiences is a man likely to have after the age of forty? Has Kennedy passed through his period of greatest personal development? Does he have any other inlets to guarantee growth?
—Margaret Laing, *The Next Kennedy*

For all of Bobby's renowned toughness and abrasiveness, he was politically conventional and timid. He wanted to be President in the "normal" way. He wanted "to put it together." Well, it isn't together anymore. It was his bad luck to be caught in a revolution he didn't understand, though he did like its rhetoric. Yet the conservative majority of the country hated him and thought him a revolutionary. I wonder what will happen when the *real* thing comes along. The two Kennedys were charming, conservative politicians, nicely suited for the traditional game but hardly revolutionaries or innovators.
—Gore Vidal, "Playboy Interview," *Playboy*

The "real" Bobby Kennedy, like matter itself, is difficult to reduce to the one significant particle. He is bright, tough-minded, competent. He can be rude, self-centered, arrogant. He has surrounded himself with an able, hard-working staff. He carries on frivolously at times like a jet-set dilettante. He has a feel for the new winds of politics. He caters to bosses in the back room. The conflicts and contradictions in his personality have forced most of those who have written about him to choose one of two lines—for or against. The dispassionate truth, if indeed it exists, is distressingly ambiguous.
—Penn Kimball, *Bobby Kennedy and the New Politics*

ℑℭ

FROM A PSYCHOHISTORICAL point of view, the most remarkable fact about Robert Kennedy was his own developing certainty that he was predestined for the White House and the shared belief of millions of Americans that the presidency was indeed his preordained fate and inheritance. Neither of these twin assumptions developed overnight. Each was the result of a complex combination of politico-historical factors, the psychological needs of masses of Americans, and the aggressive ambitions of a hugely wealthy, energetic, and psychologically hungry family.

Among all the Kennedys, Robert is surely the best example of Kennedy salesmanship. Initially, it would have been hard to imagine a young man much less suited for the roles of Cabinet officer, United States Senator, and presidential candidate. In physique, intellect, experience, and personality, Bobby was not only unimpressive but embarrassingly deficient. He was shorter than his brothers and physically awkward, dogged and unbrilliant, lacking small talk or even very large talk, and almost totally devoid of the social amenities that smooth the paths of mediocre politicians. In a word, before 1960, and even before 1963, Bobby Kennedy was almost completely unmemorable except to those who had witnessed his ruthless energy and tenacity in advancing his brother's career or who as close associates had learned to respect him for his growing liberalism. In general, Bobby was most widely judged by largely negative characteristics: his connection with Joe McCarthy's witch-hunting; his self-righteous crusade to destroy Hoffa; his vindictiveness as Attorney General; his lack of genuine identification with black suffering; and his aggressive enthusiasm for the Vietnam war. Then came Dallas, and almost overnight the national outpouring of shock, sorrow, and irrational guilt enveloped Bobby Kennedy in nearly universal pity and compassion. His own grief was clearly overwhelming. Yet eventually, after months of agony, he rose above it, and public sympathy and admiration for his great courage wiped away the harsh outlines of his past history and helped prepare the way for his popular transformation.

When President John F. Kennedy was shot on November 22, 1963, something vital seemed to be temporarily killed in Robert Kennedy. That something, in a strong sense, could be interpreted as his own identity—the self that he had projected onto his older brother. From all appearances, most of Bobby's drives, anxieties, energies, and ambitions had by 1963 gone into serving and protecting Jack. In addition, Jack had probably filled the supportive role of an unconscious all-accepting father figure to Bobby, the kind of father he had never really had. With Jack gone, Bobby understandably felt totally lost.

Yet, in a paradoxical way, the death of the parental older brother also freed Bobby to become more himself and to seek his own independent identity. The Kennedy family's feudal concept of primogeniture, which was emotionally echoed in the psychic needs of much of the American public, also supported Robert Kennedy in the search for himself, although at the same time it narrowed that search to a specific direction. Bobby was now the heir apparent to a growing legend; millions looked to him for the national leadership and emotional outlet they had found in his brother, as well as the assuagement of irrational mass guilt for JFK's murder. But the immediate months after Jack's murder were almost unbearably black for the stricken Bobby. It is clear from all accounts that he suffered an agonizing "dark night of the soul." As one journalist observed, "The assassination punctured the center of Robert Kennedy's universe. It removed the hero-brother for whom he had submerged all of his own great competitive instincts. It took away, in one instant of insanity, all of the power they had struggled together for ten years to achieve, and gave it to another, whom they both mistrusted. It thrust a man trained for the shadows into the sunlight. It made Robert Kennedy, a man unprepared for introspection, think for the first time in his life what *he* wanted to do, and what *he* stood for."

For months Bobby worked half-heartedly in a state of recurrent despondency. President Johnson helped ease his depression by sending him on a short diplomatic trip to the Far East in January, 1964. Gradually, Bobby's interest in life and work revived, but he never fully recovered from the murder of the brother who had been so much of a substitute father and projected identity for himself. After Dallas, he was clearly an older man who had endured much pain. Yet the frequent claims of concomitant wisdom and maturity in Bobby Kennedy are at least partially contradicted by his subsequent political behavior, which followed a familiar Kennedy pattern of opportunism and ruthless ambition, most notably in his 1964 election to the U.S. Senate from New York and in his ambivalent position on Vietnam, which seemed to change more from political need than from genuine conviction.

Regarding the dynamics of Bobby's relationships with the other male Kennedys, William Shannon has offered a suggestive interpretation of Bobby's constant emotional stress. Shannon saw how Kennedy's "silent, internal struggles turned upon his relationships with his demanding, domineering father, his dead hero brother Joe, and his older brother Jack. Love was central in those relationships but resentment and rivalry had also to be accommodated. No one has ever reported hearing him speak a word of criticism of his father or his brothers. Any negative emotions he experienced doubled back upon themselves and found expression in rigid identification with his family and intense, aggressive championship of its values. Crucial to this process was his sublimation of all his energies to his brother Jack's interests. He wanted nothing for himself; everything for his brother. This emotional transfer provided him a moral license for the expression of his natural driving aggressiveness. Any resentment he unconsciously felt at being the little brother or in second place he relieved by directing it outward at the slothful politicians, irreverent columnists, and disobedient bureaucrats who in one way or another obstructed his brother's wishes."

From all indications, Bobby spent the last four and a half years of his life largely searching for a meaning to Jack's death and for an atonement

through personal action that would give his brother's death the dignity of
justification and relieve his own intense inner guilt. But toward the end of
his life, Bobby seemed to come out from Jack's shadow and begin to feel that
he might live his life mainly—or at least equally—for himself. Professor
Robert Jay Lifton, a pioneering psychohistorian, has written of the "survivor guilt" felt by Hiroshima survivors, who identify with the dead victims
and may devote their lives to helping the poor, whom they see as live
victims. Dr. Lifton wrote that "the embrace of the identity of the dead may,
paradoxically enough, serve as the means of maintaining life. For in the
face of the burden of guilt the survivor carries with him, particularly the
guilt of survival priority, his obeisance before the dead is his best means of
justifying and maintaining his own existence. But it remains an existence
with a large shadow cast across it, a life which, in a powerful symbolic
sense, the survivor does not feel to be his own." It is interesting to see how
Bobby unconsciously assumed Jack's identity. Bobby quoted his murdered
brother obsessively; he unconsciously adopted Jack's mannerisms of expression, cigar smoking, longer hair; he also began wearing or carrying an
old tweed coat of Jack's, which he frequently left behind in various towns
but always remembered to retrieve. One senses here Bobby's deep inner
conflict and ambivalence, the desire both to cling to the past and to leave it
behind.

Yet despite the psychic bonds, interwoven with guilt and grief, that bound
Bobby so closely to his lost brother, there were also increasing signs that he
was trying to shake loose from the shackles of a pseudo-identity and achieve
his own. The qualities which Jack's death seemed to bring to the surface in
Bobby were not new ones, but they found different outlets and less harsh
expression. The old devils of communism and corruption were replaced by a
war on poverty, racism, and violence. As Bobby gradually returned to the
world of the living, he also returned to his old massive attack on time, space,
and the vagaries of less driven humanity. If now and then the deep inner
sadness he never lost momentarily halted him, it was just for an instant. The
hyperactive man still appeared to control Robert Kennedy, although the
fatalist within now dared mock him more openly.

Jack's death forced Bobby to find a substitute rationalized embodiment
upon which to project his neurotic needs and anxieties. This embodiment,
it seems to me, took the form of the so-called Kennedy legend, which Bobby
gradually incorporated into his own person. Thus on the deepest level of
Bobby's emotions he apparently clung to the image of "victor" created by
his father (and his father's father). The chief difference with the past was
that the image, which before had been Jack's, was now his own to fulfill.
In the process of this neurotic fulfillment, Bobby seemed to take some hesitant steps toward developing a genuine identity of his own.

To summarize Robert Kennedy's post-1963 career: Bobby remained as

Attorney General under Johnson from November, 1963, until August, 1964. In the summer of 1964, he wanted LBJ to give him the Democratic vice presidential nomination for the 1964 elections, but on July 29, 1964, Johnson told Kennedy this would be impossible. Disappointed, but determined to stay in politics, Bobby won the New York Democratic U.S. Senate nomination, and defeated the Republican incumbent in November, 1964. Through 1965, 1966, and 1967, RFK (now widely seen as the Kennedy "heir apparent") spoke out often on national issues and traveled frequently abroad. From 1966 onward, his growing anti-Vietnam position became more pronounced. Kennedy also increasingly addressed the problems of the Negroes, the poor, and the young student radicals, whom he visited often.

In the winter of 1967 and early spring of 1968, the antiwar feeling against the President grew into a widespread desire among Democratic liberals to "dump Johnson." Many Democrats and antiwar leaders wanted Bobby to run against LBJ because he would be the strongest antiwar candidate, but Kennedy refused. Finally, on March 16, 1968, after Democratic Senator Eugene McCarthy had beaten Johnson in the New Hampshire primary on March 12, Kennedy declared his candidacy for the presidency. During the next eighty-five days, RFK conducted a whirlwind campaign back and forth across the country in both primary and nonprimary states. On May 7, Bobby captured both the Indiana and the District of Columbia Democratic primaries; on May 14 he won again in Nebraska; but on May 28, he lost the Oregon primary to McCarthy. Then on June 4, RFK surged forward again with victories in both the vital California primary and in South Dakota. That night, while leaving a victory celebration in a Los Angeles hotel, Robert Kennedy was shot in the head by a young Jordanian. He died early in the morning of June 6, 1968, leaving the nation in sudden emotional shock and disbelief over this second Kennedy murder.

I will now examine in more detail some of the salient psychohistorical events and their possible interpretations during this important and tumultuous period. In the midst of Bobby's deep mourning in the winter of 1963–1964, President Johnson, as a kindly effort at distraction, sent Kennedy on a brief diplomatic trip to Japan to work out an Indonesia-Malaysia cease-fire. The overwhelming adulation met by RFK in the Far East in this January, 1964, trip—in contrast to past hostility—awoke in him a recognition of his dead brother's tremendous emotional impact among the world's youth. While Bobby's severe melancholia lingered through the early spring of 1964, his energies and zest for living gradually returned, and he began to think of his own future. Continuing as Attorney General under Johnson seemed impossible. A latent hostility had long existed between Bobby and LBJ, and now to have the disliked Johnson in Jack's place was emotionally agonizing for Kennedy. It seems probable, as many have commented, that

Bobby's strong identification with the brother he had long served and his guilt over that brother's death turned increasingly into a conviction that he himself must fulfill the dead President's shattered life—his personal promise as well as his public promises, which Bobby now saw in idealized form.

Before Jack's death, Bobby had planned to leave the Justice Department for a new role—perhaps as Assistant Secretary of State for Latin America. In the grayness of early 1964, he made two confused efforts to find a new direction. First he offered himself to LBJ as Ambassador to South Vietnam; then he indicated his desire to be Vice President on the 1964 ticket. Both suggestions were politically and personally unrealistic. Bobby and LBJ had never gotten along well; and Johnson, who had been virtually ignored by the Kennedy Administration as Vice President (and according to JFK's personal secretary would have been dropped in 1964), clearly wanted now to establish his own power structure and presidential identity. There could be no room for Kennedy rivals. It is suggestive of Bobby's deep feelings of aloneness and need for a father figure to substitute for Jack that he should have turned, even briefly, to so unlikely an older man as LBJ. Yet, curiously, even after Kennedy's emergence as a national leader in his own right in 1964–1967 and his strong open opposition to Johnson on Vietnam, Bobby still showed an excessive sensitivity to charges of a personal vendetta against Johnson, almost as though he unconsciously hoped to retain an emotional link with the hated LBJ. Johnson, in turn, often showed the same persecution feelings about Bobby.

Late in June, 1964, Bobby went to West Germany to unveil a JFK memorial, then continued to Poland where he was mobbed and applauded by students and the general populace. But Johnson was unmoved by Polish cheers for Bobby. Soon after Kennedy's return, LBJ summoned him and directly rejected Bobby's vice presidential fantasy. The President did ask him to stay on temporarily as Attorney General and perhaps later take another Cabinet or sub-Cabinet post, but Bobby refused. He knew now that he would have to chart his own course back to national power; Johnson was offering no coattails for an easier ride. In August, Bobby finally reluctantly accepted the urgings of many politicians and advisers that he run for the U.S. Senate from New York against incumbent Republican Kenneth Keating, who was up for reelection in November, 1964.

Two highly practical reasons propelled RFK's candidacy: New York, the country's most important state, would give Kennedy a new political base from which to establish a national identity; and New York was wide open for conquest. The Democratic party bosses would endorse him, and freshman Senator Keating was not a formidable opponent. The Senate itself did not appeal to Bobby, but it offered the only immediate route to important political action. Teddy was already Senator from Massachusetts;

and a governorship was even less appealing as a springboard to higher office, since most governors were largely bogged down in their own state affairs. Thus on August 25, 1964, Bobby announced his candidacy for the Senate.

Bobby Kennedy's 1964 New York campaign, although lavishly financed, was not nearly as well organized as the campaigns he had directed for Jack. The main reason was the suddenness of the decision to run (a pattern he would strangely repeat in 1968, although by then his presidential ambitions would have been evident for years). Two of Kennedy's aides later wrote that "his abrupt decision to run had not allowed time either to build a campaign organization or to permit him and his staff to familiarize themselves with the complex problems of a state where few of them had ever worked politically." They noted that Bobby himself lacked an intimate knowledge of New York problems and relations with local leaders and organizations. "Personal tragedy had induced him to find the political haven of New York, but he came without preparation, without the rudiments of a campaign organization, with a research staff that had only begun to find its way through the relevant issues." Here we see the ambivalence of Kennedy's self-defeatist strain, a repressed side of his personality that often led him either to act impulsively or not at all. The Kennedys all wanted to win; but, being as human as anyone, part of their natures secretly revolted against the internalized imperatives of competitive success. Thus their successes were often far more limited in fact than in appearance.

But Bobby also had many advantages in running for the Senate. First and foremost, of course, were his enormous notoriety and emotional appeal as the Kennedy heir. Money was a second huge asset. His Senate campaign reportedly cost close to $2 million, more than half going to an advertising agency for television commercials to erase the illiberal, ruthless McCarthy-Hoffa era image that had dismayed so many New Yorkers. A new Kennedy image was projected, one of warmth, concern, and statesmanship. Even so, many New Yorkers were stunned by Bobby's obvious power grab in a state he scarcely knew and against a Republican Senator who had worked hard to establish a progressive record. A group of prominent liberals, headed by writer Gore Vidal and television reporter Lisa Howard, established "Democrats for Keating" and announced, "We cannot, in good conscience, support Robert Kennedy for the Senate seat from New York. We believe that one of the great myths of current American politics is the widespread belief that Robert Kennedy is a liberal. We believe he is anti-liberal and disturbingly authoritarian. . . . In the weeks ahead, our Committee will work to bring these facts to the attention of New York voters."

The New York Times was equally disenchanted in an editorial entitled

"But Does New York Need Him?": "Why he has any special claim on New York to rescue him from non-office is a mystery. His sponsorship is hardly the cream of the party. . . . After some arm-twisting, apparently, Mayor [Robert F.] Wagner and State Democratic Chairman William H. McKeon are being cajoled into adding at least the lip-service of more respectability to the list of those willing to go along with a Kennedy candidacy. . . . The constitutionality of Mr. Kennedy's running in New York does not seem to be in doubt; the question of state law is being raised, but is not likely to disqualify him. His utter innocence as to New York State problems should. The cold fact is that Mr. Kennedy appears to have decided that his ambitions will be best and most immediately served by finding a political launching pad in New York state. If his brother were not already representing Massachusetts in the Senate, Mr. Kennedy undoubtedly would have run in that state. But to run now would mean that he would have to elbow out another Kennedy. Thus Mr. Kennedy apparently needs New York. But does New York really need Bobby Kennedy?"

Bobby responded with a typically hard-hitting campaign of whirlwind handshaking, massive publicity, wise-cracking appearances, and, as the deadline neared and opposition mounted, a direct attack on Keating's record which was cleverly distorted to make Keating—a certified liberal—appear as a reactionary. Keating came back with some innuendoes of his own, and the campaign hit a dismal low of mutual name-calling. Far more important than this political sniping was the fact that Keating refused to repudiate Barry Goldwater in an anti-Goldwater state, while Johnson warmly endorsed Kennedy. In the end, Bobby won by some 700,000 votes, but his margin was only a quarter of Johnson's New York landslide. Without LBJ, it is highly doubtful that Bobby would have won. But in his victory statement, Bobby refused to acknowledge Johnson's help, and instead claimed, "We started something in 1960, and the vote today is an overwhelming mandate to continue." The first step back to Camelot had been taken.

Robert Kennedy in his three years as U.S. Senator—1965 through 1967 and early 1968—seemed to work primarily on building up his national reputation. He spoke often on national and international issues, traveled widely, and was lavishly publicized. In 1965, he criticized LBJ's intervention in the Dominican Republic; gave a major speech on nuclear proliferation (regarded coolly by the White House); and supported both political and military action in Vietnam. But Kennedy avoided an open break with Johnson. On the domestic scene, the junior Senator proposed an amendment to extend Appalachian antipoverty aid into New York; worked to give voting rights to Spanish-speaking Puerto Ricans; testified for a bill to curb interstate firearms shipments; and conducted a one-man campaign against the cigarette industry. None of these issues, of course, could be regarded as major national concerns or ones of great controversy. Yet despite his general caution, Bobby's statements were gradually becoming more liberal in the broader realms of poverty, racial discrimination, and student activism. He began speaking out on the right to dissent and on black problems. The jungle of New York's Bedford-Stuyvesant captured his imagination and became a major Kennedy project.

In the Senate, Bobby was in many ways a maverick who aroused different responses in his associates, ranging from envy of his celebrity status as a probable future President to warm welcome for an active colleague. One Senator commented, "With all due respect to the kind of President Jack turned out to be, Bob is going to be a hell of a lot better senator. He's a harder worker than his brother was when he was here." Others, however, resented Kennedy's free-wheeling style of interrogation in committee hearings and his obvious lack of interest in the tedious business of making laws. As another legislator put it, "Bobby is not a senator's senator. He understands very well the limitations of achieving a national identity if you keep your nose close to the legislative grindstone. I would call Bobby a hit-and-run senator. He'll come into a committee room where the TV cameras are, take a slug at General Motors, and leave. The drudgery of writing and shepherding a bill is left to someone else." A third colleague similarly viewed Kennedy's travels as politically motivated. "Wherever the action is, he goes. Like Capetown, where he denounced *apartheid*, and Cracow, where he talked about freedom. His interests are outside the Senate. I would call him a first-act politician. You know it's easy to write the first act. And it's relatively easy to write the third act. Lyndon Johnson was a good third-act man. He liked to wrap things up. But it's the second act that is toughest to write. In Congress, that's where the drudgery and hard work come."

Bobby, in turn, was impatient with the Senate's slow pace. "They only take about one vote a week here," he said, "and they never can tell you in advance when it is going to be so you can schedule other things. If I am not going to be working here, I want to go somewhere I can do something." So, in 1965, the Senator climbed 13,900-foot Mt. Kennedy in Alaska (with the help of a helicopter and professional guides), a dubious exploit that gained him wide publicity, although his personal reasons were probably more cathartic than political. He traveled through Latin America, where he argued with hostile students, visited a Chilean coal mine ("If I worked in this mine I'd be a Communist too," said the sometimes empathetic Bobby), waded piranha-infested waters in Brazil, and toured poverty-stricken areas of Peru, Chile, Argentina, Brazil, and Venezuela. Everywhere Bobby went, he was viewed as the next Kennedy President by the Latins and as a compulsively hard-running candidate by the American press, which featured him prominently on magazine covers and in lead articles. There was no doubt that Bobby Kennedy continued to be big news.

In the fall of 1966, Bobby's personal popularity soared to a peak that was never repeated. Candidates everywhere wanted his endorsement and presence. In state after state, wherever Kennedy spoke, the crowds were huge and loudly admiring. The press and magazines helped build up and spread his political stardom; wherever he went, he was applauded as a future President. Things started going wrong for Bobby in the November elections. His greatest failure was in New York, where he had fumbled in producing a liberal and electable candidate for governor. In the end, the Democratic bosses nominated a political hack, who Kennedy felt could not attract the essential liberal and independent votes, and the Senator campaigned half-heartedly for the loser. Several Kennedy-backed candidates in other states also lost.

In addition, Bobby's continued hedging on Vietnam began to produce sharp liberal criticism. The Senator had given a speech in February, 1966, calling for a negotiated settlement which included the National Liberation Front (the political arm of the Vietcong). But Kennedy remained largely silent in the following months, claiming a reluctance to have his views distorted as partisan politics and a personal attack on Johnson. In late October, I. F. Stone wrote in "While Others Dodge the Draft, Bobby Dodges the War" that "to be a trimmer, to put career ahead of duty, to be all but silent on the greatest moral and political issue of our times is to be no different from the other politicians. . . . Kennedy in the U.S. Senate has at his disposal a forum second only to that of the Presidency. But he hasn't said a word about the war in the Senate since his one speech last February. . . . Kennedy did not support [Fulbright's] effort to rescind the Tonkin Bay resolution nor to alert the country on the danger in Thailand. He even achieved the feat of delivering a speech on peace in New York (October 11, 1966) without mentioning Vietnam! Kennedy thinks of himself as a moral man. He proclaims it in South Africa and in Latin America but at home, where thousands are being drafted every month, he says as little as he can about the one issue that matters most."

The growing American disillusion with the bloody Vietnam war above every other issue offered Bobby a chance to establish himself as a national statesman and an alternative to the increasingly unpopular Johnson. Finally, on March 2, 1967, more than a year after his first Senate speech on Vietnam, Kennedy again addressed the Senate on U.S. policy in Southeast Asia. This second speech was a great disappointment to those who wanted Kennedy to lead the way toward a major shift in policy. Although still favoring negotiations and opposed to widening the war, Bobby stuck to the

Cold War line that the Communists were the sole aggressors: "The fault for no peace rests largely with our adversary. He has pursued relentless and unyielding conquest with obdurate unconcern for mounting desolation. . . . If our enemy will not accept peace, it cannot come." While pointing out the devastating costs of the war to both South Vietnam and America, Kennedy asserted, "Of course we are willing—we must be willing—to pay all these costs if the alternative is surrender or defeat. We cannot dishonor our commitments, nor yield the lawful interests of the nation at any price." Bobby also praised LBJ, while calling for renewed efforts at negotiations: "For years, President Johnson has dedicated his energies in an effort to achieve an honorable peace." He did, however, break with the Administration in one particular, by calling for an unconditional halt in the bombing of North Vietnam which, he added, could be resumed if negotiations failed. Kennedy also offered tentative blueprints for entering discussions and what issues to resolve. While far from radical, Kennedy's suggested solutions were increasingly distant from the military course which the Johnson Administration doggedly continued to follow.

Probably the major weakness in Bobby's argument was the belief, which he never seemed to change, that the United States could actually impose a democratic structure on a separate South Vietnam which both the Southerners and Northerners would honor. We must remember, as JFK, Johnson, and Nixon did not, that it was the United States, not the Vietnamese, who initially divided their ancient land. Even with the massive American troop presence in the South, the United States had not achieved free elections in South Vietnam (as Bobby himself noted in his caustic assessment of the September 3, 1967, Vietnamese elections). Yet by the time of his death in mid-1968, Kennedy, although calling the war immoral, still did not support unilateral withdrawal (an ultimate withdrawal that, by 1969, a Republican Administration had virtually conceded as necessary behind the cloak of "Vietnamization"). Certainly on Vietnam, Bobby Kennedy, from everything he ever said or did, never became the "radical beyond liberalism" whom romantic-minded liberals professed to see. On the contrary, Kennedy's assertions and positions on Vietnam showed a still fairly solid conservative who believed, by and large, in the existing structure of Establishment laws and attitudes. While Bobby grew to denounce the war as immoral, he never admitted—or perhaps never saw—that to refuse to be a part of immorality, it may also be necessary to refuse to obey laws, such as draft orders. Kennedy, even to radical students in 1968, condemned draft evaders who went to Canada, although he continued to proclaim himself against the war.

Late 1966 and early 1967 became increasingly difficult for Bobby Kennedy in many ways. He felt himself out of power and ignored by LBJ's

Administration. In fact, he often showed signs of feeling actively persecuted by Lyndon Johnson and this reached the point where he justified his own caution on Vietnam because of Johnson's alleged vindictiveness. In December, 1967, Bobby told a friend, "I'm afraid that by speaking out I just make Lyndon do the opposite, out of spite. He hates me so much that if I asked for snow, he would make rain, just because it was me. But maybe I will have to say something. The bombing is getting worse all the time now." Johnson seemed to be equally obsessed with Bobby. While there were concrete reasons for these mutual fears and hostilities, the extreme intensity of feelings on both sides suggested elements of paranoia. Bobby's rationalizing on Vietnam caused at least one supporter (Jack Newfield) to feel deeply ambivalent about him: "His personal qualities of decency, anguish, and intelligence remained immensely appealing. But his reluctance to speak was unforgivable. . . . Kennedy, although he wasn't verbalizing it, was placing his own political future above the dead, burned, and homeless of Vietnam. He was still a good and decent man, but trapped by the conventional ambitions of conventional politics. How harshly to judge him for his compromises about the war remained a dilemma that troubled me the rest of his life."

That the Kennedys above all intended a return to presidential power was deeply believed by the Johnson Administration and certainly suspected by much of the populace. An LBJ associate expressed this feeling bluntly: "The entire post-assassination series of events has been a calculated, contrived, emotional build-up, not for the sake of paying honest respect to, and showing genuine grief for, John F. Kennedy, but to enhance the image of the Kennedy family and the Kennedy name. The Kennedys have the attitude that this is not an honor that the American people conferred on Jack Kennedy, but that the Kennedy family as a whole achieved a position of power in American society—and the important thing is to retain that position for which the family fought so long ago starting with Joe Kennedy. With the Kennedys the White House is still their house—and Jacqueline Kennedy is the widowed queen in exile, awaiting a return of the dynasty to the throne."

Yet the troubled months of 1967 brought many problems for Bobby, whose personal popularity was declining from its 1966 peak. The controversy over William Manchester's book, *The Death of a President*, damaged Kennedy's public image, although it was Jackie Kennedy who wanted the book suppressed. But Bobby himself had written the unclear contract between Manchester and the Kennedys, and he could not go against the wishes of his brother's widow. In the end, the suit against Manchester was settled out of court, and the book was published. But by then the old suspicions of Bobby's ruthlessness had been rekindled. The reputation for authoritarianism was also revived by a furious press argument at about the same time between J. Edgar Hoover and Kennedy over the FBI's wire-tapping when Bobby was Attorney General. Hoover said the electronic eavesdroppers had been cleared through Kennedy; Bobby denied knowledge of such practices. Either way, Bobby was hurt, looking like a poor administrator or an antiliberal. The public feud antagonized both liberals and conservatives.

Kennedy's three-year record in New York politics also raised serious doubts about his ability to "turn the country around" as Chief Executive. For those interested in fuller accounts, two pro-Kennedy biographers who followed state developments have given revealing details: Jack Newfield in *Robert Kennedy: A Memoir* and William V. Shannon in *The Heir Apparent: Robert Kennedy and the Struggle for Power*. Without going too deeply into the 1964–1967 New York rivalries between reform-minded Democrats and their entrenched opponents, we may usefully review some general conclusions. As New York's only Democratic Senator, Bobby failed to give effective support to the more liberal Democrats who might have successfully opposed the victorious liberal Republicans (Mayor John Lindsay and Governor Nelson Rockefeller). In only one instance did RFK decisively intervene, in his vigorous campaign for a nonmachine surrogate judge in 1966. This upset triumph gave Kennedy the temporary momentum and prestige for some genuine party changes, but he failed to use them.

Jack Newfield, who became a passionate RFK supporter, wrote, "During his three years as New York's junior Senator, Robert Kennedy lost every factional fight he engaged in, except one. And he won that one because it was the only opportunity he had to go above the heads of the party leaders, directly to the voter, in a primary." Actually there were two Democratic primaries, one for the surrogate judgeship, which Kennedy won, and one for the New York mayor's nomination, where Kennedy failed to enter or support a liberal candidate. The governor, however, was nominated by a party convention. Newfield also commented, "As in so many realms, Robert Kennedy remained only a potential in New York politics. He kept getting better, but he had not yet taken his stand." One wonders, however, if Kennedy did keep getting better. Newfield's own chapter on New York politics seems to lead to an opposite conclusion.

Bobby's first failure to exert himself in New York was in the early 1965 struggle for control of the state legislature after the Democratic sweep of November, 1964. Two mediocre and conservative Democrats had held the minority leadership posts. Reform-minded Democrats, secretly aided by Kennedy, tried to bring in more liberal candidates for the majority posts. For five weeks the legislature remained in a voting deadlock over Assembly and Senate leaders, until finally the old-line Democrats made a deal with

Governor Rockefeller to exchange sales-tax support for Republican votes. Kennedy, who had supported the reformers so covertly that many were unaware of it, had been outmaneuvered.

In the important mayoralty primary contest of September, 1965, Kennedy again failed to take a strong stand for a progressive candidate, while the reformers typically split their efforts. Again, the conservative bosses pushed their candidate to victory in the primary and lost the general election to the Republicans. "Robert Kennedy, who was supposed to be the second most powerful Democrat in the nation," observed Newfield, "spent an unhappy and grouchy autumn, trapped between the tawdry, old-fashioned Beame campaign, and the exciting, threatening candidacy of John Lindsay." Despite the Democrats' superiority in party registration, Lindsay was elected, and Bobby, having failed to gain another powerful patronage base, City Hall, was identified with a loser.

But the next year, having failed to fight for liberal and personal control of the state legislature and City Hall, the junior Senator suddenly emerged to do open battle for the Manhattan surrogate judgeship. According to Newfield, Kennedy's wrath was aroused by a press report that the judge who was supported for this post by both political parties (who routinely divided judicial patronage) had underworld ties. The former Attorney General found a new candidate, secured the support of the reformers, and launched an attack, including ten days of hard personal campaigning. Kennedy's upset victory abruptly put him at the top of the New York power pyramid within his party. With the Democratic convention to nominate a gubernatorial candidate set for September, Bobby now had a strong chance to make the choice. But once again he hesitated and temporized, and again the Democrats lost the election, despite Rockefeller's large drop in popularity. As in 1965, Kennedy had to campaign unhappily for a loser.

There was one other incident indicative of Bobby's curious indecisiveness and apparent self-defeatism. In March, 1967, the leader of Tammany Hall resigned, and the Democratic factions rushed to elect a new county chairman. The reform bloc divided into pro-Humphrey East Side and pro-Kennedy West Side factions; Kennedy secretly gave tentative support to the West Side candidate, Mrs. Ronnie Eldridge. Although Mrs. Eldridge led the reform caucus, her opponent refused to withdraw. Meanwhile the old-line faction had managed to secure a majority for its candidate. Kennedy flew back from a Montreal holiday to cajole the delegates, but it was too late. One vote short, Mrs. Eldridge withdrew, and Tammany remained with the conservatives. Bobby told Mrs. Eldridge, "If I had had forty-eight hours we could have put it together. But two hours just wasn't enough time. I didn't even connect on half my phone calls. I have no clout with politicians. My only chance comes in primaries. . . . But your reform friends are sick. They hate each other so much. They really could have put me on the spot, if they had just gotten together. . . ."

The surprising lameness of this familiar excuse (projecting hostility and ineffectiveness on others) again suggests the anxiety and insecurity behind the Kennedy façade. Like his brothers, Robert Kennedy often showed himself emotionally incapable of being the "strong man" he wished to be. Thus he had to fall back on blaming others and circumstances, when it was clear that many of the circumstances were largely of his own creation. Newfield himself, although able to rationalize and forgive Kennedy's actions, did see through to Bobby's basic lack of concern with New York when he said, "He did not fight the barons when to fight would conflict with his own self-interest. His involvement in New York was sporadic: Vietnam, poverty, and Presidential politics remained his abiding concerns."

William Shannon also made several significant observations about Kennedy's New York record. Before the gubernatorial election of 1966, RFK said, "Win or lose, changes should be made in the party." After the Democratic defeat, the press speculated, "Kennedy was now in a position to 'pick up the pieces,' take charge of the Democratic Party, and rebuild its organization." Shannon, however, from a longer range, commented, "His record as a politician in New York provides little support for these assumptions. The guerrilla warfare for the leadership of the legislature ending in an ambush, the erratic interventions in the mayoralty campaign, the refusal to offer open battle for the governorship—this is a record of defeat, inconsequence, and confused purposes. Aside from his own election to the Senate, his one success was the Surrogate primary, which was a lightning-swift sortie rather than a major, prolonged effort. That success accorded with the nature of his previous political experience. Before coming to New York, Kennedy had gained all his experience managing his brother's campaigns. . . . On the morning after one of those campaigns, he could walk away and leave Massachusetts as he found it, having no responsibility for its party organization. As his brother's political agent during the presidential years, he had political influence on a national scale and so diverse in its nature that it was not comparable to state party-building. Kennedy is a superb campaign organizer, the political equivalent of a hundred-yard-dash man, but reorganizing a party is slow, time-consuming work, more like a ten-mile cross-country run."

Shannon concluded, "Unlike John Kennedy, who coolly kept his distance from the misgovernment of Massachusetts and from most of his party's factional fights, Robert Kennedy has a recurrent impulse to dabble and dominate. This is to his credit; he cares more and more passionately about electing an honest judge and an effective governor than his brother did.

His involvement is also a reflexive response; he is a combative man with an itch to run things. But he does not persist day in and day out in the struggle to reshape the Democratic Party into a serviceable instrument of reform government and social idealism. At bottom, he lacks the patience and the interest to rebuild a party at the state and local level. And there is good reason to doubt whether it is to his own advantage to devote a major portion of his time and energy to it. His personal horizon extends far beyond the Hudson River. A man who wants to be President can get closer to his goal traveling to South Africa or Berkeley, California, than he can addressing party meetings in Great Neck or Gloversville. To win the presidential nomination, all that Kennedy needs to control is New York's delegation to the national convention, and that control is reasonably assured." But for New York, the state which Kennedy represented in the U.S. Senate, "The outlook is for more Democratic defeats and more Kennedy frustration. . . . Unless Kennedy evinces a willingness in the future to break with the party regulars, fight them openly for control, and devote much more time consistently to party affairs, the momentum of mediocrity will run on."

In this account, William Shannon used phrases that directly contradicted the Kennedy mystique of victory, energy, and direction. He called RFK's New York record one of "defeat, inconsequence, and confused purposes." Regarding the state constitutional convention, "Once again, Kennedy's reach considerably exceeded his grasp." The suggestion of a lack of realism and of self-defeatism is unmistakable. While Shannon commended Bobby for being more emotionally involved and concerned than Jack, he also pointed out RFK's "recurrent impulse to dabble and dominate," his impatience and lack of persistence, and his cautious refusal to break with the party regulars to achieve reform. These are not qualities that citizens desire in a President. While one could argue that the presidency might well have aroused Bobby's deepest interests and strongest executive talents, there was never any guarantee of such a decisive change. It is true that people are often largely stifled in constricted environments and do not show their real abilities until their circumstances significantly change. Yet it is hard to view the position of United States Senator, no matter what its realistic limitations, as a predominantly confining role.

It is also hard to imagine that the personal leadership qualities that Bobby demonstrated, or failed to demonstrate, as Senator would have undergone a dynamic transformation once he became President. Even in Kennedy's seemingly radical campaign of 1968, he often reverted to conservative postures and rhetoric directly reminiscent of the 1950s. While the presidency offered a scope for personal action far beyond that of a Senator, Kennedy would still have been working with many of the political realities he found in New York, although on a vaster and more complex scale. His older brother had used these "realities" to excuse his own mediocre presidential performance. Although Bobby often seemed to care more and want to do more than Jack, the historical record in New York casts a long shadow of doubt on his psychological ability to break away from the deep-rooted past.

We come now to the final period of Robert Kennedy's life, his half-year of indecisiveness over whether to enter the 1968 presidential race, and the hectic eighty-five days of his presidential campaign which ended with his shooting and death on June 5–6, 1968. Bobby's long wavering on announcing his candidacy has often been portrayed as untypical of the man and largely the result of circumstances beyond his control. Jules Witcover, in *85 Days: The Last Campaign of Robert F. Kennedy*, called his first chapter, "Fateful Delay: The Decision Not to Run." Some passages indicate both Kennedy's intense inner battle as viewed by close observers and Witcover's interpretation of Kennedy's ambivalence. When reporters asked RFK on January 30, 1968, if there were any circumstances under which he might run against Johnson, the Senator replied, "No, I can't conceive of any circumstances." As newsman Witcover described the scene, "Robert Kennedy clearly was a man in turmoil." Kennedy expressed "deep concern about the Vietnam War and about the alienation abroad in the land—the disquiet among whites and Negroes, the young and elderly, the wealthy and poor. . . . But in all the compassionate words, there was an overriding sense of futility, of personal helplessness. 'If I thought there was anything I could do about it,' Kennedy said near the end, 'I would do it.' He was trying to persuade them that there wasn't, but at the same time he was trying to persuade himself. As one of the witnesses said later, 'It was like seeing a man do battle with himself right there before your eyes.' . . . For Robert Kennedy, whose whole life had been a series of strong positive responses to personal, physical and political challenge, it was the greatest irony to find himself thus in the grip of such uncharacteristic uncertainty and inaction."

What Witcover and so many Kennedy observers overlooked was how often Bobby (and his brothers) had been precisely in the grip of "uncertainty and inaction." Although Kennedy's 1968 political dilemma was a very real one, it was also true, as we have seen, that Bobby had shown much past evidence of political indecisiveness. Kennedy feared that any challenge to Johnson would be judged only as a personal vendetta, part of the undeniable Kennedy-Johnson feud. He may also have been inhibited by a deeply unconscious "father-image" link to LBJ, as previously suggested. Thus Bobby could have wished both to be accepted as a "son" by Johnson (as Ambassador or Vice President), and at the same time want to destroy Johnson, the hated "rejecting father." All of these overlapping desires, it may seem superfluous to repeat, would have been at a totally unrecognized level of Bobby's repressed emotions. These, of course, are merely psycho-historical speculations, but they seem to help explain Bobby's unusual ambivalence about Johnson and his own presidential candidacy.

On the conscious level, in the fall and winter of 1967–1968, RFK felt, and certainly with some justification, that if he challenged the incumbent President, he would only split the Democrats, assure the election of Nixon and a hostile Republican Congress, and ruin himself. There was also the handicap of Bobby's lingering reputation for arrogant self-aggrandizement. But in many ways much of this thrashing about seems like the old Kennedy caution, a caution that tended to be exaggerated when a direct benefit to the Kennedys was highly questionable (such as the Kennedys' laggardness about civil rights). Probably foremost in RFK's mind, behind all the questions and apprehensions faced by every politician, was the overriding fear that he would be sacrificing an inevitable rise to presidential power for nothing.

In a sense, the enormous political uses of mass and instant communi-cations had boomeranged on Bobby: his every move now could be seen as part of the Kennedy-Johnson enmity. Thus Kennedy, in some ways, was a victim of his own fantastic publicity. Living in a glass house, he felt he had to be very careful about throwing rocks. While Kennedy often tried to keep the focus of his speeches and actions on issues, the public was far more attuned to personalities (a preference the Kennedys themselves had greatly encouraged; Bobby frequently campaigned far more on "style" than on substance). In retrospect, RFK can be seen as worrying too much about himself and the effect of trivia and incalculable factors on his career. In the final analysis, Bobby—like the other Kennedys—had been raised to believe that winning was the most important thing in life. Unless they stood a good fighting chance in a race, Kennedys wouldn't enter ("Don't play unless you can be captain," their father had told them). The Kennedys failed to understand that sometimes the mere fact of entering a race is the most important thing one can do. As Jack Newfield clearly saw, "by the end of January, there was no excuse for Robert Kennedy not joining the race. The moral imperative was clear, and the evidence was all there. He simply miscalculated. As a Kennedy, *his fear of defeat paralyzed him.* And so, as if acting out a tragic drama by his great favorite Aeschylus, Robert Kennedy again violated his best self, and chose caution rather than courage." (Italics added.)

In such frequent indications that caution was a stronger character trait in Bobby Kennedy than courage, this third Kennedy son was denying his own words in *To Seek a Newer World:* "Only those who dare to fail greatly can ever achieve greatly." Like his older brother Jack, Bobby was verbally fascinated with a moral courage and daring that he too rarely expressed in actions. Physical risks held the appeals of heroism, family approval, and even potential destruction; moral risk-taking on the other hand, was not bred into the Kennedy sons, and held the immense threat of failure and humiliation. Thus neurosis, in Kennedys as in other mortals, led to moral incapacity and paralysis.

In the end, President Johnson was first challenged by a man who would have liked to be President but didn't emotionally need it, Democratic Senator Eugene McCarthy of Minnesota, a liberal Catholic intellectual. Compared to Kennedy, McCarthy was largely unknown; but his candidacy, announced on November 30, 1967, although low-key and handicapped by McCarthy's personal pride and diffidence, soon attracted an army of activist students who worked hard and effectively for him. Later, after Kennedy became a candidate, Bobby would ruefully envy McCarthy what he called the "A kids," saying he had the B and B-minus ones. Senator McCarthy was ahead of Kennedy in sensing the country's changing mood and depth of frustration. Also he did not have a coterie of conservative advisers, such as Sorensen and Ted Kennedy, urging him to wait. So McCarthy went in, won twenty out of New Hampshire's twenty-four Democratic delegates on March 12, and suddenly Bobby Kennedy knew he would have to run hard and fast to catch up with his own national constituency.

It seems now, as it definitely did not at the time, that Kennedy's candidacy, coming on the heels of McCarthy's startling victory, was largely the result of Bobby's impatience rather than any ruthless desire to undercut McCarthy. Men fairly close to Kennedy, such as Jack Newfield, William vanden Heuvel, and Milton Gwirtzman, claim that Bobby had already decided to run before the New Hampshire primary. A great deal of ink has been used to draw the thin line between the decision and the announcement. But decision is often a shifting and tenuous affair. Whatever the exact truth of the effect of McCarthy's victory, the fact remains that Bobby did not enter the race before the New Hampshire primary; McCarthy did, beating Johnson there; and only four days later Kennedy jumped in, making his declaration in the same Senate Caucus Room where Jack had announced in 1960. Bobby's use of the same opening words (drafted by Sorensen) openly exposed his personal, emotional identification with Jack.

The long delay and then abrupt entry probably alienated more liberals than any other episode in Bobby's often brash and controversial career. Some potential supporters, like Newfield, wanted Kennedy so much they could overlook and "understand" anything. Others could not. Many felt, with Arthur Krock, that when Kennedy "required the evidence of the New Hampshire Democratic Primary that President Johnson's renomination and official record, particularly with respect to the war in Vietnam, could be challenged from within the Democratic Party (and as it turned out successfully), Bobby Kennedy blurred his image as a politician who would risk an excellent chance eventually to be President on an issue he had proclaimed as the fundamental obstacle to the social progress of the American people—the war in Vietnam." As the authors of *An American Melodrama* wrote, "The irony was clear. The contemplative McCarthy, mired in complexity, had known how to act. The supposedly existential Kennedy, who sought to create himself by action, had hesitated too long."

Bobby needed to win all the party primaries open to him, as had Jack, to impress the convention bosses and delegates that he could win the election and that Johnson could not. He came close to succeeding, racing to victory in Indiana (May 7), Nebraska (May 14) and California (June 4), with added side-wins in the District of Columbia and South Dakota. But Oregon, lost to McCarthy on May 28, cast a large shadow over the ultimate outcome, even with Johnson out of the picture after the President's March 31 withdrawal speech. Many commentators felt that the California win put Kennedy back in the race as a frontrunner; others disagreed, seeing Humphrey as LBJ's probable successor.

A British television critic has questioned both Bobby's securing of the Democratic nomination and his use of television. In *The Half-Shut Eye: Television and Politics in Britain and America,* John Whale commented on RFK, "One of the numberless ironies of his death in Los Angeles a week later, on the night of his close win in the California primary, was that he had already virtually lost his chance of being elected president in 1968. Although the antagonisms he aroused in life were washed away in his death, they had been so strong that the delegates to the Democratic convention could only have agreed on him as their candidate for one reason: their belief that no Kennedy could lose an election. This faith had been borne out by Senator Kennedy's wins in the Indiana and Nebraska primaries, but it was made groundless when he lost to Senator McCarthy by six percentage points in Oregon; and the Kennedy victory in California by a smaller margin was not enough to recover the family reputation."

While Bobby based his primary campaigns on television, Mr. Whale felt that "television never did Robert Kennedy the service he needed. Throughout his four primaries, television was his chief campaign instrument. The question he had to meet was not so much about his views as about his character. There were as many people who thought it astonishing that he should be considered fit for the presidency as there were who thought it obvious. This was an argument which paid, partisan television should have been able to settle, or at any rate to influence. Even though television may not always present character and capacity accurately, it can at least be used to present them plausibly and coherently. Yet the division of opinion among the voters of the four primary states remained as fierce as in the country at large . . . Robert Kennedy was a difficult man to present as an intellectual force. He did not talk well. He seemed aware of it himself. It was painful to him to finish a paragraph: he was always left with the sense that his thought could be better put. So he talked on, and fast: too fast for lucidity."

There were other difficulties in presenting Bobby as a strong, clear-headed, stable, forceful, yet mature, personality. The intense reactions to Kennedy's speeches, especially in the highly emotional conditions of his enormous student rallies, sometimes led Bobby to make statements bordering on the demagogic. Jules Witcover noted several instances in which Kennedy actually distorted issues when he must have known the facts (such as accusing the Vietnamese of having the United States defend Khe Sanh for them—the decision was American—and not drafting eighteen- and nineteen-year-olds, which was untrue). Bobby's volatile emotions even led him at one point to attack Johnson for "calling upon the darker impulses of the American spirit," a line he hastily dropped after adverse press reactions. Television hurt as well as helped Bobby, especially in the high-pitched, wild, early campaigning. As Theodore White described him in *The Making of the President, 1968,* "Carried away by his own emotions and their echo among the volatile cheering young, he could not quite grasp how television outlined his figure on the forty-second and one-minute snatches of evening news shows where the larger, national, mature audience saw him: hysterical, high-pitched, hair blowing in the wind, almost demoniac, frightening. In short, the ruthless, vindictive Bobby Kennedy again, action without thought, position without plan."

Witcover also pointed out Bobby's personal vulnerability to crowd emotions: "Specific references to Johnson were trimmed, but when the California mobs began to work their passions on the candidate, he was increasingly carried away. Although Robert Kennedy had the reputation of being a cold and blunt individual, he was a much more emotional and reachable man than his brother John had been as a campaigner for high public office. John Kennedy, especially in the late stages of the 1960 campaign, could fire up a crowd, but seldom did the playback get to him. Robert was not so emotionally insulated; that was one of the reasons his compassion for the poor was accepted as genuine by the mass of underprivileged with whom this rich and privileged young man came into contact. But this same emotionalism—and the intentional playing on it, to the edge of demagoguery—could also produce a negative counterreaction among those who, in times of national distress, longed for more placid times. A soft-sell candidate like Gene McCarthy, who actually was assaulting the political status quo much more basically than Kennedy was, nevertheless did not project a very frightening image."

The reaction to Bobby's "darker impulses" speech led to greater caution, although campaign planning still had to proceed on a hectic day-to-day basis. The second Kennedy presidential campaign, in fact, had started out totally unlike the first. Jack's 1960 race had been preceded by years of careful organization and personal appearances. Bobby's sights, and those of most of his entourage, had been fixed on 1972. Only the dramatic unveiling of Vietnam realities by the January-February, 1968, Tet offensive, followed by McCarthy's upset of Johnson in New Hampshire, had brought Kennedy in on the spur of the moment. But the Kennedy "old hands" rallied quickly, as well as a number of talented newcomers. Kennedy's advance men were especially good, and his scheduling was generally far superior to McCarthy's, who at times acted like a noncandidate. While the Kennedys often failed to understand popular sentiment, they understood thoroughly the manifold ways to go about putting a complex campaign together. Like his strong showing in a crisis, Bobby also knew how to mount and operate a political "blitz." It was essentially this ability, as well as a rigging of sails to pick up the prevailing Midwestern conservative winds, that brought Kennedy first across the finish line in Indiana and Nebraska.

In conservative Indiana, Kennedy retailored his liberalism, stressing law and order, the need for jobs instead of "welfare handouts," and local self-government. Soon newsmen were comparing Kennedy to Barry Goldwater. But the pitch was effective. As Witcover summed it up, "the conservative approach and the personal campaigning in rural Indiana had paid off." Kennedy won ten of eleven congressional districts and fifty-seven of the state's ninety-two counties. When McCarthy conceded defeat on television, he emphasized that what mattered was what a candidate stood for, not how he came in. Bobby, watching, summed up the Kennedy attitude: "That's not the way I was brought up. We were brought up to win." Indiana also provided an amusing instance of Kennedy humor. The Kennedys, although sensitive to outside criticism, enjoyed poking fun at themselves. This was an appealing quality—and good politics. After Bobby's first victory, he held a press conference. As Witcover described it, "The press session had been routine, except for the participation of an attractive blonde who asked, if Kennedy were elected President, 'would you appoint your brother as Attorney General?' The candidate answered, 'No, we tried that once.' Then he asked the blonde: 'Whom do you represent?' She wouldn't say. It was Joan Kennedy, wife of Teddy."

Nebraska was easier than Indiana. David Halberstam called it "a triumph of imported organization and style." Kennedy had the money to send a second team into Nebraska even while he campaigned with his main force in Indiana. Hence the ground was prepared, the scheduling set up, and Bobby was able to whirl through in a short but effective week-long campaign. While the Negro-blue-collar vote that had carried Indiana was much smaller in Nebraska, it gave Kennedy a base of some 20 percent. Bobby also had Ted Sorensen's brother, a former Nebraska lieutenant governor, to set up an effective organization. Bobby had planned on routing McCarthy completely in Nebraska, but instead the Minnesotan had campaigned only a few days, then flown west to prepare for Oregon and California. Again, Kennedy campaigned strenuously through Democratic centers, this time using an old-fashioned train—dubbed by the press "The Ruthless Cannonball"—which added a great deal of color and gaiety to his generally relaxed speech-making. Again, Kennedy's low-key, conservative slant brought victory: a clear majority of 51.5 percent, with 31 percent for McCarthy, 5.6 percent going to Johnson, and 8.4 percent on write-ins to Humphrey, who had announced his candidacy on April 27.

Oregon was different. Although liberal and presumably a Kennedy-type state, it lacked the ethnic and racial minorities that usually supported Kennedy. Oregon was, in Kennedy's view, "one giant suburb," affluent, peaceful, and largely untouched by the inflammatory issues that divided the rest of the country, except for Vietnam. Oregonians were against the war before most Americans, and McCarthy had entered as a peace candidate before Kennedy. Also McCarthy's subdued style, good-mannered liberalism, and "safe look" appealed more to Oregonian Democrats than Kennedy's seeming radicalism, although Bobby's positions were often the more conservative. The Minnesotan's air of quiet confidence reassured Oregon voters; Kennedy's flamboyance, passion, and hint of discordance often dismayed them. In Oregon, McCarthy was better organized and spent heavily on television. Kennedy, on the other hand, was poorly organized; and his refusal to debate McCarthy in a state that valued debates hurt him. Kennedy looked like a pushy Eastern millionaire to many Oregonians, and they handed him his first defeat: 38.8 percent to McCarthy's 44.7 percent (with Johnson taking 12.4 and Humphrey 4 percent).

Bobby's reaction to his first defeat—the first Kennedy defeat in twenty-six campaigns—was typically personal: Humphrey, not McCarthy, he said, was the big gainer; "I think what he [McCarthy] wanted most was to knock me off. I guess he may hate me that much." As usual, Bobby felt that any-one who opposed him did so out of personal hostility and spite. Kennedy also admitted the Oregon defeat would make his nomination far more difficult. In San Francisco on May 21, Bobby had carelessly told a press club, "If I get beaten in a primary, I'm not a viable candidate. I might be a nice man. . . . I'd return to being unruthless if I lose in Oregon." Now he would have to disprove his own remark by a huge win in California.

California made Kennedy feel at home again, with its roaring, excited crowds of young people and enthusiastic minorities, including the Mexican-

American grape pickers he had made special efforts to encourage. Kennedy's spirits rose as he flew and motorcaded around the enormous state and its three great population centers of San Francisco-Oakland, Los Angeles-Long Beach, and San Diego. Because of its vastness, California is known as a "media state," and so Bobby concentrated on maximum visibility to attract widely broadcast television coverage. Yet while Kennedy drew the tumultuous crowds, McCarthy appeared on dozens of quiz and interview shows, which provided both free time and the kind of quiet setting in which he could best demonstrate his articulate casualness.

The famous Kennedy-McCarthy "debate" just before California's primary vote has been portrayed by pro-Kennedy reporters as a skillful and effective attack by Bobby on a diffident and unprepared McCarthy. The three British authors of An American Melodrama saw it differently. In their detailed account, McCarthy is quoted at length as expressing views on housing and poverty which were significantly more radical than those held by Kennedy. The basic difference was that Kennedy advocated improving the ghettos by attracting private industry, while McCarthy emphasized the need to get black people out of the ghettos and integrate them into society as a whole. Bobby attacked McCarthy with more rhetoric than accuracy in what the British reporters saw as a "blatant perversion of the record." They pointed out "the strange contrast between Kennedy's famous concern for the black man and his willingness to use white prejudice as a demagogue's device." Kennedy also distorted McCarthy's views on Vietnam, falsely implying that McCarthy was surrendering to the Communists. Unfortunately for McCarthy, he did not counterattack effectively, and the moment passed for a genuine exchange. In California, Kennedy had a natural ethnic-black-youth base of citizens enthralled by the emotionalism of his "charisma" despite the intellectual fuzziness of his liberalism. RFK made his political comeback in California, although his victory was not a decisive majority: 46.3 percent to McCarthy's 41.8 percent, with the rest voting for a pro-Administration slate. But Humphrey still had the party regulars, the Democratic professionals, and the union leaders largely locked up.

There is no need to repeat the details of Robert Kennedy's murder on the night of his California victory celebration. They have been movingly recounted in such books as Jules Witcover's firsthand account. Kennedy's inner emotional conflicts did not cause his death, although there was a certain death fascination and very possibly a considerable death pull within him. Bobby did refuse to have any effective bodyguard protection, which conceivably could have saved him. Yet all the security forces of the U.S. government had not saved his brother. The fact remains that politicians and leaders in America must be publicly visible and exposed, and a determined assassin can often succeed.

We must return to the task of appraising Kennedy as a potential United States President in the hope of gaining greater insights in order to appraise other leaders of the present and future. During Robert Kennedy's campaign, while millions of voters rallied to the excitement of a second Kennedy candidacy, and millions were attracted by the dynamism of Bobby himself, there remained other millions who continued to doubt RFK's fitness for high office. To the end of his life, Bobby's long-standing reputation as the hatchetman behind his benign brother worried many citizens who wondered about the wisdom of entrusting him with great power.

One leading New York editorial writer put it this way: "I don't hate Bobby Kennedy. I simply don't trust him. Part of it, I suppose, is the picture I have of him going up the aisles at the 1960 convention, whispering to delegates behind his hand, just the way Roy Cohn whispered to Joe McCarthy. It annoys me that memories are so short about Bobby going to work for the McCarthy Committee. I haven't forgotten either how Jack Kennedy, with Bobby's help, clawed his way to the Presidency. The machinations of that campaign have all been glossed over in the instant histories on the bestseller lists. Bobby, to me, is the epitome of the smart maneuverer. I have an instinctive distrust of someone with unbridled ambition who calculates every move for political advancement. Now I am in trouble with myself, I have to admit. Bobby's positions on public policies in the last year or two have been damn good. I agree with him on almost every important issue— Vietnam, Latin America, Negroes in the ghetto. And yet I can't get over the feeling that he's not a man to be trusted with power."

A friendlier newspaperman, commented, "If he offered to help an old woman across the street, someone would accuse him of soliciting the votes of senior citizens." And a third observed, "Even politicians are entitled to a statute of limitations on the sins of their past." As Bobby himself told reporters, "I can't do anything without somebody questioning my motives. Perhaps I do what I do just because I think it is the right thing for a United States Senator to be doing. Did you ever think of that?" An instance that supported Bobby's claim to moral spontaneity was his public criticism of his own handpicked successor as Attorney General, Nicholas Katzenbach, who had refused to let a dead Communist veteran be buried in Arlington Cemetery. Bobby's support of sending blood to the Vietcong has been mentioned as another example of his spontaneous unselfishness.

Others felt that while Kennedy often acted from political motives, he also had a personal sincerity which many politicians lack. Charles Evers, the black mayor of Fayette, Mississippi, and brother of murdered civil rights leader Medgar Evers, said in 1970, "I respected Bobby Kennedy because he seemed to respect me. He was the only politician who ever telephoned me when he didn't want anything. Now maybe he was ruthless and calculating. Maybe he called me only because some secretary had looked in a memorandum book and reminded him that it was time to call me again. But he didn't sound that way. Maybe it would be 10 o'clock at night and I'd pick up the phone and it would be Bobby. Not some secretary but Bobby himself. Just calling to ask me how I was getting along. Maybe he did it because we both had had brothers shot. But he made me think he respected me and my work and because he really wanted to know how I was getting along. That's why I took a month's leave of absence to work for him all over the country." Evers's comments are typical of the faith and hope black Americans came to place in Bobby Kennedy. As Halberstam put it, "Kennedy had the Negroes, there was no doubt—it was one of the few remaining love affairs in American politics. In part it was the product of the John Kennedy years. At the beginning of the campaign a poll showed that while only 39 percent of the general population believed that Robert Kennedy 'has the same outstanding qualities of his brother,' 94 percent of the black people felt that way, an astonishing and quite revealing statistic."

Bobby's deep concern for deprived minorities and his strong emotional ties with them seemed in many ways to spring from his personal identifications with "underdogs," a sensitivity I have traced from his often anxious childhood. The dispossessed American Indians and the high suicide rate among Indian youths also haunted Kennedy. Perhaps unconsciously their thwarted and self-destroyed lives reawakened his own deeply buried fears. For while Bobby apparently dreaded losing elections—which had become his family's greatest achievement and status symbol—he often showed far less concern over losing his life. This is really not surprising, when we realize that conflicted people often show extraordinary outer inconsistencies in attitudes and behavior, although inwardly there is a powerful, if tragic, logic. I have already suggested elements of self-defeat, bordering at times on semi-suicidal impulses, in both of RFK's older brothers. Bobby displayed an even stronger intermittent dare-deviltry which could go beyond the normal desire to prove oneself in action.

Robert Kennedy's impulsive moments came not in politics, where we have examined his repeated caution, but in personal risk-taking. A notable example was the time in Kenya when he walked to within twenty feet of a rhinoceros, with Ethel and a guide begging him to come back. The rhino looked at Bobby, snorted, and galloped off—but he could as easily have charged and killed the unarmed Kennedy. When asked about that possibility, Bobby merely said, "I'd have thought about that then." Another example of Bobby's compulsive courting of danger was his paddling out, with two companions, into an intense rainstorm in the midst of Brazilian jungle and without a guide. Kennedy also flew over the jungle in a vintage 1939 floatplane, and that, at last, caused him to reflect, "I must be crazy to get on this thing." As a reporter wrote of this South American visit, "He repeatedly plunges into hostile situations so potentially dangerous that he seems at times to be courting disaster." It is hard not to feel that some usually repressed part of Robert Kennedy desired to be dead, just as his two older brothers were dead. Certainly a fully rational man with a large family, total financial security, loving human relationships, a significant career, and a glowing future does not hazard his life so carelessly. Kennedy had everything going for him, except his own emotions. He had to keep proving over and over that he was really the man he inwardly so doubted.

Bobby had one other personal habit worth noting: his compulsive cleanliness. During the same South American trip, a reporter noticed that he changed his shirt often, up to ten times a day. Other writers have commented on this Kennedy habit (shared by both Jack and Teddy). While the same compulsion can have different meanings for different people, a cleanliness compulsion commonly suggests unconscious feelings of personal self-disgust, of being in some way guilty or worthless and hence "dirty."

A final question remains, perhaps never to be answered with certainty: Did Robert Kennedy really change from his undoubted initial conservatism to a final genuine liberalism? By his "initial conservatism" I mean a type of authoritarian-mindedness which found purpose and compatibility in working for a man like Senator Joseph McCarthy, in trespassing well-defined boundaries of civil liberties in order to prosecute those judged evil and criminal, in the moralistic simplicities of Cold War demonology, and in the general concept that the end justifies the means. This was by and large the Bobby of the 1950s and early 1960s. By "genuine liberalism" I mean the type of social concern that puts people above property, human values above political aims, and sees the United States as a nation more concerned with global moderation and communication than with global policing. This was the image RFK increasingly sought to convey in the years 1967–1968, and the sort of liberal (or radical) whom many came to see in Kennedy when he demonstrated concern for peace, the poor, the black, and the alienated young.

Political expediency is often a debatable subject. One of RFK's interpreters, Douglas Ross, who undertook the useful task of reviewing Kennedy's public record in *Robert Kennedy: Apostle of Change*, has given a good working definition: "The relevant issue concerns the nature of the accommodation involved. Is it the minimum required to retain an influential voice in the decision-making process and further the politician's ideals and programs without sacrificing his principles in the process? Or has the man compromised himself to advance his own career at the expense of his professed reasons for wanting to hold political office? This is the distinction between unavoidable accommodation to political realities and opportunism. Unfortunately, it is a distinction which is not always easy to draw, given the confusion and furtiveness of the American political arena. Furthermore, no simple *a priori* criteria exist. Each case must be judged in its own context, with the reader attempting to weigh the relative costs and benefits of a public statement to the politician's programs and personal position." This is, in short, the political application of situational ethics.

In Robert Kennedy, as in the other Kennedys (and undoubtedly in many politicians), the legitimate outward struggle for power progressed simultaneously with an invisible inward struggle for power, for the mastery of his own purposes and convictions. In Bobby, as with Jack, both struggles were often simultaneously manifest. He was constantly seen as at war with himself, even to the very end of his abruptly terminated life; and he was only, we should remember, forty-two. We will never know what the next forty-two years might have wrought in him. As the authors of *An American Melodrama* shrewdly assessed Kennedy, "At forty-two, he had not yet been forced by life, or had not yet consented, to make those final choices which set a man's character in what we call maturity. His personality could only be described by listing pairs of opposites, all of which might be true, but which still did not add up to a final or a satisfying answer to the question: What sort of a man is this, and how will he act?"

Some observers saw, or felt they saw, or wanted to see, a genuine change in Robert Kennedy from ultraconservative to ultraliberal, or something beyond liberalism—an "existentialist man" in the process of making himself. But, in fact, we are all existentialists, for we all exist and are in the process of making our lives, either by growth or stagnation or retrogression. Waving a magic wand of romantic labels does not invalidate the simple fact of Kennedy's common humanity. He lived, he suffered, he died, and perhaps he changed in important ways en route; but there was no deifying process involved. He may have seemed larger than life, but it is doubtful that he really was. No one, as yet, has called him a genius. Many others remain skeptical of basic change. Bobby, as they viewed him, did not really grow out of his essential arrogance and blindness to the needs of others. The context of his pseudo-liberalism had changed, they argue, so that he could appear ultraliberal, but the essential opportunism of Bobby's narrow power drive remained the same.

We may never reach a really satisfactory answer. To my mind, the known lessons of human behavior and Robert Kennedy's personal history, set within the context of his socio-political environment, suggest that the answer may well lie somewhere between extreme idealization and total skepticism. Bobby gave much evidence of a capacity to grow. His very instabilities and uncertainties were hopeful signs of a personality more open to change than a rigidly self-protective one. It seems true that a considerable amount of opportunism remained in his character. A close study of the all-important Vietnam issue, for example, reveals Kennedy's recurrent turning to self-interest as his most trustworthy and consistent touchstone for action. In such shortsightedness he betrayed himself; for our greatest self-interest lies in our ability to see and reach beyond our own immediate self-centeredness. Yet there was also the impression that Kennedy was beginning to do just this. But again, doubt obtrudes. Bedford-Stuyvesant and multitudinous other Kennedy projects, for example, posed the question of Bobby's seriousness and how many commitments one human being could realistically hope to assume and sustain. As Victor Navasky described Bobby's compulsive activism, "A part of Robert Kennedy, perhaps the most important part, was committed to movement *per se*, to action *qua* action. He wasn't result-oriented as the cliché had it. He was action-oriented. Slowness was more irritating than incompetence, goofing off a greater sin than failure."

Beyond the immediate issues and Bobby Kennedy's real or claimed belief in his assertions, I must raise once more the continuing factor of his disequilibrium. Not even Kennedy's most eloquent and glorifying interpreters have totally denied RFK's inner turmoil, his indecisiveness, and his repeated self-defeatism (two examples being his morally and politically disastrous ambivalence on Vietnam and his New York political failures). All these seem expressions of a profound self-doubt which was strange in a man so utterly determined to succeed, and one who had so often succeeded so well. Self-doubt, above all, appeared to be the unshakable tiger on Robert Kennedy's back. It was not a self-doubt engendered by the tragedy of Jack's death, although this increased his fatalism. Bobby's self-doubt had clearly been with him since early childhood. And it made him often prey to ignorant or self-serving advisers, as well as to his own fears. As Halberstam noticed, "He lacked Jack Kennedy's absolute confidence in himself and his charm, and most important, his confidence that he could project that charm. . . . The people around Robert Kennedy were regularly telling him to loosen up, but it did not come easily: his knuckles would be cracking away, his hands wrestling with each other—he was not a loose man. He was less graceful and more committed than his brother."

Self-doubt and an apparent unease with abstractions also made Kennedy highly dependent on others. Margaret Laing gave an interesting view of Bobby's intellectual dependency: "He relies almost totally on other people for ideas. His is not a creative mind, but a picking-up mind. When he is well-advised, and when reason and instinct prompt him to take the advice, he can produce effective and workable plans from a synthesis of other people's polished material. It is the type of mind that works particularly well in times of crisis, when sense, speed, and decisiveness are usually the three main solvents, and the ability to simplify becomes an automatic advantage. It is not the kind of mind that enjoys thought for its own sake, or that can pursue a truly independent line. He is dependent." This analysis seemed to be borne out by Kennedy's confident behavior during the Cuban missile crisis in October, 1962—although we have seen the dangers of his narrow outlook—and by his protracted indecision during the politically complex winter of 1967–1968. In the second case, Kennedy's dependency on conservative advisers almost ruined his chance to enter the election; while in the missile crisis, Bobby himself was turned to as a chief adviser by his brother, the President.

To sum up, while Robert Kennedy may have been in some ways a very different man in 1968 from the man he was in 1958, a considerable amount (perhaps the major part) of his apparent personality neurosis seemed to remain: a gnawing self-doubt, significant elements of self-defeat, and a difficulty in making genuine and sustained commitments to ideals beyond the context of immediate political need. The presidency might have changed Kennedy further; but then again, it might not have. Much would have depended on the nature of the crises he faced, the good sense and human relevance of his advisers, the judgment he could have summoned, and the emotional identifications he might have felt.

Much has been made of the legendary Kennedy courage, of which Bobby had an ample amount. In the broadest psychohistorical sense, courage is a somewhat irrelevant matter. We all wish to be courageous; yet in the name of courage many evils have been committed (any war gives endless examples). It also takes great courage to wish to change and to find the tenacity to endure the pain that emotional change entails. But courage is not always available to those who desperately desire or need it. It may have been ground out at an early age; it may not succeed in sustaining sanity; it may be inhibited by the uncertainty and defeatism against which we all struggle.

Bobby Kennedy, like the rest of his family, had great physical courage as well as courage in the face of crisis and personal tragedy. But something more is needed in our leaders (and ourselves): a sense of human kinship, human outrage, and human limits. Compassion is a large part of it; and Robert Kennedy undeniably had much compassion. But there is something beyond that all-encompassing word that is not easy to express. Perhaps "reality" best sums it up: an essential sense of human reality—the genuine scope and potentials, yet limits and mysteries, of the human condition, which only largely non-neurotic people seem able to reconcile into humanly useful living. None of the Kennedys gave much evidence of sensing the human reality behind their enormous demands on life, themselves, and others. Family pride was part of their irrationalities: a refusal to feel the difference between artificial pride based on emotional insecurity and the pride of simple self-worth latent in all people. There was, in a word, nothing really that different about the overrated Kennedys.

Robert Kennedy, like his kinfolk, seemed to lack a basic balance which might have carried him beyond the pitfalls of his compulsions. Unbalanced, neurotically at war with himself, he might yet have accomplished much; balanced and at ease, he could have accomplished much more.

Chapter 11

THE TARNISHED HEIR:
THE MAKING OF TEDDY, 1932-1969

You boys have what you want now, and everybody else helped you work to get it. Now it's Ted's turn. Whatever he wants, I'm going to see he gets it.

Look, I spent a lot of money for that Senate seat. It belongs in the family.

—Joseph P. Kennedy to Jack and Bobby Kennedy

He's very ambitious, and naturally he wants to do what the other boys did.

—Rose Fitzgerald Kennedy

Like my three brothers before me, I pick up a fallen standard. Sustained by the memory of our priceless years together, I shall try to carry forward that special commitment to justice, to excellence, to courage that distinguished their lives.

—Edward Moore Kennedy, 1968

Even sophisticates follow tribal custom, and the dominant tribal custom in the family of Joseph Patrick Kennedy Sr. was a sort of primogeniture, which Webster defines as "an exclusive right of inheritance . . . belonging . . . to the eldest son." Joe Kennedy's children would inherit his driving political ambition, but until the family had become entrenched as an American political power, the inheritance was to remain with the oldest.

—Jack Olsen, *The Bridge at Chappaquiddick*

ↃC

NOT UNTIL THE Chappaquiddick tragedy of July, 1969, did the full impact of the Kennedy family's strange and ironic history strike the American

323

people. President John F. Kennedy's assassination on November 22, 1963, shocked the nation and the world. The murder of Senator Robert F. Kennedy four and a half years later, on June 5, 1968, further stunned all Americans. This second murder filled even political foes with compassion for the Kennedys' recurrent misfortunes.

But it took a third great Kennedy disaster to jolt the country into a realization that something was terribly wrong somewhere. Something was wrong not only with the Kennedy luck; something was also seriously wrong with the Kennedys. When United States Senator Edward Moore Kennedy, the fourth and last son, apparently drove his car off the Chappaquiddick Island bridge into Poucha Pond on the night of July 18–19, 1969, not only Mary Jo Kopechne was drowned. His own presidential ambitions were also drowned, at least temporarily. After Chappaquiddick, it seemed to people that some mysterious curse did indeed afflict the ill-fated clan. Even Senator Edward Kennedy himself voiced this superstitious fear when he wondered aloud after the accident "whether some awful curse did actually hang over all the Kennedys."

In earlier chapters, I have explored the essential nature of the "curse": that the Kennedys' repeated misfortunes are traceable in many ways to deep-rooted emotional conflicts, or neuroses, which affected all the children in different degrees. To be sure, neither Jack's nor Bobby's murder was caused by a Kennedy neurosis. But each showed in his life and career strong symptoms of the similar unconscious attitudes and anxieties that may actually have helped bring about the wartime death of Joe Kennedy, Junior, and the accidents that have plagued the only surviving son, Teddy.

In some ways, Teddy Kennedy has been the most overtly symptomatic of all four sons. As the last and most favored child, he inevitably grew up with greater expectations that life would be handed to him on a silver platter. Yet he also came under the influence of the strenuous Kennedy pressures, which were really simply exaggerations of the primary values of an over-achieving American society. Ted's election to the U.S. Senate was, at the time, probably meant to be the height of both his ambition and personal gratification, a calm post in which he could fulfill the demands of Kennedy pride and yet relax to a considerable degree. It was Teddy's bad fortune and his personal disaster that the deaths of two older brothers abruptly thrust him to the forefront. To trace the path of Teddy's ascendancy and his individual development, we must go back into his childhood and trace his growth to manhood.

Teddy Kennedy's childhood was outwardly happy. He was born on the two-hundredth anniversary of George Washington's birthday, on February 22, 1932, in a two-story frame house in Brookline, Massachusetts. Edward Moore Kennedy (named for his father's trusted secretary, Eddie Moore) was the last of Joe and Rose Kennedy's nine-child brood. By 1932, Joseph P. Kennedy was already a multimillionaire and strongly supporting FDR for the presidency, a political effort that would win him appointments as the first head of the new Securities and Exchange Commission in 1934, the Maritime Commission in 1936, and Ambassador to Great Britain in 1937, the most prestigious of all diplomatic posts.

Teddy was the family's "baby," a rosy-cheeked, chubby, friendly little boy. However sturdy and winning in his ways, any ninth child would find life suffocating in many respects and filled with rivalrous and competitive problems. When the chief rivals were a brother seventeen years older and clearly his father's favorite (Joe Junior), another brother fifteen years older and next in line as the contender for family honors (Jack), a third brother seven years older (Bobby), and five boisterous sisters, the child in position nine must often have felt small and vulnerable. The parents, too, by this time were somewhat weary of perpetual parenthood. As Rose Kennedy candidly admitted, "We tried to keep everything more or less equal, but you wonder if the mother and father aren't quite tired when the ninth one comes along. You have to make more of an effort to tell bedtime stories and be interested in swimming matches. There were seventeen years between my oldest and my youngest child, and I had been telling bedtime stories for twenty years. When you have older brothers and sisters, they're the ones that seem to be more important in a family, and always get the best rooms and the first choice of boats and all those kinds of things, but Ted never seemed to resent it." Teddy may have minded more than he let on, for years later he told one writer that his clearest memory of Kathleen, the oldest, was when she took him shopping.

Yet this parental weariness brought mixed blessings. Although Teddy might sometimes feel ignored, he also suffered from less parental pressure to triumph on all occasions. The Kennedy women tended to pamper and spoil the youngster. As his mother later said, "I admit that with Teddy I did things a little differently than I did with the other children. He was my baby and, I think every mother will understand this, I tried to keep him my baby." Teddy's sisters also seem to have often mothered him. Ted once commented, "It was like having a whole army of mothers around me. While it seemed I could never do anything right with my brothers, I could never do anything wrong so far as my sisters were concerned." This female protectiveness in childhood and youth very likely contributed to Ted's evident need as an adult for constant female attention and support. This factor in his personality development, together with the masculine mystique taught by his father, would easily explain Teddy Kennedy's well-known interest in attractive women.

But life as a Kennedy was not all nectar and honey. Especially for the males, even the youngest, there were high standards of achievement. Teddy himself recalled the rigors of his childhood, later commenting, "I remember that we always kept a tight ship. We had a clear idea of what we could do and what we could not do. You could ride your bike on the property, but not off. You had to be in the house when the lights went on. We had to pick up our clothes." Clear boundaries of permitted and unpermitted behavior are necessary for all children, if they are based on reasonable expectations and loving concern. Unfortunately, the Kennedys' expectations went far beyond those useful for growing children. A comment by the mother indicates the demanding spirit bred into the children. "My husband," said Rose, "was quite a strict father. He liked the boys to win at sports and everything they tried. If they didn't win he would discuss their failure with them. But he did not have much patience with the loser."

Those who failed to come in first were severely lectured and often sent to eat in the kitchen after a losing race. In such an atmosphere, it is hardly surprising that Ted Kennedy, like his older brothers, early realized that the only important thing in life was winning, no matter how. The spirit of fair play and good sportsmanship was totally lacking, as it had been in Joe Kennedy's own youth. There was little love of play itself. Victory was the only goal. Unless you came in first, you didn't come in at all. The only alternative to winning was failing; no in-between was permitted.

Such an upbringing takes a toll in a child's emotional growth. Since the child views the parents as the all-important judges, only their opinion counts. In order to be accepted—and loved—by the parents, a Kennedy child had to work constantly at being a winner. There could never be any final victory. Acceptance had to be won again and again, a demand that would inevitably produce deep-rooted anxieties. Outwardly, however, Teddy was physically strong and active. As his sister Jean, the next youngest Kennedy, recalled, "Even as a child, Ted had a terrific animal energy. You never had to push Ted—you always had to hold him back."

Teddy, although the family underdog, has generally been regarded as the most amiable Kennedy son. Many have commented on Ted's charm and personal magnetism and, above all, on his unfailing "niceness." While Jack was often described as a quizzical smiler and Bobby as a moody scowler, rosy-cheeked Teddy has usually been pictured as a happy-go-lucky grinner, a nice, overgrown "broth of a lad." Long-lost brother Joe was also the "happy type," but while Teddy was most like Joe Junior in handsome looks and outgoing temperament, his extroversion generally lacked Joe's argumentativeness.

Conversely, Teddy was also a far less impressive personality than the others. As the youngest in a huge tribe, he naturally tended to get rather lost in the general picture except as the cuddlesome "baby." Unlike skinny

Bobby, the "runt" who determinedly fought to make an impression and assure his place in the pecking order, Teddy always seemed the most emotionally passive member of the family, the happy boy who took orders and accepted whatever he was given. His closest sister, Jean, later said of Teddy, "If there were five people in a room, I might not like two of them. He'd find something in all five of them." Such compliance can also be a neurotic defense operation to avoid further conflict and rejection. The source and genuineness of Teddy's amiability must be set against the contrast of his erratic, bizarre behavior over the years. Although good-mannered and pleasant when caught in misbehavior by authority figures, Teddy's repeated rule-breaking, accidents, and occasional temper tantrums seem to indicate an undercurrent of rage beneath his winning exterior.

Joseph Kennedy's fabulous financial success provided his children with the physical settings and amenities for a comfortable, busy childhood. Yet the irrationality of the father's extreme philosophy of winning must have often thwarted and distorted his offsprings' spirits even as their bodies grew increasingly strong and supple. As the Kennedy muscles stretched, the evidence suggests, the Kennedy emotions grew into patterns of rigidity, repression, and inner conflict.

When Teddy was born, the family had already owned the house at the Cape Cod village of Hyannis Port for four years. More than any other place, this rambling white frame house, with ample space for a large and active family, was to be a psychological home to the Kennedys. With two and a half acres of lawn sloping down to the beach and breakwater, there was plenty of room for growing children. A Kennedy biographer has described the strenuous regimen which the patriarch laid out for his offspring: "During days filled with ceaseless activity, he shaped his children. Long before the much publicized mass gambols on the playing fields of Hyannis, the Fourth of July softball games and the bruising touch football scrimmages, he thrust each child into individual sports, such as swimming and sailing, believing these would best develop initiative and self-reliance. Firmly he implanted his conviction that playing the game was not as important as winning."

Self-reliance is notably a major quality that none of the Kennedy children developed more than superficially. Initiative and self-reliance thrive only in freedom and encouragement, not in an atmosphere of dominance and humiliation. To be obsessed with winning is to be obsessed with failure. A child whose self-esteem is constantly battered by parental scoldings and a regimen of compulsive competition will inescapably develop intense inner feelings of anxiety, guilt, frustration, rebellion, and self-hate. Outer rebellion in such an all-absorbing, close-knit family would be nearly impossible, and no Kennedy child exhibited much outward rebellion in his childhood. All competed according to the parental dictates, except Rosemary, who was retarded from birth. And all the Kennedys were physically and mentally sturdy enough to bring home frequent trophies. These trophies must have provided Joseph Kennedy with glittering proof that his family had indeed arrived as achieving Americans. Unfortunately, such misplaced pride exacts an enormous toll in the psyches of children.

A sample of remembered indignities and childhood cruelties was provided by Teddy himself when, at twelve, he volunteered a contribution to the printed collection about his dead brother, Joe Junior. Teddy was young Joe's favorite, but even he did not escape his brother's sometimes violent temper. As Teddy wrote down the incident, "I recall the day the year before we went to England. It was in the summer and I asked Joe if I could race with him. He agreed to this so we started down to the pier about five minutes before the race.

"We had our sails up just as the gun went for the start. This was the first race I had ever been in. We were going along very nicely until suddenly he told me to pull in the jib. I had know Idea what he was talking about. He repeated the command again in a little louder tone, meanwhile we were slowly getting further and further away from the other boats. Joe suddenly leaped up and grabbed the jib. I was a little scared but suddenly he zeized me by the pants and through me into the cold water. I was scared to death practualy. I then heard a splash and I felt his hand grab my shirt and he lifted me into the boat. We continued the race and came in second. On the way home from the pier he told me to be quiet about what happened in that afternoon. One falt Joe had was that he got very easily mad in a race as you have witnessed. But he always meant well and was a very good sailor and swimmer."

Teddy was only five at the time of this terrifying dunking. It seems indicative of his repressed rage that seven years later the boy chose this one incident to add to a commemoration of the dead hero-brother. The story was a subtle exercise in revenge; Joe's cruelty had been recorded for posterity.

Suggestive of the extreme obedience required of the Kennedy children is the story told about Teddy when he was six. In 1938, his father received the coveted appointment of Ambassador to Great Britain from President Roosevelt. The "Nine-Child Envoy" arrived in London amid much fanfare. The Kennedys were bound to attract great attention with their wealth, good looks, boundless energy, and, of course, numbers. The press publicized their every move. Teddy at that time was a sturdy, apple-cheeked little fellow who won almost every heart. Yet even at this early age there was a strong indication of a rigid compliance with parental dictums. One day Teddy came home from school and asked permission to punch a classmate. When his mother asked why, the little boy replied, "He's been hitting me every day and you tell me I can't get into fights because Daddy is the Ambassador!" At dinner that night, the Ambassador gave Teddy permission to fight back.

Although ultimately the Kennedy boys learned how to fight the world with startling success, in their growing years their ways of fighting were often inappropriate and self-defeating. The outside authorities spasmodically resisted by bad marks and misbehavior at school were actually shadow enemies. The real enemies were the authoritarian, overbearing, and rejecting parents.

But since overt recognition of parental rejection and of one's own worthlessness in the eyes of that parent (and therefore of oneself) are intolerable to any human being, children are forced to defend themselves by developing neurotic character patterns. I have explored this idea at some length in previous chapters. The threatened neurotic not only builds outer defenses; he also incorporates the parental authorities into his own identity, so that their demands come to seem his own demands. Psychologists call this process "internalization." (This is part of what Freud called the "superego," although he used this term to cover many questionable theories.) Thus although at first the demands and orders come from outside the child, from the parent, they gradually become part of the child himself. In neurosis, the individual moves further away from his own real needs and suffers increasing guilt, anxiety, and rage. But when the tyrant has become oneself, there is no escape. Resistance and rebellion against these internalized commands become increasingly blind and misdirected, since the enemy is now felt to be everywhere. The individual is further tyrannized by his internal conflict between demands to obey and demands to disobey. The result is emotional chaos, confusion, and spasmodic lashing out at authority figures who substitute for the parents.

Harvard marked the beginning of Ted Kennedy's serious outward troubles. By the time the youngest Kennedy followed his father and three brothers within those hallowed walls, the emotional turmoil inside Edward Moore seems to have reached a high pressure point. At age eighteen, his psychic volcano must have been ready to let off a blast, or several blasts. Until then, Teddy had obediently followed the pattern of secular schooling laid out by his socially ambitious father. In 1939, after World War II had caused Rose to bring the children home from England, Teddy was enrolled in the Lawrence Park West Country Day School in Bronxville, the exclusive suburb outside New York City in Westchester County, where the Kennedys had bought a splendid mansion in 1929. Like brother Bobby, Teddy also attended the prestigious Milton Academy near Boston. Then, in 1950, he followed father Joseph and brothers Joe, John, and Robert into Harvard.

Teddy was never considered the family's brightest member, but he had one advantage over his two remaining elder brothers. At six feet two and two-hundred pounds, Ted was bigger than Jack and towered over Bobby. At Harvard, he decided to make his mark by going out for intercollegiate sports. By the second semester of his freshman year, Ted seemed to have won himself a place as end on the next fall's football varsity eleven. But there was one problem: he was flunking Spanish, a course essential to maintaining his athletic eligibility. Fearful of failing, Teddy persuaded a friend to take a Spanish examination for him. Both boys were caught and expelled from Harvard. The punishment was severe, although the university did promise readmission in two years if they spent the interim usefully.

The Kennedys were stunned. It may be doubted, however, whether they were as stunned by Teddy's cheating as by his expulsion. After all, Father Joe had drilled into his children the importance of winning, no matter how. It was failure and loss of status that were intolerable, not unethical behavior in winning. Ted's behavior seems both unconsciously self-defeating and vengeful toward the Kennedy ethos and the parents who had put him in an emotional straitjacket. It was an especially bad year for a family disgrace: brother Jack, then a U.S. Congressman, was on the verge of running for the U.S. Senate against powerful Republican Senator Henry Cabot Lodge. But Kennedy influence hushed up the incident, and the public learned nothing of it until 1962, when Teddy himself was running for the Senate.

Expulsion from Harvard must have been a severe blow to both Ted and his perfectionist family, although one from which they were unlikely to draw helpful lessons. A former Kennedy maid (interviewed in 1969 following the Chappaquiddick incident) recalled Ted's acute depression at that time:

"Teddy had just left Harvard after the cheating scandal and I felt he was under a tremendous strain. He would sit brooding, sometimes for hours, and it was at that time that he began to plan to join the Army. When he did sign up, apparently he didn't bother to read the enlistment papers—something the family thought quite typical of him—and he enlisted for four years instead of two. His father, Ambassador Kennedy, was horrified at the thought of his baby son having to spend four years in the service with a good chance of being sent into combat in Korea. The Ambassador shouted: 'Don't you ever look at what you're signing?'

"The Ambassador got on the telephone and talked to a man he called Captain Finnerty. It was quite obvious from the conversation that Captain Finnerty had managed to get hold of Teddy's papers. When the conversation was over, the Ambassador looked relieved. He said Teddy would only have to serve two years and he would be sent to Europe, not Korea. I like to think that Teddy was so upset by the Harvard affair that he deliberately signed up for four years with the intention of trying to vindicate his name in Korea. Anyway, when the family saw him off, I remember they were all singing, 'Bye, bye, baby, remember you're our baby, when the girls give you the eye.' "

This version of Teddy's Army tour contradicts another story which has it that Teddy's enlistment was a careful plan to get an embarrassing offspring out of the way at a politically opportune moment. But the maid's account of Father Joe's handling of the enlistment rings true. It is noteworthy that Teddy did not volunteer to serve in Korea, where war was then raging, although such a desperate wish for either honor or oblivion may well have existed, consciously or unconsciously. Apparently Army life did not inspire him, for in two years he rose no higher than private. This period spent in France and Germany was probably relatively painless, given the family's financial and diplomatic resources. A temporary absence from his high-pressure family may also have eased Teddy's psychic pain. But that the youngest Kennedy continued to harbor unconscious feelings of frustration and rage would again soon come to light.

In the fall of 1953, Ted Kennedy reentered Harvard. This time there could be no question of sliding through. The external and internal demands to keep his marks up must have been great, and very likely increased Teddy's inner anger. In 1954, the outward provocation of a rugby game brought some of Teddy's hostility into the open. While playing in a rugby match between Harvard and the New York Rugby Club, Teddy got into three fist fights with opposing players and was finally thrown out of the game. According to referee Frederick Cosstick, Kennedy was the only player he had expelled from a game in thirty years of officiating.

As Cosstick later recalled, "I've thought a lot about that game since. Rugby is a character-building sport. Players learn how to conduct themselves on the field with the idea that they will learn how to conduct themselves in life. Rugby, like life, can be rough. Knocks are given and taken, but you must play by the rules. When a player loses control of himself three times in a single afternoon, to my mind, that is a sign that, in a crisis, the man is not capable of thinking clearly and acting rationally. Such a man will panic under pressure."

Cosstick's opinion was offered after the Chappaquiddick incident, when the question of Teddy's tendency to "panic under pressure" was foremost in everyone's minds. Of particular relevance here is the referee's comment on the value of rugby as a "character-building sport." It contrasts vividly with the Kennedy view of sports as an arena for victory rather than controlled competition and pleasure. For the Kennedys, the game itself and the playing of the game to the best of one's abilities were not the important values. Only being on top could bring a temporary feeling of safety.

As we have seen, Teddy's upbringing had taught him little about playing by the rules. The opposite belief was drummed into the Kennedy children: the rules don't matter; the only essential thing is to win. Intermittently, such incidents as this rugby game revealed how well Joe Kennedy's lessons had taken. The Kennedys played largely by their own rules, which they could change at will. (For example, guests at Bobby Kennedy's home touch-football games were disconcerted by their host's casual changing of the rules if his side was losing.) While these lessons served to make highly successful politicians out of the Kennedy sons, we have seen how opportunism and self-serving limited their real opportunities and contributions.

Teddy's outburst on the Harvard playing field seems to have been an expression of frustration at not being allowed to win by his own rules. It was the temper tantrum of a youngster blocked in his emotional development. We are reminded of Joe Kennedy's ferocious battles with baseball umpires in his own Harvard days, Joe Junior's bickering in games, and Jack's arguments over football rules. Ted's aggressiveness could also logically be interpreted as a sign of rage against overbearing parental authority, a rage which inevitably turns against the sufferer. Antisocial behavior, whether cheating on an exam or fighting in a rugby game, can be viewed on two psychological levels. On the shallower level, it suggests a desperate attempt to win by any means. On a deeper level, it reveals elements of self-defeat, for such actions are almost certain to rebound against the neurotic in increased humiliation and pain.

The neurotic is doubly humiliated, both by failing and by having to succumb to punishment and further apology and shame. The neurotic is saying both "I deserve to win, no matter how" and "I deserve to be punished." This is really an acting-out of his basic feelings of worthlessness: "I deserve everything" (neurotic omnipotence) and "I deserve nothing" (neurotic powerlessness). Superficially, he can feel justified in having tried to follow the parental dictum of success above everything. In reality, he has avenged himself on the parents by frustrating their desires for his success. He has punished the parents by punishing himself. And only by failing can he overcome his sense of total powerlessness, for by disappointing others he can express at least a negative kind of power. But such a destructive power operation only increases the neurotic's inner rage, which is bound to reappear in one form or another. At Harvard, Ted Kennedy briefly showed the emotional explosiveness building up beneath his façade of good manners and "niceness."

In his last year at Harvard, Teddy managed to buckle down to his studies. He also captured a moment of glory on the football field in the 1955 game with Yale when he caught a pass for Harvard's only touchdown. Playing in the Harvard-Yale game secured Ted the coveted letter, an achievement denied to brothers Joe and John. Better yet, by the time of his graduation in 1956, he had also earned honors in government and history. Ted next applied to Harvard Law School, but was refused admission, a deep disappointment. Instead, he spent a year at The Hague's International Law Institute in the Netherlands. During 1956, Teddy also did some news-gathering in North Africa for William Randolph Hearst's International New Service (now UPI). In the 1930s, Joe Kennedy had reorganized and salvaged Hearst's debt-ridden empire, and Hearst remained a good friend.

When Teddy returned home, Bobby suggested that he enter the less-demanding University of Virginia Law School, where Bobby had earned his own degree. Ted entered the school in 1957 and was graduated in 1959. Meanwhile, brother John, elected to the U.S. Senate for a six-year term in 1952, was planning his 1958 campaign for reelection. With Ted now a serious law student, it seemed a good time for the youngest Kennedy to start learning his ultimate profession. Jack asked Teddy to be his campaign manager, and Ted delightedly agreed. By now the Kennedy political machine was a smooth-running professional organization, with father Joe as its invisible helmsman. (In effect, Jack was then already running for the presidency, having lost out on the Democratic vice presidential nomination in 1956 but thereby gaining national stature.) Ted was enlisted by the family as a student-in-training. He performed with such enthusiasm and drive that afterwards Jack called Teddy "the best politician in the family," welcome praise indeed from a previously doubting family. Jack, as expected, won easily against his unknown Republican opponent, scoring a landslide victory.

Meanwhile, Teddy's psychic conflicts were finding outlets in repeated antisocial behavior, this time of a more serious kind. As a law student in Virginia, Ted was caught no less than four times in extremely reckless driving. These violations—three in 1958 and one in 1959—included running red lights and driving with his own lights off at ninety miles an hour in a suburban area. Teddy was convicted of three violations and fined, but Kennedy influence apparently came to bear and his driver's license was never revoked.

At the time, Teddy was unmarried and living off campus in Charlottesville with Gene Tunney's son, John (now a U.S. Senator from California). One spring night, Teddy headed off to an unknown destination in his Oldsmobile convertible. The Albemarle County police lieutenant who first ticketed Teddy for reckless driving in March, 1958, later recounted his impressions: "Yes, I'm the policeman who brought young Mr. Kennedy down to earth. I didn't know who he was at the time, but it wouldn't have made any difference if I did. The fact that he was a Senator's brother couldn't have had any influence on me. I would have ticketed him just the same.

"I was on routine highway patrol just outside the limits of Charlottesville, which are policed by the county force. Young Kennedy—and I didn't know who he was then—ran a red traffic light on 250 Bypass, then sped to Image Street, which leads into the city. He shot across this street, and then at the next traffic light he cut his lights off and made a right turn which goes out into the Barracks Road—that's where he lived, on the Barracks Road. He was staying with a private family, but I don't remember their name. I was driving a Ford patrol car, but it was no match for that high-powered Oldsmobile convertible. He left me far behind. But the way I found the car was by spotting the marks on the road from his tires and the touches of dust, things like that. But by the time I found the car, he had gotten into the house. [The car was parked outside Ted's residence.] I knew it was the car. I felt the hood, and the motor was warm." But since the police officer hadn't seen the driver, he couldn't write a ticket. A license check on the car showed Ted Kennedy as the registered owner.

The policeman began watching for the erratic Oldsmobile. On the next Saturday night, Teddy repeated the pattern, this time at ninety miles an hour. "I just happened to be at this same intersection," related the officer, "and here comes this car—the same car—and I knew it was the one because it seems to me the top was torn up some, the back plastic window was missing, and the car was sort of rough looking. And to my surprise, he did exactly the same thing he did before. He raced through the same red light, cut his lights when he got to that corner and made the right turn. But I knew exactly where he was going this time. So I pulled in right on him. And before he could get out of the car, I was out of the patrol car. I knew he hadn't had time to get out, but I couldn't see him behind the wheel. He had laid down in the seat so I couldn't see him. I just walked to the car and told him to get up—and then I wrote him up." Kennedy's ticket listed the following violations: "Reckless driving. Racing with an officer to avoid arrest. Operating a motor vehicle without an operator's license." As the lieutenant wrote the ticket, Teddy "came out meek as a cat. He gave me no lip."

The trial was mysteriously postponed for about three months. "Usually these ticket things are squared in a couple of days," commented the policeman, "but Kennedy seemed to be able to get postponement after postponement." Newsmen later discovered that the local court officials never filed the mandatory notice of the case in the public docket drawer, thus keeping it out of the Charlottesville press.

Teddy's second driving ticket for speeding came only three weeks later from another county policeman. In the university's summer recess, Ted and his fiancée, Joan Bennett, flew down from Connecticut for the trial, where, according to the police, "He was as nice as could be." Ted was convicted and paid fines, but his license was never suspended for these serious violations.

In November, 1958—the month of brother Jack's reelection to the Senate —Ted married Joan Bennett. He had met her in October, 1957, at Manhattanville College of the Sacred Heart (Rose Kennedy's alma mater). That fall, Teddy brought his bride to live with him in Charlottesville. Marriage, as psychologists know, does not change a neurotic's inner conflicts. It may temporarily lessen or aggravate them, but nothing is essentially altered by acquiring a mate for self-approval or self-condemnation. Ted Kennedy's peculiarly erratic behavior continued. In 1959, not long before graduation, he was again caught for running a stop light. Teddy was alone in the car when he was stopped and ticketed by an Albemarle County patrolman. Again Kennedy was convicted and paid a fine. Then the new attorney-to-be went home with his law degree.

This series of driving incidents hardly needs further comment, except to observe the obvious: repeatedly driving through red lights at night at ninety miles an hour is clearly compulsive behavior, with overtones of rebellion, hostility, and self-destructiveness. Teddy's actions, of course, endangered other lives as well, but this probably scarcely occurred to him. A person caught in the grip of unconscious self-hate and rage is too obsessed with the expression of his own needs to be able to empathize satisfactorily with others.

Teddy's explosive temper, which was usually concealed behind his grinning, boyish face, friendly handshake, and general ease of manner, had already flashed into the open from time to time. One incident which surfaced in the Kennedy literature relates how the "boisterous" Teddy overreacted to mild teasing from a probably intoxicated yachtsman. According to biographer Joe McCarthy, in *The Remarkable Kennedys*, "One summer David Hackett was invited to join Bobby and Ethel, Teddy, Jean, and Red Fay and his wife, Anita, on a ten day cruise from Cape Cod to Maine. They anchored their boat, one afternoon, near Northeast Harbor and Teddy and Hackett rowed ashore in a dinghy to get supplies. As Teddy was paddling past a large and luxurious yacht, where several couples were enjoying a cocktail party, a man leaning over the rail of the costly craft called to him to row a little faster. Teddy advised him to mind his own business. 'Come back here, and say that again,' the man yelled.

" 'Teddy spun the dinghy around so fast I almost fell out of it,' Hackett told Red Fay later. 'The next thing I knew, Teddy was on the yacht and the man was being thrown overboard and all the women were screaming and running below to hide in the cabins. Their husbands were running with them, to see that they were safely tucked away, I guess. By this time, I'm on the yacht with Teddy. The men start to come back up to the deck to deal with us, but it's a narrow hatchway and they have to come up through it one at a time. As each guy appears, I grab him and spin him around and throw him to Teddy, and Teddy throws him overboard. In no time, all of the men—there were about eight of them—were in the water. I never saw anything like it.' "

Other recorded reckless behavior in Teddy's youth included diving from the top of a dangerously high cliff into the Mediterranean (at the urging of Joe Junior), where he narrowly missed serious injury, if not death, when his forehead scraped the bottom; and racing down a steep Canadian ski run, although he was neither skillful nor experienced. Like the three brothers before him, young Ted had constantly to test his courage in order to prove himself a real man. Such recurrent foolhardiness is inevitably the result of deep unconscious insecurities. Lives genuinely valued are not risked so lightly.

In 1959, however, these incidents, as well as Teddy's wild driving in Virginia, were unknown to the Massachusetts voters. When Teddy arrived home from law school, he was swept up in the planning for Jack's 1960 presidential campaign. A Hyannis Port meeting of October 28, 1959, which included Teddy, launched the Kennedy strategy. Every Kennedy had a part in the all-out effort. Teddy did his duty by campaigning vigorously for Jack in eleven Western states. His energetic efforts included barnstorming through the West in a partially self-piloted plane, despite little flying experience; riding a bucking bronco in a Montana rodeo; and making a first ski jump on a dangerous slope, managing somehow to land on his feet. These highjinks, however, did not substitute for effective political organizing. Jack lost all but three of Ted's eleven states. But for Teddy himself, reckless flying, riding, and skiing could serve an unconscious purpose: they might have injured or killed him, even as he appeared a hero.

Shortly after Jack's inauguration, Ted was sworn in as an assistant district attorney of Massachusetts' Suffolk County on February 7, 1961. Such a modest yet significant post could hardly have been earned on his own, since Teddy had never even practiced law up until then. The assistant D.A.'s job was unglamorous, but it served to fill time until Teddy turned thirty a year later, when he would be constitutionally eligible for Jack's vacated Senate seat. This reserved sinecure was being held by a reliable family friend and former roommate of Jack's, Ben Smith, formerly the obscure mayor of Gloucester. Meanwhile the newlyweds had set up housekeeping in a seventy-thousand dollar townhouse on Boston's exclusive Beacon Hill, while Teddy half-heartedly fulfilled the duties of his appointment. Soon his fellow attorneys were complaining about Kennedy's lack of interest and failure to prepare his cases. One of them griped, "Look, we all know what he's doing, he doesn't keep it a secret. He's running for office already. He almost never takes a case, and he's out night after night making speeches and running around the state meeting people, and who's with him all the time, whispering in his ear and giving him advice? Frank Morrissey, his father's old crony, the absolute epitome of the Boston politician. If this is the Kennedys' idea of how to prepare somebody for national office, he should never be elected dogcatcher!"

Teddy seemed to be repeating his early Harvard pattern of taking the easy way out. Rather than building a real record through hard work and perseverance, Teddy ambled through his chores. As another employee recalled: "He had no feeling for the job, none whatever, and he didn't try to develop any. He wouldn't work; he was listless and uninterested, and he tried cases only when he felt like it, which was seldom. I think he had certain natural talents, especially when it came to arguing cases. He could convince a jury, sway a jury, especially if there were women on it, but the pick and shovel work on the law he never bothered to learn. They said he won the moot court competition in law school, even while he was getting average grades. I can understand that. He was exactly the same here. A great arguer, a great showman, a politician all the way—and that's what you are when you're arguing a case, a politician. But the rest of the time you're supposed to be a craftsman, and Kennedy was one of the worst. . . . He was as bad on his last day as he was on his first; he learned nothing in a year and a half. He would ask a question and stammer around and rephrase the question and make long, omnibus statements and wind up convincing everybody that he had no case because he was putting words in the mouth of the witness. Still he won some cases, partly because he could argue, and partly because he was Edward M. Kennedy."

Teddy's colleagues also resented what they felt was a superior attitude toward them. One co-worker said, "He was not only a Kennedy and a Harvard man, but a prep school boy on top of it, and around the courthouse he always acted condescending toward the rest of us, as though we were all a bad influence and he'd been advised to stay away from us. He made us feel inferior. No one was unhappy to see him go." Such resentments and jealousies would have naturally been heightened by Ted's obvious political activities, such as his trip to Africa with two U.S. Senators on a supposed fact-finding mission for his President brother, which helped build his public image and international qualifications for high office. Teddy's travels, which included Ireland, Italy, and Israel, would also be useful for winning votes among Massachusetts' Irish-Americans, Italian-Americans, and Jews, a technique he later used with good effect. In addition, Teddy began developing his speaking experience by appearing often at Rotary clubs, veterans groups, and other organizations. Though not an eloquent or polished speaker, despite his argumentative talents, Teddy was especially impressive in person-to-person relations where his Irish charm and joke-telling won him many friends. By his side hovered Boston Municipal Court Judge Frank Morrissey, Joe Kennedy's old friend, who had earlier tutored Jack Kennedy in politics.

On February 22, 1962, Teddy Kennedy reached the age of thirty. The congressional elections would take place that fall. There is a divergence of opinion on who wanted most to see Ted in the U.S. Senate at this early age, Teddy himself or his parents. While Joe and Rose Kennedy claimed that Teddy was simply following his own ambitions with parental backing, some writers tell a different story. Ted had reportedly thought about going after the Massachusetts governorship, but father Joe had urged him to head for national office (a more likely steppingstone to the White House). It is also said that Teddy thought of waiting for the 1964 congressional elections when he would be a more mature thirty-two, but his father urged his immediate entry. Both Jack and Bobby, then President and Attorney General, were reportedly at first against Teddy running so soon. His youth and lack of experience would immediately lay the whole family open to charges of arrogance and nepotism. But Ted had always turned to his father first for advice. Clearly Joe saw no reason not to go ahead. As Rose put it, "This wasn't a sudden decision. It was all thought about and discussed, like the Presidency. Ted's father said he should run for the Senate, that he was up to it, and we must encourage him." Above all, it seems amply evident that a high-level political career for the youngest son had long been planned by the patriarch. A suspiciously exact *Saturday Evening Post* article had predicted this triumvirate as early as 1957. And as the Kennedys' nurse later wrote in her memoirs, "I once sympathized when a financial adviser fretted about the cost of Ted Kennedy's first campaign for the Senate. 'The money for his political career was set aside long ago, you understand,' the adviser explained to me. 'It's just that we weren't expecting him to use it so soon.' "

Whatever the exact background, the well-primed Kennedy machine went into immediate operation for Teddy's Senate race. Brother-in-law Stephen Smith, Jean Kennedy's husband and one of the family's most effective behind-the-scenes manipulators, headed Teddy's campaign. Some voters were shocked by this openly opportunistic use of family prestige, power, and money. A group of Harvard professors stated publicly that "Teddy has been aptly described as a 'fledgling in everything except ambition.' " Yet their protests were futile against Irish enthusiasm and the well-oiled, well-practiced Kennedy organization. One writer has summarized the techniques used so successfully in repeated Kennedy campaigns, which included "recruitment of an army of volunteers, lavish publicity and advertising, and constant exposure of the candidate to the voters. Teddy's campaign revived the nighttime street-corner rally, well suited to the candidate's outgoing personality. ('Teddy,' said Bobby, 'is a better natural politician than any of us.') At the state Democratic convention, Teddy's managers strong-armed reluctant party professionals, advising them to get aboard the bandwagon before they were run over. Word came from Washington that Teddy, win or lose, would control the state's federal patronage. The McCormack forces cracked and the delegates endorsed Teddy's candidacy on the first ballot."

Teddy's Democratic opponent was State Attorney General Edward McCormack, a seasoned, hardworking, and liberal officeholder; he was also a nephew of U.S. House Speaker John McCormack. Eddie was stunned and infuriated by Teddy's triumph. Carrying the contest to the primary, he needled Teddy into two televised debates. Then McCormack blew his last chance by overaggressively attacking Kennedy. "And I ask you," said McCormack, "if his name was Edward Moore—with his qualifications, with your qualifications, Teddy—if it was Edward Moore your candidacy would be a joke. Nobody's laughing, because his name is not Edward Moore, it's Edward Moore Kennedy." This was a case of the lid, if not the entire pot, calling the kettle black, since the name McCormack had clearly proved politically useful to Eddie. The charge was also so obviously true that it created unexpected sympathy for Teddy. In addition, McCormack suffered from a lack of funds, while Teddy's treasury was well-nigh bottomless, and McCormack's image was less projectable than Teddy's clean-cut boyishness.

The Harvard cheating incident was uncovered during this campaign by a diligent newspaperman, who it was said resisted pressure from President Kennedy and his aides in reporting it. Teddy made the best of an overripe herring by a public and humble admission of guilt. "What I did was wrong," Teddy confessed. "I have regretted it ever since. The unhappiness I caused my family and friends . . . has been a bitter experience for me, but it also has been a very valuable lesson." (This supposed lesson, as we have seen, did not prevent fistfights with rugby opponents or wild driving through stoplights at night.) The majority of voters, however, viewed this revelation as simply a youthful mishap that made Teddy even more humanly appealing.

Eddie McCormack's hand-lettered signs had little effect against Teddy's expensive campaign and Kennedy aura. As one writer put it, ". . . Kennedy was seen by hundreds of thousands of Democrats as very special, unusually magnetic if not electrifying. Where he campaigned, not only did large crowds cheer him enthusiastically, scream at him as they do at the Beatles, and want to touch him, but a peculiar kind of titillation swept over the people." The *Berkshire Eagle* commented, "There is a sort of 'princely' effect in the Ted Kennedy campaign. In any dynasty the king is respected and obeyed, but everyone loves the prince, and Ted Kennedy seems to have that attraction, wherever he goes." A veteran Irish ward politician who supported McCormack clearly spelled out the Kennedy appeal: "I honestly believe the Americans of Irish extraction look up to the Kennedys as royal blood . . . .They like John Kennedy because he's Irish and Catholic and has taken them up a few steps socially. . . . Everybody realizes and recognizes the Kennedys are all wealthy. Now, a lot of people say, if I had a lot of money I'd be enjoying myself, I'd be over in the Riviera, I'd be cutting out coupons, but these people want to serve the public. And this is the great thing they have going for them. They are not ones to sit back and enjoy the money that they've inherited or compiled over the years; they want to do something useful. And this in the Irish makes them proud. I'm sure this is the basic thing among the Irish, to know the Kennedys is a social step upward."

Teddy's victory was predictable. He beat McCormack in the primary election by taking 69 percent of the vote. Then he went on to defeat Republican candidate George Lodge, son of Henry Cabot Lodge, Jr., who had been dethroned by Jack Kennedy in 1958. While Joseph Kennedy, the first family member Teddy talked to after his victory, was "extremely excited," according to the new Senator, other observers were less entranced. *The New York Times* called Teddy's election "demeaning to the dignity of the Senate and the democratic process." The distinguished Washington correspondent of *The New York Times*, James Reston, wrote an unsparing criticism: "The Kennedys have applied the principle of the best man available for the job to almost everyone but themselves. Teddy's victorious headlines are resented here . . . because he is demanding too much too soon on the basis of too little. . . . What is particularly surprising about all that is that the Kennedys do not see this line of criticism at all, and in fact deeply resent it. They have invoked the new pragmatism, but cannot see that, where the family was concerned, they applied the old nepotism." But Massachusetts' Irish voters were indifferent to such considerations. One of their own had won, and that was what counted.

The new freshman Senator arrived on Capitol Hill with becoming modesty. As the "nicest" Kennedy, the most naturally friendly and outgoing (other than dead brother Joe, a popular extrovert), Teddy fitted into the Senate's slow-moving protocol far more easily than had brother Jack, who had been frankly bored by the legislature. Ted soon became well liked by the other Senators for his deference to Senate veterans, general friendliness, good manners, and diligence in Senate business. Teddy's first Senate speech was devoted to denouncing a Civil Aeronautics Board decision to cut off Northeast Airlines' New York–Miami run. The Bay State had over

1,200 voters employed by Northeast. (Brother Bobby went further; as Attorney General, he had the Justice Department petition for a reargument of the case.) The new Massachusetts Senator, who would later proclaim his belief in Senate reform, also followed an old practice of bypassing the archaic 1925 Corrupt Practices Act which called for disclosure of campaign spending. Merely by using campaign committees, Teddy was able to state that his high-priced campaign had cost him nothing.

During 1963, Teddy labored quietly to build strong political fences in his home state. His interests remained provincial, and he typically took no chances on the Senate floor. As an aide recalled, "I'd talk to him about the national interest, and all he'd talk about was the Springfield, Mass., arsenal." Then on November 22, 1963, John F. Kennedy was shot. For Teddy, this meant the loss of a second brother, a huge reduction in Kennedy power, and an increase in his own family and political responsibilities. Although Teddy had never been as close to Jack as to Bobby, the President's assassination was a stunning blow to all the Kennedys as well as to the nation and the world. Two out of four sons were gone, and Robert Kennedy soon emerged as the next "heir apparent." Bobby had always been a second father figure to kid brother Teddy. Separated by age and rank of succession from the oldest boys, the two youngest Kennedy sons, despite a seven-year age difference, had stuck closely together. When Bobby failed to get the vice presidential nomination from Lyndon Johnson in 1964 and ran for the Senate from New York, the two brothers became even closer. Although Teddy was the senior Senator, the nation's gaze was focused on Bobby, whose presidential aspirations became increasingly clear.

Meanwhile Teddy had come close to death himself. Only seven months after the President's murder, the thirty-two-year-old Senator crashed in a light plane flying from Washington, D.C., to Springfield, Massachusetts. In June, 1964, Teddy was en route to receive the 1964 Democratic nomination for a full, six-year Senate term. The six-seat airplane approached the field in a heavy fog. According to a later Associated Press account, Teddy, "the only one who didn't have his seat belt fastened, turned in his seat, half standing." Then the plane tore into trees and an apple orchard. The pilot was killed outright and a Kennedy aide died later. The Senator was thrown in the aisle and severely injured. With six spinal fractures, two broken ribs, and numerous cuts and bruises, Teddy's condition was listed as critical. "It's amazing he is alive," said a doctor. Kennedy's other two companions, Senator and Mrs. Birch Bayh of Indiana, were only bruised. Kennedy was soon off the critical list, but he spent eight months in the hospital. From there he successfully campaigned for reelection to the Senate, although the family's usual energetic efforts were scarcely needed. A vast flood of sympathy swept Ted back into office. But even after he could walk again, Teddy spent more painful months with a back brace and cane as he slowly regained his strength. Had Ted fastened his safety belt like the Bayhs, it is probable he would have escaped serious injury. The two men killed were in the crushed cockpit. Was this carelessness another instance of Teddy's unconscious self-destructive forces at work?

The next blow to Ted's psychic security came four years later, when Bobby was shot in California on June 5, 1968. The brothers had grown increasingly close in the intervening years. As one Kennedy commented earlier, "Teddy has become to him [Bob] now what Bob was to Jack. They talk every morning and every night, wherever they are. They're like crossed fingers." The growing feebleness of Joe Kennedy, on whom Teddy had previously relied, had also increased his dependence on Bobby. The founding father had suffered a serious stroke in late 1961 and had only partially recovered. By 1968 he was a shadow of his former imperious self. Teddy had at first opposed Bobby's desire to enter the 1968 presidential election, but once the decision was made, he threw all his considerable energies and talents behind the next Kennedy. With Bobby gone, only one political heir remained.

In Chicago that tumultuous summer of 1968, it became apparent that the Democratic convention would offer the presidential nomination to Edward Kennedy if he would accept it. But Kennedy's advisers, as well as himself, felt that while he could win the nomination, he couldn't win the election. It was too soon and he was too young. Teddy was also still despondent over Bobby's death and too emotionally incapacitated for an all-out campaign. So he turned down this chance, as well as a vice presidential offer from Hubert Humphrey. He needed time to reconcentrate his personal and political powers. Nineteen-seventy-two seemed time enough.

In 1969, a recovered Teddy Kennedy began taking long strides toward the White House. In January, he astonished the nation by winning a Senate fight for Assistant Majority Leader or party "Whip" when he adroitly outmaneuvered Louisiana's Senator Russell Long, a twenty-year Senate veteran. Kennedy was strongly supported by Majority Leader Mike Mansfield. With Mansfield aging and nearing retirement, this surprise move brought Kennedy into a position of national authority and next in line for party leadership. From his new platform, Ted now began strengthening his national image by speaking out on popular issues. He concentrated on sharp attacks against the continuing war in Vietnam, on Administration spending for expensive military projects such as the ABM missiles program, and against Republican lagging in civil rights and poverty programs. Almost overnight—and with typical Kennedy speed—Teddy was magically transformed from the boy Senator to the leading man of the hour. Being suddenly at the top of the family heap must have felt gratifying—and dizzying—to the former underdog. The world had become his personal oyster. All he had to do was carefully extract the pearl of political power; but six months later, as American spacemen journeyed to the moon, Teddy dropped his oyster in the bottom of Poucha Pond. Whether he can fish it out again is still a question. While 1972 at first seemed beyond consideration, by early 1971 Teddy's tarnished image had, in the minds of many, recovered its former luster.

Let us briefly review the known actions of Teddy's life which support the thesis of a Kennedy neurosis. There may, of course, be other incidents not known, such as additional driving violations. The two years of his Army service in Europe are veiled in silence. But even if no similar incidents occurred, the existing incidents and the implications regarding their motivations are serious enough.

(1) He was expelled from Harvard for cheating on an exam.

(2) He was thrown out of a rugby game after three violent arguments with opposing team members. (The referee in thirty years of officiating had never before expelled a player, so this was not an ordinary incident.)

(3) Infuriated by teasing, he threw eight men off a yacht without knowing whether they could swim.

(4) As a graduate law student, he was three times convicted of reckless driving, which included running through red lights at night at excessive speeds. He also tried to hide from a police officer.

(5) As a campaign manager, he piloted a plane without adequate experience, rode bucking broncos, and made his first ski jump off a dangerous slope.

(6) On a hazardous night plane landing in foggy weather, he failed to buckle his seat belt and was seriously injured when the plane crashed.

(7) He confessed to causing the accidental death of a passenger in his car by driving off a narrow bridge at night and to failing to report the accident for nine hours.

Seen in such stark terms, Teddy Kennedy's record is unmistakably erratic and frightening. Throughout the past fifteen years, his actions have intensified from a self-defeatism often seen in somewhat disturbed young (and older) people up to the level of apparently destructive urges, which have actually resulted in the death of another person and serious injuries to Kennedy himself. To date, Ted's greatest self-injury has been to his career and his public reputation rather than to his body. This is perhaps the cruelest self-destruction of all, and it reveals the mercilessness of self-hatred. Physical destruction could have canonized Teddy, as it did brother Jack and Bobby and, to a lesser degree (because he was not a public figure), brother Joe. But moral destruction does just the opposite, and casts into shadow Teddy's life and actions, including those resulting from healthy impulses. Public condemnation is also a revenge on the parents, who are a basic part of the neurotic's self-hate.

Without knowing any facts of Teddy's life other than those of his early childhood, one would still expect from the pattern of that childhood to find neurotic character defenses developing. These defenses would unavoidably include self-defeating impulses. It would also be surprising—although such exceptions sometimes occur—for Kennedy to be able to shake off or outgrow the effects of his early years without a major change in his life. This has not happened.

Unless Ted Kennedy should now begin to change the direction of his life, it is highly probable that his neurosis will not only continue but increase. The chances of another serious "accident" seem high. For the last Kennedy son is not only a victim of outside pressures and extreme expectations. Far more disastrously, these pressures and expectations now have been internalized and come from within, from his own unconscious emotions, as well as from outside influences.

I will now explore more closely the psychological implications of the Chappaquiddick accident, the long shadow it has cast over Teddy's life and family, and the possible future career of Edward Moore Kennedy as the last Kennedy son.

Chapter 12

CHAPPAQUIDDICK AND AFTER:
BACK TO CAMELOT?

... the man most closely involved in the incident with her also appeared ordinary in most matters. Certainly he was not reputed to be an intellectual giant, an "egghead." His own name, Edward Moore (Ted) Kennedy, was not closely associated with any cultural or scientific advances, nor had he made any significant contributions in the areas of statesmanship or diplomacy. There was, nonetheless, a touch of *noblesse oblige* about him. He was that rarest of noblemen: a future king in a land that had purged kings. For millions of people whose daily lives were lacking in any semblance of high romance or grandeur, he satisfied deep anachronistic longings: to bow before purple robes, to idolize, to lift up and carry above the heads of the mob, to cheer and cheer.
—Jack Olsen, *The Bridge at Chappaquiddick*

We suggest that Edward Kennedy's rise to power and subsequent political stardom, and that of many other candidates, was based partly on the public's extravagant expectations—their need for heroes and illusions, albeit illusions of a particular kind—and on Kennedy's ability to pay for the services of men expert in the business of creating and selling pseudo events. His success was also based on the fact that he possesses some attributes, some substance, and some presence which makes it not difficult for him and his employees to create and sell an attractive public profile.
—Professor Murray B. Levin, *Kennedy Campaigning: The System and the Style as Practiced by Senator Edward Kennedy*

You know, it isn't enough just to be a Kennedy. There is a *time* for Kennedys ... and you have to know when that time is. You have to know what the country is ready for.
—Senator Edward Moore Kennedy

345

I regard as indefensible the fact that I did not report the accident to the police immediately.
—Senator Edward Kennedy's statement of July 28, 1969

Edward Kennedy showed signs of a boy who had been born the youngest son. There was a certain strain in him, the result, doubtless, of having to compete with older and perhaps more brilliant brothers. . . .
—Pearl S. Buck, *The Kennedy Women*

In the recent past I suppose I've had more than my share of tragedy and disappointment. The pendulum swings wide, and when it does, you develop an ability to live with these changes. You take life in short bursts. Right now I look forward to the next few years in the Senate. I have important work to do.
—Senator Edward Kennedy

ॐ

BY THE EARLY summer of 1969, Edward Moore Kennedy, then thirty-seven years old, seemed well on his way to repeating the political victories of his two older brothers in their rapid climb to, or near, the presidency of the United States. As we have seen, Ted Kennedy could possibly have had either the presidential or vice presidential place on the Democratic ticket in 1968, shortly after Bobby's murder. But both Teddy's intense grief and his own political caution kept him out of a questionable and premature race. Nineteen-seventy-two would be a different matter. Teddy would be an apparently more mature forty, and he would have time to build up an impressive record in the Senate.

It seems clear that from early 1969 on, Teddy was definitely in the unannounced running for the presidency. His surprise election as Majority Whip—the youngest in the Senate's history—in January, 1969, was a spur-of-the-moment prize which Ted seized only when he suddenly realized the incumbent's weakness. This prominent post significantly boosted Teddy's already strong image of popularity and leadership, although the Whip's actual duties were burdensome. Senator Kennedy said that he viewed his victory "as expressing the sense of the Democratic senators in favor of an aggressive and creative program in the upcoming Congress." Ironically, two years later, Teddy himself would be unseated in a surprise upset, largely brought about by his dilatory inattention to the thankless duties of Whip. We can see repeatedly, in Ted Kennedy's Senate career and elsewhere, how difficult it is for a person who has literally coasted into every job to assume genuine responsibility, develop initiative, and produce hard, often unpublicized, and unrewarded work. The Kennedys have not been people who worked very much out of the limelight for the good of others at the sacrifice of themselves.

In early 1969, Ted Kennedy's fast-rising political star was at its zenith. In a cover story on Teddy in January, *Time* rhapsodized that "the last of the clan rekindled a beacon of courage and change—one that should certainly brighten his party and the Senate and may yet achieve the full promise of a haunted dynasty." *Look* called Teddy "the 'different' Kennedy, the 'nice' Kennedy, the 'easygoing' Kennedy. He is the husky, hearty, quick-to-chuckle kid brother who grew up but never forgot his pals or his manners." There was little doubt that the fourth Kennedy son was at that time generally regarded by both friend and foe as the Democrats' most likely presidential nominee in 1972. Campaign buttons declaring for Ted had appeared even before President Nixon's inauguration. Teddy's beautiful blond wife, Joan, was obviously being pushed forward in a preliminary First Lady buildup.

The latest Kennedy "heir" now became the focus of intense public attention. Having succeeded to the chairmanship of the Senate subcommittee on Indian education—formerly headed by Bobby—Ted went to Alaska in April, 1969, to fulfill a pledge made by his murdered brother to investigate personally the Eskimos' living conditions. Teddy toured in a hard-hitting style reminiscent of Bobby, with the press boring in on every move. Finally the Republican members—apparently on directions from the White House—declared the trip a political publicity stunt and went home. The Republican assault against their number-one enemy had started.

A month later, in a continued spirit of adventurousness, the Massachusetts Senator impulsively flew West to join California's grape strikers. It is interesting to note that both forays were in directions followed earlier by the brother Teddy had felt closest to, Bobby Kennedy. As Bobby had done before him, Teddy seemed to be gathering strength from the image of his dead brother, and shaping himself in the likeness of the dead in order to assume the mantle of succession. The media, always eager for a new hero both to exploit, and even, optimistically, to believe in, enthusiastically endorsed the newest Kennedy. To those who wanted so desperately to believe, Teddy looked increasingly solid, liberal, and responsible. The White House began briefing its field deputies on Teddy, as "EMK in 1972" buttons and "Happiness Is Ted Kennedy in '72" placards flooded Washington streets and offices.

Popular magazines extolled the Edward Kennedys as the epitome of married bliss, although Washington gossips and insiders laughed knowingly over the young Senator's little-concealed flirtations with beautiful women. After the Chappaquiddick disaster, *Time* would print what had remained publicly unspoken before: "As for women, there are countless rumors in Washington, many of them conveyed with a ring of conviction. Some who have long watched the Kennedys can say with certainty that he often flirts with pretty girls in situations indiscreet for someone named Ted Kennedy. At the same time, he and his wife, Joan, are rumored to have had their troubles. There is no question that they are frequently separated. On one journey alone last summer, he was seen in the company of another lovely blonde on Aristotle Onassis' yacht. Such incidents might be recounted about innumerable people in Washington and elsewhere." Yet in the early summer of 1969, only the social circles of the large cities were aware of Teddy's wandering eye, just as Jack's and Bobby's sexual adventures had been kept out of the news media in America's main streets.

Then in mid-July, 1969, Ted Kennedy's car was found submerged in the waters of Chappaquiddick Island with a young blond woman drowned inside. Suddenly nothing seemed too bad to say about the Kennedys, as the nation went through a curious convulsion of outrage, malice, and frustration. For those who had set such high hopes on the last Kennedy son and invested so much of their emotional needs in him, the shock and disappointment were irrationally excessive. For the few who had always seen Ted Kennedy as merely human, with a plentiful share of human problems and weaknesses, the accident was far less surprising.

The details of Chappaquiddick are so well known that the briefest summary should serve the reader. The known—or revealed—facts of the accident are remarkably few. On the night of July 18–19, 1969, Senator Kennedy and a young Kennedy political worker, Miss Mary Jo Kopechne, drove away together from an isolated cottage on Chappaquiddick Island, off Martha's Vineyard in Massachusetts. In the cottage, they had spent the evening with ten other friends—five men and five women—celebrating the regatta weekend and their own political adventures as Kennedy campaigners. Senator Kennedy, according to later testimony, was giving Miss Kopechne a ride back to her hotel in Edgartown on Martha's Vineyard, connected to Chappaquiddick by a ferry.

Early the next morning, the Senator's car was found submerged in a pond a mile and a quarter from the cottage. The car had apparently run off a dangerously narrow and angled bridge which led over the pond to a beach beyond. Soon after this discovery, the body of Mary Jo Kopechne was recovered from the car. A short time later, Ted Kennedy entered the police station at nearby Edgartown and made a statement that he had been driving the car when the accident occurred. Kennedy said he had mistakenly turned onto the road leading to the bridge, instead of taking the road to the Edgartown ferry. When the car came to the bridge over the pond, it went off the side into the water. The Senator claimed he had no recollection of how he got out, but that he repeatedly dived for the other passenger, not knowing if she had escaped or not. Then, exhausted and in a state of shock, he had returned to the cottage and climbed into the back seat of a car. After a while someone drove him back to Edgartown, where he walked around a little and finally returned to his hotel. In the morning, Kennedy said he realized what had happened and went to the police.

A full statement was submitted by Kennedy to Edgartown Police Chief Arena on that morning of July 19, 1969. Chief Arena did not release the statement to the press for three hours, two hours longer than Kennedy's attorney, Paul Markham, had requested, but within minutes of the release of the statement Markham telephoned from Hyannis Port, where he and Ted had flown to confer with the rest of the family, asking that it be held up. The call came too late. Thus an important document only narrowly escaped concealment from the public view. Had the statement been delayed, the Kennedys might have managed to change this irretrievably damaging testimony and so have saved Teddy from the worst of the ensuing repercussions. The strong possibility that Teddy fumbled badly in making the best of a poor case is supported by his record as a mediocre lawyer both in and out of school. Unfortunately for the Kennedys, there was no better lawyer on hand.

In this first statement, Ted Kennedy testified, "On July 18, 1969, at approximately 11:15 P.M., on Chappaquiddick Island, Martha's Vineyard, I was driving my car on Main Street on my way to get the ferry back to Edgartown. I was unfamiliar with the road and turned onto Dyke Road instead of bearing left on Main Street. After proceeding for approximately a half mile on Dyke Road I descended a hill and came upon a narrow bridge. The car went off the side of the bridge. There was one passenger in the car with me, Miss Mary Jo Kopechne, a former secretary of my brother Robert Kennedy. The car turned over and sank into the water and landed with the roof resting on the bottom. I attempted to open the door and window of the car but have no recollection of how I got out of the car. I came to the surface and then repeatedly dove down to the car in an attempt to see if the passenger was still in the car. I was unsuccessful in the attempt.

"I was exhausted and in a state of shock. I recall walking back to where my friends were eating. There was a car parked in front of the cottage and I climbed into the back seat. I then asked for someone to bring me back to Edgartown. I remember walking around for a period of time and then going back to my hotel room. When I fully realized what happened this morning, I immediately contacted the police."

After giving this statement to Chief Arena, Kennedy flew by private plane to Hyannis Port, and went into seclusion. Soon he was joined there by other family members and trusted Kennedy advisers, both obscure and illustrious: sister Eunice Kennedy Shriver, wife of Ambassador to France J. Sargent Shriver (JFK's former Peace Corps head); Frank O'Conner, one of Teddy's advisers; David Burke, Kennedy's administrative assistant; former Defense Secretary Robert McNamara; Theodore Sorensen, former special assistant to President Kennedy; Burke Marshall, former Assistant Attorney General; brother-in-law and family business manager Stephen Smith (Jean Kennedy's husband); and former JFK adviser Richard Goodwin. Other top Kennedy Democrats were reportedly contacted, including John Kenneth Galbraith, the Harvard economist and former Ambassador to India; and Connecticut Senator Abraham Ribicoff, former HEW Secretary. As always, a Kennedy could call upon an impressive array of top-level advisers to help solve his political and personal problems.

But this problem would not be easily solved. Commentators throughout the nation immediately noticed the "credibility gaps" in Senator Kennedy's hasty statement. Most shocking of all to people everywhere was his admitted failure to report the accident immediately. Not only had Kennedy admitted leaving the scene without summoning help, but he had failed to notify the authorities until eight to ten hours after the tragedy. This was and continues to be his greatest failure, one for which there seems to be no satisfactory explanation. As one newspaper put it, "The crime in the tribunal of public opinion was going for a lawyer instead of a scuba diver." To millions, it seemed incredible that Kennedy could have gone through all the actions he claimed without himself or his friends ever calling for help or reporting the accident to the police. The stark impression of cowardly selfishness was impossible to avoid.

Another dubious point in Kennedy's statement, which struck many people as an outright lie, was his claim to be "unfamiliar" with the main road on Chappaquiddick Island. The clearly marked paved road leading to the ferry went almost due west; the unmarked, rutted dirt road leading to the bridge where the disaster occurred led almost due east. It seemed impossible for anyone to mistake the two, even a stranger to the island. Kennedy had not only driven over the paved road the day before, but, island residents pointed out, he had visited the island since youth. In the later inquest, however, Teddy claimed that the fatal weekend was his first visit to Chappaquiddick Island. But Mary Jo herself must have realized their destination. The narrow, hump-backed Dyke Bridge led over Poucha Pond to a deserted beachfront section of the island. The six girls from the party, including Mary Jo Kopechne, had gone swimming there the day before. All the evidence points to the likelihood that Teddy knew where he was going. At that time of night, there seemed only one reason for a man to take a young, attractive, unmarried woman to a deserted stretch of beach.

Whatever his exact intentions, it appeared almost undeniable to the world that Kennedy intended to indulge in some romantic dalliance.

This conclusion was entirely in character, despite the beauty and loyalty of the Senator's young wife, Joan. As noted, both Ted Kennedy and his older brother Jack were well known among intimates for their amorous proclivities (as was Joe Junior; Bobby seems to have bloomed late in life). After the accident, *Newsweek* asserted that "the senator's closest associates are known to have been powerfully concerned over his indulgent drinking habits, his daredevil driving, and his ever-ready eye for a pretty face. . . ." *Time* partly supported the drinking contention. On August 1, 1969, it commented, "Kennedy has been drinking more heavily since his brother was murdered last year, but he is far from being a drunkard . . . in short, no proof either way." *Life* also commented that "some thought his drinking had got beyond the strains it was supposed to relieve, and there were parties for tightly knit Kennedy loyalists—similar to the one out on Chappy that week. 'The possibility of heavy drinking by Senator Kennedy will fall within the scope of this investigation,' Dukes County Prosecutor Walter Steele said, but finally leveled no charges of that nature." Many observers noted also that no such investigation was made. The American public speculated widely that Teddy had not reported the accident sooner to avoid the more serious charge of driving while intoxicated, which could bring a manslaughter charge. This is one of several crucial questions which have never been satisfactorily answered.

Most damaging was the constant question in everyone's mind: Why didn't Kennedy rush to the nearest house for help? A house only 100 yards away had its lights on, and he passed others in his mile-and-a-quarter hike back to his friends in the rented cottage. Teddy testified later that he saw no lights. Despite Kennedy's assertions of shock, confusion, and exhaustion, even his staunchest supporters found it hard to defend his search for legal and political help instead of making every effort to save the girl in his car.

In the week following the accident, Teddy remained silent. After his first sketchy statement, the flurries of doubts and rumors began to build into an incriminating blizzard of blood-chilling questions. Only once did the Senator leave Hyannis Port, when he and his wife Joan and sister-in-law Ethel Kennedy attended the funeral of Mary Jo Kopechne at Plymouth, Pennsylvania. The Kennedy debacle, which occurred forty hours before man's first lunar landing, began to eclipse the moon in national interest. It became increasingly imperative that Kennedy break his silence and explain the mystery of those eight to ten hours lost between the accident and the statement.

Meanwhile, the legal tangle had grown. Teddy's lawyers at first opposed the misdemeanor proceedings filed against him, but then waived a hearing. On Friday, July 25, a week after the fatal accident, Senator Kennedy appeared in the Edgartown District Court and pleaded guilty to leaving the scene of the accident. His guilty plea cut short plans for a public hearing and forestalled testimony from any of the other ten party guests. All of them had disappeared from Martha's Vineyard shortly after the accident and had made few comments. None had been summoned to testify. Because of his guilty plea, Kennedy was not required to undergo cross-examination. The prosecuting attorney, Walter Steele, who had worked with Ted Kennedy in 1961 as an assistant state prosecuting attorney, asked for the minimum verdict: a two-month suspended sentence. This was granted by Judge Boyle. About nine minutes after he walked into the courthouse, Senator Kennedy walked out a free man. But the American public did not miss the irony of the trial: nine minutes of questioning for nine hours of silence.

The examination of Kennedy's conduct, however, continued; and the Senator knew it. That same evening, Ted went on a nationwide television hookup in a desperate attempt to restore his reputation. Ostensibly, his plea was to the voters of Massachusetts to help him decide if he should resign from the Senate (which no one had suggested). Clearly, Kennedy's appeal was to the nation to understand, forgive, and forget. The country had forgiven and forgotten Teddy's early misadventures. Would the old Kennedy magic once more dispel shame and scandal? Here is Ted Kennedy's second statement of July 25, 1969:

"My fellow citizens: I have requested this opportunity to talk to the people of Massachusetts about the tragedy which happened last Friday evening. This morning I entered a plea of guilty to the charge of leaving the scene of an accident. Prior to my appearance in court, it would have been improper for me to comment on these matters. But tonight I am free to tell you what happened and to say what it means to me.

"On the weekend of July 18 I was on Martha's Vineyard Island participating with my nephew Joe Kennedy—as for thirty years my family has participated—in the annual Edgartown sailing regatta. Only reasons of health prevented my wife from accompanying me.

"On Chappaquiddick Island, off Martha's Vineyard, I attended on Friday evening, July 18, a cookout I had encouraged and helped sponsor for a devoted group of Kennedy campaign secretaries. When I left the party, around 11:15 P.M., I was accompanied by one of these girls, Miss Mary Jo Kopechne. Mary Jo was one of the most devoted members of the staff of Senator Robert Kennedy. She worked for him for four years and was broken up over his death. For this reason, and because she was such a gentle, kind and idealistic person, all of us tried to help her feel that she still had a home with the Kennedy family.

"There is no truth, no truth whatever, to the widely circulated suspicions of immoral conduct that have been leveled at my behavior and hers regarding that evening. There has never been a private relationship between us of any kind. I know of nothing in Mary Jo's conduct on that or any other occasion—the same is true of the other girls at that party—that would lend any substance to such ugly speculation about their character. Nor was I driving under the influence of liquor.

"Little over one mile away, the car that I was driving on an unlit road went off a narrow bridge which had no guardrails and was built on a left angle to the road. The car overturned in a deep pond and immediately filled with water. I remember thinking as the cold water rushed in around my head that I was for certain drowning. Then water entered my lungs and I actually felt the sensation of drowning. But somehow I struggled to the surface alive. I made immediate and repeated efforts to save Mary Jo by diving into the strong and murky current but succeeded only in increasing my state of utter exhaustion and alarm.

"My conduct and conversations during the next several hours to the extent that I can remember them make no sense to me at all. Although my doctors informed me that I suffered a cerebral concussion as well as shock, I do not seek to escape responsibility for my actions by placing the blame either on the physical, emotional trauma brought on by the accident or on anyone else. I regard as indefensible the fact that I did not report the accident to the police immediately. Instead of looking directly for a telephone after lying exhausted in the grass for an undetermined time, I walked back to the cottage where the party was being held and requested the help of two friends, my cousin Joseph Gargan and Paul Markham, and directed them to return immediately to the scene with me—this was some time after midnight—in order to undertake a new effort to dive down and locate Miss Kopechne. Their strenuous efforts, undertaken at some risks to their own lives, also proved futile.

"All kinds of scrambled thoughts—all of them confused, some of them irrational, many of them which I cannot recall and some of which I would not have seriously entertained under normal circumstances—went through my mind during this period. They were reflected in the various inexplicable, inconsistent and inconclusive things I said and did, including such questions as whether the girl might still be alive somewhere out of that immediate area, whether some awful curse did actually hang over all the Kennedys, whether there was some justifiable reason for me to doubt what had happened and to delay my report, whether somehow the awful weight of this incredible incident might in some way pass from my shoulders. I was overcome, I'm frank to say, by a jumble of emotions—grief, fear, doubt, exhaustion, panic, confusion and shock.

"Instructing Gargan and Markham not to alarm Mary Jo's friends that night, I had them take me to the ferry crossing. The ferry having shut down for the night, I suddenly jumped into the water and impulsively swam across, nearly drowning once again in the effort, and returned to my hotel about 2 A.M. and collapsed in my room. I remember going out at one point and saying something to the room clerk. In the morning, with my mind somewhat more lucid, I made an effort to call a family legal adviser, Burke Marshall, from a public telephone on the Chappaquiddick side of the ferry and belatedly reported the accident to the Martha's Vineyard police.

"Today, as I mentioned, I felt morally obligated to plead guilty to the charge of leaving the scene of an accident. No words on my part can possibly express the terrible pain and suffering I feel over this tragic incident. This last week has been an agonizing one for me and the members of my family, and the grief we feel over the loss of a wonderful friend will remain with us the rest of our lives.

"These events, the publicity, innuendo and whispers which have surrounded them and my admission of guilt this morning raise the question in my mind of whether my standing among the people of my state has been so impaired that I should resign my seat in the United States Senate. If at any time the citizens of Massachusetts should lack confidence in their senator's character or his ability, with or without justification, he could not in my opinion adequately perform his duty and should not continue in office.

"The people of this state, the state which sent John Quincy Adams and Daniel Webster and Charles Sumner and Henry Cabot Lodge and John Kennedy to the United States Senate, are entitled to representation in that body by men who inspire their utmost confidence. For this reason, I would understand full well why some might think it right for me to resign. For me this will be a difficult decision to make. It has been seven years since my first election to the Senate. You and I share many memories—some of them have been glorious, some have been very sad. The opportunity to work with you and serve Massachusetts has made my life worthwhile. And so I ask you tonight, people of Massachusetts, to think this through with me. In facing this decision, I seek your advice and opinion. In making it, I seek your prayers. For this is a decision that I will have finally to make on my own.

"It has been written a man does what he must in spite of personal consequences, in spite of obstacles and dangers and pressures, and that is the basis of all human morality. Whatever may be the sacrifices he faces, if he follows his conscience—the loss of his friends, his fortune, his contentment, even the esteem of his fellow man—each man must decide for himself the course he will follow. The stories of past courage cannot supply courage itself. For this, each man must look into his own soul. I pray that I can have the courage to make the right decision. Whatever is decided and whatever the future holds for me, I hope that I shall be able to put this most recent tragedy behind me and make some further contribution to our state and mankind, whether it be in public or private life. Thank you and good night."

Although the palpable phoniness of this mock-heroic "plea" was criticized by many, thousands of other Americans—especially the Kennedys' steadfast Massachusetts supporters—responded with an outpouring of sympathy and a readiness to "live and let live." It is hard to believe that Teddy ever genuinely intended to resign from the Senate. Instead, his speech was so packed with public-relations-type references and exaggerations that it seemed evident the underlying aim was to restore the badly tarnished Kennedy image. Above all, behind Teddy's maudlin appeal for courage and prayer lay the fact of his self-serving cowardice in a crisis. No mention of confused emotions and tribute to past political greatness seemed to explain away those lost hours when Teddy went to bed instead of reporting the accident. Yet millions of Americans refused to look closely into the Kennedy mystique. Instead, Ted's statement was hailed as "manful" and a satisfactory explanation of his behavior. But some critics, such as David Halberstam, found the statement "of such cheapness and bathos as to be a rejection of everything the Kennedys had stood for in candor and style." A *Life* writer commented, "He was simply hustling heartstrings, using words, cashing in on the family credibility. For the first time ever, I felt embarrassed for a Kennedy." Most Edgartown residents also rejected Teddy's apologia. As a newsman found, "Edgartown got sick to its stomach watching him on TV. People here know this area and they know the Dyke Bridge, and they can't be conned. They sat in front of their screens and listened to Ted Kennedy tell stories that made him sound like Superman, and they laughed and said, 'Come on, Teddy, you've got to be kidding!' "

But Teddy was not kidding; he was urgently striving to salvage his career. Never before had a Kennedy been both attacked and defended so emotionally in waves of outrage and apology. Kennedy's second statement gave ammunition to each camp. For once again, Teddy had failed to answer the key question: Why had he not looked for immediate help? A walk of one and a quarter miles back to get his two lawyer friends could hardly be viewed as the action of a man desperately trying to rescue an accident victim. It seemed, all too obviously, the act of a man desperately trying to save his own political life. The remaining mysteries paled into insignificance beside this one overwhelming fact: Kennedy's primary drive had been to save his political future, not another person's life.

Teddy's statement also contained a judgmental irony. Above all, the young Senator needed to establish himself in the public mind as a mature.

self-controlled individual. If elected in 1972, Edward Kennedy would be the nation's youngest President. Yet his need to avoid a serious manslaughter charge by pleading physical and emotional incapacity had seriously jeopardized a carefully created profile of cool, confident, responsible maturity. Teddy's easy legal escape—a suspended sentence and a year's suspension of his driving license—also raised in many minds the question of the law's double standard and the Kennedys' use of power and influence to subvert justice. As one observer saw the case, "The irony of it is that Senator Kennedy's political career has been characterized by persistent pleas that law enforcement should apply with equal weight to all citizens." Another critic commented, "I ask you to consider what would happen to a private citizen who, heading 'out to the dunes' after a party with a girl in his car, drove off the road and killed the girl—and then crept quietly away from the scene without saying anything to anyone, leaving car and corpse to be discovered the next day without his assistance. The laws covering a situation like this are stringent—nay, merciless. Such a private citizen would pay a very stiff price indeed for his irresponsible behavior. Yet it seems that Edward Kennedy intends to pay no price at all."

The Senator remained silent under the blasts of criticism and returned to his home in McLean, Virginia, on July 30. That afternoon his office released a statement that "Senator Edward M. Kennedy is returning to Washington to resume his duties as United States Senator and assistant majority leader. He is grateful to the people of Massachusetts for their expressions of confidence and expects to submit his record to them as a candidate for re-election in 1970. If re-elected, he will serve out his entire six-year term." It was clear that the Kennedys intended to weather the storm, as they had in the past. And as every experienced politician knows, the public can be surprisingly willing to forgive, forget, or rationalize away past lapses. The Senate welcomed Teddy back warmly and closed ranks around him. Although Ted had obviously suffered from his ordeal, he gradually regained strength and self-confidence as he continued his senatorial duties, including public speech-making. Kennedy also began his campaign for Senate reelection more than a year before the November, 1970, vote. If Massachusetts returned him to power with an overwhelming vote, much of the stain would be erased from his name.

Meanwhile, public hopes of further revelations about Chappaquiddick were renewed when an inquest was announced for the fall, then postponed until early 1970. Finally, on January 5, 1970, the inquest opened in Edgartown to ascertain "whether or not any crime has been committed." As Judge James A. Boyle of the Edgartown District Court pointed out, an inquest is not a prosecution or trial, but simply a fact-finding investigation. Kennedy was the first witness, and essentially corroborated his previous testimony. The other men and women present at the Chappaquiddick party were also called to testify. After the three-day hearing, Judge Boyle issued a summary in which his final conclusions were severely critical of Teddy's truthfulness. The judge concluded in this statement of February 18, 1970, "I infer a reasonable and probable explanation of the totality of the above facts is that Kennedy and Kopechne did *not* intend to return to Edgartown at that time; that Kennedy did *not* intend to drive to the ferry slip and his turn onto Dyke Road was intentional. Having reached this conclusion, the question then arises as to whether there was anything criminal in his operation of the motor vehicle.

"From two personal views, which corroborate the Engineer's statement (Exhibit 29), and other evidence, I am fully convinced that Dyke Bridge constitutes a traffic hazard, particularly so at night, and must be approached with extreme caution. A speed of even twenty miles per hour, as Kennedy testified to, operating a car as large as this Oldsmobile, would at least be negligent and, possibly, reckless. If Kennedy knew of this hazard, his operation of the vehicle constituted criminal conduct.

"Earlier on July 18, he had been driven over Chappaquiddick Road three times, and over Dyke Road and Dyke Bridge twice. Kopechne had been driven over Chappaquiddick Road five times and over Dyke Road and Dyke Bridge twice.

"I believe it probable that Kennedy knew of the hazard that lay ahead of him on Dyke Road but that, for some reason not apparent from the testimony, he failed to exercise due care as he approached the bridge. I, therefore, find there is probable cause to believe that Edward M. Kennedy operated his motor vehicle negligently on a way or in a place to which the public have a right of access and that such operation appears to have contributed to the death of Mary Jo Kopechne."

Despite Judge Boyle's finding, however, no further charges were made against the Senator. A brief flurry of excitement was rearoused when the Dukes County grand jury announced in late March, 1970, that it would conduct a new investigation. The new inquiry was quickly cut off, however, when a Superior Court judge, dispatched from Boston, lectured the jury for an hour on the narrow guidelines it could follow. After less than three and a half hours of deliberation on April 6, the grand jury closed. The long arm of Kennedy influence seemed once again to have reached out to forestall further embarrassment.

Let us return briefly to the accident itself. What are we to make of all the conflicting and ambiguous testimony? One ingenuous reporter, Jack Olsen, after a detailed study, evolved the theory that Mary Jo herself had accidentally driven the large car off the unfamiliar bridge while the Senator hid in the bushes back down the road when a car seemed about to follow them.

Thus Kennedy would have known nothing of the accident. Although he worriedly summoned his aides to search for the missing girl, he would not have learned of the tragedy until the following morning.

While plausible in many respects, this theory appears untenable when set beside the testimony at the inquest. Teddy and his two companions, Gargan and Markham, gave graphic descriptions of their efforts to dive for the girl they believed still trapped in the submerged car. While the heroic dimensions may well have been enlarged, the greater part of their testimony sounds genuine. "Covering up" for Kennedy's failure to report the accident is evident throughout the inquest report, but the basic facts seem to be that he did indeed drive off the bridge, escape through the window open on his side, and finally return to his hotel in a confused emotional state, knowing Mary Jo must be dead, but frantically wanting to believe that she was still alive and that there was a way for him to escape the infamy of such an extraordinary accident.

When all the available facts are studied, the conclusion I find most likely is the simplest one: The accident happened basically as Teddy testified—he did, in fact, unwittingly drive off the dangerous bridge. When one accepts this, it is easier to understand how Kennedy can accept and live with his guilt, for accidents happen to everyone. As the Senator later said, "I can live with myself. I feel the tragedy of the girl's death. That's on my mind. That's what I will always have to live with. But what I don't have to live with are the whispers and innuendos and falsehoods, because these have no basis in fact." Since Teddy and his aides did make efforts to find Mary Jo in the submerged car, Kennedy's guilt over her death would understandably be limited. The bridge was admittedly dangerous, and Kennedy himself had nearly been killed. After the vain attempts to find the girl in the car, the three men must have concluded that she was dead. According to the testimony of Joseph Gargan (Ted's cousin) and Paul Markham, they insisted that the accident should be reported at once. The two left Teddy swimming back to Edgartown across the narrow channel, no large feat for such an experienced swimmer. Both Gargan and Markham said they believed that the Senator would immediately report the accident.

The inquest testimony highlighted the dreadful confusion and anguish in Kennedy's mind over the predicament in which he suddenly found himself. For a young man who had had his way largely "paid" through life and who had always had the lavish resources of his family to help him out of scrapes, the enormity of his dilemma, with no other Kennedy present to help, must indeed have seemed strangely unreal and unbelievable.

Gargan's testimony brings out the neurotic conflict in Teddy's emotions over his need to face reality and his deep desire to wish it away. After their failure to get inside the car, the three men started back up the dirt road:

"Senator Kennedy was very emotional, extremely upset, very disturbed, and he was using this expression which I have heard before, but he was using it particularly that night, 'Can you believe it, Joe, can you believe it, I don't believe it, I don't believe this could happen, I just don't believe it,' and it continued in this way." After Kennedy described driving off the bridge and struggling to the surface, "he started to go into this thing about, 'I don't believe this, I don't believe this could happen to me, I don't know how this could have happened, I don't understand it,' and this again. . . ." In Kennedy's agony of stunned disbelief we can sense the immaturity of his response to the crisis and his childish retreat into amazed disbelief.

Teddy's own testimony also supports the impression that his predominant emotional need was to wish away the shocking accident, rather than to cope with the reality of it. As the Senator drove back down the road with Markham and Gargan, he worried about how he could call Mrs. Kopechne and his own parents and wife in the middle of the night about Mary Jo: ". . . and I even—even though I knew that Mary Jo Kopechne was dead and believed firmly that she was in the back of that car I willed that she remained alive. As we drove down that road I was almost looking out the front window and windows trying to see her walking down that road. I related this to Gargan and Markham and they said they understood this feeling, but it was necessary to report it. And about this time we came to the ferry crossing and I got out of the car and we talked there just a few minutes. I just wondered how all of this could possibly have happened. I also had sort of a thought and the wish and desire and the hope that suddenly this whole accident would disappear, and they reiterated that this has to be reported and I understood at the time that I left that ferry boat, left the slip where the ferry boat was, that it had to be reported and I had full intention of reporting it, and I mentioned to Gargan and Markham something like, 'You take care of the girls, I will take care of the accident,'—that is what I said and I dove into the water."

Teddy then related how he nearly drowned a second time as he found himself caught in an unexpected current which pulled him out into the darkness. However, Markham watched Kennedy swim halfway across and had no concern for his safety. But the Senator at this point needed to stress his physical exhaustion in order to explain his mental confusion and difficulty in reporting the accident. Another explanation is more probable: A favored child of fortune who had never grown up in many important emotional respects was now, for the first time in his life, faced with a serious personal crisis that he had to handle primarily alone. Emotionally, Ted Kennedy was simply unable to respond adequately to the situation. This failure was not, however, the result of the accident, but rather the result of his lifetime conditioning and neurotic defense structure. It is indicative that Teddy retreated to his bed—a prevalent symbol of the protective womb—rather than face the truth about what had happened, with its deeply feared consequences of judgment and punishment. Teddy stated that he was shaking with chill and suffering from head, neck, and back pains, that he collapsed on his bed, then later arose to ask about the hotel noise that "seemed around me, on top of me, almost in the room. . . ." The Senator then returned to his room until around eight o'clock in the morning, when he went to the lobby, ordered some papers, conversed briefly with several guests, and then met in his room with Gargan and Markham.

The aides asked Kennedy if he had reported the accident. Ted Kennedy's reply is revealing: "Well, they asked, had I reported the accident, and why I hadn't reported the accident; and I told them about my own thoughts and feelings as I swam across that channel and how I [had] always willed that Mary Jo still lived; how I was hopeful even as that night went on and as I almost tossed and turned, paced that room and walked around that room that night that somehow when they arrived in the morning that they were going to say that Mary Jo was still alive. I told them how I somehow believed that when the sun came up and it was a new morning that what had happened the night before would not have happened and did not happen, and how I just couldn't gain the strength within me, the moral strength to call Mrs. Kopechne at 2:00 o'clock in the morning and tell her that her daughter was dead."

Only a deep emotional disturbance could explain this extraordinary attitude. Ted Kennedy's distorted feelings seemed to have clouded his view of reality. There was no final proof that Mary Jo was dead or still in the car, for none of the men had actually seen or felt her body through the black, swirling waters. The possibility remained that she had somehow escaped, but might be lying unconscious along the shore. Yet no fire engine, scuba diver, ambulance, policeman, or Chappaquiddick resident had been summoned. Gargan and Markham had abdicated their own responsibility by relying on their all-powerful Senator to carry out what they knew had to be done. But Ted Kennedy, as they must have realized the next morning with cold inner shock, had been incapable of acting responsibly. Instead of a stunned but essentially mature man, they found they were dealing with an immature youth—though a youth whose power and family intimidated them at every step. Suddenly, action was imperative. Looking for a private phone, the three men crossed over to the Chappaquiddick ferry house, where Kennedy tried to telephone one of the family's most brilliant and trusted aides, former Assistant Attorney General Burke Marshall. While at the ferry, a local resident told them about the discovery of Kennedy's wrecked car. With the accident now known to the world, the Senator returned to the Edgartown police station and made his belated first "confession."

One final comment is perhaps necessary. Judge Boyle in his summary stated his belief that "Kennedy knew of the hazard that lay ahead of him on Dyke Road but that, for some reason not apparent from the testimony, he failed to exercise due care as he approached the bridge." From the knowledge we now have of Teddy's past reckless driving and other dangerous behavior, the reasons for his carelessness are not hard to guess. At heart, Ted Kennedy showed every sign of unconsciously feeling a personal omnipotence, as did all the Kennedys. Despite all his scrapes and narrow escapes, no real retribution had ever befallen him. Perhaps in his innermost feelings, part of Teddy longed for such retribution to assuage his deep childhood guilt and the heavy burden of being the only surviving Kennedy son, with all the massive implications of fantastic achievement and triumph which that survival carried. I have already explored some of the probable semi-suicidal impulses in the four Kennedy sons, as well as their latent hostility and destructiveness. All of these complex emotions could easily have helped propel Teddy into carelessly driving to Dyke Bridge without realistic caution, simply because his personal sense of existence was so ambivalent and unrealistic. The struggle within every neurotic person between life and death, between self-realization and self-defeat, is ever-present, and will manifest itself according to outer circumstances as well as inner conditions. In my view, Kennedy drove off the bridge because part of him secretly wanted it to happen, while at the same time part of him didn't believe it could happen; and when it did happen, he tried to wish away with childhood magic the adult realities of chance, gravity, violence, and death.

We can now return to the post-Chappaquiddick consequences of Kennedy's emotional and moral failure. Once he had been accepted back by the familiar world of political power and manipulation, Ted Kennedy seemed to feel his feet again on solid ground. Very likely he soon repressed his inner knowledge of exactly what had happened, just as he had tried to repress his knowledge of having to report the accident. As far as the sexual implications of the episode went, there seemed no reason for Teddy to feel any more shame than he had over past escapades. Nothing had really happened, because Poucha Pond had intervened. And he had intended no harm to Mary Jo; on the contrary, Kennedy probably felt that he was flattering her with his attention. Of course, it was politically essential to deny any personal relationship, America being as puritanical as it is. But in essence, the Senator was doing nothing that millions of other men—and hundreds of other Senators in their time—hadn't done and would continue to do. One simply lied a little to one's wife and went on living successfully. That such a view of human relationships bears within it the seed of mutual defeat and nonlove is something which apparently has not occurred much—if at all—to the Kennedy family. Different social standards based on sex only produces mutual hostility and guilt between the sexes. But the Kennedys have never understood this human reality, and it has been a large part of the neurotic patterning so evident in all their lives.

That same year, a fresh blow hit the Kennedys. Joseph P. Kennedy, long an invalid, suffered a final stroke and died at eighty-one on November 18, 1969. The patriarch's death contained an element of relief, for he had long been incapacitated. But his passing also removed the last male emotional prop in the family for Teddy. The mantle of ascendancy was now the youngest son's alone. At the funeral, Ted behaved in the stoical Kennedy tradition by reading the eulogy written by Robert Kennedy, as well as a tribute by his mother. Yet the "glue" of the family remained—the matriarch. There was still a determined Kennedy coach on hand to keep Teddy racing toward a political touchdown.

Back in the Senate, Ted Kennedy suffered what one writer called "a sort of instant political decompression." His prestige and power dropped rapidly over the next months. In this period, Kennedy failed to gain Senate approval of ammunition control, to halt the closure of a NASA research complex in Massachusetts, or to speed the end of the current draft law. Yet on the surface the Senators welcomed Teddy back warmly, and Majority Leader Mike Mansfield opined that "It's preordained. With Ted, I'm afraid it's not a question of choice, but a matter of destiny." Meanwhile, Kennedy concentrated on rebuilding his damaged reputation by working hard on draft reform and Indian relief, as well as speaking out against Vietnam and Nixon's policies.

Despite Teddy's public composure, intense speculation continued about the extent of family pressure on this remaining son to be President and his own inner reluctance to assume such an enormous responsibility and personal risk. Teddy's fears of assassination were reportedly strong, as were those of his wife. According to one journalist, it was Rose Kennedy who kept Teddy from dropping out of politics entirely in the fall of 1969, when the storm of criticism and calumny was breaking over his head. After Joseph P. Kennedy's death in November, Rose became "Chief of the Clan" and the parent solely responsible for maintaining the family political dynasty founded by the patriarch. During a reported confrontation between mother and son allegedly related by Eunice Kennedy Shriver, "Mother put her foot down—hard!" At first Teddy was stubborn, but Rose told him that fear must never dominate his life, and that he had a responsibility to his parents and dead brothers. As the writer interpreted the episode, "To Rose, the whole thing was the dynasty, and Ted was the dynasty, at least until her grandsons were of age. Rose posed a question: Would a Royal

Family forfeit its right to the throne because one of its kings and one of its princes had fallen to murderous lunatics?"

This highly ambitious and vigorous woman has lived her entire eighty-plus years in the limelight of successes achieved by the male surrogates for her intense desires—her father, husband, and sons. Through these men Rose has achieved enormous prestige and praise. It is hard to imagine that such a regal, strong-willed, dominating woman, who has so clearly shaped her self-image in the ideal portrait of a "queen," would relinquish this deeply gratifying role. Rose has achieved the rare position of becoming a national figure embodying noble motherhood, martyrdom, and matriarchy, but only through the lives and deaths of her sons. In a country where politically ambitious women who seek election for themselves are still largely considered jokes, a political queen cannot exist without a king. For Rose Kennedy, her last son had now become that irreplaceable monarch.

However, more recent reports indicated that Rose definitely did not want Teddy to run in 1972. In a May, 1972, interview, the matriarch expressed relief that Teddy had decided not to run for President that year: "I think there is too much risk now. If he wants to, it would be much better to run a little later. . . . No, Teddy really is not going to run this time. . . . A President has so little time for family matters. . . . He says I can campaign until I'm ninety, and that's still almost ten years away. I am sure it is Teddy's present intention not to run. I think it is a wise intention." Assassination is uppermost in her mind, as it is for Ted's wife, Joan. As Rose said elsewhere, "We all know he might be assassinated . . . but it's never discussed."

In the late fall of 1969, Teddy had begun his campaign for reelection to the Senate, apparently bolstered by new resolve and filial obedience. Massachusetts polls showed a large majority still in favor of Kennedy (78 percent in November), and his return seemed assured. But to regain a footing as a potential national candidate, Teddy needed to win by a large majority. Through 1970, as his senatorial campaign picked up speed, it became obvious that the Kennedys were going all-out for the kind of win that would restore the "heir apparent" to his former place. In 1964, Ted had been elected by 71 percent, a landslide victory. But as his aides pointed out, unusual circumstances had boosted his popularity—his brother's assassination, his own plane crash, and the Goldwater candidacy. While the setting was far less hopeful in 1970, in the wake of Chappaquiddick, the Kennedy machine launched an intensive, lavishly financed campaign, using the customary techniques of personal and technological politicking which had been polished by several generations of Kennedys. Teddy worked furiously to show himself personally to as many voters as possible. "The voters need reassurance," the Senator said. "They need to see me, to be convinced that I'm reliable and mature. You can't counter the Chappaquiddick thing directly. The answer has to be implicit in what you are, what you stand for and how they see you." Joan Kennedy campaigned tirelessly with her husband, filling the prescribed role of loyal and devoted helpmate in which she has always evidently believed. Of Chappaquiddick, Joan said simply that she believed everything Teddy said, although he should have gone to the police sooner.

In November, 1970, the Massachusetts voters demonstrated their continued faith in the Kennedys by giving Teddy an impressive majority of 62 percent. While not quite the overwhelming victory the family had hoped for, the win was still a considerable success, and Teddy's national prestige shot upward. Commentators began viewing him again as the only potential presidential candidate who might win the nomination without entering the primaries. As one political associate phrased what many were thinking, "The intellectual side of him tells him it's impossible to seek it in '72. But the emotional side tells him that this is what he's been trained for; it's his goal in life, he owes it to his brothers." Teddy himself seemed to feel a great upsurge of self-confidence, stating, "I look forward to being a voice for peace in the U.S. Senate . . . a voice of reconciliation . . . that appeals to the best within people. I return to the U.S. Senate to give voice to the powerless groups that exist within our society."

But a new shock, this one political, struck Teddy a few months later in January, 1971, when he lost his Senate post of Majority Whip to West Virginia conservative Robert Byrd, by a vote of 31 to 24. Contrary to many reports, Kennedy had lobbied hard for votes among the Senators and received the assurances of a majority. But with five other presidential hopefuls maneuvering in the Senate, some devious tactics seem to have been used. Also, Kennedy had lost favor with many Senators because of his lack of energy in responding to personal requests. Long absences and inattention to the boring but politically necessary details of his post had eroded Teddy's support. Byrd, on the other hand, was popular for the personal favors he rendered his legislative colleagues. The liberal press was more horrified at Byrd's election than Kennedy's defeat. Doubts over EMK's presidential potential, at least for 1972, were temporarily revived. Teddy himself was clearly disappointed, but made the best of this surprise blow by commenting that he would now have more time to devote to essential matters, such as a major draft reform.

Kennedy had already achieved a highly liberal voting rating in the Senate. In 1969, he had voted for ABM restrictions; for the shift of research funds from the Defense Department to the National Science Foundation; against state restrictions on legal services in poverty programs; for increased urban renewal funding; for the self-regulation of campuses; and against the removal of oil/gas drilling costs from taxable items. In 1970, Senator Kennedy had voted for a ceiling on defense expenditures; for congressional seniority reform; for the use of education funds to further desegregation; against "no-knock" warrants; against the nomination of G. Harrold Carswell to the Supreme Court; and for the withdrawal of troops from Vietnam by December 31, 1971.

As chairman of the Senate Judiciary Committee's Subcommittee on Refugees, Ted Kennedy had been concerned for many years with the treatment of Vietnamese civilians. In the summer of 1965, his subcommittee had held its first hearings, and these were followed by further investigations in 1966 and 1967. In January, 1968, the Senator and his staff visited South Vietnam and in May issued a report that denounced the inadequate treatment of refugees and the mounting civilian casualties in Vietnam. In December, 1969, the Senator reported estimates of over 1 million civilian casualties since 1965, including 300,000 dead, most by U.S. and South Vietnamese firepower.

On the national scene, Kennedy concentrated on a widescale health insurance program to help correct the disgraceful state of American medicine. As chairman of the Senate Health Subcommittee, the Senator held hearings in the early spring of 1971. Viewing health insurance as a right, not a charity, Kennedy said, "Every individual residing in the United States will be eligible to receive benefits." Although Kennedy's plan was far ahead of the feeble, privately-geared Nixon program in meeting real needs, Teddy was also criticized for shying away from the thorny question of how medical costs can be kept down when doctors and hospitals keep raising fees. Kennedy also strongly opposed further federal funding of the SST, calling the supersonic transport "the fastest flying Edsel" and "a flying toy for the jet set." He severely criticized the SST program for its excessive costs, nonproductivity, and pollution hazards. He also introduced a bill "to provide for retraining scientists and engineers to direct their talents to social needs."

In general, we can detect in Kennedy's senatorial concerns, despite their merits, a frequent repetition of the apparently liberal, yet politically cautious, political patterns followed by the other Kennedy brothers. Vietnam, the draft, refugees, and American health costs are all essentially safe issues which build Teddy's national reputation but do not threaten either his seat or his political future. On equally important, but politically risky issues, he falls back into a familiar conservative and even reactionary position. Kennedy opposed the Equal Rights Amendment, which would guarantee American women equal rights and opportunities under the Constitution, although he tried to disguise his opposition by offering an unpassable rider for D.C. enfranchisement. Only in late 1971 did Kennedy come out for the amendment in return for help from the women's lobby on his own bills. But

Teddy's real attitudes were revealed in his remark to the president of the National Organization for Women when she testified before the Senate Judiciary subcommittee on the Equal Rights Amendment: "Do you really think this is important?" the allegedly liberal Senator asked scornfully. As feminist Gloria Steinem's new magazine *Ms.* noted in its critical rating of the 1972 presidential candidates, "Though young people may think Kennedy is a civil libertarian, half of them (the females) may be in for a rude awakening. . . . Kennedy's staff situation reflects a sexist attitude. Women held 77 per cent of the jobs on his Senate staff during the first six months of 1971 but received only 58 per cent of the total payroll. Men hold all but one of the top staff positions in his office. Hard-working women— called 'Boiler Room Girls'—keep the Kennedy machine going at the lower levels, but they get rewarded with parties, not promotions." Kennedy is also, as one would expect, a staunch opponent of any abortion reform. Even many of his apparently liberal policies do not touch on the basic problems, such as his draft reforms, which avoid outright termination, and his national health insurance policy, which is vague about who sets limits on medical costs.

The main fact of life for Edward Kennedy as a possible President, however, is not his intellectual or moral stance, but his continuing attraction as the Kennedy magician, the symbol of power and potency to whom so many Americans turn in the anguish of their own feared impotence. Only a year after Chappaquiddick, a new Kennedy momentum was getting underway. As one person close to the Senator said, "Of all the possible candidates, Teddy is the only one with charisma, glamour. He is a Kennedy, and the Kennedy name packs tremendous power. . . . Subconsciously, Teddy is keeping his options open. It's almost impossible to believe that, at the subconscious level, he is not really thinking of the Presidency. Consciously, he does not want to run."

Some observers still agreed with *The New Republic*'s TRB that "somehow or other we have always felt that he did not really seek the Presidency; that the role was being forced upon him by a kind of morbid national speculation. He could not reject it because, if he turned his back, he would feel he was somehow a traitor to his family, like one of the royal pretenders in Europe. Now he's out of the race, at least for 1972, we think; his mortifying defeat for Senate whip by reactionary Robert Byrd removes him for a time at least and he can get on with serious matters like health insurance. It may have been the best thing that ever happened to him." Many, however, felt with California's Democratic leader Jesse Unruh that "If you're a Kennedy, you don't have to be a candidate to be a candidate."

Speculations on Teddy's candidacy increased as the polls showed his rising popularity, and *Look* asked, "Will He or Won't He?": ". . . he is a man of destiny, like it or not. And he does not like it, he does not want it. Deep down, he is trapped in his own Gethsemane. He would like the chalice to pass, yet he approaches what must be with resignation. Fulfilling such a destiny will be a long and excruciating ordeal, and he shrinks from it. But when the time comes he is resolved to do his best . . . in the minds of millions of Americans, he has no choice. The White House is his legacy, his ultimate responsibility, even his debt to society. One brother was there and another was on his way there, and both were cut down by assassins' bullets. It is up to him, goes the argument of these millions, to finish the work that they began. If not in 1972, then in 1976 or 1980 or thereafter."

Whether or not Teddy will ever reach for, or win, the Democratic presidential nomination and then the election is beyond anyone's knowing at this writing. But one final view is relevant: Should Edward Kennedy ever occupy the White House, there is no reason to believe that he will be more successful than his brothers in moving beyond the self-protective imitations of action into the initiation of genuine change, which requires a broad human vision and an inner strength that only the self-actualized person can summon. In addition, as pressures increase upon Ted Kennedy—from the public, his ambitious family, and the retinue of associates who still dream of "Camelot"—the possibility increases that other Kennedy disasters, even self-inflicted accidents, may occur. Neurosis can be forgotten, but it does not vanish—either from an individual or from the national psyche—at the wave of a publicist's wand.

Chapter 13

KENNEDYISM AND AMERICA:
NATIONAL NEUROSIS
AND LEADERSHIP

ANDREA: "Unhappy is the land that breeds no hero."
GALILEO: No, Andrea. "Unhappy is the land that needs a hero."

—Bertolt Brecht, *Galileo*

. . . it is difficult to see—at least at this close range—wherein John F. Kennedy was a great President. The actual achievements of his three brief years in office were minimal. . . . Almost certainly President Kennedy will be remembered more for what he said and proposed than for what he accomplished. Unlike the Lincoln Legend, the Kennedy legend-in-the-making will be based on attributes, not achievements, on what he personified rather than on what he did. With Lincoln the legend was the man; with President Kennedy the legend is the image.

—Carey McWilliams, "The Making of the Legend," *Book World*

. . . in their unimaginative fierce way, the Kennedys continue to play successfully the game as they found it. They create illusions and call them facts, and between what they are said to be and what they are falls the shadow of all the useful words not spoken, of all the actual deeds not done. But if it is true that in a rough way nations deserve the leadership they get, then a frivolous and apathetic electorate combined with a vain and greedy intellectual establishment will most certainly restore to power the illusion-making Kennedys.

—Gore Vidal, "The Holy Family," *Esquire*

For unfortunate reasons, the nature of the man and the official record of the surviving Kennedy male are going to be irrelevant to the election process . . . in the current stage of the development of

368

the national psyche a segment of the public herd harbors a belief in the mystique of nobility. The Kennedys are the American nobility. They are judged by different standards.
—Ronald Van Doren, *Charting the Candidates '72*

ↈ

AFTER ONE HAS read some two hundred books and articles on the Kennedys and then quietly reflected on how this massive literature fits the political and psychosocial realities of the 1960s and 1970s, a general impression of the family's character begins to take shape. The over-all impression is of financial genius, total unscrupulousness, and huge ambition in the father; political brilliance and manipulative proficiency in both father and sons; and glorious rhetoric and stylish manner in all the family. But there is no lingering memory of imagination or of concern for others. There is no trace of originality in thought or action to change the nation or to transcend old patterns of leadership. Ideas that occurred to American social thinkers and activists a century before seem almost unknown to the Kennedys. Only when the *political* necessity became strong—when survival in the area of political competition and struggle came into question—did the Kennedys react to ideas in any way. And their actions, because they were not based on genuine commitment and wisdom, were nearly always reactions—superficial and limited. Caution and conventionality remained the touchstones of Kennedy politics.

The sentimentalizing of the Kennedys has largely obscured the basic immorality both of what they did (the Bay of Pigs, the arms race, the Berlin crisis, the missile crisis, the Vietnam war) and of what they left undone (racial and sexual discrimination, poverty and hunger, unfair distribution of wealth and government benefits). While the Kennedys often had compassion for individual victims, they blindly and callously created thousands of new victims (as, for instance, in Vietnam) or perpetuated old victimizations (sex, race, poverty). This immorality grew out of their individual and socially-engendered neurosis, and it was shared to a large degree by most of American society. (Thus we find similar immoralities throughout American history.) Conditioned to the acceptance of inhumanity, contemporary commentators, with few exceptions, have been unable to transcend themselves to see the underlying wrongness of so much that the Kennedys did.

Yet by words the Kennedys offered themselves as idealistic prophets of impending change that only they could effect. As Ronald Steel perceptively saw, ". . . the Kennedy record was one of great expectations rather than inspiring accomplishments . . . if ever there was a politics of hope, it was that practiced by the Kennedys. Our hope that they had a remedy for the social ills they described so graphically, their hope that we would be patient while they figured out what to do. The legacy they left is the enduring hope that somehow things would have been better were they still here."

This legacy seems to be shared by fewer Americans in the disillusionment of the 1970s than in the imperialistic optimism of the 1960s. From the growing vantage of distance, the Kennedy dynastic fantasy (which was not necessarily fantastic in its attainment, but contained large elements of unreality, both national and personal) begins to seem curiously dreamlike and extraordinary, although this fantasy has since been partially revived. While essentially the same national political and social realities are with us, we have generally grown more skeptical, even pessimistic; we no longer believe quite so readily in myths of knights on white chargers riding out to slay dragons. The constant din of Kennedy and Kennedy-like rhetoric has dulled our credulity and sharpened our skepticism. As John Kenneth Galbraith wrote in *Who Needs the Democrats?*,". . . evasion, however disguised by rhetoric, moral purpose, or soaring phrase, comes over increasingly as crap." National leadership, we are perhaps beginning to learn, must be constantly reaffirmed by a realistic scrutiny by the led.

Yet the price of liberty is not only eternal vigilance, but also sufficient emotional health and maturity to distinguish between imposed and voluntarily accepted leadership, between authoritarianism—no matter how elegant—and recognized competence. That authoritarian leadership may result even more from the inner neurotic need of the followers than from the outer pressure of self-ordained leaders makes the authority no less irrational. If the Kennedys have taught us anything in their historic rekindling of mankind's latent desire to "escape from freedom" (as Fromm put it), it is that the knights who assume magical infallibility may themselves become the dragons. Ronald Steel observed, "The last journey of Robert Kennedy marked more than the death of a leader; it was the end of a whole era of American politics—one in which it was possible to believe that good government could come from good style, that society could be changed if only the right rhetoric could be found, that a single man could correct everything that was wrong, that things would be all right if we just loved one another. It was not that the Kennedys said it would be easy. They often evoked sacrifice, hard work, and endurance. Rather it was that they nurtured our fantasies. The last fantasy was shattered with the murder of Robert Kennedy."

Unfortunately, fantasies are not so suddenly dispelled. American society is still affected by a considerable neurosis, and millions await the return of the Kennedy promise of Utopia. For the Kennedys did indeed nurture American fantasies and arouse a response from the neurotic, as well as the healthy, elements of the American character. It is healthy to want dynamic, intelligent, competent, compassionate, imaginative leaders; but it is neurotic to find such leaders among those who so patently lack these qualities. Yet a large part of the American public refused—and still refuses—to see or believe the Kennedys' flaws, even when the evidence was beyond question. For, as Steel wrote, "Kennedyism, like the Beatle-mania of the Sixties that was its cultural counterpart, was not a plot foisted on the public, but an audience response—a response that could never have occurred, whatever the public relations effort involved, had there not been a need for it." The reaction to President Kennedy was a psychohistorical parallel to the public enthusiasm aroused by Martin Luther in the sixteenth-century Reformation. As historian William Langer described the reaction to Luther, "It is inconceivable that he should have evoked so great a popular response unless he had succeeded in expressing the underlying, unconscious sentiments of large numbers of people and in providing them with an acceptable solution to their religious problem." Simply substitute "social" for "religious" and we have a true picture of the Kennedy dynamic.

Unless we understand something of the neurotic compulsions of our society, the Kennedys themselves will be incomprehensible. It is only because so many Americans to a large degree, and nearly all of us to some degree, lack a national and personal sense of certainty and self-identity that we ever turned to such quite transparent pseudo-sorcerers as the Kennedys. They have always pursued overtly their headlong quest for social affirmation and security. Yet somehow only the cold shock of Chappaquiddick, more than two decades after their unobtrusive entry into our lives (discounting the father's sporadic public career), literally washed away the cobwebby mask that had so blinded us. The public reaction to Chappaquiddick suggests how fully and furiously we unconsciously realized the extent of our self-deception. In a way, then, it is meaningless to blame the Kennedys for their superb supersalesmanship. They did not create the market; they reshaped themselves into the latest model to suit the consumer appetites of the time, and they plugged their product (Jack, Bobby, Teddy) for all it was worth—and a good deal more.

This book can hardly presume to be an analysis of the American psyche, although one is sorely needed, but it is possible to separate out from the American characterology at least a dozen strains of neurotic obsessiveness that are directly mirrored in the Kennedys, as a family and as individuals. Just as neurotic persons usually marry other neurotic persons who directly play into their neuroses, so, too, did a majority of American voters choose and delight in the all-triumphant Kennedys, who seemed to reaffirm the meaning of the qualities they sensed, consciously or unconsciously, in themselves. The list can only be drawn simply in this space, but it should suggest pertinent areas in which all of us—as individuals, voters, citizens—

should reflect more deeply. Nor should these traits be seen as separate strands of national and individual personality, for all are interwoven in action and reaction to form the over-all individual and national personality that has come to seem most typically American.

(1) *Compulsiveness:* to fight, dominate, win, be triumphant and heroic, often with a terribly intense self-destructive physical testing. This is part of the exaggerated work ethic, and also a part of

(2) *The cult of toughness* or *machismo:* an overvaluation of physical aggressiveness, force, hardihood, recklessness, violence, and sexual virility, with a concomitant scorning of the humanistic qualities of love, tenderness, gentleness, compassion, concern, nurturing. Again, this is part of the dominant element of

(3) *Sexism:* the belief that men are inherently superior to women and that women are by nature passive nurturers of males and their children. A neurotic relationship between the sexes is the direct result.

(4) *Obsessive competitiveness:* closely linked with *machismo* and the compulsiveness, especially for material success, found in many Americans. This fosters an inability to see beyond competitive triumph over others to the self-actualization that can occur only in cooperative situations of trust and spontaneity, rather than distrust, hatred, secrecy, and suspicion. As a nation, this has resulted in

(5) *The certainty of superiority* (formerly, *the White Man's Burden*): a direct cause of the intellectual and nationalistic arrogance of American foreign policy toward the Third World nations through the five postwar Administrations, culminating in the Vietnam tragedy; part of the unrealistic feeling that American technology and efficiency can do anything, resulting in acute impatience and patronizing attitudes that contain their own defeat. All the above have brought about

(6) *A lack of moral vision and courage* in acting beyond the purely selfish aims of American interests. This attitude has predominated in American policy toward Asian and Latin American countries. It is reflected in

(7) *The greed and hyperacquisitiveness* of so much of American life. Examples are rampant in the focus of most Administrations upon American business interests rather than on the welfare of the general public. Greed for money and power were also basic motivations in the Kennedys, resulting in a ruthless and often dishonest self-centeredness.

(8) All the foregoing result in *acutely disturbed human relations* and the inability to relate warmly and spontaneously to others. Closely linked is

(9) *The inability to relate creatively to oneself* and thus to achieve a strong inner identity and ultimate self-actualization and maturity. These lacks lead to

(10) *Anxiety, insecurity, depression, feelings of worthlessness*, both conscious and unconscious, which result in

(11) *Further neurotic patterns of defense*, including psychosomatic illnesses, belief in illusions (such as the Cold War demonology), images, irrational desires and fears, the feeling that constant motion equals accomplishment, and the superstition that words have magical powers. Such vicious circles cause more

(12) Self-defeat, punishment of self and others, and *the failure to achieve one's human potential*.

An underlying question is, What makes a good society? Dr. Ruth Benedict, the distinguished anthropologist who valiantly pioneered in this area, left us with one succinct idea about humanizing social arrangements: "Societies where nonaggression is conspicuous, have social orders in which the individual, by the same act and at the same time, serves his own advantage and that of the group. . . . Nonaggression occurs, not because people are unselfish and put social obligations above personal desires, but when social arrangements make these two identical. . . . Their institutions insure mutual advantage from their undertakings." The destructive societies she found to be societies "where the advantage of one individual becomes a victory over another, and the majority who are not victorious must shift as they can."

While America largely created the Kennedys, the Kennedys have helped perpetuate these neurotic national characteristics, although they had the opportunity to lead America away from many of its neurotic preoccupations. Many of the qualities that the Kennedys so amply displayed could have been used in healthy ways rather than for their own neurotic triumphs, such as their energy, self-confidence, concentration, assertiveness, physical courage, resourcefulness, informality, wit, intelligence, and exuberance. The greatest tragedy of the Kennedy neurosis was that John Kennedy had qualities that aroused the hopes of the world for change and a better life, yet his own emotional shortcomings doomed these rekindled dreams to disappointment. More than any American President since Franklin Roosevelt, Kennedy possessed the personal dynamism and visionary rhetoric, plus great personal sympathy and charm, which set human pulses quickening and imaginations soaring. His appearance was so captivating and his abilities seemed so evident that even today many refuse to recognize his great failures of leadership. Of course, his assassination inflated and enshrined Kennedy's image and made many people reluctant to think about his shortcomings.

As I. F. Stone put it with his customary forthrightness, "Of all the Presidents, this was the first to be a Prince Charming. To watch the President at press conferences or at a private press briefing was to be delighted by his wit, his intelligence, his capacity and his youth. These made the terrible flash from Dallas incredible and painful. But perhaps the truth is that in some ways John Fitzgerald Kennedy died just in time. . . . For somehow one has the feeling that in the tangled dramaturgy of events, this sudden assassination was for the author the only satisfactory way out. The Kennedy Administration was approaching an impasse, certainly at home, quite possibly abroad, from which there seemed no escape. . . . Abroad, as at home, the problems were becoming too great for conventional leadership, and Kennedy, when the tinsel was stripped away, was a conventional leader, no more than an enlightened conservative, cautious as an old man for all his youth, with a basic distrust of the people and an astringent view of the evangelical as a tool of leadership. It is as well not to lose sight of these realities in the excitement of the funeral; funerals are always occasions for pious lying. . . . In the clouds of incense thus generated, it is easy to lose one's way, just when it becomes more important than ever to see where we really are."

The saddest thing of all about the Kennedys was that they seemed to, but did not, offer the wise and compassionate leadership that America—and the world—so desperately needs. The Kennedys, and President Kennedy in particular, could have been a huge force for good around the earth, for the enlightenment and education of millions to their own real needs and highest human potentials. But because the Kennedys were not themselves genuinely self-actualizing people—because their own neurotic conflicts kept them selfish and petty and narrowly focused on themselves—they were quite unable to meet this historic challenge.

Thus it seems clearer with each passing year that the Kennedys were highly accomplished craftsmen-salesmen in the art of winning elections and creating images—and very little else. Like many modern manufacturers, the Kennedys sold a "product"—themselves—that had more shape and color than substance. Like marketing experts, they substituted glamor and psychological-sensory appeal at the point of purchase for genuine quality and durability. In the Kennedys, the American free-enterprise industrial-republic ethic culminated in the absurdity of national leaders fabricated specifically to garner the greatest gain from the existing voting market. Although political manufacturers lack the precision of a Ford assembly line, foresight and luck brought the Kennedys to a temporary high level of accuracy in meeting public specifications. Although this "market appeal" might be said to be a necessity for all politicians, those who venture into the life-and-death responsibilities of high national leadership should be reasonably equipped to bear the burden of their triumphs. In addition, the electorate should be prepared to see through inflated claims of leadership. Today's voter-consumer must become as sophisticated and rationally skeptical as today's buyer-consumer.

The Kennedys, as we have seen, were not skillful in envisioning, forming, and implementing policies, for their interests did not lie primarily in that direction. Theirs were the skills of the corporate manager who does not question his product and lives largely by group consultation, rather than the skills of the great national leader who constantly questions human priorities and values above all else, and has more confidence in his own wisdom and experience than in the expertness of too-narrow technocrats. One of John F. Kennedy's deepest failures in this respect was his acceptance of Defense Secretary McNamara's supertechnocratic and nonhumanistic guidance, a counseling that led Kennedy and his successors into the quagmire of Vietnam. Recent revelations of the secret *Pentagon Papers* have shown the voters of the 1970s just how wary a President must be in following the analyses of too-detached and too-narrow counsellors.

Neither JFK nor his brothers truly displayed the vision or the grasp of reality that can carry politics into the realm of inspired statesmanship. Trained in the techniques of manipulation and instant image, they could not see beyond immediate self-centered gain. In the psychohistorical sense, however, this first basis of Kennedy power was rational, in that it involved specific, concrete skills which, if not often admirably used, were at least understandable and could conceivably be countered by equally adroit opponents. The truth of this is suggested by the fact that eight years later Richard Nixon skillfully used the techniques of television imagery that had eluded him in 1960. This does not mean that Nixon became a better person or leader, but he definitely became a better politician. (*The Selling of the President, 1968*, by Joe McGinniss is a dismaying firsthand study of these techniques and their inherent artificiality.) As master manipulators of public opinion, the Kennedys were following an age-old tradition, although with new technologies and advanced techniques.

As McGinniss clearly saw, "Politics, in a sense, has always been a con game. The American voter, insisting upon his belief in a higher order, clings to his religion, which promises another, better life, and defends passionately the illusion that the men he chooses to lead him are of finer nature than he. It has been traditional that the successful politician honor this illusion. To succeed today, he must embellish it. Particularly if he wants to be President. 'Potential presidents are measured against an ideal that's a combination of leading man, God, father, hero, pope, king, with maybe just a touch of the

avenging Furies thrown in,' an adviser to Richard Nixon wrote in a memorandum late in 1967. Then, perhaps aware that Nixon qualified only as
father, he discussed improvements that would have to be made—not upon
Nixon himself, but upon the image of him which was received by the voter.
. . . It is not surprising, then, that politicians and advertising men should
have discovered one another. And, once they recognized that the citizen
did not so much vote for a candidate as make a psychological purchase of
him, not surprising that they began to work together."

The "psychological purchase" of the Kennedys by the American public
was also based on the undeniable fact that the Kennedy brothers have had
an enormous appeal to widely differing strata of American society. To
understand the causes and nature of that appeal, we must look critically at
our society and at ourselves as individuals. A large part of the Kennedy
magnetism, it seems evident, has been primitively emotional and on the
unconscious level of superstitious spirit-worship. The Kennedys have been
felt by millions of Americans to possess the magical powers that most of us,
in some unevolved recess of our beings, still want to find in the world. And
the more neurotically powerless we feel ourselves to be, the more we look to
objects, persons, and creeds outside ourselves to provide us with the powers
and certainty we feel we lack. This partly explains both the contemporary
fascination with astrology and with such "stars" as the Kennedys.

On a similar level, many of us look both to the stars and to such human
luminaries as the Kennedys to provide the excitement and glamor that we
feel so lacking in our monotonous, pressurized, uncertain, and anxious lives.
It is no accident that astrology and the worship of movie stars, or political
figures cast in the guise of movie stars (such as the Kennedys), have reached
parallel heights of popularity. Both are "above us," yet each offers to show
us the path to true enlightenment and direction in our daily lives, as well as
to provide a frequent stimulus for our dulled minds and senses. But such
emotional displacement cannot truly fulfill people, for the dynamic behind
such star-gazing is an inner emptiness and boredom. Human beings naturally hunger for color, meaning, change, a joy in living. Yet the imitation of
life—the glittering image—provided by the Kennedys can only increase
emotional hunger, rather than satisfying it with the means of self-actualization. A closely related and often noted element in the Kennedy fascination
is a widespread American need to live vicariously among the famous,
wealthy, and powerful. The Kennedys have supplied in abundance all the
ingredients of an American-grown royal-family-out-of-Hollywood, aided
by the sensation-starved mass media that both arouse and benumb the
general public.

The manifold roots of America's psychohistorical compulsions as a nation
can hardly be explored in this book. Indeed, we are all well aware of many

of them from our common knowledge and experience (Vietnam being only the most recent and dramatic example). But that America was ripe and ready for the Kennedys when they appeared has been widely remarked upon. Daniel Boorstin wrote in *The Image*, "We have become so accustomed to our illusions that we mistake them for reality. We demand them. And we demand that there be always more of them, bigger and better and more vivid. . . . In the last half-century we have misled ourselves . . . about men . . . and how much greatness can be found among them. . . . The deeper problems connected with advertising come less from the unscrupulousness of our 'deceivers' than from our pleasure in being deceived, less from the desire to seduce than from the desire to be seduced. . . ."

The basis of JFK's magical appeal as a growing legend was irrational in that it did not rest on the reason and judgment of the electorate, but rather on the citizens' own irrational fears and doubts. The increasing "charisma" of the Kennedy sons was not an indication of their personal growth, but rather a gauge of the troubled dimensions of what might be seen as a national neurosis. The Kennedys, in effect, became a new religion and opiate for much of America. Only this diagnosis can fully explain the deification of Jack Kennedy and the subsequent transformation of his brothers, Bobby and Teddy, into demi-gods. The less faith Americans had in themselves, the more irrational faith they invested in the Kennedys.

As Fawn Brodie described this psycho-political phenomenon, "The choice of qualities of a nation's heroes is a reliable index to that nation's health. This is particularly true of political heroes rather than poets or actors or even the first men on the moon. For it is the statesmen who have made an impact on the nation's political and emotional life, men who have been followed with passionate idolatry and attacked with consuming hatred—heroes of the quality of Washington, Jefferson, Lincoln, and Franklin Roosevelt, and men of potential heroic stature like John and Robert Kennedy—who have a continuing vitality in the fantasies of a large segment of the American people."

A New York public relations firm expressed during the 1968 campaign the leadership mystique which is so imbued in the American people: "The American crisis is not the war in Vietnam, nor rioting in the cities, nor inflation, nor deterioration of respect among our friends, nor any specific. It is a failure of leadership. WHAT IS A LEADER? A leader is bold, aggressive, positive, creative. . . . Despite the computerized complexities of modern life, the leader in his field is still the emergent hero. And America is, has been and (God willing) always will be hungry for heroes. Her treatment of them . . . from Lincoln to Babe Ruth to Martin Luther King amounts almost to canonization, so deeply is the need felt. Who among us is up to this?"

Who indeed? A former White House assistant, George Reedy, has cast a refreshingly cool and critical eye on the nature of our country's most august office and what it does to its occupant. In *The Twilight of the Presidency*, Reedy wrote bitingly, "The White House does not provide an atmosphere in which idealism and devotion can flourish. Below the president is a mass of intrigue, posturing, strutting, cringing, and pious 'commitment' to irrelevant windbaggery. It is designed as the perfect setting for the conspiracy of mediocrity—that all too frequently successful collection of the untalented, the unpassionate, and the insincere seeking to convince the public that it is brilliant, compassionate, and dedicated. . . . It is not that the people who compose the menage are any worse than any other collection of human beings. It is rather that the White House is an ideal cloak for intrigue, pomposity, and ambition. No nation of free men should ever permit itself to be governed from a hallowed shrine where the meanest lust for power can be sanctified and the dullest wit greeted with reverential awe."

Apropos of Reedy's observations on the White House, we should be more aware of the astonishing naiveté and intimidation of the Kennedy-watchers and the vast ignorance of the Kennedy historians—including those in residence. Reporters and writers have swooned in print over the Kennedys, but is it really so impressive and awe-inspiring when a Senator or a President supports a good bill or gives an intelligible speech or behaves charmingly at a social function? Is this not what one would routinely expect of any sort of leadership? Is it so amazing that a leader should write a respectable book or talk knowledgeably to heads of nations or win elections or travel to different countries? One of the most astonishing aspects of the Kennedy literature is how awestruck the authors generally seem to be. It is as though they expected most leaders to be stupid, dishonest, and lazy; and when a mortal politician acts halfway intelligent and decent, they applaud him as a superman. If he is good-looking, brave, and eccentric (surely not rare characteristics in either sex), the awe turns to outright veneration. The Kennedy literature, in general, is a good example of mediocrity in social observation and a curious revelation of childlike expectations. Perhaps a large part of the problem is that there was not all that much to report upon. If the subject matter is lacking in depth, so, too, is apt to be the reporting.

The gaps in historical awareness surrounding the Kennedys have also been striking. (For a general antidote I can recommend a quick taste of E. H. Carr's fruit of much observation, *What Is History?*) While John Kennedy's court historians painstakingly traced the accumulation of presidential wisdom, they resolutely ignored half the country's population, as did Kennedy himself. I am referring, of course, to Women, Child Care, Sex Discrimination, the Equal Rights Amendment, and other subjects that do not appear in the indexes to books about the Kennedys, although they are part of American social reality. In the Kennedy historiography these subjects are never mentioned. Similarly, it was only when the black leadership forced the Negro presence on the Kennedys—and society as a whole—that our social and political history began to include the 11 percent of America that happened to be black. The poor have yet to achieve a voice.

Underlying America's continuing need for hero-worship is the fact that humanity has largely lost—or perhaps never discovered—a rational faith in the natural goodness, reason, and powers innate in ourselves and other human beings. Instead, people continually turn to irrational faith in superior authority figures, such as the Kennedys. Erich Fromm clearly stated our modern dilemma in *Man for Himself:* "Man cannot live without faith. The crucial question for our own generation and the next ones is whether this faith will be an irrational faith in leaders, machines, success, or the rational faith in man based on the experience of our own productive activity."

Behind their heroic postures, the Kennedys, too, suffered from this widespread lack of rational faith in humanity and in themselves. Historic developments as well as their personal psychology made the Kennedy sons both victors and victims. Like the rest of us, they could not escape the revolutionary degree to which contemporary thought and feeling have broken away from the past dependence on moral absolutes. The eighteenth-century belief in the power of reason and the inevitability of progress gave way to the nineteenth-century belief in materialistic and commercial values, undergirded by theological certainties. But with the advent of Darwin, Marx, Freud, and Einstein, these certainties collapsed into a moral relativism shored up by a dependence on scientific-industrial technology, but prey to great doubt as to where that technology was taking us. Thus we have looked increasingly to our leaders, rather than to ourselves, and especially to leaders felt to possess some godlike, magical powers with which to lead us out of our anxieties and profound uncertainties into a glorious future.

Yet I believe that today we have reached a point in psychohistorical knowledge where we can turn with a certainty never before possible to the strengths and inherent powers that we possess as individuals. If it seems like flying in the face of reality to talk of individual strength at a time when individuals seem to feel increasingly helpless, I can only respond that appearances are often extraordinarily deceiving. The vital genuine advances made in bringing more people into the mainstream of American life—such as universal education, work safeguards and limitations against exploitation by employers, legal and political rights for women, and the semi-leisure that has accompanied our relative affluence—have made it truly possible for the first time in history for a majority of citizens to participate in a nation's processes of power. That this has not yet come to pass does not mean that it will not.

The theme of equality must underlie all great social changes. But dependence upon mythical "leaders" such as the Kennedys will not lead the dispossessed to the land of equal opportunity, unless the leaders show themselves to be genuinely part of the people, and genuinely capable of leadership based on a concern for others and for equality. This the Kennedys never did. They were not raised to have broad social imaginations and did not undergo the experiences which might have developed such outlooks. While the Kennedys rightly felt bitterly dispossessed in one sense—as social equals of the ruling upper classes—this feeling of inferiority led to a neurotic passion for prideful assertion and dominance that was always focused most intensively upon themselves. In a word, the Kennedys saw power as a means of raising themselves; not, in any meaningful degree, as a means of raising the people. Despite all the Kennedys said they wanted to do, there has been very little in their actions to prove the integrity of their social language.

We should all emerge from this study of the Kennedys, whether we agree with it or not, with an increased desire to study ourselves and our leaders. I hope that I have suggested some specific methods to make our analyses more relevant to reality. If we approach our leaders with the moral relativism of "all politicians make promises they can't carry out," we will get nowhere. While it is true that politicians cannot speak their minds fully on all occasions (as can none of us) and must constantly balance the desirable against the possible, it is also true that there are specific standards of honesty and consistency that should be demanded of them. Truth may have to be tempered with discretion, but it does not have to be hidden, distorted, or destroyed. In the long run, if a politician has no specific truth to uphold his views and sustain his policies, then assuredly he is not the sort of politician who will make his country more livable and more human.

We must demand deeds as well as words, and base our judgments more upon records than upon rhetoric. The cult of personality that has hypnotized Americans so often will disappear when we begin to use the lessons of psychology and history to assess the maturity of candidates for office. We must demand evidence and proof, the empiricism used so successfully by the physical sciences, and dismiss as "very nice but hardly relevant" the fashionable glamor of certain candidates. We must, in short, have the emotional maturity to see through and reject the style and blandishments of leaders and candidates who have little else to offer. For only as we grow and mature ourselves, I believe, can American democracy truly "come of age." Louis Gottschalk expressed a similar thought in *Understanding History:* "A better and more lasting patriotism can be inculcated by a frank and unabashed preaching of democratic ideals as a faith. . . . Our ideals, not a series of frail mortals, ought to be held up to our school children as the foundation of our national creed. . . ."

Yet a grave danger remains. This is simply the possibility that time may run out before we learn to weigh our leaders and Presidents more rationally. The President of the United States has incredible power over the world, a power which we are only beginning to apprehend dimly. The President—with enough nuclear power at his disposal to blow up the world or to propel this country into a mutual suicidal nuclear holocaust with another nation—has become far more than the Chief Executive. Richard Neustadt describes the essence of contemporary presidential power: "The President remains our system's Great Initiator. When what we once called 'war' impends, he now becomes our system's Final Arbiter. He is no less a clerk in one capacity than in the other. But in the second instance those he serves are utterly dependent on his *judgment*—and judgment then becomes the mark of 'leadership.' Command may have a narrow reach but it encompasses irreparable consequences. Yet persuasion is required to exercise command, to get one's hands upon subordinate decisions. With this so-nearly absolute dependence upon presidential judgment backed by presidential skill, we and our system have no previous experience. Now in the Sixties we begin to explore it. Hopefully, both citizens and Presidents will do so without fear or histrionics, or withdrawals from reality, or lurches toward aggression. Regardless of the dangers, presidential power even in this new dimension still has to be sought and used; it cannot be escaped. We now are even more dependent than before upon the mind and temperament of the man in the White House."

This is a frightening picture when we consider how limited was the experiential and emotional background of a President such as John F. Kennedy, a man who dawdled and played his way through three terms as a U.S. Congressman and only grew serious when the presidency became a prize to be won. But the Kennedy aim was always a Kennedy political victory, not social justice for America's forgotten majority. Yet the Kennedy mystique can also be seen as essentially the outcome of some four thousand years of the Graeco-Judeo-Christian ethos which has directed and energized Western civilization, and which has now spread over the world. This philosophy embodies—with good and bad results—the ideas of the conquest of nature and death through obsessive activism and human competition. The only significant difference between the Kennedys and most of their contemporaries has been the Kennedys' wealth and their singleness of purpose. And an obsession with wealth, power, and status is the logical outcome of the irrationalities of Western civilization as a whole. While wealth and singleness of purpose are neither good nor bad per se, they must be accompanied by a maturity of spirit, which sets limits, evaluates priorities, and values human life and relationships far more than material and social conquest. But it is just these mature qualities which I believe both Western civilization and the Kennedys—as the epitome of the most dominant aspects of that civilization—have so sorely lacked.

Our national malady was perceptively diagnosed by Daniel Boorstin: "Nowadays everybody tells us that what we need is more belief, a stronger and deeper and more encompassing faith. A faith in America and in what we are doing. That may be true in the long run. What we need first and now is to disillusion ourselves. What ails us most is not what we have done with America, but what we have substituted for America. We suffer primarily not from our vices or our weaknesses, but from our illusions. We are haunted, not by reality, but by those images we have put in place of reality." All neurotics unconsciously substitute illusion for reality in an effort to gratify childish needs. When neurotic nations are led by neurotic leaders, the illusions only grow worse, the irrationalities more difficult to penetrate, understand, and outgrow. In place of real leadership, a large number of Americans eagerly accepted the image handed to them by the self-serving Kennedys. In this respect, millions of Americans have shared (and probably continue to share) with the Kennedys their appetite for illusion.

Throughout this book I have used the words "obsession" and "compulsion," and tried to indicate the manifold ways in which such unconscious emotional drives influenced and even determined the behavior of individual Kennedys in power. Both Western civilization as a whole and the Kennedys as a product of that civilization have suffered—and continue to suffer—profound emotional conflicts and ambivalences that have led to profoundly neurotic and self-defeating patterns of attitude and behavior. In this century alone, we have seen and lived through the terrible wars engendered by underlying psychopathological trends that exist in many—perhaps most—human cultures, and today we live under the threat of instant nuclear annihilation.

The great patterns of history are too large for any of us to grasp in more than a limited sense, either intellectually or emotionally. Yet we must continually make the effort to understand their effects on our lives and our era. By studying the lives of national leaders, such as the Kennedys, we can find reflections of our own search for identity and confirmation, and help change both ourselves and our nation toward maturity and health rather than neurosis. In short, we must refuse to be intimidated by power, glamor, and wealth, refuse to surrender to our immature needs for total security and all-protective parental authority figures. As citizens, we must be far more willing to live with and endure our personal anxieties if we are to develop greater personal strengths and the capacity to select more mature, responsive, and responsible national leaders. We must be willing and able to give up our own childhoods and demand that our leaders do likewise.

NOTES

1 The Kennedys and Psychohistory, pages 1–19

For the general psychological background to this chapter I am most indebted to the late Karen Horney, a brilliant and compassionate pioneering psychoanalyst of great literary as well as analytic gifts; to the humanistic psychology of the late Abraham Maslow; and to the continuing insights and lucid phrasing of Erich Fromm, who has applied his psychoanalytic understandings so profoundly to social and political realities.

PAGE

1   *"In the White House"*: George E. Reedy, *The Twilight of the Presidency* (New York: New American Library, 1970), 30.

1   *"The psyche of the President"*: Michael Harrington, "Does Nixon Have the Stuff?" Washington *Evening Star* (May 19, 1970).

1   *"The public wants to know"*: William V. Shannon, *The Heir Apparent: Robert Kennedy and the Struggle for Power* (New York: Macmillan, 1967), 41.

1   *"The sins of the fathers"*: Ronald V. Sampson, *The Psychology of Power* (London: Heinemann, 1965), 113.

1   *"Daddy was always"*: qtd in Richard J. Whalen, *The Founding Father: The Story of Joseph P. Kennedy* (New York: New American Library, 1964), 95.

2   *"today Kennedy dead"*: Gore Vidal, "The Holy Family," *Esquire* (April, 1967), 99.

5   *"The moral law"*: Sampson, *op. cit.*, 1–2.

6   *"When we speak"*: Erich Fromm, *Man for Himself: An Inquiry into the Psychology of Ethics* (New York: Holt, 1947), 19.

6   *"craving for prestige"*: Samuel J. Warner, *Self-Realization and Self-Defeat* (New York: Grove, 1966), 62–63.

8   *"the desire to become"*: qtd in Frank Goble, *The Third Force: The Psychology of Abraham Maslow* (New York: Grossman, 1970), 41.

9   *"no accidents in politics"*: Whalen, *op. cit.*, 451.
9   *"examples to demonstrate"*: Hannah Arendt, *On Violence* (New York: Harcourt, 1970), 86.
10   *"these contradictions"*: Karen Horney, *The Neurotic Personality of Our Time* (New York: Norton, 1937), 289–90.
13   *"If any organism"*: Rollo May, *Man's Search for Himself* (New York: Norton, 1953), 95.
14   *"Only the individual"*: Karen Horney, *Neurosis and Human Growth* (New York: Norton, 1952), 18.
15   *"In his* Castle": Erich Fromm, *Escape from Freedom* (New York: Avon, 1965), 154.
17   *"the effort to make psychiatry"*: Arnold A. Rogow, *The Psychiatrists* (New York: Putnam, 1970), 147–48.
18   *"Clinton as an adult"*: William B. Willcox, *Portrait of a General: Sir Henry Clinton in the War of Independence* (New York: Knopf, 1964), 511.

2 Growing Up Competitive, pages 20–44

Biographical material on Joseph P. Kennedy and his forebears is drawn largely from Richard J. Whalen, *The Founding Father: The Story of Joseph P. Kennedy*, and Joseph F. Dinneen, *The Kennedy Family*. Mr. Whalen's carefully written book remains the single best source on the Kennedys and an indispensable study for all Kennedy historians. Mr. Dinneen's book, while superficial and highly laudatory, contains interesting supplemental material that unwittingly supports the thesis of egregious Kennedy competitiveness. William F. Duncliffe's *Life and Times of Joseph P. Kennedy* was also useful. These sources have been supplemented by William V. Shannon's insightful *American Irish* and by more general works.

20   *"I don't think much"*: qtd in Victor Lasky, *JFK: The Man and the Myth* (New York: Macmillan, 1963), 26.
20   *"The measure of a man's success"*: qtd in Richard J. Whalen, *The Founding Father: The Story of Joseph P. Kennedy* (New York: New American Library, 1964), 31.
20   *"Remember"*: qtd in William J. Duncliffe, *The Life and Times of Joseph P. Kennedy* (New York: Macfadden, 1965), 34.
20   *"For the Kennedys"*: qtd in Whalen, *op. cit.*, 440.
20   *"the true virtue of human beings"*: John Stuart Mill, *The Subjection of Women*; reprinted in *On Liberty, Representative Government, The Subjection of Women* (Oxford: Oxford University Press, 1952), 479.
20   *"the founding father"*: Kenneth Lamott, *The Moneymakers: The Great Big New Rich in America* (New York: Bantam, 1970), 105, 106.
21   *Hobbesian-Darwinian core*: The effects of Hobbesian and Darwinian thought in America are discussed in Richard Hofstadter, *Social Darwinism in American Thought* (Boston: Beacon, 1967).

23 *"Three generations"*: Joseph F. Dinneen, *The Kennedy Family* (Boston: Little, Brown, 1959), 3–4.
23 *"A severe look"*: Whalen, *op. cit.*, 28.
24 *"this egocentric assumption"*: Ronald V. Sampson, *The Psychology of Power* (London: Heinemann, 1965), 97.
24 *ward heelers*: Whalen, *op. cit.*, 29.
24 *Boston Latin School*: *Ibid.*, 31–32.
25 *"The first time I saw Joe"*: qtd in *Ibid.*, 33.
25 *"Joe was the kind of guy"*: qtd in *Ibid.*, 37.
26 *learning the inside ways of business*: *Ibid.*, 40–117.
29 *"I am not ashamed"*: Joseph P. Kennedy, *I'm for Roosevelt* (New York: Reynal and Hitchcock, 1936), 3.
29 *"He had no political philosophy"*: Whalen, *op. cit.*, 115–16.
32 *"I can't take criticism"*: qtd in *Ibid.*, 347.
32 *according to one Cape Cod historian*: Leo Damore, *The Cape Cod Years of John Fitzgerald Kennedy* (Englewood Cliffs, N.J.: Prentice-Hall, 1967), 24–25.
33 *"Rose Kennedy showed"*: Pearl S. Buck, *The Kennedy Women: A Personal Appraisal* (New York: Cowles, 1970), 176.
35 *"With the thought"*: Lamott, *op. cit.*, 108.
35 *"the most elaborate"*: Whalen, *op. cit.*, 389.
36 *"When you've beaten him"*: qtd in *Ibid.*, 408.
36 *the patriarch supplied the campaign's . . . direction*: qtd in *Ibid.*, 409, 411.
37 *"the most methodical"*: qtd in *Ibid.*, 411.
37 *"At last, the Fitzgeralds"*: qtd in *Ibid.*, 423.
37 *"I knew Adlai"*: qtd in *Ibid.*, 431.
37 *"God was still with him"*: qtd in *Ibid.*, 433.
38 *"Jack is the greatest"*: qtd in *Ibid.*, 434.
38 *"If we can get"*: qtd in *Ibid.*, 436.
38 *"but I'm seventy-two"*: qtd in *Ibid.*, 438.
38 *"Jack and Bob"*: *Ibid.*, 444.
39 *"I didn't think"*: qtd in *Ibid.*, 449.
39 *key Cabinet appointments*: *Ibid.*, 454.
39 *"What the hell"*: qtd in *Ibid.*, 456.
39 *Kennedy . . . was paralyzed*: *Ibid.*, 467, qtd 468.
40 *"Look I spent"*: qtd in *Ibid.*, 461.
40 *election night*: *Ibid.*, 465.
41 *tribute*: *New York Times* (November 21, 1969).
42 *"You always had to hold"*: qtd in Whalen, *op. cit.*, 173.
42 *"I like Joe Kennedy"*: qtd in *Ibid.*, 461.
42 *"Am I"*: Karen Horney, *Neurosis and Human Growth* (New York: Norton, 1952), 188.
42 *"He may be"*: *Ibid.*, 193.
42 *"Kennedy had a pessimistic view"*: Whalen, *op. cit.*, 375.
43 *"If Joe liked you"*: qtd in *Ibid.*, 374.

3 Growing Up Disciplined, pages 45–70

The only full-length biography of Rose Kennedy to date is Gail Cameron's *Rose: A Biography of Rose Fitzgerald Kennedy*, a highly laudatory account, in general, although it does not reach the ecstatic absurdities of Pearl S. Buck's *The Kennedy Women: A Personal Appraisal*. Miss Cameron does provide significant and little-known facts about Rose's father and her childhood that underline the neurotic psychodynamics of her upbringing. Although she avoids any real analysis, she is one of the few writers to mention the possibility of a harmful obsessive control over the children and how Rose helped "program" them toward hyperactive competition.

Essential to an understanding of Rose's background is John Henry Cutler's biography of her father, *"Honey Fitz": Three Steps to the White House; The Life and Times of John F. (Honey Fitz) Fitzgerald*. Cutler, a veteran Boston political reporter, followed Boston politics and Fitzgerald's flamboyant career closely.

Other useful sources are Richard J. Whalen, *The Founding Father: The Story of Joseph P. Kennedy*; James MacGregor Burns, *John Kennedy: A Political Profile*; Joe McCarthy, *The Remarkable Kennedys*; Joseph Dinneen, *The Kennedy Family*; and Mary Barelli Gallagher, *My Life with Jacqueline Kennedy*.

45   *"I grew up"*: qtd in Victor Lasky, *J.F.K.: The Man and the Myth* (New York: Macmillan, 1963), 69.

45   *"We would try"*: qtd in Gail Cameron, *Rose: A Biography of Rose Fitzgerald Kennedy* (New York: Putnam, 1971), 86.

45   *"Whatever his religion"*: Rose Kennedy, "Giving Children the Gifts of Faith and Courage," *Ladies' Home Journal* (December, 1969), 60.

45   *"In the America of today"*: Erik Erikson, *Young Man Luther* (New York: Norton, 1958), 65.

46   *"I'm going to be eighty"*: qtd in Fred Sparks, "Rose Kennedy's Determined Coaching Kept Ted in Ball Game," *Hartford Courant* (July 12, 1970).

46   *"The authentic child"*: Alan DeWitt Button, *The Authentic Child* (New York: Random House, 1969), 13.

46   *"at last"*: qtd in James MacGregor Burns, *John Kennedy: A Political Profile* (New York: Harcourt, 1960), 21.

49   *pathetic incident*: John Henry Cutler, *"Honey Fitz": Three Steps to the White House; The Life and Times of John F. (Honey Fitz) Fitzgerald* (New York: Bobbs-Merrill, 1962), 170–73.

50   *"a bundle of dynamos"*: *Ibid.*

50   *"I want my home"*: *Ibid.*

50   *an amusing anecdote*: *Ibid.*, 170.

51   *Rose's childhood*: Cameron, *op. cit.*, 38–39.

51   *"dear old North End"*: Cutler, *op. cit.*, 43.

52   *"chokingly sentimental details"*: *Ibid.*, 42.

52   *"Work harder"*: *Ibid.*, 51.

52   *"The President must deceive"*: qtd in Cutler, *op. cit.*, 93.
53   *"According to . . . Doyle"*: qtd in Lasky, *op. cit.*, 33.
53   *"I am preparing three addresses"*: qtd in *Ibid.*, 34.
53   *"Fitzie discovered"*: qtd in Joseph F. Dinneen, *The Kennedy Family* (Boston: Little, Brown, 1959), 7–8.
54   *to meet President William McKinley*: Cutler, *op. cit.*, 66.
56   *"On pleasant days"*: qtd in Dinneen, *op. cit.*, 35.
56   *"I used to have a ruler"*: qtd in Richard J. Whalen, *The Founding Father: The Story of Joseph P. Kennedy* (New York: New American Library, 1964), 65.
56   *"Hot water"*: qtd in *Ibid.*, 93.
57   *"She would leave"*: qtd in *Ibid.*, 64–65.
57   *"I don't think I know anyone"*: qtd in *Ibid.*, 430.
58   *"Years ago"*: qtd in *Ibid.*, 164.
58   *"Tell me"*: qtd in *Ibid.*, 392.
58   *the Kennedys' new importance*: *Ibid.*, 252, 202.
59   *"She was terribly religious"*: qtd in Burns, *op. cit.*, 21.
59   *"If anybody"*: qtd in Joe McCarthy, *The Remarkable Kennedys* (New York: Dial, 1960), 54.
59   *"reserved and shy"*: Hank Searls, *The Lost Prince: Young Joe, the Forgotten Kennedy* (New York: New American Library, 1969), 33.
59   *"If I tried to tell you"*: qtd in McCarthy, *op. cit.*, 55.
60   *"obviously disoriented"*: qtd in Burton Hersh, "The Thousand Days of Edward M. Kennedy," *Esquire* (February, 1972), 152.
62   *"there was not a more resourceful"*: Cutler, *op. cit.*, 83.
62   *"Now, let me tell you"*: qtd in McCarthy, *op. cit.*, 135.
62   *Rose gave one of her . . . "speeches"*: qtd in Leo Damore, *The Cape Cod Years of John Fitzgerald Kennedy* (Englewood Cliffs, N.J.: Prentice-Hall, 1967), 114.
62   *"She's a natural politician"*: qtd in Theodore C. Sorensen, *Kennedy* (New York: Harper, 1965), 37.
63   *"She damn well knows"*: qtd in Cameron, *op. cit.*, 53.
63   *"But for Rose"*: *Ibid.*
63   *"There is no more rewarding career"*: qtd in Murray B. Levin, *Kennedy Campaigning: The System and the Style as Practiced by Senator Edward Kennedy* (Boston: Beacon Press, 1966), 157, n. 20.
65   *Rose Kennedy's philosophy for meeting tragedy*: "The Durable Matriarch," *Time* (August 8, 1969), 15.
65   *irreverent reporter*: Deedee Moore, "Joan Kennedy Grows Up," *Cosmopolitan* (November, 1970), 138.
66   *"Ann-Margret"*: qtd in Fred Sparks, "Rose Has Ted Counting Calories, Drinks in Search for New Image," *Hartford Courant* (July 16, 1970).
66   *"Whenever there are older boys"*: qtd in *Ibid.*
68   *"I will never allow myself to be vanquished"*: Rose Kennedy, *op. cit.*, 120.

4 Joseph Patrick Kennedy, Jr., pages 71–97

Two books have been invaluable for biographical information on Joseph P. Kennedy, Jr., and his disastrous final flight: Hank Searls, *The Lost Prince: Young Joe, the Forgotten Kennedy*, and Jack Olsen, *Aphrodite: Desperate Mission*. Neither explores Joe's psychology in any depth, but both provide ample grounds for such speculation.

The impressions these books give of Joe Junior are supported and supplemented by material in Richard J. Whalen, *The Founding Father: The Story of Joseph P. Kennedy*; Joe McCarthy, *The Remarkable Kennedys*; Joseph F. Dinneen, *The Kennedy Family*; Bruce Lee, *JFK: Boyhood to White House*; Leo Damore, *The Cape Cod Years of John Fitzgerald Kennedy*; and James MacGregor Burns, *John Kennedy: A Political Profile*.

71 *"The pyramid"*: Richard J. Whalen, *The Founding Father: The Story of Joseph P. Kennedy* (New York: New American Library, 1964), 350.

71 *"It was Joe"*: qtd in William V. Shannon, *The Heir Apparent: Robert Kennedy and the Struggle for Power* (New York: Macmillan, 1967), 43.

71 *"I think that"*: qtd in Whalen, *op. cit.*, 365.

71 *"He had a pugnacious personality"*: James MacGregor Burns, *John Kennedy: A Political Profile* (New York: Harcourt, 1960), 28.

72 *"I always felt"*: qtd in Joseph F. Dinneen, *The Kennedy Family* (Boston: Little, Brown, 1959), 37–38.

74 *"hell-raiser"*; *"couldn't pass a hat"*: qtd in Leo Damore, *The Cape Cod Years of John Fitzgerald Kennedy* (Englewood Cliffs, N.J.: Prentice-Hall, 1967), 26.

76 *"She doesn't need one"*: qtd in Gail Cameron, *Rose: A Biography of Rose Fitzgerald Kennedy* (New York: Putnam, 1971), 86.

76 *"he was very good"*: qtd in Hank Searls, *The Lost Prince: Young Joe, the Forgotten Kennedy* (New York: New American Library, 1969), 96.

77 *"rugged and fearless"*: qtd in Damore, *op. cit.*, 26.

78 *"Behind his flashing smile"*: Searls, *op. cit.*, 60.

78 *"He was roughhousing"*: qtd in *Ibid.*, 63.

78 *"Joe is still"*: qtd in *Ibid.*, 64.

79 *The Laskis on Joe Junior*: qtd in *Ibid.*, 71, 77.

80 *"In a room full of experts"*: qtd in *Ibid.*, 72, 77.

81 *"the kind of guy"*: qtd in *Ibid.*, 83.

83 *"Today Joe would be"*: *Ibid.*, 94.

83 *"a slight detachment"*: qtd in *Ibid.*, 97.

83 *"Nobody's going to high-pressure me"*: qtd in *Ibid.*, 102.

85 *"Joe liked the racetrack"*: qtd in *Ibid.*, 120.

85 *"Joe—like all of the Kennedys"*: qtd in *Ibid.*, 125.

86 *career at Harvard Law School*: qtd in *Ibid.*, 148, 149, 153.

88 *"as previously undefeated contender"*: *Ibid.*, 181–82.

88 *"he stood for perfection"*: qtd in *Ibid.*, 194.

89 *"almost too handsome"*: *Ibid.*, 16.

89   *Joe's . . . amorous reputation*: *Ibid.*, 149, qtd 149–50.
89   *training . . . for ocean and English Channel duty*: qtd in *Ibid.*, 200, 201.
90   *a tactless toast that omitted Joe*: qtd in *Ibid.*, 202–3.
91   *"the girl with the sky-blue eyes"*: *Ibid.*, 207.
92   *"Never did anyone"*: qtd in *Ibid.*, 230.
92   *"no-nonsense guy"*: qtd in *Ibid.*, 234.
93   *"volunteered immediately"*: *Ibid.*, 238.
94   *Jack Olsen's account*: Jack Olsen, *Aphrodite: Desperate Mission* (New
        York: Putnam, 1970), 219–20, qtd 222, 224.
97   *"You may not have heard"*: qtd in *Ibid.*, 315.

5 The Making and Selling of Jack, pages 98–122

For the details of John F. Kennedy's early years, wartime experiences, and
election to Congress, I have relied primarily on Richard J. Whalen, *The
Founding Father: The Story of Joseph P. Kennedy*; James MacGregor Burns,
John Kennedy: A Political Profile; Joe McCarthy, *The Remarkable Kennedys*;
Bruce Lee, *JFK: Boyhood to White House*; Joseph F. Dinneen, *The Kennedy
Family*; William R. Manchester, *Portrait of a President: John F. Kennedy in
Profile*; Victor Lasky, *JFK: The Man and the Myth*; Robert J. Donovan,
PT-109: John F. Kennedy in World War II; and Paul B. Fay, Jr., *The Pleasure
of His Company*.

98   *"Jack hates to lose"*: qtd in Victor Lasky, *JFK: The Man and the
         Myth* (New York: Macmillan, 1963), 68.
98   *"I thought everybody"*: qtd in Joe McCarthy, *The Remarkable Ken-
         nedys* (New York: Dial, 1960), 19.
98   *"I got Jack into politics"*: qtd in Richard J. Whalen, *The Founding
         Father: The Story of Joseph P. Kennedy* (New York: New American
         Library, 1964), 392.
98   *"It was like being drafted"*: qtd in *Ibid.*, 392.
98   *"We're going to sell Jack"*: qtd in *Ibid.*, 434.
99   *"The children argued"*: qtd in Joseph F. Dinneen, *The Kennedy
         Family* (Boston: Little, Brown, 1959), 37.
99   *"Neither Jack nor Joe"*: qtd in Bruce Lee, *JFK: Boyhood to White
         House* (New York: Crest, 1964), 17.
100   *"You had to remember"*: qtd in *Ibid.*, 28.
100   *headfirst into a barbed-wire fence*: Dinneen, *op. cit.*, 168.
100   *plowed into a rose bush*: William Manchester, *Portrait of a President:
         John F. Kennedy in Profile* rev. ed. (Boston: Little, Brown, 1967),
         179.
100   *"By and large"*: qtd in Lasky, *op. cit.*, 67.
101   *Jack's carelessness with personal possessions*: Manchester, *op. cit.*, 97;
         Lasky, *op. cit.*, 104.
101   *"careless in keeping track of things,"* *"He was always forgetting things"*:
         Evelyn Lincoln, *My Twelve Years with John F. Kennedy* (New
         York: McKay, 1965), 21–23.

103   *"stream of words and ideas"*: *Ibid.*, 20.
104   *impatience with his wife*: *Ibid.*, 36.
104   *"The Senator liked to take the wheel"*: *Ibid.*, 31–32.
104   *At Canterbury School*: qtd in James MacGregor Burns, *John Kennedy: A Political Profile* (New York: Harcourt, 1960), 25, qtd 24.
105   *"he is casual and disorderly"*: qtd in Whalen, *op. cit.*, 166.
105   *"His letters home"*: Burns, *op. cit.*, 26.
105   *"Maybe Dad thinks I am alibing"*: qtd in *Ibid.*, 26–27.
105   *"definitely decided"*: qtd in *Ibid.*, 27.
105   *"great satisfaction"*: qtd in *Ibid.*, 27.
107   *"almost reached the German level"*: A. J. P. Taylor, *English History 1914–1945* (New York: Oxford, 1965), 410.
107   *"You would be surprised"*: qtd in Whalen, *op. cit.*, 289.
110   *"Wherever he was"*: Burns, *op. cit.*, 26.
110   *"who was driving"*: Lee, *op. cit.*, 47–48.
111   *"once received a low rating"*: Manchester, *op. cit.*, 48.
111   *shafting the dock*: Robert J. Donovan, *PT-109: John F. Kennedy in World War II* (New York: McGraw-Hill, 1961), 74–75.
112   *a Japanese destroyer rammed his boat*: *Ibid.*, 142–45.
113   *"there were . . . sceptics"*: Lasky, *op. cit.*, 84.
114   *Kennedy's political pep talk*: Paul B. Fay, Jr., *The Pleasure of His Company* (New York: Harper, 1966), 17–21.
115   *"Kennedy did not feel"*: Donovan, *op. cit.*, 216.
115   *"Working against Jap barges"*: qtd in McCarthy, *op. cit.*, 100–101.
117   *"What do you want to do?"*: qtd in Donovan, *op. cit.*, 158.
117   *"Kennedy is bland"*: Manchester, *op. cit.*, 143.
117   *"If that human Kennedy"*: Tom Wicker, *Kennedy without Tears* (New York: Morrow, 1964), 23.
117   *"was even less committed"*: Burns, *op. cit.*, 263–64.
118   *"in his family"*: *Ibid.*, 35.
119   *"there was an elusive detachment"*: qtd in Lasky, *op. cit.*, 5.
120   *the political mantle fell . . . upon Jack*: Fay, *op. cit.*, 152.
120   *"Kennedy! How can he lose?"*: qtd in Dinneen, *op. cit.*, 123.
121   *Joe Kennedy ran the show*: qtd in Whalen, *op. cit.*, 387–89.
121   *"It takes three things"*: qtd in *Ibid.*, 390.
121   *"Even on this safe ground"*: *Ibid.*
121   *"the kind of progressive representative"*: qtd in *Ibid.*, 390–91.
121   *"That reception"*: qtd in *Ibid.*, 392.

6 Steppingstone to the White House, pages 123–153

For information on John Kennedy's career in Congress I have relied mainly on Theodore C. Sorensen, *Kennedy*; Richard J. Whalen, *The Founding Father: The Story of Joseph P. Kennedy*; James MacGregor Burns, *John Kennedy: A Political Profile*; and Evelyn Lincoln, *My Twelve Years with John F. Kennedy*.

123   *"After all, I wasn't equipped"*: Victor Lasky, *JFK: The Man and the Myth* (New York: Macmillan, 1963), 99.

123   *"His performance"*: Theodore C. Sorensen, *Kennedy* (New York: Harper, 1965), 27.

123   *"John Kennedy was not one"*: *Ibid.*, 43.

123   *"Just as I went into politics"*: qtd in Joe McCarthy, *The Remarkable Kennedys* (New York: Dial, 1960), 116.

124   *"shy, boyish smile"*: James MacGregor Burns, *John Kennedy: A Political Profile* (New York: Harcourt, 1960), 71.

125   *"intellectual blood bank"*: qtd in Theodore H. White, *The Making of the President 1960* (New York: Atheneum, 1961), 61.

125   *"Massachusetts Democrat"*: Richard J. Whalen, *The Founding Father: The Story of Joseph P. Kennedy* (New York: New American Library, 1964), 393.

125   *"Kennedy seems to feel honestly"*: qtd in *Ibid.*

125   *"In two years"*: *Ibid.*

125   *"How long can we"*: qtd in *Ibid.*, 402–3.

126   *"At the Yalta conference"*: qtd in *Ibid.*, 403.

126   *"cannot reform the world"*: qtd in *Ibid.*

126   *"railed against expanding government"*: *Ibid.*, 404.

126   *Of Jack's years in the House*: Sorensen, *Kennedy*, 17, 26, 27.

127   *more explicit criticism*: Theodore C. Sorensen, *The Kennedy Legacy* (New York: Macmillan, 1969), 42–43.

127   *"a recognition"*: *Ibid.*, 43.

127   *"far more often his positions"*: *Ibid.*

127   *"Soon after I went to work"*: Evelyn Lincoln, *My Twelve Years with John F. Kennedy* (New York: McKay, 1965), 5–6.

128   *"He wanted people"*: *Ibid.*, 6.

129   *"unfailing devotion"*: Sorensen, *Kennedy*, 55.

129   *"stern protectiveness"*: Patrick Anderson, *The President's Men* (Garden City, N.Y.: Doubleday, 1968), 247.

129   *"The White House was a man's world"*: qtd in *Ibid.*, 246.

130   *"I think we are heading for a major disaster"*: qtd in Burns, *op. cit.*, 81.

130   *"Many of us feel"*: qtd Lasky, *op. cit.*, 123.

130   *"showed itself sporadically"*: Burns, *op. cit.*, 88.

130   *In a later review*: Sorensen, *Kennedy*, 26.

131   *"I'll bet he talked"*: qtd in Burns, *op. cit.*, 100.

131   *"Back there in 1948"*: qtd in Lasky, *op. cit.*, 138.

131   *"You're driving with Jack"*: qtd in Joe McCarthy, *The Remarkable Kennedys* (New York: Dial, 1960), 31–32.

131   *"Jack's keyed-up, almost compulsive, competitiveness"*: *Ibid.*, 30.

132   *"Jack's success"*: qtd in *Ibid.*, 31.

132   *"I didn't know whether I would run"*: qtd in Lasky, *op. cit.*, 137.

132   *"This may be the key"*: qtd in *Ibid.*, 138.

132   *"The pros wait too long"*: qtd in *Ibid.*

132   *"The Ambassador worked around the clock"*: qtd in *Ibid.*, 140.

133   *"tried to carry water on both shoulders"*: qtd in *Ibid.*, 171.

134   *"the image was created early"*: Gore Vidal, "The Holy Family," *Esquire* (April, 1967), 102, 201.

134   *"But he was a man of action"*: Sorensen, *Kennedy*, 80–81.
134   *"because that's where the power is"*: Whalen, *op. cit.*, 426.
135   *"His best-selling book"*: Sorensen, *Kennedy*, 81.
136   *"The ease"*: Theodore Draper, *Abuse of Power* (New York: Viking, 1967), 50–51.
137   *"The Attorney General"*: qtd in Burns, *op. cit.*, 202–4.
137   *"mindful of the watching eyes"*: qtd in *Ibid.*, 204.
138   *"showed a profile in caution and moderation"*: qtd in *Ibid.*
139   *"There was no fundamental clash"*: Whalen, *op. cit.*, 425–26.
140   *"This was the investigation"*: Clark R. Mollenhoff, *Tentacles of Power: The Story of Jimmy Hoffa* (Cleveland: World, 1965), 3–4.
140   *"Out of that convention loss"*: *Ibid.*
141   *"he knew Joe pretty well"*: qtd in Burns, *op. cit.*, 133.
142   *"I'd rather die"*: McCarthy, *op. cit.*, 151.
142   *"The doctors had recommended"*: Lincoln, *op. cit.*, 56.
142   *Kennedy's favorite poem*: Arthur M. Schlesinger, Jr., *A Thousand Days: John F. Kennedy in the White House* (Boston: Houghton Mifflin, 1965), 98.
142   *"the national interest"*: John F. Kennedy, *Profiles in Courage* (New York: Harper, 1955), 203–4.
143   *"what then caused the statesmen"*: *Ibid.*, 209–10.
144   *"In spite of a life"*: *Ibid.*, 29.
145   *"William Lamb"*: David Cecil, *Lord M* (London: Constable, 1954), 1–2.
146   *"What Jack Kennedy thought and did"*: Whalen, *op. cit.*, 426.
146   *Lord M, according to Cecil*: Cecil, *op. cit.*, 3–6.
147   *"I was struck by the impersonality"*: Schlesinger, *op. cit.*, 17.
147   *"He was a partisan"*: Kennedy, *op. cit.*, 100.
148   *"the day after his 1952 campaign ended"*: Sorensen, *Kennedy*, 74.
148   *"the hardest campaign ever"*: qtd in Schlesinger, *op. cit.*, 11.
149   *"the religious issue"*: Walt Anderson, *Campaigns: Cases in Political Conflict* (Pacific Palisades, Cal.: Goodyear, 1970), 169–70.
150   *"first completely packaged products"*: qtd in Schlesinger, *op. cit.*, 64.
150   *"He has no taste"*: qtd in *Ibid.*, 65.
150   *"sharp, ambitious, opportunistic"*: qtd in *Ibid.*, 64.
152   *"a President governing the United States"*: White, *op. cit.*, 443.

7 Camelot Revisited I, pages 154–223

Two recent books contain excellent analyses of John F. Kennedy's foreign policy: Richard J. Walton's *Cold War and Counterrevolution* and Louise FitzSimon's *The Kennedy Doctrine*. Both are highly critical of the Kennedy Administration and can be commended for scholarship and readability. Each was useful throughout this chapter, excepting "The Moon Project," which Walton and FitzSimons curiously omit.

For "The Bay of Pigs," I found two books especially useful: Tad Szulc and Karl E. Meyer, *The Cuban Invasion: The Chronicle of a Disaster*, and Arthur Schlesinger, Jr., *A Thousand Days: John F. Kennedy in the White House*.

Theodore Sorensen's *Kennedy* provides interesting supplementary detail.

"The Arms Race" was drawn largely from two books by Ralph E. Lapp, *The Weapons Culture* and *Arms Beyond Doubt: The Tyranny of Weapons Technology*; Chalmers M. Roberts, *The Nuclear Years: The Arms Race and Arms Control 1945–70*; and I. F. Stone's articles in the *New York Review of Books*.

For little known details on "The Moon Project" I am indebted to "Why We Went to the Moon," by Hugo Young, Bryan Silcock, and Peter Dunn, which was excerpted from their *Journey to Tranquility*. Comments by I. F. Stone, printed originally in *I. F. Stone's Weekly* and reprinted in *In a Time of Torment*, were insightful and to the point.

"The Berlin Crisis" was researched in many sources. FitzSimons and Walton were particularly helpful, as was Schlesinger's mixed account in *A Thousand Days*. (Schlesinger is constantly pulled between his training as a scholarly historian and his concern to avoid damage to the reputation of his presidential patron—which produces some odd results.)

For "The Missile Crisis" the most absorbing single account is Elie Abel's *The Missile Crisis*. But Abel must be supplemented by a reading of Schlesinger and Sorensen, and by the commentary of more critical observers, such as Walton, FitzSimons, Stone, and Louis Heren. Roger Hilsman's *To Move a Nation* contains interesting background information.

My research on "Vietnam" goes back many years—too far for me to credit only a few sources. Several works, however, are indispensable to a thorough understanding of the war: *The Pentagon Papers*; Theodore Draper's *Abuse of Power*; and David Halberstam's *The Making of a Quagmire*. A first-rate general account is *The United States in Vietnam* by George McT. Kahin and John W. Lewis.

154   *"It has been lately"*: qtd in Richard K. Cralle, ed., *The Works of John C. Calhoun* (New York: Appleton, 1854), IV, 416, 420.

154   *"As missionaries"*: Hans J. Morgenthau, *A New Foreign Policy for the United States* (New York: Praeger, 1969), 81.

154   *"Reflecting and speaking"*: Robert Lekachman, "Money in America: The End of the Economists' Dream," *Harper's* (August, 1970), 32–33.

155   *"Kennedy began where Dulles"*: Louis Heren, *No Hail, No Farewell* (New York: Harper, 1970), 251.

155   *"it would be wise"*: I. F. Stone, "We All Had a Finger on That Trigger," *I. F. Stone's Weekly* (December 9, 1963); reprinted in Stone, *In a Time of Torment* (New York: Random House, 1967), 14–15.

156   *the exaggerated rhetoric of Kennedy's inaugural address*: qtd in Edmund S. Ions, *The Politics of John F. Kennedy* (New York: Barnes & Noble, 1967), 49–52.

157   *"When you look around"*: qtd in Hugh Sidey, *John F. Kennedy, President* (New York: Atheneum, 1964), 128.

157   *"What gets me"*: qtd in *Ibid.*

158   *"The idea that the power"*: George Kateb, "Kennedy as Statesman," *Commentary* (June, 1966), 54–60.

I. The Bay of Pigs

159   *"The folly of the American"*: Herbert L. Matthews, *Fidel Castro* (New York: Simon & Schuster, 1969), 210.

160   *"the incident on"*: Tad Szulc and Karl E. Meyer, *The Cuban Invasion: The Chronicle of a Disaster* (New York: Ballantine, 1962), 7–8, 10.

160   *"The ill-fated"*: Theodore Draper, *Castro's Revolution: Myths and Realities* (New York: Praeger, 1962), 59.

160   *"Thank God"*: qtd in Theodore C. Sorensen, *Kennedy* (New York: Harper, 1965), 644.

160   *"in Western Europe"*: Arthur M. Schlesinger, Jr., *A Thousand Days: John F. Kennedy in the White House* (Boston: Houghton Mifflin, 1965), 291–92.

162   *"Of the so-called"*: Matthews, *op. cit.*, 197–98.

163   *Senator Kennedy . . . criticized the embargo*: qtd in Szulc and Meyer, *op. cit.*, 67–68.

163   *Nixon struck back*: qtd in *Ibid.*, 68.

163   *"the campaign's low"*: *Ibid.*, 71.

164   *"wary and reserved"*: Schlesinger, *A Thousand Days*, 238.

164   *"a now-or-never choice"*: *Ibid.*, 240.

164   *"After June 1"*: *Ibid.*

164   *"this would be your first"*: *Ibid.*

165   *"Kennedy tentatively agreed"*: *Ibid.*, 242.

165   *"the President, listening somberly"*: *Ibid.*, 243.

166   *"When I asked the President"*: Sorensen, *op. cit.*, 295.

166   *"The President knew better"*: Schlesinger, *A Thousand Days*, 214.

166   *"enormous confidence"*: *Ibid.*, 259.

167   *"showed that the Cuban"*: qtd in *Ibid.*, 291.

167   *"The primary cause"*: Daniel M. Rohrer, Mark G. Arnold, and Roger L. Conner, *By Weight of Arms: America's Overseas Military Policy* (Skokie, Illinois: National Textbook Co., 1969), 44–45.

168   *Fulbright wrote . . . to argue against*: qtd in Schlesinger, *A Thousand Days*, 251.

168   *"it was a brilliant memorandum"*: *Ibid.*

168   *"wildly out of proportion"*: *Ibid.*, 252.

168   *Schlesinger wrote . . . of his opposition*: *Ibid.*, 253, 254.

169   *The President . . . made up his mind*: qtd in *Ibid.*, 257–58.

169   *"his own mistakes were"*: Sorensen, *op. cit.*, 306.

170   *"Both had in common"*: Szulc and Meyer, *op. cit.*, 97.

171   *"In spite of the news"*: Schlesinger, *A Thousand Days*, 275–76.

172   *"When it happened"*: qtd in Sidey, *op. cit.*, 118.

172   *"Let the record show"*: qtd in Schlesinger, *A Thousand Days*, 287–88.

172   *"Having uttered this obscure"*: *Ibid.*, 288.

173   *"Although it seemed a transient"*: Richard J. Walton, *Cold War and Counterrevolution: The Foreign Policy of John F. Kennedy* (New York: Viking, 1972), 58–59.

II. The Arms Race

174   *"In the area"*: Ralph E. Lapp, *The Weapons Culture* (New York: Norton, 1968), 32.

174   *"In the opinion"*: Louise FitzSimons, *The Kennedy Doctrine* (New York: Random House, 1972), 215–17.

174   *"Some observers have"*: Chalmers M. Roberts, *The Nuclear Years: The Arms Race and Arms Control 1945–70* (New York: Praeger, 1970), 56–57.

175   *"This deterrent concept"*: John F. Kennedy, *Public Papers of the President 1961* (Washington, D.C.: GPO, 1962), 402.

176   *"We arm not just"*: Ralph E. Lapp, *Arms Beyond Doubt: The Tyranny of Weapons Technology* (New York: Cowles, 1970), 193.

177   *contradictory words of his inaugural speech*: John F. Kennedy, Inaugural Address (January 20, 1961), *Public Papers, 1961*, 2.

177   *"Basically the opportunity"*: I. F. Stone, "Theatre of Delusion," *New York Review of Books* (April 23, 1970), 20.

178   *State of Union message*: John F. Kennedy, *Public Papers, 1961*, 19–28.

178   *"It has been publicly"*: qtd in Walton, *op. cit.*, 68.

178   *McNamara's candid retrospection*: qtd in Lapp, *The Weapons Culture*, 209, 211.

178   *"In terms of total"*: qtd in *Ibid.*, 49.

179   *"In 1961 at the start"*: qtd in FitzSimons, *op. cit.*, 232–33.

180   *"The strategic nuclear power"*: qtd in Urs Schwarz, *John F. Kennedy, 1917–1963* (London: Hamlyn, 1964), 148–50.

181   *"all delusion"*: I. F. Stone, "The Test Ban Comedy," *New York Review of Books* (May 7, 1970), 14.

181   *McNamara . . . outlined steps*: qtd in *Ibid.*, 18.

182   *"Indeed, Mr. President"*: qtd in *Ibid.*, 19.

182   *"that appears to be"*: *Ibid.*, 19.

III. The Moon Project

183   *"A Soviet success"*: Lapp, *The Weapons Culture*, 43–44.

183   *"Kennedy, who had promised"*: H. L. Nieburg, *In the Name of Science* (Chicago: Quadrangle, 1966), 169.

184   *"The need to triumph"*: Philip Slater, *The Pursuit of Loneliness: American Culture at the Breaking Point* (Boston: Beacon Press, 1970), 133.

184   *"Some sociologists agree"*: James Tracy Crown and George P. Penty, *Kennedy in Power* (New York: Ballantine, 1961), 108.

185   *"In one extraordinary convulsion"*: Hugo Young, Bryan Silcock, and Peter Dunn, "Why We Went to the Moon," *Washington Monthly* (April, 1970), 28–29; an excerpt from *Journey to Tranquility* (Garden City, N.Y.: Doubleday, 1970).

186   *"The pressure on Kennedy"*: Sidey, *op. cit.*, 99.

186   *"manifested an almost bottomless ignorance"*: Young, Silcock, Dunn, *op. cit.*, 34.

186   *"was already halfway to the moon"*: qtd in *Ibid.*

186   *"whose tone was that"*: *Ibid.*, 34–35.

187   *"In accordance with"*: qtd in *Ibid.*, 35.

187   *"If scientists had"*: qtd in *Ibid.*, 36.

187   *"never to refer"*: qtd in *Ibid.*, 37.

187   *Webb and . . . McNamara wrote in their report*: qtd in *Ibid.*, 38.

188   *"Why, some say"*: qtd in I. F. Stone, "Mr. Kennedy's Speech on

Space Nationalistic Soap Ad Hoopla," *I. F. Stone's Weekly* (September 24, 1962); reprinted in Stone, *In a Time of Torment,* 9.

188 *"to reflect a family"*: *Ibid.,* 9–10.
188 *"We have vowed that"*: qtd in *Ibid.,* 10.
188 *The Camelot Administration presented the moon*: qtd in Sorensen, *op. cit.,* 526.
189 *"For industry"*: Stone, "Mr. Kennedy's Speech . . . ," *Ibid.,* 10–11.
189 *"there is no strife"*: qtd in *Ibid.,* 10.
189 *"the success of our leadership"*: qtd in Schwarz, *op. cit.,* 150.
189 *"Even in our space program"*: qtd in *Impact of the War in Southeast Asia on the U.S. Economy: Hearings Before the Committee on Foreign Relations, United States Senate, April 28 and 29, May 13 and 19, June 2, and August 13, 1970* (Washington, D.C.: GPO, 1970), 142.
190 *"If space has produced"*: Young, Silcock, Dunn, *op. cit.,* 57.

IV. The Berlin Crisis

191 *"The admirers"*: Walton, *op. cit.,* 93.
191 *"President Kennedy's"*: Frederick L. Schuman, *The Cold War: Retrospect and Prospect* (Baton Rouge: Louisiana State University Press, 1967), XIV–XV.
191 *"That same year"*: Sidney Lens, *The Military-Industrial Complex* (Philadelphia: Pilgrim Press, 1970), 90–91.
191 *"how tenuous"*: qtd in Schlesinger, *A Thousand Days,* 397.
192 *"President Kennedy"*: FitzSimons, *op. cit.,* 97–98.
192 *"suggested the messianic"*: *Ibid.,* 80.
193 *"Our most somber"*: John F. Kennedy, *Public Papers of the President 1961,* 444.
194 *militaristic hardliners*: Schlesinger, *A Thousand Days,* 380–81.
194 *"For Acheson"*: *Ibid.,* 383.
195 *"a peaceful settlement"*: qtd in Walton, *op. cit.,* 83.
195 *"the peace and"*: Kennedy, *Public Papers, 1961,* 476–77.
195 *"West Berlin"*: *Ibid.,* 533ff.
196 *"For whatever reason"*: Walton, *op. cit.,* 88.
196 *"If Khrushchev wants"*: qtd in Schlesinger, *A Thousand Days,* 391.
196 *"We do not intend"*: qtd in Walton, *op. cit.,* 92.
196 *"It had been Bob"*: Sidey, *op. cit.,* 203–4.

V. The Missile Crisis

197 *"It has been"*: Walton, *op. cit.,* 103–4.
197 *"The world"*: Heren, *op. cit.,* 251.
197 *"In October"*: FitzSimons, *op. cit.,* 126–27.
198 *"The Cuban missile"*: Lens, *op. cit.,* 91.
198 *"Through thirteen"*: Elie Abel, *The Missile Crisis* (Philadelphia: Lippincott, 1966), jacket.
199 *As Sorensen pointed out*: Sorensen, *op. cit.,* 678.
199 *"The real stake"*: I. F. Stone, "What If Khrushchev Hadn't Backed Down?" *I. F. Stone's Weekly* (April 14, 1966); reprinted in Stone, *In a Time of Torment,* 19.

199   *"A missile is a missile"*: qtd in Roger Hilsman, *To Move a Nation* (Garden City, N.Y.: Doubleday, 1967), 195.

200   *"If at any time"*: qtd in Sorensen, *op. cit.,* 671.

200   *two options were available:* Ibid., 682–83.

201   *the military implications:* Ibid., 683.

201   *"The fact of the matter"*: Hilsman, *op. cit.,* 196–97.

201   *"There might have been"*: Stone, "What If Khrushchev . . . ," *Ibid.,* 20–21.

202   *conversation related by Robert Kennedy:* Robert F. Kennedy, *Thirteen Days: A Memoir of the Cuban Missile Crisis* (New York: Norton, 1969), 67.

202   *"obsolete, unreliable"*: Hilsman, *op. cit.,* 202.

203   *"that the United States"*: Ibid., 216.

203   *"If the Soviets"*: Ibid., 221.

204   *"The President then"*: Ibid., 224.

204   *"The continuation of"*: Sorensen, *op. cit.,* 715.

204   *"with a strong verbal message"*: Ibid.

204   *"We all agreed"*: qtd in Schlesinger, *A Thousand Days,* 829–30.

205   *"Now it can"*: qtd in Hilsman, *op. cit.,* 224.

205   *"If we had invaded"*: qtd in Schlesinger, *A Thousand Days,* 830.

205   *"And above all"*: qtd in Walton, *op. cit.,* 142.

205   *"The only conceivable time"*: FitzSimons, *op. cit.,* 172.

206   *"What worried him"*: qtd in Schlesinger, *A Thousand Days,* 391.

VI. Vietnam

206   *"The Pentagon's study"*: Hedrick Smith, "The Kennedy Years: 1961–1963," in Sheehan *et al., The Pentagon Papers* (New York: Bantam, 1971), 79.

206   *"Characteristically, the world"*: Gore Vidal, "The Holy Family," *Esquire* (April, 1967), 201.

207   *"As early as 1956"*: Ronald Steel, a review of *The Lost Crusade: America in Vietnam* by Chester L. Cooper, *New York Times Book Review* (November 8, 1970), 1.

207   *"Kennedy assumed"*: Henry Brandon, *Anatomy of Error: The Inside Story of the Asian War on the Potomac, 1954–1969* (Boston: Gambit, 1969), 30.

209   *"I am frankly"*: qtd in Theodore Draper, *Abuse of Power* (New York: Viking, 1967), 37.

210   *"Of the close"*: Townsend Hoopes, *The Limits of Intervention* (New York: McKay, 1970), 16.

210   *"an extraordinarily tolerant"*: Brandon, *op. cit.,* 40.

211   *"armed attacks"*: qtd in Schlesinger, *A Thousand Days,* 333.

212   *"a whole new kind"*: qtd in Hilsman, *op. cit.,* 415.

212   *"The name of the game"*: Stanley Karnow, "A Grim Notebook on Our Asian Tragedy," *Washington Post Outlook* (June 28, 1970), C1.

213   *"Eventually South Vietnam"*: David Halberstam, *The Making of a Quagmire* (New York: Random House, 1965), 52.

213   *"The Kennedy Administration's"*: Ernest Gruening and Herbert W.

Beaser, *Vietnam Folly* (Palo Alto, Cal.: National Press, 1968), 201.

213 *"Kennedy, who had"*: Arthur Schlesinger, Jr., *The Bitter Heritage: Vietnam and American Democracy, 1941–1966* (Boston: Houghton Mifflin, 1966), 20.

214 *"It expressed a conscious"*: Schlesinger, *A Thousand Days*, 545.

215 *The military view was backed up*: qtd in *Ibid.*, 548.

215 *Kennedy never . . . made a final decision*: Sorensen, *op. cit.*, 654–55.

215 *Kennedy sealed his new policy*: *Ibid.*, 655.

215 *"primary responsibility would"*: qtd in *Ibid.*

215 *"In a brilliant analysis"*: Karnow, *op. cit.*, C2.

216 *"In place of a serious"*: Schlesinger, *A Thousand Days*, 548–49.

216 *"Every quantitative measurement"*: qtd in *Ibid.*, 549.

216 *"The spearpoint of aggression"*: qtd in *Ibid.*, 550.

217 *President Kennedy in a . . . interview stated*: qtd in Sorensen, *op. cit.*, 658–59.

218 *"had never felt"*: David Halberstam, *The Unfinished Odyssey of Robert Kennedy* (New York: Bantam, 1969), 22.

219 *In a prophetic piece*: I. F. Stone, "Lost Chances for Peace in Indochina," *I. F. Stone's Weekly* (October 28, 1963); reprinted in Stone, *In a Time of Torment*, 181–82.

220 *"The study also observes"*: *The Pentagon Papers*, *op. cit.*, 84.

220 *"a stable government"*: qtd in Schlesinger, *A Thousand Days*, 989.

220 *"I can't do it"*: qtd in Kenneth O'Donnell, "L.B.J. and the Kennedys," *Life* (August 7, 1970), 51.

221 *Kennedy had . . . ordered*: Sorensen, *op. cit.*, 654.

VII. A Crisis-Oriented President?

221 *"Kennedy spent so much"*: Walton, *op. cit.*, 203.

222 *"But John F. Kennedy"*: Theodore H. White, *The Making of the President 1960* (New York: Atheneum, 1961), 452.

222 *"A president"*: George E. Reedy, *The Twilight of the Presidency* (New York: New American Library, 1970), 40–41.

8 Camelot Revisited II, pages 224–259

For information on the racial situation, the civil rights movement, and the reactions of the Kennedy Administration, I am most indebted to Arthur Schlesinger, Jr., *A Thousand Days: John F. Kennedy in the White House*; William Robert Miller, *Martin Luther King, Jr.*; Louis E. Lomax, *The Negro Revolt*; Walter Lord, *The Past That Would Not Die*; Martin Luther King, Jr., *Why We Can't Wait*; and Victor S. Navasky, *Kennedy Justice*.

Regarding the state of the American economy, poverty, and the Kennedy policies, most useful were Bernard D. Nossiter, *The Mythmakers: An Essay on Power and Wealth*; Arnold Schuchter, *White Power, Black Freedom*; Ben Seligman, *Permanent Poverty: An American Syndrome*; Thomas Gladwin, *Poverty U.S.A.*; Edgar May, *The Wasted Americans*; Nicholas Kotz, *Let Them Eat Promises: The Politics of Hunger in America*; and David T. Bazelon, *The Paper Economy*.

Kennedy's tax policies are well explained in both Nossiter and Schuchter. Robert Lekachman's "Money in America: The End of the Economists' Dream," *Harper's*, was also helpful.

224 *"As Mr. Kennedy defined"*: Robert Lekachman, "Money in America: The End of the Economists' Dream," *Harper's* (August, 1970), 33.

224 *"Presidents are supposed"*: Gore Vidal, "Playboy Interview," *Playboy* (June, 1969), 84.

225 *"as Congress saw things"*: Tom Wicker, *J.F.K. and L.B.J.: The Influence of Personality upon Politics* (New York: Morrow, 1968), 146.

225 *"Just as the road to hell"*: qtd in Evelyn Lincoln, *My Twelve Years with John F. Kennedy* (New York: McKay, 1965), 130.

226 *"Whether as a result"*: Wicker, *op. cit.*, 88.

227 *"During the activist Kennedy regime"*: Paul Goodman, *People or Personnel* and *Like a Conquered Province* (New York: Vintage, 1968), 47–48.

228 *Green report*: *Discrimination against Women: Hearings before the Special Subcommittee on Education of the Committee on Education and Labor, House of Representatives, on Sec. 805 of H.R. 16098, June 17, 19, 26, 30, 1970.*

I. Black America

228 *"At the time"*: Wicker, *op. cit.*, 88–89.

229 *"The forlorn Mississippi engagement"*: Ronald Segal, *The Americans: A Conflict of Creed and Reality* (New York: Viking, 1969), 241–42.

229 *"Only a President"*: qtd in Arthur Schlesinger, Jr., *A Thousand Days: John F. Kennedy in the White House* (Boston: Houghton Mifflin, 1965), 929.

229 *"In the decade that lies ahead"*: qtd in Arnold Schuchter, *White Power, Black Freedom* (Boston: Beacon, 1968), 591.

230 *King . . . petition*: qtd in William Robert Miller, *Martin Luther King, Jr.* (New York: Weybright, 1968), 128–29.

232 *"People are dying"*: qtd in Walter Lord, *The Past That Would Not Die* (New York: Harper, 1965), 3.

232 *"King was highly critical"*: Miller, *op. cit.*, 144–45.

233 *"If tokenism were our goal"*: *Ibid.*, 133.

233 *"in at least 193 counties"*: Arthur Schlesinger, Jr., *op. cit.*, 935.

233 *King described 1962*: qtd in *Ibid.*, 950.

234 *"I attacked John Kennedy"*: qtd in *Ibid.*

234 *"a great many very bad things"*: qtd in *Ibid.*, 952.

234 *interim report*: qtd in *Ibid.*

235 *"subject to misunderstanding"*: qtd in *Ibid.*, 953.

235 *"the Federal Government would have found a way"*: qtd in Miller, *op. cit.*, 156.

236 *"Despite the formal expressions"*: I. F. Stone, "The Wasteland in the White Man's Heart," *I. F. Stone's Weekly* (September 30, 1963); reprinted in Stone, *In a Time of Torment* (New York: Random House, 1967), 125.

236   *"The cause of desegregation"*: qtd in James L. Sundquist, *Politics and Policy: The Eisenhower, Kennedy and Johnson Years* (Washington, D.C.: Brookings Institution, 1968), 261.
236   *"The great need now"*: qtd in *Ibid.*
237   *"It was clear"*: *Ibid.*, 263.
237   *"was looking"*: qtd in *Ibid.*
237   *John Lewis . . . original speech*: qtd in Joanne Grant, *Black Protests: History, Documents, and Analyses* (Greenwich, Conn.: Fawcett, 1968), 375–76.

II. Kennedy and the Economy

238   *"Of all the myths"*: Bernard D. Nossiter, *The Mythmakers: An Essay on Power and Wealth* (Boston: Houghton Mifflin, 1964), 40.
238   *"As of mid-1959"*: qtd in David T. Bazelon, *The Paper Economy* (New York, Random House, 1963), 337.
238   *"By proper application"*: Theodore J. Lowi, *The End of Liberalism: Ideology, Policy, and the Crisis of Public Authority* (New York: Norton, 1969), 79, n. 27.
239   *"In a country of such opulence"*: Bazelon, *op. cit.*, 353.
240   *"With this single concession"*: Schuchter, *op. cit.*, 455.
241   *"by enabling"*: *Ibid.*, 460.
241   *"Negroes have shown"*: *Ibid.*, 489–90.
241   *"If, to borrow"*: Thomas Gladwin, *Poverty U.S.A.* (Boston: Little, Brown, 1967), 58–59.
242   *"In the five-year period"*: Schuchter, *op. cit.*, 451.
242   *"The arsenal of tools"*: *Ibid.*, 451.
243   *"Moved by the poverty"*: Nicholas Kotz, *Let Them Eat Promises: The Politics of Hunger in America* (Englewood Cliffs, N.J.: Prentice-Hall, 1970), 24.
244   *"attitude that had become pervasive"*: Sundquist, *op. cit.*, 113–14.
244   *"to bring six million"*: Ben B. Seligman, *Permanent Poverty: An American Syndrome* (Chicago: Quadrangle, 1968), 36.
244   *"by 1967 a transfer"*: Norman Macrae, *The Neurotic Trillionaire: A Survey of Mr. Nixon's America* (New York: Harcourt, 1970), 78.
245   *"The New Economists"*: Lekachman, *op. cit.*, 34.

III. Kennedy's Tax Bill

247   *"The President"*: Nossiter, *op. cit.*, 34–36.
248   *"The legacy"*: Lekachman, *op. cit.*, 34.
248   *"Economic growth"*: John Kenneth Galbraith, "An Agenda for American Liberals," *Commentary* (June, 1966), 29–34.
249   *"tax dodger's delight"*: qtd in Nossiter, *op. cit.*, 33.
249   *"The bill"*: qtd in *Ibid.*
249   *"This is an important bill"*: qtd in *Ibid.*, 33–34.
249   *"the suggested rates"*: *Ibid.*, 34–35.
250   *The projected economic expansion"*: Schuchter, *op. cit.*, 460.
250   *"The Kennedy Administration"*: *Ibid.*

IV. The Steel Crisis

251 *"While Kennedy's treatment"*: Nossiter, *op. cit.*, 14.
251 *"Rather than being anti-business"*: qtd in *Ibid.*, 41.
252 *"The steel union"*: qtd in *Ibid.*, 19.
252 *"Had U.S. Steel"*: *Ibid.*, 20.
252 *"are not incompatible"*: qtd in *Ibid.*, 22.

V. The High Cost of Neurosis

254 *"sons-of-bitches"*: qtd in Schlesinger, *op. cit.*, 635.
254 *"He had the most wonderful life"*: qtd in Dick Schaap, *R.F.K.* (New York: New American Library, 1967), 13.
257 *"A President is limited"*: Schuchter., *op. cit.*, 592.

VI. JFK's Health

258 *"Shortly before polling day"*: Hugh L'Etang, *The Pathology of Leadership* (New York: Hawthorn, 1970), 187.
259 *"in the dose range"*: *Ibid.*
259 *Kennedy's presidential behavior*: *Ibid.*, 188.

9 Robert Francis Kennedy, pages 260–290

The details of Robert Kennedy's youth, early career, and term as Attorney General are drawn largely from Margaret Laing, *The Next Kennedy*; William Nicholas (pen name of William Johnson and Nick Thimmesch), *The Bobby Kennedy Nobody Knows*; William V. Shannon, *The Heir Apparent: Robert Kennedy and the Struggle for Power*; Ralph De Toledano, *R.F.K.: The Man Who Would Be President*; Dick Schaap, *R.F.K.*; and Victor S. Navasky, *Kennedy Justice*.

260 *"He was the smallest"*: qtd in William V. Shannon, *The Heir Apparent: Robert Kennedy and the Struggle for Power* (New York: Macmillan, 1967), 43.
260 *"Bobby has been a great joy"*: qtd in *Ibid.*, 52.
260 *"If one of you guys"*: qtd in *Ibid.*, 50.
260 *"I was the seventh"*: qtd in *Ibid.*, 43.
260 *"Once he identifies"*: *Ibid.*, 54–55.
261 *"It is the conjunction"*: qtd in William vanden Heuvel and Milton Gwirtzman, *On His Own: RFK, 1964–68* (Garden City, N.Y.: Doubleday, 1970), 25.
261 *"Kennedy's emotionalism"*: Jack Newfield, *Robert Kennedy: A Memoir* (New York: Dutton, 1969), 36.
262 *"Humanity remains"*: qtd in Margaret Laing, *The Next Kennedy* (New York: Coward-McCann, 1968), 290.
262 *"the most thoughtful"*: qtd in *Ibid.*, 64–65.
263 *"a nice freckled-faced little kid"*: qtd in *Ibid.*, 75–76.

263   *"He was very gentle"*: qtd in *Ibid.*, 66.
263   *"Bobby was"*: qtd in American Heritage Editors, *RFK: His Life and Death* (New York: Dell, 1968), 41.
263   *"He's feisty"*: William Nicholas (pseud.), *The Bobby Kennedy Nobody Knows* (Greenwich, Conn.: Fawcett, 1967), unpaged.
263   *"He grew up"*: qtd in *Ibid.*
263   *"What I remember"*: qtd in Newfield, *op. cit.*, 45.
263   *"As an adult"*: *Ibid.*
263   *"either a lot of guts"*: qtd in American Heritage, *op. cit.*, 40.
264   *"He was the little brother"*: qtd in Victor Lasky, *Robert F. Kennedy: The Myth and the Man* (New York: Trident, 1968), 45.
264   *"[he] became heir apparent"*: Arthur Krock, *Memoirs: Sixty Years on the Firing Line* (New York: Funk & Wagnalls, 1968), 354.
264   *"When I first knew Bobby"*: qtd in Laing, *op. cit.*, 82.
265   *"He was not outstandingly brilliant"*: qtd in *Ibid.*, 94.
265   *Milton classmates*: qtd in *Ibid.*, 95.
266   *"To tell you the truth"*: qtd in Ralph De Toledano, *R.F.K.: The Man Who Would Be President* (New York: Putnam, 1967), 39.
266   *"I can't think of anyone"*: qtd in Laing, *op. cit.*, 100.
266   *"Except for war"*: qtd in *Ibid.*, 99.
267   *"very shy"*: qtd in *Ibid.*, 101.
267   *"In college"*: qtd in De Toledano, *op. cit.*, 39.
267   *"Nobody who ever went"*: qtd in *Ibid.*, 38.
267   *"He was different"*: qtd in Laing, *op. cit.*, 101.
268   *"more, much more spirit"*: qtd in Laurence Swinburne, *RFK: The Last Knight* (New York: Pyramid, 1969), 33.
269   *Fay . . . remembered him*: Paul B. Fay, Jr., *The Pleasure of His Company* (New York: Harper, 1966), 157–58.
271   *"With Bobby"*: qtd in Shannon, *op. cit.*, 54.
271   *"keep that fresh kid"*: qtd in Richard J. Whalen, *The Founding Father: The Story of Joseph P. Kennedy* (New York: New American Library, 1964), 410.
271   *"My brother Jack"*: De Toledano, *op. cit.*, 49.
272   *"Bobby works at high tempo"*; *"These politicians"*: qtd in Laing, *op. cit.*, 132.
272   *"work that needed to be done"*: qtd in Dick Schaap, *R.F.K.* (New York: New American Library, 1967), 67.
273   *"Kennedy had shown"*: Clark R. Mollenhoff, *Tentacles of Power: The Story of Jimmy Hoffa* (Cleveland: World, 1965), 128–29.
274   *"The Labor Committee"*: qtd in *Ibid.*, 146.
274   *"Hoffa's personal morality"*: Ralph and Estelle James, *Hoffa and the Teamsters: A Study of Union Power* (Princeton, N.J.: Van Nostrand, 1965), 68.
275   *"With Mr. Kennedy in the lead"*: qtd in Newfield, *op. cit.*, 74–75.
275   *"no one seriously believes"*: Paul Jacobs, *The State of the Unions* (New York: Atheneum, 1963), 86.
275   *"It called for"*: qtd in *Ibid.*, 86.
275   *"Jimmy Hoffa and the Teamsters Union"*: *Ibid.*, 86–87.
276   *"From the day"*: qtd in Victor Navasky, *Kennedy Justice* (New York: Harper, 1972), 395.

276   *"Two men pervaded his life"*: Schaap, *op. cit.*, 67.
276   *"Bobby is more direct"*: qtd in *Ibid.*, 50.
277   *"This was the investigation"*: Mollenhoff, *op. cit.*, 3.
278   *"I'll never forget"*: qtd in Laing, *op. cit.*, 169.
278   *"It really struck me"*: qtd in *Ibid.*, 170.
278   *"learned by direct experience"*: Mollenhoff, *op. cit.*, 3–4.
279   *"He directed"*: Newfield, *op. cit.*, 30.
279   *"Robert Kennedy had been the tough guy"*: David Halberstam, *The Unfinished Odyssey of Robert Kennedy* (New York: Bantam, 1969), 1–2.
279   *His father commented*: qtd in Schaap, *op. cit.*, 85.
280   *"at the moment"*: Theodore H. White, *The Making of the President 1960* (New York: Atheneum, 1961), 127.
280   *"deserves to be spanked"*: qtd in Laing, *op. cit.*, 173.
280   *"Once the issue"*: White, *op. cit.*, 127.
280   *"angry and high-strung"*: Nicholas, *op. cit.*, unpaged.
281   *"We're not out here"*: qtd in Laing, *op. cit.*, 176.
281   *"Hubert, we want"*: Nicholas, *op. cit.*, unpaged.
281   *"This is it"*: *Ibid.*
282   *a tight grip on every detail*: Schaap, *op. cit.*, 84.
282   *ruled his political army*: *Ibid.*, 85.
282   *"Nepotism"*: qtd in Whalen, *op. cit.*, 454.
283   *"dedication to excellence"*; *"No aspect"*: Navasky, *op. cit.*, 244–45.
283   *"As civil rights activists"*: Newfield, *op. cit.*, 24.
284   *"I don't think"*: qtd in Lasky, *op. cit.*, 181.
284   *"This 'Wait' "*: qtd in Arthur M. Schlesinger, Jr., *A Thousand Days: John F. Kennedy in the White House* (Boston: Houghton Mifflin, 1965), 957.
285   *"The crusade"*: Schaap, *op. cit.*, 76.
285   *Navasky's view*: Navasky, *op. cit.*, 436.
285   *"When he first decided"*: Schlesinger, *op. cit.*, 700–701.
286   *"I know now"*: qtd in *Ibid.*, 803.
286   *analyzed his own attitude*: Robert F. Kennedy, *Thirteen Days: A Memoir of the Cuban Missile Crisis* (New York: Norton, 1969), 37–39.
287   *"We all agreed"*: qtd in Schlesinger, *op. cit.*, 829–30.
287   *"freely attacked"*: *Ibid.*, 702.
288   *"The solution"*: qtd in Douglas Ross, *Robert F. Kennedy: Apostle of Change* (New York: Harper, 1968), 500.
289   *"Being number one"*: Sylvan Priest, "How Bob Kennedy's Children Are Growing Up without Him," *The Woman* (August, 1970), 18–19.
289   *"swing higher"*: qtd in Laing, *op. cit.*, 263.

10 The Importance of Being President, pages 291-322

For information on Robert Kennedy's career as a U.S. Senator from New York and his subsequent presidential campaign, I have relied most heavily on William V. Shannon, *The Heir Apparent: Robert Kennedy and the Struggle for Power*; Jack Newfield, *Robert Kennedy: A Memoir*; Douglas Ross, *Robert F. Kennedy: Apostle of Change*; Dick Schaap, *R.F.K.*; Margaret Laing, *The Next Kennedy*; William vanden Heuvel and Milton Gwirtzman, *On His Own: RFK, 1964–68*; Jules Witcover, *85 Days: The Last Campaign of Robert Kennedy*; Theodore H. White, *The Making of the President 1968*; David Halberstam, *The Unfinished Odyssey of Robert Kennedy*; Penn Kimball, *Bobby Kennedy and the New Politics*; Lewis Chester, Godfrey Hodgson, Bruce Page, *An American Melodrama: The Presidential Campaign of 1968*; Victor Lasky, *Robert F. Kennedy: The Myth and the Man*; and Ralph De Toledano, *R.F.K.: The Man Who Would Be President*.

291   *"Robert Francis Kennedy was"*: Arthur Krock, *Memoirs: Sixty Years on the Firing Line* (New York: Funk & Wagnalls, 1968), 345.
291   *"There is a mysterious"*: William V. Shannon, *The Heir Apparent: Robert Kennedy and the Struggle for Power* (New York: Macmillan, 1967), 41–42.
292   *"Fresh challenges"*: Margaret Laing, *The Next Kennedy* (New York: Coward-McCann, 1968), 308.
292   *"For all of Bobby's renowned toughness"*: Gore Vidal, "Playboy Interview," *Playboy* (June, 1969), 82.
292   *"The 'real' Bobby Kennedy"*: Penn Kimball, *Bobby Kennedy and the New Politics* (Englewood Cliffs, N.J.: Prentice-Hall, 1968), 75.
294   *"The assassination"*: Jack Newfield, *Robert Kennedy: A Memoir* (New York: Dutton, 1969), 31.
294   *"silent, internal struggles"*: Shannon, *op. cit.*, 68–69.
295   *"the embrace of the identity of the dead"*: Robert Jay Lifton, *History and Human Survival* (New York: Random House, 1970), 171.
298   *"his abrupt decision"*; *"Personal tragedy"*: William vanden Heuvel and Milton Gwirtzman, *On His Own: RFK, 1964–68* (Garden City, N.Y.: Doubleday, 1970), 40.
298   *"We cannot, in good conscience"*: qtd in Victor Lasky, *Robert F. Kennedy: The Myth and the Man* (New York: Trident, 1968), 216.
299   *"Why he has any special claim"*: qtd in *Ibid.*, 203.
299   *"We started something"*: qtd in *Ibid.*, 232.
300   *responses in his associates*: qtd in Dick Schaap, *R.F.K.* (New York, New American Library, 1967), 113, 117.
300   *"They only take"*: qtd in *Ibid.*, 116–17.
300   *"If I worked"*: qtd in Laing, *op. cit.*, 291–92.
301   *"to be a trimmer"*: I. F. Stone, "While Others Dodge the Draft, Bobby Dodges the War," *I. F. Stone's Weekly* (October 24, 1966); reprinted in Stone, *In a Time of Torment* (New York: Random House, 1967), 105.
302   *stuck to Cold War line*: qtd in Douglas Ross, *Robert F. Kennedy: Apostle of Change* (New York: Harper, 1968), 517–18.

303   *"I'm afraid that"*: qtd in Newfield, *op. cit.*, 140.
303   *"His personal qualities"*: *Ibid.*
303   *"The entire post-assassination series"*: qtd in Louis Heren, *No Hail, No Farewell* (New York: Harper, 1970), 129.
304   *"During his three years"*: Newfield, *op. cit.*, 156.
304   *"As in so many realms"*: *Ibid.*, 181.
305   *"Robert Kennedy"*: *Ibid.*, 163.
305   *"If I had had forty-eight hours"*: qtd in *Ibid.*, 179.
306   *"He did not fight the barons"*: *Ibid.*, 181.
306   *"Win or lose"*: qtd in Shannon, *op. cit.*, 201.
306   *"Kennedy was now"*: qtd in *Ibid.*
306   *Shannon commented*: *Ibid.*, 201–4.
308   *"No, I can't conceive"*: qtd in Jules Witcover, *85 Days: The Last Campaign of Robert Kennedy* (New York: Putnam, 1969), 15.
308   *"Robert Kennedy clearly was a man in turmoil"*; *"deep concern"*: *Ibid.*, 16–17.
309   *"by the end of January"*: Newfield, *op. cit.*, 223.
309   *"Only those who dare"*: Robert F. Kennedy, *To Seek a Newer World* (New York: Bantam, 1969), 234.
310   *"required the evidence"*: Krock, *op. cit.*, 347.
311   *"The irony was clear"*: Lewis Chester, Godfrey Hodgson, and Bruce Page, *An American Melodrama: The Presidential Campaign of 1968* (New York: Viking, 1969), 126.
311   *"One of the numberless ironies"*: John Whale, *The Half-Shut Eye: Television and Politics in Britain and America* (New York: St. Martin's, 1969), 169.
311   *"television never did"*: *Ibid.*, 169, 172.
312   *"calling upon the darker impulses"*: Witcover, *op. cit.*, 116.
312   *"Carried away"*: Theodore H. White, *The Making of the President 1968* (New York: Atheneum, 1969), 195.
312   *"Specific references"*: Witcover, *op. cit.*, 117.
313   *"the conservative approach"*: *Ibid.*, 181.
313   *"That's not the way"*: qtd in White, *op. cit.*, 204.
313   *"The press session"*: Witcover, *op. cit.*, 180.
313   *"a triumph of imported organization"*: David Halberstam, *The Unfinished Odyssey of Robert Kennedy* (New York: Bantam, 1969), 158.
314   *"a giant suburb"*: *Ibid.*, 175.
314   *"I think what he wanted most"*: qtd in Witcover, *op. cit.*, 221.
314   *"If I get beaten"*: qtd in *Ibid.*, 207.
315   *"blatant perversion"*; *"the strange contrast"*: Chester, Hodgson, and Page, *op. cit.*, 345.
316   *"I don't hate Bobby"*: qtd in Kimball, *op. cit.*, 62–63.
316   *"If he offered"*: qtd in *Ibid.*, 63.
316   *"Even politicians are entitled"*: qtd in *Ibid.*
316   *"I can't do anything"*: qtd in *Ibid.*
316   *"I respected Bobby"*: William Bradford Huie, "A Black Mayor Fails," *True* (May, 1970).
317   *"Kennedy had the Negroes"*: Halberstam, *op.. cit.*, 198.
317   *"I'd have thought"*: qtd in Kimball, *op. cit.*, 64.
317   *"I must be crazy"*: qtd in Shannon, *op. cit.*, 46.

318   *"He repeatedly plunges"*: Andrew J. Glass, "The Compulsive Candidate," *Saturday Evening Post* (April 23, 1966), 36.

318   *"The relevant issue"*: Ross, *op. cit.*, xviii.

319   *"At forty-two"*: Chester, Hodgson, and Page, *op. cit.*, 113.

320   *"A part of Robert Kennedy"*: Victor S. Navasky, *Kennedy Justice* (New York: Harper, 1972), 177.

320   *"He lacked"*: Halberstam, *op. cit.*, 127.

320   *"He relies"*: Laing, *op. cit.*, 203.

11 The Tarnished Heir, pages 323–344

Details of Edward Kennedy's childhood are taken mainly from Richard J. Whalen, *The Founding Father: The Story of Joseph P. Kennedy*; Joe McCarthy, *The Remarkable Kennedys*; and Jack Olsen, *The Bridge at Chappaquiddick*. An extremely useful study of Kennedy's first Senate campaign is Murray B. Levin, *Kennedy Campaigning: The System and the Style as Practiced by Senator Edward Kennedy*. Periodicals and newspapers have provided the information on the Senator's activities from 1969 to 1972.

323   *"You boys have what you want"*: qtd in Richard J. Whalen, *The Founding Father: The Story of Joseph P. Kennedy* (New York: New American Library, 1964), 461.

323   *"He's very ambitious"*: qtd in "The Ascent of Ted Kennedy," *Time* (January 10, 1969), 14.

323   *"Like my three brothers"*: qtd in Jack Olsen, *The Bridge at Chappaquiddick* (Boston: Little, Brown, 1970), 48.

323   *"Even sophisticates"*: *Ibid.*, 9.

324   *"whether some awful curse"*: *New York Times* (July 26, 1969).

325   *"We tried"*: qtd in Olsen, *op. cit.*, 10.

325   *"I admit"*: qtd in E. M. Byro, "Joan and Ted Separate," *Photo Screen* (December, 1969), 55.

325   *"It was like having"*: qtd in *Ibid.*, 56.

326   *"I remember"*: qtd in Victor Lasky, *JFK: The Man and the Myth* (New York: Macmillan, 1963), 65–66.

326   *"My husband"*: qtd in Bruce Lee, *JFK: Boyhood to White House* (New York: Crest, 1964), 20.

326   *"Even as a child"*: qtd in George Carpozi, Jr., "The Ted Kennedy Story," *National Enquirer* (August 31, 1969), 15.

327   *"If there were five people"*: qtd in *Ibid.*

327   *"During days"*: Whalen, *op. cit.*, 95.

328   *"I recall the day"*: qtd in Joe McCarthy, *The Remarkable Kennedys* (New York: Dial, 1960), 107.

328   *"He's been hitting me"*: qtd in Whalen, *op. cit.*, 252.

330   *"Teddy had just left Harvard"*: Elizabeth Cameron as told to *National Enquirer* (September 21, 1969).

331   *"I've thought a lot"*: qtd in Roger Langley, "Rugby Referee Says: Ted Kennedy Is Only Player I've Had to Throw Out of a Game in 30 Years," *National Enquirer* (September 13, 1969), 21.

333   *"the best politician in the family"*: qtd in Carpozi, *op. cit.* (September
        7, 1969).
333   *"Yes, I'm the policeman"*; *"I just happened"*; *"Usually these ticket things"*:
        qtd in Carpozi, *op. cit.* (September 21, 1969), 18–19.
335   *"One summer"*: McCarthy, *op. cit.*, 143–44.
337   *"Look, we all know"*: qtd in Olsen, *op. cit.*, 20.
337   *"He had no feeling"*: qtd in *Ibid.*, 21.
337   *"He was not only"*: qtd in *Ibid.*, 21–22.
338   *"This wasn't a sudden decision"*: qtd in Gail Cameron, *Rose: A Biog-
        raphy of Rose Fitzgerald Kennedy* (New York: Putnam, 1971), 193.
338   *"I once sympathized"*: Rita Dallas, "My Eight Years as the Kennedys'
        Private Nurse," *Ladies' Home Journal* (February, 1971), 164.
338   *"Teddy has been aptly described"*: Whalen, *op. cit.*, 463.
338   *"recruitment of an army"*: *Ibid.*
339   *"And I ask you"*: qtd in Murray B. Levin, *Kennedy Campaigning: The
        System and the Style as Practiced by Senator Edward Kennedy* (Boston:
        Beacon Press, 1966), 182.
339   *"What I did was wrong"*: qtd in *Ibid.*, 14.
339   *"Kennedy was seen"*: *Ibid.*, 121.
340   *"There is a sort of 'princely' effect"*: qtd in Levin, *op. cit.*, 26.
340   *"I honestly believe"*: qtd in *Ibid.*
340   *"extremely excited"*: qtd in Whalen, *op. cit.*, 465.
340   *"The Kennedys have applied"*: qtd in Olsen, *op. cit.*, 29.
341   *"I'd talk to him"*: qtd in *Ibid.*, 31.
341   *"the only one"*: Associated Press, *Triumph and Tragedy: The Story of
        the Kennedys* (New York: Associated Press, 1968), 211.
341   *"It's amazing"*: *Ibid.*
342   *"Teddy has become"*: *Ibid.*

12 Chappaquiddick and After, pages 345–367

For my analysis of the Chappaquiddick tragedy, its political implications,
and the discussion of Edward Kennedy's post-Chappaquiddick career, I am
especially indebted to Jack Olsen's sleuthing in *The Bridge at Chappaquiddick*,
to the publishers of *The Kennedy-Kopechne Inquest*; and to the reporters of
*Time, Newsweek, Life, Look, The New Republic, U.S. News & World Report, The
New York Times, The Washington Post*, and the *Washington Evening Star*.

345   *"the man most closely involved"*: Jack Olsen, *The Bridge at Chippaquid-
        dick* (Boston: Little, Brown, 1970), 3.
345   *"We suggest"*: Murray B. Levin, *Kennedy Campaigning: The System
        and the Style as Practiced by Senator Edward Kennedy* (Boston: Beacon
        Press, 1966), 293.
345   *"You know, it isn't enough"*: qtd in Olsen, *op. cit.*, 60.
346   *"I regard as indefensible"*: qtd in *New York Times* (July 28, 1969).
346   *"Edward Kennedy showed signs"*: Pearl S. Buck, *The Kennedy Women:
        A Personal Appraisal* (New York: Cowles, 1970), 147.
346   *"In the recent past"*: qtd in *Time* (March 1, 1971), 13.

346   *"as expressing the sense"*: qtd in Olsen, *op. cit.*, 54–55.

347   *"the last of the clan"*: *Time* (January 10, 1969), 13.

347   *"the 'different' Kennedy"*: Warren Rogers, "Ted Kennedy Talks about the Past, and His Future," *Look* (March 4, 1969), 38.

348   *"As for women"*: Olsen, *op. cit.*, 66.

349   *Ted Kennedy testified*: *New York Times* (July 20, 1969).

350   *"The crime"*: Richard Harwood and Laurence Stern, "Recirculation of Testimony Certain to Damage Sen. Kennedy Further," *Washington Post* (September 3, 1969), A23.

351   *"the senator's closest associates"*: *Newsweek* (July 28, 1969), 33.

351   *"Kennedy has been drinking"*: *Time* (August 1, 1969), 12.

351   *"some thought his drinking"*: Brock Brower, "The Incident at the Dyke Bridge," *Life* (August 1, 1969), 25.

352   *Kennedy's second statement*: *New York Times* (July 26, 1969).

355   *"of such cheapness and bathos"*: qtd in Olsen, *op. cit.*, 249.

355   *"He was simply hustling heartstrings"*: qtd in *Ibid.*

355   *"Edgartown got sick"*: qtd in *Ibid.*, 250.

356   *"The irony of it is"*: Robin P. Hartmann, "Letters to the Editor," *Life* (August 22, 1969), 20A.

356   *"I ask you to consider"*: Gordon N. Walker, "Letters," *Time* (August 15, 1969), 9.

356   *Kennedy office statement of July 30*: Olsen *op. cit.*, 277.

356   *"whether or not any crime"*: *The Kennedy-Kopechne Inquest* (New York: EVR Production and Lincoln Graphic Arts, 1970), 1.

357   *"I infer a reasonable and probable explanation"*: qtd in *Ibid.*, 126.

358   *"I can live with myself"*: qtd in *Time* (August 22, 1969), 13.

358   *Gargan's testimony*: *The Kennedy-Kopechne Inquest*, 35–36.

359   *Teddy's own testimony*: *Ibid.*, 9–11.

361   *Judge Boyle in his summary*: *Ibid.*, 126.

362   *"a sort of instant political decompression"*: William H. Honan, "The Enemy Within the Kennedy Family," *Pageant* (September, 1970), 133.

362   *"It's preordained"*: Brower, *op. cit.*, 25.

362   *"Mother put her foot down — hard"*: qtd in Fred Sparks, "Rose Kennedy's Determined Coaching Kept Ted in Ball Game," *Hartford Courant* (July 12, 1970), 12.

362   *"To Rose, the whole thing was the dynasty"*: *Ibid.*

363   *"I think there is too much risk now"*: qtd in Lenore Hershey, "How Rose Keeps Growing," *Ladies' Home Journal* (May, 1972), 141.

363   *"We all know"*: *Ibid.*

363   *"The voters need reassurance"*: qtd in R. W. Apple, Jr., "Kennedy Is Running Hard Against 1964 Vote Total," *New York Times* (August 27, 1970), 28c.

364   *"The intellectual side of him"*: *Newsweek* (November 16, 1970), 34.

364   *"I look forward"*: *Ibid.*

365   *"Every individual"*: TRB, "Here We Come, Otto," *New Republic* (February 27, 1971), 8.

366   *"Do you really think this is important?"*: Told to author by member present at the hearings.

366   *"Though young people may think"*: Brenda Feigen Fasteau and Bonnie

Lobel, "Rating the Candidates: Feminists Vote the Rascals In or Out," *Ms.* (December 20, 1971), 78.

366   *"of all the possible candidates"*: qtd in "What Kennedy Is Up To," *U.S. News & World Report* (May 24, 1971), 20.

366   *"somehow or other"*: TRB, *op. cit.*, 8.

366   *"If you're a Kennedy"*: Frances Spatz Leighton, "Why Ted Kennedy Can Never Live by the Rules," *Coronet* (May, 1971), 18.

366   *"he is a man of destiny"*: Warren Rogers, "Kennedy's Comeback: Will He or Won't He?", *Look* (August 10, 1971) 13, 20.

13 Kennedyism and America, pages 368–382

The conclusions and suggestions of this chapter grew out of many books and conversations. Two especially provocative books can be recommended for further reading: Daniel J. Boorstin, *The Image: A Guide to Pseudo-Events in America*, and Frank Goble, *The Third Force: The Psychology of Abraham Maslow*. I also strongly urge the reader to become acquainted with the thought of the late Karen Horney through her five best works — *The Neurotic Personality of Our Time, New Ways in Psychoanalysis, Self Analysis, Our Inner Conflicts*, and *Neurosis and Human Growth*.

368   *"it is difficult to see"*: Carey McWilliams, "The Making of the Legend," *Book Week*, (May 3, 1964), 3.

368   *"in their unimaginative fierce way"*: Gore Vidal, "The Holy Family," *Esquire* (April, 1967), 204.

368   *"For unfortunate reasons"*: Ronald Van Doren, *Charting the Candidates '72* (New York: Pinnacle, 1972), 99.

369   *"the Kennedy record"*: Ronald Steel, "The Kennedy Fantasy," *New York Review of Books* (November 19, 1970), 3.

370   *"evasion, however disguised"*: John Kenneth Galbraith, *Who Needs the Democrats and What It Takes to Be Needed* (Garden City, N.Y.: Doubleday, 1970), 59.

370   *"The last journey"*: Steel, *op. cit.*, 3.

371   *"Kennedyism"*: *Ibid.*, 4.

371   *"It is inconceivable"*: qtd in Bruce Mazlish, ed., *Psychoanalysis and History* (New York: Grosset, 1971), 105.

373   *"Societies where nonaggression is conspicuous"*: qtd in Frank Goble, *The Third Force: The Psychology of Abraham Maslow* (New York: Grossman, 1970), 108–9.

374   *"Of all the Presidents"*: I. F. Stone, "We All Had a Finger on That Trigger," *I. F. Stone's Weekly* (December 9, 1963); reprinted in Stone, *In a Time of Torment* (New York: Random House, 1967), 12–13.

375   *"Politics, in a sense"*: Joe McGinniss, *The Selling of the President 1968* (New York: Pocket Books, 1970), 19–20.

377   *"We have become"*: Boorstin, *op. cit.*, 5–6, 45, 211.

377   *"The choice of qualities"*: Fawn M. Brodie, "The Political Hero in America," *Virginia Quarterly Review* (Winter, 1970), 46.

377   "*The American Crisis*": qtd in Lewis Chester, Godfrey Hodgson, and Bruce Page, *An American Melodrama: The Presidential Campaign of 1968* (New York: Viking, 1969), 384.

378   "*The White House*": George E. Reedy, *The Twilight of the Presidency* (New York: New American Library, 1970), xii.

379   "*Man cannot live*": Erich Fromm, *Man for Himself: An Inquiry into the Psychology of Ethics* (New York: Holt, 1947), 212.

380   "*A better and more lasting patriotism*": Louis Gottschalk, *Understanding History* (New York: Knopf, 1950), 7.

381   "*The President remains*": Richard E. Neustadt, *Presidential Power* (New York: Wiley, 1964), 189.

382   "*Nowadays everybody tells us*": Daniel J. Boorstin, *The Image: A Guide to Pseudo-Events in America* (New York: Atheneum, 1971), 6.

SELECTED BIBLIOGRAPHY

Abel, Elie. *The Missile Crisis*. Philadelphia: Lippincott, 1966.

Alsop, Joseph. "Nixon Picks Kennedy." *Washington Post*, March 27, 1972.

American Heritage Editors. *RFK: His Life and Death*. New York: Dell, 1968.

Anderson, Patrick. *The President's Men*. Garden City, N.Y.: Doubleday, 1968.

Anderson, Walt. *Campaigns: Cases in Political Conflict*. Pacific Palisades, Cal.: Goodyear, 1970.

Apple, R. W., Jr. "Despite His Lead in the Gallup Poll, Kennedy Insists He Won't Run for President in 1972." *New York Times*, May 23, 1971.

_____. "Kennedy Is Running Hard Against 1964 Vote Total." *New York Times*, August 27, 1970.

_____. "Kennedy Urges Democratic Alternative." *New York Times*, June 13, 1970.

Arendt, Hannah. *On Violence*. New York: Harcourt, 1970.

"The Ascent of Ted Kennedy." *Time*, January 10, 1969.

Associated Press. "JFK Lacked Depth, Acheson Tells BBC." July 18, 1971.

_____. *Triumph and Tragedy: The Story of the Kennedys*. New York: Associated Press, 1968.

Baldrige, Letitia. *Of Diamonds & Diplomats*. Boston: Houghton Mifflin, 1968.

Barber, James D. "The Presidency: What Americans Want." *Center Magazine*, January/February, 1971.

Barnet, Richard J. *Intervention and Revolution: America's Confrontation with Insurgent Movements around the World*. New York: World, 1968.

Bazelon, David T. *The Paper Economy*. New York: Random House, 1963.

Beecher, Williard, and Marguerite Beecher. *Beyond Success and Failure: Ways to Self-Reliance and Maturity*. New York: Julian, 1966.

Belser, Lee. "What Ted Kennedy and Those Chappaquiddick Girls Are Up to Now." *Coronet*, August, 1970.

Bishop, James A. *The Day Kennedy Was Shot*. New York: Funk & Wagnalls, 1968.

Boorstin, Daniel J. *The Image: A Guide to Pseudo-Events in America*. New York: Atheneum, 1971.

Brandon, Henry. *Anatomy of Error: The Inside Story of the Asian War on the Potomac, 1954–1969.* Boston: Gambit, 1969.

Broder, David S. "Sen. Kennedy Is Nominated for 2d Term." *Washington Post,* June 13, 1970.

———. "Kennedy Campaigns Like Underdog. Nothing Left to Chance in Massachusetts Re-election Drive." *Washington Post,* September 20, 1970.

Brodie, Fawn M. "The Political Hero in America." *Virginia Quarterly Review,* Winter, 1970.

Brogan, Denis. "Has Teddy Ended the Kennedy Dynasty?" *Esquire,* November, 1969.

"Brother Quotes LBJ as Calling RFK 'Runt.' " *Washington Evening Star,* November 30, 1969.

Brower, Brock. "The Incident at the Dyke Bridge." *Life,* August 1, 1969.

Buck, Pearl S. *The Kennedy Women: A Personal Appraisal.* New York: Cowles, 1970.

Burns, James MacGregor. *John Kennedy: A Political Profile.* New York: Harcourt, 1960.

Button, Alan DeWitt. *The Authentic Child.* New York: Random House, 1969.

Byro, E. M. "Joan and Ted Separate." *Photo Screen,* December, 1969.

Cameron, Gail. *Rose: A Biography of Rose Fitzgerald Kennedy.* New York: Putnam, 1971.

Carpozi, George, Jr. "The Ted Kennedy Story." *National Enquirer,* August 31, September 7, and September 21, 1969.

Cecil, David. *Lord M.* London: Constable, 1954.

Chester, Lewis; Godfrey Hodgson; and Bruce Page. *An American Melodrama: The Presidential Campaign of 1968.* New York: Viking, 1969.

Clawson, Ken. "Constant Threat of Death Affects Kennedy's Life, Family, Career." *Washington Post,* February 7, 1971.

Conroy, Sarah Booth. "Touring the Kennedys' House on the Potomac—a Private View." *New York Times,* May 10, 1970.

Corry, John. *The Manchester Affair.* New York: Putnam, 1967.

Cralle, Richard K., ed. *The Works of John C. Calhoun.* New York: Appleton, 1854.

Crown, James Tracy, and George P. Penty. *Kennedy in Power.* New York: Ballantine, 1961.

Cutler, John Henry. *"Honey Fitz": Three Steps to the White House; The Life and Times of John F. (Honey Fitz) Fitzgerald.* New York: Bobbs-Merrill, March, 1962.

Dallas, Rita. "My Eight Years as the Kennedys' Private Nurse." *Ladies' Home Journal,* February, March, 1971.

Damore, Leo. *The Cape Cod Years of John Fitzgerald Kennedy.* Englewood Cliffs, N.J.: Prentice-Hall, 1967.

David, Lester. *Ethel: The Story of Mrs. Robert F. Kennedy.* New York: World, 1971.

———. *Ted Kennedy: Triumphs and Tragedies.* New York: Grosset, 1972.

Davis, John H. *The Bouviers: Portrait of an American Family.* New York: Farrar, 1969.

De Toledano, Ralph. *R.F.K.: The Man Who Would Be President.* New York: Putnam, 1967.

Dinneen, Joseph F. *The Kennedy Family*. Boston: Little, Brown, 1959.

Donovan, Robert J. *PT-109: John F. Kennedy in World War II*. New York: McGraw-Hill, 1961.

Draper, Theodore. *Abuse of Power*. New York: Viking, 1967.

_____. *Castro's Revolution: Myths and Realities*. New York: Praeger, 1962.

Duncliffe, William J. *The Life and Times of Joseph P. Kennedy*. New York: Macfadden, 1965.

"The Durable Matriarch." *Time*, August 8, 1969.

Erikson, Erik H. *Childhood and Society*. New York: Norton, 1963.

_____. *Young Man Luther*. New York: Norton, 1958.

Fasteau, Brenda Feigen, and Bonnie Lobel. "Rating the Candidates: Feminists Vote the Rascals In or Out." *Ms.*, December 20, 1971.

Fay, Paul B., Jr. *The Pleasure of His Company*. New York: Harper, 1966.

FitzSimons, Louise. *The Kennedy Doctrine*. New York: Random House, 1972.

Foster, Frank. "Joan Kennedy: I Don't Want Ted to Run for President." *National Enquirer*, June 13, 1971.

Frischauer, Willi. *Onassis*. New York: Meredith, 1968.

Fromm, Erich. *Escape from Freedom*. New York: Avon, 1965.

_____. *Man for Himself: An Inquiry into the Psychology of Ethics*. New York: Holt, 1947.

Fulbright, J. William. Introduction to *The Vietnam Hearings*. New York: Random House, 1966.

Fuller, Helen. *Year of Trial: Kennedy's Crucial Decisions*. New York: Harcourt, 1962.

Galbraith, John Kenneth. "An Agenda for American Liberals." *Commentary*, June, 1966.

_____. *Who Needs the Democrats and What It Takes to Be Needed*. Garden City, N.Y.: Doubleday, 1970.

Gallagher, Mary Barelli. *My Life with Jacqueline Kennedy*. New York: McKay, 1969.

Girling, J. L. S. *People's War: Conditions and Consequences in China and Southeast Asia*. New York: Praeger, 1969.

Gladwin, Thomas. *Poverty U.S.A.* Boston: Little, Brown, 1967.

Goble, Frank. *The Third Force: The Psychology of Abraham Maslow*. New York: Grossman, 1970.

Goldston, Robert. *The Negro Revolution*. New York: New American Library, 1969.

Goodman, Paul. *People or Personnel* and *Like a Conquered Province*. New York: Vintage, 1968.

Gottschalk, Louis. *Understanding History*. New York: Knopf, 1950.

Grant, Joanne. *Black Protest: History, Documents, and Analyses*. Greenwich, Conn.: Fawcett, 1968.

Gruening, Ernest, and Herbert W. Beaser. *Vietnam Folly*. Palo Alto, Cal.: National Press, 1968.

Guiles, Fred Lawrence. *Norma Jean: The Life of Marilyn Monroe*. New York: McGraw-Hill, 1969.

Halberstam, David. *The Making of a Quagmire*. New York: Random House, 1965.

_____. *The Unfinished Odyssey of Robert Kennedy*. New York: Bantam, 1969.

Hall, Gordon Langley, and Ann Pinchot. *Jacqueline Kennedy: A Biography.* New York: Fell, 1964.

Harrington, Michael. "Does Nixon Have the Stuff?" Washington *Evening Star*, May 19, 1970.

―――. *The Other America: Poverty in the United States.* New York: Macmillan, 1962.

Harwood, Richard, and Laurence Stern. "Recirculation of Testimony Certain to Damage Sen. Kennedy Further." *Washington Post*, September 3, 1969.

Heren, Louis. *No Hail, No Farewell.* New York: Harper, 1970.

Hershey, Lenore. "How Rose Keeps Growing." *Ladies' Home Journal*, May, 1972.

Hicks, Glen. "Kennedy-Shriver Marijuana Case." *National Enquirer*, September 6, 1970.

Hilsman, Roger. *To Move a Nation.* Garden City, N.Y.: Doubleday, 1967.

Hoffman, Betty Hannah. "Joan Kennedy's Story." *Ladies' Home Journal*, July, 1970.

―――. "Joan Kennedy Today." *Ladies' Home Journal*, August, 1970.

Hofstadter, Richard. *Social Darwinism in American Thought.* Boston: Beacon, 1967.

Honan, William H. "The Enemy Within the Kennedy Family." *Pageant*, September, 1970.

Hoopes, Townsend. *The Limits of Intervention.* New York: McKay, 1970.

Hope, Paul. "Humphrey Charts Kennedy Gains." Washington *Evening Star*, March 30, 1970.

Horney, Karen. *Neurosis and Human Growth.* New York: Norton, 1952.

―――. *The Neurotic Personality of Our Time.* New York: Norton, 1937.

―――. *New Ways in Psychoanalysis.* New York: Norton, 1939.

―――. *Our Inner Conflicts.* New York: Norton, 1945.

―――. *Self-Analysis.* New York: Norton, 1942.

Houghton, Neal D. *Struggle against History: U.S. Foreign Policy in an Age of Revolution.* New York: Washington Square Press, 1968.

Huie, William Bradford. "A Black Mayor Fails." *True*, May, 1970.

Ions, Edmund S. *The Politics of John F. Kennedy.* New York: Barnes & Noble, 1967.

Jacobs, Paul. *The State of the Unions.* New York: Atheneum, 1963.

James, Ralph, and Estelle James. *Hoffa and the Teamsters: A Study of Union Power.* Princeton, N.J.: Van Nostrand, 1965.

"JFK, as Student, Was Caught with Woman." *Washington Post*, August 3, 1971.

Kaiser, Robert Blair. *"R.F.K. Must Die!" A History of the Robert Kennedy Assassination and Its Aftermath.* New York: Dutton, 1970.

Karnow, Stanley. "A Grim Notebook on Our Asian Tragedy." *Washington Post Outlook*, June 28, 1970.

Kateb, George. "Kennedy as Statesman." *Commentary*, June, 1966.

Kennedy, Edward M. "Sen. Kennedy Replies to a Letter." *Washington Post*, May 17, 1970.

Kennedy, John F. *Profiles in Courage.* New York: Harper, 1955.

―――. *Public Papers of the President, 1961, 1962, 1963.* 3 vols. Washington, D.C.: GPO, 1962, 1963, 1964.

――――. *The Strategy of Peace.* New York: Harper, 1960.

――――. *While England Slept.* New York: Funk & Wagnalls, 1940.

Kennedy, Joseph P. *I'm for Roosevelt.* New York: Reynal and Hitchcock, 1936.

Kennedy, Robert F. *The Enemy Within.* New York: Harper, 1960.

――――. *Thirteen Days: A Memoir of the Cuban Missile Crisis.* New York: Norton, 1969.

――――. *To Seek a Newer World.* New York: Bantam, 1969.

Kennedy, Rose. "Giving Children the Gifts of Faith and Courage." *Ladies' Home Journal,* December, 1969.

The Kennedy-Kopechne Inquest. New York: EVR Production and Lincoln Graphic Arts, 1970.

Kevles, Barbara. "An Intimate Portrait of Joan Kennedy." *Good Housekeeping,* September, 1969.

Kimball, Penn. *Bobby Kennedy and the New Politics.* Englewood Cliffs, N.J.: Prentice-Hall, 1968.

King, Martin Luther, Jr. *Where Do We Go from Here: Chaos or Community?* New York: Harper, 1967.

――――. *Why We Can't Wait.* New York: Harper, 1964.

Kotz, Nicholas. *Let Them Eat Promises: The Politics of Hunger in America.* Englewood Cliffs, N.J.: Prentice-Hall, 1970.

Krock, Arthur. *Memoirs: Sixty Years on the Firing Line.* New York: Funk & Wagnalls, 1968.

Laing, Margaret. *The Next Kennedy.* New York: Coward-McCann, 1968.

Lamott, Kenneth. *The Moneymakers: The Great Big New Rich in America.* New York: Bantam, 1970.

Langley, Roger. "Rugby Referee Says: Ted Kennedy Is Only Player I've Had to Throw Out of a Game in 30 Years." *National Enquirer,* September 13, 1969.

Lapp, Ralph E. *Arms Beyond Doubt: The Tyranny of Weapons Technology.* New York: Cowles, 1970.

――――. *The Weapons Culture.* New York: Norton, 1968.

Lasky, Victor. *JFK: The Man and the Myth.* New York: Macmillan, 1963.

――――. *Robert F. Kennedy: The Myth and the Man.* New York: Trident, 1968.

Lee, Bruce. *JFK: Boyhood to White House.* New York: Crest, 1964.

Leighton, Frances Spatz. "Why Ted Kennedy Can Never Live by the Rules." *Coronet,* May, 1971.

Lekachman, Robert. "Money in America: The End of the Economists' Dream." *Harper's,* August, 1970.

Lens, Sidney. *The Military-Industrial Complex.* Philadelphia: Pilgrim Press, 1970.

Lerner, Max. "Joe Kennedy: Pathos in Success." Washington *Evening Star,* November, 1969.

L'Etang, Hugh. *The Pathology of Leadership.* New York: Hawthorn, 1970.

Levin, Murray B. *Kennedy Campaigning: The System and the Style as Practiced by Senator Edward Kennedy.* Boston: Beacon Press, 1966.

Lifton, Robert Jay. *History and Human Survival.* New York: Random House, 1970.

Lincoln, Evelyn. *Kennedy and Johnson.* New York: Holt, 1968.

――――. *My Twelve Years with John F. Kennedy.* New York: McKay, 1965.

Lindley, Ernest K. "Will Kennedy Run for President? (1938)." *Liberty*, Fall, 1971.

Lomax, Louis E. *The Negro Revolt*. New York: Harper, 1963.

Lord, Walter. *The Past That Would Not Die*. New York: Harper, 1965.

Lowi, Theodore J. *The End of Liberalism: Ideology, Policy, and the Crisis of Public Authority*. New York: Norton, 1969.

Lundberg, Ferdinand. *The Rich and the Super-Rich*. New York: Lyle Stuart, 1968.

McCarthy, Joe. *The Remarkable Kennedys*. New York: Dial, 1960.

Macrae, Norman. *The Neurotic Trillionaire: A Survey of Mr. Nixon's America*. New York: Harcourt, 1970.

McGinniss, Joe. *The Selling of the President 1968*. New York: Pocket Books, 1970.

McManus, George. *The Inside Story of Steel Wages and Prices, 1959–1967*. Philadelphia: Chilton, 1967.

MacPherson, Myra. "Joan Kennedy: No Cracks in Family Image." *Washington Post*, November 1, 1970.

McWilliams, Carey. "The Making of the Legend." *Book Week*, May 3, 1964.

Manchester, William R. *Death of a President*. New York: Harper, 1967.

———. *Portrait of a President: John F. Kennedy in Profile*, rev. ed. Boston: Little, Brown, 1967.

Mankiewicz, Frank, and Tom Braden. "Meaning of Kennedy's Defeat." *Washington Post*, January 26, 1971.

Marvin, Richard. *The Kennedy Curse*. New York: Belmont, 1969.

Maslow, Abraham H. *Motivation and Personality*. New York: Harper, 1964.

Matthews, Herbert L. *Fidel Castro*. New York: Simon and Schuster, 1969.

May, Edgar. *The Wasted Americans*. New York: Harper, 1964.

May, Rollo. *Man's Search for Himself*. New York: Norton, 1953.

Mazlish, Bruce, ed. *Psychoanalysis and History*. New York: Grosset, 1971.

Mill, John Stuart. *The Subjection of Women*. Reprinted in *On Liberty, Representative Government, The Subjection of Women*. Oxford: Oxford University Press, 1952.

Miller, William Robert. *Martin Luther King, Jr*. New York: Weybright, 1968.

Mollenhoff, Clark R. *Tentacles of Power: The Story of Jimmy Hoffa*. Cleveland: World, 1965.

Moore, Deedee. "Joan Kennedy Grows Up." *Cosmopolitan*, November, 1970.

Morgenthau, Hans J. *A New Foreign Policy for the United States*. New York: Praeger, 1969.

"A Mother's Day Tribute to Ethel Kennedy." *Lady's Circle*, May, 1970.

Navasky, Victor S. *Kennedy Justice*. New York: Harper, 1972.

Neustadt, Richard E. *Presidential Power*. New York: Wiley, 1964.

Newfield, Jack. *Robert Kennedy: A Memoir*. New York: Dutton, 1969.

Nicholas, William, pseud. (William Johnson and Nick Thimmesch). *The Bobby Kennedy Nobody Knows*. Greenwich, Conn.: Fawcett, 1967.

Nieburg, H. L. *In the Name of Science*. Chicago: Quadrangle, 1966.

Nossiter, Bernard D. *The Mythmakers: An Essay on Power and Wealth*. Boston: Houghton Mifflin, 1964.

O'Donnell, Kenneth. "L.B.J. and the Kennedys." *Life*, August 7, 1970.
Opotowsky, Stan. *The Kennedy Government*. London: Harrap, 1961.
Olsen, Jack. *Aphrodite: Desperate Mission*. New York: Putnam, 1970.
_____. *The Bridge at Chappaquiddick*. Boston: Little, Brown, 1970.
Pachter, Henry M. *Collision Course: The Cuban Missile Crisis and Coexistence*. New York: Praeger, 1963.
Parenti, Michael. *The Anti-Communist Impulse*. New York: Random House, 1969.
Philosophers and Kings: Studies in Leadership. *Daedalus*, Summer, 1968.
Priest, Sylvan. "How Bob Kennedy's Children Are Growing Up without Him." *The Woman*, August, 1970.
Putney, Snell, and Gail J. Putney. *Normal Neurosis: The Adjusted American*. New York: Harper, 1964.
Reedy, George E. *The Twilight of the Presidency*. New York: New American Library, 1970.
Roberts, Chalmers M. *The Nuclear Years: The Arms Race and Arms Control 1945–70*. New York: Praeger, 1970.
Robertson, Nan. "1965 Tribute by Robert Kennedy Read at Funeral of His Father." *New York Times*, November 21, 1969.
Rogers, Warren. "Kennedy's Comeback: Will He or Won't He?" *Look*, August 10, 1971.
_____. "Ted Kennedy Talks about the Past, and His Future." *Look*, March 4, 1969.
Rogow, Arnold A. *The Psychiatrists*. New York: Putnam, 1970.
Rohrer, Daniel M.; Mark G. Arnold; and Roger L. Conner. *By Weight of Arms: America's Overseas Military Policy*. Skokie, Ill.: National Textbook Co., 1969.
Ross, Douglas. *Robert F. Kennedy: Apostle of Change*. New York: Harper, 1968.
Sabin, Francene. "Kathleen Kennedy: Like Father, Like Daughter." *Catholic Digest*, December, 1970.
Sable, Martin H. *A Bio-Bibliography of the Kennedy Family*. Metuchen, N.J.: Scarecrow Press, 1969.
Salinger, Pierre. *With Kennedy*. Garden City, N.Y.: Doubleday, 1966.
Sampson, Ronald V. *The Psychology of Power*. London: Heinemann, 1965.
Schaap, Dick. *R.F.K.* New York: New American Library, 1967.
Schlesinger, Arthur M., Jr. *The Bitter Heritage: Vietnam and American Democracy, 1941–1966*. Boston: Houghton Mifflin, 1966.
_____. *A Thousand Days: John F. Kennedy in the White House*. Boston: Houghton Mifflin, 1965.
Schoenbrun, David. *Vietnam: How We Got In, How to Get Out*. New York: Atheneum, 1968.
Schuchter, Arnold. *White Power, Black Freedom*. Boston: Beacon Press, 1968.
Schuman, Frederick L. *The Cold War: Retrospect and Prospect*. Baton Rouge: Louisiana State University Press, 1967.
Schwartz, H. L., III. "Kennedy-Dole Duels Have Old-West Air." Washington *Evening Star*, November 30, 1970.
Schwarz, Urs. *John F. Kennedy, 1917–1963*. London: Hamlyn, 1964.
Searls, Hank. *The Lost Prince: Young Joe, the Forgotten Kennedy*. New York: New American Library, 1969.

Segal, Ronald. *The Americans: A Conflict of Creed and Reality*. New York: Viking, 1969.

―――. *The Race War*. New York: Viking, 1967.

Seligman, Ben B. *Permanent Poverty: An American Syndrome*. Chicago: Quadrangle, 1968.

Shannon, William V. *The American Irish*. New York: Macmillan, 1966.

―――. *The Heir Apparent: Robert Kennedy and the Struggle for Power*. New York: Macmillan, 1967.

Shaplen, Robert. *The Lost Revolution: The U.S. in Vietnam*. New York: Harper, 1965.

Shaw, Maud. *White House Nannie*. New York: New American Library, 1966.

Sheehan, Neil; Hedrick Smith; E. W. Kenworthy; and Fox Butterfield. *The Pentagon Papers*. New York: Bantam, 1971.

Shulman, Irving. *"Jackie"! The Exploitation of a First Lady*. New York: Trident, 1970.

Sidey, Hugh. *John F. Kennedy, President*. New York: Atheneum, 1964.

Slater, Philip. *The Pursuit of Loneliness: American Culture at the Breaking Point*. Boston: Beacon Press, 1970.

Sorensen, Theodore C. *Kennedy*. New York: Harper, 1965.

―――. *The Kennedy Legacy*. New York: Macmillan, 1969.

Sparks, Fred. "Marrying into the Family Means Adopting the Kennedy Life-Style." *Hartford Courant*, July 15, 1970.

―――. "Rose Has Ted Counting Calories, Drinks, in Search for New Image." *Hartford Courant*, July 16, 1970.

―――. "Rose Kennedy at 80 Is a Best-Dressed Celebrity of the Jet Set." *Hartford Courant*, July 13, 1970.

―――. "Rose Kennedy Finds Presidential Prospects in 27 Grandchildren." *Hartford Courant*, July 14, 1970.

―――. "Rose Kennedy's Determined Coaching Kept Ted in Ball Game." *Hartford Courant*, July 12, 1970.

―――. *The $20,000,000 Honeymoon: Jackie and Ari's First Year*. New York: Geis, 1970.

Steel, Ronald. A review of *The Lost Crusade: America in Vietnam*, by Chester L. Cooper. *New York Times Book Review*, November 8, 1970.

―――. "The Kennedy Fantasy." *New York Review of Books*, November 19, 1970.

Stillman, Edmund, and William Pfaff. *The Politics of Hysteria: The Sources of 20th-Century Conflict*. New York: Harper, 1964.

Stone, I. F. *In a Time of Torment*. New York: Random House, 1967.

―――. "The Test Ban Comedy." *New York Review of Books*, May 7, 1970.

―――. "Theatre of Delusion." *New York Review of Books*, April 23, 1970.

Sundquist, James L. *Politics and Policy: The Eisenhower, Kennedy, and Johnson Years*. Washington, D.C.: Brookings Institution, 1968.

Swinburne, Laurence. *RFK: The Last Knight*. New York: Pyramid, 1969.

Szulc, Tad, and Karl E. Meyer. *The Cuban Invasion: The Chronicle of a Disaster*. New York: Ballantine, 1962.

"A Talk with Kennedy." *Time*, March 1, 1971.

Taylor, A. J. P. *English History 1914–1945*. New York: Oxford, 1965.

Taylor, Telford. *Nuremberg and Vietnam: An American Tragedy*. New York: Bantam, 1971.

"Teddy Cracks the Whip." *Newsweek*, January 13, 1969.

Thompson, Clara, and Patrick Mullahy. *Psychoanalysis: Evolution and Development. A Review of Theory and Therapy*. New York: Grove, 1957.

Travell, Janet. *Office Hours: Day and Night*. New York: World, 1968.

TRB. "Here We Come, Otto." *New Republic*, February 27, 1971.

Van Doren, Ronald. *Charting the Candidates '72*. New York: Pinnacle, 1972.

Vanden Heuvel, William, and Milton Gwirtzman. *On His Own: RFK, 1964–68*. Garden City, N.Y.: Doubleday, 1970.

Vidal, Gore. "The Holy Family," *Esquire*, April, 1967.

_____. "Playboy Interview." *Playboy*, June, 1969.

Wagner, Liz. "The Only Four People Who Know the Truth about Ted Kennedy." *Woman's Home Companion*, February, 1970.

Walton, Richard J. *Cold War and Counterrevolution: The Foreign Policy of John F. Kennedy*. New York: Viking, 1972.

Warner, Samuel J. *Self-Realization and Self-Defeat*. New York: Grove, 1966.

Warren, Sidney. *The Battle for the Presidency*. Philadelphia: Lippincott, 1968.

Weintal, Edward, and Charles Bartlett. *Facing the Brink: An Intimate Study of Crisis Diplomacy*. New York: Scribner's, 1967.

Whale, John. *The Half-Shut Eye: Television and Politics in Britain and America*. New York: St. Martin's, 1969.

Whalen, Richard J. *The Founding Father: The Story of Joseph P. Kennedy*. New York: New American Library, 1964.

_____. "Joseph Kennedy: 'He Called on the Best That Was in Us.' " *New York Times*, November 23, 1969.

White, Theodore H. *The Making of the President 1960*. New York: Atheneum, 1961.

_____. *The Making of the President 1968*. New York: Atheneum, 1969.

White, William S. "Kennedy Gains Political Power." *Washington Post*, May 19, 1971.

Wicker, Tom. *J.F.K. and L.B.J.: The Influence of Personality upon Politics*. New York: Morrow, 1968.

_____. *Kennedy without Tears*. New York: Morrow, 1964.

Willcox, William B. *Portrait of a General: Sir Henry Clinton in the War of Independence*. New York: Knopf, 1964.

Witcover, Jules. *85 Days: The Last Campaign of Robert Kennedy*. New York: Putnam, 1969.

Young, Hugo; Bryan Silcock; and Peter Dunn. "Why We Went to the Moon." *Washington Monthly*, April, 1970.

INDEX

NANCY GAGER CLINCH, Co-Director of
the Center for Women Policy Studies
in Washington, D.C., is also a member
of the American Historical Association and the Association for Women in
Psychology. Since her graduation from
Wellesley College and completion of
studies at Oxford University, she has
worked in the areas of historical evaluation and military affairs as a writer
and editor. Her articles and reviews
have appeared in *Military Affairs,
Armed Forces Journal, Military Collector & Historian,* and other periodicals. For her political analysis while in
Korea, Nancy Gager Clinch received
a Department of the Army citation.
The Kennedy Neurosis is her first full-
length historical study. She now lives
in Bethesda, Maryland, with her two
daughters.

DATE DUE

JUL 9 '73	FEB 8 '77	SEP 3 0 '87	
E H	FEB 7 '77		
AUG 8 '73	JAN 10 '78		
E H	DEC 6 '77		
NOV 12 '73	OCT 3 1 '78		
H E	NOV 10 '78		
FEB 1 2 '74	NOV 2 8 '78		
H E	NOV 14 '78		
SEP 1 3 '74	SEP 25 '78		
E H	NOV 12 '79		
MAR 27 '75	NOV 4 '80		
	OCT 22 '80		
NOV 1 1 '75	NOV 8 '83		
	NOV 2 1983		
FEB 2 4 '76	MAY 8 '84		
	MAY 2 1 1984		
NOV 3 0 1976	NOV 2 0 '84		
NOV 1 9 '76	NOV 8 '84